THE SEXUAL PREDATOR

LAW AND PUBLIC POLICY

CLINICAL PRACTICE

Volume III

Edited by

Anita Schlank, Ph.D.

Civic Research Institute

4478 U.S. Route 27 • P.O. Box 585 • Kingston, NJ 08528

Printed in the United States of America

Library of Congress Cataloging in Publication Data
The sexual predator/Anita Schlank

ISBN 1-887554-53-X

Library of Congress Control Number 2006922587

Acknowledgements

I am extremely grateful for the hard work of the authors of the individual chapters, and give grateful acknowledgement to our publisher, Art Rosenfeld. Special thanks also go to Deborah Launer, Executive Vice President of Civic Research Institute, her editorial assistant, Leslie Gwyn (for her excellent proofreading), and to Lori Jacobs, our copy editor. In addition, I would like to give special thanks to Bill Plum (for his never-ending emotional support), and to my whole family, especially my parents (for their continued support with this project despite the unappealing title of this series), and Judy Gardner (my sister and best friend). My appreciation also continues to go to Jeanne Morrow, Robin Lagerquist, John Bergman, Sue Persons, Janis Bremer, Glenn Ferguson, and Merrill Berger for their friendship and support, and to Craig Nelson, Janice Marques, Barbara Schwartz, Bill Marshall, Richard Laws, Connie Isaac, and Jim Haaven for inspiring others through their dedication and excellent work in the field.

About the Authors

John Bergman, M.A., R.D.T.
John Bergman is a registered dramatherapist and master teacher in dramatherapy. He is the Founding Director of Geese Theatre, Stonewall Arts Project, Inc. Geese USA and Geese UK were affiliated for many years, and Geese USA is currently partners with Transcena in Romania. He has extensive experience providing training to staff of treatment programs and correctional facilities and conducts dramatherapy with sexual offenders, violent offenders, chemical abusers, and juvenile offenders in treatment programs located in many different countries, including Australia, Bulgaria, and Romania and throughout Europe and the United States. Mr. Bergman has also authored many articles and book chapters on the use of dramatherapy with offenders.

Janis F. Bremer, Ph.D.
Janis F. Bremer is currently the clinical director for Adolescent Services at Project Pathfinder, Inc., which serves male and female juveniles with sexual concerns in the seven county metropolitan Minneapolis/St Paul area. Dr. Bremer continues in the juvenile sex abuse field after two plus decades. She has worked in outpatient, correctional residential, and court assessment arenas. She has published internationally in professional journals and as a book contributor. She gives presentations and workshops on the national and international levels. Dr. Bremer participated on the APN National Task Force for Guidelines on Juvenile Sex Offender Treatment. She is currently on the advisory board revising these guidelines. She is a member of the Association for the Treatment of Sexual Abusers and helped found the Minnesota chapter of this organization.

C. Justin Brown, J.D.
C. Justin Brown graduated in 2005 from the University of Maryland School of Law, where he was an articles editor for the *Maryland Law Review*. He is currently a law clerk for U.S. District Court Judge Andre M. Davis. Prior to entering the legal field, Mr. Brown was a journalist.

John Kip Cornwell, J.D.
John Kip Cornwell received his A.B., with honors, from Harvard University, his M.Phil. in International Relations from Cambridge University, and his J.D. from Yale Law School where he was an editor of the *Yale Law Journal*. He clerked for the Honorable Mariana R. Pfaelzer of the U.S. District Court, Central District of California, and the Honorable Dorothy W. Nelson of the U.S. Court of Appeals for the Ninth Circuit. He is currently is a Professor of Law at Seton Hall University School of Law in Newark, New Jersey, where he teaches criminal law, criminal procedure, employment law, and mental health law. He is also the director of New Jersey's Institute of Law and Mental Health. Prior to joining Seton Hall in 1994, he was a senior trial attorney in the Civil Rights Division of the U.S. Department of Justice and an adjunct professor at the National Law Center of George Washington University. In

1993, he received a Special Achievement Award from Attorney General Janet Reno for "sustained, superior performance" at the Justice Department. He has published a number of articles in scholarly journals in the areas of mental health law and criminal procedure, with particular emphasis on juveniles and the civil commitment of sex offenders, incompetent criminal defendants, and competent defendants acquitted by reason of insanity.

Dennis M. Doren, Ph.D.

Dennis M. Doren received his doctorate in clinical psychology with a subspecialty in crime and delinquency studies from the Florida State University in 1983. Since mid-1994, Dr. Doren has conducted and testified about sex offender civil commitment evaluations, served as a consultant, and/or done training on risk assessment of sex offenders in fifteen of the seventeen states with active sex offender civil commitment laws, as well as other places where civil commitments were not the main issue. His more recently published book, his second, was entitled *Evaluating Sex Offenders: A Manual for Civil Commitments and Beyond.* His other publications concerning sex offender assessments include numerous book chapters and articles in professional periodicals. Dr. Doren has presented at various national and international conferences on topics related to the assessment of sex offenders.

Joel Dvoskin, Ph.D., A.B.P.P.

Joel Dvoskin has worked as a clinician, researcher, scholar, and administrator in the fields of mental health and criminal justice. He received his doctorate in clinical psychology from the University of Arizona and completed an internship at McLean Hospital and Harvard Medical School, followed by a fellowship in forensic psychology at the Harvard Medical School. Dr. Dvoskin served as the president of Division 18 of the American Psychological Association. He has won awards for scholarship and service from the American Academy of Psychiatry and the Law, the National Coalition for the Mentally Ill in the Criminal Justice System, the American Psychological Association (Division 18), and the Arizona Psychological Association. Dr. Dvoskin presided over the forensic and correctional mental health systems of the New York State, later serving as Acting Commissioner of Mental Health for New York State. Dr. Dvoskin has worked with and evaluated some of the most violent individuals in America, and has provided consultation to more than thirty state governments, numerous Fortune 100 companies, and various professional organizations. Dr. Dvoskin also routinely provides expert testimony and consultation in regard to other class actions involving prisons, jails, psychiatric hospitals, and juvenile justice systems, as well as other criminal and civil forensic cases. Currently, Dr. Dvoskin serves on the faculties of the medical schools at Louisiana State University, New York University, and the University of Arizona. He is affiliated with the Threat Assessment Group and Park Dietz and Associates and maintains a clinical, forensic, and consulting psychology practice in Tucson, Arizona.

John Edens, Ph.D.

John Edens is a licensed psychologist (Texas) and associate professor in the psychology department at Southern Methodist University. He received his Ph.D. in clinical psychology from Texas A&M University in 1996 and then completed a two-year postdoctoral fellowship in forensic psychology at the University of South Florida. His research and clinical interests primarily revolve around psychological assessment and legal decision making in relation to both criminal and civil matters. Dr. Edens is an associate editor of the journal *Assessment*, and is a coauthor (along with Mark Ruiz, Ph.D.) of the Personality Assessment Inventory Interpretive Report for Correctional Settings (PAI-CS).

Kim English, M.A.

Kim English is the research director for the Colorado Division of Criminal Justice. She manages a staff of researchers who conduct policy analysis, program evaluation, and research in all areas of the justice system. She has a bachelor of arts degree in corrections and sociology from Washburn University in Topeka, Kansas, and an master's degree in sociology from the University of Colorado, Boulder. She has been conducting research on the use of the polygraph with adult and juvenile sex offenders since 1993. In 1999, Ms. English was awarded the G. Paul Sylvestre Award for outstanding achievement in advancing criminal justice statistics in the states, conferred by the U.S. Bureau of Justice Statistics. She is on the editorial board of *Polygraph* and the *Journal of Offender Rehabilitation*.

Glenn Ferguson, Ph.D.

Glenn Ferguson is the clinical director of the Division of Mental Health Services/Special Treatment Unit in Kearny and Woodbridge New Jersey. This program is the secure inpatient treatment center designated for individuals civilly committed under the New Jersey Sexually Violent Predators Act. Dr. Ferguson is also a professor of forensic psychology at the College of New Jersey. Prior to opening the Special Treatment Unit in 1999, Dr. Ferguson worked as a psychology consultant for the New Jersey State Parole Board, where he performed psychological evaluations on high-risk violent offenders in the New Jersey prison system. He is an active member of the New Jersey Association for the Treatment of Sexual Abusers and a former member of their board of directors.

W. Lawrence Fitch J.D.

W. Lawrence Fitch is director of forensic services for the Mental Hygiene Administration in Maryland, clinical associate professor of psychiatry at the University of Maryland Medical School, and adjunct associate professor of law in the University of Maryland Law School. From 1982 to 1994, Mr. Fitch was associate professor of law at the University of Virginia, where he served as director of the Forensic Evaluation Training and Research Center at the University's Institute of Law, Psychiatry and Public Policy and taught in both the law school and the medical school. From 1978 to 1982, Mr. Fitch was an attorney with the Institute on Mental Disability and the Law at the National Center for State Courts.

Vince Gollogly, Ph.D.

Vince Gollogly received his doctorate from the Union Institute in Cincinnati, Ohio, in 1991. Prior to joining the Special Commitment Center in Washington, Dr. Gollogly directed substance abuse treatment programs in Alaska and worked at an addictions hospital in Saudi Arabia as director of rehabilitation services. He was formerly the clinical director at the Special Commitment Center. He is now a licensed psychologist in private practice in Washington where he undertakes forensic evaluations and treats sex offenders.

Andrew J. Harris Ph.D.
Andrew J. Harris serves as deputy director of health and criminal justice programs and is an assistant professor of family medicine and community health at the University of Massachusetts Medical School. He has helped to establish the institution's program of service to the commonwealth's criminal justice agencies, including the university's program providing comprehensive health, mental health, and substance abuse services to the Massachusetts inmate population. Prior to that, Dr. Harris served as associate executive director for Correctional Health Services in New York City's Health and Hospitals Corporation; he also served as assistant commissioner in the New York City Department of Corrections. Dr. Harris received his master's degree from Columbia University's School of International and Public Affairs and his doctorate from New York University's Robert F. Wagner Graduate School of Public Service.

Ian Heath, M.D., C.M.
Ian Heath pursued his medical training at the McGill University Faculty of Medicine in Montreal, Canada, and he completed both his internship and residency training in general psychiatry at the Hennepin-Regions Psychiatry Training Program in Minneapolis and St. Paul, Minnesota. After completing his residency, Dr. Heath obtained additional training in the subspecialty of forensic psychiatry, completing the Charles E. Steinberg Fellowship in Psychiatry and the Law in Rochester, New York. Dr. Heath is employed by State Operated Forensic Services, a division of the Minnesota Department of Human Services; initially, he provided psychiatric services to both the Minnesota Security Hospital and Minnesota Sex Offender Program. Currently, Dr. Heath is the clinical director of the Minnesota Security Hospital.

Peggy Heil, L.I.C.S.W.
Peggy Heil is a licensed clinical social worker. She developed and directed the Sex Offender Treatment and Monitoring Program at the Colorado Department of Corrections for nineteen years. Currently, she works in the Office of Research and Statistics at the Colorado Division of Criminal Justice and has a private practice. In addition, she is the mountain region representative on the Association for the Treatment of Sexual Abusers' executive board, a therapist representative on the Colorado Sex Offender Management Board, and a member of the executive board of the Colorado Coalition Against Sexual Assault.

Merrill Main, Ph.D.
Merrill Main is a licensed clinical psychologist. He is currently the director of psychology for the New Jersey Department of Human Services Special Treatment Unit in Kearny and Avenel. In that role, he supervises clinical staff, including approximately twenty psychologists in the delivery of sex offender-specific and mental health treatment to civilly committed sexual offenders. Dr. Main received his training in the assessment and treatment of sexual offenders at the New Jersey Adult Diagnostic and Treatment Center where he was employed as a staff psychologist and a unit director.

Randy K. Otto, Ph.D.

Randy K. Otto is an associate professor in the Department of Mental Health Law & Policy at the Louis de la Parte Florida Mental Health Institute at the University of South Florida. Dr. Otto's research and writing focuses on forensic assessment. He has served as president of the American Academy of Forensic Psychology, the American Psychology–Law Society, and the American Board of Forensic Psychology. He currently is chair of the committee revising the *Specialty Guidelines for Forensic Psychologists*, which are published jointly by Division 41 of the American Psychological Association and the American Board of Forensic Psychology.

John Petrila, J.D., L.L.M.

John Petrila is a professor in the Department of Mental Health Law & Policy at the Louis de la Parte Florida Mental Health Institute at the University of South Florida. He served as chair of the department from 1992 to 2004. He is coauthor of *Psychological Evaluations for the Courts* (2nd ed., 1997) and writes frequently on mental health law and policy issues. He is currently coeditor of *Behavioral Sciences & the Law*. Mr. Petrila is also president of the International Association of Forensic Mental Health Services (2005–2007).

William Plum, L.A.D.C.

William Plum is program director of the Center for Alcohol and Drug Treatment in Duluth, Minnesota, and an associate with the Institute for the Study of Therapeutic Change. He is also an adjunct instructor for the University of Minnesota Medical School. Mr. Plum is an experienced international trainer throughout Eastern Europe, Scandinavia, and Russia and is author and coauthor (with Scott Miller, Ph.D., and David Mee-Lee, M.D.) on several articles and book chapters on client-directed and outcome-informed substance abuse treatment.

Anita Schlank, Ph.D.

Anita Schlank is a licensed clinical psychologist who received her doctorate with a forensic specialty from the law–psychology program at the University of Nebraska-Lincoln. She has worked evaluating and treating sexual offenders since 1986, and was the clinical director of the civil commitment program for Minnesota (the Minnesota Sex Offender Program) from 1995 to 2003. She was also past president of the Minnesota chapter of the Association for the Treatment of Sexual Abusers. In addition to editing *The Sexual Predator* series, Dr. Schlank is author of several journal articles and chapters about the assessment and treatment of sexual offenders. She currently maintains a clinical, forensic, and consulting practice in Duluth, Minnesota, is clinical supervisor for the Human Development Center, a not-for-profit agency/ community mental health center, and is director of the Center for Forensic Mental Health, a program of the Human Development Center,

Jennifer Schneider, Ph.D.

Jennifer Schneider received her doctorate in criminal justice at Rutgers University. She is presently the director of research and quality improvement at the Special Treatment Unit, New Jersey's sexually violent predator civil commitment facility. She served as the project coordinator on a federally funded sex offender reentry study that

provided counseling and case management to sex offenders recently released from
incarceration in collaboration with the Department of Corrections and State Parole
Board. In addition, Dr. Schneider worked as a program development specialist for the
New Jersey Department of Corrections, where she supervised the release processes
and monitored prosecutor notification. She also taught a variety of undergraduate
criminal justice classes at Rutgers University.

Introduction

Sexual offenders tend to be viewed as the most objectionable type of criminal offender and are assumed by many to be untreatable and more likely to recidivate (Farkas & Stichman, 2002). Because of that view, many laws have been developed specifically for this subgroup of offenders. For example, in Jacksonville, Florida, officials approved legislation requiring sexual offenders who seek emergency shelter during a hurricane to notify shelter operators of their sex crime history, and sheriffs in another county in Florida proposed passing legislation that would ban them from public hurricane shelters altogether, forcing them to be evacuated to a separate shelter (Associated Press, 2005).

Special laws providing for the civil commitment of sexual offenders following the termination of their prison sentences are currently enacted in seventeen states and the District of Columbia. Like other laws which are aimed at monitoring and controlling sexual offenders, the passing of these statutes was precipitated by several high-profile horrendous crimes. However, these statutes, of all the sex offender-related laws, appear to stir the most controversy. Those in favor of the statutes argue that it will incapacitate the most dangerous sexual offenders until they can be successfully treated and returned to the community when they present a much lower risk. They point to recent crimes that are believed to be committed by released sexual offenders, such as the case of Dru Sjodin, who was kidnapped from a mall parking lot in South Dakota and murdered (Associated Press, 2003) and the kidnapping and murder of Jessica Lunsford in Florida (Associated Press, 2005), as the evidence of the need for such statutes. Others argue that the laws are unconstitutional, that there is no accurate method for identifying those most likely to offend, and that there are more economical ways to prevent sexual offenders from reoffending.

The emotion surrounding these arguments can be quite intense. For example, one author (Sarker, 2003) noted that the sexually violent predator (SVP) laws are similar to serial slasher movies in that both tend to shock, test human rationality to the limit, have incredible twists and turns, and get worse with each sequel. Janus (2004) compared the passing of these statutes to the opening of Pandora's Box, noting that they initially seemed attractive but now seem excessive. And, the New York Civil Liberties Union (n.d.) indicates that, in its opinion, identifying people who have a disorder that makes it more likely to commit a crime is dangerous, adding, "Who is next?" People with a family history of alcoholism and a driver's license?

Other authors (including myself) believe that despite the continuing controversy about their existence, it is unlikely that these statutes will disappear. Therefore, it may be that the more useful focus will be on ensuring that evaluators do the most accurate job possible in identifying the subgroup that presents the highest risk to society, and assisting treatment providers to identify the most effective methods for treating this very difficult population.

These varying views can all be found among the collective authors in *The Sexual Predator* series. Not everyone will agree with the viewpoints outlined in the chapters. However, it is just this variety of opinions that provides a crucial balance to the overall picture of this highly complex issue.

I am grateful to the authors for their excellent contributions to this volume. I believe that this book will be useful for psychologists involved in the evaluation of sexual offenders for possible civil commitment, attorneys either defending or prosecuting such cases, treatment providers in those states that have or are considering such statutes, and those individuals who are addressing related public policy issues.

References

Associated Press. (2003, December 1). *Police arrest Minnesota man in disappearance of missing college student.*

Associated Press. (2005, April 20). *Prosecutors: Lunsford raped, buried alive.*

Associated Press. (2005, June 3). *Separate hurricane shelter for sex offenders?*

Farkas, M. A., & Stichman, A. (2002). Sex offender laws: Can retribution, public safety and treatment be reconciled? *Criminal Justice Policy Review, 27*(2), 256–283.

Janus, E. (2004). Closing Pandora's box: Sexual predators and the politics of sexual violence. *Seton Hall Law Review, 34*(4), 1233–1253.

New York Civil Liberties Union. (n.d.). *Legislative memo: Civil commitment of "sexually violent predators.* Available: *www.nyclu.org/violent_off.html.*

Sarker, S. P. (2003). From *Hendricks* to *Crane:* The sexually violent predator trilogy and the inchoate jurisprudence of the U.S. Supreme Court. *Journal of the American Academy of Psychiatry and the Law, 31*(2), 242–248.

Table of Contents

PART 1: LEGAL AND PUBLIC POLICY ISSUES

Chapter 1: Enforcing the Right to Treatment for Civilly Committed Sex Offenders
C. Justin Brown, J.D. and W. Lawrence Fitch, J.D.

Chapter 2: Admissibility of Expert Testimony Regarding Recidivism Risk in Sexually Violent Predator Proceedings
Randy K. Otto, Ph.D. and John Petrila, J.D., L.L.M.

Chapter 3: Inaccurate Arguments in Sex Offender Civil Commitment Proceedings

Dennis M. Doren, Ph.D.

Chapter 4: The Right to Community Treatment for Mentally Disordered Sex Offenders
John Kip Cornwell, Ph.D.

Chapter 5: Cost and Resource Allocation in the Implementation of SVP Civil Commitment Policies—A Guide for Policymakers
Andrew J. Harris, Ph.D.

Chapter 6: The Model for Considering Release of Civilly Committed Sexual Offenders
Dennis M. Doren, Ph.D.

PART 2: CLINICAL ISSUES

Chapter 7: Similar Statutes, Different Treatment Needs—A Comparison of SVP and Mentally Ill Populations
Anita Schlank, Ph.D. and Joel Dvoskin, Ph.D., A.B.P.P.

Chapter 8: Medical Interventions for Paraphilias

Ian Heath, M.D., C.M. and Anita Schlank, Ph.D.

Chapter 9: The Need for Complete Information Leads to the Polygraph Examination

Kim English, M.A. and Peggy Heil, L.C.S.W.

Chapter 10: The Use of Ethics and Drama-Based Techniques to Modify Security Staff's Beliefs About Working With Sex Offenders
John Bergman, M.A., R.D.T., M.T.

Chapter 11: Assessing Treatment Progress in Civilly Committed Sex Offenders—The New Jersey Approach

Glenn Ferguson, Ph.D., Merrill Main, Ph.D. and Jennifer Schneider, Ph.D.

Chapter 12: Implications of Cognitive Rigidity in the Civilly Committed Sex Offender Population

Anita Schlank, Ph.D.

Chapter 13: Evolution of the Special Commitment Center Program

Vince Gollogly, Ph.D.

PART 3: SPECIAL POPULATIONS

Chapter 14: Psychopathy in the Civilly Committed Population of Sexual Offenders—Treatment Issues

Anita Schlank, Ph.D., and John Edens, Ph.D.

Chapter 15: Juvenile Hazards—What About Civil Commitment?

Janis F. Bremer, Ph.D.

Chapter 16: Substance Abuse—Euphoric Recall and Deviant Sexual Fantasy

William Plum, L.A.D.C.

Appendices

Index

Part 1

Legal and Public Policy Issues

The sexually violent predator (SVP) statutes continue to raise many legal and public policy questions, from the types of expert testimony that should be allowed into evidence at the hearings, the methods for releasing these residents, and the costs of maintaining such programs. This section addresses the most recent legal and public policy concerns raised by these controversial laws.

In Chapter 1, Justin Brown and W. Lawrence Fitch provide a current overview of civil commitment laws throughout the United States, with a particular emphasis on the issues related to the right to treatment in the SVP programs. They perceive a need for a change in the way courts have approached complaints regarding the SVP treatment programs.

Those involved in testifying at SVP commitment hearings will find Chapters 2 and 3 particularly useful. In Chapter 2, Randy K. Otto and John Petrila keep us updated on the evidentiary standards for expert testimony in SVP commitment hearings. In Chapter 3, Dennis M. Doren provides some valuable information regarding the common erroneous arguments made in such proceedings.

In Chapter 4, John Kip Cornwell provides an argument for the constitutional right for SVP patients to have a transition period of community treatment as part of their discharge plan. This chapter is likely to be particularly useful for those states struggling with the problems posed by an inability to provide a slow, gradual reintegration back into the community for their SVP commitments.

In Chapter 5, Andrew J. Harris provides a comprehensive overview of cost issues relevant to this type of commitment. He identifies concerns related to the evaluation process, cost of facilities and facility expansion, and costs related to individualized treatment, including transition stages and release.

Many people have mistakenly believed that civil commitment as a sexual offender meant institutionalization for life, when instead it provides for treatment until the offender is capable of returning to the community with a lowered risk for reoffending. Some offender advocates have been outraged at the slow pace of releases from civil commitment programs, while others note that in Wisconsin (where releases are more rapid), more that fifteen of forty-three offenders released from the civil commitment program have already had their supervised release revoked. Some of those revocations were for unauthorized contact with minors, including one individual who was charged with "enticing a minor" (L. Sinclair, personal communication, February 10, 2005). Thus, some may believe that these offenders were released too quickly. However, another way of looking at that data is to say they suggest that nearly two-thirds of those offenders released are apparently doing well in a less restrictive environment. Dennis M. Doren addresses this complicated issue in Chapter 6, where he details the differences in release procedures for those states that have SVP laws and offers his opinion regarding what he believes to be the best model for determining when to release a civilly committed sexual offender.

Chapter 1

Enforcing the Right to Treatment for Civilly Committed Sex Offenders

by C. Justin Brown, J.D. and W. Lawrence Fitch, J.D.

INTRODUCTION

Seventeen states and the District of Columbia have laws for the special civil commitment of sex offenders completing a term of imprisonment.[1] Although nearly all these laws were enacted in the last fifteen years, they have roots dating back more than sixty years.[2] At that time, sex offenders were subject to civil commitment in many states as a therapeutic alternative to prison. The state would have to choose: Prosecute the crime and punish the offender, or seek civil commitment for treatment.[3] Under today's statutes, however, no such choice need be made. These new laws provide for commitment only after an offender has completed his or her sentence and otherwise would be eligible for release.[4]

To critics, these laws are nothing more than an indefinite extension of an offender's criminal sentence. The conditions of confinement in many facilities mirror those in correctional settings,[5] they contend, and treatment programming is not always robust. Professional organizations have been particularly vocal in their objection to these laws. In 1999, a task force of the American Psychiatric Association declared: "[S]exual predator commitment laws represent a serious assault on the integrity of psychiatry. . . . [B]y bending civil commitment to serve essentially non medical purposes, sexual predator commitment statutes threaten to undermine the legitimacy of the medical model of commitment. . . . [T]his represents an unacceptable misuse of psychiatry."[6]

Despite doubts about their purpose and therapeutic value, these laws enjoy broad support among citizens and legislatures concerned about sex offender recidivism. Indeed, many of these laws were enacted in response to heinous crimes committed by released sex offenders.[7]

SEX OFFENDER COMMITMENT STATUTES

A New Breed

The first of this new breed of sex offender commitment statutes—and the statute that has served as the model for legislation in other states—was enacted in Washington State in 1990.[8] Part of a larger bill aimed at protecting the public from dangerous sex offenders, Washington's law targets individuals who would not be candidates for commitment under the state's ordinary (psychiatric) civil commitment law:

> The legislature finds that a small but extremely dangerous group of sexually violent predators exists that do not have a mental disease or defect that renders them appropriate for the existing Involuntary Treatment Act. . . . In contrast to persons appropriate for [ordinary] civil commitment, sexually violent predators generally have antisocial personality disorder features which are unamenable to existing mental illness treatment modalities.[9]

The Washington law provides for the indeterminate commitment of individuals found to be "sexually violent predators."[10] Under the law, a sexually violent predator is "a person who has been convicted of . . . a crime of sexual violence who suffers from a mental abnormality or personality disorder which makes the person likely to engage in predatory acts of sexual violence."[11] "Mental abnormality" is defined as "a congenital or acquired condition affecting the emotional or volitional capacity which predisposes the person to the commission of criminal sexual acts."[12] "Personality disorder" is not defined.

Under Washington law, the commitment process begins when a sex offender is about to be released from prison and an "end-of-sentence review committee" refers the case to a prosecutor.[13] If the prosecutor seeks the offender's commitment, a hearing is held. Upon a finding of probable cause to believe that the offender is a sexually violent predator (SVP), the court commits the offender to the state's Special Commitment Center (SCC) for evaluation.[14] When the evaluation is completed, the case goes back to court and a hearing is held (within forty-five days).[15] The judge (or jury) must decide beyond a reasonable doubt whether the individual is an SVP.[16] If the individual is found to be an SVP, he or she is returned to the SCC.[17] Once committed, the offender is entitled to an annual review.[18]

Confinement Indeterminate

Despite the opportunity for an annual review, few civilly committed sex offenders are released. The result is a system in which those convicted of certain sex crimes face the prospect of continued, indeterminate confinement following service of their criminal sentences. A 2002 survey (of the sixteen jurisdictions with SVP laws in effect at that time) found that 2,478 people were confined in SVP facilities nationally.[19] Only eighty-two people had been released after commitment.[20] Some states with these laws have never released a civilly committed SVP.[21] It has been suggested that the extended commitment of sex offenders reflects either the failure of treatment (to prepare the offender for release) or political pressure not to release even in the face of treatment success.[22]

Ordinary Civil Commitment

Sex offender commitment statutes find their basis in laws for civil commitment of people with mental illnesses. Every state has such a law. There are two legal justifications for involuntary civil commitment: the notion of *parens patriae,* and the state's inherent police power.[23]

Parens Patriae. Under the *parens patriae* rationale, states may hold people against their will in civil confinement for their own protection and safety. Such is the duty of the state as the "parent of the country."[24]

States' Inherent Police Power. Under its police power, a state may commit someone because of the risk he or she poses to public safety. In the context of civil commitment, however, the state's police power has significant constitutional limitation.[25] Indeed, the Supreme Court has ruled that dangerousness alone will not justify an individual's civil commitment to a psychiatric hospital; there must also be a showing of mental illness causing the dangerousness.[26] If the mental condition that led to the individual's confinement no longer exists—or if the individual is no longer a danger to society—he or she may no longer be held.[27]

CHALLENGES TO SPECIAL CIVIL COMMITMENT

Laws for the special civil commitment of sex offenders have been challenged on the ground that they allow commitment without a finding of mental illness—that a "mental abnormality" or "personality disorder" does not constitute the kind of mental disorder that justifies commitment to a mental health facility. In 1997, however, the U.S. Supreme Court in *Kansas v. Hendricks*[28] held otherwise, rejecting the idea that the mental health community should decide which mental conditions are appropriate:

"[W]e have never required State legislatures to adopt any particular nomenclature in drafting civil commitment statutes. Rather, we have traditionally left to legislators the task of defining terms of a medical nature that have legal significance."[29]

Other challenges to the validity of sex offender commitment statutes have centered on constitutional prohibitions against double jeopardy and ex post facto lawmaking. Leroy Hendricks (the first person committed under the Kansas Sexually Violent Predator Act) argued that the law in Kansas had the effect of punishing him for past conduct for which he already had been convicted and served a prison term.[30] If Hendricks's argument was correct, and the law was punitive, then it could not be classified as civil, and the ex post facto and double jeopardy protections would apply.

In a 5–4 decision upholding Hendricks's commitment, however, the U.S. Supreme Court determined that the law was civil based on its legislative intent.[31] Writing for the majority, Justice Thomas concluded that the act had neither of the two objectives of criminal punishment: retribution or deterrence.[32] The majority, moreover, were unmoved by the fact that Hendricks had received "essentially no treatment during this period of commitment."[33] The majority attributed that apparent shortcoming to the novelty of the treatment program, pointing out that treatment was a stated purpose of the commitment. Indeed, Justice Thomas declared, "We have never held that the Constitution prevents a state from civilly detaining those for whom no treatment is available, but who nevertheless pose a danger to others."[34]

In a dissenting opinion, Justice Breyer identified aspects of the statute that made it appear more punitive than civil. In addition to the apparent lack of treatment for committed patients, he noted that the state's concerns about an offender's treatment needs were absent altogether prior to the offender's release from prison, suggesting that the motivation for commitment was not to ensure treatment but, rather, to ensure continued confinement.[35] He also noted the state's failure to provide for alternative, less restrictive forms of treatment,[36] routinely available for individuals subject to ordinary civil commitment.

The Supreme Court's decision in *Hendricks* gave states extraordinary latitude in the construction and use of their SVP laws. First, states were free to define the mental conditions warranting commitment in whatever terms they desired; no longer did an individual need to be "mentally ill." Second, the demands for treatment programming were minimal. Rather than provide services meeting professional standards, states would have only to profess in their statutes that treatment was among the purposes of commitment. Those who were committed would face an uphill battle to enforce their right to treatment.

Hendricks stands today as good law, with one caveat. In 2002, the Court in *Kansas v. Crane*[37] slightly refined the mental condition requirement for commitment, ruling that it must be one that causes the defendant to have "serious difficulty in controlling behavior."[38] Although the implications of this ruling have yet to become clear, early reports suggest that commitments have not been overturned and rates of commitments have not slowed.[39]

THE RIGHT TO TREATMENT

Despite language in Justice Thomas's opinion in *Hendricks,* it is well settled that civilly committed people have a right to treatment. That right, although not clearly and uniformly defined by the courts, is necessary to ensure that confinement is civil rather than punitive and that the conditions of confinement are related to its purpose.

First, without treatment—or at least the guise of treatment—a commitment statute could not pass the test established by the Supreme Court in *Kennedy v. Mendoza-Martinez* to determine if a measure is civil or punitive. Two inquiries from that test apply to the sex offender statutes: (1) whether a law is connected to another assignable purpose, and (2) whether the measure appears excessive considering its other purpose.[40] One stated purpose of every SVP statute is treatment.[41] Without offering the treatment promised, it would be difficult for states to justify the other aspects of commitment that more closely resemble punishment.

Second, the Supreme Court acknowledged in *Youngberg v. Romeo* that civilly committed people retain a protected Fourteenth Amendment liberty interest.[42] In *Youngberg,* the Court considered a Section 1983 (title 42 of the U.S. Code) claim put forth by the mother of a severely retarded man named Romeo who was injured on numerous occasions during his stay in a Pennsylvania facility for people with mental retardation.[43] The Court held that despite the lenient standard for Romeo's placement in the institution, he retained a residual liberty interest under the due process clause.[44] Implicit in that interest was the right to safety and freedom from undue restraint.[45] However, Romeo was asking for more: He wanted at the very least a "minimal" amount of training.[46] The Court agreed, concluding that training was necessary so Romeo could learn to reduce his aggressive behavior, which in turn would promote Romeo's safety and freedom from restraint.[47]

Although the *Youngberg* Court stopped short of declaring a per se right to treatment,[48] other courts have held that the principle on which Romeo was decided ensures a treatment right for persons under civil commitment, including civilly committed sex offenders.[49] Like Romeo, a civilly committed sex offender has a liberty interest manifested in a freedom from undue restraint. Treatment for the sex offender—just like training for Romeo—would promote that freedom. Without treatment, on the other hand, it would be highly probable that the sex offender would remain in the same psychiatric condition indefinitely, never to leave confinement. If effective treatment were possible but was not provided, that restraint would be undue.

The *Youngberg* Court also ruled that judges, when assessing a civil commitment scheme, should defer to the professionals who designed it and give them the benefit of doubt.[50] A hospital or other facility could be held liable for inadequate treatment or conditions only when "the decision by a professional is such a substantial departure from accepted professional judgment, practice, or standards as to demonstrate that the person responsible actually did not base the decision on such a judgment."[51] The Court elaborated that a professional could not be held liable for inadequate standards if shortcomings were caused by budgetary constraints—although this notion was not relied on in subsequent cases.[52]

Finally, under the "duration principle,"[53] put forth in *Jackson v. Indiana,* "due process requires that the nature and duration of commitment bear some reasonable relation to the purpose for which the individual is committed."[54] If the sex offender was committed at least partially for the purpose of treatment, and not purely punitively, then the nature of confinement would have to be therapeutic, providing some opportunity for treatment. The duration of confinement specified by law is tied to treatment as well: "until such a time as the person's mental abnormality or personality disorder has so changed that the person is safe to be at large."[55] Without treatment, the "change" that delimits commitment is not likely to occur.

While the courts seem to recognize a right to treatment for committed sex offenders, two vexing issues remain: (1) determining the quality and extent of treatment that is due; and (2) devising a method by which this treatment right can be enforced.

A LAW UNDER FIRE

Andre Brigham Young was convicted of rape six times over a twenty-two-year period.[56] The day before his release from a Washington State prison in October 1990, the state filed a petition to commit him to the SCC in Monroe, Washington.[57] For the next eleven years, his case was heard in a variety of courts on a variety of issues. Finally, in 2001, it reached the U.S. Supreme Court, in the case *Seling v. Young* (see Appendix 3, this volume).[58]

Seling v. Young

The issue before the Supreme Court in *Young* was whether the Washington sex offender commitment law should be held unconstitutional—not on its face but as it was applied in his case.[59] Young argued that his confinement at the SCC was "too restrictive, that the conditions [were] incompatible with treatment, and that the system [was] designed to result in indefinite confinement."[60] Therefore, he claimed, his confinement was incompatible with the law's stated purpose and had the effect of punishment, in violation of the double jeopardy and ex post facto clauses of the U.S. Constitution.

The Court, however, denied Young's claim, on the ground that as-applied challenges "would prove unworkable."[61] The majority noted that treatment facilities, such as the one in which Young was held, had changing conditions that made it difficult for federal courts to assess their constitutionality.[62] The result was that even if Young was receiving de facto punishment in the SCC, the Supreme Court was in no position to provide the relief Young sought. Rather, the court suggested, Young's remedy lay elsewhere.

Turay v. Seling

Prior to the Court's ruling in *Young*, committed sex offenders in Washington had scored a number of victories in the lower courts, leading to a long-standing injunction against the state's commitment facility.[63] The federal district court in *Turay v. Seling* ordered Washington to improve its SVP facility and established guidelines for how the facility should be run in order to comply with the law.[64] The Supreme Court in *Young* cited these civil actions as the primary recourse for sex offenders objecting to the conditions of their confinement.[65] "It is for the Washington courts to determine whether the Center is operating in accordance with state law and provide a remedy," Justice O'Connor wrote in her majority opinion.[66] In addition, the Court noted, confined sex offenders might have causes of action under federal civil rights law, through Section 1983.[67]

Turay v. Seling produced rulings from both state and federal courts in Washington. Neither had difficulty finding inadequacies in the administration of Washington's commitment law. Indeed, the federal district court found that the state had departed from professional standards to such a degree that the *Youngberg* standard was violated—that "the person responsible actually did not base the [treatment] decision on [professional] judgment."[68]

The SCC was first enjoined in 1994. The court ordered the state to "take certain steps to make constitutionally adequate mental health treatment available at the SCC."[69] In 1998, fifteen inmates sought damages, and the state agreed to pay each claimant $10,000 as well as $250,000 in lawyers' fees.[70] Among the complaints at that time were that the facility was located within a state prison rather than a civil mental health facility, that treatment was inadequate, and that staffing was insufficient.[71] One resident alleged that he was placed in solidary confinement for more than two months and was severely beaten by a counselor.[72]

Later court rulings regarding conditions at the SCC suggested that the facility was making some progress, although not enough. Orders issued in 1998 and 1999 called for further improvement at the SCC.[73] In a 1999 evidentiary hearing, the state conceded that it still had not met professional standards as required under *Youngberg*.[74] Later that year, a federal district court found the state and the SCC guilty of "foot-dragging which had continued for an unconscionable time."[75] The court admonished the state for failing to provide sufficient staff training, failing to provide individualized treatment programs, failing to make adequate provisions for the participation of the residents' families in treatment, failing to distinguish the facility from the state prison, failing to improve the treatment environment by providing for resident grievances and vocational training, failing to institute more oversight, and failing to take "all reasonable steps to bring a constitutionally adequate program into reality rather than merely describing it on paper."[76]

After years of litigation, and rulings in their favor, however, the people held at the Washington SCC still did not have the adequate treatment they were due under the Fourteenth Amendment.[77] Yet it was the promise of a remedy under actions of this type that the Supreme Court pointed to in *Seling v. Young,* when it foreclosed consideration of an as-applied analysis of the law's constitutionality.[78] Reliance on Section 1983 actions was endorsed not only by Justice O'Connor, in her majority opinion, but also by Justice Scalia in his concurrence.[79] By recognizing the availability of such claims, the Court effectively silenced critics who claimed that SVPs had no legal recourse.

STANDARDS FOR TREATMENT

The injunction issued against Washington State for the shortcomings of its SVP treatment facility is something of an aberration. Other courts have not been so willing to make judgments about state treatment programs, and when they have, they have not set such a high bar.[80] The injunction, however, is highly instructive for states responsible for sex offender commitment programs, as it set forth useful guidelines for the establishment and operation of programs.[81] These guidelines were based largely on recommendations made by the Association for the Treatment of Sexual Abusers.[82]

The injunction in *Turay* begins with the requirement that the facility have a staff of trained professionals.[83] Rather than act as prison guards, the staff must be qualified to provide residential care and treatment.[84] The treatment itself should be individualized,[85] as sex offenders may have a wide variety of problems and treatment needs. The treatment should have phases, so that SVPs can mark their progress and work toward community release.[86]

The injunction also provides that civil commitment for sex offenders must be clearly nonpunitive.[87] This can be partially achieved by housing the program outside the confines of a prison, the court observed. The facility should provide space for living, treatment, and other activities,[88] rather than simply confining residents in cells. Residents should be treated with respect, and they should have an outlet for grievances.[89] Finally, there should be some type of external oversight to ensure that the program is being run fairly.[90]

THE FAILURE OF EFFORTS TO GAIN TREATMENT RIGHTS FOLLOWING *SELING V. YOUNG*

In the years following the Supreme Court ruling in *Seling v. Young,* committed sex offenders have filed countless lawsuits asserting their rights to treatment or release under federal and state law. The success of these suits has been limited. Federal courts have shown great deference to the treatment centers and their experts, as the Supreme Court said they could in *Youngberg.* Only the most extreme violations of treatment standards have elicited sympathy from the bench. Second, some states that enacted their SVP laws after the rulings in *Turay* employed language that, although no more lenient, proved less vulnerable to challenge. Finally, Section 1983 claims have been hindered by a fundamental limitation in the civil rights statute: Release from confinement is not a possible remedy.

By relying on *Youngberg,* courts assessing treatment standards for SVPs have been slow to question the judgment of professionals who design and run state programs. To clear this hurdle, a plaintiff with a Section 1983 claim must first present expert testimony that the treatment provided for the plaintiff was insufficient. Second, the plaintiff must overcome the presumption that the state's judgment regarding the adequacy of its program was correct.

Thielman v. Leean

In *Thielman v. Leean,*[91] a federal claim under Section 1983, the plaintiff argued that the Wisconsin sex offender commitment law violated his rights by placing him in full restraints every time he was transported to the hospital, randomly searching his room, requiring him to have contact with prisoners in residential and dining areas, requiring him to provide full disclosure of his sexual offenses in order to receive treatment, and failing to provide overall adequate treatment.[92] Thielman pointed out that sentenced prisoners routinely were considered for different security levels for transport, whereas sex offenders were automatically put in the highest level of security.[93] That alone, Thielman argued, violated due process because the state was not considering less restrictive alternatives.[94] Thielman compared his treatment to that of Leroy Hendricks, the sex offender whose commitment was at issue in *Kansas v. Hendricks.*[95] He noted that Hendricks, in a minimal treatment program, received more than thirty hours of treatment per week, whereas he had received only four to six hours a week of group therapy.[96]

The court, however, was not moved by Thielman's arguments and dismissed his claims because he did not present an expert witness to testify that the state's treatment program was inadequate.[97] The judge wrote: "Plaintiff cannot expect this court to find that defendants are providing constitutionally inadequate treatment just because he says so."[98]

West v. Schwebke

In *West v. Schwebke,* the Court of Appeals for the Seventh Circuit considered an appeal for immunity from the officials who ran the Wisconsin Resource Center.[99] Plaintiffs, civilly committed sex offenders, had filed a claim under Section 1983. At issue was a form of treatment that the Wisconsin Resource Center called "therapeutic seclusion,"[100] in which residents were sometimes kept in a solitary confinement cell that contained only a concrete platform (for use as a bed), a toilet, and a sink.[101] Residents were allowed out of the cell only in shackles, and only one hour per weekday.[102] Sometimes the residents were deprived of clothing.[103] One plaintiff was submitted to "therapeutic seclusion" for eighty-two consecutive days.[104] All sex offenders in the program had been in seclusion at one time or another for at least twenty days.[105] The plaintiffs presented affidavits from two respected psychiatrists stating the treatment was in clear violation of professional standards.[106]

Although the court of appeals did not rule on the adequacy of treatment at the Wisconsin Resource Center, its written opinion highlighted the uphill battle sex offenders face in bringing federal civil rights claims. As Judge Easterbrook wrote for the court: "We grant the proposition . . . that states are entitled to experiment. Detainees need not receive optimal treatment, and the Constitution does not immediately fall into line behind the majority view of a committee appointed by the American Psychiatric Association."[107] The case was sent back to the trial court, and the state settled with the four plaintiffs for $365,000.[108] Wisconsin officials admitted no wrongdoing and attributed the poor conditions at their facility to the fact that the state was still in the early stages of developing its sex offender program.[109]

Munoz v. Kolender

States also have defended their sex offender programs against allegations of punitiveness by contending that restrictive conditions were necessary for safety. In *Munoz v. Kolender*,[110] an SVP challenged his detentions in the San Diego County Jail while he was "awaiting civil proceedings related to his SVP status."[111] His detentions were for periods of three months (twice), five months, and four months.[112] During these detentions, Munoz was handcuffed while talking with his lawyer, submitted to strip searches, and locked down for extended periods of time.[113] The claim, under Section 1983, called for damages and injunctive relief.[114]

The Court rejected Munoz's claim, noting that the conditions of his confinement were not so different from those accepted in *Seling v. Young* and *Kansas v. Hendricks.* The judge noted that those Courts concluded that "Acts permitting segregated confinement in such 'secure facilities' were appropriate and non-punitive because the persons confined were dangerous to the community."[115] If the conditions were considered civil rather than punitive for Young and Hendricks, then they must be considered the same for Munoz. The court also examined the mechanics of a Section 1983 claim, declaring that the plaintiff would have a successful claim only if he identified a "policy so deficient that the policy itself is a repudiation of constitutional rights and is the moving force of the constitutional violation."[116] Facing such a high bar, it was not surprising that the defendant's motion for summary judgment was granted. Not only did Munoz not recover damages, but the state was allowed to continue putting other civil committees in jail for extended periods.

People v. Ciancio

A California appeals court faced a similar issue in *People v. Ciancio.*[117] In *Ciancio,* the state appealed the order of a lower court that required it to provide treatment for alleged SVPs who were in jail awaiting hearings to determine their committability.[118] While in jail, the alleged SVPs were classified in the highest security level.[119] They could not participate in programs that they had been a part of in prison, such as Alcoholics Anonymous.[120] One alleged SVP was assaulted by an inmate, and another was denied medications that he had been prescribed while he was incarcerated.[121] In determining whether these detainees were entitled to treatment, the California court again turned to *Hendricks.*[122] Offering an interpretation of language in Justice Thomas's opinion at odds with interpretations in other court decisions, the Court held that California was not required to provide treatment to SVPs.[123] The court having reached the conclusion that there was no constitutionally protected right to treatment, the plaintiffs then turned to state law for support to their claim. But because they could point to no part of the California statute that required treatment prior to determination of SVP status, their claim failed here as well.[124]

Allison v. Snyder

Second generation statutes for sex offender commitment—those differing from the Washington template—have incorporated new features that also have been challenged under Section 1983. Under the Illinois Sexually Dangerous Persons Act, people charged with sex offenses may be subject to civil commitment before a criminal conviction.[125] In *Allison v. Snyder,* the plaintiffs challenged their commitments on three grounds: (1) they were confined in the wing of a prison, (2) they were required to confess their crimes and submit to polygraph tests, and (3) they received group rather than individual treatment.[126]

The Court of Appeals for the Seventh Circuit, employing a *Youngberg* analysis, sought to determine whether the Illinois officials used reasonable professional standards in devising and implementing their program.[127] The court even considered the treatment recommendations put forth by the Association for Treatment of Sexual Abusers, which differed from those used by Illinois.[128] In the end, however, the plaintiffs could not meet the high bar of proving that the state officials "depart[ed] from accepted professional judgment, practice or standards as to demonstrate that the person responsible actually did not base the decision on such a judgment."[129] The claim against the state of Illinois failed.

Flowers v. Thornton

In *Flowers v. Thornton,*[130] it was the very nature of Section 1983 that doomed the plaintiff's claim. Flowers, who had been diagnosed as "personality disorder, not otherwise specified,"[131] argued that his diagnosis was "experimental" and not one that justified his commitment under the law.[132] Flowers asked the court for money damages and an injunction that would require the state of Wisconsin to cease his treatment[133] The court rejected Flowers's claim not because it doubted that Flowers had been unfairly diagnosed but because it concluded that Flowers was essentially challenging the conditions of his confinement.[134] Therefore, the court held, Flowers's claim would have to fall under Section 2254 (title 28 of the U.S. Code) for habeas corpus relief.[135]

CORRECTIVE MEASURES NECESSARY TO GIVE SEX OFFENDERS LEGAL RECOURSE

The cases discussed above make it clear that committed sex offenders have difficulty enforcing their legal rights to fair treatment. With the Supreme Court having denied offenders ex post facto and double jeopardy protections, the only recourse currently available to SVPs is under state law or a federal Section 1983 claim. These claims, however, have proven ineffective in all but the most extreme circumstances. One reason these claims have failed is that the federal courts defer broadly to states' judgment in implementing treatment programs. Given the nature of sex offender commitment, however, this deference may be short-sighted.

The professional judgment standard established in *Youngberg v. Romeo* may have made sense for Romeo, who was mentally retarded, but it may make no sense in the case of a violent sex offender. Approaches to serving individuals with mental retardation are well established. Moreover, they are almost universally based on a *parens patriae* rationale. People with mental retardation have strong advocates, and sometimes family, who carefully monitor the conditions in which they live. The same cannot be said for SVPs, who are held primarily under the state's police power. SVPs are among the most despised people in society. Even in prison settings, they are shunned. Some people working in facilities for sex offenders admit that they view themselves as jailers rather than therapists.[136] Many sex offenders lack the outside support of friends and family, who may be too embarrassed to associate with them.

Accordingly, deference to the state's experts, as approved by *Youngberg,* may be the wrong approach to take in assessing the suitability of programs for committed SVPs. Clearly, alternative remedies are needed if sex offenders are to receive fair treatment in state commitment programs.

NEW REMEDIES UNDER *ZADVYDAS* AND *JACKSON*

When states fail to provide adequate treatment, people held in civil commitment should have viable claims for release based on the liberty interests they retain as civil detainees.[137] Until recently, enforcement of these rights has been sought on ex post facto and double jeopardy grounds—grounds the Supreme Court denied in *Hendricks*. An alternative remedy, however, may be derived from the Supreme Court's decisions in *Zadvydas v. Davis*[138] and *Jackson v. Indiana.*[139]

Kestutis Zadvydas was a resident alien of Lithuanian descent who, in 1994, was ordered deported by the Immigration and Naturalization Service (INS) on the grounds of a criminal conviction.[140] When the INS tried to ship Zadvydas to another country, however, the agency ran into a problem: It could find no country willing to take him.[141] Zadvydas, therefore, remained in U.S. custody.

In 2001, when the U.S. Supreme Court considered Zadvydas's case, it looked to the INS removal statute to determine whether it contained any time limitation on the detention of a deportee.[142] Because the statute was silent on that issue, the Court offered a constitutional limitation: "In our view, the statute, read in light of the Constitution's demands, limits an alien's post-removal-period detention to a period reasonably necessary to bring about that alien's removal from the United States."[143] Ultimately, for the purpose of administrative efficiency, the Court set a period of six months for the agency to complete removal.[144] After this time has expired, if the alien shows good reason to believe that he or she will not be removed in the reasonably foreseeable future, the government must respond with evidence to rebut that showing or the alien must be released.[145]

Although the basis for detaining an alien pending deportation is significantly different from that underlying the commitment of a sex offender, the duration of confinement for either may be subject to the same constitutional test. Just as the deportable alien cannot be held indefinitely without hope for release, a committed sex offender should not be subject to continued confinement if the treatment for which he or she was committed is unavailable or ineffective, leaving the offender with no meaningful hope for recovery and release.

The *Zadvydas* opinion has its roots in the U.S. Supreme Court's 1972 decision in *Jackson v. Indiana.*[146] In *Jackson,* the Supreme Court ruled that commitment of a criminal defendant for purposes of restoring his or her competency to stand trial is constitutional only as long as there is a substantial probability that the defendant will regain trial competency in the foreseeable future. The nature of confinement must be related to its purpose, the Court declared. Thus, if it becomes apparent that a defendant committed for purposes of competency restoration is unrestorable, any continued confinement must be justified by a different purpose (e.g., civil commitment).

As discussed earlier, it is generally accepted that treatment is one essential purpose of sex offender civil commitment. But treatment is meaningless—and serves no purpose—unless the recipient stands to benefit from the treatment. Unless an individual committed as an SVP has some prospect of improvement and eventual release, what can be the purpose of his or her confinement? It must be punishment or incapacitation for the sake of public safety. But neither purpose provides justification for confinement in a treatment facility.[147] Accordingly, under the principles in both *Zadvydas* and *Jackson,* such an individual should be released.

For many sex offenders, treatment and other services have much to offer. If a state's treatment programs are deficient, however, there may be no benefit to commitment. As states struggle to meet budgets, unpopular programs, like those for SVPs, stand to receive insufficient support. If only as a means of incentivizing states to offer quality services for committed sex offenders, with a goal of community reintegration, the courts would be well advised to give serious consideration to constitutional claims based on *Zadvydas* and *Jackson.*

CONCLUSION

Beginning with its 1997 ruling in *Kansas v. Hendricks,* the Supreme Court has gradually stripped away the constitutional protections afforded people subject to civil commitment. After the Court's ruling in *Seling v. Young,* it appeared there was virtually nothing left to prevent the indeterminate confinement of sex offenders. *Young* offered only one possible recourse: claims under Section 1983.

In the years since *Young*, however, most Section 1983 claims have failed, as the courts have shown great deference to state authorities. New approaches are needed to ensure fair treatment for committed sex offenders. One such approach is outlined in this chapter. Should the courts hold sex offender commitment to the standards they have applied to the detention of aliens pending deportation (under *Zadvydas*) and the commitment of defendants found incompetent to stand trial (under *Jackson*), limiting the state's authority to confine these individuals indefinitely, the challenge to provide therapeutic benefit for committed sex offenders should take on a new urgency and the business of commitment a new respectability.

Footnotes

[1] Arizona, California, District of Columbia, Florida, Illinois, Iowa, Kansas, Massachusetts, Minnesota, Missouri, North Dakota, New Jersey, Pennsylvania (only for individuals leaving confinement in the state's juvenile justice system), South Carolina, Texas (outpatient commitment only), Virginia, Washington, and Wisconsin.

[2] W. Lawrence Fitch, "Sexual Offender Commitment in the United States, Legislative and Policy Concerns," 989 *Ann. N.Y. Acad. Sci.* 489 (2003). Pennsylvania also has a similar provision, but it applies to sex offenders aging out of the juvenile system.

[3] Id.

[4] Id. Note, however, that statutes in some states may also be used for the commitment of individuals charged with a criminal offense but found to be incompetent to stand trial or not guilty by reason of insanity and not otherwise subject to confinement.

[5] *See, e.g.*, Thielman v. Leean, 140 F. Supp. 2d 982, 989, 1000 (W.D. Wis. 2001) (describing the Wisconsin Resource Center for sex offenders, in which full shackles were placed on offenders while they were transported and offenders' treatment consisted of group therapy twice a week for two or three hours—or 2 percent of their time at the Center).

[6] American Psychiatric Association, *Dangerous Sex Offenders: A Task Force Report of the American Psychiatric Association* 173–174 (1999).

[7] Washington State enacted its law following the sexual mutilation of a 7-year-old Tacoma boy by a paroled sex offender. Measures to crack down on sex offenders received even broader support following the 1994 rape and murder of 7-year-old Megan Kanka in New Jersey by a repeat sex offender who lived across the street from the unsuspecting Kanka family.

[8] Wash. Rev. Code § 71.09.010.

[9] Id.

[10] Id.

[11] Wash. Rev. Code § 71.09.030

[12] Wash. Rev. Code § 71.09.020(2).

[13] Roxanne Lieb & Scott Matson, *Sexual Predator Laws in the United States: 1998 Update* 7 (1998), available: *http://www.wsipp.wa.gov/rptfiles/sexcomm_98.pdf* (last checked April 9, 2004).

[14] Id.

[15] Id.

[16] Id.

[17] Lieb & Matson, *supra* note 12, at 7.

[18] Id.

[19] Fitch, *supra* note 2, at 492.

[20] Id.

[21] Bruce J. Winick, Ken Kress & John Q. La Fond, "Outpatient Commitment's Next Frontier: Sexual Predators," 9 *Psychol. Pub. Pol'y & L.* 159 (2003).

[22] Bruce J. Winick, "Sex Offenders: Scientific, Legal, and Policy Perspective: Sexually Violent

Predator Laws and Registration and Community Notification Laws: Policy Analysis: Sex Offender Law in the 1990s: A Therapeutic Jurisprudence Analysis," 4 *Psychol. Pub. Pol'y & L.* 505, 544 (1998).

[23] David DePugh, "The Right to Treatment for Involuntary Committed Sex Offenders in the Wake of *Kansas v. Hendricks*," 17 *Buff. Pub. Interest L.J.* 71, 73–74 (1999).

[24] Id.

[25] Eric S. Janus & Wayne A. Logan, "Substantive Due Process and the Involuntary Confinement of Sexually Violent Predators," 35 *Conn. L. Rev.* 319, 344 (2003).

[26] Foucha v. Louisiana, 504 U.S. 71 (1992).

[27] *See* Jones v. United States, 463 U.S. 354, 369 (1983) ("Thus . . . no matter how serious the crime committed by the aquittee, he may be released . . . if he has recovered").

[28] 521 U.S. 346 (1997).

[29] Id. at 357.

[30] Id. at 361.

[31] To make this determination, the Court relied partially on the civil-punitive test put forth in Kennedy v. Mendoza-Martinez, 372 U.S. 144 (1963). The test asked whether (1) the sanction produced an affirmative disability, (2) the measure was historically punitive, (3) it required a finding of scienter, (4) its application promoted traditional forms of punishment, (5) it applied to behavior that was already a crime, (6) it was connected to another assignable purpose, and (7) it appeared excessive when compared to its other purpose. Id. at 168–169.

[32] *Hendricks, supra* note 28, at 361–362.

[33] Id. at 384 (Breyer, J., dissenting) (quoting Hendricks's program director).

[34] Id. at 359

[35] Id. at 385 (Breyer, J., dissenting).

[36] Id. at 387 (Breyer, J., dissenting).

[37] Kansas v. Crane, 534 U.S. 407 (2002).

[38] Id. at 412.

[39] Discussion among members of the Forensic Division of the National Association of State Mental Health Program Directors during a session captioned "C3I," at the Division's annual meeting, in Savannah, GA, September 2004.

[40] Kennedy v. Mendoza-Martinez, 372 U.S. 144, 168–169 (1963). These are the last two inquiries in a seven-part test.

[41] Janus & Logan, *supra* note 25, at 348.

[42] 457 U.S. 307, 317–318 (1982).

[43] Id. at 310.

[44] Id. at 317–318.

[45] Id.

[46] Id. at 317.

[47] Id. at 320.

[48] Id. at 318. The court said it would not consider "the difficult question whether a mentally retarded person, involuntarily committed to a state institution, has some general constitutional right to training *per se.*" Id.

[49] *See* Allison v. Snyder, 332 F.3d 1076, 1079 (7th Cir. 2003) (noting that, based on *Youngberg*, Allen v. Illinois, 478 U.S. 364 (1986) (challenging the Illinois Sexually Dangerous Persons Act) and Seling v. Young, 531 U.S. 250 (2001) (challenging the Washington Act), "detainees are entitled to some kind of treatment.")

[50] *Youngberg, supra* note 42, at 323.

[51] Id.

[52] Id. In *Turay v. Seling,* the U.S. District Court for the Western District of Washington noted that states could not justify their treatment failures by citing a lack of funds or staff. 108 F. Supp. 2d

1148, 1151 (2000) (citing to Ohlinger v. Watson, 652 F.2d 775, 778–779 (9th Cir. 1980)).

[53] *See* Janus & Logan, *supra* note 25, at 351 (describing the "duration principle," which requires, as the goal of treatment, "reasonable progress toward release").

[54] 406 U.S. 715, 738 (1972).

[55] Wash. Rev. Code § 71.09.100.

[56] Young v. Weston, 898 F. Supp. 744, 748 (W.D. Wash. 1995).

[57] Id.

[58] Seling v. Young, 531 U.S. 250 (2001).

[59] Id. at 263.

[60] Id. at 262.

[61] Id. at 263.

[62] Id.

[63] 108 F. Supp. 2d 1148, 1160 (2000).

[64] Id.

[65] *Young, supra* note 58, at 265.

[66] Id.

[67] Id. Section 1983 makes it possible for people to sue state officials in federal court, so long as a constitutional right has been violated and the official acted under color of state law.

[68] *Turay, supra* note 52, at 1152 (citing Youngberg v. Romeo, 457 U.S. 307, 323 (1982)).

[69] Id. at 1152.

[70] Id.

[71] Carter, *supra* note 9.

[72] Id.

[73] Turay, *supra* note 52, at 1153.

[74] Id.

[75] Id.

[76] Id. at 1154–1158.

[77] 531 U.S. 250, 277 n.3 (Stevens, J., dissenting) ("In this case, those detained pursuant to Washington's statute have sought an improvement in conditions for almost seven years. Their success in the courts, however, has had little practical impact.").

[78] Id. at 265.

[79] Id. at 269–270 (Scalia, J., concurring).

[80] *See infra,* notes 114–157 (showing the courts' deference to states in determining what kind of treatment is appropriate for sex offenders who were civilly committed).

[81] When assessing treatment schemes, it is helpful to appreciate the difference—or lack of difference—between treatment and conditions. Most courts do not make a clear distinction, for the reason that conditions of confinement often have a direct impact on the treatment itself.

[82] The suggested guidelines from the Association for the Treatment of Sexual Abusers can be found at the organization's web site, www.atsa.com. The ATSA guidelines are included as an appendix to the decision issued in Turay v. Seling, 108 F. Supp. 2d 1148, 1160–1161 (2000).

[83] *Turay, supra* note 52, at 1160–1161 (2000).

[84] Id.

[85] Id.

[86] Id.

[87] Id.

[88] Id.

[89] Id.

[90] Id.

91 140 F. Supp. 2d 982 (W.D. Wis. 2001). The court eventually determined that this claim was moot because the plaintiff was allowed to advance in his treatment program without making such disclosures. Id. at 986.

93 Id. at 984.

93 Id. at 991.

94 Id.

95 Id. at 1000.

96 Id.

97 Id. at 1001.

98 Id.

99 333 F.3d 745, 748 (2003).

100 Id. at 747.

101 Id.

102 Id. They were not allowed out of solitary on weekends because of lower staffing levels. Id.

103 Id.

104 Id.

105 Id.

106 Id.

107 Id. at 748.

108 Reid J. Epstein, "State Settling 4 Men's Suit over Seclusion," *Milwaukee J. Sentinel*, Oct. 3, 2003, at 1B (available at 2003 WL 58663872). The men each received $500 for each day they spent in seclusion.

109 Id.

110 208 F. Supp. 2d 1125 (2002).

111 Id.at 1130.

112 Id. at 1144.

113 Id.

114 Id. at 1130.

115 Id. at 1143. The court failed to point out, however, that a major point of contention in the *Seling* injunctions was the fact that the SVP facility was housed within the state prison. *See supra* notes 78–82 (explaining the inadequacies of the Washington program and pointing out the state's failure to distinguish the SVP facilities from the prison facilities).

116 Id. at 1151–1152 (citing Mackinney v. Nielsen, 69 F.3d 1002, 1008 (9th Cir. 1995)).

117 109 Cal. App. 4th 175 (2003).

118 Id. at 181.

119 Id. at 188.

120 Id.

121 Id.

122 Id. at 195.

123 Id. The court reached this conclusion by following the holding of another California court that interpreted *Hendricks* to hold that SVPs were not entitled to treatment. Id. (citing Hubbart v. Superior Court, 19 Cal. 4th 1138 (1999)). *But see* Allison v. Snyder, 332 F.3d 1076, 1079 (7th Cir. 2003) (pointing out that "detainees are entitled to some kind of treatment.").

124 Id. at 196.

125 *Allison, supra* note 49, at 1078.

126 Id.

127 Id. at 1080–1081.

128 Id. at 1081.

129 Youngberg v. Romeo, 457 U.S. 307, 323 (1982).

[130] 2001 WL 34373017 (W.D. Wis.)

[131] Id. at 2.

[132] Id.

[133] Id. at 3.

[134] Id.

[135] Id.

[136] Winick, *supra* note 22, at 545.

[137] *See supra* notes 52–57 (explaining the liberty interest retained by a civil detainee under *Youngberg*).

[138] *See* 533 U.S. 678, 683 (2001) (holding that a statute allowing detention of aliens awaiting deportation contained an implicit "reasonable time" limitation). For a discussion of the application of *Zadvydas* to sex offenders, *see also* Janus & Logan, *supra* note 25, at 354–356.

[139] 406 U.S. 715, 738 (1972).

[140] Id. at 684.

[141] Id. He was rejected by Germany, Lithuania, and the Dominican Republic—three countries to which he had ties but no claim of citizenship. Id.

[142] Id. at 688–689.

[143] Id. at 689.

[144] Id. at 701.

[145] Id.

[146] 406 U.S. 715, 738 (1972).

[147] Foucha v. Louisiana, 504 U.S. 71 (1992).

Chapter 2

Admissibility of Expert Testimony Regarding Recidivism Risk in Sexually Violent Predator Proceedings

by Randy K. Otto, Ph.D. and John Petrila, J.D., LL.M.

INTRODUCTION

Contemporary sexually violent predator (SVP) laws, which typically provide for the indeterminate civil commitment of persons with a history of sexual offending upon completion of their criminal sentences, have been in existence for approximately fifteen years. Although SVP laws vary across the seventeen states in which they have been implemented, they have a fair number of similarities (Janus & Walbeck, 2000; Miller, Amenta, & Conroy, 2005). SVP statutes typically require (1) an established history of sexual offending (demonstrated by a conviction for or plea to some type of sexual offense), (2) the presence of an underlying mental disorder (broadly defined and conceptualized), which (3) places the offender at increased risk for committing another sexual offense (with the likelihood of or risk for reoffending required varying across jurisdictions), that (4) necessitates some type of commitment (some states allow for outpatient or inpatient commitment—e.g., Washington, others allow only for inpatient commitment—e.g., Florida, and at least one state—Texas—provides only for outpatient commitment).

Adoption and implementation of this type of legislation have been controversial. Proponents have argued that SVP laws provide for the protection of the public and control and treatment of offenders (e.g., Held, 1999; Shaw & Funderburk, 1999), while critics have suggested that SVP legislation does little more than provide for extended confinement of a particularly unsympathetic and repugnant class of offenders (Cohen, 1997; Morse, 1998; Schwartz, 1999). SVP laws are here to stay, however, as legal challenges posed by the defense bar have generally met with little success (Janus, 2000). Specifically, arguments that SVP laws constitute double jeopardy, are ex post facto, violate substantive and procedural due process concerns, and are inappropriate given limitations in the ability of mental health professionals to accurately assess reoffense risk have consistently been rejected by the courts (La Fond, 2005; Kozlowski, 2001). As we predicted a little more than four years ago (Petrila & Otto, 2001), because the more general legal challenges to SVP laws have been unsuccessful, defense attorneys have subsequently focused their attention on mental health professionals' ability to assess recidivism risk and identify that subset of offenders who qualify for commitment as a result. It is this body of appellate litigation that we review with the goals of better understanding how the courts are treating this body of risk testimony and providing direction to attorneys and mental health professionals who practice in this forum.

PRELIMINARY ISSUES

Before embarking on a review of cases, some preliminary issues need to be elaborated.

Limitations of Reviewing Appellate Cases

There are limitations in analyzing appellate cases as a way of surveying the legal landscape. Although describing and understanding the decision making of appellate courts is important because of the direction such decisions provide to trial courts, it must be remembered that only select cases are set for appeal. As a result, such decisions do not necessarily reflect what is occurring on a regular basis in the trial courts. But because trial courts' judgments and rulings are not consistently reported, we are left to review the work of the appellate courts and advise the interested reader of this caveat. But such reviews are not without merit. As noted previously, and as the discussion that follows will make clear, appellate opinions ultimately control trial court decision making; thus, these opinions do reflect the current state of law and what is likely occurring on a day-to-day basis.

Admissibility Rulings

We are struck by how frequently commentators in this and related areas, when discussing such cases, make reference to courts "ruling inadmissible" particular assessment techniques or analytic approaches. Strictly speaking, a court never offers a judgment about whether a particular approach or technique is admissible. Rather, trial and appellate courts reach decisions about whether certain testimony, based in full or in part on a particular approach or technique, is admissible under applicable rules of evidence. The end result of such decisions, of course, is that experts are likely to abandon use of assessment techniques when expert opinions based on them have been ruled inadmissible.

Varying Rules of Evidence and Tests for Admissibility

In considering the courts' treatment of expert testimony regarding recidivism risk, it is important to keep in mind the law that controls such testimony. Although a complete review of evidentiary law that controls the admissibility of expert testimony in SVP proceedings is beyond the scope of this chapter and is offered elsewhere (see, e.g., Petrila & Otto, 2001), some review is merited.

When questions about the scientific foundation of proffered testimony are raised, courts typically rely on the rules of evidence in operation in the jurisdiction, usually applying one of two legal standards or "tests" that shape the judge's consideration of the evidence that has been proffered. The oldest standard—the *"Frye* test"—was devised by a federal circuit court in 1923 in its ruling about the (in)admissibility of expert testimony based on an early version of the polygraph. The *Frye* court instructed trial judges considering whether expert testimony based on scientific evidence should be admitted to determine whether "the thing from which the deduction is made . . . [is] sufficiently established to have gained general acceptance in the particular field in which it belongs."[1] Many states subsequently adopted and employ legal tests akin to *Frye*. For example, California courts developed and adopted a *Frye*-like standard in *People v. Kelly*,[2] while Florida's version of *Frye* appears in *Ramirez v. State*.[3]

The "general acceptance" standard enunciated in *Frye* has been criticized on several grounds. For example, some have described it as vague and not providing direction to the fact finder in its use of terms such as "sufficiently established," "general acceptance," and "particular field in which it belongs." Others have criticized the test as one that abdicates judicial decision-making responsibility, by directing judges to defer to the relevant scientific community when ruling on the admissibility of challenged expert opinion (Faigman, Kaye, Saks, & Sanders, 1997).

In 1993, the Supreme Court rejected the general acceptance standard enunciated in *Frye* in its decision in *Daubert v. Merrell Dow Pharmaceuticals*.[4] Although some state courts have continued to employ the general acceptance test, federal courts and a large number of state courts now base decisions regarding the admissibility of challenged expert testimony on a consideration of four factors identified by the Supreme Court in *Daubert*: (1) the testability or falsifiability of the method, (2) the error rate of the method (if known), (3) whether the matter at issue has been subjected to peer review and publication, and (4) general acceptance of the method in the relevant fields. Providing further insight into the Court's reasoning about this issue is commentary it offered in a case elaborating on the standard established by *Daubert*. In *Kumho Tire Co. v. Carmichael*,[5] the Supreme Court observed that the judicial gatekeeper is to "make certain that an expert . . . employs in the courtroom the same level of intellectual rigor that characterizes the practice of an expert in the relevant field."[6]

CASE ANALYSES

The large majority of states that have considered admissibility of expert testimony regarding recidivism risk in SVP proceedings are *Frye* jurisdictions. Regardless of the standard involved, the trial judge is required to make a threshold determination regarding the admissibility of the testimony and opinion offered; this puts the judge in the position of having to make some determination regarding the scientific merit of the evidence—a challenging task when a field is evolving and is in a comparatively early stage, which is the case with the risk assessment instruments developed for use in SVP proceedings.

A review of the relevant appellate cases indicates that courts have take a variety of approaches when asked to determine the admissibility of expert testimony regarding the reoffense risk of sex offenders in the context of SVP proceedings. A handful of appellate courts have ruled that the threshold determination of admissibility under *Frye* or *Daubert* is not relevant because *Frye* or *Daubert* analyses do not apply to expert testimony offered by mental health professionals. In contrast, the majority of appellate courts have ruled that such proffered testimony is subject to such considerations and analysis. In some cases, however, the courts have chosen to address the issue from a quite broad perspective, and they have concluded that the question of admissibility of expert testimony of mental health professionals regarding future risk has been long decided. Other courts, however, have distinguished expert testimony regarding risk for sexual reoffending from other types of expert risk testimony (e.g., general offending and violence). This section offers a representation of these cases.

Expert Testimony Regarding Risk in SVP Proceedings Is Not Subject to *Frye* or *Daubert* Analysis

In some cases in which the admissibility of mental health professionals' expert testimony regarding risk is at issue, the courts have ruled that such evidence is not subject to consideration via *Frye* or *Daubert*-like tests. Although the courts have come to this conclusion in two very different ways, the end result of this body of decisions, not surprisingly, is that such testimony is ultimately allowed.

Expert Testimony of Mental Health Professionals Is "Different." After distinguishing expert testimony offered by psychologists and psychiatrists from "science-based testimony," some appellate courts have ruled that tests like *Frye* or *Daubert* are not applicable. For example, in *People v. Ward*,[7] Ronald Ward appealed his commitment as a sexually violent predator, in part, based on the trial court's decision to admit the expert testimony of a psychologist and psychiatrist regarding his risk for reoffending. Ward argued that this decision constituted reversible error because there was no scientifically accepted way of making such predictions. In upholding Ward's commitment and the trial court's decision to admit the testimony, the appellate court concluded that expert psychiatric and psychological testimony in such cases was not subject to *Kelly-Frye* analysis.[8] Of particular interest is the court's citation of case law related to this issue[9] and its explanation that "California distinguishes between expert medical opinion and scientific evidence; the former is not subject to the special admissibility rule of *Kelly-Frye* . . . [which] applies to cases involving novel devices or processes, not to expert medical testimony, such as a psychiatrist's prediction of future dangerousness of a diagnosis of mental illness. Similarly, the testimony of a psychologist who assesses whether a criminal defendant displays signs of deviance or abnormality is not subject to *Kelly-Frye*."[10]

Michael Therrian appealed his California commitment as a sexually violent predator based, in part, on his claim that the trial court wrongfully denied his request for a pretrial hearing to consider the admissibility of expert testimony offered by a psychologist and psychiatrist called by the state, and that their testimony was wrongfully admitted as a result.[11] At trial, both professionals opined that Therrian suffered from a mental disorder that made him likely to engage in sexually violent criminal behavior. These experts' opinions were based on the examinee's score on the Static-99 (Hanson & Thornton, 2000), a six-item actuarial measure designed to identify groups of sexual offenders at greater and lesser risk for sexual reoffending, as well their clinical assessments of case-specific factors. In affirming the trial court's decision, the appellate court reviewed California evidence law and cited *People v. Stoll*,[12] in which the Supreme Court of California offered that only novel expert testimony that appears "both in name and description to provide some definitive truth which the expert need only accurately recognize and relay to the jury" such as "machines or procedures which analyze physical data" was subject to the *Frye*-like general acceptance test the same court adopted in *People v. Kelly*.[13] The Court's decision in *Stoll* was based on the court's concern that "lay minds might easily, but erroneously, assume that [machine-based techniques] are objective and infallible."[14] The court ruled that because the mental health professionals' expert risk testimony about the appellant was based, at least in part, on their clinical evaluations of him, it was not subject to evidentiary review via *Kelly-Frye*. The *Therrian* court left undecided whether a *Kelly* hearing would have been required if the experts' testimony was based solely on the results of the Static-99.

A similar outcome was reached in *Westerheide v. State*.[15] The Florida appellate court, while noting that Westerheide had abandoned that portion of his appeal challenging the admissibility of testimony offered by two psychologists regarding his risk for reoffending, found that risk testimony of mental health professionals that is based on training and experience, and which is therefore "pure opinion" testimony, is not subject to analysis under the *Frye* standard (also see this same appellate court's ruling in *Pedroza v. State*[16]).

Expert Testimony of Mental Health Professionals Regarding Risk Is Not New or Novel. Other appellate courts have concluded that the threshold analyses required by *Frye* or *Daubert* are unnecessary because mental health professionals' expert testimony regarding violence risk has long been admitted, rendering such assessments and opinions in SVP cases, and the techniques on which such opinion testimony is based, anything but "new" or "novel." In reaching this conclusion, appellate courts have chosen for analysis and consideration violence risk assessment testimony broadly, rather than expert testimony regarding assessment for risk for sexual reoffending, or assessment of reoffense risk using a particular technique, such as one of the following actuarial measures: the Minnesota Sex Offender Screening Tool (MnSOST-R; Epperson, et al., 1999), the Violence Risk Appraisal Guide (VRAG; Webster, Harris, Rice, Cormier, & Quinsey, 1994), or the Static-99 (Hanson & Thornton, 2000). Had the courts chosen as the focus for analysis testimony based on use of specific instruments, rather than risk assessment more generally, it is possible that some of these cases would have reached a different conclusion, because assessing the risk of sexual offending is a much newer enterprise than risk assessment more broadly defined.

The best example of such an approach is provided by the Supreme Court of Washington. In *In re Young*,[17] the appellant challenged his commitment as a sexually violent predator, in part, based on the claim that the trial court wrongfully admitted testimony by two mental health professionals regarding his reoffense risk. With support from the Washington State Psychiatric Association, Young argued that testimony regarding his recidivism risk was grounded in theory that was not generally accepted in the relevant scientific community. In rejecting the appellant's argument, the Court concluded: "The sciences of psychology and psychiatry are not novel; they have been an integral part of the American legal system since its inception."[18] The Court also noted that it had already determined that such testimony was sufficiently accurate and reliable in a previous case—*In re Harris*[19]—a civil commitment case in which the admissibility of mental health professionals' expert testimony regarding violence risk was unsuccessfully challenged. Of particular interest is the *Young* court's acknowledgment, via its citation of part of its *Harris* decision, that ruling to the contrary had the potential to preclude SVP commitments, "Petitioner's argument would eviscerate the entire law of involuntary commitment as well as render dubious the numerous other areas where psychiatry and law intersect. There is no question that prediction of dangerousness has its attendant problems. . . . But we are not prepared to abandon the possibility of conforming the law of involuntary civil commitment to the requirements of the Constitution."[20]

The Washington Supreme Court used similar reasoning in a later case as well.[21] In considering the appeal of Elmer Campbell, who challenged his commitment as an SVP on grounds that mental health professionals could not offer "expert opinions" regarding dangerousness generally and risk for sexual reoffending more specifically, the Court ruled that its decision in *Young* had decided the question of the admissibility of expert testimony regarding dangerousness. Concerns about the accuracy of such professional judgments could be addressed at trial via cross-examination and would ultimately go to the weight accorded the evidence, ruled the court.

Expert Testimony Regarding Risk in SVP Proceedings Is Subject to *Frye* or *Daubert* Analysis

In contrast to the foregoing, a number of courts have ruled that mental health professionals' expert testimony regarding risk for sexual reoffending is subject to review using a *Frye*- or *Daubert*-like analysis because the techniques underlying the opinion may be new or novel. In these cases, with few exceptions, the courts have ruled that expert testimony about recidivism risk is admissible, and expert opinion based on any kind of assessment technique, tool, or approach has been allowed.

For example, In *In re Holtz*,[22] the appellant challenged the trial court's decision to admit expert testimony based, in part, on actuarial measures including the Rapid Risk Assessment for Sex Offender Recidivism (RRASOR), MnSOST, and MnSOST-R. The Iowa Court of Appeals ruled that the trial court's decision to admit this testimony was not reversible error, and that concerns about the accuracy of such techniques should go to the weight of the evidence. Of some interest, however, is the court's commentary that "we are not concluding that actuarial risk assessment instruments are reliable *per se* or have our approval when used alone and not in conjunction with a full clinical evaluation. We note this was not the situation or issue presented in the instant case. The instruments were used in conjunction with a full clinical evaluation and their limitations were clearly made known to the jury."[23]

The Wisconsin Court of Appeals reached a similar conclusion when it considered the admissibility of expert testimony regarding reoffense risk in SVP proceedings in two cases. In *State v. Tainter*,[24] the court ruled that the trial court's decision to admit expert testimony regarding reoffense risk based, in part, on actuarial measures was appropriate given that such measures employed "the type of information commonly and reasonably relied upon by experts in the field of sex offender risk assessment."[25] Similarly, in *State v. Lalor*,[26] the same court ruled that expert testimony regarding reoffense risk based, in part, on instruments including the MnSOST, MnSOST-R, VRAG, and Psychopathy Checklist—Revised (PCL-R; Hare, 1991) was admissible. Also of interest is the *Lalor* court's response to the appellant's claim that the expert opinion offered at trial was not "personalized" insofar as the actuarial measures employed by the testifying experts referenced group data rather than information or data regarding the appellant himself. In rejecting this argument, the court noted that the trial court "could not predict Lalor's propensities to reoffend in a vacuum. The court required the assistance of the expert testimony and the studies that such experts employ. The court then applied such evidence to Lalor's particular situation."[27] It is worth noting that other judges on occasion have asserted that probabilistic risk assessment tools offend the core criminal law principle that *individual* guilt is to be adjudicated; however, this view has not persuaded a majority of an appellate court to date (Petrila & Otto, 2001).

In *Jackson v. State*,[28] the Fourth District Court of Appeals in Florida ruled that the trial court did not err in determining that the actuarial measures relied on by the examiners were generally accepted by the relevant scientific community with respect to assessment of reoffense risk. More recently, the Second District Court of Appeals in Florida ruled that testimony based on the RRASOR and the PCL-R met *Frye* requirements, while testimony based on use of the Sexual Violence Risk-20 (SVR-20; Boer, Hart, Kropp, & Webster, 1997), a structured professional judgment approach, was "pure opinion" and so not subject to *Frye* scrutiny.[29]

The Illinois Supreme Court recently resolved a conflict within Illinois courts regarding the admissibility of this type of evidence. In *In re Commitment of Simons*,[30] the Court ruled that testimony based on the MnSOST-R, the Static-99, the VRAG, and the Sex Offender Risk Appraisal Guide (SORAG; Quinsey, Harris, Rice, & Cormier, 1998) was admissible regardless of whether it specifically met *Frye* standards. The Court offered that actuarial risk assessment "is generally accepted by professionals who assess sexually violent offenders and therefore is perfectly admissible in a court of law. As of this writing, experts in at least nineteen other states rely upon actuarial risk assessment in forming their opinions on sex offenders' risk of recidivism."[31] Before the state supreme court's ruling, the Illinois courts had been split on the question. In *People v. Taylor*,[32] the Second District Court of Appeals had concluded that *Frye* applied to testimony flowing from a number of sex offender risk assessment instruments and that the instruments were too novel to pass muster under *Frye*. The appellate court wrote: "Whether these tools are viewed as psychological tests or actuarial instruments, they certainly constitute a scientific methodology for predicting sex offender recidivism. As such a methodology has yet to be adopted in a court proceeding in Illinois, the court was obligated to show that these instruments have gained acceptance in the relevant scientific community required under *Frye*."[33] This same court reached a similar conclusion in *In re Detention of Hargett*.[34] A year later, the same appellate court ruled that a trial court had erred in admitting expert testimony regarding reoffense risk based on sex offender risk assessment instruments under *Frye* in an SVP proceeding, but that the error was harmless to the defendant because other evidence before the court and unrelated to use of the instruments supported the opinions of the state experts.[35] Two panels of the Illinois Fourth District Court of Appeals reached different conclusions about admissibility *on the same day*. In *In re Detention of Bolton*[36] the court reached in a 2–1 decision that actuarial instruments instilled a "false sense of confidence" in the decision maker's reliance on what was essentially the subjective opinion of the expert and that therefore testimony based on use of these instruments did not satisfy the *Frye* test. In contrast, in *In re Detention of Erbe*[37] a different panel of the same court ruled that (1) actuarial assessment tools were not scientific approaches, (2) even if actuarial approaches were scientific approaches they were not new or novel, and (3) even if they were considered to be new or novel scientific approaches, actuarial approaches like those used in SVP proceedings were generally accepted by the relevant scientific community. Judge Myerscough sat on both panels and was the deciding vote in the *Bolton* opinion ruling that these instruments did not meet *Frye* standards; in *Erbe* he was the dissenting vote. Given the conflicting views among appellate courts in Illinois on the admissibility question, it is not surprising that the Illinois Supreme Court eventually decided the question in *Simons*.

In *In re Commitment of R.S.*[38] the Superior Court of New Jersey was asked to consider the admissibility of expert testimony in SVP proceedings that was based on actuarial measures that included the RRASOR, MnSOST, and MnSOST-R. Upon reviewing the testimony of the state's and respondent's experts, as well as the decisions of other states' court, the New Jersey court concluded that use of such actuarial measures was generally accepted by professionals who assessed sex offenders for risk of reoffense, and that arguments that their probative value was outweighed by their prejudicial effects were unpersuasive.

Significant because of the fact that it goes against the courts' clear tendency to admit any and all risk-based testimony in SVP proceedings is the decision in *Collier v. State*,[39] in which a Florida appellate court upheld the appellant's challenge to his commitment based on claims that the assessment technique relied on by the two testifying psychologists—the SVR-20—was experimental. The court, noting that one of the psychologists who employed the technique testified that he could not testify that the SVR-20 had gained general acceptance, ruled that the state failed to meet its burden, the testimony of the two psychologists was admitted in error, the error was not harmless, and the defendant had to be granted a new trial. This case stands as a clear exception to the general willingness of the courts to admit risk testimony regardless of the evidentiary standard applied; whether it will stand or be reversed on appeal is yet to be determined.

SUMMARY

At the time this chapter was written, the general trend among the courts was clearly to admit essentially all expert testimony regarding reoffense risk in SVP proceedings. Although it is clear that a consensus has emerged among the courts, regardless of the reasoning employed, it is our view that those courts that do not apply either *Frye* or *Daubert* or comparable state rule to this testimony are abdicating an important judicial role in scrutinizing testimony that in fact is comparatively novel. The use of actuarial instruments *in general* appears to sharpen clinical decision making on the issue of risk beyond unstructured or wholly clinical risk assessments. However, the instruments applied in SVP proceedings are still comparatively untested: A *Frye* or *Daubert* hearing can sharpen judicial thinking about the applicability of such instruments, just as the use of such instruments by clinicians can sharpen clinical decision making. As Judge Myerscough wrote in his dissent in *Erbe,* application of *Frye* moves the court beyond asking "the questions of 'Is this an actuarial test?' or 'Is the actuarial test being used by many psychologists?' The question becomes the following: 'What is the theory upon which the tests base their prediction of future behavior—the method of selecting factors, the determination of the numeric scale, the revision of testing instruments, etcetera?'"[40] In our view, this more in-depth inquiry by the court has merit not simply in putting the state to its proof, but as important, in causing experts to not become casual about the testimony and methods they use which ultimately are the primary tools for the deprivation of liberty.

Footnotes

[1] Frye v. United States, 293 F. 1013, 1014 (D.C. Cir. 1923).

[2] 549 P.2d 1240 (Cal. 1976).

[3] 651 So. 2d 1164 (Fla. 1995).

[4] 503 U.S. 579 (1993).

[5] 526 U.S. 137 (1999).

[6] Id. at 152.

[7] 83 Cal. Rptr. 828 (4th Dist. 1999).

[8] *Supra* note 2.

[9] People v. McDonald (1984); People v. Mendibles (1988).

[10] *Supra* note 2.

[11] People v. Therrian, 6 Cal Rptr 3d 415 (3d Dist. 2003), *review denied*, People v. Therrian, 2004 Cal. LEXIS 1277 (2004).

[12] 783 P.2d 698 (Cal. 1989).

[13] *Supra* note 2.

[14] *Supra* note 12, at 710.

[15] 767 So. 2d 637 (Fla. 5th Dist. 2000).

[16] 773 So. 2d 639 (Fla. 5th Dist. 2000).

[17] 857 P.2d 989 (Sup Ct. Wash. 1993).

[18] Id. at 1017.

[19] 654 P.2d 109 (1982).

[20] Young, *supra* note 17, at 1017.

[21] In re Detention of Campbell, 986 P.2d 771 (Wash. 1999).

[22] In re Holtz, 653 N.W.2d 613 (Iowa Ct. App. 2002).

[23] Id. at 620–621.

[24] State v. Tainter, 655 N.W.2d 538 (Wis. App. 2002).

[25] Id. at 544.

[26] State v. Lalor, 661 N.W.2d 898 (Wis. App. 2003).

[27] Id. at 905.

[28] 833 So. 2d 543 (Fla. 4th Dist. 2002).

[29] Burton v. State, 884 So. 2d 1112 (Fla. 2d Dist. 2004).

[30] 821 N.E.2d 1184 (Ill. 2d Dist. 2004).

[31] Id. at 1192.

[32] 782 N.E.2d 920 (Ill. 2d Dist. 2002).

[33] Id. at 977.

[34] 786 N.E.2d 557 (Ill. 3d Dist. 2003).

[35] People v. Field, 813 N.E.2d 319 (Ill. 2d Dist. 2004).

[36] 800 N.E.2d 128 (Ill. 4th Dist. 2003).

[37] 800 N.E.2d 137 (Ill. 4th Dist. 2003).

[38] 773 A.2d 72 (Sup. Ct. N.J., 2001).

[39] 857 So. 2d 943 (Fla. 4th Dist. 2003).

[40] *Supra* note 37 at 158.

References

Boer, D. P., Hart, S. D., Kropp, P. R. & Webster, C. D. (1997). *The Sexual Violence Risk–20 Guide (SVR-20)*. Burnaby, British Columbia, Canada: The Mental Health, Law and Policy Institute, Simon Fraser University.

Cohen, F. (1997). Sexually dangerous persons/predators legislation. In B. K. Schwartz & H. R. Cellini (Eds.), *The sex offender: New insights, treatment innovations, and legal developments* (pp. 22-1–22-12). Kingston, NJ: Civic Research Institute.

Epperson, D. L., Kaul, J. D., Huot, S. J., Hesselton, D., Alexander, W., & Goldman, R. (1999). *Minnesota Sex Offender Screening Tool—Revised (MnSOST-R): Development, performance, and recommended risk level cut scores* [Online]. Available: *www.psychology.iastate.edu/faculty/ epperson/mnsost_download.htm*.

Faigman, D. L., Kaye, D. H., Saks, M. J., & Sanders, J. (1997). *Modern scientific evidence. The law and science of expert testimony* (Vol. 1). St. Paul, MN: West.

Hanson, R. K., & Thornton, D. (2000). Improving risk assessments for sex offenders: A comparison of three actuarial scales. *Law and Human Behavior, 24,* 119–136.

Hare, R. D. (1991). *The Hare Psychopathy Checklist—Revised.* Toronto, Ontario, Canada: Multi-Health Systems.

Held, A. (1999). The civil commitment of sexual predators—Experience under Minnesota's law. In A. Schlank & F. Cohen (Eds.), *The sexual predator: Law, policy, evaluation, and treatment* (pp. 2-1–2-54). Kingston, NJ: Civic Research Institute.

Janus, E. S. (2000). Sexual predator commitment laws: Lessons for law and the behavioral sciences. *Behavioral Sciences and the Law, 18,* 5–21.

Janus, E. S., & Walbeck, N. H. (2000). Sex offender commitments in Minnesota: A descriptive study of second generation commitments. *Behavioral Sciences and the Law, 18,* 343–374.

Kozlowski, K. (2001). In the wake of *Hendricks*—States seem "committed" to SVP programs. In A. Schlank & F. Cohen (Eds.), *The sexual predator: Law, policy, evaluation, and treatment* (pp. 4-1–4-24). Kingston, NJ: Civic Research Institute.

La Fond, J. (2005). *Preventing sexual violence: How society should cope with sex offenders.* Washington, DC: American Psychological Association.

Miller, H. A., Amenta, A. E., & Conroy, M. A. (2005). Sexually violent predator evaluations: Empirical evidence, strategies for professionals, and research directions. *Law and Human Behavior, 29,* 29–54.

Morse, S. J. (1998). Fear of danger, flight from culpability. *Psychology, Public Policy, and Law, 4,* 25–54.

Petrila, J., & Otto, R. K. (2001). Issues in admissibility of expert testimony in sexually violent predator evaluations. In A. Schlank (Ed.), *The sexual predator: Legal issues, clinical issues, and special populations* (pp. 3-1–3-25). Kingston, NJ: Civic Research Institute.

Quinsey, V. L., Harris, G. T., Rice, M. E., & Cormier, C. A. (1998). *Violent offenders: Appraising and managing risk.* Washington, DC: American Psychological Association.

Schwartz, B. (1999). The case against involuntary commitment. In A. Schlank & F. Cohen (Eds.), *The sexual predator: Law, policy, evaluation, and treatment* (pp. 4-1–4-22). Kingston, NJ: Civic Research Institute.

Shaw, T., & Funderburk, J. R. (1999). Civil commitment of sex offenders as therapeutic jurisprudence—A rational approach to community protection. In A. Schlank & F. Cohen (Eds.), *The sexual predator: Law, policy, evaluation, and treatment* (pp. 5-1–5-8). Kingston, NJ: Civic Research Institute.

Webster, C. D., Harris, G. T., Rice, M. E., Cormier, C. A., & Quinsey, V. L. (1994). *The violence prediction scheme: Assessing dangerousness in high risk men.* Toronto, Ontario, Canada: Centre of Criminology, University of Toronto.

Chapter 3

Inaccurate Arguments in Sex Offender Civil Commitment Proceedings

by Dennis M. Doren, Ph.D.

INTRODUCTION

Few, if any, forensic areas in which psychologists and psychiatrists do assessments are more contested than sex offender civil commitments. Seventeen states currently have laws that require the evaluation of certain sex offenders for possible commitment. Conducting a civil commitment evaluation can result in the clinician's being required to give days of court testimony, with scores of arguments being tested during each occasion.

Despite, or maybe because of, the highly contested nature of sex offender civil commitment proceedings, there are some common arguments that are completely inaccurate. As the reader will see, some of these inaccuracies are regularly made by attorneys on either side of the litigation, and many are made by the expert witnesses themselves. This chapter is designed to describe many of those inaccurate arguments as well as to expose these errors and indicate instead what is accurate.

Most of the delineated arguments can be found in various court proceedings, meaning that no one expert witness or attorney seems ultimately responsible for the persistence of the error. In those situations, this chapter avoids naming any single individual as accountable for the fallacious argument. To single out one or two people from the many who make a common error would not be fair to those few people. The fact is that most of the following inaccurate arguments cannot be found anywhere in professional writings. Maybe that is a good thing, but it also means that the reader may not easily find a published reference for the error being discussed. On the other hand, when a publication is known to exist espousing the inaccurate argument, the publication is noted. Either way, the philosophy behind this chapter is that we are each fully responsible for what we offer to the courts, and we need to be as accurate as possible in our testimony. It is hoped that this chapter will facilitate that process.

As a caveat, this chapter should not be considered comprehensive in setting out all the inaccuracies made in sex offender civil commitment arguments and testimony. Selected here are simply what I consider to be the most common and most fundamental errors of a conceptual, statistical, and/or factual nature within sex offender civil commitment proceedings around the country.

This chapter covers four rubrics, each with its own set of multiple inaccurate arguments.

☐ *Diagnostic issues.* Common inaccurate statements include the following:

- Paraphilia not otherwise specified (NOS), nonconsent does not exist.
- Anyone who rapes has a paraphilia.
- Paraphilia NOS, nonconsent is not in DSM-IV-TR.
- Everyone who molests a child is pedophilic.

☐ *Conceptual issues related to risk assessment.* Common inaccurate statements include the following:
  - Prediction is the same thing as risk assessment.
  - Flawed instrument developmental procedures equate to "meaningless" outcomes.
  - All sexual recidivism base rates are the same.
  - Revisions of instrumentation mean they are not ready to be used.
  - Actuarial means based on historical (unchangeable) data only.

☐ *Statistical issues.* Common inaccurate statements include:
  - Correlations and their derivatives are equal to predictive accuracy.
  - The ROC equates to accuracy of a risk assessment within civil commitment arena.

☐ *Actuarial instrument usage issues.* Common inaccurate statements include the following:
  - The instruments have not been shown to have interrater reliability.
  - The instruments lack validity.
  - The instruments represent a novel principle.
  - Actuarial risk percentages below statutory threshold mean the person does not meet commitment criteria.
  - Structured clinical judgments are better than actuarial data.
  - The instruments are only good for screening purposes.
  - His category has 50 percent likelihood, but which half is he in?
  - The instruments are not "good enough," and nothing else is either.

DIAGNOSTIC ISSUES

The sex offender civil commitment process involves two main areas appearing to require expert testimony: diagnostic assessment and risk assessment. This first section addresses some commonly made inaccurate arguments involving diagnostic issues.

Paraphilia NOS, Nonconsent Does Not Exist

The diagnosis of paraphilia NOS, nonconsent is probably the only commonly made diagnosis within sex offender civil commitments that is attacked based on the argument that the condition does not exist, as opposed to the more obvious idea that a given diagnosis does not apply to the subject of the commitment or reexamination petition. (Hereafter, throughout this chapter, the subject, detainee, patient, resident, etc., will be referred to as the respondent, though it is recognized that the subject could also be the person who filed for reexamination of his or her commitment. This simplification is purely to make the chapter easier to read, rather than mixing terms or regularly listing multiple terms.) The argument also differs from the one in the fourth edition, text revision of *Diagnostic and Statistical Manual of Mental Disorders* (DSM-IV-TR; American Psychiatric Association, 2000) by asserting that the diagnosis is not in the manual, an issue addressed later in this chapter.

The bottom-line assertion in this first argument is that there is no paraphiliac condition (i.e., disorder of sexual arousal) specifically involving sexual arousal to nonconsensual interactions with others. To test the accuracy of this assertion, that a certain condition does not exist, all we need to find is a single example to the contrary.

There are, in fact, various places where one can document the existence of people who show sexual arousal specific to nonconsenting interactions within a sexual context (cf. Doren, 2002; Lalumière, Quinsey, Harris, Rice, & Trautrimas, 2003). Treaters commonly describe cases in which the person has acknowledged ongoing sexual fantasies, urges, and historical behaviors involving raping others. One such case example is briefly described here, for the reader who may not have met such a person: The person was middle aged at the time I became familiar with him. He had already been incarcerated for some years, most recently for a sexual assault of an adult. He was not psychopathic based on the Psychopathy Checklist—Revised score of 18 (PCL-R; Hare, 1991), and he expressed a good deal of upset about his repetitive history of rape. Penile plethysmograph (PPG) data and his self-report concurred in showing him to become far more sexually aroused with depictions of rape compared to consensual sexual contact. Even so, there was no indication that the specific infliction of pain or injury to others was sexually arousing for him. He complained of ongoing sexual fantasies of raping, fantasies that bothered him but over which he felt a significant lack of control. Occasionally, he also expressed urges to rape, though he was able to deal with those without actual raping while in institutions. In treatment, he described having had these thoughts and desires since he was an adolescent, a report substantiated by his recorded criminal history.

Given that examples like this exist, demonstrating a paraphilia related to raping, it is inaccurate to say the condition does not exist. It should also be noted that sex offender treatment providers have seen many similar examples in their work.

Anyone Who Rapes Has a Paraphilia

The flipside to the foregoing argument is that instead of no one having a paraphilia related to raping, everyone who rapes has such a condition. This argument is just as inaccurate as the previous one.

Again, this issue raises an empirical question. The aforementioned question was, Can anyone document such a condition? With this argument, the empirical issue is whether anyone who rapes can be found who does not show signs of a paraphilia.

In fact, research results with such a finding can be located without trouble. In Marshall and Barbaree (1995), only about 30 percent of convicted rapists showed sexual arousal to depictions of rapes while still showing arousal to depictions of consensual adult sexual contact. Lalumière et al. (2003) found that about 65 percent of rapists showed clear arousal to depictions of raping, meaning that 35 percent did not. The fact of having committed rapes does not properly translate to the automatic conclusion that the perpetrator is paraphilic.

Paraphilia NOS, Nonconsent Is Not in DSM-IV-TR

If the first inaccuracy represents a faulty defense expert's statement, and the second error above represents a faulty prosecution expert's statement, then the issue here is one from defense attorneys themselves. The argument typically comes from cross-examination of prosecution witnesses when the diagnosis has been made concerning a respondent. The relevant questioning is usually put in the form something like the following: "Isn't it true that the diagnosis 'paraphilia NOS, nonconsent' does not exist in DSM-IV-TR?"

The accurate answer is that of course it does, on page 576 of the hard-cover version of DSM-IV-TR. The inaccuracy made here confuses the diagnosis of paraphilia NOS with a descriptor called "nonconsent." The diagnostic title is paraphilia NOS, with this phrase standing alone as the diagnosis. When the descriptor "nonconsent" is included, it is for the purpose of clarity in professional communication. (The general explanation of an NOS diagnostic determination is on page 4 of DSM-IV-TR. In this case, the descriptor, "nonconsent," indicates that the NOS diagnosis was made for the second reason enumerated on page 4: "The presentation conforms to a symptom pattern that has not been included in the DSM-IV Classification but that causes clinically significant distress or impairment," as opposed to three other possible reasons listed for an NOS diagnosis.) Other examples of possible descriptors listed for the same reason include hebephilia, pornography, and autoasphyxiation. Saying that the phrase "paraphilia NOS, nonconsent" does not exist in the manual in its complete form obfuscates the distinction between the diagnosis and a descriptor added for clarity.

Arguments made about the manual's lack of inclusion of the diagnosis sometimes will acknowledge the paraphilia NOS as the essential diagnosis but then point out the lack of inclusion of "nonconsent" in the enumeration of possible types within the paraphilia NOS description (on page 576). To be clear, the term "nonconsent" initially appears in the first sentence defining paraphilias overall: "The essential features of a Paraphilia are recurrent, intense sexually arousing fantasies, sexual urges, or behaviors generally involving 1) nonhuman objects, 2) the suffering or humiliation of oneself or one's partner, or 3) children or other *nonconsenting* persons that occur over a period of at least 6 months . . ." (p. 566, emphasis added). It is, in fact, a defining characteristic of various paraphilias.

Everyone Who Molests a Child Is Pedophilic

This argument, most typically heard by implication in what prosecutors ask, represents the same faulty logic as the first two arguments presented (involving "all" or "none" statements). Again, the only thing necessary to demonstrate the inaccuracy of an "everyone" statement is a single exceptional case. In fact, there are many such cases including some to be found in the professional literature. PPG studies with child molesters typically find many offenders who show sexual arousal to children (the essential meaning of pedophilia) but a portion who do not (e.g., Barbaree & Marshall,

1989). An argument can be made that the sensitivity of PPGs is not perfect, so some pedophiles are missed through this method of testing. Missing some, however, cannot be meaningfully interpreted as saying that everyone who fails on a PPG to show sexual arousal to children is really a pedophile despite the lack of evidence.

Likewise, just as described previously concerning paraphilia related to raping, sex offender treaters and evaluators quite regularly work with people who have molested a child without qualifying for the diagnosis of pedophilia. Reasons for such offending, besides being driven by paraphilic desire, include loneliness coupled with a sense of inadequacy with adults, psychopathic lack of concern about who is the partner, desire to hurt the child's parent, psychotic delusion, and others.

CONCEPTUAL ISSUES RELATED TO RISK ASSESSMENT

This is the first of three sections in this chapter related to the risk assessment portion of civil commitment proceedings. This section covers general conceptual issues, whereas the next two sections relate to more specific topics within the risk assessment overall rubric.

Prediction Is the Same Thing as Risk Assessment

There is a very common but fundamental confusion between the process of making predictions and the process of making a risk assessment. The two different concepts are frequently used interchangeably as if they mean the same thing. This error leads to various other arguments that are then inaccurate as well.

First, to be clear, we need to describe the difference between the two terms. A prediction is a forecasting of an event or outcome. A person states that what is projected *will* occur in the future (in some specified time period, location, etc.). A risk assessment is an estimate of the likelihood for an event or outcome. (Risk assessments, in general, typically also involve estimates of harm or severity, frequency, and imminence, though those considerations do not typically apply within the civil commitment evaluation process.) The risk assessor states what is the estimated likelihood for a future event or outcome (again within a specified time period, etc.).

The difference can be described metaphorically. If we have a standard, evenly balanced coin and are going to flip it, there are two possible outcomes (ignoring the coin's landing on its edge): its landing on side A or its landing on side B. If we make a prediction for the coin to land on side A upon (the first) flipping, we cannot know if that prediction is correct or not until the coin is actually flipped. In other words, our accuracy in making a prediction can necessarily only be known in the future, after the predicted event did or did not happen. Then, and only then, can we determine whether we were completely correct or completely incorrect, with no in between possibility. If, however, before flipping the coin, we were to do a risk assessment, we would look at the fact that there are two equal outcomes upon any flipping of the coin. This would lead us to conclude that there is 50 percent likelihood that the coin will land on side A (for instance) upon flipping. In contrast to the predictive process, we do not need to flip the coin, or go into the future at all to find out if we are accurate in our risk assessment. All we have to do is verify that our assessment of two equal possible outcomes is correct, again something that could be done without ever flipping the coin (by studying the characteristics of the coin itself). We can conclude that we are perfectly correct without ever flipping the coin. In fact, flipping the coin after the risk assessment to see a single outcome would not tell us that our risk assessment was correct or incorrect. The coin's landing on side A would not tell us that we were correct and its landing on side B would not indicate that we were incorrect. We would always have been correct, before any flipping of the coin, when the risk assessment concluded with 50 percent likelihood for landing on side A, no matter what the result from the next flip of the coin.

We deal with probability in our lives all the time and know better than to view such circumstances as predictions. We do not (typically) predict that a bad thing will happen to us when we buy insurance. Instead, we buy insurance because we are aware of the probability (or at least possibility) of a bad thing happening to us and wish to lower the degree to which that bad thing will hurt us if it happens. We take an umbrella with us when the meteorologist states there is a 75 percent chance of rain not because we heard "it will rain" but because it costs us little to carry an umbrella compared to an assessed high likelihood for rain. We require licensure for someone to practice medicine not because we see this as guaranteeing fine medical practice but because the requirements for a license are viewed as lowering the likelihood that bad medical practice will occur.

With all this being said, how the described conceptual inaccuracy occurs within civil commitment proceedings can be explicated. Sometimes, the confusion is stated straightforwardly in a single comment, such as the statement by Janus and Prentky (2003), "Risk assessment—the prediction of sexual recidivism . . ." (p. 1443) or even within an article title by Berlin, Galbreath, Geary, and McGlone (2003): "The use of actuarials at civil commitment hearings to predict the likelihood of future sexual violence" (p. 377). Most typically, the initial confusion causes a compound set of subsequent errors. Campbell (2000, 2004) is the main proponent for this degree of confusion between prediction and risk assessment. He states his argument in the following ways:

> . . . risk assessments made for sexual predator hearings will lead to one of the following four outcomes:
>
> (i)   The offender is correctly classified as an individual who would commit future sexually violent offenses if released into the community.
>
> (ii) The offender is correctly classified as an individual who would not commit future sexually violent offenses if released into the community.
>
> (iii) The offender is incorrectly classified as an individual who would commit future sexually violent offenses if released into the community, but in fact would not commit such offenses.
>
> (iv) The offender is incorrectly classified as an individual who would not commit future sexually violent offense if released into the community, but in fact would commit such offenses. (Campbell, 2000, p. 114)

Arguments regarding a "likelihood threshold for sexual reoffending" are also disingenuous. Civil commitment proceedings reach decisions that ultimately amount to one of four outcomes: (1) true positive, (2) false positive, (3) true negative, or (4) false positive [sic: clearly the phrase "false negative" was meant, but not written here]. In other words, the outcomes of civil commitment proceedings do not equate to a continuum of "more or less likely" to reoffend. Instead, these outcomes assume one of two dichotomous events occurring—The offender will, or will not, reoffend. (Campbell, 2004, p. 122)

Dr. Campbell may find the argument against his statements as disingenuous, but the fact is that his statements are contrary to each and every one of the current seventeen sex offender civil commitment statutes. In none of them do the commitment criteria include the assessment or determination of whether or not the offender will offend. Instead, all of them describe that a specified degree of likelihood is required for commitment (Doren, 2002).

To emphasize how the espoused "prediction model" ignores the relevant statutory language, we can look at how the various commitment laws (coupled with related case law) describe differing degrees of risk as their commitment thresholds. For example, (1) California and North Dakota's commitment thresholds have been determined specifically to be lower than "more likely than not" (e.g., North Dakota's definition for "likely" is "propensity toward sexual violence is of such a degree as to pose a threat to others," a threshold specifically not as high as "more likely than not"); (2) Iowa and Washington's thresholds are "more likely than not"; and (3) Arizona, Illinois, and Minnesota's thresholds have been determined specifically to be beyond "more likely than not" (i.e., described as "highly probable," "much more likely than not," and "high probability"). Is it even reasonable to say that all these are really just saying the same thing: will or will not reoffend? In any other arena, these widely different risk levels would be seen for what they are: widely different.

The differentiation between predictions and risk assessments is far more than semantic or minor. Various errors stem from this initial confusion, with resultant inaccurate arguments being brought into the courtroom.

One of the main secondary errors pertains to the discussion of the sensitivity and specificity of the actuarial instruments (cf. Campbell, 2004). Sensitivity and specificity refer to the degrees to which discriminations are made without error. Within the civil commitment realm, the supposed discrimination of interest is between people who would actually reoffend and those who actually would not reoffend (sensitivity meaning the degree to which all future reoffenders are included in the selection process and specificity meaning the degree to which all future nonreoffenders are excluded in that same process). If one believes that evaluators are really making predictions about which offender "will, or will not, reoffend," then a discussion about sensitivity and specificity might make some sense (though it really still does not, as explicated later). Without making predictions of who will and will not reoffend, however, computations concerning sensitivity and specificity cannot even be made, no less be argued accurately as relevant.

To put the above another way, let's go back to the coin-flipping metaphor. If we devised a system for making predictions concerning the coin's landing on side A, and we implemented that system, we could test how accurate our system is by making the predictions and flipping the coins hundreds of times. We could then also compute how many times side A came up that you correctly and incorrectly predicted (to determine the sensitivity of our system), and how many times side B came up that we correctly and incorrectly predicted (thereby determining the specificity). On the other hand, if we conducted a risk assessment of the likelihood that side A would come up when the coin was flipped, we would have determined that there was a 50 percent probability without ever flipping the coin. If we then flipped the coin, its outcome would not have made us right or wrong. We could not count the outcome as a "positive" or "negative," our original assessment as a "true" or "false" positive or negative, and we could not compute sensitivity and specificity figures based on our original assessment. All these concepts do not apply, and the numbers cannot be computed because we did not make a prediction in the first place. (For the record, the proper statistical measure for accuracy of a risk assessment is the confidence interval, or probability interval.)

The reason any of this is important is because discussions about sensitivity and specificity within the civil commitment context usually occur for the purpose of concluding that there is too much error, that the evaluators are using faulty instrumentation. Using improper statistics to make a conclusion, any conclusion is the real error here.

As an aside, there is another common inaccurate argument made by people who talk about the sensitivity and specificity of civil commitment "predictions." The error is in believing that society is necessarily interested in minimizing both of these types of error and both are of equal importance. Within the civil commitment realm, this is demonstrably not accurate. Given how selections are made for commitment referrals across the country, the real concern is solely that the respondents *assessed as meeting criteria* for commitment are accurately assessed (Doren, 1998, 2001), not that subjects not referred will not reoffend. Translating that into (improper) predictive terms, the real issue is that those predicted to reoffend would have really reoffended if released into the community. This is not the same as sensitivity (which in this context means the degree to which all actual future recidivists are correctly predicted as such), but a statistic called positive predictive power (PPP): the degree to which predictions of future recidivism are accurate. It means high accuracy for those about whom the evaluators say "commit" but does not address whether all future recidivists are predicted as such. The data are available demonstrating that no state tries to commit each and every future recidivist (Doren, 1998, 2001), meaning that discussions about inadequate sensitivity (Campbell, 2004; Lloyd & Grove, 2002) are improper even within the view that evaluators make predictions; representing error upon error.

There are other errors that flow from the original failure to differentiate predictions from risk assessments. Rather than belabor this main point, however, only some of these are discussed, with these discussions occurring later in this chapter.

Flawed Instrument Developmental Procedures Equate to "Meaningless" Outcomes

An argument typically made concerning the Minnesota Sex Offender Screening Tool—Revised (MnSOST-R; Epperson et al., 1999), but sometimes generalized to other risk assessment instruments, is that the instrument's developmental process was flawed, and hence, the resultant product is, at best inadequate. The most poignant description of this argument has been written by Lloyd and Grove (2002). (Unpublished works are rarely cited in this chapter, but an exception was made here because Lloyd and Grove have been cited elsewhere within a published work; Grisso,

2003, as discussed by Knight.) In their paper, Lloyd and Grove argue that the MnSOST-R had a flawed developmental process which caused the instrument's accuracy to be "meaningless" compared simply to predictions made using recidivism base rates.

Issues related to using a "prediction" accuracy model were described earlier, and although applicable here, they do not need to be reiterated. What is new here is the idea that "flawed developmental" procedures automatically lead to a meaninglessness resultant product. (The issue whether suboptimal procedures were used in the development of the MnSOST-R, or any other instrument, is not addressed here, as that issue is only tangential to the inaccurate argument being discussed in this section.)

Metaphorically, we can think of the utility of penicillin. Not only was the development of penicillin suboptimal, it was accidental. Yet, the outcome was phenomenally positive. Of course, improvements could and have been made to the original product since the original development, but the fact that the developmental process was suboptimal did not result in a "meaningless" product.

The point is that something useful can be developed without optimal or even scientifically standard procedures. Flawed developmental procedures lower the *likelihood* that a new instrument will be useful, but the real test for the meaningfulness of the instrument is whether it works in the way it should when tested with various new samples. If an instrument is empirically found to work consistently across various samples (i.e., consistently shows results supportive to validity), the fact that there may have been suboptimal developmental procedures only means that some potential improvement can be made to the instrument as it currently exists. Despite such a shortcoming, the current instrument is anything but "meaningless."

All Sexual Recidivism Base Rates Are the Same

There are various statistical reasons why recidivism base rates are important within a risk assessment (Doren, 2002). Only one of these issues seems to be brought up regularly in sex offender civil commitment testimony. That one concerns a comparison of the supposedly "true" sexual recidivism base rate and the risk threshold for commitment. The purpose for testimony concerning this topic is in an attempt to show how unlikely it is that the specific respondent actually meets the commitment threshold criterion. The usual comparison of this type shows that "the" sexual recidivism base rate is much lower than the commitment threshold, such that the rarity of recidivism makes it very difficult to predict accurately who will be a recidivist. In this argument, the base rate that is used is also presented as the risk assessment of the individual respondent, at least by implication.

There are three flaws with the argument as typically made.

Ignoring Descriptive Parameters. First of all, "the" sexual recidivism base rate presented is regularly not an accurate portrayal of the base rate of relevance to sex offender civil commitment proceedings. There are three parameters in defining a sexual recidivism base rate with accuracy: (1) the relevant time period, (2) the outcome measure employed, and (3) the types of sex offenders included in the computation. Inaccurate arguments involving recidivism base rates quite regularly ignore one, two, or all three of these parameters.

Concerning the time period of relevance, the current implementation of all seventeen civil commitment statutes involves the working definition of risk as pertaining to (certain) sexual reoffending over the respondent's remaining lifetime. In contrast, Lloyd and Grove (2002) make their statistical arguments using a five-year sexual recidivism rate (borrowed from Hanson & Bussière, 1998). In reality, the typical respondent across the country has far longer than an average five years remaining to his or her expected lifespan. Average respondent ages across the states do not tend to go beyond the offenders' mid-40s, with some states such as North Dakota and Pennsylvania having a far lower median respondent age. The portrayal of "the" relevant sexual recidivism rate using shorter-term estimates ignores the empirically demonstrated fact that different follow-up periods regularly demonstrate different average sexual recidivism figures, with recidivism rates (using any one specific type of measure) continuing to rise as the time period for follow-up is extended (Doren, 1998). For instance, five-year sexual recidivism rates are only about half of the twenty-five-year rate using the same outcome measure (of reconviction or rearrest) (Doren, 2002). This means that, on average, using a five-year rate to represent lifetime risk represents an underestimation by at least half of the true rate.

Concerning the outcome measure employed to derive the base rate figure, the Hanson and Bussière (1998) average sexual recidivism figure (like virtually all such research-derived recidivism rates) was derived almost completely from studies of reconviction and rearrest rates, not actual reoffending rates. No commitment statute requires the assessment that the respondent will be caught and legally processed, however—only the likelihood for certain sexual reoffending. We know reconviction figures are lower than rearrest rates (e.g., Doren, 1998; Langan, Schmitt, & Durose, 2003), and we tend to believe that both are underestimates of the true reoffending rates (Doren, 1998; Hanson et al., 2003). Inaccurate statements about recidivism base rates result from ignoring the effects of these differences in outcome measurements.

Concerning the inclusion of statutorily ineligible offenders, some studies are cited that include a large proportion of probationers, incest offenders, exhibitionists, and so on. These subpopulations of the sex offender population are typically ineligible for commitment (though exceptions exist, such as for exhibitionists). Probationers and purely incest offenders typically show lower sexual recidivism rates than do child molesters and rapists (with time period and outcome measures controlled; Doren, 1998). Exhibitionists show the opposite (Doren, 2002). Citing a base rate from a study that disproportionately includes probationers and incest offenders compared to populations eligible for commitment represents a seriously flawed argument. (For example, Adkins, Huff, and Stageberg, 2000, have been cited various times even though the study involves only a three-year follow-up period with a large proportion of the sample being probationers.)

Analogously, the the previous description of errors in defining base rates is similar to describing the amount of interest one will earn based on a bank deposit. We can talk about the average interest earned across a lot of people, but what would the figure mean? If we said that the average interest earned was $250, would that be good, bad, or indifferent? If that interest were earned within six months, would that be good? If we knew nothing more than that interest was earned based on an average deposit of $5,000, might that not be seen as good—that is, until we learn that it took twenty years to earn that interest? Without knowing the period over which the interest was earned, the specific interest rate, and the initial amount of the deposits, meaningful statements about the average interest people earn can be seriously misleading. A simple figure, without qualifiers, has no inherent meaning and can be very misleading.

The Base Rate Equals the Accuracy of the Risk Assessment. The second flaw involving testimony concerning recidivism base rates stems from the use of a base rate as the determinant of the degree of accuracy in a risk assessment. This flaw is a carryover from the inaccurate argument described earlier where the process of prediction is confused with the process of a risk assessment. As applied here, the inaccurate argument is of the following type. If we make the prediction that no one will reoffend, we will be wrong equal to the base rate. (For example, if we say the relevant base rate is 15 percent, and we predict that no one will reoffend, then our predictions would be in error 15 percent of the time.) Improvements on that error rate can be very difficult due to the relative rarity of the recidivism acknowledged. (People who use the argument involving the accuracy of predictions almost invariably cite rather low sexual recidivism base rates for their computations; cf. Campbell, 2004; Lloyd & Grove, 2002). Besides the issue of using base rate figures that are too low, the discussion of predictive accuracy is flawed in its assumption. As explicated previously, sex offender civil commitment laws do not require that predictions be made, and evaluators of respondents do not make predictions of recidivism. The use of base rates to compute potential prediction error rates represents an improper process.

Applying Nonspecific Base Rates to Every Respondent. Third, the use of even a well-defined and statutorily applicable base rate to describe a respondent can represent an inaccuracy. The issue here is that the most proper "well-defined and statutorily applicable" base rate needs to be applied to the respondent. People with different characteristics can be members of subgroups with different base rates. Research has shown, for example, that first-time molesters of girls have lower average sexual recidivism base rates (over various time periods) than do people convicted several separate times for sex offenses at least sometimes against boys (e.g., Hanson & Thornton, 2000). The most accurate base rate for the first subgroup would not include members of the latter subgroup, and vice versa. Ultimately, these differences in base rates based on respondent characteristics are the basis for actuarial instrument score interpretations. The recidivism percentage corresponding to each instrument score represents a separate base rate for subgroups of sexual offenders.

As described, there are various ways in which inaccurate statements about sexual recidivism base rates make their way into inaccurate arguments in the courtroom. Essentially, if a statement about a sexual recidivism base rate does not include some descriptors related to the amount of time postincarceration, the type of outcome measure, and the type of sexual offender involved, the statement has set the stage for inaccurate arguments to follow.

Revisions of Instrumentation Mean They Are Not Yet Ready to Be Used

The Static-99 (Hanson & Thornton, 2000) was developed by borrowing from the earlier instrument called the Rapid Risk Assessment for Sexual Offense Recidivism

(RRASOR; Hanson, 1997). The MnSOST-R (Epperson et al., 1999) was developed borrowing from the MnSOST.

The inaccurate argument made that uses the foregoing facts states that because the instruments have only "recently" been revised, they cannot yet be good enough to be applied to real-life decision making. This argument makes two assumptions that are faulty: (1) once science finds something that works, all work on improving that thing stops, and (2) anything that can be improved is not sufficient for practical use. Of course, these assumptions are quite regularly false, including in the area of risk assessment. The fact that improvements can be found does not imply that earlier forms were not appropriate to be applied to real life, or that current forms are insufficient if work to improve those forms is ongoing.

Again, metaphorically, one can think of any number of medical procedures that were useful and important in their time, even though improvements on those procedures have since been made and implemented in real-life medical practice. The fact is, we all hope improvements will always continue to be made, both in medical practice and in sex offender risk assessments.

Actuarial Means Based on Historical (Unchangeable) Data Only

There is a common misconception concerning actuarial instrumentation: that actuarial data are synonymous with historical and essentially unchangeable information. To be fair, this misunderstanding may stem from the fact that most current sexual reoffense risk actuarial instruments commonly used in sex offender civil commitment assessments do largely, sometimes solely, use historical data.

Actuarial scales, however, do not necessarily have to use historical information, in total, or even at all. The Level of Service Inventory—Revised (LSI-R; Andrews & Bonta, 2001), for instance, involves numerous changeable characteristics. The Sex Offender Needs Assessment Rating (SONAR; Hanson & Harris, 2001) consists almost solely of characteristics that can show change over time. Actuarial assessment simply implies the use of data that are specifically delineated, involve specific coding rules, and involve specific interpretive schemes. Whether or not an actuarial instrument contains solely historical information was simply a reflection of how it was developed.

As a further comment, actuarial assessment procedures actually represent the basis for all empirically developed psychological testing. This is true for intelligence tests, personality tests, attitudes tests, and so on. A review of existing psychological tests will show that a vast majority of what is tested within any of those measures is not historical in nature.

STATISTICAL ISSUES

Testimony concerning statistical issues may be the most difficult for judges and juries to follow. The terms used are strange, are technical, and do not easily translate naturally into life experience. It is not surprising, then, that some inaccurate arguments creep into sex offender civil commitment proceedings when it serves someone's purpose to use them, or out of ignorance.

There are probably a wide variety of inaccurate arguments made involving statistical concepts. Because of the technical nature of statistical analysis, this chapter concentrates on just two of the most common errors, beyond what has already been described previously.

Correlations and Their Derivatives Are Equal to Predictive Accuracy

The General Issue. A vast majority of empirical studies trying to delineate risk and protective factors related to sexual reoffending have offered a correlational statistic in their summary of findings. Maybe that is why there is a common misconception about the meaning of that statistic in relation to the predictive accuracy of those same risk and protective factors. The fact is, as Quinsey stated (as quoted in Grisso, 2003), "correlations and percent variance accounted for are not measures of predictive accuracy; they are measure of association" (p. 245). Given the frequency at which inaccurate arguments are made regarding this same concept, however, one can only surmise that this concept is not well understood.

The inaccurate arguments seem to come in one of two forms: (1) in terms of the correlation figure itself not being high enough, or (2) in terms of the derived "variance accounted for," again this derived figure being deemed not high enough. We can sometimes find both of these forms within the same testimony and written work (cf. Campbell, 2004; Wollert, 2002), as the thinking behind one is the same as behind the other.

The first argument states that (1) the correlation between supposed risk factor X and sexual recidivism is "just" a certain figure, (2) because correlational figures essentially go from 0.0 through 1.0 and the correlation described is far closer to 0.0, (3) this shows that the predictive accuracy of risk factor X still leaves far too much to be desired (i.e., is not showing enough predictive accuracy). This argument wrongly assumes that a correlational statistic is a measure of predictive accuracy, as will be explained later.

The second form of the argument takes the correlational statistic, multiplies it by itself (i.e., squares it), describes the resultant figure as a percentage (of variance accounted for), and compares that percentage to the full range from 0 to 100 percent. For example, through this process, a correlation of .30 would be multiplied by itself (to equal .09), put into percentage form (changing .09 to 9%), and compared to the range 0–100 percent. Using this type of process, the user is allegedly computing the degree to which the variability found in sexual recidivism outcomes (i.e., whether someone was found to be an actual recidivist or not) can be accounted for (i.e., explained by the variability in risk factor X). This argument (cf. Berlin et al., 2003) again wrongly assumes that a correlational statistic is a measure of predictive accuracy. An additional fault is the assumption that the best measure of "variance accounted for" is the square of the correlation, an assumption that is statistically questionable (Ozer, 1985).

Understanding the Gender Issue. Two not-so-technical methods are used here to demonstrate the impropriety of viewing a correlation as equal to predictive accuracy. More statistical methods for this demonstration exist but are not offered here. The

Figure 3.1
Illustrating a Correlation Does Not Equate to Predictive Accuracy

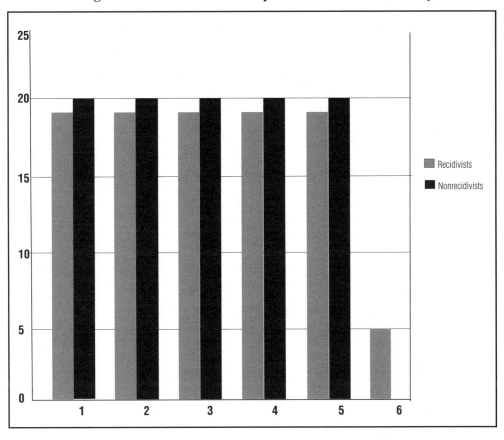

explication here is of a type thought more useful in courtroom testimony, where sophisticated statistical analysis might not otherwise be well understood.

The more analytical method of the two for demonstrating that a correlation does not equate to predictive accuracy uses Figure 3.1. (In a courtroom, like elsewhere, a picture can be worth a thousand words.) In this figure, the risk measure is divided into six categories, numbered 1 through 6. The different columns represent the proportion of actual recidivists and nonrecidivists who multiple large pieces of research have consistently found to have scored in each category. If we run a correlational analysis on these findings, we would discover only a small correlational relationship between the risk measure scores and the differentiation between actual recidivism and nonrecidivism (if $n = 200$, $r = .16$).

The (inaccurate) argument often made would involve looking at this correlational figure and drawing the conclusion that this risk measure shows poor predictive accuracy. Likewise, if squaring the correlation were believed to be telling us something meaningful, the conclusion would again be drawn that this risk measure is virtually useless (that squared figure being described as representing less than 3 percent of the variance).

The actual predictive accuracy can be quite the opposite from those conclusions, however. In explanation, predictive accuracy, like the predictive process on which it is determined, needs to have a division drawn between what will lead to a prediction in the affirmative (recidivism) versus a prediction in the negative (lack of recidivism). The determination of where the "line" should be drawn is crucial. Importantly, the process of deciding on a "cut-score" is not in keeping with what a correlational statistic typically does. A correlation describes the relationship between the whole measure and the outcome of interest (i.e., a correlation measures the degree of association). A cut-score treats a whole scale as if it has only two levels, above and below the cut-score.

In addition, predictive accuracy is often viewed as if its determination must include all types of predictions made; that is, it must be computed including predictions made for both recidivism and nonrecidivism. In practical circumstances, however, this is not always correct, in particular in the sex offender civil commitment realm.

The current implementation of every sex offender civil commitment statute involves some type of screening process by which not every offender thought to represent some recidivism risk is pursued for commitment. In fact, most of the actual future recidivists are knowingly not pursued (cf. Doren, 1998, 2001). Virtually all states screen out from any individual evaluator's consideration the majority of the people who will go on to recidivate sexually. Counting such "errors" in prediction (what some would improperly term "false negatives") as relevant to evaluators' judgments highly distorts what evaluators are in a position to do. Given the real-life screening that occurs, the (improperly described) predictive issue for evaluators is not whether the risk measure is fully accurate in differentiating all future nonrecidivists from all future recidivists. The real issue is specifically and solely the degree to which "predictions" of recidivism are accurate. In other words, when respondents are recommended for commitment because they are "predicted" to recidivate, how accurate are those predictions? (This issue was described earlier, in reference to the concept of positive predictive power.) This is the (predictive) question posed to courts in all sex offender commitment hearings, and it is the real predictive accuracy of importance.

Within that context, and using the data from Figure 3.1, if we draw our predictive differentiation line (cut-score) at a score of 6 versus anything lower, we can see that the predictive accuracy is *perfect*. Every positive prediction for recidivism would have been accurate. An evaluator using this risk measure and this cut-score would be correct 100 percent of the time. The evaluator opining "will reoffend" (or more accurately, does meet criteria in terms of the risk assessment) would be perfectly correct. Of course, in this illustration, most of the actual recidivists would not have been predicted to be such (i.e., there is low sensitivity), but this is simply analogous to how respondents are selected from among the complete sex offender population in the real world. (In this example, 5 percent of the actual future recidivists would have been assessed as such whereas 95 percent of the recidivists would not have been differentiated from the complete set of nonrecidivists. This 5 percent, or what represents 2.5 percent of the total set of recidivists and nonrecidivists, may seem like a small percentage, but the fact is that most states do not refer a much larger proportion of their convicted sex offenders for commitment; Doren, 1998, 2001.) The issue for the court in sex offender civil commitment proceedings is whether or not the referred individual (the respondent) meets criteria, not what portion of actual future recidivists were never referred for commitment. Referred respondents find themselves in that position at least partially because someone assessed them as meeting criteria, so the question for the court is whether or not that assessment, and that specific assessment, is correct.

Real-Life Examples. In summary, within the real-life context, a measure showing a low correlation can still be a fine measure, even a perfect measure in terms of the predictive accuracy of relevance. The correlational statistic is simply the wrong one with which to make the determination of the predictive accuracy of a measure.

A second way to demonstrate the "degree of association" nature of correlations versus their supposed relatedness to "accuracy of prediction" comes from real-life examples. Meyer et al. (2001) conducted a review of research in which a large number of correlational findings were summarized from a wide variety of contexts. As illustration, here are some of the findings that were summarized, with the correlations listed after each set of variables:

(1) Aspirin and reduced risk of death by heart attack: .02

(2) Chemotherapy and surviving breast cancer: .03

(3) General batting skill as a Major League baseball player and hit success on a given instance at bat: .06

(4) Coronary artery bypass surgery for stable heart disease and survival at 5 years: .08

(5) Effect of nonsteroidal anti-inflammatory drugs (e.g., ibuprofen) on pain reduction: .14

(6) Graduate Record Exam Verbal or Quantitative scores and subsequent graduate GPA in psychology: .15

(7) Scholastic Aptitude Test scores and subsequent college GPA: .20

(8) Sleeping pills (benzodiazepines or zolpidem) and short-term improvement in chronic insomnia: .30 (Meyer et al., 2001, cited from portions of pp. 130–137)

One can see that even the highest of the aforementioned correlations (i.e., .30) would still represent less than 10 percent of the variance accounted for if computed by squaring that figure, despite the fact that this figure stems from a relationship that most people probably consider obvious: Taking sleeping pills helps you get to sleep.

To put the foregoing correlations into a real-life context to see how inappropriate this summary statistic is concerning predictive accuracy, we can take the smallest of the figures rather than the largest. In a study by the Steering Committee of the Physicians' Health Study Research Group (1988), the researchers found part way through the planned study that the number of people dying from heart attacks from among the people taking aspirin was about half the rate from among people not taking aspirin—about a 50 percent relative improvement rate! The researchers were so impressed by these early findings that they felt it unethical to continue denying aspirin to people in the control group (i.e., the group not taking aspirin). The original study was halted for this reason. Such a dramatic finding, a 50 percent lower mortality rate, would seem to suggest that aspirin can be of high importance in lowering one's risk for dying from a heart attack, the conclusion drawn by the researchers. Still, the correlation between taking aspirin and the reduction in heart attacks was only .02, tiny by anyone's measure. How can the correlation between taking aspirin and the risk of death from a heart attack be so low given the dramatic results?

The answer lies in the fact that a vast majority of the approximately total group of 22,000 people did not die from a heart attack during the length of the study. The "great" improvement in reducing risk by taking aspirin stemmed from a comparison of a the very small proportion of people who died from heart attacks in both groups, with the aspirin-taking group showing only half the other group's number. Statistically, however, when one takes into consideration all the people in both groups who did not die from a heart attack, the *degree of association* between taking aspirin and death from heart attack was very small. After all, it was only a very small subset of people who died from heart attacks in either group, and the vast majority of the "variance" (i.e., varying outcomes) in the correlational analysis was contributed by the people who did not die from heart attacks. This results in a very small correlation, despite an effect the researchers considered so dramatic that it was thought unethical to continue to withhold potentially life-saving treatment.

The point is that a correlational statistic looks at the degree of association between two complete set of variables. Under various circumstances, the degree of association is a poor surrogate for the true degree of predictive accuracy or utility of a measure or intervention.

The ROC Equates to Accuracy of a Risk Assessment Within the Civil Commitment Arena

The receiver operating characteristic (ROC) is another statistic often mentioned in sex offender civil commitment testimony. ROC figures are typically mentioned when an expert witness is discussing the relative utility of actuarial risk assessment instruments. Flawed arguments begin when an instrument's ROC figure is described as synonymous with the accuracy of a sex offender civil commitment risk assessment derived from the use of that same instrument. That argument is not correct, for two reasons.

The ROC statistic is computed by comparing the sensitivity and specificity of predictions made using cut-scores at each successive level of a measure, and then summing those comparisons across the complete scale. In other words, the ROC represents a statistic that can only be computed by presuming that it is proper to make predictions using cut-scores as thresholds. As described previously in some detail, predictions of any kind are not the same thing as a risk assessment. Because ROCs are completely based on predictions, this statistic is improper for evaluating the accuracy of a risk assessment.

In addition, the sex offender civil commitment evaluation does not involve specifically the determination of some absolute degree of risk. In other words, these evaluations do not necessarily involve determining if the respondent's relevant risk is at 22 percent, or 47 percent, or 52 percent. The relevant statutory question across the country is whether or not the respondent's risk is above or below a specified threshold; that is, above or below "more likely than not," for instance. A sex offender civil commitment risk assessment is therefore accurate to the degree that determinations are on target concerning whether respondents are above or below the specified legal threshold. Differentiations among "low"-risk percentages (say of 12 percent, 22 percent, or 33 percent) do not matter relative to the conclusion of "below threshold" in a state where the legal threshold for commitment is above those figures (e.g., where the threshold is "more likely than not"). Likewise, discriminations among 55 percent, 67 percent, and 82 percent (again, for example) do not matter in that same state. Specific absolute levels of risk are not of primary relevance in a civil commitment risk assessment but only the discrimination of above or below the legal threshold.

The ROC statistic does not tell us the accuracy of risk assessments of this type. This statistic adds up the degrees of error found across all possible cut-scores, or risk levels of a measure. Because a lot of this summation includes error that is not relevant to the specific risk assessment question at hand (i.e., above or below one threshold only), the ROC statistic necessarily gives a statistical summation of error that is not in keeping with the evaluator's task, or what the court needs to know.

For the record, the proper computation of the accuracy of a risk assessment within this context needs to consider the dichotomous nature of the determination using a threshold for risk as the differentiation point, something that is conceptually and statistically different from both the process of making predictions and the process of making determination of respondents' absolute degree of risk.

ACTUARIAL INSTRUMENT USAGE ISSUES

Probably the most contested aspect of current risk assessment procedures within sex offender civil commitment proceedings is the use of and findings from actuarial risk assessment instruments. Maybe this is because courts are not used to methodical risk assessments beyond what is typically labeled "clinical judgment." Perhaps, the degree of contention concerning actuarial instruments simply reflects that making arguments against them (i.e., the more methodical process) is a lot easier than making arguments against a professional's general clinical judgment. Actuarial figures can be proven to be incorrectly computed, misinterpreted, or otherwise in error, whereas clinical judgments are less open to scrutiny concerning how the opinions are derived and how much error is included in the conclusion drawn.

No matter the reason, the fact is that numerous arguments have been raised about the use of actuarial risk assessment instruments in sex offender civil commitment proceedings. This section describes many such arguments that are regularly made but are nevertheless inaccurate. Some are technical arguments, whereas others reflect more conceptual matters of relevance to courts.

In the following, the reader can assume that the phrase "commonly used" in regard to actuarial instruments within the sex offender civil commitment evaluation setting refers to at least these three specific instruments: (1) the RRASOR (Hanson, 1997), (2) the Static-99 (Hanson & Thornton, 2000), and (3) the MnSOST-R (Epperson et al., 1999). Each topic being discussed also typically applies equally as well to other actuarial instruments not used as commonly as the above in commitment evaluations, such as the Violence Risk Appraisal Guide (VRAG; Webster, Harris,

Rice, Cormier, & Quinsey, 1994) and Sex Offender Risk Appraisal Guide (SORAG; Quinsey, Harris, Rice, & Cormier, 1998).

The Instruments Have Not Been Shown to Have Interrater Reliability

Two sets of authors have made negative statements about the interrater of commonly employed actuarial risk assessment instruments. Campbell (2004) reviews a select set of research and makes a distinction between "field reliability" (i.e., among people working in real-life settings) versus "research reliability" (i.e., within research studies) to draw the conclusion that adequate research on interrater reliability is lacking for all actuarial instruments. Otto and Petrila (2002) state that "interrater reliability and measurement error are unknown for these instruments . . . " (p. 14). Both of these views are flawed.

By definition, interrater reliability is a *characteristic of the device* being tested, not of the raters employed. To test a device meaningfully, one must use raters well trained in the scoring system. The issue concerning interrater reliability is whether or not an instrument's coding rules are sufficiently precise, given real-life data input, for trained raters largely to agree on instrument scores. The use of poorly trained or untrained raters cannot represent a meaningful empirical test of an instrument's interrater reliability. Such raters' errors all too easily reflect the raters' lack of knowledge of scoring rules and not the sufficiency of the scoring rules themselves.

With this understanding in mind, the distinction between "research reliability" and "field reliability" is artificial and of no meaning. If the distinction were simply to point out that there are inadequately trained people who will use instruments anyway, then that point is granted. The fact that improperly trained people use an instrument does not reflect on the instrument, though. It only reflects on the people who use an instrument when they are not trained to do so. If the distinction between "field" and "research" reliability is to reflect something inherent about real life versus research settings, then the distinction is fictitious. Virtually every piece of interrater reliability research concerning the commonly used actuarial instruments has involved real-life cases with real-life file materials.

This brings us to the second inaccurate argument: that the interrater reliability for the instruments is unknown. In fairness to Otto and Petrila, they wrote their article before some of the more recent research was conducted and published. Their article, however, is cited in more current literature (cf. Janus & Prentky, 2003) as if that same assessment is still current as well.

An enumeration of empirical tests of interrater reliability for three of the most commonly used risk assessment instruments has already been published. (See Doren, 2004, concerning the RRASOR and Static-99; and Doren & Dow, 2003, concerning the MnSOST-R.) The first two instruments show interrater reliability figures ranging between .88 and .94 stemming from about eight studies each. The latter instrument shows figures ranging from .80 to .86 across five studies. Although someone may argue that the number of empirical tests completed to date is still insufficient (a general criticism discussed later), the various studies documenting interrater reliability figures clearly demonstrate the inaccuracy of any statement suggesting that the interrater reliability of these instruments is unknown. In addition, any argument that there are insufficient numbers of studies of interrater reliability must also account for the fact that the dozens of validity studies of these instruments (described in the next section) demonstrate interrater reliability each time validity is supported.

One other comment should be made here. Janus and Prentky (2003, 2004) point out that no matter how one looks at the current actuarial instruments, their interrater reliability must be better than the other type of expert assessments regularly accepted by the courts: clinicians' judgments unstructured by empirical findings. To say that the interrater reliability of actuarial instruments is insufficient is also to say that *all* types of evaluators' testimony concerning risk are insufficient in this same regard. The interrater reliability of actuarial instruments is the highest we have within the context of a risk assessment. If the instruments are not good enough in this regard, nothing else is either. The argument that nothing is good enough is discussed later.

The Instruments Lack Validity

This argument, that instruments lack validity, comes in various forms. The most straightforward says that the commonly used instruments, or even all actuarial risk assessment instruments, lack sufficient demonstrations of their validity to be used (e.g., Campbell, 2004). "Sufficient" is a judgment call, not a scientific standard. The judgment is based on the degree to which the instrument has been empirically demonstrated to work as it should, especially within the context to which it is to be applied.

To make a judgment about sufficiency, one needs to be aware of the empirical findings that exist. Over two dozen validity studies have been conducted with the RRASOR and Static-99 (each), with the results nearly uniformly supportive in both cases. Those studies stem from at least eight different countries, including various U.S. states (again, for each instrument). Although someone may fault single pieces of research, the consistency of the findings across samples and jurisdictions seems clear. A recent meta-analysis including most of these studies' results found very supportive results as well (Hanson & Morton-Bourgon, 2004). The MnSOST-R has been investigated fewer times, using about eight different samples from three different countries and four different states within the United States. Although people will sometimes cite three different published works as showing nonsupportive results for the instrument's validity, only one accurately represents such a finding (Bartosh, Garby, Lewis, & Gray, 2003). The conclusion of nonsupport by Barbaree, Seto, Langton, and Peacock (2001) was altered by follow-up work by Langton (2003) using the same subject sample. Wollert's (2002) conclusion was found to be incorrect by Doren and Dow (2003), though Wollert (2003) argues otherwise.

Thus, is this sufficient to demonstrate validity? A vast majority of the country's state- and court-appointed sex offender civil commitment evaluators think so, as determined by a series of informal surveys concerning which instruments are used in these assessments (contact the author, Dennis Doren, for details).[1]

A second form of "the instruments lack validity" argument states that only a portion of the aforementioned research has been published, and unpublished works should not be considered (i.e., if the study has not gone through a peer review process, we cannot be so certain of its scientific merit). There are, of course, smaller numbers of published studies for the instruments testing their validity compared to the number of studies both published and unpublished. (To see an enumeration of published works for each instrument, see the reference list found at *www.atsa.com.*) Again, the determination of "sufficient" is a judgment call, this time being made within the context of another judgment call that only published works matter in determining the validity of an instrument. The issue for people making this judgment is whether they make the same kind of judgment in other professional areas (such as evaluations related to competency, criminal responsibility, and child custody). A discrepancy in the standard used (in defining sufficient validity for using an instrument within a forensic context) indicates a bias that needs to be explained.

A third form of the validity argument concerns the degree to which the individual risk percentages associated with each scale risk category remains stable across different samples of sex offenders. Wollert (2002) made an argument for insufficient stability specific to one of the commonly used instruments (the MnSOST-R). As mentioned earlier, Doren and Dow (2003) found otherwise by reanalyzing the data. The stability of the risk percentages for the RRASOR and Static-99 were both found to be well supported with large samples by Doren (2004).

Of course, someone can argue that these findings are not enough, that more is needed. As described above, no matter how much research there may be, the argument there is not yet enough research can literally always be made. The issue then becomes whether or not the person's threshold for "enough" is consistent across various types of evaluations and applications.

In contrast to the foregoing problematic arguments, there is one accurate argument that very rarely makes it into the courtroom during sex offender civil commitment proceedings. This argument was stated most eloquently by Quinsey, as cited in Grisso (2003): "The accuracy of a particular instrument is underestimated in follow-up research by the unreliability of the outcome measure" (p. 245). We know that reconviction and rearrest rates (the usual instrument outcome measure) are only surrogates for what we are trying to measure, the true reoffending process. To the extent that reconviction and rearrest rates are in error in measuring true reoffense rates, the actuarial risk assessment instruments are constrained in their potential accuracy—not because of the design of the instrument, but because the instrument was developed with a flawed outcome measure. Error in measurement necessarily interferes with the demonstration of accuracy. From these points, we can conclude that the demonstrations of accuracy of our current risk assessment instruments are underestimations of what would be found if our outcome measure were more accurate.

The Instruments Represent a Novel Principle

This argument is typically offered when issues of evidentiary admissibility are raised. A consideration in some states for the admission of scientific information as evidence is that it does not represent a novel scientific principle. Unfortunately, there are some people who argue that the instruments represent just such a principle.

The fact is that the psychological assessment of individuals by comparison to systematically obtained group data goes back nearly a century. The first such process may have been the Stanford-Binet intelligence test. (Developed in 1916, this test actually was a revision by Lewis M. Terman of the 1908 Binet-Simon Scale.) Data from a group of people were obtained against which individual test scores were compared, and interpreted. Modern-day psychological testing of virtually all types (intelligence, personality, attitude, etc.) maintains this same exact process. There is no basis in reality for saying it is a novel principle to assess an individual by comparing that person's scores to actuarial group data.

Of course, the application of this principle to risk assessment procedures is newer than 100 years old. Even so, the application of actuarial procedures to risk assessments is older than what various people describe in testimony. Of actuarial risk assessment instruments that are still regularly used (at least in revised forms), probably the earliest were two instruments developed about the same time: (1) the Statistical Information on Recidivism scale (SIR; Nuffield, 1982); and (2) the LSI (Andrews, 1982). Both were developed about twenty-two years ago at the time this chapter was written. Of actuarial risk assessment instruments still very popular in their original form, the VRAG (Webster et al., 1994) may be the oldest, having been developed over a decade ago. Although some people may argue that "only" ten years, or even twenty-two years of application is still novel (an argument that seems questionable on its face), the typical interpretation of the legal issue is actually not how novel the specific application of the scientific principle is, but how novel the principle is. The principle of comparing individuals to group data from which conclusions about the individual are drawn has a century-long history in psychology, with even the application to risk assessment procedures approaching a quarter century. It would seem that arguments about the instruments representing a novel scientific principle either ignore the aforementioned facts or push the time factor inherent in the concept of "novel" to the point of incredulity.

Actuarial Risk Percentages Below Statutory Threshold Mean the Person Does Not Meet Commitment Criteria

A common argument heard in civil commitment proceedings, by attorneys and expert witnesses alike, takes an actuarial risk percentage, compares it to the legal threshold for commitment, and finds it insufficient. At times, this conclusion can be perfectly accurate. There is an inaccuracy in the comparison, however, that can make the resultant conclusion also inaccurate.

The percentages attached to actuarial risk instrument scores describe empirical findings using specific outcome measures. Those outcome measures virtually always involved the subjects being reconvicted and/or rearrested. In contrast, none of the relevant statutes describes the issue of risk in terms of the person being reconvicted or rearrested for relevant crimes but solely the likelihood for recommitting such a crime. There is already documentation that rearrest rates differ from reconviction rates within the same samples of sex offenders (Doren, 1998) and professional literature describing the accepted idea that true reoffense rates (over the same time periods) have to be larger than either of these surrogate measures. For example, Hanson et al. (2003) state: "The observed rates underestimate the actual rates because not all offenses are detected . . ." (p. 154). Likewise, the current actuarial instruments go out no further than fifteen years in recidivism percentages, but research indicates that new first-time sexual recidivism can still occur beyond that time period (cf. Doren, 1998; Hanson et al., 2003), meaning that a person's risk even for being reconvicted or rearrested can also be underestimated by the current set of actuarial figures.

These differences between what actuarial figures represent and what the laws indicate is of relevance are ignored by some people. Wollert (2002), for example, uses the phrase "recidivism risk" both in relation to an actuarial instrument's risk percentages and to the statutory risk threshold for commitment, as if there is no differentiation between the two. Campbell (2004) does the same thing.

The process of ignoring these definitional differences between what is measured and what the laws require for commitment allows for the potentially inaccurate argument to be made that any actuarial figure below the legal threshold means the respondent does not meet commitment criteria. That argument is flawed whenever proper consideration of factors beyond what any single actuarial scale measures moves the assessed risk to above the commitment threshold despite a risk percentage that falls below.

Structured Clinical Judgments Are Better Than Actuarial Data

Some people argue that the current set of actuarial instruments are simply not yet good enough to be used in forensic evaluations, an argument that is discussed later. Within that set of people, many then go on to say a different method of risk assessment, using structured lists of risk factors (otherwise called structured clinical judgment), is better and can be used.

The flaw in this argument stems from a mischaracterization of the relative utility and support for the two risk assessment methodologies. If the assertion is made that actuarial procedures are not yet good enough, but structured clinical judgments are, there should be research showing the latter to perform better (either in risk assessments or in predictions of recidivism, both over the long term). Although a few research results of that type can be found (e.g., deVogel, deRuiter, van Beek, & Meed, 2004), most empirical findings indicate that actuarial assessment is more accurate (Hanson & Morton-Bourgon, 2004). This is not to say that structured clinical procedures should be avoided, as they clearly have an important role in various types of risk assessments outside the sex offender civil commitment realm (Doren, 2005). It is only that asserting that structured clinical judgments are better than actuarial procedures in conducting sex offender civil commitment risk assessments is empirically very questionable.

The Instruments Are Only Good for Screening Purposes

Berlin et al. (2003) appear to be the main proponents of the view that instruments are only useful for screening. The argument stems from the initial conclusion they draw that the instruments are not sufficiently accurate in determining who will and who will not reoffend (i.e., predictions of sexual reoffending). If the actuarial instruments are not good enough in their predictive abilities, the instruments can only be used within a screening process in assessing who should be committed and who should not.

The first flaw in their argument stems from the view that predictions need to be made. This issue was discussed in detail previously, so it will not be reiterated here except to point out that without this flawed assumption, the inaccurate argument that the sole use for actuarials is for screening goes away. In other words, the rationale for saying the instruments can only be used for screening purposes stems from the flawed view that risk assessments and predictions are the same thing.

There is a corollary within this "only for screening purposes" argument that is also in error. Proponents of this argument state that because most of the people referred for commitment have a repetitive sexual offending history, extrafamilial victims, other (nonsexual) criminal histories, and other such characteristics that are on current actuarial scales, the scales cannot differentiate among these referred people who will and who will not reoffend. From this argument comes the conclusion the instruments can only be used to screen potential commitment candidates and not beyond that point in the assessment.

This corollary argument lacks statistical meaning once placed back into the realm of risk assessment. To explain by analogy, it is similar to saying that once we screen a group of people for all the high-risk signs for cancer, we cannot differentiate between those with high risk for cancer and those with lesser risk for cancer. Of course, we cannot differentiate any further, because we already selected all the high-risk people in our "screening" process. If our task was to determine the complete group of high-risk people, we already accomplished the task. No further work is needed. Our original differentiation process was all that was needed, whether we call it a "screening" or a complete assessment.

His Category Has 50 Percent Likelihood, But Which Half Is He in?

I give credit to Harris (2003) for the title to this section, and quickly point out that the inaccurate argument in this regard certainly does not represent Harris's view. The flawed argument states something like "the respondent may be in the 70 percent category for risk, but we cannot tell if he is in the 70 percent group that will reoffend or the 30 percent group that will not."

Again, this argument confuses prediction and risk assessment. If it is a fact that that respondent is accurately assessed within a certain risk category (let us say, in keeping with the example, 70 percent), then the risk assessment in that regard is complete. Any argument from that point on concerning whether or not the respondent will reoffend falls into the set of inaccurate arguments that stem from the confusion between risk assessment and prediction, what Harris (2003) describes as "not knowing the technical meaning of the word 'risk'" (p. 391). Unfortunately, this permutation on the inaccurate arguments can be found even in recent professional literature (cf. Berlin et al., 2003; Hart, 2003).

The Instruments Are Not "Good Enough," and Nothing Else Is Either

This argument has been mentioned in various earlier sections due to its representing the bottom line to all arguments of "insufficiency" in risk assessment methodology. Nothing is good enough. As stated previously as well, this argument ultimately represents a value judgment about what is "good enough," not a statement with an empirical basis. If a person sets the proverbial bar high enough, no risk assessment methodology, in fact no aspect of psychological science, will be able to jump high enough to qualify as "good enough."

The reason this value-laden argument is included here, among others that are more clearly simply inaccurate, is because there appears to be confusion even within the value-laden argument. The confusion is in defining "good enough" for what.

Campbell (2004) argues that "good enough" is what is defined by admissibility standards for scientific evidence (as often defined by *Frye v. United States*[2] and *Daubert v. Merrell Dow Pharmaceuticals*[3]). In his opinion, nothing science has to offer concerning risk assessments yet meets either of these evidentiary standards.

The view is certainly debatable and in fact is not in keeping with the very large proportion of the country's courts that have already adjudicated relative to the admissibility of actuarial instrument testimony. Of importance here, however, is a completely different standard of relevance in determining "good enough for what." To my knowledge, there are no or at least virtually no evaluators who solely rely on actuarial information in making conclusions about respondents' risk within the sex offender civil commitment context. Actuarial instruments typically serve as an anchor, or foundation on which final clinical opinions are determined, but the instruments do not stand alone. The question, then, is the degree to which the instruments are "good enough" for this purpose.

The fact is that the courts are regularly willing, even determined, to hear opinions about risk from expert witnesses. This is true apparently despite concerns about the accuracy of those opinions (cf. *Barefoot v. Estelle*[4]). Therefore, the question, "Are the instruments good enough?" does not pertain to legal standards for admissibility in court, but to professional standards in forming the basis for a forensic opinion.

Again, if the bar in making this determination is set high enough, the answer will always be no. The placement of "the bar" is a judgment call, not an empirically based determination. If we place the bar's level by (1) considering the fact that the courts need to elicit such testimony from someone (in order to conduct these matters of law), and (2) the fact that actuarial procedures represent the best we have to offer the courts in such elicited testimony, then the answer of yes to the question "are they good enough?" would seem quite reasonable professionally.

SUMMARY

The sex offender civil commitment process represents a very serious public policy. Individuals' life freedoms over potentially long periods of time are threatened, while society attempts to protect itself from the most dangerous sex offenders. Within this context, it would seem that professionals owe it to the courts, and to society in general, to give only the most accurate information to those people who are making the decisions in these cases. Inaccurate arguments should be avoided, and if made, corrected.

This chapter was designed to describe a number of the commonly made inaccurate arguments, ones that are repeated all too many times. Maybe Yogi Berra had it right when he said: "We made too many wrong mistakes." My hope is that this chapter will help diminish the degree to which this remains true.

Author's Note

The opinions expressed in this chapter do not necessarily reflect those of the Wisconsin Department of Health and Family Services.

Footnotes

[1] Dennis Doren, Ph.D., 301 Troy Drive, Madison, Wisconsin 53704; DMDOREN@prodigy.net.
[2] Frye v. United States, 293 F. 1013, 1014 (D.C. Cir. 1923).

[3] Daubert v. Merrell Dow Pharmaceuticals, 113 S. Ct. 2786 (1993).

[4] Barefoot v. Estelle, 463 U.S. 880 (1983).

References

American Psychiatric Association. (2000). *Diagnostic and statistical manual of mental disorders* (4th ed., text rev.). Washington, DC: Author.

Andrews, D. A. (1982). *The Level of Supervision Inventory (LSI): The first follow-up.* Toronto, Ontario, Canada: Ontario Ministry of Correctional Services.

Andrews, D. A., & Bonta, J. L. (2001). *The Level of Service Inventory—Revised user's manual.* North Tonawanda, NY: Multi-Health Systems.

Adkins, G., Huff, D., & Stageberg, P. (2000). *The Iowa Sex Offender Registry and recidivism.* Des Moines: Iowa Department of Human Rights, Division of Criminal and Juvenile Justice Planning and Statistical Analysis Center.

Barbaree, H. E., & Marshall, W. L. (1989). Erectile responses among heterosexual child molesters, father-daughter incest offenders, and matched non-offenders: Five distinct age preference profiles. *Canadian Journal of Behavioural Science, 21,* 70–82.

Barbaree, H. E., Seto, M. C., Langton, C., & Peacock, E. (2001). Evaluating the predictive accuracy of six risk assessment instruments for adult sex offenders. *Criminal Justice and Behavior, 28*(4), 490–521.

Bartosh, D. L., Garby, T., Lewis, D., & Gray, S. (2003). Differences in the predictive validity of actuarial risk assessments in relation to sex offender type. *International Journal of Offender Therapy and Comparative Criminology, 47*(4), 422–438.

Berlin, F. S., Galbreath, N. W., Geary, B., & McGlone, G. (2003). The use of acturials at civil commitment hearings to predict the likelihood of future sexual violence. *Sexual Abuse: A Journal of Research and Treatment, 15*(4), 377–382.

Campbell, T. W. (2000). Sexual predator evaluations and phrenology: Considering issues of evidentiary reliability. *Behavioral Sciences and the Law, 18,* 111–130.

Campbell, T. W. (2004). *Assessing sex offenders: Problems and pitfalls.* Springfield, IL: Charles C. Thomas.

Doren, D. M. (1998). Recidivism base rates, predictions of sex offender recidivism, and the "sexual predator" commitment laws. *Behavioral Sciences and the Law, 16,* 97–114.

Doren, D. M. (2001). Analyzing the analysis: A response to Wollert (2000). *Behavioral Sciences and the Law, 19,* 185–196.

Doren, D. M. (2002). *Evaluating sex offenders: A manual for civil commitments and beyond.* Thousand Oaks, CA: Sage.

Doren, D. M. (2004). Stability of the interpretative risk percentages for the RRASOR and Static-99. *Sexual Abuse: A Journal of Research and Treatment, 16*(1), 25–36.

Doren, D. M. (2005). Recidivism risk assessments: Making sense of controversies. In W. Marshall, Y. Fernandez, L. Marshall, & G. Serran (Eds.), *Sexual offender treatment: Issues and controversies* (pp. 3–16). West Sussex, UK: Wiley.

Doren, D. M., & Dow, E. A. (2003). What "shrinkage" of the MnSOST-R? A response to Wollert (2002). *Journal of Threat Assessment, 2*(4), 49–64.

Epperson, D. L., Kaul, J. D., Huot, S.J., Hesselton, D., Alexander, W., & Goldman, R. (1999). *Minnesota Sex Offender Screening Tool—Revised (MnSOST-R): Development, performance, and recommended risk level cut scores* [Online]. Available: *www.psychology.iastate.edu/faculty/epperson/mnsost_download.htm.*

Grisso, T. (2003). Risk assessment: Discussion of the section. In R. A. Prentky, E. S. Janus, & M. C. Seto (Eds.), *Understanding and managing sexually coercive behavior* (Vol. 989, pp. 236–245). New York: Annals of the New York Academy of Sciences.

Hanson, R. K. (1997). *The development of a brief actuarial risk scale for sexual offense recidivism* [Online]. Ottawa, Ontario: Department of the Solicitor General of Canada. Available: *www.psepc-sppcc.gc.ca/publications/corrections/199704_e.pdf.*

Hanson, R. K. & Bussière, M. T. (1998). Predicting relapse: A meta-analysis of sexual offender recidivism studies. *Journal of Consulting and Clinical Psychology, 66*(2), 348–362.

Hanson, R. K., & Harris, A. J. R. (2001). A structured approach to evaluating change among sexual offenders. *Sexual Abuse: A Journal of Research and Treatment, 13*(2), 105–122.

Hanson, R. K., & Morton-Bourgon, K. E., (2004). Predictors of sexual recidivism: An updated meta-analysis. Ottawa, Ontario, Canada: Public Works and Government Services. Available: *www.psepc.gc.ca/publications/corrections/pdf/200402_E.pdf.*

Hanson, R. K., Morton, K. E., Harris, A. J. R. (2003). Sexual offender recidivism risk: What we know and what we need to know. *Annals of the New York Academy of Sciences, 989*, 154–166.

Hanson, R. K., & Thornton, D. (2000). Improving risk assessments for sex offenders: A comparison of three actuarial scales. *Law and Human Behavior, 24*, 119–136.

Hare, R. D. (1991). *The Hare Psychopathy Checklist—Revised.* Toronto, Ontario, Canada: Multi-Health Systems.

Harris, G. (2003). Men in his category have a 50% likelihood, but which half is he in? Comments on Berlin, Galbreath, Geary, and McClone. *Sexual Abuse: A Journal of Research and Treatment, 15*(4), 389–392.

Hart, S. D. (2003). Actuarial risk assessment: Commentary on Berlin et al. *Sexual Abuse: A Journal of Research and Treatment, 15*(4), 383–388.

Janus, E. S., & Prentky, R. A. (2003). Forensic use of actuarial risk assessment with sex offenders: Accuracy, admissibility and accountability. *American Criminal Law Review, 40*(4), 1443–1499.

Janus, E. S., & Prentky, R. A. (2004). Forensic use of actuarial risk assessment: How a developing science can enhance accuracy and accountability. *Sex Offender Law Report, 5*(5), 55–56 & 62–63.

Lalumière, M. L., Quinsey, V. L., Harris, G. T., Rice, M. E., & Trautrimas, C. (2003). Are rapists differentially aroused by coercive sex in phallometric assessments? In R. A. Prentky, E. S. Janus, & M. C. Seto (Eds.), *Understanding and managing sexually coercive behavior* (Vol. 989, pp. 211–224). New York: Annals of the New York Academy of Sciences.

Langan, P. A., Schmitt, E. L., & Durose, M. R. (2003, November). *Recidivism of sex offenders released from prison in 1994* (NCJ 198281). Washington, DC: U.S. Department of Justice, Office of Justice Programs, Bureau of Justice Statistics.

Langton, C. M. (2003). *Contrasting approaches to risk assessment with adult male sexual offenders: An evaluation of recidivism prediction schemes and the utility of supplementary clinical information for enhancing predictive accuracy.* Unpublished doctoral thesis, University of Toronto, Toronto, Ontario, Canada.

Lloyd, M. D., & Grove, W. M. (2002). *The uselessness of the Minnesota Sex Offender Screening Tool—Revised (MnSOST-R) in commitment decisions.* Manuscript submitted for publication.

Marshall, W. L., & Barbaree, H. E. (1995). *Heterogeneity in the erectile response patterns of rapists and nonoffenders.* Unpublished manuscript, Queen's University, Kingston, Ontario, Canada.

Meyer, G. J., Finn, S. E., Eyde, L. D., Kay, G. G., Moreland, K. L., Dies, R. R., et al. (2001). Psychological testing and psychological assessment. *American Psychologist, 56*(2), 128–165.

Nuffield, J. (1982). *Parole decision making in Canada: Research towards decision guidelines.* Ottawa, Ontario: Solicitor General of Canada.

Otto, R. K., & Petrila, J. (2002). Admissibility of testimony based on actuarial scales in sex offender commitments: A reply to Doren. *Sex Offender Law Report, 3*(1), 1, 14–16.

Ozer, D. J. (1985). Correlation and the coefficient of determination. *Psychological Bulletin, 97*, 307–315.

Quinsey, V. L., Harris, G. T., Rice, M. E., & Cormier, C. A. (1998). *Violent offenders: Appraising and managing risk.* Washington, DC: American Psychological Association.

Steering Committee of the Physicians' Heath Study Research Group. (1988). Preliminary report: Findings from the aspirin component of the ongoing physicians' health study. *New England Journal of Medicine, 318*, 262–264.

Vogel, V. de, Ruiter, C. de, Beek, D. van, & Mead, G.(2004). Predictive validity of the SVR-20 and the Static-99 in a Dutch sample of treated sex offenders. *Law and Human Behavior, 28*(3), 235–251.

Webster, C. D., Harris, G. T., Rice, M. E., Cormier, C., & Quinsey, V. L. (1994*). The violence prediction scheme: Assessing dangerousness in high risk men.* Toronto, Ontario, Canada: University of Toronto, Centre of Criminology.

Wollert, R. W. (2002). The importance of cross-validation in actuarial test construction: Shrinkage in the risk estimates for the Minnesota Sex Offender Screening Tool–Revised. *Journal of Threat Assessment, 2,* 87–102.

Wollert, R. W. (2003). Additional flaws in the Minnesota Sex Offender Screening Tool—Revised: A response to Doren and Dow (2002). *Journal of Threat Assessment, 2*(4), 65–78.

Chapter 4

The Right to Community Treatment for Mentally Disordered Sex Offenders

by John Kip Cornwell, J.D.

INTRODUCTION

In 1990, Earl Shriner, a released pedophile, raped a 7-year-old boy, severed the boy's penis, and left him to die.[1] The public outrage that followed this horrific incident in Tacoma, Washington, led to the passage of that state's sexually violent predator (SVP) law. The law provides for postincarceration psychiatric commitment of sex offenders who suffer from a "mental abnormality or personality disorder" that makes them sexually dangerous.[2] State officials deemed the legislation necessary to protect the public against individuals such as Shriner, whom they had been unable to detain under the state's involuntary psychiatric commitment standard following release from prison.[3] Legislators believed that the adoption of a standard that specifically targeted sexual dangerousness while incorporating ambiguous mental impairment language would facilitate the commitment of sex offenders.

They were right. In the first twelve years of enforcement, 164 individuals were committed under the law.[4] But Washington is not alone. Fifteen states and the District of Columbia have enacted SVP statutes patterned closely on Washington's[5] (while two other states have somewhat unique variations to their SVP statutes, with Texas committing individuals only to outpatient treatment and Pennsylvania committing only those referred from the juvenile system). As of the spring of 2002, some 2,229 individuals, virtually all of them men, were civilly detained or committed nationally as SVPs.[6]

Commentators have debated both the constitutionality of these statutes and their merit as a matter of public policy.[7] Whatever their pros and cons, the Supreme Court's vindication of this approach to managing the risks posed by mentally disordered sex offenders in *Kansas v. Hendricks*[8] presages the continuation of the practice for the foreseeable future. As such, our attention must now focus on the issues of statutory implementation[9] and release from confinement. The latter is especially critical.

Statutory Implementation and Release From Confinement

While state and local prosecutors have been very successful in securing commitments, detainees have been profoundly unsuccessful in gaining releases. For example, in Washington State, fewer than ten civilly committed SVPs have been granted conditional release from institutional confinement due, in large part, to the refusal of state officials to recommend discharge in any form.[10] Likewise, in Minnesota, only one patient gained conditional discharge over a twenty-year period under that state's SVP and sexual psychopath commitment statutes.[11]

This intransigence on the part of state officials with respect to release must ultimately give way, however, if the commitment of SVPs is to remain constitutionally viable. In *Hendricks,* where the U.S. Supreme Court split 5–4 on the issue of whether Kansas's SVP law was unconstitutionally punitive, Justice Kennedy recognized the statute's potential to convert civil detention into "confinement for life."[12] To this end, his concurrence warned state officials not to use the civil system "to impose punishment after the State makes an improvident plea bargain on the criminal side"[13]; while incapacitation is a legitimate objective of psychiatric hospitalization, deterrence and retribution are not.

The indefinite detention of all those committed as SVPs would promote the conflation of civil and criminal incapacitation of which Justice Kennedy warns. Recognizing, perhaps, the untenability of this result, some jurisdictions have begun to release SVPs into the community in greater numbers. For example, whereas only forty-nine SVPs had gained release by the year 2000,[14] sixty-nine were released by 2002—an increase of over 40 percent.[15]

The Need for Community-Based Treatment

As these numbers increase, the need for community-based treatment will grow as well. This eventuality will create a significant problem because of the critical shortage of clinicians qualified to treat this unique patient population.[16] Indeed, given the difficulty jurisdictions have had in securing resources to hire and train psychologists and social workers to staff their inpatient programs, it is hard to imagine how burgeoning outpatient needs will be satisfied. For example, at the time of his initial commitment as a sexually violent predator, Leroy Hendricks was receiving treatment that was nonexistent at worst and "meager"[17] at best. Even ten months later, the facility's clinical director testified that SVPs were receiving essentially no treatment and that the program was woefully understaffed.[18]

Washington State has encountered similar problems in implementing its SVP statute. In 1994, a superior court judge found that the state's Special Commitment Center (SCC) for SVPs was failing to provide constitutionally adequate treatment based, inter alia, on the "[l]ack of sufficient staff trained, experienced and certified in [the] treatment of sex offenders."[19] That same year, a federal court also found the treatment program to be constitutionally inadequate.[20] The court entered an injunction requiring improvements in a host of areas, including staffing, in order to bring the SCC into constitutional compliance.[21] Five years later, however, the SCC remained noncompliant, principally because of the state's failure to allocate sufficient resources for necessities such as staffing and training.[22] Only after an order of contempt was entered against the state in November 1999, which assessed significant monetary penalties for each day the SCC remained noncompliant, did the state allocate the resources necessary to provide adequate staffing and treatment.[23]

The problems associated with resource availability for inpatient treatment are even more pronounced in the outpatient context. Consider, for example, the situation in New Jersey. New Jersey is relatively unusual in that it has a separate correctional facility in Avenel for repetitive and compulsive sex offenders.[24] Inmates housed at this facility receive therapy throughout their period of incarceration. Those who are civilly committed as SVPs at the end of their sentence, whether or not they had served their time at Avenel,[25] would also receive therapy at state expense. Once released into the community from either criminal or civil detention, however, state-sponsored treatment is available only at the correctional facility in Avenel.

Parolees who are unable to access those services are seriously disadvantaged. They may look to the state's network of community mental health centers, but few have expertise in sex offender therapy and many will not accept sex offenders as clients. Conversely, paroled sex offenders may attempt to locate qualified therapists on their own, but, even if successful, the cost will ultimately prove prohibitive to many. A federal grant funded aftercare services at selected district parole offices for sex offenders whom the court ordered to participate in community supervision for life[26]; thus, at least some released sex offenders who cannot access Avenel have treatment options available to them.

As the foregoing illustrates, even in New Jersey, which is among the most proactive states with respect to providing sex offender treatment, individuals released from SVP commitment have no guarantee of continued access to therapeutic intervention. Ironically, because individuals released from SVP commitment are less likely than paroled sex offenders to be subject to community supervision for life, they would be far less likely, as a group, to benefit from the treatment services provided through the federal grant. As mentioned previously, even if released SVPs manage to find treatment providers on their own, their ability to pay for these services over the long term is questionable. Of course, the converse is equally true. In areas far from Avenel and the state's urban centers, SVPs are likely to find it difficult to find clinicians qualified to treat them, whether or not they can pay for those services.

For the time being, these problems are speculative as no one has yet been released from SVP commitment in New Jersey, other than by court order. In other jurisdictions, where SVPs have been conditionally discharged, treatment policies vary. In Wisconsin, for example, the state does pay for (and require) outpatient treatment.[27] In Minnesota, by contrast, the state will pay for Depo-Provera, an antiandrogen medication, but expects offenders eventually to take over the responsibility for paying for their group therapy sessions after release.[28] As time passes and SVPs are released in greater numbers, current policies introduce the alarming notion that mentally disordered sex offenders may be released into the community without necessary therapeutic supports. The specter of relapse is troubling not only for the individual but for ordinary citizens as well, as they must confront the risk to public safety occasioned by this eventuality.

I believe that not only is this result undesirable from a policy perspective, but it offends federal constitutional principles. Due to the unique nature of SVP commitment, and the representations states have made to justify it, substantive due process requires state-sponsored outpatient treatment for all those who gain release. This argument does not presuppose a right to postrelease treatment for civilly committed individuals, nor does it address directly the right of the state to detain sex offenders without treatment in a nonpsychiatric facility, though I would consider such a practice to raise serious constitutional questions. My focus is squarely on the treatment rights upon release of individuals civilly committed as SVPs under statutory schemes similar to the Kansas statute addressed by the U.S. Supreme Court in *Kansas v. Hendricks.*

RIGHT TO INPATIENT TREATMENT

Scope

A right to community treatment would be illogical if there were not a preexisting right to treatment while housed as an inpatient. Thus, we must first explore the parameters of inpatient treatment requirements. Although the U.S. Supreme Court has never squarely addressed the right to treatment, the Justices have noted on several occasions that the nature of psychiatric detention must be tailored to its purpose.[29] This mandate would not be met in the case of sexual predators if they were confined in a psychiatric hospital without treatment addressing the mental abnormality that makes them sexually dangerous.

Contrarians may point to Justice Thomas's embrace in *Hendricks* of civil incapacitation as a legitimate goal of civil detention.[30] This fact does not suggest, however, that a failure to provide suitable treatment over time would be acceptable as a matter of substantive due process. On the contrary, Justice Thomas noted that confining SVPs to an institution "expressly designed to provide psychiatric care and treatment" clearly "satisfied *its obligation to provide available treatment.*"[31]

This choice of words is informative, because the statutory language, relied on elsewhere in the opinion,[32] nowhere references the phrase "available treatment." It would seem, therefore, that the majority are promoting a free-standing duty of state officials toward those whom they choose to confine in mental health facilities.

Moreover, Justice Kennedy warned that while lifelong detention may be the "practical effect" of SVP commitment, if it is the statute's very *intention*, the confinement it prescribes is indistinguishable from criminal incarceration and is therefore impermissible.[33] A contrary purpose is demonstrated most persuasively by the provision of treatment. In this regard, the "presently available treatment" standard referenced by the *Hendricks* majority has significant roots. For example, in the seminal case of *Rouse v. Cameron*,[34] the Court of Appeals for the District of Columbia held that, to justify psychiatric detention, a state must endeavor to provide treatment that is "adequate in light of present knowledge."[35] To demonstrate that they are fulfilling this obligation in good faith, state officials must monitor a patient's status by making "initial and periodic inquiries" to facilitate the creation of a therapeutic program "suitable to his particular needs."[36]

Rouse provides a ready framework for interpreting the treatment standard forwarded in *Hendricks*. Its emphasis on patients' needs and the development of individualized treatment programs precludes long-term reliance on nonspecific treatments, such as "milieu" therapy, that may not prove beneficial. *Rouse* is also consistent with *Youngberg v. Romeo*,[37] the U.S. Supreme Court's leading right-to-treatment case. There, in the context of institutionalized mentally retarded individuals, the Justices required not only that treatment be made available but also that it be "minimally adequate . . . to ensure safety and freedom from undue restraint."[38] The Court added that lower courts should bestow "presumptive validity" to the judgments of "qualified professionals" in this regard.[39] In determining whether the exercise of professional judgment was proper in a given case, *Youngberg* accommodates the use of certain factors, including periodic patient reevaluation and the development of individualized treatment programs.[40] Incorporating these considerations serves not to usurp medical judgment but rather "to ensure that professionals . . . apply their knowledge and skills" in determining the sufficiency of the state's treatment efforts.[41]

In sum, the foregoing uncovers that individuals who are involuntarily committed to psychiatric hospitals have, at a minimum, a right to presently available treatment, reasonably tailored to the their disorder(s), and informed by professional judgment. Although a necessary precondition to any subsequent right to community-based treatment, this entitlement to inpatient treatment does not incorporate such a right in and of itself, in light of the lesser liberty infringement associated with conditional release. I believe, however, that SVPs who are conditionally discharged from civil confinement do, in fact, have such a right. As I explain in the next section, this right derives from a fusion of the justification proffered by state officials in committing SVPs initially and the theoretical underpinnings of the right-to-treatment case law.

Theoretical Underpinnings

Having examined the potential scope of a right to treatment, we must now consider its historical foundations. Among the various theories that courts and commentators have forwarded to justify a right to treatment, two have particular relevance in the case of SVPs[42]: the statutory guarantee of treatment and the quid pro quo theory.

Statutory Guarantee of Treatment. In *Rouse*, the Court of Appeals for the District of Columbia cited language in the federal 1964 Hospitalization of the Mentally Ill Act specifying that "[a] person hospitalized in a public hospital for a mental illness shall, during his hospitalization, be entitled to medical and psychiatric care and treatment."[43] Likewise, in *Welsch v. Likins*,[44] the district court derived a treatment mandate from statutory authority permitting state officials to hospitalize involuntarily any "mentally deficient" individual who "requires treatment or supervision for his own good or the public welfare."[45] Because hospitals were defined in the statute as places "equipped to provide care and treatment," when state officials choose to place citizens in hospitals against their will, those citizens have a right to receive treatment.[46]

The SVP statutes also reference treatment, as this prototypical provision from Washington State illustrates:

> The legislature finds that a small but extremely dangerous group of sexually violent predators exist who do not have a mental disease or defect that renders them appropriate for the existing involuntary treatment act . . . which is intended to be a short-term civil commitment system that is primarily designed to provide short-term treatment to individuals with serious mental disorders and then return them to the community. [By] contrast, sexually violent predators generally have personality disorders and/or mental abnormalities which are unamenable to existing mental illness treatment modalities and those conditions render them likely to engage in sexually violent behavior. The legislature further finds that sex offenders' likelihood of engaging in repeat acts of predatory sexual violence is high. . . . The legislature further finds that the prognosis for curing sexually violent offenders is poor, the treatment needs of this population are very long term, and the treatment modalities for this population are very different than the traditional treatment modalities for people appropriate for commitment under the involuntary treatment act.[47]

In *Hendricks,* the U.S. Supreme Court acknowledged that Kansas's SVP law, which is fundamentally similar to Washington's, obligates state officials to provide treatment.[48] It does not matter that the primary purpose of these laws is to separate those committed under them from society. Even if treatment is merely an "ancillary" goal, having declared that the state will provide it, it cannot fail to do so.[49]

Quid Pro Quo Theory. A second justification for a right to treatment, known as the quid pro quo theory,[50] posits that the state must give individuals who are involuntarily civilly committed something in exchange for their loss of liberty.[51] If the restraint on freedom is based on a need for treatment, the quid pro quo is the provision of that treatment. It does not matter if treatment is not the primary motivation for detention; even if the deprivation of liberty is based only in part on the promise of treatment, the representation is sufficient to force the state's hand.[52]

LOCATING A RIGHT TO POSTRELEASE COMMUNITY TREATMENT FOR SVPS

While the foregoing identifies a right to presently available treatment for civilly committed SVPs based on a statutory guarantee and a quid pro quo theory, these considerations do not suggest that SVPs have any right to state-sponsored treatment once they are discharged into the community. State constitutions may provide certain community-treatment rights for mentally ill individuals.[53] There may also be some entitlement to community-based services based on state statutes. These provisions are likely, however, to provide only short-term treatment[54] and to face practical challenges based on funding shortages.[55]

Statutory and Quid Pro Quo Imperatives

Significantly, no court has yet to embrace any federal constitutional obligation to provide treatment once discharged from institutional confinement. I believe, however, that such a right does exist for individuals committed under modern SVP statutes. This obligation derives principally from the legislative "findings" highlighted earlier. Those findings specify that SVPs subject to civil commitment (1) are extremely sexually dangerous, (2) are likely to reoffend, and (3) have "very long-term" treatment needs that are different from those of other individuals subject to involuntary psychiatric detention.[56] Because SVPs typically do not have a mental disorder sufficient to qualify them for commitment under preexisting standards for involuntary psychiatric detention, "special" laws are necessary and should be specifically tailored to SVPs' unique mental impairment and the resulting dangers it produces.[57]

Drawing a distinction between SVPs and other psychiatric patients makes sense. Many of the latter have mental illnesses that, based on pharmacological advances, do not require long-term confinement. Accordingly, involuntary psychiatric commitment is ordinarily intended "to provide short-term treatment to individuals with serious mental disorders and then return them to the community."[58] Once in the community, these individuals can receive follow-up services through the network of clinical providers available privately or through community mental health centers.

SVPs, however, are very differently situated. Unlike other psychiatric patients, their mental "abnormalities"[59] require *specialized, long-term* treatment.[60] The goal of treatment for this "small group of extremely dangerous"[61] mentally disordered sex offenders is not to "cure" them; indeed, the state has acknowledged that these individuals have little chance of being "cured" of their disorders.[62] Instead, treatment is designed to achieve a degree of recovery sufficient to allow them to reenter the community.

Because discharged SVPs are not "cured," it would be unrealistic at best, and disingenuous at worst, to expect that they would be able to sustain their progress without therapeutic reinforcement. As previously indicated, however, the willingness to provide this treatment varies widely among the states.[63] This problem is compounded when SVPs relocate to areas away from urban centers where clinicians experienced in providing sex-offender therapy are in especially short supply or, when services are available but released SVPs cannot afford them.

It is my belief that states are obligated, as a matter of constitutional due process, to provide these services to discharged SVPs. States cannot justify their authority to confine SVPs in a psychiatric facility indefinitely to address their unique, long-term treatment needs and then refuse, upon conditional release, to provide the very treatment that they have acknowledged is necessary to allow them to gain their freedom. The state would be effectively saying: "You have a special condition that makes you dangerous and, because of it, we are going to confine you for a long time during which you will be treated to reduce that risk. At the point at which your therapy has succeeded such that you can begin to re-integrate into the community, we can stop providing treatment so that you can regress and return to inpatient hospitalization for another indefinite period."

In addition to contravening the state's statutory guarantee, this result would also violate quid pro quo principles. The state would, on the one hand, justify the restraint of liberty by the need for ongoing, long-term treatment to restore it and, on the other hand, take that treatment away the moment its success became manifest. As Judge Becker of the U.S. Court of Appeals for the Third Circuit noted, "due process dictates that the benefit to which the civilly committed are entitled is the habilitation to enable them to leave their commitment."[64] By denying SVPs the right to state-sponsored, outpatient treatment, the state would be nullifying this entitlement.

This is not only unjust, it invokes the kind of animus that Justice Kennedy warned of in *Hendricks*. There, the Justice noted that when civil confinement becomes a mechanism for retribution or general deterrence, it loses its constitutional moorings. The problem is not that committed SVPs face potentially lifelong commitment[65]; the difficulty lies, instead, with structuring a civil commitment system to promote that result.

Role of Treatment Efficacy

Critics may argue against my position on the ground that treatment is insufficiently effective to obligate the state to provide it upon conditional release. Indeed, treatment efficacy remains a controversial topic among commentators and researchers.[66] Arguably, the most comprehensive review of the psychological treatment for sex offenders is that conducted by the Collaborative Outcome Data Project Committee. In 2002, the project's first report positively associated treatment with reductions in both sexual and general recidivism.[67] In four to five years of follow-up, sexual recidivism in the treatment group was 10 percent versus 17 percent in the non-treatment group. In addition, general recidivism was at 32 percent for those receiving treatment versus 51 percent for the untreated.[68] The significance of these findings has been challenged, however, based on alleged flaws in the research design, including (1) that the comparison groups were not comparable, and (2) that the evidence was contaminated by the inclusion in the comparison groups of higher-risk offenders who would have refused or quit treatment if they had had the choice.

Fortunately, it is not necessary to resolve this ongoing debate about treatment efficacy to vindicate a constitutional right to community treatment because the states have chosen, in their legislative findings, to declare that treatment is necessary to reduce the risks of recidivism posed by this population. By denying treatment upon release, the states would, by their own admission, be setting SVPs up for failure and recommitment. In addition, by denying SVPs the proverbial "benefit of the bargain," the state would extinguish the possibility of SVPs living in a less restrictive setting than that of the institution, a result which raises distinct constitutional concerns. In litigation over Washington's SVP statute, a federal judge has held that providing for community transition to a less restrictive setting is a vital and necessary part of professional minimum standards. "Without LRAs [least restrictive alternatives]," the court commented, "the constitutional requirement of treatment leading, if successful, to cure and release cannot fully be met."[69]

Advocating Affirmative Rights

Another potential criticism of my proposal is that it impermissibly imposes on the states affirmative obligations where the state does not assume full custody and control over the individuals to whom services are provided. In *DeShaney v. Winnebago County*

Department of Social Services,[70] the U.S. Supreme Court held that the state has no constitutional duty to protect a child from his parent after receiving reports of possible abuse. In reaching this conclusion, the Court noted that "[a]lthough the liberty protected by the due process clause affords protection against unwarranted government interference, it does not confer an entitlement to government aid as may be necessary to realize all the advantages of that freedom."[71]

The context of *DeShaney* is distinguishable, however, from that with which this chapter is concerned. Most significantly, *DeShaney* dealt with purely private conduct; the deprivation of liberty to which the complainant was subjected was not created by the state, nor was the minor in state custody when the violence occurred. By contrast, even when SVPs are no longer confined institutionally, the state still restrains their freedom substantially. Common conditions of discharge include, for example, mandatory supervision when outside the residence, electronic monitoring, no drug or alcohol use, no access to pornography, and restricted access to "vulnerable" populations.[72] Thus, the state impedes the liberty of sexual offenders but does offer, in exchange, treatment to allow targeted SVPs to gain freedom. By creating this interest in treatment as part of the commitment process, states should not be permitted to abandon it by removing some restrictions on liberty.[73]

Moreover, *DeShaney* itself recognizes that affirmative duties of care may exist in certain circumstances in which individuals face less than total deprivation of liberty. The Court opined that if state officials had removed Joshua DeShaney from his home and placed him in a foster home run by "its agents," the situation might be "sufficiently analogous to incarceration or institutionalization to give rise to an affirmative duty to protect."[74] Like foster care, community placement of an SVP is less restrictive than institutional care, though the state imposes conditions and retains substantial oversight that permits restoration of institutional custody if the situation warrants. Thus, in both instances, this exercise of state authority and control is sufficient to give rise to affirmative obligations on the part of the state to provide care and treatment.[75]

Equal Protection

Because the community treatment rights that I am advocating would apply only to SVPs discharged from civil commitment, some might argue that the rights of other individuals discharged from involuntary psychiatric detention are violated under the equal protection clause of the Fourteenth Amendment. To evaluate this claim, it is first necessary to identify the appropriate level of scrutiny. This task is challenging, as the U.S. Supreme Court has not spoken with clarity about the standard of review it applies in cases involving involuntary commitment classifications.

Early cases seemed to require only that these classifications be rationally or reasonably related to legitimate government interests.[76] However, the 1992 case of *Foucha v. Louisiana*[77] suggested greater scrutiny, mandating that the state provide a "particularly convincing reason" for continuing to commit insanity acquittees who had regained mental health. The Court's two most recent decisions, both concerning Kansas's SVP law, do not explicitly reference any particular standard of review. In *Hendricks,* the Court stated simply that involuntary civil commitment statutes that "narrow the class of persons eligible for confinement to those who are unable to control their dangerousness" are constitutional.[78] Five years later, *Kansas v. Crane*[79] specified that proof of a "serious difficulty in controlling behavior" is an essential requirement of substantive due process.[80]

By mandating proof of a volitional impairment not specified in the Kansas statute, *Hendricks* and *Crane* suggest a level of scrutiny higher than the rational basis test, which would have required upholding the statute as written. In addition, because the stigmatizing effect of mental illness undermines respect and dignity and promotes social isolation,[81] I have repeatedly advocated for heightened scrutiny in evaluating classifications affecting involuntary civil commitment.[82]

That being said, I believe that there is a "particularly convincing reason" or "exceedingly persuasive justification"[83] for treating SVPs differently from other individuals discharged from involuntary psychiatric detention with respect to community treatment. As discussed earlier, individuals committed as SVPs have treatment needs that are distinct from those of other patients in terms of modality and duration, a fact states have acknowledged in enacting this legislation. Moreover, because the failure to provide necessary treatment carries specific risks to public safety that are unique and deeply troubling, the state may use different procedures to guard against those risks.

ALTERNATIVE APPROACHES TO SEX OFFENDER COMMITMENT

Because the constitutional right to community treatment that I am vindicating relies on legislative findings specific to SVP commitment laws, the entitlement to such services would not necessarily apply to discharge from other systems of civil detention. Should we worry, therefore, that states will create alternative means of civilly confining SVPs to avoid providing community treatment upon release?

The experience in New Jersey is instructive in this regard. In 1994, New Jersey declared that certain sex offenders "suffer from mental illness which renders them dangerous to others."[84] The legislature then facilitated their detention under the *existing* civil commitment law by redefining mental illness as "a current, substantial disturbance of thought, mood, perception or orientation which significantly impairs judgment, *capacity to control* behavior or capacity to recognize reality. . . ."[85] This "clarification" of the state's mental illness standard was subsequently held constitutional by the state Supreme Court in a case brought by a sex offender detained under it.[86] In so finding, the justices also overturned the decision of the appellate court that the petitioner was insufficiently mentally ill to warrant ongoing detention. Medical testimony concluding that he suffered from an antisocial personality disorder and had fantasies of sexual sadism were adequate to support the trial court's order for continued psychiatric detention.[87]

The foregoing suggests that states need not resort to novel commitment standards to manage mentally disordered SVPs. It is curious, therefore, that more have not chosen to alter their existing commitment standards, instead of creating a new, controversial commitment formula. Faced, for example, with a definition of mental illness similar to that of the unamended New Jersey statute, Wisconsin[88] chose to enact a separate SVP statute, patterned after Washington's, rather than altering the definition of mental illness to achieve the same result.

Wisconsin's reluctance may reflect a tension between the nature and purposes of "ordinary" psychiatric commitment and that provided under SVP statutes. Normally, the state's civil commitment authority is based on its *parens patriae* power to "provid[e] care to its citizens who are unable because of emotional disorders to care for themselves" and its police power "to protect the community from the dangerous tendencies of those who are mentally ill."[89] Because the commitment of SVPs is primarily—some would say exclusively—an exercise of states' police power,[90] the "profile" of committed SVPs differs markedly from that of most psychiatric inpatients in that the former do not typically suffer from mental disorders that pose a danger to themselves or impair their ability to live day-to-day in a community setting. In addition, whereas involuntary commitment is designed to be short term,[91] the treatment needs of the SVP population are necessarily long term.[92]

Because of these differences, attempting to force mentally disordered sex offenders into preexisting commitment schemes that do not naturally fit seems unwise. To that end, notwithstanding the aforementioned expansion of its mental illness standard, New Jersey enacted a *Hendricks*-style SVP statute in 1998.[93] The law was urged by the Task Force for the Review of the Treatment of the Criminally Insane created by then-Governor Christine Todd Whitman in 1996.[94] When members of the task force invited me to meet with them to discuss *Hendricks* and its implications for the care and management of sexual predators, I inquired as to why New Jersey would need an SVP statute in light of the changes made to accommodate sex offender commitment in its existing civil commitment statute. Those who responded opined that offenders committed under the expanded mental illness standard were gaining release too easily because judges, psychiatrists, or both did not consider them sufficiently mentally ill to justify indefinite detention. Thus, special standards and procedures were necessary to identify more specifically the particular dangers and disorders presented by mentally disordered sex offenders.

These remarks illustrate the difficulty in managing SVPs within the traditional civil commitment framework. It is for this reason, perhaps, that states have not favored this approach and New Jersey abandoned it. Parenthetically, inasmuch as those who promoted adopting an SVP law in New Jersey were motivated by the desire to lengthen the duration of civil detention for sex offenders, they should be pleased with the results. According to a survey conducted in the summer of 2002, New Jersey had an inpatient SVP population of 223 with only 2 gaining release in the first three years the statute went into effect.[95]

CONCLUSION

Prior to the 1990s, the psychiatric commitment of sex offenders was largely moribund. Statutes that existed were little enforced, and new initiatives were not on the horizon.[96] The *Shriner* case, and others like it,[97] changed all this. They ushered in a new wave of legislation that allowed mentally disordered sex offenders to be committed at the expiration of their criminal sentences based on mental impairments otherwise insufficient for involuntary detention. As these laws proliferated in the 1990s, the legal debate focused on the constitutionality of this novel approach to sex offender containment. To this end, the U.S. Supreme Court considered challenges based on SVP laws three times between 1997 and 2002.[98] Thus, in 2004, we have a much clearer picture of the constitutional landscape with respect to SVP commitment than we did a few years ago.

Because the U.S. Supreme Court has all but foreclosed challenges based on the ex post facto and double jeopardy clauses, our focus must now be on whether the implementation of these laws satisfies due process, ever mindful of Justice Kennedy's admonition that "[i]f . . . civil confinement were to become a mechanism for retribution or general deterrence . . . [the Court's] precedents would not suffice to validate it."[99] Persistent refusal on the part of state officials to afford release would provide persuasive evidence of this impermissible purpose, but simply allowing discharge is not enough. Because SVPs have unique, long-term treatment needs which state officials acknowledged as a basis for confinement and affirmatively obligated themselves to treat, the state must continue to provide that treatment in the community in fulfillment of their statutory guarantee and corresponding constitutional mandate.

Some discharged SVPs may already be receiving state-sponsored treatment; others may not. Some may be able to find qualified sex offender therapists on their own; others may not. Some may be able to pay for such treatment; others may not. By recognizing the obligation of state officials to provide therapeutic services to *all* SVPs discharged into the community from civil commitment, the opportunity to retain their freedom will be equally available to all.

Footnotes

[1] Roxanne Lieb, "State Policy Perspectives on Sexual Predator Laws," in *Protecting Society From Sexually Dangerous Offenders: Law, Justice and Therapy* 41–59 (Bruce J. Winick & John Q. La Fond, eds., 2003).

[2] Wash. Rev. Code Ann. § 71.09.020 (West 2004).

[3] Gary Gleb, "Washington's Sexually Violent Predator Law: The Need to Bar Unreliable Psychiatric Predictions of Dangerousness From Civil Commitment Proceedings," 39 *UCLA L. Rev.* 213, 247 (1991).

[4] W. Lawrence Fitch, "Sexual Offenders in the United States: Legislative and Police Concerns," 989 *Annals N.Y. Acad. Sci.* 489, 492 (2003).

[5] Eric S. Janus & Wayne A. Logan, "Substantive Due Process and the Involuntary Confinement of Sexually Violent Predators," 33 *Conn. L. Rev.* 319, 321 n. 7 (2003).

[6] Lieb, *supra* note 1, at 45.

[7] Alexander D. Brooks, "The Constitutionality and Morality of Civilly Committing Violent Sexual Predators," 15 *U. Puget Sound L. Rev.* 709, 751–754 (1992); John Q. La Fond, "Washington's Sexually Violent Predator Law: A Deliberate Misuse of the Therapeutic State for Social Control," 15 *U. Puget Sound L. Rev.* 655, 691–701 (1992). Compare Bruce J. Winick, "Sexually Violent Predator Laws and Registration and Community Notification Laws: Policy Analysis," 4 *Psychol., Pub. Pol'y & Law* 505 (1998) (urging, as a matter of constitutional law, stricter limits on the use of involuntary civil commitment) and Janus & Logan, *supra* note 5 (positing that statutes which authorize confinement beyond what is a reasonable time for the accomplishment of treatment goals contravene the doctrine of substantive due process) with John Kip Cornwell, "Protection and Treatment: The Permissible Civil Detention of Sexual Predators," 53 *Wash. & Lee L. Rev.* 1293 (1996) (arguing that sexual predator legislation is constitutional).

[8] 521 U.S. 346 (1997).

[9] John Kip Cornwell, John V. Jacobi, & Philip H. Witt, "The New Jersey Sexually Violent Predator Act: Analysis and Recommendation for the Treatment of Sexual Offenders in New Jersey," 24 *Seton Hall Legis. J.* 1, 36–41 (1999).

[10] Sarah Duran, "Expert Faults McNeil Plan for Sex Predators," *The News Tribune*, p. A1 (2001, July 10).

[11] Eric S. Janus, "Preventing Sexual Violence: Setting Principled Constitutional Boundaries on Sex Offender Commitments," 72 *Ind. L.J.* 157, 205–206 (1996).

[12] *Hendricks, supra* note 8, at 372 (Kennedy, J., concurring).

[13] Id. at 373 (Kennedy, J., concurring).

[14] John Q. La Fond, "The Costs of Enacting a Sexual Predator Law and Recommendation for Keeping Them From Skyrocketing," in *Protecting Society From Sexually Dangerous Offenders: Law, Justice and Therapy* 283, 288 (Bruce J. Winick & John Q. La Fond, eds., 2003).

[15] Fitch, *supra* note 4, 2003, at 492.

[16] Robert M. Wettstein, "A Psychiatric Perspective on Washington's Sexually Violent Predator Statute," 15 *U. Puget Sound L. Rev.* 597, 624 (1992).

[17] *Hendricks, supra* note 8, at 367.

[18] Id. at 392–393 (Breyer, J., dissenting).

[19] Orders on Motions to Dismiss Because of Unconstitutional Conditions of Confinement at 4, In re Detention of Pedersen, 93-2-09933-9 (King County Super. Ct. March 7, 1995).

[20] Order and Injunction, Turay v. Weston, No. C91–664WD (W.D. Wash., June 3, 1994).

[21] Id.

[22] Turay v. Seling, 108 F. Supp. 2d 1148, 1152–1153 (W.D. Wash. 2000).

[23] Id. at 1154, 1160.

[24] N.J. Stat. Ann. § 2C:47–1 (West Supp. 2004) states:

[w]henever a person is convicted of the offense of aggravated sexual assault, sexual assault, aggravated criminal sexual contact, kidnapping pursuant to paragraph (2) of subsection c. of N.J. Stat. Ann. § 2C:13–1, endangering the welfare of a child by engaging in sexual conduct which would impair or debauch the morals of the child pursuant to subsection a. of N.J. Stat. Ann. § 2C:24–4, endangering the welfare of a child pursuant to paragraph (4) of subsection b. of N.J. Stat. Ann. § 2C:24–4, or an attempt to commit any such crime, the judge shall order the Department of Corrections to complete a psychological examination of the offender, except the judge shall not require a psychological examination if the offender is to be sentenced to a term of life imprisonment without eligibility for parole. The examination shall include a determination of whether the offender's conduct was characterized by a pattern of repetitive compulsive behavior and, if it was, a further determination of the offender's amenability to sex offender treatment and willingness to participate in such treatment. The court's order shall contain a determination of the offender's legal settlement in accordance with subdivision D of article 3 of chapter 4 of Title 30 of the Revised Statutes.

[25] That is, not all sex offenders are separately housed at Avenel. Some are excluded because they do not meet the "repetitive and compulsive" standard; others are ineligible because, although they satisfy these criteria, they refuse to engage in treatment and thus must remain in the general prison population.

[26] State v. L.P., 800 A.2d 207, 209 (N.J. Super. Ct. App. Div. 2002) (affirming a sentence that included community supervision for life).

[27] Wis. Stat. Ann. §§ 980.08(5), 980.12(1) (West 2004).

[28] Dr. Anita Schlank, personal communication, April, 2004.

[29] *E.g.,* Foucha v. Louisiana, 504 U.S. 71, 87–88 (1992) (O'Connor, J., concurring); Jackson v. Indiana, 406 U.S. 715, 738 (1972).

[30] Hendricks, *supra* note 8, at 365–366.

[31] Id. at 368 n.4 (emphasis added).

[32] Id. at 367.

[33] Id. at 372–373 (Kennedy, J., concurring).

[34] 373 F.2d 451 (D.C. Cir. 1966).

[35] Id. at 456.

[36] Id.; Mahoney v. Lensink, 569 A.2d 518, 527 (Conn. 1990) (stating that "meaningful" treatment requires individualized effort to help each patient by "formulating, administering and monitoring a 'specialized treatment plan'").

[37] 457 U.S. 307 (1981).

[38] Id. at 319.

[39] Id. at 322–323.

[40] *E.g.*, Janet D. v. Carros, 362 A.2d 1060 (Pa. Super. Ct. 1976).

[41] Id. at 320; John Kip Cornwell, "Understanding the Role of the Police and Parens Patriae Powers in Involuntary Civil Commitment," 4 *Psychol., Pub. Pol'y & Law* 377, 408–412 (1998).

[42] A third theory relies on the state's authority as parens patriae to provide care and treatment for those citizens who are unable to care for themselves. Accordingly, due process requires treatment when citizens are deprived of liberty "upon the altruistic theory that the confinement is for humane therapeutic reasons." Wyatt v. Stickney, 325 F. Supp. 781, 785 (D. Ala. 1971). Because the civil confinement of sexual predators is based overwhelmingly on the state's police power authority to protect its citizens rather than its beneficent parens patriae powers, this theory has little relevance in this context.

[43] Rouse, *supra* note 34, at 453.

[44] 373 F. Supp. 487 (D. Minn. 1974).

[45] Id. at 500 (quoting Minn. Stat. Ann. § 253A.02 subd. 5).

[46] Id. (quoting Minn. Stat. Ann. § 253A.02 subd. 8).

[47] Wash. Rev. Code Ann. § 71.09.010 (West 2004); see also 1995 Ariz. Sess. Laws § 10; Cal. Welf. & Inst. Code § 6606 (West 2004).

[48] Hendricks, *supra* note 8, at 367.

[49] Id.

[50] *E.g.*, Susan Stefan, "Leaving Civil Rights to the Experts: From Deference to Abdication Under the Professional Judgment Standard," 102 *Yale L.J.* 639, 687–688 (1992).

[51] *E.g.*, Gary W. v. Louisiana, 427 F. Supp. 1209, 1216 (E.D. La. 1976) (holding that where an individual is confined against his will for reason other than commission of criminal offense, the state must provide a benefit in exchange for loss of liberty); Donaldson v. O'Connor, 493 F.2d 507, 522 (5th Cir. 1974) (stating that outside the criminal context, "there must be a quid pro quo extended by the government to justify confinement").

[52] Youngberg, *supra* note 37, at 326 (Blackmun, J., concurring).

[53] Anthony B. Klapper, "Finding a Right in State Constitutions for Community Treatment of the Mentally Ill," 142 *U. Pa. L. Rev.* 739–835 (1993).

[54] *E.g.*, Mont. Code Ann. § 53–21–185 (1991) (obligating state mental health department "to provide adequate transitional treatment and care for all patients released after a period of involuntary confinement").

[55] Klapper, *supra* note 53, at 816.

[56] See *supra* text accompanying note 47.

[57] Not all SVP statutes explicitly contain the legislative findings referenced above. However, the statutes are fundamentally similar in all significant respects in terms of content, sentiment and intent; all provide for treatment; and all are patterned after the Washington statute which did contain such findings. Thus, it is appropriate to give the findings full force when construing SVP statutes.

[58] Wash. Rev. Code Ann. § 71.09.010 (West 2004).

[59] Id.

[60] Id.

[61] Id.

[62] Id.

[63] See *supra* notes 24–27 and accompanying text.

[64] Clark v. Cohen, 794 F.2d 79, 94 (3d Cir. 1986) (Becker, J., concurring).

[65] *Hendricks, supra* note 8, at 372 (Kennedy, J., concurring).

[66] Compare Robin Fretwell Wilson, "Cradles of Abuse: Evaluating the Danger Posed by a Sexually Predatory Parent to the Victim's Siblings," 51 *Emory L.J.* 241, 298–299 (2002) (arguing that treatment can lower the risk of future offenses and courts should take into account an offender's par-

ticipation in treatment) and James A. Billings & Crystal L. Bulges, "Maine's Sex Offender Registration and Notification Act: Wise or Wicked?" 52 *Me. L. Rev.* 175, 243–245 (2000) (highlighting flaws in research techniques that measure treatment efficacy, but concluding that "[t]reatment is also integral to sex offense solutions"), with R. Karl Hanson, "What Do We Know About Sex Offender Risk Management?" 4 *Psychol., Pub. Pol'y & Law* 50, 68 (1998) (noting that research regarding whether SVPs benefit from treatment is inconclusive) and Kirk Heilbrun, Michelle Kenney, Christine Maguth Nezu, Susie Chung, & Adam L. Wasserman, "Sexual Offending: Linking Assessment, Intervention, and Decision Making," 4 *Psychol., Pub. Pol'y & Law* 138, 169 (1998) (concluding that "[p]rogress in treatment is not a powerful risk-reduction indicator").

[67] R. Karl Hanson, Arthur Gordon, Andrew J. R. Harris, Janice K. Marques, William Murphy, Vernon L. Quinsey, & M. C. Seto, "First Report of the Collaborative Outcome Data Project on the Effectiveness of Psychological Treatment for Sex Offenders," 14 *Sexual Abuse: A Journal of Research & Treatment* 169–194 (2002).

[68] Id.

[69] Turay v. Seling, 108 F. Supp. 2d 1148, 1156 (W.D. Wash. 2000).

[70] 489 U.S. 189 (1989).

[71] Id. at 196 (quoting Harris v. McCrae, 448 U.S. 297, 317–318 (1980)).

[72] Fitch, *supra* note 4, at 492.

[73] Compare Cleveland Bd. of Educ. v. Loudermill, 470 U.S. 532 (1985) (holding that creating constitutionally protected property interest obligates the state to support that interest adequately).

[74] DeShaney, *supra* note 70, at 201 n.9.

[75] Hasenfus v. LaJeunesse, 175 F.3d 68 (1st Cir. 1999) (stating that public school officials may have affirmative duties to render aid to school children under the Due Process Clause); *accord* Freeman v. Ferguson, 911 F.2d 52 (8th Cir. 1990); compare Dwares v. New York, 985 F.2d 94 (2d Cir. 1994) (positing that affirmative duties may arise in the absence of state custody where state actors play a part in the liberty deprivation).

[76] *E.g.*, Jones v. United States, 463 U.S. 354, 364 (1983) (concluding that it was not "unreasonable" for Congress to provide for the "automatic" commitment of a defendant found not guilty by reason of insanity); Jackson v. Indiana, 604 U.S. 715, 729 (1972) (requiring a "reasonable justification" for involuntary commitment classification); Baxstrom v. Herold, 383 U.S. 107, 114 (1966) (stating that "classification of patients for involuntary commitment . . . may not be wholly arbitrary").

[77] 504 U.S. 71 (1992).

[78] *Hendricks, supra* note 8, at 359.

[79] 534 U.S. 407 (2002).

[80] Id. at 413.

[81] Linda J. Skinner, Kenneth K. Berry, Sue Ellen Griffith, & Brenda Byers, "Generalizability and Specificity of the Stigma Associated With the Mental Illness Label: A Reconsideration Twenty-five Years Later," 23 *J. Community Psychol.* 1 (1995).

[82] *E.g.*, John Kip Cornwell, "Confining Mentally Disordered 'Super Criminals': A Realignment of Rights in the Nineties," 33 *Houston L. Rev.* 651, 677–689 (1996); John Kip Cornwell, "Sex Offenders and the Supreme Court: The Significance and Limits of *Kansas v. Hendricks*," in *Protecting Society From Sexually Dangerous Offenders: Law, Justice and Therapy* 197 (Bruce J. Winick & John Q. La Fond, eds., 2003); John Kip Cornwell & Raymond Deeney, "Exposing the Myths Surrounding Preventive Outpatient Commitment for Individuals With Chronic Mental Illness," 9 *Psychol., Pub. Pol'y & Law* 209, 209 (2003).

[83] United States v. Virginia, 518 U.S. 515, 529 (1996) (defining heightened scrutiny standard in context of gender-based discrimination).

[84] Act of Oct. 31, 1994, ch. 134, § 1(a), 1994 N.J. Sess. Law Serv. 542, 542 (West).

[85] N.J. Stat. Ann. § 30:4–27.2(r) (West 1994) (emphasis added to denote amended language).

[86] In re D.C., 679 A.2d 634 (N.J. 1996).

[87] Id. at 649.

[88] Wis. Stat. Ann. § 51.01(13b) (West 1987) ("'Mental illness,' for purposes of involuntary commitment, means a substantial disorder of thought, mood, perception orientation, or memory which grossly impairs judgment, behavior, capacity to recognize reality, or ability to meet the ordinary demands of life, but does not include alcoholism.").

[89] Addington v. Texas, 441 U.S. 418, 426 (1979).

[90] Cornwell, *supra* note 41, at 403; Eric S. Janus, "*Hendricks* and the Moral Terrain of Police Power Commitment," 4 *Psychol., Pub. Pol'y & Law* 297, 302 (1998).

[91] *See supra* text accompanying note 47.

[92] Id.

[93] Cornwell et al., *supra* note 9, at 2.

[94] Report of the Task Force for the Review of the Treatment of the Criminally Insane 3 (Oct. 1997) (unpublished report, on file with author).

[95] Fitch, *supra* note 4, at 492.

[96] Cornwell, *supra* note 7, at 1297; Gleb, *supra* note 3, at 215.

[97] *E.g.*, Kelly A. McCaffrey, "The Civil Commitment of Sexually Violent Predators in Kansas: A Modern Law for Modern Times," 42 *U. Kan. L. Rev.* 887 (1994) (discussing the rape and murder of Stephanie Schmidt by a released sex offender that inspired the passage of the Kansas SVP law).

[98] Kansas v. Crane, 534 U.S. 407 (2002); Seling v. Young, 531 U.S. 250 (2001) (hearing claim that SVP statute violated ex post facto and double jeopardy clauses requires proof that law is punitive "on its face" rather than as applied in practice); Kansas v. Hendricks, 521 U.S. 346 (1997).

[99] Hendricks, *supra* note 8, at 373 (Kennedy, J., concurring).

Chapter 5

Cost and Resource Allocation in the Implementation of SVP Civil Commitment Policies—A Guide for Policymakers

by Andrew J. Harris, Ph.D.

INTRODUCTION

In 1990, Washington State adopted the nation's first contemporary civil commitment law for sexually violent predators (SVPs).[1] In the ensuing decade and a half, sixteen other states have passed similar laws, with states holding more than 2,000 committed individuals as of mid-2004 (Fitch & Hammen, 2004).

Reviews of SVP civil commitment policies have identified significant costs associated with prosecution of SVP cases, estimated at up to $100,000 per case, and with custody and treatment programming, estimated at between $60,000 and $107,000 annually for each committed individual (La Fond, 2003). These incremental costs per case, coupled with the steady growth of the committed population and a range of legal and operational requirements, have produced growing pressure on state budgets (Harris, 2005).

Considering the significant price tag associated with implementing these policies, the matter of cost emerges as a critical variable in assessing the policies' long-range viability. As such, states contemplating SVP civil commitment as a policy strategy, as well as those managing existing policies, must consider the full spectrum of organizational, legal, and political factors that drive costs and apply this knowledge to their implementation practices.

Drawing on state experiences to date, this chapter analyzes the drivers and cost patterns associated with SVP civil commitment and sets forth a framework through which to analyze these factors. The chapter's focus is ultimately a prospective one: examining the role of cost in establishing the viability and direction of SVP civil commitment as a policy strategy. Specifically, the framework presented focuses on three main questions:

1. What are the key variables and drivers associated with program cost?

2. What are the observable patterns and trajectory of costs over time as the policies evolve and mature?

3. How can state experiences to date inform the future direction of SVP civil commitment policies?

The chapter begins by presenting a model for evaluating SVP civil commitment costs, followed by an analysis focused on the aforementioned questions. Much of the data presented are drawn from a series of six state case studies conducted by the author between late 2001 and early 2003, with these data supplemented by with more recent information.[2]

A MODEL OF SVP CIVIL COMMITMENT COSTS

The current assessment is built around patterns of resource investment within three systems associated with the implementation of SVP civil commitment policies:

- Case selection systems, encompassing activities leading to commitment, from initial evaluation to the completion of legal proceedings;

Figure 5.1
Model for Assessing Policy Implementation Costs

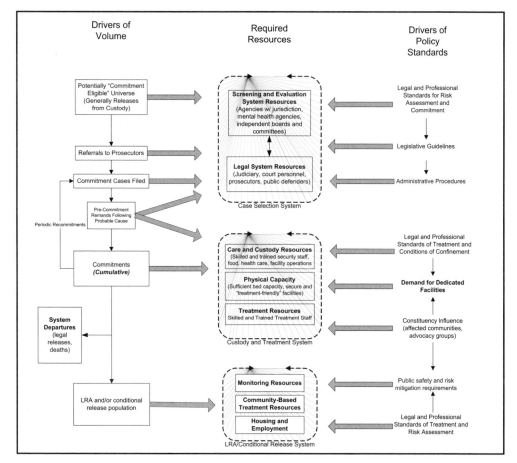

• Custody and treatment systems, including programming, facility operations, development of bed capacity, and general care for the committed population; and

• Conditional release/less restrictive alternative (LRA) systems, including community-based treatment, supervision and monitoring, and operation of transitional facilities.

Figure 5.1 presents a model for assessing the costs associated with implementing the policies and provides a framework for the remainder of this analysis.

The model depicts the three systems described previously with the level of resources in each driven by two sets of factors—service volume, associated with the number of cases that must be handled within each system, and policy standards, linked to the legal, professional, organizational, and political environment in which the policies operate.

Service volume drivers are represented by the left side of the diagram, which depicts the standard case flow associated with civil commitment, and in turn the "universe" of cases that must be addressed at each stage of the process. Policy standards are reflected to the right, which contains a range of variables affecting the scope of activity—and in turn the required resource levels—associated with implementing SVP civil commitment policies. In a rudimentary sense, service volume tells us how many units of service are required, and the policy standards dictate the general "costs per unit." Combined, these two sets of factors serve as the primary determinants of overall program costs.

With the general model specified, we now turn to a review of each of the three systems, with specific focus on the general resource requirements associated with each system; the primary cost drivers within each system, including a review of observed trends; and a long-range prognosis of cost growth within each system

CASE SELECTION SYSTEMS

Overview of Resource Demands

Systems of case selection generally consist of two sets of activities—a *screening process,* which separates potential commitment candidates from the broader population of sex offenders, and a *legal process,* intended to identify the group for which civil commitment is legally supported.

States vary in their approaches to the resource intensity and organizational locus of initial screening evaluations. From an organizational vantage, some delegate authority to mental health agencies, others centralize screening activities with correctional officials, and still others rely on independent multiagency boards or commissions. Regarding resource levels, states have adopted a range of approaches, ranging from streamlined reviews using in-house staff specialists to more resource-intensive systems requiring multiple levels of review and consensus and extensive use of contracted evaluators (Harris, 2005).

Similarly, states adopting civil commitment laws have employed various models regarding the locus of prosecutor jurisdiction and funding mechanisms for prosecutors, public defenders, and the courts to handle the legal processing of cases. Approaches include decentralized systems relying solely on regional or county prosecutors, centralized legal activities in the office of state attorneys general, and hybrid approaches combining both attorney general involvement and selected county prosecutors. Regarding funding structure, some states have effectively insulated counties and regional prosecutors from costs either through legislative appropriations or mandate relief, while others have required counties to absorb some or all of the costs associated with the commitment process.

Primary Cost Drivers

As noted in the model, the required service volume for case selection systems is a product of two variables—the number of individuals representing the potential universe of civil commitments and the proportion of cases that proceed through each key decision point (referrals to prosecutors, decisions to file, and judicial probable cause determinations).

Regarding the universe of prospective cases, the assumed effects of tougher sen-

Figure 5.2
Shifting Case Selection Burden

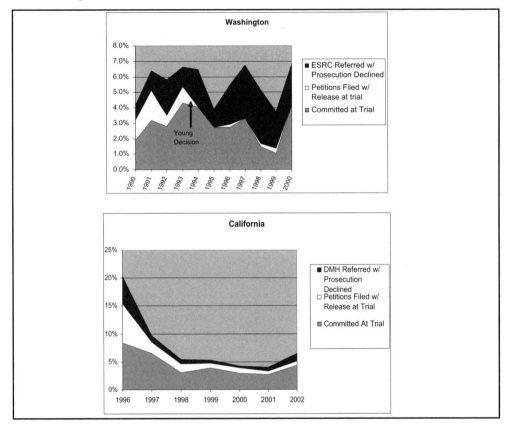

tencing laws on reducing the number of sexual offenders discharged from U.S. prisons have not appeared to taken hold. In fact, national data indicate that the number of sex offenders released from prison each year has shown some increase over the past decade.[3] Consistent with this finding, the author's analysis of case selection processes in six states indicated that states have seen no decline in the raw number of cases handled by initial case screening systems (Harris, 2005).

Significant changes, however, can be observed over time in the outcomes of the initial screening processes and in the proportion of cases proceeding through each stage of the case selection process. Specifically, it appears that the parties involved in case selection—from screening evaluators to prosecutors to judges and juries–appear to adjust their decision practices over time as the policies mature. Examples of these changes may be noted in Figure 5.2, which depicts the shifting distribution of the "case selection burden" in Washington and California.[4]

The Washington data, drawn from aggregate data provided by the End of Sentence Review Committee (ESRC; a multiagency board functioning as the state's primary screening entity) and case-level information provided by the Office of the Attorney General, indicates the disposition of cases as of the end of 2001.[5] While the data indicate significant fluctuations in the proportion of cases referred by the ESRC it appears that prosecutors have been fairly consistent in the proportion of cases selected for petition. Of particular note is the significant reduction in the proportion of cases resulting in release at trial following a key 1994 court decision validating the state's civil commitment law.[6]

The pattern observed in California, extrapolated from monthly case-flow data compiled by the Department of Mental Health (DMH),[7] highlights the relative surge of commitment activity upon commencement of the policy, and increased selectivity over time exercised by the key parties involved in the commitment decision process, including DMH screeners, prosecutors, and the courts. Perhaps most critically for the current analysis, the case of California indicates a process of adaptive "policy learning" that brings organizational decisions, and in turn the volume of cases handled across the system, into a general state of equilibrium.

Organizational Factors

In both the screening and the legal arenas, states must make a range of choices regarding the structure and funding of case selection systems—choices including which agencies will carry out key functions, how resources are balanced across systems, and the alignment of budgetary incentives to achieve policy goals. In turn, these choices may directly affect the efficiency with which cases flow through the system, the rates at which commitments are pursued, and ultimately the "downstream" resource demands associated with custody and treatment.

Prereferral Screening Systems. First, we consider the organizational locus and relative efficiency of the prereferral screening process. Although state models are varied, the contrasts between two particular approaches illuminate the potential role of organizational factors on overall resource demands and system efficiency.

The first such approach, adopted by Minnesota and Wisconsin, bases prereferral screening activities within correctional agencies, relying on in-house resources consisting of licensed psychologists or other individuals trained in the application of assessment instruments. In adopting this approach, these states essentially draw on fixed pools of resources to manage a relatively stable number of new cases each year. In 1998, Minnesota reported the cost of its corrections-based screening system, which processed approximately 450 cases discharged from the Department of Corrections (DOC) each year, at $188,000, projecting costs to increase to approximately $239,000 in 2005 (Minnesota Department of Corrections, 1999). A 1999 legislative analysis pegged the cost of Wisconsin's DOC-based screening program, handling an estimated 150 cases annually, at $286,000 (Wisconsin Legislative Fiscal Bureau, 1999).

In contrast, larger states such as California and Florida require mental health authorities to oversee evaluations prior to referral. Under this model, resource requirements involve both internal agency staff allocated for case screening and management of the process and contracted evaluator services that are used for the formal evaluations required by the policies.[8] In the case of California, the process also involves initial screenings performed by both the Department of Corrections and the Bureau of Prison Terms, the state's parole agency.

The costs associated with the latter approach are significantly higher than those linked to DOC-based screening models. California's 2003–2004 budget included $5.9

million for evaluation services, of which approximately $3.9 million may be allocated for initial evaluations (California Legislative Analyst's Office, 2004).[9] This figure is beyond the $346,000 allocated to the California Department of Corrections to staff its prereferral screening activities (California Department of Finance, 2004), and a similar amount allocated for staff resources at the Board of Prison Terms.[10] During calendar year 2003, the state's DMH received 558 cases from the Bureau of Prison Terms for review, of which 283—approximately half—were referred for independent evaluations. In the case of Florida, the state's 2002–2003 budget allocated $2.9 million to the Department of Children and Families (DCF) for contracted evaluation services, with the agency handling approximately 2,000 referrals per year.[11]

Comparing the two models described raises certain critical issues for policymakers. First, as a matter of relative efficiency, one might speculate that the more expensive and intricate screening process adopted by California and Florida might be justified by a more refined universe of cases referred to prosecutors (La Fond, 2003). Theoretically, a higher-cost screening program might be supported through a higher proportion of referrals ultimately resulting in commitment, and in turn a more efficient system. A comparative multistate examination of legal dispositions of cases referred to prosecutors, however, provided no evidence to this effect (Harris, 2005). In fact, while the commitment rates in California were roughly comparable to those in other states, Florida's relatively resource-intensive screening process was associated with a *significantly higher* rate of subsequent case dismissals than in many other states.[12]

Yet Minnesota's experience in recent years, notably a significant shift in its screening practices beginning in late 2003, highlights the volatile nature of case selection practices. Largely due to one tragic case—a high-profile rape and murder committed by an individual who had "slipped through the cracks" of the Minnesota DOC's screening system—the state witnessed a nearly fifteenfold increase from 2002 to 2003 in the number of cases referred to prosecutors for potential commitment, as noted in Table 5.1.

Table 5.1
Minnesota Referrals and Commitments, 1997–2004

Year	DOC Referrals	New Commitments
1997	58	25
1998	43	18
1999	32	26
2000	30	23
2001	24	13
2002	13	12
2003	246	18
2004	170	28

Source: Minnesota Department of Corrections

A further matter for consideration regarding screening responsibility pertains to incentive and resource alignment. In both California and Florida, evaluation activities are coordinated by the agencies ultimately responsible for managing services to the committed population. While the placement of referral decisions in the hands of mental health authorities rather than correctional agencies may carry certain legal benefits, the practice also brings the risk that evaluation and referral practices may be tainted by organizational or resource factors associated with the agencies' custodial functions (for example, budgetary pressures or incentives).

Certainly, state practices regarding the prereferral screening process may be a product of many variables. Factors such as the size of the state, the magnitude and geographic distribution of the potential commitment universe, and the vagaries of each state's legal and political landscape all contribute in some form to the choices that states make in this regard. However, considering the capacity for organizational structure and incentives to drive costs and policy utilization, further comparative review of state practices in this area, analyzing both efficiency and policy outputs, appears warranted.

Legal Systems. As mentioned earlier, there is evidence to suggest some level of organizational adaptation on the part of prosecutors and the courts as SVP civil commitment policies mature. Whether prosecutors initiate their policies in a tentative fashion and gradually ramp up utilization, or conversely whether they begin with relatively high rates of filing and scale back over time, it appears that practice within most systems stabilizes over time, as organizational actors reach requisite "comfort levels."

From a structural vantage, there is no particular evidence of significant differences in direct resource requirements between centralized prosecution models that place filing decisions in the hands of attorneys general and decentralized approaches relying on local or regional prosecutors. One pivotal organizational issue that *does* appear to have some basis, however, pertains to the funding mechanisms that states have employed to address the incremental costs of SVP civil commitment to the justice system, and how those mechanisms have affected policy practice. These issues are highlighted by the comparative experiences of two states—California and Florida.

As previously noted, these two states have adopted similar models for the prereferral process, centralizing activities with their respective mental health authorities. In addition, both states have placed filing decisions and responsibility for case prosecution in the hands of county or regional prosecutors, rather than centralizing the function with the attorney general, as is the practice in several other states. Yet despite these similarities, practices in Florida and California differ in one critical respect. Where the California system effectively provides uncapped state reimbursement to counties for legal expenses, the circuit-based legal system in Florida—states attorneys, public defenders, and the courts—remain dependent on limited state appropriations to address incremental resource needs.

Comparing data from California and Florida, there is little to suggest a relationship between availability of funding and prosecutor decisions to file. A review of cumulative figures to date indicate that Florida's state attorneys had filed cases on 91 percent of referrals by the DCF through September 2004, whereas California's counties had filed petitions on 85 percent of DMH referrals through that date, providing no indication that resource availability is a factor in filing decisions.

Yet, although funding constraints appear to have no effect on decisions to file, they do appear to bring operational impacts with potentially substantial cost implications. Notably, Florida has experienced a significant and persistent backlog within its pre-screening evaluation and its legal systems virtually since the inception of its policy. Of 723 petitions filed through September 2004, only 185 had proceeded to trial. Moreover, the thirty cases proceeding to trial during the first nine months of 2004 averaged 1,179 days from the date of the initial referral (Florida Legislature, 2004). While the state has seen some recent improvement in its case backlog, the program has yet to come into compliance with mandated timeframes for the disposition of cases.

One result of this backlog—a substantial proportion of cases being held in pre-commitment detention—carries potentially significant financial implications. A recent legislative report from Florida estimated that combined delays in the state's evaluation and legal systems had contributed to $15 million in pretrial detention costs related to individuals who were ultimately released by the courts (Florida Office of Program Policy Analysis and Governmental Accountability, 2004). These findings not only call into question the efficacy of the state's screening systems but also illustrate the significant interdependency between sufficient investment in screening and legal systems and the effective management of custody and treatment costs. Whether the delays may be attributed to system inefficiency, lack of sufficient funding, or a combination of these factors, the Florida experience highlights the potential financial implications of failing to effectively balance and manage resources across systems.

Prognosis

Volume-driven costs associated with legal case processing and screening, while indeed significant, appear to ultimately stabilize over time. In contrast with custody and treatment, which must contend with cumulative growth in the population, case selection costs are moderated by the universe of potential commitments (e.g., sex offenders released from custody) in a given year. Yet, although state experiences indicate that systems of case selection may become more discriminating and more efficient as the policies mature, the experience of Minnesota—a state that had apparently refined its case identification process until one tragic case led to a dramatic re-examination of its practice—points to the significant trade-offs involved in tighter gatekeeping practices.

Ultimately, the resource demands associated with case selection appear to be less associated with issues of volume and more linked to structure and organization. In this regard, policymakers must consider matters such as the relative efficiency of their screening systems, whether financial incentives impede or encourage certain programmatic decisions, and whether resources and funding mechanisms linked to case selection systems effectively align with implementation requirements.

CUSTODY AND TREATMENT

Overview of Resource Demands

Costs associated with managing the committed SVP population are driven by the joint demands of providing secure care and custody and maintaining a therapeutic environment consistent with the policies' underlying legal rationale. As illustrated by

Figure 5.3, drawn from Washington, these costs represent the most significant proportion of SVP program costs.[13]

Custody and treatment costs may be grouped into two categories: *operating costs* associated with program and support of institutional operations and *capital costs* linked to provision of sufficient bed capacity.

Operating costs, reflected in the survey data presented earlier in this chapter, may consist of direct staffing resources, service contracts for functions such as treatment or health care, and costs of general facility operations. As noted earlier, estimates of these costs have ranged from $60,000 to $107,000 per person. Notably, the author's six-state analysis found no relationship between per-person program spending and a program's ability to engage individuals in treatment and effectuate treatment progress (Harris, 2005).

Capital costs are more sporadic in nature but appear to be an invariable part of implementing an SVP civil commitment program (Lieb, 2003). Of the six states evaluated in Harris's review, Washington, Minnesota, and Wisconsin had undertaken multiple stages of facility development during the first decade of their policies, California and Florida had embarked on a construction of major new facilities, and Kansas had initiated plans to build a new mental health facility to house the patient population displaced by its growing number of committed SVPs. Construction costs per bed ranged from $130,000 in Wisconsin (Wisconsin Building Commission, 2001) to double that level ($260,000 per bed) in California (California Legislative Analyst's Office, 2004). The debt service costs of such construction, generally omitted from SVP program cost analyses, add significantly to the total cost per bed.[14]

Figure 5.3
Allocation of Washington SVP Program Costs

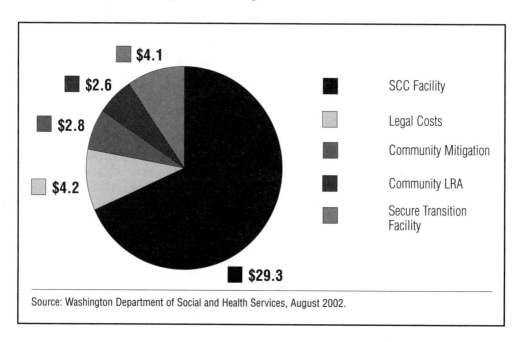

Source: Washington Department of Social and Health Services, August 2002.

Primary Cost Drivers

Evaluating custody and treatment costs over time, three main factors may be cited: population growth, legal and professional standards associated with commitment and treatment, and operational demands tied to facility expansion. To illustrate the effects of these factors, the graphs presented in Figure 5.4 illustrate the patterns of spending on custody and treatment over time in four states—Minnesota, Wisconsin, Washington, and California. The data presented in these graphs were pulled from the 2003 survey of state agencies and budget authorities.

Population Growth

As noted by Dennis Doren (Chapter 6, in this volume), states have achieved very limited success in moving individuals toward release—a factor that, coupled with a continued inflow of new commitments, produces a steadily growing number of individuals to be serviced through commitment programs. Hence, in contrast with costs linked to case selection systems, which eventually may level off or perhaps decline in accordance with relatively stable workloads, custody and treatment demands are linked to a population volume that is inherently cumulative in nature.

The graphs presented in Figure 5.4 point toward population size as a readily apparent driver of custody and treatment expenses. The most direct such relationship may be observed in California, where we see a direct correlation between DMH funding and population growth. This pattern may be attributed to that state's funding model that links legislative appropriations directly to the size of the SVP population under the care of the state's DMH.[15] Of the states presented here, the one exception to the

Figure 5.4
Custody and Treatment Spending and Population Levels in Selected States

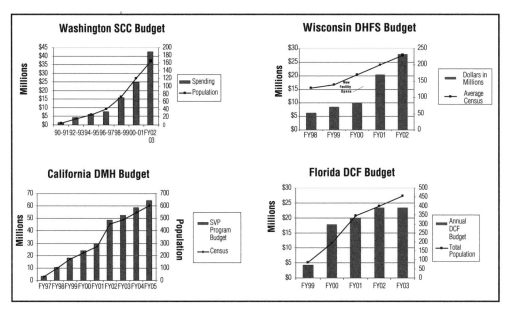

rule appears to be Florida, where the majority of the population in DCF custody has been composed of precommitment detainees, and where the DCF's budget allocation has been essentially level-funded for three years.[16]

Facility Expansion

Whereas states implementing SVP civil commitment policies typically begin by consolidating SVPs within existing correctional or mental health facilities, legal and capacity requirements almost invariably lead states to develop stand-alone facilities for the SVP population.

In terms of assessing resource viability, the implications of new facility investment are threefold. First and most apparent, states almost invariably incur significant capital construction costs associated with implementation of their civil commitment policies. Further, the experiences of "early adopting" states (e.g., Washington, Minnesota, and Wisconsin) that appear to embark on new phases of facility expansion every five to seven years seems to indicate that facility demands may be easily underestimated.

Second, beyond the direct costs associated with facility construction, the seemingly inevitable shift from "piggy-back" to "stand-alone" status for SVP facilities appears to bring with it substantial increases to operating costs. This phenomenon may be illustrated by the case of Wisconsin, which indicates a substantial surge in its spending levels in the year following the opening of the state's new SVP facility at Sand Ridge. Similar patterns may be observed in Minnesota and Washington in the years following their moves to new facilities. California, meanwhile, has already begun to accrue significant operational expenses far in advance of opening its new facility (California Legislative Analyst's Office, 2004).

Third and finally, facility investment may also carry a range of less tangible implications for the implementation of SVP civil commitment policies. On the political front, the continued patterns of facility investment in states such as Minnesota, Wisconsin, Washington, and California may be viewed as an indicator of the policy's significant level of support from lawmakers and the executive. It may also, under certain circumstances, generate renewed political support for the policy by mobilizing affected constituencies, as in the case of Coalinga, California, which lobbied hard for the state's SVP facility and the jobs that it stands to bring to the community (Rainey, 2000).

Legal Standards

The emergence of stand-alone facilities may at least in part be attributed to policymakers' recognition that civil commitment's legal foundations necessitate unique programming and conditions of confinement. The impact of legal requirements on program costs can be observed most readily through the cost graph presented for Washington (in Figure 5.4), which has operated its SVP civil commitment program under federal court oversight since 1994. In the years since the injunction was imposed, the state experienced a series of surges in its spending on custody and treatment services, coinciding with a range of court-driven facility and program improvements.

Whereas Washington's case is exceptional in the magnitude of legal oversight involved, the outcome of a similar case challenging conditions of confinement remains pending in Illinois,[17] and Florida—which has level-funded its program for three years—faces a similar legal challenge.[18] Moreover, whether conditions for treatment and confinement are imposed directly by the courts or are self-imposed due to states' tacit recognition of underlying requirements, the effect is essentially the same: States must invest considerable resources to ensure that policies are carried out in a manner consistent with their fundamental legal rationale and to forestall similar challenges.

Prognosis

Considering the cumulative nature of the committed population, it can be expected that the demands for volume-driven incremental resources will continue to expand over time. Further, considering baseline legal requirements regarding treatment and conditions of confinement, it would appear that states are somewhat limited in their ability to effectuate savings based on reduced scopes of service.

From an operational vantage, states may still have some room for system improvements that might mitigate some of the cost impacts. As discussed earlier, for example, states such as Florida that have experienced backlogs in their screening and legal systems might achieve significant custody-related savings through initiatives that reduce the pretrial detainee population. Along these lines, California has recently proposed shifting responsibility for pretrial housing from the state DMH to the counties.[19]

Ultimately, however, such operational modifications will not address the fundamental issues of structural growth related to the population. In this area, cost containment will depend either on a slowing of inflow through pursuit of alternative strategies that divert potential civil commitments or on the development of treatment approaches that can safely effectuate discharge and provide requisite public safety assurances. Based on the current landscape, both of these potential solutions remain only marginally tractable means of addressing the core issue of population growth. In the absence of such an approach, it remains probable that costs will continue their upward climb.

CONDITIONAL RELEASE/LRA SYSTEMS

Overview of Resource Demands

An individual's designation as an SVP for purposes of commitment considerably raises the stakes associated with transitional release. To mitigate against this, authorities planning and implementing LRA programs are often required to go to extraordinary lengths to ensure public safety and to address community demands (Lieb, 2003). Resource requirements associated with LRAs may include costs associated with siting, constructing and operating specialized transitional facilities, establishing and supporting community-based treatment capacity, monitoring individuals in the community, and providing mitigation funds to affected communities.

As with case selection systems, one may observe considerable state practice variation in the design and utilization of community-based release programs for SVPs. Of the states operating confinement programs for SVPs, Arizona has developed the most extensive means of integrating supervised release programming into its core program model, moving 49 of 117 committed individuals into these programs. At the other end of the spectrum is California, where less than 1 percent of committed SVPs to date have progressed to the community release stage of treatment, and Florida, where annual agency requests for resources to create a structured supervised release program have repeatedly been omitted from the state's executive budget submission.[20]

Primary Cost Drivers

LRA and supervised release (SR) programming can be extremely expensive, often far exceeding the costs of facility-based commitment. This is illustrated in Figure 5.5, based on information provided by the Washington Department of Human Services, comparing the costs per person associated with incarceration, civil commitment, and the state's LRA, and indicating that the average cost of community-based supervision may be greater than four times the cost of commitment.

Although the magnitude of costs reflected in Figure 5.5 may not be broadly representative of all state experiences, examining the circumstances surrounding these costs provides a useful framework for evaluating key cost drivers in this area. Four factors in particular require particular attention: caseload growth driven by legal requirements, the "cost of entry" associated with establishing LRA capacity, requirements driven by communities and key constituencies, and the variability associated with the individualized nature of supervised release programs.

Figure 5.5
Washington's Relative Costs of Commitment and Transition

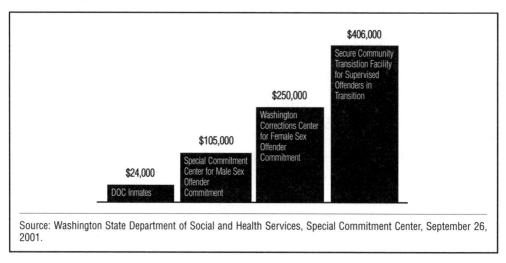

Source: Washington State Department of Social and Health Services, Special Commitment Center, September 26, 2001.

Legally Driven Population Growth

Treatment professionals have long maintained that provisions for supervised release represent an essential component of any civil commitment program (Association for the Treatment of Sexual Abusers, 2001). Consistent with this, the

Turay injunction that has been so pivotal in shaping the Washington program has stipulated provision of a "light at the end of the tunnel" as an essential part of the state's civil commitment program. The court has required that the state employ whatever means necessary to create a viable LRA for any individual who complies with and successfully progresses through institutional treatment.

Although practices in other states are not directly guided by such an injunction, most states implicitly recognize that the legal foundations on which civil commitment is based require that provision of an adequate treatment program consistent with professional standards regarding LRA availability. Hence, it should be expected that states that have not already done so must eventually transition from a purely institution-based model to a blended model including both institutional and community-based systems of treatment and supervision. Moreover, it remains likely that those states that do not proactively address this requirement will eventually be compelled to do so by the courts.

Cost of Entry and Economies of Scale

Washington's per-person cost cited in Figure 5.5 in part reflects the relatively high "cost of entry" that states experience during the initial deployment of their LRA programs. In Washington's case, the state elected to centrally house its program in a transitional facility, with the initial cases in the system providing few economies of scale. In a state such as California, which has adopted a more individualized approach to addressing its limited number of cases, per-case annual costs may in fact greatly exceed the roughly $406,000 cited by Washington.[21]

Individual Treatment Plan Requirements

Considering the political issues surrounding release, the provision of supervised release programs does not easily lend itself to a "one-size-fits-all" approach. While treatment services provided in an institutional setting may be provided with relative uniformity, the broad range of treatment and monitoring conditions, typically stipulated by the court granting release, contribute to make resource requirements connected to transitional programming highly variable.

Reflecting this variability, a Wisconsin legislative fiscal bureau report notes that the cost in that state's supervised release program may range from $2,600 per month ($31,000 annually) to $10,800 per month ($130,000 annually) (Wisconsin Legislative Fiscal Bureau, 2001).

Constituency and Community Demands

As noted previously, the designation of an individual as a "sexually violent predator" significantly raises the stakes surrounding release. Considering the substantial role that victims' groups have played in the development of SVP civil commitment policies, requirements set forth by affected constituencies play a major role in defining general provisions for LRAs. Washington's experience in particular indicates the potentially significant resource demands associated with meeting community and constituency-driven public safety demands. From the siting of its transitional facility to the allocation of resources to sufficiently monitor the activities of individuals in the LRA program, the Department of Human and Social Services has been required to invest considerable funding in response to concerns raised by victims groups and adjacent communities (Washington Department of Social and Health Services, 2000, 2002, 2003).

Prognosis

Considering the factors described earlier, the emergent challenge to the financial viability of transition and release hinges on programs' capacity to balance individual treatment demands with the policies' fundamental public safety mandate. Specifically, can transition and release systems be structured to both create a viable and cost-effective means for release *and* to provide the requisite level of community protection?

Based on states' experience to date, it appears premature to draw firm conclusions surrounding this question. With the numbers of release eligible individuals comparatively small, LRA and SR programmatic demands have more typically driven by case-specific requirements than by any type of broader strategic focus. Accordingly, while some states are gradually gaining experience in this area, their capacity to develop cost-effective and stable systems of community reintegration for committed SVPs remains a largely open question.

Despite this broader uncertainty, three key things do appear clear:

1. The demands for more structured systems of transition and release are likely to grow over time, as states are pressured by the courts to release committed SVPs nearing the end of their treatment.

2. The prevailing *modus operandi* for transition and release is one of caution, focusing first and foremost on community protection and only secondarily on facilitating pathways of societal reintegration for SVPs.

3. This cautious approach to community risk reduction comes with a substantial and highly unpredictable price tag, requiring resources that in many cases may in fact exceed the costs of commitment. The potential variability and magnitude of costs associated with housing, supervision, and treatment for individuals in transition significantly are likely to complicate future planning and development.

4. Whether the prevailing risk-averse approach to transition and release will diminish over time and whether it will continue to serve as an impediment to successful release programming remain to be seen. Ultimately, the operational viability of transition and release depends on whether programs can become more resource-efficient over time, without sacrificing public safety or (perhaps more critically) the *public perceptions* of public safety at the core of the policies' political rationale.

CONCLUSIONS/POLICY IMPLICATIONS

The extent of resource support over time represents a critical indicator of both a policy's relative level of political support and its ability to withstand socioeconomic change—variables directly related to the policy's long-term viability (Mazmanian &

Sabatier, 1989). Given that SVP civil commitment policies generally emerged during a time of economic growth and associated state budget surpluses, their level of sustenance during the current period of economic contractions becomes an especially critical factor.

Harris's 2005 analysis indicated that legislatures and governors had shown a fairly robust level of support for the policies, even in the face of growing costs and shrinking state revenues. States have exhibited a fairly consistent willingness to invest in new facilities, and to appropriate funds to meet legal requirements and to accommodate population increases. Yet considering projected cost growth and mounting strains within the target population, it remains quite likely that SVP custody and treatment costs will invite growing scrutiny in the years ahead.

The material presented in this chapter indicates that the policies' resource sustainability depends on a range of factors, including states' ability to effectively align incentives and resources across systems and a consistent focus on seeking cost-effective means of managing the size of committed populations. Although program costs to date have been concentrated in the area of custody and treatment, the policies' future depends largely on program investment in effective reintegration efforts.

Footnotes

[1] Wash. Laws. ch. 3 §§ 1001–1013 (1990).

[2] The six case studies focused on the experiences of Washington, Minnesota, Wisconsin, Kansas, California, and Florida (Harris, 2005).

[3] Data collected from the National Corrections Reporting Program indicates that individuals with rape or other sex offenses listed as their highest-level offense has remained relatively stable (fluctuating between 4.6 percent and 4.9 percent of total prison releases between 1992 and 2001). Bureau of Justice Statistics data indicate that total U.S. releases from state prison increased by 46 percent between 1990 and 2001.

[4] The universe of cases screened by Washington's End of Sentence Review Committee may not be directly comparable to that referred to the California Department of Mental Health, where the case universe is refined by initial screenings performed by the Department of Corrections and the Board of Prison Terms.

[5] Data include cases initiated in the designated year for which final disposition had been established by the end of 2001.

[6] In re Young, 857 P.2d 989 (Wash. 1993).

[7] Monthly activity reports are available at *www.dmh.cahwnet.gov/SOCP/facts-figures.asp.*

[8] Both states require the performance of more than one clinical evaluation, with referral determinations in California dictated by statutorily defined consensus rules, and decisions in Florida mediated by a multidisciplinary review committee guided by administrative policies.

[9] California law requires recommitment proceedings every two years. A recent legislative proposal to eliminate this requirement pegged potential evaluation-related savings at approximately $2 million per year. Based on this, approximately two-thirds of the $5.9 million figure may be linked to initial evaluation activities.

[10] Although official state budget documents do not break out SVP-related costs at the Board of Prison Terms (BPT), a cost analysis applying state salary schedules to a staffing resource plan provided by the BPT estimated annual BPT costs related to SVP screenings at approximately $300,000 (Harris, 2003).

[11] The significant difference between the Florida Department of Children and Families caseload and that handled by the California DMH may be attributed to Florida's lack of an intermediate prescreening system such as that provided by the California Department of Corrections and BPT.

[12] Forty-two percent of cases filed by prosecutors that were disposed of as of September 2004 had

resulted in dismissal, release, or release at trial (Florida Department of Children and Families, 2004).

[13] Washington data are presented for illustration purposes, considering that legal expenses associated with commitment flow through and are tracked by the Department of Social and Health Services, presenting the most complete overall picture of cost allocation across systems. For more detailed analysis of relative costs across systems in other states, *see* Harris (2005).

[14] To provide some context, California's 1,500-bed facility—currently estimated at a construction cost of $380 million, translates into a rough annual debt service cost of $20,000 per bed, assuming that the facility operates at full capacity. Based on the states current population projections, however, the functional cost per bed on an annual basis may be far greater, perhaps double this level.

[15] Until 2004, California's cost growth noted in the chart was accompanied by a steady decline in the overall proportion of those costs associated with "level of care" at Atascadero State Hospital—a multipurpose forensic facility. This trend suggests that state appropriations were progressively exceeding the incremental costs of care, producing a budgetary windfall for the DMH for every newly committed SVP (Harris, 2005). However, with the phase-in of Coalinga State Hospital—the state's new SVP commitment facility scheduled to begin operation in September 2005—it appears likely that the $107,000 per patient will not fully meet the new facility's full operating costs.

[16] Florida's level funding strategy has apparently come at a cost. A legal challenge has maintained that the state has rationed treatment services, providing access to only one-third of FCCC residents, and is challenging conditions of confinement within the facility (Canupp v. Liberty Behavioral Health (complaint filed in M.D. Fla., May 7, 2004)). Moreover, two inspector general reports in 2004–2005 identified significant system failures and instances of staff and managerial misconduct associated with the state's contracted vendor (Florida Office of Inspector General, 2004, 2005).

[17] Hargett et al. v. Baker et al. (complaint filed in N.D. Ill., Feb. 27, 2002).

[18] Canupp v. Liberty Behavioral Health (complaint filed in M.D. Fla., May 7, 2004).

[19] Although the state ultimately bears responsibility for county costs, the presumption behind this cost-savings measure is that county-based custody will be significantly less expensive than the cost of maintaining individuals in a psychiatric inpatient setting prior to commitment (California Legislative Analyst's Office, 2004).

[20] For greater detail on state utilization of supervised release, refer to Doren (Chapter 6, in this volume).

[21] A report out of California indicates that the state plans to spend approximately $1 million in fiscal 2004 to cover the costs of its new contracted supervised release program for SVPs, which as of March 2003 was planning for only one client (Associated Press, 2003). Since that time, three individuals have been released from custody into community supervision

References

Associated Press. (2003, March 15). *State to pay $1 million for sex predator oversight.*

Association for the Treatment of Sexual Abusers. (2001). *Practice standards and guidelines for members of the Association for the Treatment of Sexual Abusers.* Beaverton, OR: Author.

California Legislative Analyst's Office. (2004). *Analysis of 2004–05 budget bill: Department of Mental Health.* Sacramento, CA: Author.

Fitch, W. L., & Hammen, D. (2004, September). *Sex offender commitment in the United States.* Paper presented at the conference of the National Association of Mental Health Program Directors—Forensic Division, Atlanta.

Florida Department of Children and Families. (2004, September). *Monthly caseflow report.* Tallahassee, FL: Author.

Florida Legislature. (2004). *Sexually violent predator program—Time from referral to DCF to trial.* Tallahassee, FL: Office of Economic and Demographic Research.

Florida Office of Inspector General. (2004). *Report Summary, Case #2004–0043-WB.* Tallahassee, FL: Department of Children and Families.

Florida Office of Inspector General. (2005). *Report Summary, Case #2004–0083.* Tallahassee, FL: Department of Children and Families.

Florida Office of Program Policy Analysis and Governmental Accountability. (2004). *Sexually violent predator program is reducing backlog, but still not timely* (Report # 04–63). Tallahassee, FL: Author.

Harris, A. (2005). *Civil commitment of sexual predators: A study in policy implementation.* New York: LFB Scholarly Publications.

La Fond, J. Q. (2003). The costs of enacting a sexual predator law and recommendations for keeping them from skyrocketing. In B. J. Winick & J. Q. La Fond (Eds.), *Protecting society from sexually dangerous offenders: Law, justice and therapy* (pp. 283–300). Washington, DC: American Psychological Association.

Lieb, R. (2003). After *Hendricks*: Defining constitutional treatment for Washington State's civil commitment program. *Annals of the New York Academy of Science, 989*(1), 474–488.

Mazmanian, D. A., & Sabatier, P. A. (1989). *Implementation and public policy; with a new postscript.* Lanham, MD: University Press of America.

Minnesota Department of Corrections. (1999). *Civil Commitment Study Group 1998 report to the legislature.* St. Paul, MN: Author.

Rainey, J. (2000, August 3, 2000). Coalinga gets its wish. *Los Angeles Times,* p. A3.

Washington Department of Social and Health Services. (2000). *Special commitment center: Secure community housing criteria and site selection process.* Olympia, WA: Author.

Washington Department of Social and Health Services. (2002). *Allocation of Additional Secure Transition Facility Beds Per RCW 71.09.250 (6) and ESSB 6594.* Olympia, WA: Author.

Washington Department of Social and Health Services. (2003, April 4, 2003). *DSHS adds a forest area location as a potential sex offender housing site* (Press release). Olympia, WA: Author.

Wisconsin Building Commission. (2001). *2001–2003 capital budget recommendations.* Madison: Wisconsin Department of Administration.

Wisconsin Legislative Fiscal Bureau. (1999). *Sexually violent person evaluation unit (Paper 335).* Madison, WI: Author.

Wisconsin Legislative Fiscal Bureau. (2001). *Supervised and conditional release (Paper 502).* Madison, WI: Author.

Chapter 6

The Model for Considering Release of Civilly Committed Sexual Offenders

by Dennis M. Doren, Ph.D.

INTRODUCTION

Since 1990, seventeen states in the United States have passed and are currently using some form of civil commitment specifically for sexual offenders (Arizona, California, Florida, Illinois, Iowa, Kansas, Massachusetts, Minnesota, Missouri, New Jersey, North Dakota, Pennsylvania, South Carolina, Texas, Virginia, Washington, and Wisconsin). Some of these states have been employing such a commitment law for a decade or longer (i.e., Kansas, Minnesota, Washington, and Wisconsin), whereas other states just very recently started implementing this type of specialized civil commitment law (e.g., Pennsylvania, in February 2004). A survey from February 2004, described in this chapter, found that more than 2,100 people have been committed under these laws across the United States, not counting the scores more who were detained still awaiting commitment hearings.

In more typical "mentally ill and dangerous" civil commitment situations commitments occur for relatively short periods, measured in weeks and months. Within the realm of sex offender civil commitments, however, longer periods of commitment are both expected and demonstrable. Statutorily, the time period for commitment within California's current law is two years (with possible two-year extensions), with every other relevant statute leaving the period completely open ended (i.e., no automatic expiration time period). The effect of that open-ended type of commitment has been for people to remain committed for many years. An average length of commitment in Wisconsin, for example, a state in which the law has existed for about ten years, is about four years (Amy Ahler, personal communication, January 2004).

This chapter explores how committed sex offenders get released either from their secure facility placement or from their commitment in total. For instance, Table 6.1 (at page 6-3) presents data showing that relatively few committed individuals have been released from the locked facilities to date. Most states have released few to none of their secure-placement patients even though those states have been committing sex offenders for many years (e.g., Iowa, Minnesota, Missouri, and North Dakota). Only a few states have made movement to lesser restrictive placements outside the main locked facility something beyond a rare event.

Complete discharges from commitments were found to be even more rare. At the time a 2004 survey was completed, nine of the seventeen states had yet to discharge a single individual, with another three states having discharged only one or two patients.

There can be many reasons why these laws are being implemented the way they are. Some among us might presume the answer can be summed up with the word "politics." Society generally wants sex offenders to be locked up and to "go away," such that there is little honest desire to administer over them like patients to be treated and released, and far more desire just to keep them locked up. There is no advocacy group working hard for sex offenders, the argument goes. Hence, once a sex offender is committed, he is essentially going to be locked up for life, or at least for a very long time.

Even if this argument has merit, the argument does not explain differences documented among the states. Apparent differences, even statistically significant differences, can be found when comparing how the seventeen states are implementing their commitment laws. (See analysis of data.) Differences can be found in the rates at which people are committed, rates at which they are released with imposed conditions, and the states' discharge rates. "Politics" is too simple a concept to explain the differences to be described.

The purpose of this chapter is to explicate other factors that may be influencing how committed individuals get released and to make recommendations based on the findings. This chapter was not written to address concerns about such things as (1) the constitutional appropriateness of the sex offender commitment laws, (2) ethical issues beyond the release process, or (3) commitment procedures. This chapter focuses purely on what has been happening in the process of releasing committed individuals from secure facilities and their commitments and what factors seem to explain the cross-state differences that are found.

The chapter initially offers data from a national survey describing each state's experience through February 2004 in committing and releasing sexual offenders. Differences among the states are enumerated based on those data. The bulk of the chapter then describes the factors that may have brought about those differences. Conclusions are then drawn based on the findings overall, including a few recommendations based on the interstate trends discovered.

THE SURVEY

The Data

When sex offender civil commitment laws began to be passed and implemented, one could commonly hear (in courtrooms and in general discussion) that once committed "no one" would ever "get out." Ultimately, the accuracy of this prediction is an empirical question.

To test that prediction, I conducted a survey involving each of the seventeen states with sex offender civil commitment laws as of the end of February 2004. I personally contacted people in each state who were in a position to know (or compute) the exact data for their state's commitment history. At times, I contacted more than one person within a state to ensure that complete information was obtained, or because one person in the state served as a facilitator to help me find the person with the data.

Table 6.1 lists the survey results. A few things about the data in this table need to be explained for the reader to have a clear picture. The column "Year Begun" refers to the year the commitment process was actually implemented in the listed state. For some states, this was the same year the law was passed. For other states, the law had been "on the books" but not yet enacted for some while prior to its implementation (compare "Year Passed" with "Year Begun").

The column "Number Ever Committed and Commitment Not Overturned" gives the total number of commitments in each state excluding all commitments that were overturned by the courts (either through appeal or reconsideration at the trial court level). In other words, this column lists the number of effective commitments in each state through February 2004, as compared to the start date (year) for the commitment process in the previous column.

Of greatest relevance to this chapter are the numbers in the three remaining columns. They are, in order, the number of committed individuals who (1) were granted a release into the community while still under some commitment status, (2) died while under a commitment, and (3) were completely discharged from their commitment in a manner other than through winning a court appeal or death. The number of people listed in each of these columns represents subsets of the total number of committed offenders in the column "Number Ever Committed and Commitment Not Overturned," not people in addition to that total amount. On the other hand, the numbers in each of these three last columns are not necessarily related to one another; nor do they represent subsets of one another. For instance, people can be (and have been) discharged from their commitment without having also been people who were released with conditions into the community (i.e., they were discharged directly from a secure facility).

Analyzing the Data

These data show some clear differences across the states in how they have implemented their commitment laws. Some analyses, and summary statements follow to describe the trends found in these differences. All figures have been derived from Table 6.1. It should be understood that these data clearly reflect a snapshot in time and may not project accurately into a future time when this chapter might still be read.

Table 6.1

Sex Offender Civil Commitments in the United States as of February 2004

State	Statute Number	Year Passed	Year Begun	Number Ever Committed & Commitment Not Overturned	Number Released With Conditions	Number Died While Committed	Number Discharged From Commitment
Arizona	36-3701 et seq.	1995	1997	117	49	5	27 (includes 2 to DOC)
California	6600 et seq.	1995	1996	451	1	7	23
Florida	394.910 et seq.	1998	1999	163	6	1	4
Illinois	725 ILCS 207	1997	1998	149	11	3	1
Iowa	229A	1998	1998	38	1	0	0
Kansas	59-29a	1994	1994	123	9*	5	1
Massachusetts	123A	1998	1999	52	7*	0	0
Minnesota	253B.185 et seq.	1994	1994	131 (+ 70 SPP**)	0 (+ 1 SPP)	0 (+ 5 SPP)	0
Missouri	632	1998	1999	48	N/A	0	0
New Jersey	30:3-27.25 et seq.	1998	1998	310	12	3	2
North Dakota	25.03.3	1997	1997	14	0	0	0
Pennsylvania	42	2003	2004	0	0	0	0
South Carolina	44-48-10 et seq.	1998	1998	78	N/A	3	5
Texas	841	1998	1999	35	35	1	0
Virginia	37.1	1999	2003	7	2	0	0
Washington	71.09	1990	1990	138	13	6	0
Wisconsin	980	1994	1994	269	39	12	11
TOTALS				2123 (+ 70 MN SPP)	185 (+ 1 MN SPP)	46 (+ 5 MN SPP)	74

Note. All numbers were obtained through direct communication with people in that state.

* The number of seven under conditional release represents the number of committed people who were at some point placed into a transitional residence on the same grounds as the secure facility, though not all of those people actually had community access.

** Minnesota has two commitment statutes. The more recent statute is the most like that found in the other states listed. An earlier statute, the Sexual Psychopathic Personality (SPP) law, however, is still used, such that numbers for those people are listed here for comprehensiveness sake. Although some people are committed under both statutes and not just one, the numbers for SPP include people committed solely under that statute. People committed under both are included in the regular numbers listed.

The Number of People Committed. The absolute numbers of people committed across the various states range from 0 (in Pennsylvania) to 451 (in California), a wide range. Clearly and obviously, however, these numbers are affected at least by (1) the length of time the commitment law was in use and (2) the population size of the states involved. Pennsylvania had literally just started using its law weeks before this survey was conducted. Sex offender civil commitments rarely occur within that short a time period, so Pennsylvania's zero tells us nothing about the future frequency of commitments in that state. California's commitment number reflects both the length of time that state has been committing sex offenders (since 1995) as well as its population size compared to the other states.

Meaningful comparisons concerning the number of people committed across the states must take these two factors of time frame and population size into consideration. When doing so, the findings can be summarized as shown in Table 6.2. The relative values of the numbers in the last column of this table give a different impression from a review of the absolute numbers of commitments in the earlier column. To be clear, the use of a state's population only serves as a surrogate for the total number of

Table 6.2
Number of Commitments Considering Time and Population Size

State	Years Enacted	Population Size (in Millions)*	Absolute Number of Commitments (From Table 6.1)	Commitments per Year per Million People
Arizona	7	5.3	117	3.15
California	9	34.5	451	1.45
Florida	5	16.4	163	1.99
Illinois	6	12.5	149	1.99
Iowa	6	2.9	38	2.18
Kansas	10	2.7	123	4.56
Massachusetts	5	6.4	52	1.63
Minnesota	10	5.0	131**	2.62
Missouri	5	5.6	48	1.71
New Jersey	6	8.5	310	6.08
North Dakota	7	0.6	14	3.33
Pennsylvania	0	12.3	0	___
South Carolina	6	4.1	78	3.17
Texas	5	21.3	35	0.33
Virginia	1	7.2	7	0.97
Washington	14	6.0	138	1.64
Wisconsin	10	5.4	269	4.98

* Based on figures from July 2001 from the U.S. Census Bureau.

** MN's SPP population was ignored in this analysis as virtually all people committed under SPP in the past ten years are included already given they were also committed under the State's SDP commitment law.

incarcerated sex offenders in a state. A state's commitment rate for sex offenders would most properly be computed by using that latter figure, and not simply the total population size. Obtaining a state's number of incarcerated sex offenders, however, is a very problematic task. The definition concerning who should be counted and who not would actually vary from state to state, depending on (1) its sexual offense laws and (2) the relevant criteria within the commitment laws. In addition, to get the most exact figure, numbers from beyond the prison system would need to be counted in most states to include (1) people found "insane" for sex crimes and in psychiatric facilities, (2) in a notable minority of the states, juveniles who were adjudicated delinquent for sexual offenses and who were incarcerated in a facility for such juveniles, and (3) in some states, people who are incompetent to proceed to trial while facing any of certain sexual offense charges. Getting accurate counts of these sets of people would be very difficult. Therefore, while acknowledging the surrogate nature of the state populations for computing relative commitment rates across the states, the population figures were thought to serve sufficiently for the analysis herein.

The figures in the last column of Table 6.2 show something different compared to what may have been suggested by the data in Table 6.1. The mean figure in Table 6.2's last column is 2.6 (with Pennsylvania excluded, something that will be true for all analyses in this section), with a standard deviation of 1.54. These numbers indicate that any figure in the last column of Table 6.2 that falls between 1.06 and 4.14 (i.e., the mean rate plus or minus 1 standard deviation) is clearly in the average range among the different states' commitment rates. States with figures falling outside that range are more atypical.

That analysis showed that Texas and Virginia are the states with commitment rates lower than expected, given the typical commitment rate of the remaining states. New Jersey, Wisconsin, and Kansas showed rates higher than expected, with New Jersey actually falling a notable 2 standard deviations higher than the other states' mean [i.e., 6.08 > 2.6 + 2(1.54)], a true statistical extreme (i.e., outlier).

There seem to be some statutory/procedural reasons that present themselves to explain why these states stand out in their commitment rates compared to the rates in the bulk of the other states. Some of these reasons, although plausible, are demonstrably not accurate in explaining these findings. Other explanations remain plausible after critical review. This section discusses the different possible reasons.

One possible explanation is that states that require either a higher demonstration of recidivism risk (i.e., statutory risk threshold for commitment) and/or more criteria to be met (e.g., statutory requirement that the risk be of a "predatory" nature, a factor in only a portion of the current statutes) would show lower rates of commitment, and vice versa. This hypothesis does not hold up under inspection, however. For instance, the risk thresholds for commitment in Texas, Virginia, and Kansas, are all statutorily the same: "likely" (as are the statutes from various other "average rate" states). Although New Jersey's commitment risk threshold is arguably lower than most other states ("likely to engage in acts of sexual violence means the propensity of a person to commit acts of sexual violence is of such a degree as to pose a threat to the health and safety of others," this being a description that appears lower than the manner by which the term "likely" is interpreted in many of the other states), Wisconsin's risk threshold (at the time of the survey being "much more likely than not") was higher than found in these other states, not lower. Likewise, the statutory requirement that the relevant risk be "predatory" in nature was found in the Virginia and Kansas statutes (the latter only in the early years of the statute) and not in the other listed states' laws (though in the laws from other "average" states such as Iowa and Washington).

An alternative explanation for commitment rates differing across the states stems from more unique considerations in the various states. Consider the two states with the lower commitment rates. The Texas rate reflects a commitment process that is quite unique among all the others. All the commitments in Texas are outpatient, meaning there is no inpatient commitment facility and no inpatient commitment status. As discussed later when considering conditional releases from secure facilities, the process of labeling people "sexually violent" and then placing them in the community is problematic. The low commitment rate in Texas may reflect the problems inherent in this process. Virginia's low commitment rate may simply reflect the fact that the commitment law was implemented only one year earlier. In a vast majority of the states, the first year of enactment involves many people being detained but relatively few actual commitments due to the need to work out the numerous procedural and statutory issues.

The states with the higher rates also show some potential individual explanatory procedures. New Jersey is the one state in which the commitment process necessarily begins with a simple certificate from a psychiatrist (or other physician), with this certificate being based statutorily on an interview of the subject. Only after probable cause is found is a more standard (actuarially based) risk evaluation completed, unlike most other states in which the referral process to a prosecutor already involved a more standard risk assessment. Research has shown that general clinical judgments about risk tend to see far more recidivism risk than actuarial assessment procedures do (e.g., Nicholaichuk, Templeman, & Gu, 1999). Certainly when added to the fact that the commitment risk threshold is lower than for many other states, it may not be surprising that New Jersey referred a greater number of people for commitment than did other states, when controlling for population size and years of enactment.

Wisconsin's high rate may reflect the combination of two factors. One is that Wisconsin prosecutors file commitment petitions for nearly every case referred to them (Thomas Fallon, personal communication, multiple dates spanning years), this being unlike the practice in some other states in which a greater degree of prosecutory discrimination has been found. For example, only about one-third of referred cases have been prosecuted in Iowa (Michael Ferjak, personal communication, September 2004) and Washington (Milloy, 2003). The second factor is that Wisconsin initially showed a referral rate for sex offenders leaving prison at the high end of what was typical (Doren, 1998), though that referral rate has declined since.

Overall, the explanation for why some states have disproportionately higher or lower commitment rates seems to be based on factors unique to each such state. Simple explanations such as differences in risk thresholds or statutorily defined commitment requirements are insufficient in this regard.

The Number of People Released With Conditions. The nation's sex offender civil commitment statutes describe differing ways by which committed individuals can be released from a secure facility while still under a commitment into the outside community with imposed restrictions. Terms such as "conditional release," "transitional release," "supervised release," and "less restrictive alternatives" are used in the statutes to describe this process. The issues being explored here are how often this occurs and under what circumstances.

The numbers in Table 6.1 concerning the people released with conditions are found in the third column from the end. Like the foregoing, however, these numbers of people need to be converted to a common metric to compare across the states and their varying number of years and rates of civil commitments. Table 6.3 shows that conversion.

One can easily see that the 100 percent figure from Texas clearly stands as very discrepant compared to all the other states. The explanation for this is straightforward, as it is statutory. As mentioned earlier, all the commitments in Texas are conditional releases into the community, with no inpatient commitments allowed. If the figures from Texas were included in computing average percentages of conditionally released individuals, then the mean proportion across the fourteen states (excluding Missouri, Pennsylvania, and South Carolina) would equal 16.7 with a standard deviation of 26.8. (Missouri and South Carolina would be excluded because their statutes do not allow for conditionally released committed people. Pennsylvania would be excluded because no one had yet been committed at the time these data were gathered.) The fact

Table 6.3
Number of Conditional Releases Considering Number Committed

State	Number Committed (From Table 6.1)	Number Released With Conditions (From Table 6.1)	Percentage Who Were Conditionally Released
Arizona	117	49	41.88
California	451	1	0.02
Florida	147	6	4.08
Illinois	149	11	7.38
Iowa	38	1	2.63
Kansas	123	9	7.32
Massachusetts	52	7	13.46
Minnesota	131	0	0.00
Missouri	48	——*	——
New Jersey	310	12	3.87
North Dakota	14	0	0.00
Pennsylvania	0	0	——
South Carolina	78	——*	——
Texas	35	35	100.00
Virginia	7	2	28.57
Washington	138	13	9.42
Wisconsin	269	39	14.50

* Conditional releases are not allowed by statute in these states.

the Texas figure stands as such an outlier, however (over 3 standard deviations above the mean), suggests that a more appropriate analysis would exclude Texas when drawing conclusions about the other states' figures.

When Texas is also excluded, the mean proportion of conditionally released people across the remaining thirteen states is 10.2, with a standard deviation of 12.4. These figures show that of those thirteen states, Arizona and Virginia showed disproportionately high proportions. (Arizona's proportion was over 2 standard deviations above the mean, while Virginia's was over 1 standard deviation above the mean.) Although still within 1 standard deviation from the mean, it may seem notable that Minnesota had only one conditional release (a resident committed under an earlier commitment statute), North Dakota had literally no conditional releases, with California virtually with the same result. (For the record, if Arizona were also excluded from this analysis as representing another outlier (besides Texas), the mean proportion of conditionally released people across the remaining twelve states would have been 7.6 with a standard deviation of 8.25. The net effect of this analysis compared to the one including Arizona is only to portray Virginia as more of an outlier, as no new state is found to fall into the range beyond one standard deviation from the new mean.)

The concept mentioned at the beginning of this chapter, that once people are committed they will "never" get out, already has an "it depends" attached to it, even before we explore the issue of complete discharges from commitment. The numbers related to conditional releases showed as wide a divergence as can be, from 0 to 100 percent. Even when Texas is excluded from this analysis due to its unique process of placing all committed individuals in the community, the proportion of committed people who obtain placements in lesser restrictive environments varies from 0 to 42 percent. Exploring why the extremes are as they are is very telling.

The first potential explanation for the variability in states' results is that the conditional release process requires people to make treatment progress and hence takes some time to occur. With that logic, states conducting civil commitments longer than others would disproportionately show higher conditional release rates than states with newer laws, everything else being equal. This explanation does not hold up under scrutiny, however. Among the higher proportion states, Arizona's law had been functioning for seven years (as of the time of the survey), but Virginia's had been functioning for only one. Likewise, among the lowest proportion states are Minnesota and North Dakota, both of which had been doing civil commitments at least seven years, compared to a majority of states that had their laws for a shorter period of time.

A second potential explanation for the variability is related to the number of people who have been committed: It is easier to have a high proportion of conditionally released people from a small total number of committed people, with higher number of committed people resulting in lower proportions receiving conditional releases. Again, the data do not support that explanation. The highest number of committed people, in absolute terms, was found in California, but that state did not have even close to the absolute number of conditionally released people as various other states. New Jersey had committed both a high absolute number of people, and (as was demonstrated earlier) a high proportional number relative to its population, but its proportion of conditional releases was found to be in the average range. On the flipside, North Dakota had the smallest number of committed people (in absolute terms), but it had yet to conditionally release a single patient from its secure hospital commitment setting.

Something more complicated than these simple hypotheses appears to be needed to explain the high degree of interstate variability in conditional releases. To discover what it may be, each "extreme" state's process is explored.

Arizona clearly showed the greatest degree of placing committed people outside the secure environment compared to other states besides Texas. The process used in Arizona, however, is not as risky as may first appear by this statement. In Arizona, many patients are moved from the locked forensic hospital setting (i.e., the Arizona State Hospital) to a less restrictive alternative (LRA) facility on the same grounds as the state hospital and still in a locked building. This situation is sometimes referred to as a locked quarterway house (i.e., halfway house on the grounds of a hospital). (In fact, Arizona's law allows for a person to be placed in the LRA facility immediately following his commitment hearing, instead of necessarily going to the secure facility first. This situation is currently unique among the seventeen states, though Wisconsin had such a statutory option as well for the first five years of its law.) Committed individuals in the LRA facility can go into the community for certain purposes, but the patients do not live in the community and their community trips are supervised (to varying degrees). Of the forty-nine people listed in Table 6.3 who obtained a release with conditions, only about seven were actually released to live in the community (Judith Becker, personal communication, February 2004), making Arizona's number of truly released into the community far more in keeping with what we found in the other states, though with a unique transitional process out of the secure facility.

Virginia's proportion also was found to stand out compared to that of the other states. The fact that the state had been using its commitment law for only one year prior to the data collection, however, coupled with the very small numbers of people involved, makes any conclusion here about real trends questionable.

There are also interesting findings from the states that showed essentially no conditional releases (even when allowed by statute). Minnesota stands out as a state that has been civilly committing sex offenders (even under their newer such law) for a long time, ten years, has had an average number of commitments (per year per million in the state population; i.e., as shown in Table 6.2), but only had one conditional release, of a resident committed under an older commitment law. (Minnesota actually has two active sex offender civil commitment statutes. The conditionally released person was committed under the older but still existent commitment law, the Sexual Psychopathic Personality Statute (SPP).) However, no person committed in Minnesota under the newer law, the Sexually Dangerous Person Statute (SDP), has obtained a conditional release through the time of this survey. The SDP statute uses language more typical to that found in other states' current sex offender civil commitment laws and therefore was thought the more appropriate for comparison to other states in this analysis. Any analysis including the SPP commitments who are not also committed under the SDP law would need to lengthen the number of years the Minnesota law has been enacted beyond the SDP law. North Dakota is similar, though with a far smaller absolute number of committed people. Despite differences in procedures, the reason these two states have yet to conditionally release anyone may overlap.

As stated in the North Dakota law at the time the survey was conducted (§ 25-03.3-17): "A committed individual must remain in the care, custody, and control of the executive director until, in the opinion of the executive director, the individual is safe to be at large" (i.e., eligible to be discharged). In other words, the person with complete responsibility for the decision for conditional releases is the head of the treatment facility. The courts are not involved. It is a given that the executive director of a treatment facility will obtain a significant degree of input from the treatment staff.

In Minnesota, the process of obtaining a conditional release is more obtuse. First, there is the statute that states: "The head of the treatment facility may provisionally discharge any patient without discharging the commitment. . . . Each patient released on provisional discharge shall have a written aftercare plan. . . . The provisional discharge shall terminate on the date specified in the plan unless specific action is taken to revoke or extend it" (§ 253B.15). In other words, once a secure facility placement is ordered by the court, the head of the treatment facility may take the responsibility for approving and placing a committed patient into the community. This process of placing a committed patient into the community by the head of the treatment facility necessarily needs to involve a plan for discharging the patient completely, including a time frame by which this is expected to happen given no "specific action is taken to revoke or extend" the plan. The process of releasing a patient at the treatment facility's initiation has yet to occur.

Minnesota patients can also apply for conditional discharge without the formal approval of the head of the treatment facility (Stephen Huot, personal communication, January 26, 2005). The patient starts the process by petitioning the Special Review Board (SRB; a panel of attorneys, psychiatrists, and psychologists under contract to the Department of Human Services). That panel addresses petitions from patients, by taking testimony from the treatment team, the state's attorney general (who represents the Department of Human Services), the county attorney, the patient, and in some cases, the victim. The SRB either denies or grants the petition. Either way, there is a second review stage by the Commissioner of the Department of Human Services. No matter what the commissioner decides, to agree or disagree with the SRB recommendation, any of the parties can appeal the commissioner's decision to a three-judge panel. That panel may again hear testimony. Appeals of that panel's decision can be made to higher courts.

Having a staged process for obtaining a conditional release may not be the issue. Possibly most telling is that the treatment team, a clear contributor to the process, does not recommend conditional releases until someone is deemed to have completed all prior phases of the treatment program. Through the date of the survey, this had never happened for those committed under the newer generation of SDPs (once for the older generation of SPPs). In other words, patients petitioning for conditional release to date have had to face the SRB and the commissioner with active lack of support for the petition from their treatment staff and implied lack of support from the head of the treatment facility. The courts then get the case only after the treatment staff, the head of the treatment facility, the SRB, and the commissioner have gone on record, at least most of the time against the petition.

The ultimate outcome seems clear: Decisions in favor of conditional releases never happen even after years of commitments with average numbers of committed people. Maybe this should not be surprising, as forensic hospital administrators and department commissioners can be expected to listen to what their hospital treatment staff members tell them. Quite typically, the first is strongly governed by the idea that patients need to complete the treatment program before being released into the community, as opposed to using a more objective risk management assessment (cf. Doren, 2005, concerning the accuracy of treatment staff risk judgments). It can also be expected that the director's superiors, departmental personnel high in state government, will be influenced by strong concerns to avoid any community incident harmful to state citizens. That is their job. No matter why, both of these influences then serve to diminish the likelihood that a patient will receive a conditional release decision. (In contrast, judges are regularly required to balance individual rights with society's need for protection, without having to answer to superiors in the same way when things go wrong. On the other hand, it seems reasonable to presume that judges will pay attention to a list of prior reviewers at least most of whom are not supportive to the petition.)

In both North Dakota and Minnesota, the determination of who can be conditionally released seems heavily influenced by the apparent necessity first to complete the treatment program. As we shall see, this necessity seems to differentiate the states with very low numbers of conditional releases and those with higher numbers.

California's experience overlaps this issue but adds its own unique statutory commitment structure affecting the decision as well. Concerning the latter point first, all commitments are for a maximum period of two years, with an ongoing chance for renewal at the end of each two-year period. (The prosecutor needs to demonstrate that the person meets commitment criteria for each two-year period.) Conditional release applications can only be made after a year of secure facility placement. Then, as stated in the California statute (§ 6604): "Time spent on conditional release shall not count toward the two-year term of commitment, unless the person is placed in a locked facility by the conditional release program . . . on the grounds of an institution under the jurisdiction of the Department of Corrections." Because the court will not consider discharge for at least a year after a conditional release has occurred (which was at least a year into his commitment), a patient on conditional release cannot shorten his current commitment time to less than two years, and he may not even lessen the time for which he is in a locked facility by getting on a conditional release. This structure would seem to represent a disincentive for someone whose option is simply to wait until the two-year commitment period has passed and the state has to re-prove that the commitment criteria are met. As the discussion concerning Table 6.5 will show later in this chapter, this latter option is clearly more favored by, and more successful for, the patients.

There is a second factor apparently influencing the numbers of conditionally released patients in California. As of the date of this survey, the California treatment program had yet to recommend conditional release for any patient, despite being in place for about nine years. The treatment staff apparently makes such a recommendation only when the person completes the program (Amy Phenix, personal communication, October 27, 2004), a factor found to be potentially important in explaining North Dakota's and Minnesota's lack of conditional releases.

Overall, there appear to be four reasons that some states show relatively extreme numbers concerning the conditional release process:

1. A lack of statutory approval for any such releases (i.e., in Missouri and South Carolina);

2. Statutory procedures that either determine high numbers of conditional releases (i.e., in Texas) or set up contingencies against conditional releases (i.e., in California);

3. The use of an LRA program on hospital grounds to serve as a transitional process between the secure facility and conditional release into the outside community (as is done in Arizona); and

4. The effect of having departmental administrators responsible for the decisions concerning those conditional releases coupled with a philosophy from the treatment staff of not recommending conditional releases until the person completes the treatment program (as is true in Minnesota and North Dakota).

Despite the widely divergent frequencies of conditional releases across the states, the above four reasons appear to account for nearly all extreme numbers found.

The Number of People Who Died While Committed. This category may seem odd to the reader to compare across the states, given that every patient who died while committed did so from natural causes (which is true). The original issue raised in this chapter, however, was the idea that people had to die to get out of their commitments. It therefore seems prudent to inspect the rate at which people are dying while committed, and if that rate differs in different jurisdictions.

The proportion of each state's set of patients who died while still committed can be found in Table 6.4. The mean proportion of patients who died across the states (excluding Pennsylvania, again due to the lack of commitments in that state through the timing of the survey) was 1.82, with a standard deviation of 1.86. This means that

Table 6.4
Number of Deaths Considering Number Committed

State	Number Committed (From Table 6.1)	Number Who Died While Committed (From Table 6.1)	Percentage Who Died While Committed
Arizona	117	5	4.27
California	451	7	1.55
Florida	147	1	0.68
Illinois	149	3	2.01
Iowa	38	0	0.00
Kansas	123	5	4.07
Massachusetts	52	0	0.00
Minnesota	131	0	0.00
Missouri	48	0	0.00
New Jersey	310	3	0.97
North Dakota	14	0	0.00
Pennsylvania	0	0	——
South Carolina	78	3	3.85
Texas	35	1	2.86
Virginia	7	0	0.00
Washington	138	6	4.35
Wisconsin	269	12	4.46

five states were found with proportions greater than one standard deviation higher than the mean (Wisconsin, Washington, Arizona, Kansas, and South Carolina, in decreasing order), while no states showed rates lower than the average range (because a proportion of zero was still within one standard deviation from the mean). No state showed a rate that was two standard deviations from the mean, so no state's rate stood out as an outlier in this regard.

There appears to be a straightforward explanation for why the enumerated states showed higher than average rates of death among committed individuals. The mean length of time these states have been committing sex offenders is 9.4 years, while the mean for the remaining states (excluding Pennsylvania) is 5.9 years, less than two-thirds the time. Logic would suggest that the longer a state holds a group of people, the greater the number of natural deaths will occur among those people. The fact that no state stands as a true statistical outlier also suggests that nothing significant differentiates one state from the others in regards to their patient death rates.

The Number of People Who Were Discharged From Their Commitments. This last category may be of greatest importance in addressing the original issue raised about whether people ever get out of a commitment. As the numbers in the last column of Table 6.1 showed, some people do get discharged (without overturning their commitment through legal appeals). As has been true for the other analyses, to make the most sense from these discharge figures, they need to be viewed in comparison to the total number of committed people in each state. For this tabulation, see Table 6.5.

The mean percentage of patients discharged from their commitments was 4.62 with a standard deviation of 8.5 (excluding Pennsylvania, for the usual reason). These numbers demonstrate that Arizona represents an outlier in this regard (i.e., its discharge rate was beyond two standard deviations from the mean). If Arizona were simply considered an outlier and excluded from the analysis, the mean of the remaining fifteen states in this regard is 3.13 with a standard deviation of 6.27. This means that none of those fifteen states was found to discharge patients at a rate beyond the average range (i.e., none showed a rate beyond 1 standard deviation, a rate beyond 9.4).

The central issue to this chapter concerns if and how people get out of their commitments short of dying. Because this section pertains most directly to that issue, the results found in Table 6.5 are explicated state by state rather than solely by discussing the one statistically extreme case of Arizona.

On point to the central concern of this chapter is the fact that eight states (excluding Pennsylvania, which would have made nine) have, in fact, not discharged a single committed individual through means other than a court overturning the commitment or the patient's dying. Put another way, only eight states have discharged anyone, and only five states have discharged even 1 percent of the total number of people they committed (though this rate is still over twice the rate of patient deaths in those same states; seventy vs. twenty-eight).

For committed individuals in the eight states without discharges, the original concern that once people are committed they will remain committed has complete support through the time of the survey. On the other hand, this finding of no discharges was almost regularly documented in states with relatively younger laws. The states with the five newest laws (Florida, Massachusetts, Missouri, Texas, and Virginia; besides Pennsylvania, which would have made six) all were found with no discharges to date except one (Florida).

Table 6.5
Number of Discharged Patients Considering the Number of Commitments

State	Number Committed (From Table 6.1)	Number Who Were Discharged (From Table 6.1)	Percentage Who Were Discharged
Arizona	117	27	23.08
California	451	23	5.10
Florida	147	5	3.40
Illinois	149	1	0.67
Iowa	38	0	0.00
Kansas	123	1	0.81
Massachusetts	52	0	0.00
Minnesota	131	0	0.00
Missouri	48	0	0.00
New Jersey	310	2	0.65
North Dakota	14	0	0.00
Pennsylvania	0	0	——
South Carolina	78	5	6.41
Texas	35	0	0.00
Virginia	7	0	0.00
Washington	138	0	0.00
Wisconsin	269	11	4.09

Importantly, there is some reason to believe that the process of discharging patients from their commitment should not be expected during the initial set of years of a commitment law's implementation. Specifically, discharges in Wisconsin have shown a clear but nonlinear trend over time. In a state that has been conducting sex offender civil commitments since 1994, most discharges occurred in 2003 (the last full year before the survey), about nine years after the law was initially implemented. While the Wisconsin's first two discharges occurred in 1996, both involved patients already living in the community on conditional release after being placed into that status immediately at the time of their commitment (a possibility that has existed in very few states). The first discharge directly from the secure facility occurred in 2000, six years after the law's implementation. If Wisconsin's experience represents what can be expected in other places, then all the states whose law was still just five years old at the time of this survey have yet to reach the time when discharging patients would start to become expected.

Still, even Wisconsin's experience does not explain what is happening in the four states (Iowa, Minnesota, North Dakota, and Washington) with relatively older laws but still no discharged individuals. All four states have at least two things in common: (1) their treatment programs have community reintegration as their final treatment stages, and (2) members of treatment teams write the statutorily required annual reexaminations and have not recommended any type of release (conditional or through discharge) for any patient who has failed to reach that final stage in the program. Treatment programs with that design (including a community reintegration final stage) are found elsewhere (e.g., Wisconsin), but at least in some of those other states the annual reexaminations are written by people other than members of the treatment teams. It may be that the combination of the foregoing two factors is the telling characteristic that results in no commitment discharges even in states with relatively older laws.

This brings us to the states that have discharged people from their commitments. Do they have something to tell us in this regard, especially those that have discharged more than one or two people (i.e., Arizona, California, Wisconsin, South Carolina, and Florida)?

The process of discharge even in some of these states does not appear to represent what might be most desired: the determination that a higher-risk individual has lowered his risk through efforts and became ready for release. In Arizona, the state with the highest absolute number and statistically far greater proportion of discharges at the time of the survey, the vast majority of discharges resulted from a change in the commitment risk threshold (as determined by that state's supreme court) midway through that state's years of committing people. Many patients had been committed with a working understanding by evaluators and trial courts that the risk threshold (described in the statute as "likely") was equal to "more likely than not." That changed when the Arizona Supreme Court determined the meaning of "likely" to be higher than that. This resulted in reexaminers finding a set of "about 20" (Judith Becker, personal communication, February 2004) patients "no longer" met commitment criteria and effectively recommended discharge for those patients. This reevaluation process clearly demonstrated integrity, but at the same time it did not represent a general model for other states for discharging people from their commitments without changing commitment criteria. (To explain a note in Table 6.1, another two Arizona patients were considered "unsuccessful" discharges, having been sent to prison following new charges.)

An analogous situation is found in California, the state with the second largest number of discharges. Literally all the discharges listed in Table 6.5 for California were the result of the fact that California's commitments need to be renewed after each two-year period or they expire. The complete set of discharged patients for California through the time of the survey obtained their discharge either because prosecutors decided not to petition to renew the commitment or because they failed in the renewal attempts. None of the discharges were the result of a person working his or her way through the treatment program with recommendations from the treatment staff (George Bukowski, personal communication, February 2004). (For the record, California has had one discharge of the latter type between the time the survey was completed and the writing of this chapter. Also for the record, nontreatment staff reexaminers had recommended discharge prior to treatment program completion, but these recommendations were never supported by the treatment program (Amy Phenix, personal communication, October 27, 2004).) Again, the available information suggests that a relatively large number of discharges stem from a situation unique to one state, and not from a model more generally applicable to the other states with commitment laws.

Wisconsin is the state with the next largest number of discharges (in absolute terms, not relative to the number of commitments). The discharges in this state largely reflect two different circumstances involving recommendations from reexaminers for discharge: (1) the patient was living in a conditional release status within the (outside) community for some period of time without significant incident, and/or (2) the recidivism risk the patient represented was assessed at reexamination as lower than the commitment threshold even without the patient necessarily having worked to reach that goal (this finding being despite the prior court adjudication the person met commitment criteria). Some lowering of risk from treatment participation was relevant in a few cases as well, even though no patient had yet completed the treatment program.

Putting these three considerations into the context of Wisconsin's documented conditional release process, Wisconsin's model for discharging patients might be viewed as involving three different (though potentially overlapping) components, and may be the most useful for other states to consider. The three components for that state's model are:

1. Placing people on conditional release status in the outside community when the person's risk is thought sufficiently manageable with reasonable community resources, and then if the person does well long enough (including with ongoing treatment participation) to recommend discharging the person from the commitment;

2. Reassessing each committed person's recidivism risk annually and making recommendations for discharge if the person was essentially thought never to have met criteria despite a court's adjudication otherwise (this happening, for instance, when newer risk assessment procedures and knowledge lowered the assessed risk compared to earlier assessments); and

3. Reassessing each committed person's recidivism risk annually with the idea

that clear demonstration of treatment gain can be sufficient for recommending discharge (depending on the patient's initial risk level) even if the patient had not yet completed the available treatment program.

Although the numbers shown in Table 6.5 demonstrate that, for instance, California and Wisconsin do not have a significant difference in the proportions of people who have completely discharged their commitments (chi square = .03, df = 1, $p > .05$), Wisconsin's reasons for discharging people from their commitment may be more transferable to other jurisdictions compared to California's.

South Carolina and Florida had each discharged five people from their commitments, though this number represented a higher proportion of committed people in South Carolina compared to Florida (or even Wisconsin). In both states, these discharges reportedly occurred mostly due to the impending death of the person or other significant changes in his physical status (Geoffrey McKee, personal communication, February 2004; Gregory Venz, personal communication, November 2004). In neither state did a person get discharged based on his completion of the treatment program. Notably, some of these discharges occurred with recommendations for such from appointed reexaminers.

CONCLUSIONS

The original issue of interest herein was whether or not people committed under sex offender commitment laws ever "get out." The survey reviewed showed that the current answer is "sometimes, but not often." For some states, conditional releases and discharges are not common but not unusual either. For other states, they are both non-existent.

The reasons behind these differences seemed to differ. Although some structural statutory factors were clearly of relevance, simple explanations concerning differing risk thresholds for commitment and additional prongs for commitment (such as the risk being "predatory" in type) did not serve.

Of relevance in explaining cross-state differences in conditional release and discharge rates appeared to be the underlying philosophy by which reexaminations were conducted, especially if conducted by treatment staff. When there was a requirement that the person complete the secure facility treatment program prior to any type of release, then the numbers of releases were zero, or virtually so. When the philosophy underlying the reexamination is to have the person placed into the community when his risk and its manageability allow it, then some conditional releases and discharges occurred.

Treatment designed to lower the sexual reoffense risk in high-risk sex offenders obviously takes a long time. The two different philosophies, concerning whether or not treatment programming needs to be completed prior to any type of release, do not disagree on that fact, however. Instead, the issue comes down to whether or not it is necessary and appropriate to keep people in a locked facility to complete a program when their risk is sufficiently manageable under imposed conditions outside the secure facility. From a public safety perspective, one can always argue that keeping potential reoffenders locked up is safer. From a civil commitment perspective, however, where we talk about concepts such as least restrictive environments and individual rights, the expectation is that most people will move from the secure environment to less secure placements when they are ready, with readiness not always being determined by the completion of treatment. From this perspective, completion of treatment can occur while someone is living well supervised in a less restrictive placement.

Specific to the issue of discharge, the difference between the two philosophies becomes potentially even more prominent. Where the "treatment completion" philosophy rules, the person must go through a transitional process, sometimes a very slow one, to obtain a recommendation for discharge. In contrast, the more "traditional" civil commitment philosophy leads to a recommendation for discharge when the person's situation warrants it, no matter where he is in the treatment program. In other words, the "treatment completion" philosophy mandates the view that people can only reach discharge criteria upon completion of a treatment program coupled (in most cases) with a transitional period under supervision. The "traditional" model indicates that someone should be discharged when he no longer meets criteria for commitment, period. Statutorily, the "treatment completion" model is supportable only if one assumes that (1) initial risk level differences among patients do not matter in terms of the effectiveness of current treatment program designs; (2) everyone who completes a program has necessarily reached a risk level below the commitment threshold, no matter what the statutory risk threshold may be; and (3) this occurs just as they complete the program and not before. There is little logic to these assumptions, and no evidence that these ideas are true.

The analysis of the described survey results indicates that the "treatment completion" philosophy is associated with a near-zero release rate, while the "traditional" approach has resulted in some (though not a great deal of) conditional and unconditional releases. As described in the previous paragraph, the "treatment completion" philosophy also appears to ignore the statutorily defined timing for when someone should be discharged from his commitment. To the extent that we are really enacting civil commitment procedures, we apparently need to keep in mind as well that the release process from that civil commitment is based in the individual and not the stage in a treatment program.

Author's Note

Dennis M. Doren, Ph.D., is the Evaluation Director for the Sand Ridge Secure Treatment Center–Evaluation Unit in Madison, Wisconsin. The opinions expressed herein do not necessarily reflect those of the State of Wisconsin Department of Health and Family Services.

Thanks go to many people for their help in gathering and communicating their states' data for this project: in Arizona, Judith Becker, Steven Gray, Lyn Kane; in California, George Bukowski, Michelle Lawson; in Florida, Jill Levenson, Ted Shaw, Gregory Venz; in Illinois, Tim Budz, Corinne Davis-Corr; in Iowa, James Gardner, Kate Schapman; in Kansas, Austin DesLauriers; in Massachusetts, Nancy Connolly; in Minnesota, Stephen Huot; in Missouri, Richard Gowdy; in New Jersey, Glenn Ferguson; in North Dakota, Joseph Belanger; in Pennsylvania, Diane Dombach; in South Carolina, Geoffrey McKee; in Texas, Maria Molett; in Virginia, Mario Dennis, Stephen Wolf; in Washington, Robert Wheeler, Daniel Yanisch; and in Wisconsin, Deborah McCulloch.

References

Doren, D. M. (1998). Recidivism base rates, predictions of sex offender recidivism, and the "sexual predator" commitment laws. *Behavioral Sciences and the Law, 16,* 97–114.

Doren, D. M. (2005). What weight should courts give to treaters' testimony concerning recidivism risk? *Sex Offender Law Report, 6*(1), 1–2 & 15.

Milloy, C. (2003). *Six-year follow-up of released sex offenders recommended for commitment under Washington's Sexually Violent Predator law where no petition was filed.* Olympia: Washington State Institute for Public Policy.

Nicholaichuk, T., Templeman, T. L., & Gu, D. (1999, May). *Empirically based screening for sex offender risk.* Paper presented at the conference of the Correctional Services of Canada, Ottawa, Ontario.

Part 2

Clinical Issues

In the midst of the ongoing legal and public policy debates concerning civil commitment of sexual offenders, the clinicians in the programs continue to work diligently to provide the best possible treatment under less than desirable circumstances. In those states that have sexually violent predator (SVP) laws, many of the offenders confined to the treatment programs have begun filing lawsuits[1] arguing that their conditions are more like a prison or that their treatment is substandard (American Civil Liberties Union, 2004; Associated Press, 2004). Given the high-risk nature of these individuals, and the fact that these civilly committed residents do not resemble the patients typically committed under mental health laws, there does appear to be some uncertainty about how the treatment program should appear. This section discusses a wide variety of issues related to the provision of treatment in SVP facilities.

Joel Dvoskin and Anita Schlank have both been involved as expert witnesses in class action lawsuits concerning the provision of treatment in SVP facilities. In Chapter 7, they correct some common misunderstandings about the nature of the SVP population. In particular, they contrast the traits and treatment needs of this population with the population of the committed mentally ill.

Ian Heath is a psychiatrist who has worked treating sexual offenders both in the prison setting and in the SVP program in Minnesota. In Chapter 8, he and Anita Schlank help clarify answers to the many questions treatment providers might have about the role of medical interventions in addressing the disordered sexual arousal so often seen in this population.

Kim English and Peggy Heil are coauthors of Chapter 9, which focuses on the use of the polygraph. Given the high risk this population presents, it is extremely important that treatment providers can find methods for ensuring that treatment progress is genuine. It appears that the polygraph is a very important tool to assist in that goal, and they discuss its role and also some cautions regarding potential misuse.

John Bergman has consulted to numerous sex offender treatment programs, including outpatient, civil commitment, and prison programs, both throughout the United States and in many different countries. Chapter 10 offers insightful observations about the importance of the climate of the treatment environment and, particularly, the training needs of the line staff.

Much attention has been paid to methods for assessing treatment progress in civil commitment programs, particularly with the recent scrutiny regarding the release rates for these programs. In Chapter 11, Glenn Ferguson, Merrill Main, and Jennifer Schneider provide one state's solution to this very difficult task.

In Chapter 12, Anita Schlank discusses the implications of specific neuropsychological deficits on the progress of sexual offenders in civil commitment programs. This chapter discusses the prevalence of cognitive rigidity in repeat sexual offenders, along with its effect on treatment progression. Finally, Schlank offers suggestions for addressing this deficit.

In the final chapter of this section, Chapter 13, Vince Gollogly describes the evolution of a high-profile SVP program, the Washington Special Commitment Center. This program gained national attention when the state supreme court found that the treatment program did not meet constitutional standards, and a special master was appointed to oversee improvements to the program. Many other states heard periodic updates about the ongoing effort to improve the program, but this chapter provides a detailed chronology.

Footnotes

[1] Hargett v. Adams, Case No. 02 C 1456 (op. U.S. District Court, 2005).

References

American Civil Liberties Union. (2004). *Class action complaint challenges failure of Illinois officials to provide adequate mental health treatment under the state's Sexually Violent Persons Act.* Available: *www.aclu-il.org/news/press/000064.shtml.*

Associated Press. (2004, February 16). *Two sex offenders sue over confinement: Terms over, treatment continues in NJ.*

Chapter 7

Similar Statutes, Different Treatment Needs— A Comparison of SVP and Mentally Ill Populations

by Anita Schlank, Ph.D. and Joel Dvoskin, Ph.D., A.B.P.P.

INTRODUCTION

In June 1997, the U.S. Supreme Court upheld the constitutionality of the use of civil commitment statutes to continue to confine sexually violent criminal offenders after the end of their sentence, provided that they have a "mental abnormality" that causes them to pose a danger to others.[1] These statutes arose out of a perception that some inmates who posed a very high risk of violent sexual recidivism would be released, in many cases without any supervision at all, in the community upon the expiration of their sentences. Because they had already been sentenced, more severe sentences would not be legally permissible for these offenders, so states began to look for ways to preventively detain them.

To avoid the constitutional prohibition against ex post facto laws and double jeopardy, the first efforts to confine sex offenders after expiration of their sentence looked toward other examples of preventive detention that are allowed under constitutional law. Those seeking to confine these offenders might have relied on public health quarantine laws, such as those historically used to fight outbreaks of tuberculosis (Mindes, 1995–1996). Instead, they looked to and adopted the civil commitment statutes that have traditionally been used to confine persons with serious mental illness who posed an imminent danger to themselves or others. However, there were obvious differences between disorders that had traditionally been viewed as "mental illnesses" for the purposes of commitment and the predilection to commit sex offenses. Most important, traditional mental illnesses such as schizophrenia and bipolar disorder are widely accepted as squarely within the fields of clinical psychiatry and psychology. Sex offender treatment, on the other hand, is at best a small niche of the traditional mental health professions.

Second, although serious mental illnesses are believed in some cases to often overcome free will, there is no real consensus on the degree to which sexual disorders such as paraphilias diminish the offender's ability to "just say no" to his or her illegal desires; the difference between irresistible impulses and unresisted ones is often unclear. An example of this lack of consensus can be seen in the trial of serial killer Jeffrey Dahmer. During that trial, psychiatrist Fred Berlin testified that Dahmer was "insane" and not responsible for his actions; however, forensic psychiatrist Park Dietz stated that, in his opinion, "the thing that makes people willing to commit offenses for gratification of sexual arousal is exactly the same thing that makes others willing to commit robbery in order to get more money" (Keiger, 1994). Dietz testified that Dahmer was mentally disordered due to paraphilias, alcoholism, and personality disorders but not legally insane, and he noted that he draws a distinct line between psychotic mental illness and other disorders such as pedophilia or antisocial personality disorder. For the new wave of sex offender civil commitment statutes, it appears that a similar distinction was made and the term "mental abnormality" was used because most such offenders were not considered to have a "mental illness" sufficient to justify involuntary commitment under regular commitment statutes (Alexander, 2000).

Many observers and advocates have opposed the use of civil commitment statutes for those who are not mentally ill for several reasons (National Association of State Mental Health Program Directors, 1997). First, it could have severe and negative consequences for individuals with mental illnesses by increasing the stigma against them. The public already associates mental illness with dangerousness, despite that fact that people with serious mental illness are more likely to be victims than perpetrators of violence (Link & Phelan, 1999; Link, Phelan, Bresnahan, Stueve, & Pescosolido, 1999; Mulvey & Fardella, 2000). Second, we live in a time at which there are already too few resources devoted to the treatment of serious mental illness. Hospital beds are difficult to access, and community mental health services are far too few and not nearly intensive enough to prevent the most serious consequences of undertreated mental illness. As a result, jails and prisons have increasingly become unwilling and poor substitutes for more appropriate mental health treatment settings (National GAINS Center, *www.gainsctr.com*). By basing sex offender commitment statutes on mental disorders, it was feared that already thin resources would be taken from these programs and devoted to locking up sex offenders. Finally, there is the question of cost. Psychiatric hospitals are very expensive to run, far more so than prisons. To house sex offenders in psychiatric facilities, at a cost of up to $200,000 per bed per year or more, it would mean spending money on services (e.g., intensive twenty-four-hour nursing care) that have little to do with sex offender treatment.

Despite these arguments and the considerable attention that has been paid to the issue of how civilly committed sexual offenders differ from populations that are mentally ill, there continues to be considerable confusion in this area. Clinical directors for the sexually violent predator (SVP) programs frequently find that the public assumes that civilly committed sexual offenders are "mentally ill," and some advocates have assumed and asserted that their treatment programs should look just like those provided for patients with severe and persistent mental illnesses (Summit on the Treatment of Sexually Violent Predators, 2000). Others believe that sex offenders should be held in relatively inexpensive, even prison-like, circumstances, with sex offender treatment added on only to the meager extent required in *Kansas v. Hendricks*.[2] This chapter focuses on clarifying the differences between the populations of civilly committed sexual offenders and those who have been civilly committed for major mental illnesses. In addition, this chapter makes recommendations regarding specific treatment approaches that are appropriate for each type of client.

STRUCTURE OF STATUTES

Only recently have states used civil commitment statutes for sex offenders for confinement following completion of their prison sentences. Previously, in some states, statutes for mentally disordered sexual offenders (MDSO statutes) tended to divert offenders from the prison system into state hospitals or treatment centers, typically on a voluntary basis, allowing for return to the prison setting if they requested to do so, or if they showed a lack of progress in treatment (Reisner, Slobogin, & Rai, 1999). With the new postconfinement commitment arrangement, there was some confusion regarding how the statutes should be written. Some states, such as Minnesota, based the statutes on their statute for the confinement of individuals found to be mentally ill and dangerous (MI&D). This led to some aspects of the MI&D statute being applied illogically to sexual offenders. For example, the population committed as MI&D is committed initially on a temporary warrant, to be reviewed in sixty days (Minnesota Commitment Act of 1982). This sixty-day hearing is to determine whether the individual still meets commitment criteria, or whether his or her condition has changed significantly to suggest that he or she no longer meets those criteria. Because psychotropic medications can work fairly quickly, this procedure makes sense for individuals whose psychosis led them to be a danger to self or others. The Sexually Dangerous Person and Sexual Psychopathic Personality statutes in Minnesota use this same temporary warrant and sixty-day hearing, despite the fact that an individual who is committed as a dangerous sex offender will not be likely to show any significant change in sixty days. By modeling after a statute for the mentally ill, it appears that court time and tax dollars are wasted on numerous hearings that simply confirm that individuals who have been found to be repetitive, dangerous sexual offenders will not show significant improvement in only sixty days. Interestingly, in other ways Minnesota did seem aware of the differences in the two populations to some degree, as the civilly committed sexual offenders were categorically excluded from the vulnerable adult clause that applied to other committed populations.[3] By doing so, it was recognized that those individuals committed as sexual offenders are not suffering from mental illnesses that make them especially vulnerable to exploitation and abuse. In addition, Minnesota developed a special licensing rule, "Rule 26,"[4] which applied only to the program for the civilly committed sexual offenders. This separate licensing rule recognizes that the Department of Health/Department of Human Services regulations to set standards of care for the treatment of the mentally ill populations need to differ significantly from the standards for the treatment program for civilly committed sexual offenders.

PSYCHIATRIC INVOLVEMENT

Because civilly committed sexual offenders are not usually suffering from major mental illnesses, there is less need for treatment by psychiatrists. Programs have estimated that only approximately 10 percent of residents committed to SVP programs required treatment with antipsychotic medications, and most of those were well stabilized on their medications prior to their sex offender commitment (Summit, 2000). Most SVP programs have clinical psychologists as clinical directors and use a consultative model with psychiatry, which differs from the programs for the civil commitment of individuals with mental illness.

In Minnesota, a review of diagnoses among the committed sex offender population showed that none had been diagnosed solely with a major mental illness, and only 6 percent had a diagnosis of a major mental illness along with a paraphilia and/or personality disorder. Ninety-three percent had diagnoses of paraphilias and personality disorders. (And, at the SVP Summit ("Summit on the treatment . . .," 2000) other states reported similar findings.) These statistics differed greatly from the diagnoses of those patients committed as mentally ill and dangerous, even when compared to those who also had histories of sexual offenses. The agency responsible for licensing the Minnesota Sex Offender Program (MSOP) recognized this difference and approved a licensing variance for psychiatric treatment. According to the variance, residents no longer are required to have automatic assessments by a psychiatrist upon admission, or yearly follow-ups. Only those who were admitted on psychiatric medications or determined to be in need of such services by the psychology department are currently referred to the consulting psychiatrist.

It should be noted, however, that one very important role for psychiatrists is in the treatment of obsessive sexual thoughts and compulsive sexual behaviors, which are symptoms sometimes seen in this population. A variety of medications have been found to be useful in treating these symptoms, including serotonin-specific reuptake inhibitors and antiandrogens (Bradford, 1991, 1994, 1995; Stein et al., 1992; Walker & Meyer, 1981; Gagne, 1981). There is empirical evidence that these medications have a suppressing effect on disordered sexual arousal and may also enhance the arousal toward adult consensual sexual activity. Therefore, the use of these medications may be a crucial component for some offenders in a comprehensive sex offender treatment program (Heath & Schlank, Chapter 8, in this volume, examine this topic in further detail).

RESPONSE TO RESIDENT VIOLENCE

In a treatment program for patients who are committed as mentally ill, it is presumed that incidences of violence on their part are likely to be the product of their mental illness. For that reason, care is taken to ensure that patients are isolated following aggressive behavior only long enough to stabilize them and allow them to regain control over their behavior. Once the patient has regained behavioral control, (perhaps with the assistance of necessary psychotropic medication), the patient is returned to his or her living unit. Many resident advocates or hospital review boards believe these same procedures should be used with the sex offender population; however, we (Schlank and Dvoskin) disagree. Violence conducted in a sex offender population is often planned and rationally executed, with the offender often demonstrating behavioral control immediately before and following the act of violence. There is no reason to assume that violence in SVP facilities is any more or less the product of mental illness than violence in any other congregate living setting, such as military barracks or college dormitories. Isolating the individual only until he or she has "regained control" is essentially a useless gesture; there is no reason to assume that the individual has in fact lost control in the first place. Such a brief period of isolation has no therapeutic purpose for the offender and no assurance of safety for the rest of the resident population. Perhaps most important, brief periods of separation provide no natural negative consequences for violent or predatory behavior.

Some have argued that methods outside the treatment program can be used for such acts, such as pressing criminal charges and transfer to county jails. However, in reality police and sheriffs are quite reluctant to fill already crowded jail cells with offenders who are already in a secure facility. They are often unaware of the limitations that may be placed on SVP treatment staff to use methods such as segregation, which are available in prisons. In addition, when offenders are transferred to jail, they can sometimes post bail and return to the treatment center almost immediately. On at least one occasion in Minnesota, when a resident was charged and sentenced for an assault he committed against staff, he received "jail time credit" for time spent in the treatment facility prior to resolution of the charge, despite the fact that the treatment facility was not a jail. Law enforcement officials and prosecutors can also be extremely reluctant to press charges for some offenses, such as deliberate indecent exposure to staff members, without realizing that facing consequences for such behavior is an important part of treatment for these offenders.

The absence of a system of consequences for violent and predatory behavior within an SVP facility poses an unacceptable risk to staff and residents alike. Requiring a facility to follow illogical and irrelevant seclusion and restraint rules, as if the behavior were due to the symptoms of a serious mental illness, is wasteful of psychiatric and nursing resources and quite unlikely to be effective in changing the behavior. Prisons have responded to this challenge by creating disciplinary systems, with administrative due process, that have passed constitutional muster (Dvoskin, Petrila, & Stark-Riemer, 1995).[5] The primary purpose of these systems is not to punish offenders but to vindicate the state's compelling duty to maintain safe institutions; consequences for violent behavior are one essential component of this task.

Most recently, a class action suit involving the SVP program in Illinois[6] supported the view that civilly committed sexual offenders may receive different consequences for violent behavior than those individuals who are committed with serious mental illnesses. In that case it was held that the American Psychiatric Association Standards for seclusion and restraint did not "apply wholesale" to the use of secured or special management status, because the patient population was noted to be "significantly different from that found in psychiatric hospitals."[7]

CONDITIONS OF CONFINEMENT

One similarity between treatment programs for civilly committed sexual offenders and forensic mental health facilities is their shared need for security. In both cases, perimeter security systems often include two fences, with the main purpose of the inner fence to define an area beyond which patients are not allowed. Perimeter fences often have electronic alarm systems that are able to alert security staff of entrance into the area between the fences (Dvoskin & Patterson, 2000). Razor ribbon or alarm systems such as motion detectors are also often used on the outside fence. Because there is a high need for security in these programs, the external appearance of a facility can often resemble that of a prison, and the rights of residents or patients will be limited to a significant extent by the security needs of the institution and the existence of a secure perimeter. This can be somewhat concerning for family members and/or resident advocates. The residents of several SVP programs have filed class action lawsuits challenging their conditions of confinement.[8] In these cases, the residents allege that the facilities are too restrictive, and appear more like a prison than a treatment center. (American Civil Liberties Union, 2004; C. Nelson, personal communication, 2000).

Ironically, residents have also argued that they observed more rights and privileges in prison than they now have in SVP facilities. For example, even after a long sentence, a prisoner may have earned status as a minimum custody inmate or trustee. Trustees often have the freedom to move about the prison complex, perform jobs within the prison, and so on. SVP facilities, however, are likely to treat each new admission as "starting over," at the highest level of restrictiveness. There is understandable controversy about this practice. From the residents' point of view, they have earned trust, perhaps by years of good institutional behavior. From the facility's side, however, the inmate may have achieved trustee status based largely on the fact that he has little time left to serve and thus "a lot to lose" by misbehaving or escaping. In contrast, SVP committees have no fixed release date to which they are looking forward, and many believe that the state does not intend to release them, ever.[9] Thus, the facility may reasonably believe that the same person may perceive him- or herself as having more to lose as a resident than he or she did as an inmate.

At this time, the correct balance between security needs and the provision of a therapeutic environment remains unclear, and program directors for SVP programs are faced with a dilemma of providing a secure environment for offenders deemed to be highly dangerous without appearing punitive. They must ensure the safety of the surrounding community by preventing escape and ensure the safety of the staff and residents by preventing institutional violence while simultaneously giving residents the opportunity to grow and learn new, safer sexual behaviors.

In an effort to avoid having a "prison-like" setting, some programs have allowed residents to have VCRs and CD players and, in Minnesota, local restaurants and stores are allowed to deliver meals to the residents. The Minnesota program is also required to pay minimum wage to residents for any work that they do. Unfortunately, this lifestyle, which is considered comfortable by some of the residents, contributes to a tendency to become institutionalized. Some residents in the Minnesota program have even reported that they have no desire to leave the facility, and consider it their "retirement home."

In addition to the problem of potential institutionalization, an environment that is far less restrictive than a prison can allow some offenders to continue their criminal behavior. Sexual offenders who have completed their prison sentences do have their civil rights restored; however, in some cases, these rights are antithetical to the aims of sexual offender treatment. For example, most patients civilly committed to state-run hospitals have a right to privacy while making telephone calls.[10] Although this may be considered an important right, it can actually create an opportunity for further criminal behavior by a sexual offender. For example, civilly committed sexual offenders in the Minnesota program abused this right by contacting minors and engaging in sexually explicit conversations. When staff members were able to detect some of that behavior and place the offenders making the calls on individual behavior programs that allow for supervision of their calls, some offenders found ways to circumvent the supervision (Schlank & Harry, 2003). Similar problems occurred because of the restored right to privacy of communication through the mail. Some civilly committed sexual offenders continued their pattern of predation by abusing this right. Some created false letterheads in order to convince others that they ran a modeling agency, convincing parents to send pictures of their children, or vulnerable women to send identifying information including their social security numbers. In other cases, residents used phone and mail to accumulate huge debts that they had no intention of repaying. In many cases, the businesses simply wrote off the losses without prosecuting the residents, which served to reinforce this criminal behavior. One individual (in addition to defrauding several businesses) created a fraudulent company in which he listed other residents as employees and filed false tax returns obtaining thousands of dollars illegally (Oakes, 2004).

The balance between providing a secure environment and a therapeutic environment was addressed, to some degree, in *Hargett v. Adams*.[11] In that case, the court found that although the physical structure of the facility in Illinois did not facilitate a positive therapeutic environment, it was not a significant impediment to the delivery of effective treatment and the security decisions fell "under the purview of reasonable professional judgment in the administration of a hybrid detention and treatment facility."[12]

Whatever limitations are ultimately deemed appropriate for these programs, it seems clear that residents and staff alike have a right to know what the rules are. No one's interests are well served by ambiguity when it comes to resident rights; indeed, sincere misunderstandings about unclear institutional rules can pit staff against residents, detracting from the therapeutic alliance that treatment requires. Whereas residents have an understandable interest in maximizing their rights and freedoms, at the very least they have the right to know and understand the rules under which they are required to live. If SVP facilities are neither prisons nor psychiatric hospitals, then a set of rules must be developed that is unique to this new kind of institution.

In 2002, the clinical director of the Minnesota program proposed developing a revised bill of rights specifically for the SVP population that would be different from the one applied to the mentally ill populations. Central office administrators were not in favor of it at that time, stating that it would be too difficult to pass.[13] However, other states took the initiative to implement variations on the rights outlined for their SVP populations. California has restricted some parts of its patient bill of rights for the sexual offenders through policies and directives and proposed a modification of state regulations related to forensic hospital patients (Bukowski, personal communication, 2002). Florida had a specific reference in its SVP statute that provisions of its civil commitment of persons with mental illness act shall not apply to SVPs. Illinois also has a "rights" section in its Administrative Code that is specific to SVPs and allows for restrictions of rights. Missouri's statute allows for rights to be modified or denied if the facility head determines that the right "is inconsistent with the person's therapeutic care, treatment, habilitation or rehabilitation and the safety of other facility or program clients and public safety."[14] These modifications, for the most part, focus on the SVP facilities' need to supervise visits and inspect mail and packages for contraband.

ALTERNATIVES TO CIVIL COMMITMENT

There are many alternatives to civil commitment available to address the problem posed by dangerous sexual offenders. Obviously, one alternative is to dramatically increase sentences for repeat offenders of certain kinds of crimes. Though more severe sentences would do nothing to solve the problem of those offenders who have already been sentenced and whose sentences will expire soon, it might reduce and ultimately eliminate the need for such facilities in the future. Some states already have the option for judges to give lengthier sentences for those determined to be "patterned sexual offenders."[15] Other states have indeterminate sentencing (Tonry, 1999) or are considering the possibility of reintroducing open-ended sentences just for dangerous sexual offenders (Governor's Commission on Sex Offender Policy, 2005). In Florida, the Jessica Lunsford Act was recently pushed through by lawmakers and passed both the Senate and House unanimously. This act imposes tougher penalties on child molesters and requires many sexual offenders who have been released from prison to wear satellite tracking devices for the rest of their lives (Associated Press, 2005).

Minnesota has opened a prison-based site of its civil commitment program that is aimed at giving the highest-risk sexual offenders in prison a chance to obtain the same level of treatment they would receive if committed, but prior to their prison release. In past years, most of the offenders in Minnesota who were referred for civil commitment had not participated in the treatment program offered in the prison, with only approximately 4 percent of the committed population having previously completed a treatment program (Becker, Marques, Nelson, & Schlank 2001). Those who did complete the prison-based program who were still civilly committed were assessed to have participated in a program that was not intensive enough or comprehensive enough for their treatment needs. With the availability of this new program, offenders are now screened early in their prison sentence and warned if they have histories that suggest the likelihood of being civilly committed. They are then instructed that if they do not participate in treatment while incarcerated, they are highly likely to face an indeterminate period of civil commitment at the end of their sentence. Because the new prison-based site of the civil commitment program is run by the same staff as the regular site of the program and has similar comprehensiveness and level of intensity, it may prevent the need for some offenders to continue to be detained after the end of their sentence.

Colorado does not have a civil commitment statute for sexual offenders; however, in 1998 this state did pass a law allowing for the lifetime supervision of certain sex offenders. Other states have followed this model, and currently twelve states altogether provide for some type of lifetime supervision of some sexual offenders (Madigan, 2005). In these states, specially trained probation officers often work exclusively with the sexual offenders who have been released to the community. These probation officers are willing to take a more active role in monitoring the daily life and habits of those they supervise, as compared as the role they might take with other types of offenders, and must be willing to openly discuss avoidance of preoffense planning and behaviors. In addition, it is necessary that they be assigned lower caseloads in order to achieve this higher level of supervision. Intensive parole or lifetime supervision of sexual offenders appears to be a promising tool and can provide a needed therapeutic link of accountability for offense behavior management.

SUMMARY

The SVP laws may look somewhat similar to the laws for the civil commitment of persons with mental illness; however, the populations are quite different and require very different treatment programs. The diagnoses of the SVP population vary greatly from those committed individuals who suffer from mental illness, and the procedures used for isolating aggressive civilly committed patients who are mentally ill are often inappropriate when applied to the sexual offender population. Sexual offenders who complete their prison term have their civil rights restored. However, it is difficult to reconcile residents' civil liberties with the need for a secure, highly supervised setting. In addition, some of the rights that are restored may present few problems for mentally ill populations but actually appear to interfere with the provision of good sexual offender treatment and create the opportunity for the very crimes that these institutions have been created to prevent.

It is clear that the provision of treatment for the highest-risk, most disordered, and most treatment-resistant population presents many challenges. If civil commitment is to be used for sexual offenders, it is important that the treatment programs recognize the difference between this population and the population of mentally ill patients. A separate bill of rights will be crucial for such programs.

Dvoskin (1991) has argued that the absence of evidence that institutional treatment works suggests that it is better suited to prerelease and parole-based circumstances. But, that was written in 1991, prior to the wide-scale implementation of civil commitment statutes. Since that time, there have been some contradictory research findings regarding treatment outcome and inherent difficulties in attempting to evaluate the effectiveness of sex offender treatment programs (Marques, 1999). However, some recent research has found that the sexual offense recidivism rate was lower for treatment groups than for comparison groups, provided that cognitive-behavioral techniques based on the relapse prevention model were used (Hanson et al., 2002; Nagayama-Hall, 1995). In a recent study (Marques, Wiederanders, Day, Nelson, & van Ommeren, 2005), no significant effect on recidivism was found for the group of offenders randomly assigned to treatment; however, results did show that those sex offenders who were judged to have truly met the program's treatment goals did have a lower reoffense rate than those who did not. Thus, there is still disagreement about the overall effectiveness of sex offender treatment and about the ability of clinicians to determine for whom treatment has worked. All this being said, to whatever extent that institutional treatment is needed and effective in lowering risk, it would make little sense to waste the offender's entire period of incarceration only to provide it at great public expense after the sentence has expired. Thus, it may be that state dollars would be better spent on improving the quality and comprehensiveness of prison treatment programs and increasing treatment and scrutiny on parole for those sex offenders who are not civilly committed, rather than initiating any new civil commitment statutes.

States vary greatly in where they place the threshold for commitment, and many dangerous sex offenders will not be subject to civil commitment, even in the most aggressive states. Therefore, civil commitment should be only one aspect of a state's response to the problem posed by sexual offenders, and other alternatives, such as more severe or indeterminate sentencing, intensive community supervision, or life-time supervision, should be considered.

Footnotes

[1] Kansas v. Hendricks, 117 S. Ct 2072 (1997).

[2] Id.

[3] In Minnesota Statutes, a "vulnerable adult" included any person who is a resident or inpatient of a facility, as it was assumed that they must possess a physical or mental infirmity or other physical, mental, or emotional dysfunction that impaired their ability to adequately provide for their own care and places them at risk for abuse or exploitation. However, the statutes noted that a person who is committed as a sexual psychopathic personality or as a sexually dangerous person is not automatically considered to be a vulnerable adult, and is only classified as such if it is clearly demonstrated that they have a severe developmental disability or a major mental illness that inter-feres with their ability to care for themselves (Minn. Stat. § 626.557).

[4] Minn. Stat. § 256.9657, ch. 9515.3000–9515.3110.

[5] *See also* Wolf v. McDonald, 428 U.S. 539 (1974); Powell v. Coughlin, 953 F.2d 744 (2d Cir. 1991).

[6] Hargett v. Adams, Case No. 02 C 1456 (op. U.S. District Court, 2005).

[7] Id. at 36.

[8] Id.; Turay v. Seling, 108 F. Supp. 2d 1148 (W.D. Wash. 2000).

[9] Hargett v. Baker, 2002 WL 1433729 (N.D. Ill.). See Appendix 2, this volume.

[10] Cal. Welf. & Instit. Code §§ 5325–5337 (available: *www.leginfo.ca.gov/cgi-bin/displaycode? section=wic&group=05001-06000&file=5325-5337*); State of Connecticut, *Your Rights in a Psychiatric Facility* (available: www.ct.gov/opapd/cwp/view.asp?a=1756&q=277272); Minnesota Department of Human Services, *Bill of Rights for for Patients and Residents of Healthcare Facilities* (Document No. DS-2907-G) (2000).

[11] *Supra* note 6.

[12] Id. at 35.

[13] Most recently, Minnesota has finally proposed to the legislature some revisions to the rights afford-ed to civilly committed sexual offenders. Minn. Stat. ch. 134-S.F. No. 906 (signed by governor on February 17, 2004). According to these changes, residents can be placed in administrative restric-tion if suspected of committing a crime and, if charged with a crime, may continue on administra-tive restriction until the charge is resolved.

[14] Mo. Stat. § 630.110.

[15] Minn. Stat. ch. 609.108 (2004).

References

Alexander, R. (2000). Civil commitment of sex offenders to mental institutions: Should the standard be based on serious mental illness or mental disorder? *Journal of Health and Social Policy, 11*(3), 67–79.

American Civil Liberties Union. (2004). *Class action complaint challenges failure of Illinois offi-cials to provide adequate mental health treatment under the state's Sexually Violent Persons Act.* Available: *www.aclu-il.org/news/press/000064.shtml.*

Associated Press. (2005) Florida governor OK's tough child molester bill: Violators face lifetime of tracking by global positioning technology. Available: *www.msnbc.msn.com/id/7712095/print/1/ displaymode/1098.*

Becker, J. Marques, J. Nelson, C., & Schlank, A. (2001). *Best practices in civil commitment pro-*

grams. Preconference workshop presented at the 20th annual Research and Treatment Conference of the Association for the Treatment of Sexual Abusers. San Antonio, TX.

Bradford, J. M. W. (1991, October 9). *The role of serotonin reuptake inhibitors in forensic psychiatry*. Paper presented at the 4th Congress of European College of Neuropsychopharmacology, The Role of Serotonin in Psychiatric Illness, Monte Carlo, Monaco.

Bradford, J. M. W. (1994). Can pedophilia be treated? *The Harvard Mental Health Letter*, *10*(8), 3.

Bradford, J. M. W. (1995). The pharmacological treatment of paraphilias. In J. M. Oldham & M. B. Riba (Eds.), *Review of psychiatry* (Vol. 14, pp. 755–777). Washington, DC: American Psychatric Association Press.

Dvoskin, J. A. (1991). Allocating treatment resources for sex offenders. *Hospital and Community Psychiatry*, *42*(3), 229.

Dvoskin, J. A., & Patterson, R. F. (1998). Administration of treatment programs for offenders with mental illness. In R. M. Wettstein (Ed.), *Treatment of offenders with mental disorders* (pp. 1–43). New York: Guilford Press.

Dvoskin, J. A., Petrila, J., & Stark-Riemer, S. (1995). Application of the professional judgment rule to prison mental health. *Mental and Physical Disability Law Reporter,* *19*(1), 108–114.

Gagne, P. (1981). Treatment of sex offenders with medrooxyprogesterone acetate. *American Journal of Psychiatry*, *138*(5), 644–646.

Governor's Commission on Sex Offender Policy. (2005). *Final report*. Available: *www.doc.state.mn.us/commissionsexoffenderpolicy/commissionfinalreport.pdf*.

Hanson, R. K, Gordon, A., Harris, A. J., Marques, J. K., Murphy, W., Quinsey, V. L., et al. (2002). First report of the collaborative outcome data project on the effectiveness of psychological treatment for sex offenders. *Sexual Abuse: Journal of Research and Treatment,* *14*(2), 169–194.

Keiger, D. (1994). The dark world of Park Dietz. *Johns Hopkins Magazine*. (November) available at *www.jhu.edu/jhumag/1194web/dietz.html*.

Link, B. G., & Phelan, J.C. (1999). The labeling theory of mental disorder (II): The consequences of labeling. In A. V. Horwitz & T. L. Scheid (Eds.), *A handbook for the study of mental health: Social contexts, theories, and systems* (pp. 361–376). New York: Cambridge University Press.

Link, B. G., Phelan, J. C. Bresnahan, M., Stueve, A., & Pescosolido, B. A. (1999). Public concepts of mental illness: Labels, causes, dangerousness, and social distance. *American Journal of Public Health, 89*(9), 1328–1333.

Madigan, L. (2005). Madigan unveils lifetime supervision for sex offenders [Illinois Attorney General's press release]. Available: *www.illinoisattorneygeneral.gov/pressroom/2005_02/20050214c.html*.

Marques, J. K. (1999). How to answer the question, Does sex offender treatment work? *Journal of Interpersonal Violence*, *14*(4), 437–451.

Marques, J. K., Wiederanders, M., Day, D. M., Nelson, C., & van Ommeren, A. (2005). Effects of a relapse prevention program on sexual recidivism: Final results from California's Sex Offender Treatment and Evaluation Project (SOTEP). *Sexual Abuse: A Journal of Research and Treatment, 17*(1), 79–107.

Mindes, P. (1995–1996). Tuberculosis quarantine: A review of legal issues in Ohio and other states. *Journal of Law and Health, 10*(2), 403–423.

Mulvey, E. P., & Fardella, J. (2000, November/December). Are the mentally ill really Violent? *Psychology Today, 39,* 51.

Nagayama-Hall, G. C. (1995). Sexual offender recidivism revisited: A meta-analysis of recent treatment studies. *Journal of Consulting and Clinical Psychology, 63*, 802–809.

National Association of State Mental Health Program Directors. (1997). *Position statement on laws providing for the civil commitment of sexually violent criminal offenders*. Available: *www.nasmhpd.org/general_files/position_statement/sexpred.htm*.

Oakes, L. (2004). Sex offender continues crime from custody. *Star Tribune,* Dec. 13, 2004.

Reisner, R., Slobogin, C., & Rai, A. (1999*). Law and the mental health system: Civil and criminal aspects*. New York: West Group.

Schlank, A., & Harry, R. (2003). The treatment of the civilly committed sex offender in Minnesota: A review of the past ten years. *William Mitchell Law Review, 29*(4), 1221–1239.

Stein, D. J., Hollander, E., Anthony, D. T., Schneider, F. R., Fallon, B. A., & Liebowitz, M. R. (1992). Serotonergic medications for sexual obsessions, sexual addictions and paraphilias. *Journal of Clinical Psychiatry, 453,* 267–271.

Summit on the treatment of the sexually violent predator. (2000). Meeting sponsored by the Sand Ridge Secure Treatment Center, Oshkosh, WI.

Tonry, M. (1999). Reconsidering indeterminate and structured sentencing. *Sentencing and corrections* (Vol. 2). Available: *www.msccsp.org/resources/reconsidering.pdf.*

Walker, P. A., & Meyer, W. J. (1981). Medroxyprogesterone acetate treatment for paraphiliac sex offenders. In J. R. Hayes, T. K. Roberts, & K. S. Solway (Eds.), *Violence and the violent individual* (pp. 353–373). New York: SP Medical and Scientific Books.

Chapter 8

Medical Interventions for Paraphilias

by Ian Heath, M.D., C.M. and Anita Schlank, Ph.D.

INTRODUCTION

The population of civilly committed sexual offenders is generally accepted to be a very difficult population to treat, requiring a comprehensive approach. The majority of the treatment interventions usually involve group therapy, based on cognitive-behavioral techniques; however, advances in psychopharmacology offer clinicians additional means to manage disordered sexual thinking and/or arousal intrinsic to paraphilias. Paraphilias are sexual impulse disorders in which the individual experiences intensely arousing, recurrent sexual fantasies, urges, and behaviors that violate cultural norms and produce clinically significant distress and/or impairment in psychosocial functioning (American Psychiatric Association, 1994). To address this disordered arousal, clients are usually involved in both psychological treatment components and concurrent pharmacotherapy. However, it is the medical approaches to disordered sexual thinking and arousal that have undergone the most significant changes in the past twenty years.

Sexual offenders comprise a heterogenous group of individuals most often diagnosed with paraphilias and personality disorders; however, clinicians must be vigilant for additional psychopathology, whether a thought, mood, or anxiety disorder, which may be contributory to the offender's deviant thoughts and behaviors. Hence, psychopharmacological intervention commences with a thorough psychosexual interview and evaluation. This chapter proceeds under the assumption that any comorbid major mental illness is appropriately managed, and our focus comprises consideration of various pharmacological interventions designed to decrease sexually deviant thinking and arousal. Pharmacological intervention is guided by our evolving understanding of a number of biological substrates integral to sexual thinking, drive, and arousal. Primary areas for intervention include modulation of the central nervous system

(CNS) serotonergic and dopaminergic activity; manipulation of the hypothalamic-pituitary-gonadal (HPG) axis; and antagonism or altered metabolism of androgens. A comprehensive review of the biological underpinnings of sexuality is beyond the scope of this chapter, though succinct explanations regarding mechanisms believed to underlie therapeutic effects are proffered when discussing each group of agents. Contemporary theories regarding regulation of sexual behavior describe multiple agents, including the monoamine neutrotransmitters, serotonin, dopamine, and norepinephrine, as modulating hypothalamic expression of luteinizing hormone releasing hormone (LHRH). This hormone stimulates pituitary gonadotrophs, resulting in release of luteinizing hormone (LH), which, in turn, promotes testosterone synthesis in the Leydig cells of the testes (Griffin & Wilson, 2003). Testosterone is believed to be the most important steroid, in men, promoting sexual drive and behavior (Bradford & Harris, 2003). The intended goal of this chapter is to provide education to professionals from various disciplines regarding psychopharmacological intervention for sex offenders while concurrently providing practical information for prescribers. Psychopharmacological intervention with female sex offenders is not addressed. Particular emphasis is devoted to the LHRH analogues.

PSYCHOTROPICS

Psychotropic medications are frequently used in treatment of paraphilias; often, they constitute the initial pharmacological treatment intervention. Psychotropics can modulate CNS serotonergic and dopaminergic tone and affect the HPG axis, as well as diminish an individual's capacity to achieve and maintain erection and achieve orgasm. Selective serotonin reuptake inhibitors (SSRIs) are frequently used as first-line agents in the pharmacological treatment of paraphilias, and they are addressed in detail here.

SSRIs are recognized to increase CNS serotonergic activity, and increased CNS serotonin is associated with decreased sexual drive (Bradford, 1999). Many investigators postulate that certain individual's paraphilias are obsessive and compulsive in nature, and SSRIs are widely recognized as effective agents in the treatment of obsessive-compulsive disorder. Like many other psychotropics, SSRIs also affect end organ receptors, resulting in anorgasmia and/or erectile dysfunction. Essentially, capitalization on the side effect profile of psychotropics can be useful. Agents increasing dopaminergic tone are recognized to boost sexual drive; conversely, dopaminergic antagonists decrease sexual drive. Certain dopaminergic antagonists elevate prolactin, and hyperprolactinemia suppresses pulsatile GnRH secretion (Griffin & Wilson, 2003). Antipsychotic medications are not routinely used for the treatment of paraphilias, though they do decrease sexual drive and impair sexual functioning.

Since the early 1990s, SSRIs have been frequently prescribed for treatment of paraphilias. Typically, physicians prefer to begin treatment with SSRIs rather than antiandrogens or hormonal agents, given the favorable side effect profile of SSRIs. Initial reports came from very small case studies, such as Bianchi's (1990) treatment of an exhibitionist with fluoxetine (Prozac) reporting a reduction in paraphilic fantasy, and Kafka and Prentky's (1991b) report of four patients who experienced a reduction in sexual drive after use of fluoxetine. Kafka (1991) also treated one rapist who improved over a ten-month follow-up period after using that same medication.

Kafka and Prentky (1991a) studied a small group of paraphilic and nonparaphilic hypersexuals and noted that fluoxetine appeared to reduce paraphilic or hypersexual behavior while facilitating normal sexual arousal. Stein et al. (1992) found similar success with fluoxetine, as did Coleman, Cesnik, Moore, and Dwyer (1992). Sertraline (Zoloft) and fluvoxamine (Luvox) were later also found to be equally effective in reducing paraphilic urges, fantasies, and behaviors (Greenberg et al., 1996). In addition, Kafka (1996) noted that studies have suggested that lithium, clomipramine (Anafranil) and desipramine (Norpramin) may also be effective in decreasing paraphilic behaviors. However, he also noted that a client may fail to respond to one of these medications, while showing a beneficial response to a similar drug in the same class. Studies comparing SSRIs to other non-tricyclic antidepressants, such as venlafaxine and mirtazapine, note individuals taking SSRIs are more likely to experience sexual dysfunction (Fava & Rankin, 2002; Gregorian et al., 2002). SSRIs are postulated to be effective for disorders of heightened sexual drive (Kafka, 2000). SSRIs maintain a more favorable side effect profile compared to antiandrogen or hormonal medications; however, tolerance may develop to their beneficial effects (Kafka, 1994). Nonetheless, these agents comprise a less invasive means of intervention, devoid of the adverse effects characteristic of hormonal and antiandrogen agents. In many programs, SSRIs have become the primary somatic treatment intervention (Kafka, 2000).

ANTIANDROGENS AND HORMONAL AGENTS

Testosterone is considered the most important androgen effecting male sexual behavior, and medications which lower testosterone levels are frequently used in treatment of sexual offenders. To facilitate understanding of the mechanism of action of both the antiandrogens and LHRH analogues/agonists, a brief review of testosterone biosynthesis and regulation ensues. The reader is alerted that the following synopsis is reductionistic. For a comprehensive discussion of androgen synthesis and regulation, the reader is referred to Griffin and Wilson's (2003) review.

Ninety-five percent of a man's testosterone is produced by the Leydig cells of the testes. Liberation of esterified cholesterol from lipid droplets within Leydig cells, and the subsequent transport of cholesterol by steroidogenic acute regulatory protein to mitochondria of Leydig cells, constitutes the rate-limiting step in testosterone biosynthesis. Following side chain cleavage, resulting in Pregnenolone, further metabolism occurs within the endoplasmic reticulum, yielding testosterone. The major route for testosterone release into the circulation is via venous blood. During transport in plasma, testosterone is largely protein bound, both to albumin and sex hormone-binding globulin. Testosterone serves as a prohormone and, pending available metabolic pathways intrinsic to target tissues, may be converted via irreversible 5-alpha reduction to dihydrotestosterone or converted by an aromatase to estradiol. Testosterone and dihydrotestosterone bind to high affinity intracellular androgen receptors which in turn bind to hormone response elements within the cell's genetic material. Androgen receptor rich target tissues comprise the accessory organs of male reproduction, including the Sertoli and Leydig cells of the testis, and the brain. Testosterone biosynthesis is regulated by a plethora of mechanisms, including, though not limited to, the HPG axis. Pulsatile release of gonadotropin releasing hormone produced by hypothalamic cells stimulate pituitary gonadotrophs to secrete luteinizing and follicle stimulation hormone, which stimulate testosterone production in Leydig and spermatogenesis in Sertoli cells, respectively (Griffin & Wilson, 2003).

The Food and Drug Administration (FDA) has not approved either antiandrogens or hormonal agents for the treatment of paraphilic disorders; however, numerous research studies conducted over several decades demonstrate their usefulness in the reduction of male sexual aggression. The effect of these medications on sexual desire and fantasies is usually evident within four weeks after the first dose. Debate exists regarding the extent to which plasma testosterone needs be reduced to elicit the therapeutic effect (Kravitz, Haywood, Kelly, Liles, & Cavanaugh, 1996). Clients do not appear to develop a tolerance to the drugs' therapeutic effects, and, on occasion, the medication may be tapered without a rebound increase in sexual or aggressive behaviors. Kafka (1996) noted that there have been cases of antiandrogens being prescribed for more than a decade with no significant negative effects. Most men return to their previous level of sexual functioning shortly following discontinuation of the medication.

Ethical issues surrounding the use of antiandrogens include issues of informed consent. Patients must fully understand the potential risks and benefits of use of these agents, and they should retain the right to refuse such treatment. There is also obviously some concern if treating offenders whose cognitive capacity is in the subnormal range, as the functioning of these medications is quite complex. As part of the informed consent process, and in order to administer these agents in a therapeutic and safe fashion, recipients need to be informed of necessary laboratory work, imaging studies, and routine physical examinations.

Prior to prescription of antiandrogens or hormonal agents, patients need a routine physical examination. Although individual practices vary, obtaining a baseline hormone profile, inclusive of testosterone, prolactin, LH, and follicle stimulating hormone levels, is indicated. Also, a metabolic profile, lipid panel, complete blood count, and, pending choice of agent, coagulation studies must be obtained. As emergence of hyperglycemia can occur with certain agents, some investigators have obtained glucose tolerance tests to assess baseline glycemic control (Kravitz et al., 1995). Patients should be referred for a "baseline" bone density measurement, though this need not delay commencing treatment. Counseling regarding iatrogenic osteopenia and osteoporosis is indicated. Prescription of a calcium and vitamin D supplement for prophylaxis against osteoporosis should be strongly considered. Reilly, Delva, and Hudson (2000) published protocols for pretreatment testing and subsequent monitoring to guide practitioners during their management of patients treated with medroxyprogesterone acetate, cyproterone acetate, or leuprolide. It is reasonable to generalize their recommendations for leuprolide to other LHRH analogues.

Medroxyprogesterone Acetate

Medroxyprogesterone acetate (MPA) suppresses testosterone levels by the following mechanisms: (1) accelerating testosterone metabolism and clearance via induction of hepatic testosterone-alpha-reductase; (2) producing a progestational effect which reduces secretion of gonadotropins (Bradford, 1985); and (3) affecting binding of testosterone to sex hormone binding protein (American Psychiatric Association, 1999). An extensive body of literature, spanning five decades documents the efficacy of this medication in treatment of sexual deviancy (American Psychiatric

Association, 1999; Rosler & Witztum, 2000). MPA may be administered in tablet form (generally in doses up to 300 milligrams per day with a gradual tapering after approximately six months), or intramuscularly, at a rate of 150–500 mg intramuscularly weekly. Some physicians prefer the oral form because it allows for a more rapid reduction of the medication if the patient develops significant side effects (Abel, Osborn, Anthony, & Gardos, 1992). Possible side effects include weight gain, hepatotoxicity, abdominal pain, hot flashes, gynecomastia, and the possibility of sperm changes that might lead to genetic abnormalities should the patient impregnate a sexual partner during a course of treatment. There is also an increased risk of hyperglycemia and emergence of iatrogenic osteopenia or osteoporosis. Prescription of MPA is contraindicated for individuals with a history of coagulopathy or thromboembolic phenomena; LHRH analogues comprise a treatment alternative for those individuals (Reilly et al., 2000). As with other antiandrogens and hormonal agents, active pituitary pathology is a contraindication to presciption of MPA (Reilly et al., 2000).

Cyproterone Acetate

Cyproterone acetate (CPA) has antiandrogenic, antigonadotrophic, and progestational effects. Cyproterone acetate blocks intracellular uptake and metabolism of testosterone and competitively inhibits testosterone and dihydrotestosterone at androgen receptor sites (Mainwaring, 1977). Interestingly, the acetate radical bestows the progestational profile (American Psychiatric Association, 1999). Cyproterone acetate's progestational effects are one-hundredfold more potent than progesterone, resulting in further inhibition of gonadotropin activity (Rosler & Witztum, 2000). Although endocrinological changes resulting from CPA usually start to reverse within a month of its discontinuation, some sexual offenders have reported an ongoing decrease of sexual fantasies, at times spanning months or even years. The antigonadotropin and antiandrogen effects of cyproterone acetate are dose dependent. Typical oral dosages range between 50 and 200 mg a day. A depot preparation is available; dosages range between 300 and 600 mg per one to two weeks for injectables. Possible side effects include fatigue, depression, hepatotoxicity, decreased spermatogenesis, changes in body hair distribution, weight gain, gynecomastia, and possible loss of bone density (Rosler & Witztum, 2000). Close scrutiny of bone density for emergence of osteopenia or osteoporosis is warranted (see next section for further information). Prescription of CPA is contraindicated for individuals with a history of coagulopathy or thromboembolic phenomena; LHRH analogues comprise a treatment alternative for those individuals (Reilly et al., 2000). As with other antiandrogens and hormonal agents, active pituitary pathology is a contraindication to presciption of CPA (Reilly et al., 2000). Laschet and Laschet (1971, 1975) published seminal work documenting efficacy of cyproterone acetate, and a number of additional studies corroborate the efficacy of this drug. Of note, the FDA has not approved use of cyproterone acetate in the United States.

Luteinizing Hormone Releasing Hormone Analogues

LHRH agonists/analogues constitute the latest area of advance in the pharmacological management of paraphilias. These agents are analogues of the native decapeptide, gonadotropin releasing hormone (GnRH), which is produced in the medial basal hypothalamus (Griffin & Wilson, 2003). GnRH stimulates gonadotrophs, located within the anterior pituitary, to produce luteinizing and follicle stimulating hormones, which in turn drive testosterone synthesis within the testes. LHRH agonists replace the biological, pulsatile release of LHRH with chronic elevation of the hormone. Pulsatile stimulation of the pituitary gonadotrophs by LHRH results in physiological LH levels which drive testosterone production; however, chronic stimulation of pituitary gonadotrophs yields an initial elevation of testosterone production, followed by marked suppression of testosterone synthesis. This reversible, chronic suppression yields testosterone levels similar to those resulting from surgical castration. LHRH analogues are approved by the FDA for treatment of prostate cancer, endometriosis, leiomyoma, and LHRH-dependent precocious puberty; accordingly, the use of LHRH agonists in treatment of paraphilias constitutes off-label use.

Although several LHRH analogues are available, leuprolide (Lupron) and triptorelin (Trelstar) may be administered as depot agents, and goserelin (Zoladex) can be administered as an implant, all ensuring compliance. If concern exists regarding precipitating a hypersensitivity reaction, leuprolide may be administered on a daily basis, subcutaneously, prior to administration of a depot preparation. Initially, injections are administered monthly, though once the patient demonstrates an ability to tolerate the medication, injections containing up to a three-month supply may be administered. For example, 7.5 mg of leuprolide is administered per month; if the patient tolerates the medication, the clinician may opt to administer 22.5 mg every third month in lieu of continuing monthly injections. With increased use of this class of medication, a number of research articles, case reports, and reviews became available. These studies demonstrated the efficacy of these agents, as well as raised concern regarding long-term effects of these medications.

Rosler and Witztum (1998) published a cardinal study describing findings of an uncontrolled, observational study of thirty men treated with the LHRH analogue, triptorelin. The study sample comprised patients with various paraphilias, some of which had previously undergone treatment with antiandrogens and serotonergic agents. Investigators assessed clinical response by administering questionnaires and obtaining additional information from family members and partners of study participants. Adjunctive psychotherapy was provided. All thirty men experienced significant diminution of paraphilic activities, corroborated by reports of relatives, partners, and probation officers. Of six participants who failed to complete one year of pharmacotherapy with triptorelin, three discontinued due to medication side effects. No active participant recidivated during the study. Of note, suppression of serum testosterone was impressive; the mean serum testosterone level at baseline was 545 +/- 196 compared to 32 +/- 14 ng/dl following twelve monthly injections of 3.75 mg of triptorelin. Following Rosler and Witztum's work, a number of additional reports regarding use of LHRH analogues were published (Briken, Nika, & Berner, 2001; Briken, 2002: Briken, Hill, & Berner, 2003; Krueger & Kaplan, 2001; Saleh, Niel, & Fishman, 2004).

With the increase in use of LHRH agonists, practitioners must be aware of potential side effects of these potent agents. Similar to the antiandrogens, side effects are the ramification of depressed testosterone production. Possible side effects resulting from use of LHRH analogues include erectile dysfunction, testicular atrophy, hot flashes, diaphoresis, and a temporary increase in sexual drive and behaviors. The latter effect is a consequence of the initial potentiation of testosterone synthesis, a ramification of tonic stimulation of LH receptors, prior to the secondary metabolic exhaustion and suppression of testosterone synthesis. This phenomenon is typically seen within the first several weeks of treatment. Heightened monitoring may be necessitated, and, if indicated, concurrent prescription of an antiandrogen may be used to directly antagonize the temporary surge in testosterone (Reilly, 2000). Given the lack of progestational activity, side effects related to the progestational profile of antiandrogens are lacking, though clinicians are becoming increasingly aware of detrimental effects of markedly suppressing testosterone production upon bone density. As these agents are being considered for potential long-term use, and as a number of individuals prescribed these agents may be in their youth, vigilance for and active management of emerging osteopenia and osteoporosis is necessitated. Rosler and Witztum (1998) documented the main side effects as erectile dysfunction, hot flashes, and decreased bone density, and they theorized that the use of calcium, vitamin D supplementation, and possible prescription of bisphosphonates may prevent or reverse iatrogenic osteopenia or osteoporosis. Additional investigators confirmed loss of bone density as a significant side effect of treatment of paraphilias with LHRH analogues (Grasswick & Bradford, 2003); a review of literature regarding prescription of LHRH analogues for treatment of prostate cancer yields similar findings (Chang, 2003). Measurement of bone density prior to and periodically within a course of treatment with LHRH analogues, as well as any antiandrogen, is prudent. Dual-energy x-ray absorptiometry (DXA) scans comprise a noninvasive, readily available technique by which to monitor for osteopenia or osteoporosis (Brunader & Shelton, 2002). Following an initial measurement, repeat measurements may be obtained on a semiannual to annual basis. Standard sites of bone density measurement include the lumber spine, proximal femur, and the distal forearm. Prophylactic prescription of calcium, vitamin D, and counseling regarding the need for exercise and avoidance of caffeine are warranted.

SURGICAL INTERVENTIONS

It has long been hypothesized that some violent crime is based on high levels of testosterone, which has been shown to increase aggressiveness in male mammals. Surgical interventions for the treatment of sexual offenders, such as the surgical removal of the testes, have been shown to be surprisingly effective. Surgical castration has led to reductions in recidivism from over 60 percent to less than 5 percent in some studies (Heim & Hursch, 1977); one study found that the recidivism rate for offenders who had undergone surgical castration was only 2.3 percent as compared to 80 percent in the untreated group (Langeluddeke, 1963). However, the irreversibility of such treatment interventions and the many other ethical dilemmas surrounding its use make it an unlikely treatment choice (Abel et al., 1992). For example, it should not be used with juveniles and should always be voluntary. It should be noted that most sex offender treatment is somewhat coercive, with potential consequences of a probation violation or lengthy incarceration should the offender decline to participate in treatment. Therefore, if surgical castration is offered as one option that leads to increased freedom, there would be many concerns about the true "voluntariness" of a consent to such treatment. Accordingly, the Association for the Treatment of Sexual Aggressors is opposed to surgical castration of offenders.

SUMMARY

The pharmacological treatment of deviant sexual thinking and behavior has undergone significant changes over the past decades. Early efforts using surgical castration aimed to alter hormonal levels and change an offender with disordered sexual arousal into an asexual individual. Treatment also initially focused on the hormonal basis of sexuality, with "off-label" prescription of antiandrogens being used to lower disordered sexual drive and arousal. In the 1990s, SSRIs began to be used to address the hypersexuality often accompanying paraphilias, which raised the question of whether the paraphilias may be part of the obsessive-compulsive-spectrum disorders. These medications offer fewer risks of deleterious side effects compared to antiandrogens and hormonal agents, though the likelihood of eliciting a therapeutic response is less predictable. In addition, clients can develop a tolerance to their beneficial effects. For those reasons, some clinicians have suggested that antiandrogens and hormonal agents remain the treatment of choice for the most dangerous and treatment refractory sexual offenders (Kafka, 1996), including those referred for civil commitment. LHRH analogue use is increasing, and these agents appear promising and efficacious and are devoid of progestational side effects. Nonetheless, practitioners need be wary of potential side effects, especially regarding bone density, and proactive in their prevention. It is also noted that in one clinician's experience, a combination of antiandrogen medication and an SSRI was safely administered with several potential advantages, including obtaining a beneficial clinical effect from a relatively lower dose of the antiandrogen, with the ability to maintain control over disordered sexual arousal while switching from one SSRI to another (Kafka, 1996). This appears to be an option worthy of further investigation.

References

Abel, G. G., Osborn, C., Anthony, D., & Gardos, P. (1992). Current treatments of paraphiliacs. *Annual Review of Sex Research, 3*, 255–290.

American Psychiatric Association. (1994). *Diagnostic and statistical manual of mental disorders* (4th ed.). Washington, DC: Author.

American Psychiatric Association. (1999). *Dangerous sex offenders: A Task Force report of the American Psychiatric Association.* Washington, DC: Author.

Bianchi, M. (1990). Fluoxetine treatment of exhibitionism [Letter]. *American Journal of Psychiatry, 147*(8), 1089–1090.

Bradford, J. (1985). Organic treatments for the male sexual offender. *Behavioral Sciences & the Law, 3*(4), 355–375.

Bradford, J. (1999, Fall). The paraphilias, obsessive compulsive spectrum disorder, and the treatment of sexually deviant behaviors. *Psychiatric Quarterly, 70*(3). Available: *www.brainphysicis. com/ocd/research/ocpara.html*

Bradford, J., & Harris, V. (2003). *Principles and practice of forensic psychiatry* (2nd ed.). New York: Oxford University Press.

Briken, P., Nika, E., & Berner, W. (2001). Treatment of paraphilia with luteinizing hormone-releasing hormone agonist. *Journal of Sex and Marital Therapy, 27*(1), 45–55.

Briken, P. (2002). Pharmacotherapy of paraphilias with luteinizing hormone-releasing hormone agonists. *Archives of General Psychiatry, 59*(5), 469–470.

Briken, P., Hill, A., & Berner, W. (2003). Pharmacotherapy of paraphilias with long-acting agonists of luteinizing hormone-releasing hormone: A systematic review. *Journal of Clinical Psychiatry, 64*(8), 890–897.

Brunader, R., & Shelton, D. (2002). Radiologic bone assessment in the evaluation of osteoporosis. *American Family Physician, 65*, 1357–1364.

Chang, S. (2003). Exploring the effects of luteinizing hormone-releasing hormone agonist therapy on bone health: Implications in the management of prostate cancer. *Urology, 62*(Suppl. 6A), 29–35.

Coleman, E., Cesnik, J., Moore, A. M., & Dwyer, S. M. (1992). An exploratory study of the role of psychotropic medications in treatment of sexual offenders. *Journal of Offender Rehabilitation, 18*, 75–88.

Fava, M., & Rankin, M. (2002). Sexual functioning and SSRIs. *Journal of Clinical Psychiatry, 63*(Suppl. 5), 13–16.

Grasswick, L. J., & Bradford, J. M. W. (2003). Osteoporosis associated with the treatment of para-philias: A clinical review of seven case reports. *Journal of Forensic Science, 48*(4). Available: *www.astm.org.*

Greenberg, D. M., Bradford, J. M., Curry, S., & O'Rourke, A. (1996). A comparison of treatment of paraphilias with three serotonin reuptake inhibitors: A retrospective study. *Bulletin of the American Academy of Psychiatry and the Law, 24*(4), 525–532.

Gregorian, R. S., Golden, K. A., Bahce, A., Goodman, C., Kwong, W. J., & Khan, Z. M. Antidepressant-induced sexual dysfunction. *Annals of Pharmacotherapy, 36*(10), 1577–1589.

Griffin, J., & Wilson, J. (2003) *Williams textbook of endrocrinology* (10th ed.). Philadelphia: Saunders.

Heim, N., & Hursch, C. J. (1977). Castration for sexual offenders: Treatment or punishment? A review and critique of recent European literature. *Archives of Sexual Behavior, 8*, 281–304.

Kafka, M. P. (1991). Successful treatment of paraphilic coercive disorder (a rapist) with fluoxetine hydrochloride. *British Journal of Psychiatry, 158*, 844–847.

Kafka, M. P. (1994). Sertraline pharmacotherapy for paraphilias and paraphilia-related disorders: An open trial. *Annals of Clinical Psychiatry, 6*(3), 189–195.

Kafka, M. P. (1996). Therapy for sexual impulsivity: The paraphilias and paraphilia-related disorders. *Psychiatric Times, 13*(6). Available: *www.psychiatrictimes.com/p960627.html.*

Kafka, M. P. (2000). Psychopharmacologic treatments for nonparaphilic compulsive sexual behaviors. *CNS Spectrums, 5*(1), 49–59.

Kafka, M. P., & Prentky, R. (1991a). Comparative study of non-paraphilic sexual addictions and paraphilias in men. *Journal of Clinical Psychiatry, 53*, 345–350.

Kafka, M. P., & Prentky, R. (1991b). Fluoxetine treatment of voyeurism. *American Journal of Psychiatry, 148*, 950.

Kravitz, H., Haywood, T., Kelly, J., Liles, S., & Cavanaugh, J. (1996). Medroxyprogesterone and paraphiles: Do testosterone levels matter? *Bulletin of the American Academy of Psychiatry and the Law, 24*(1), 73–83.

Kravitz, H., Haywood, T., Kelly, J., Wahlstrom, C., Liles, S., & Cavanaugh, J. (1995). Medroxyprogesterone treatment for paraphiliacs. *Bulletin of the American Academy of Psychiatry and the Law, 23*(1), 19–33.

Krueger, R. B., & Kaplan, M. S., (2001). Depot-leuprolide acetate for treatment of paraphilias: A report of twelve cases. *Archives of Sexual Behavior, 30*(4), 409–422.

Langeluddeke, A. (1963). *Die Entmannung von Sittlichkeitsverbrecher.* Berlin, Germany: Aldine de Gruyter.

Laschet, U., & Laschet, L. (1971) Psychopharmacotherapy of sex offenders with cyproterone acetate. *Pharmacopsychiatric and Neuropsychopharmacological Advances in Clinical Research, 4*, 99–110.

Laschet, U., & Laschet, L. (1975) Antiandrogens in the treatment of sexual deviations in men. *Journal of Steroid Biochemistry, 6*(6), 821–826.

Mainwaring, J. P. (1977). Modes of action of antiandrogens: A survey. In L. Martini & M. Motta (Eds.), *Androgens and antiandrogens* (pp. 151–161). New York: Raven Press.

Reilly, D., Delva, N., & Hudson, R. (2000). Protocols for the use of cyproterone, medroxyproges-terone, and leuprolide in the treatment of paraphilia. *Canadian Journal of Psychiatry, 45*, 559–563.

Rosler, A., & Witztum, E. (1998) Treatment of men with paraphilia with a long-acting analogue of gonadotropin releasing hormone. *New England Journal of Medicine, 338*(7), 416–422.

Rosler, A., & Witztum, E. (2000) Pharmacotherapy of paraphilias in the next millenium. *Behavioral Sciences and the Law, 18*, 43–56.

Saleh, F. M., Niel, T., & Fishman, M. J. (2004). Treatment of paraphilia in young adults with leuprolide acetate: A preliminary case report series. *Journal of Forensic Science, 49*(6). Available: *www.astm.org.*

Stein, D. J., Hollander, E., Anthony, D. T., Schneider, F. R., Fallon, B. A., & Liebowitz, M. R. (1992). Serotonergic medications for sexual obsessions, sexual addictions and paraphilias. *Journal of Clinical Psychiatry, 453*, 267–271.

Chapter 9

The Need for Complete Information Leads to the Polygraph Examination

by Kim English, M.A. and Peggy Heil, L.C.S.W.

INTRODUCTION

The postconviction polygraph examination currently is in use in many jurisdictions across the United States (Burton, 2004).[1] Its use is a response to the need for more complete information about individual offenders. The polygraph examination is most commonly used to verify information the offender provides to the treatment provider and supervising officer, ascertain the use of force or threats, and determine the offender's compliance with treatment and supervision conditions (English, 2004). The polygraph examination may also serve as a deterrent to future crime for offenders who anticipate being asked questions about current deviant or high-risk behaviors (National Research Council, 2003).[2]

Research has established that the use of the polygraph exam results in professionals obtaining more complete information about the offender than what was available in official records, and also more than what was obtained in treatment (Ahlmeyer, Heil, McKee, & English, 2000; Emerick & Dutton, 1993; O'Connell, 1998; English, Jones, Pasini-Hill, Patrick, & Cooley-Towell, 2000; English, Jones, Patrick, & Pasini-Hill, 2003b). It also validates details about the conviction crime when the victim's version varies from the offender's version (including discrepancies between the offender's account and information in the official records). The postconviction polygraph exam provides professionals with information that is essential to public safety, and it is common for those who have used the polygraph to report that they would not work with sex offenders without it (English, Pullen, & Jones, 1996; English et al., 2000).

Despite these findings, the use of the postconviction sex offender polygraph exam remains controversial. Although many aspects of sex offender management are controversial, such as civil commitment (Janus & Prentky, 2003; Janus, 2004; La Fond, 2003; Winick & La Fond, 2003), the use of the postconviction polygraph exam continues to spur debate, even among professionals who regularly use the instrument.

This chapter discusses the use of the postconviction polygraph specifically in terms of the need for reliable information about individual offenders. It first discusses the incompleteness of official record data and problems with traditional self-report data obtained from sex offenders. It also highlights problems with overreliance on risk assessment instruments as a means of managing the sex offender population. Incomplete information on individual offenders leads to recommending the use of the postconviction polygraph examination with all convicted sex offenders. This chapter also attempts to address some of the controversial aspects of using the polygraph by considering, in part, what it means to manage this population *without* more complete information about individual offenders. For example, will treatment plans be inadequate if they are developed without information about the offender's full scope of deviant behavior, frequency of activity, duration of abusive behavior, and level of commitment to living a crime-free lifestyle? Likewise, will supervision plans have dangerous gaps without complete information about individual offenders?

OFFICIAL RECORDS ARE INCOMPLETE

Most professionals understand that official crime records are incomplete, yet many fail to incorporate this understanding into the day-to-day treatment and management of convicted sex offenders. For example, risk assessment instruments rely heavily on official record data; so do studies of recidivism and treatment efficacy.

Criminologists have a long history of lamenting the problems with the quality of official record data. In 1970, Gold summed up the problem with official records as they relate to juveniles, but the same problems exist for the official records of adults:

> [O]fficial records . . . inevitably confound delinquent behavior with other behavior. For official records also document the behavior of citizens who report the crimes; of the police who investigate and detain the alleged offenders; of the [police] officers who interview the youngsters brought in; of the juvenile court workers who interview, test, investigate and evaluate; and of the juvenile court judges and referees who dispose the cases which have reached them. (p. 1)

It is commonly understood that the primary problem with official records is that they do not reflect crimes that are never discovered or reported. As early as 1964 Sellin and Wolfgang referred to this as the "dark figure" of crime. Data quality problems associated with official records and their use in establishing recidivism rates are well documented in the scholarly literature (Gold, 1970; Farrington, 1979; Hindelang, 1974; Elliott, Ageton, & Huizinga, 1980; Hindelang, Hirschi, & Weis, 1981; Kitsuse & Cicourel, 1963; Maltz, 1977, 1999). Data quality problems persist in all types of official criminal justice records, but they are particularly acute for crimes that are rarely reported to authorities.[3] This means that the problems are especially profound in the field of sex offender treatment, management, and research.

Over thirty years ago, the problems with criminal justice records propelled the development of the National Crime Survey (NCS; later renamed the National Crime Victimization Survey, or NCVS), a telephone survey conducted since 1973 by the U.S. Department of Justice's Bureau of Justice Statistics (BJS). This survey asks respondents whether anyone age 12 or older in the household was the victim of a crime during the last six months, and if the crime was reported to the police. The NCS showed substantial underreporting of all violent crime, including rape. In 1993, BJS developed enhanced questions on rape, sexual assault, and domestic violence to get better estimates of these crimes. The redesign resulted in a 157 percent increase in the rape rate (Kindermann, Lynch, & Cantor, 1997). In 2003, the NCVS reported that 47.5 percent of rapes and sexual assaults of victims over the age of 12 were reported to the police (Catalano, 2004).

Other surveys of crime victims have found much lower sexual assault reporting rates than those reported in the NCVS. This is due in large part to the fact that 29 percent of victims are below the age of 12 (Kilpatrick, Edmonds, & Seymour, 1992), and this group is excluded from the NCVS survey. In the Women's Health Survey of a national random sample of 4,008 women, Kilpatrick et al. (1992) found a reporting rate of 16 percent for women who experienced a completed or attempted rape. Further study found 11 percent of child victims reported the crime (Smith et al., 2000). Tjaden and Thoennes (2000b) found that only 17 percent of women who were raped as adults reported the crime. Smith et al. (2000) reported that 47 percent of rape victims surveyed as adults said that they did not disclose the assault for five years, and 28 percent never disclosed the rape until the researcher asked during the telephone interview. In an earlier study of both men and women, Finkelhor, Hotaling, Lewis, and Smith (1990) found that 42 percent of the men and 33 percent of the women never disclosed the crime until the researcher asked.

Reporting rates for incest victims are even lower. Russell (1986) found that only 2 percent of victims reported the crime to law enforcement. Roesler and Wind (1994) studied 228 female incest victims and found that the victims did not disclose the abuse for, on average, twenty years from onset. Likewise, Lamb and Edgar-Smith (1994) studied sixty incest victims and found that, on average, the victims did not report the abuse for ten years. Generally, these disclosures were made to a trusted friend and not to law enforcement. Smith et al. (2000) and Hansen, Resnick, Saunders, Kilpatrick, and Best (1999) established that, for both child and adult victims, knowing the perpetrator significantly decreased the likelihood of reporting the crime to authorities.

Even when rapes and sexual assaults are reported to police, only about one-fourth result in an arrest of a suspect. Of those arrested, fewer than half are convicted of the crime. Snyder (2000) analyzed data from twelve states and found that an arrest was made in only 27 percent of reported sex crimes. A study of data from six states conducted by the BJS (1994) tracked 4,175 arrested rapists. This study found that 48 percent were convicted (29 percent of the cases were dismissed, 2 percent were acquitted at trial, and 1 percent was categorized as "other").

Tjaden and Thoennes (2000b) found that for the 17 percent of adult women who reported a rape by an intimate to law enforcement, the following occurred: 78 percent of responding police officers took a report and 47 percent arrested or detained the attacker; 7.5 percent of perpetrators were prosecuted, and of these, 42 percent were convicted.

These studies reflect an astonishing fact: Convictions for sex crimes are extremely rare events compared to the actual frequency that this crime occurs.

SELF-REPORT DATA FILL A GAP IN KNOWLEDGE

Self-Report Data and Criminology

If official crime data were incomplete, how could criminologists understand this social problem and how could public policy be designed to improve community safety?

Nearly three decades ago researchers at the Rand Corporation began to study individual crime rates by asking adult offenders about their criminal activity (Petersilia,

Greenwood, & Lavin, 1977; Peterson, 1978; Greenwood, Chaiken, Petersilia, & Peterson, 1978; Peterson & Braiker, 1980). This endeavor increased knowledge about high-risk, high-crime-rate offenders because it was significantly more complete than official record data for the same offenders (Chaiken & Chaiken, 1982; Mande & English, 1988; English, 1989; Horney & Marshall, 1991; English & Mande, 1992).

There are obvious problems with self-reported data provided by known offenders. In 1981, in his classic book *Measuring Delinquency,* Michael Hindelang summarized the core problem of using self-reported crime information from known offenders: "If people lie, cheat and steal, those using a method based on the assumption that they do can hardly claim that they do not" (Hindelang et al., 1981, p. 3). Nevertheless, criminologists pursued this approach so that they might better understand the incidence, prevalence, and causes of deviant behavior.

In fact, offender self-report data became the foundation for developing the criminal career paradigm. In the mid-1980s, the National Research Council convened an expert advisory board to study "criminal careers and 'career criminals'" (Blumstein, Cohen, Roth, & Visher, 1986). The focus was self-reported crime data. This effort included substantial discussions about the measurement problems associated with the data (Weis, 1986), along with concerns about the ethical use of the data and the accuracy of predicting the most high-crime-rate individuals (Moore, 1986).

Based entirely on data obtained from self-report studies, the criminal career was defined as composed of four dimensions: participation in a specific crime type, duration, seriousness (referring to participation in particular crime types and crime combinations, or "mix"), and frequency (Blumstein et al., 1986). The data indicated that these dimensions varied for individual offenders. This approach to criminology provided a significantly different perspective from the traditional approach of focusing on aggregate arrest rates, victim reports, or recidivism data obtained from official records, and each dimension was theoretically linked to concerns about public risk.

Self-Report Data From Sex Offenders: Unreliable

Ironically, sex offenders' self-reports were found to be unreliable during the early pretests conducted by Rand researchers (Petersilia, 1977; Petersilia et al., 1977; Peterson & Braiker, 1980). Consequently, questions about sex crimes were never included in the large-scale criminal career self-report surveys (Chaiken & Chaiken, 1982; English & Mande, 1992; Horney & Marshall, 1991).

In sum, the introduction of self-report data forever changed the criminology landscape, permanently casting doubt on the completeness and accuracy of official records and incorporating and elevating victimization information as a primary source of crime rate data. However, at the same time, this early work confirmed the unreliability of self-report data obtained from convicted sex offenders when asked by researchers about their criminal behavior, even when confidentiality was assured.

Therapists Also Seek Self-Report Data

Many sex offender therapists also sought to fill the gaps in official records with offender self-reports of deviant activity. Serin and Mailloux (2003) describe the value of self-report data for describing pre-assaultive risk situations. They worked on the assumption that offenders become more honest once a therapeutic relationship has been established (Abel, Becker, Cunningham-Rathner, Mittelman, & Rouleau, 1988). However, the extent to which offenders voluntarily disclose previously undetected crimes and ongoing risk information is suspect. Rice and Harris (2003b) discuss denial, distortion, and minimization as problems with self-reports from sex offenders. Deliberate concealment is another obvious problem. In fact, there are many more reasons to conceal this information than to reveal it. Most offenders in the community and in prison successfully masked their assaultive behaviors for years and were able to continue the behavior without apprehension (English et al., 2000; Ahlmeyer et al., 2000; English et al., 2003b). Many offenders are adept at grooming and managing the perspectives of others. This behavior generally continues in treatment, as offenders attempt to control the therapist's impressions. They may fear that disclosing information will jeopardize a positive relationship with the therapist who may—as a result of the information—develop a more negative opinion of the offender. Further, disclosing deviant behavior might lead to additional lifestyle restrictions, or a lengthier course of treatment. It could even trigger mandatory reporting.

For many sex offenders, then, the shame and fear associated with disclosing illegal paraphilic behavior interferes with attempts to assist them in creating a new, nonassaultive lifestyle. And it broadly hampers professionals' efforts to obtain the accurate information required to develop a meaningful treatment plan, determine the level of risk the offender presents, and implement safety plans that protect potential victims and offenders.[4] Anecdotal information suggests that although many offenders disclose considerable information in the course of treatment, they tend to withhold their most secret or their most secret abusive behavior and victim(s).[5] Ultimately, then, there is a pressing need for more complete information than official records or offender self-reports provide.

In sum, the discussion thus far reflects the complicated nature of sexual assault statistics and the dismal state of criminal justice records to accurately reflect occurrences of sexual assault. Efforts to obtain accurate information from offender self-reports—while an improvement over official records—result in professionals knowing what offenders want them to know.

In the end, then, it seems highly unlikely that sexual recidivism rates of sex offenders are as low as official records indicate. These data problems plague other efforts to manage sex offenders, such as studying treatment efficacy using new arrests and convictions as the outcome measures and the development of actuarial risk assessment scales.

RESEARCH ON TREATMENT EFFICACY REMAINS INCONCLUSIVE

Many research methodological problems are associated with treatment efficacy studies, such as the lack of appropriate comparison groups. But chief among the problems is the unreliability of the data on which efficacy is based: new arrest or conviction for a sex crime. In the end it is difficult, if not impossible, to determine whether there are problems with treatment or problems with measurement that have resulted in statistics reflecting a minimal impact (Hall, 1995; Hanson et al., 2002; Berliner, 2002; Hanson & Morton-Bourgon, 2004; Craig, Browne, & Stringer, 2003; Rice & Harris, 2003a).[6]

Recently, two meta-analyses reported treatment effects. Gallagher, Watson, Hirschfield, Coggenshall, and MacKenzie (1999) reviewed twenty-five studies and found a moderate reduction in recidivism, and Hanson et al. (2002) reviewed forty-three studies and reported an 8 percent reduction in recidivism. This finding led Prentky (2003) to conclude that "there is little question at this point that treatment reduces sexual recidivism" (p. 26). Although the findings from the two studies are important, meta-analysis is a controversial analytical approach because the selection of the original studies and the statistical methods employed are open to subjective bias.[7] Further, the methodological problems in the original studies are not negated by the process of meta-analysis. In fact, in a careful review of Hanson et al. (2002), Rice and Harris (2003a) found many if not most of the forty-three studies to have significant methodological problems, most commonly the lack of an adequate or appropriate comparison group. Rice and Harris (2003a) identified only six of the forty-three studies as meeting their criteria of a "minimally useful evaluation," and these studies indicated a "trend toward treatment having been detrimental" (pp. 436–437). They conclude that the impact of treatment remains unknown because the available evidence continues to be contaminated by the reliance on noncomparable groups. Incomplete recidivism data are also a problem, however.

Hanson (1997a) suggested that given the methodological problems encountered by treatment efficacy studies, measuring individual level changes may be more meaningful: "Unlike recidivism, such changes are easily observed, can be replicated across settings and individuals, and can be closely linked to specific theories of sex offender treatment" (p. 142).

Is Treatment of Individual Offenders Poorly Informed?

Perhaps research has been unable to consistently identify treatment effects because—beyond the methodological and outcome measurement problems—treatment plans are not based on an accurate account of the offender's problems. Most therapists understand that clients generally present incomplete pictures of themselves and their lives. The widespread and accepted use of the phallometric testing reflects the need for objective information about the offender's sexual preferences.

The need to obtain accurate information about sex offenders has been recognized by for many years:

> Therapists evaluating and/or treating sexual assaulters need valid, reliable information from the sex offender. Without this, the therapist is less able to identify the precise treatment needs of the patient, to evaluate precisely the impact of treatment interventions, and to quantify treatment's long-term effects. Since much valuable information is frequently unobservable by the therapist, steps must be taken to ensure valid, reliable offender reports. (Abel & Rouleau, 1990, p. 10)

These comments from Abel and Rouleau (1990) accompanied their analysis of data from over 561 male adults who self-reported, during a structured clinical interview lasting between one and five hours, committing a wide variety of paraphilic behaviors over the span of many years. The findings were remarkable: 90 percent reported a history of multiple paraphilic behaviors; half of the subjects who reported involvement with nonfamilial boys also reported involvement with nonfamilial girls; and half of the incest perpetrators (with female victims) reported molesting girls outside the home. These men reported a wide range of deviant behaviors and many types of victims. The researchers attributed the promise of confidentiality surrounding the study as a primary reason that the study participants revealed diverse and frequent deviant behaviors.

It is interesting to note that the initial response in the sex offender treatment field to the publication of these data was generally dismissive. Many professionals were critical of the study because the subjects were not apprehended by the criminal justice system and therefore the findings were not generalizable to men convicted of sex crimes. Rather, the men in the study were voluntarily seeking evaluation or treatment and so were likely to be more compulsive and were perhaps more troubled than convicted rapists and other pedophiliacs. They had to be different: The ratio of arrest to self-reported crimes of rape and child molesting was estimated to be 1:30 and the ratio of arrest to self-reports of exhibitionism and voyeurism was 1:150 (Abel et al., 1988).

Our early field research in the area of sex offender management, described in English et al. (1996), found that probation and parole officers thought the findings from Abel and his colleagues resonated with their experiences. Rather than finding the information exceptional, many officers found it consistent with what they were learning from offenders who were serving sentences in the community: This population had many undetected sex crimes, kept secrets from their therapists, regularly lied to either the officer or the treatment provider or both, were manipulative, and frequently were arrested for sexually assaulting another person while they were under supervision (English et al., 1996). In an attempt to better understand this dangerous group of men, supervising officers in locations scattered across the country began going to the local library and contacting the National Institute of Corrections to learn more about this population. Abel's work stimulated interest in finding ways of breaking into the secret world maintained by these men. As a result, the use of the polygraph for supervision and monitoring—first used by a judge in Chicago in the 1960s—began to grow (Abrams & Abrams, 1993; English et al., 1996).

Indeed, preliminary analysis of data gathered from polygraph examination files and compared with information obtained during treatment showed that half of the offenders reported a history of assaulting both adults and children compared to 10 percent reporting this behavior early in treatment (Ahlmeyer, Heil, & English, 1998). Research on data obtained during polygraph examinations underscored the extent to which offenders were maintaining secret lives. Later studies found that 80 percent of rapists in prison have a history of assaulting children (Heil, Simons, & English, 2004). Further, Heil and Simons have shown in a small but growing sample of prisoners who have successfully passed polygraph exams that actuarial scale scores do not correlate with self-reported high-risk behaviors (Heil, Simons, & English, 2004).

In another study, researchers analyzed case file data from a sample of 232 adult sex offenders under varying levels of community supervision in four states (English, et al., 2000; English et al., 2003b).[8] Information available before and after polygraph testing showed that most sex offenders revealed a significant amount of past deviant activity. For example, the number of offenders with boy victims between the ages of 6 and 9 nearly doubled from 15 to 28 of the 180 polygraphed offenders (increasing from 8 percent to 15 percent of the sample). The data *before* the postconviction treatment/polygraph process suggest that both male and female adults were at relatively low risk of victimization by this particular sex offender group because all but seven of the sample had been convicted of a sex crime against a child. But self-report data obtained from the combination of treatment and polygraph exams indicated that the proportion of the group that had assaulted adult women tripled from 13 percent to 39 percent. The proportion of offenders with girl victims ages 6 to 9 more than tripled, from 20 percent to 64 percent. And 42 percent of the group with boy victims ages 6 to 9 reported abusing boys ages 0 to five 5. Nearly all the offenders (over 95 percent) reported assaulting a female.[9] This study found an average age of onset of 12, and the majority of these assaults were committed when the offender was an adult.

Can treatment be effective without accurate information about each offender's sexual deviancy? Is it important to know the age of onset, frequency, and variety of deviant sexual behavior? If this information is not available to the therapist, is this one reason researchers are unable to consistently detect significant differences between treatment and nontreatment groups?

Is Risk Assessment the Solution to Concerns About Treatment Efficacy?

The problems associated with measuring treatment efficacy led Quinsey, Khanna, and Malcolm (1998) and Rice and Harris (2003a, 2003b) to conclude that risk assessment should be a cornerstone of sex offender management. Risk assessment has a long history in criminology.

> If one seeks to control crime behavior, one needs first to be able to predict it. Much of our behavior is guided by the principle that relations observed in the past will hold in the future even though we believe there can be no guarantee of it. Change may be expected, but science requires that we assume that nature, subject to change, will change slowly. Thus we assume that some consistency will be found over time. . . . Any prediction method can merely provide a way to summarize previous experience to guide future decisions. (Gottfredson & Tonry, 1987, p. 6)

In practice with sex offenders, risk scales can be used as a resource allocation and offender management tool. Sex offenders falling into high-risk categories, for example, can be targeted for treatment and intense supervision. They might also be identified for longer—perhaps indefinite—periods of incarceration (Janus & Prentky, 2003). Low-risk offenders, on the other hand, might be subject to lower levels of supervision in the community. But do we really know who the low-risk offenders are?

Risk assessment in criminology and mental health began as expert opinions were provided by clinicians during court testimony or at parole hearings. The field has moved away from these subjective professional judgments to determine dangerousness, however, and the use of objective risk assessment instruments has become the new standard. In fact, developing and implementing objective risk assessment tools are necessary given the findings of Grove and Meehl (1996), who concluded that empirical tools significantly and consistently surpassed clinical judgment.[10] In the past decade, significant progress has been made in the area of actuarial risk assessment for convicted sex offenders. The need for actuarial risk assessment scales increased in the mid-1990s as many states passed laws pertaining to civil commitment, the identification of sexual predators, and community notification. Systems needed methods to sort offenders into risk categories because only the most dangerous sex offenders were intended to be managed by these means.

Several risk assessment tools have been statistically validated. Many are in use in North America, most notably the Violence Risk Appraisal Guide (VRAG; Harris, Rice, & Quinsey, 1993), the Sexual Offense Risk Appraisal Guide (SORAG; Rice & Harris, 1997; Quinsey, Harris, Rice, & Cormier, 1998), the Rapid Risk Assessment for Sexual Offense Recidivism (RRASOR; Hanson, 1997b), and Static-99 (see Hanson & Thornton, 2000). The use of a validated instrument adds structure, clarity, and consistency to the risk assessment process. However, limitations in the science and application of risk prediction (Janus & Prentky, 2003), most notably the inaccuracy of low risk classifications (Hanson, 1998), may undermine public safety.

Most risk instruments rely on official records and/or self-report data to classify cases. Because official data are incomplete, does "low risk" really mean unknown risk?

What Do Recidivism Rates Really Mean?

Recidivism rates reflect the proportion of offenders who were caught and convicted for a sex crime. If getting caught and convicted is a rare event for sex offenders, it becomes clear that recidivism rates are artificially low. Also, recidivism studies are based on official record data obtained for a specific period of time, usually five or ten years. It is common for professionals to think that this reflects a lifetime risk. It is important to understand the method used to develop the risk assessment instrument so that users are clear regarding the time period of the study. In sum, then, these instruments do not reflect lifetime risk, nor do they capture unreported crimes. These limitations are critical to understand when managing this population.

Can Risk Last a Lifetime?

Even incomplete official record data show that risk can last a lifetime. Prentky, Lee, Knight, and Cerce (1997) analyzed 136 rapists and 115 child molesters who were discharged over a twenty-five-year period. These civilly committed offenders had an average of two to four known sexual offenses prior to the crime for which they were civilly committed. Over a twenty-five-year period, 74 percent of the rapists and 75 percent of the child molesters incurred new charges for any crime, and 39 percent and 52 percent, respectively, for a new sex charge. The analyses showed that this sample of sex offenders continued recidivating throughout the twenty-five-year period, and if the group had been followed for only five years, more than half of the new sex charges would have been missed. Similarly, Hanson and Harris (2000) analyzed data on 4,724 offenders in ten separate samples and used both new charge and new conviction as measures of sexual recidivism. The five-year recidivism rate was 14 percent, the ten-year rate was 20 percent, the fifteen-year rate was 24 percent, and the twenty-year rate was 27 percent. The authors note that only 3 percent recidivated during years 15 to 20. Recognizing that official data underestimate actual offending rates, the authors concluded that a reasonable estimate is an actual sexual recidivism rate in the range of 35 to 55 percent over a twenty-year period.[11]

Despite the aforementioned studies, Hanson, Morton, and Harris (2003) report that "the available data suggest that most sexual offenders do not recidivate" (p. 156). Doren (2002), on the other hand, concluded "that the lifetime sexual recidivism by previously convicted sex offenders is not a statistically 'rare event'" (p. 150). Neither is it actually a rare event. Tjaden and Thoennes (2000a) report a lifetime rape prevalence rate of 17.6 percent for women and 3.0 percent for men, meaning that at a minimum one out of six U.S. women and one out of thirty-three U.S. men have been victims of a completed or attempted rape.[12]

In sum, these findings reflect the complicated nature of sexual assault statistics and the dismal state of criminal justice records to accurately reflect occurrences of sexual assault. Therefore, it seems highly unlikely that sexual recidivism rates of sex offenders are as low as official records indicate. Clearly, additional sources of information, beyond official records, are necessary to understand and manage this population. It was this need for additional information, combined with criminal justice system reforms based on the new information, that resulted in an innovative method of managing sex offenders: the containment approach.

SEX OFFENDER CONTAINMENT AND THE POLYGRAPH

One solution to the problem of incomplete information is the use of the polygraph examination with convicted sex offenders. Many jurisdictions in the United States are using the postconviction polygraph exam as one component of sex offender risk management, commonly known as the containment approach. Information disclosed by sex offenders during polygraph examinations generally reveals that the conviction crime—the traditional criteria for case management—did not reflect the seriousness of the offender's deviant history. In fact, practitioners discovered that managing sex crime cases based on conviction crime would endanger public safety because it would underestimate the offender's risk.

The Containment Approach

The containment approach for managing sex offenders was first described by researchers in 1996 (English et al., 1996; see also English, 1998, and English, Jones, & Patrick, 2003a). Based on interviews with hundreds of progressive and concerned practitioners from across the country, the "containment model" is a promising approach to protecting victims from sex crimes committed by convicted sex offenders. The containment approach operates in the context of multiagency collaboration, explicit policies, and consistent practices that combine case evaluation, risk assessment, sex offender treatment, behavioral monitoring, and intense community surveillance. Sex offender containment requires a commitment by professionals to communicate with each other about the risk management of individual offenders. These activities are designed specifically to maximize public safety and protect past and potential victims. The five components of the containment approach are briefly described next (see also English et al., 2000).

Victim Focused. The containment approach requires a clear philosophy that prioritizes victim protection and public safety. Finkelhor (1988) explained that the harm of some sexual abuse experiences lies less in the actual sexual contact than in the process of disclosure or even in the process of intervention. Kilpatrick et al. (1992) found that victims of rape did not report the crime because they were afraid of being blamed by others, and they did not want their families or friends to know. Goodwin's (1988) following statement clarifies why the containment approach must be victim focused: "The problem now is how to develop an acceptable system of response that minimizes rather than exacerbates the traumatic effects of this kind of abuse" (p. 21). The criminal justice system must make every effort to ensure that known offenders are prohibited from harming again.

Collaboration and Communication. Professionals from multiple disciplines (psychologists, social workers, psychiatrists, lawyers, probation/parole officers, nurses, polygraph examiners, law enforcement, crime victims or their representatives) must genuinely respect each others' expertise and experience, and they must continuously collaborate and communicate in the service of systematically managing the sex offender population. Partnerships must cross agency boundaries and include cross-training and other forms of information sharing regarding each agency's responsibility and scope of authority in the process of holding offenders accountable for past and current criminal behaviors.

Case-Specific Risk Management Strategies. Containment requires the implementation of case-specific "customized" risk management strategies designed to hold individual sex offenders accountable through the combined use of the offenders' internal controls and external criminal justice controls. These strategies must include the use of specialized treatment and postconviction polygraph examinations as a method of enhancing and intensifying criminal justice supervision.

A variety of containment tools must be available to supervising officers, including specialized conditions of probation and parole, a manageable caseload size,[13] and the authority to restrict employment and living arrangements. It is critical that the court mandate an expectation that each offender fully participate in specialized treatment and supervision that incorporates regular polygraph examinations. The availability of a variety of consequences invoked quickly, then, is a vital and ongoing aspect of risk management. Without consistent pressure on the offender to adhere to the behavioral expectations detailed in the conditions of supervision and treatment contract, community safety must depend on the offender's goodwill. Dr. Judith Herman (1992) of Harvard underscores the need for enforcement and structure that are key aspects of containment: "Vigorous enforcement . . . might be expected to have some preventive effect since both the compulsive and opportunistic offenders are keenly sensitive to external controls" (p. 188).

A vital part of containment requires that therapists and supervising officers proactively establish collateral contacts for each offender. These contacts are an essential component of the supervision and treatment process because they provide invaluable information about the offender. For example, the offender's boss or neighbor might telephone the supervising officer if the offender is seen driving with children in the vehicle. Mood swings, computer use, use of illegal substances, and other important information can be provided by collateral contacts, giving officers and therapists greater access to the offender's lifestyle and potentially high-risk behaviors. It is imperative that resources be made available to supervising officers and therapists to monitor offenders' leisure time and to obtain collateral information about the offender's behavior from neighbors, friends, and family members and sometimes the victim's therapists.

Consistent Policies and Practices. Consistent policies and practices should be developed collaboratively and based on research. This component requires local criminal justice practitioners to develop consistent and reinforcing public policies at all levels of government that institutionalize and codify the containment approach. These take the form of multiagency policies and protocols developed by multidisciplinary teams. This effort creates a "seamless" response that holds offenders accountable, and to be effectively implemented in the field, it must empower those who work closely with these cases. Policies must define and structure the discretion authorities need to manage each offender individually, including the development of criteria for treatment and polygraph providers and the use of polygraph information. These policies should be based on research and best practices.

Quality Control Mechanisms.   The final component focuses on quality-control mechanisms, including program monitoring and evaluation and strict adherence to professional standards of practice. The criminal justice system typically allows broad discretion on the part of professionals. Such discretion must be systematically monitored to ensure fairness and justice. Quality-control mechanisms include, among other things, written program descriptions, methods to assess case management practices, the collection of case data that describe the characteristics of offenders who fail in treatment or commit new crimes, and videotaping of polygraph exams.

Collaboration Is Key

Clearly, collaboration is at the heart of the containment approach. Collaboration requires already busy professionals to attend regularly scheduled face-to-face meetings. Collaboration must be recognized as time intensive but critically important. At the case management level, there is simply no substitute for regular face-to-face meetings that include (at a minimum) the treatment provider, the polygraph examiner, and the supervising officer. Communication about individual cases is a priority. Frequent communication among containment professionals builds and sustains relationships over time, and it identifies gaps in case management (English et al., 1996). Frequent face-to-face meetings facilitate proper implementation and make the best use of information obtained through the collaborative process. In the end, successful collaboration requires that each team member believe that contacting each other is "100 percent my responsibility." Further, it is essential that all members of the containment team sincerely believe that the other professionals, regardless of their educational level, have expertise and experience that are critical to the decision-making process.

Effective collaboration is difficult to achieve. Interviews with professionals nationwide reveal that it is indeed a challenge for many professionals to incorporate this essential component into their everyday work life. It requires specific social and professional skills. Professional group facilitators and mediators are sometimes used to resolve inevitable conflicts that naturally emerge (English et al., 1996).

Containment Requires Local Commitment

Use of the polygraph in sex offender management requires an understanding of the political and professional environment that must be created to ensure successful implementation. It is irresponsible to consider the use of the polygraph outside the context of the larger containment approach. As with every other component of treatment and supervision, the use of the polygraph without adequate "buy-in" from key stakeholders can undermine other aspects of sex offender management by creating inconsistent expectations of offenders. The polygraph examination must be used within carefully developed protocols and the ongoing collaboration among polygraph examiners, treatment providers, supervising officers, decision makers in criminal justice agencies, and, in the case of civil commitment, officials from the department of human services. This collaboration is essential to the successful implementation of the postconviction polygraph.

Containment With the Polygraph

In 1980, professionals in Jackson County, Oregon began to integrate the use of the postconviction polygraph examination with adults and juveniles sentenced to sex offender treatment.[14] In the mid-1980s, with the support of the state department of corrections, Oregon probation and parole officers with specialized sex offender caseloads began to meet quarterly to discuss consistency in practice. Subcommittees of this group focused on training and public policy. The quarterly meetings were inclusive and the group welcomed the regular participation of the state police and treatment providers. During the same period in Phoenix, Arizona, the police department and the district attorney's office began to work together to successfully prosecute sex crimes. Officials from the district attorney's office worked closely with probation. This interaction was facilitated by the fact that the district attorney's office and the probation department were housed in the same downtown building. These professionals also worked closely with treatment providers and polygraph examiners, and the relationships were well established by 1988 when lifetime probation supervision was enacted by the state legislature. Developing implementation policies regarding lifetime supervision was simplified by the fact that these professionals had a history of collaboration and cooperation. In 1987 in Colorado—Denver, Arapahoe, and Jefferson counties—probation officers, deputy district attorneys, treatment providers, polygraph examiners, and parole officers began to meet monthly to clarify policies and attempt to ensure consistency in practice regarding sex offender supervision, treatment, and polygraph testing. These efforts led to the enactment five years later of the statewide Sex Offender Management Board. The board built on these early collaborations and the long-standing priority of offender accountability and public safety.[15]

These early demonstrations of the containment approach reflect grassroots efforts by innovative professionals who reported feeling challenged and frustrated by sex offenders' ability to manipulate gaps in the system and ultimately harm another victim. Studying and documenting the work of these and other professionals allowed researchers to articulate the five components of the containment approach (English et al., 1996). The long-standing use of containment strategies—including the use of the postconviction polygraph—in a variety of jurisdictions nationwide may encourage implementation elsewhere, particularly in communities in which the political climate discourages the community supervision of this population of sex offenders. While the containment approach is evolving and can manifest flaws in implementation, particularly in the areas of communication and collaboration, it holds some promise for interrupting offenders' propensity to reoffend while encouraging offenders and professionals to focus on risk management as priorities for sex offender treatment and supervision.[16]

HOW THE POLYGRAPH IS USED

Focus Is Information and Honesty

The postconviction sex offender polygraph examination is first and foremost a tool to help facilitate the acquisition of risk-related information and to promote offender honesty. Incorporating the polygraph test into a system of supervision, monitoring, and treatment requires a continual emphasis on honesty. The therapist and the supervising officer must continually convey to the offender the expectation of and necessity for honesty to replace a lifetime of secrets and harmful behavior.

It is common that "passing the polygraph" becomes a treatment goal (and sometimes a power struggle), but this emphasis misses the fundamental value underlying the use of the polygraph: a focus on honesty and crime-free living. Anyone who has attempted to change venerable behaviors knows that the change process is often hard and uncomfortable. The use of the polygraph over years of treatment and supervision allows the offender to integrate the positive rewards of honest living. Research in the area of substance abuse has repeatedly shown that length of time in treatment—sometimes accumulated over a lifetime—predicts client success (Anglin & Hser, 1990).[17] As in drug treatment, the focus should not be on a "clean urinalysis test" but rather the benefits related to a drug-free lifestyle.

Likewise, the polygraph is a tool to encourage honesty and treatment cooperation. The objective is to obtaining information about the offender's behavior that can be used to develop meaningful, individual-level interventions. Just as the offender's current offense may not accurately reflect his level of dangerousness, the information he self-reports will most likely reflect what he is willing to disclose rather than what professionals need to know.

This focus on information and honesty occurs within a system of supervision and treatment intended to safely integrate offenders into the community, a goal that is humane for both the public and the offender.

The containment approach provides an environment that supports offenders in making positive choices that simultaneously enhance community safety and each offender's opportunity to change. Communication among containment team members often can prevent the offender from successfully manipulating the professionals. Manipulative behavior is entrenched in most sex offenders, and it is necessary to help offenders tell the truth about their secret lives (see Groth, 1979, for a description of this secret life.

The containment approach places the onus on the offender to prove that his or her risk is manageable. Authentic cooperation is measured by the offender's honesty about the nature and extent of harm for which he is responsible. Cooperation with treatment and supervision is verified via the offender's participation in regular polygraph examinations along with more traditional methods.[18]

The postconviction polygraph examination is an important tool to gauge the validity of the offender's portrayal of past and current victims, crime frequency, offending patterns, and current or recent high-risk behaviors. Dr. Michael Knapp (1996), sex offender treatment provider in Jackson County, Oregon, describes the use of the postconviction polygraph in sex offender management:

> We believe that a triangular relationship among the therapists, the polygraph examiner and the parole/probation officer is essential to keep the offender motivated and honest. . . . Finding himself squeezed between his therapist, the victim's therapist, the polygraph examiner, and the parole/probation officer, the offender is no longer held in the traditional 'unconditional positive regard' by his therapist and other team members. Instead, the offender is valued for telling the full and complete truth and for participating fully in treatment. Respect and positive regard are to be earned and not simply given unconditionally, as in more traditional psychotherapeutic approach. . . . (pp. 13–10)

Like urinalysis testing for drug offenders, the polygraph monitors the offender's actual behavior—not future behavior, not sexual interest, not sexual attraction, and not fantasies unless the fantasies are linked to actual behavior (such as masturbation). The focus is on the offender's honest self-report of his actual behavior. This provides information regarding the offender's risk to the community and his commitment to treatment and supervision. It may also encourage offenders to remain committed to treatment and supervision. Barrett, Wilson, and Long (2003) conducted a very interesting study of motivational change among 101 sex offenders during various stages of institutional and community treatment. They found that levels of motivation decreased during the first twelve weeks of conditional release to the community. Further, acceptance of guilt and responsibility, measured at the community treatment stage, were significantly correlated with treatment outcome. The polygraph can help keep each offender's focus on responsibility and accountability.

Actual Examination

The postconviction polygraph is used to encourage offender truthfulness in the following ways (see English et al., 2000):

1. *Sexual history disclosure polygraph exams.* Sexual history disclosure polygraph examinations are used to verify the accuracy and completeness of the sexual history information a sex offender provides during treatment. This information is obtained using a very specific treatment tool: sexual history documentation. Programs frequently develop a specific journal our outline on a paper form that allows offenders to document their deviant sexual history prior to meeting with the polygraph examiner. This treatment task requires the offender to record the gender, age, method of assault, and relationship with every past victim. The sex history document can be completed within six months of commencing treatment, as offenders learn or acknowledge the variety of behaviors that constitute abuse.[19] The document is then provided to the

polygraph examiner who, after reading it carefully along with other case file information, asks the offender very specific questions about the accuracy and completeness of parts of the sex history reported by the offender. In most cases, the completed sex history document is long and includes disclosures of many prior assaults, attempted assaults, and paraphilias. The clear expectation that the offender will be accurate and truthful on the sex history assignment, coupled with the ability to verify truthfulness through polygraph exams, increases the offender's incentive to disclose this potentially embarrassing and illegal information to the treatment provider.

2. *Specific-issue, single-incident, or event-specific exams.* Specific-issue exams are focused on a single event such as a known incident or allegation. These tests are usually given when the offender's version of the crime varies from the victim's version, or the offender continues to deny committing the crime of conviction. Specific-issue exams are also used to address a single concern or suspicion that arises during an offender's probation or parole, such as suspected contact with children. Specific-issue tests are also recommended as a follow-up on one area that was found to be on deceptive on previous exams to clarify the nature of the deception.

3. *Maintenance or monitoring (compliance) exams.* Maintenance or monitoring exams are used to verify whether a probationer or parolee is complying with the terms and conditions of community supervision and cooperating with treatment expectations. These exams require the polygraph examiner, the treatment provider, and the supervising officer to work together to identify questions that target high-risk behavior related to the assault patterns described in the offender's sexual history document. In more recent years, the term "maintenance polygraph" has been used to refer to a focus on high-risk behaviors and "monitoring polygraph" refers to behaviors that would result in revocation of the offender's probation or parole.

Preparation Is Critical. Preparation for the polygraph actually begins when the treatment provider and the supervising officer emphasize the need for complete truth as a first step toward offender responsibility, accountability, and community safety. The offender must be encouraged to be honest, prior to visiting the polygraph examiner. Group discussions regarding offenders' cognitive distortions that rationalize abusive behaviors or misrepresent the victim's experience are important educational and therapeutic activities that help prepare the offender for the polygraph test. Note that research on treatment effectiveness in corrections has found that confrontations must be supportive in nature (Marshall, Thornton, Marshall, Fernandez, & Mann, 2001). Research has also found that lack of adequate preparation for the polygraph examination may decrease accuracy (Amato-Henderson, 1996).

A vital part of the preparation for a polygraph exam takes place when the offender observes others in the treatment process who are preparing for and taking the exam. This includes sex offenders watching as group members undergo the natural consequences for lying or withholding information from the containment team. Harrison and Kirkpatrick (2000) asked a sample of twenty-eight sex offenders in treatment how they first learned about the polygraph, and the most frequent response was "by talking to peers." The way each offender is treated and managed will affect the others in a treatment setting. In fact, it is arguably the most powerful message sent and received during the therapeutic process.

Other preparation also requires teamwork. Policies about how the exam information will be obtained and used must be in place prior to implementing the polygraph. Forms should be designed in advance to facilitate proper documentation of the process. These include sex history disclosure forms for use in treatment (remember, these become journal-like), all consent forms, and polygraph examiner's questionnaires. Generally, efforts to develop policies, procedures and documents in this area can be initiated by reviewing the work undertaken in other jurisdictions. For example, the Colorado Sex Offender Management Board (2004) has prepared comprehensive guidelines on this topic, and these are revised regularly to reflect updated practices. Specifying the extent of information offenders will be expected to disclose is important. Other issues that must be clarified include the frequency of exams, payment (the offender should have to pay some portion of the fee to ensure his commitment to the process) and consequences for nonparticipation.

Treatment/Polygraph Process. The postconviction polygraph examination must be completely integrated into the treatment process. The sex history document will serve to identify the offender's modus operandi. For example, a sex history document may reflect a pattern of stalking, or the use of a puppy, as part of the offender's victim identification and grooming process. Polygraph examiners will use these details to identify possible areas of focus during a monitoring test. *The objective is to obtain the information necessary to catch the offender before he commits a new crime.*

In the end, this process results in the disclosure of additional, previously unknown information provided by the offender. The amount of information disclosed through the combined use of treatment and the polygraph will be the result of many factors, but most often the amount of new information can be linked to the cohesiveness of the containment team and the consistently expressed expectation that the offender stop living a life with secrets. Ideally, the offender will disclose important information to the treatment group and not the polygraph examiner. Disclosing shameful behaviors is very difficult for everyone, and thus it is not surprising that many sex offenders wait as long as possible before they reveal new victims, deviant behaviors, or risky, pre-assaultive behaviors.

Do We Really Need *All* This Information?

Many treatment providers and supervising officers believe that it is better for them (rather than the offender) to decide what information is important and relevant to risk management. It is possible and essential to prevent new sex crimes by systematically monitoring offenders' lifestyles so that the presence of risk factors can be established and compliance with individual safety plans can be monitored. This can, in turn, avert new sex crimes. It requires that the containment team have the information they need to intervene before a new crime is committed.

Hanson and Morton-Bourgon (2004) summarized generally static historical offender characteristics that predicted recidivism (defined as new sex crime conviction). The characteristics included diverse sex crimes, victim type, deviant sexual preferences, early onset, prior sex crimes, and prior non-sex crimes as predictive of sex crime conviction, reflecting duration, frequency and "mix" as measured by official record data. Harris, Rice, and Quinsey (1998) found that sex offenders with a history of committing both rape and child molestation "exhibited near total recidivism" (p. 84) in a study of violent rearrest rates over twenty years. Additional information on criminal career dimensions can be inferred from work by Hanson and Harris (2000) who used case file and interview data to find that recidivists[20] failed relatively quickly while under supervision, reflecting the need to consider recency in deviant behavior. Moreover, recidivists did not consider themselves at risk to reoffend and "they took few precautions to avoid high risk situations" (p. 18). While under supervision, the recidivists were more likely than the nonrecidivists to engage in excessive masturbation and to report deviant sexual fantasies and urges; they were more likely to have an uncontrolled release environment and were considered by supervising officers to be disengaged in treatment. They were more likely to attempt to manipulate and deceive the officers and miss scheduled appointments, and generally they were uncooperative with supervision. They minimized and justified their crimes and lifestyle during the course of supervision.

For the risk factors to be useful in the field, they must be "observable" (Hanson & Harris, 2000, p. 5). Sometimes these behaviors are readily observable to therapists and supervising officers. But self-reports of these behaviors made during polygraph exams greatly increases our ability to observe what is really happening with the offender. The postconviction polygraph examination is the best tool available today to encourage offenders to disclose the risk factors identified by Hanson and Harris (2000), along with other more idiosyncratic risk factors that are specific to individual offenders.

Test outcomes direct future actions: Disclosures of deviant and noncompliant behavior during a polygraph exam should flag further investigation by both the therapist and the supervising officer. A finding of deceptive on any question renders the entire exam deceptive, and this event should also trigger further investigation,[21] including a retest at the offender's expense. Test findings of "inconclusive" can be the result of several things, including poor question construction or weak chart tracings. If the offender has nothing at stake during the examination, inconclusive results are more likely.[22]

Countermeasures

Sometimes polygraph examiners render a finding of inconclusive when the offender uses countermeasures (i.e., intentional behaviors that cause odd chart tracings for the purpose of manipulating or distorting the outcome of the exam). This is unfortunately common because information about executing countermeasures is readily available. For example, many anti-polygraph web sites advocate the use of countermeasures. These sites often fail to explain that many "odd tracings" are obviously countermeasures, and most examiners will terminate the examination when countermeasures are used. Some countermeasures are sophisticated, however, and all examiners should receive ongoing training on the identification of countermeasures. Further, containment team members will want to inform all offenders at the beginning of treatment and supervision that using countermeasures is counterproductive—and, if not detected, are likely to increase errors when offenders are truthful.

Research found that examination subjects who attempt to conceal important information are more likely to employ countermeasures, compared to those who are forthcoming. In one mock crime study of countermeasures, 90 percent of the guilty subjects reported the use of one or more types of countermeasures but, surprisingly, nearly half (46 percent) of the "innocent" subjects also reported the use of "mental maneuvers"[23] (Honts, Amato, & Gordon, 2001). The innocent subjects were significantly more likely to be rated deceptive by the polygraph examiner whereas the guilty subjects were still found guilty.

In another study examinees received expert countermeasure training and coaching by a lab assistant in a laboratory setting. The study was designed to model the effects of hostile intelligence officers trying to infiltrate a national security system. Efforts to beat the polygraph were successful in half of the cases (Honts, Hodes, & Raskin, 1985; Honts, Raskin, & Kircher, 1994). Honts, Raskin, Kircher, and Hodes (1988) found that providing information about countermeasures but not intense training did not affect the outcome of the examination. Even the use of prescription drugs to distort polygraph findings would require an extremely sophisticated subject because the effort must result in the suppression of a response to some questions but not others (Gaschler, McGettigan, Menges, & Waller, 2001).

It is important to consider that other assessment tools, even psychological tests, are subject to countermeasures when the questions are transparent and the subject is not truthful. In Colorado, most examiners will terminate the examination when an individual attempts countermeasure behaviors. The examiner's report to the treatment provider and supervising officer then includes all the information learned during the pretest interview and a final note that the offender was not cooperative during the exam, describing the offender's attempt to manipulate the examination. Episodes like this should result in requiring the offender to take another examination as soon as possible, and again they should pay for the additional exam.

Consequences for Deceptive Exams

One of the controversies regarding the use of the polygraph relates to consequences invoked for inconclusive findings resulting from countermeasures and deceptive exam results.[24] Because the polygraph is not 100 percent accurate, should major case decisions be based on deceptive results, especially when there are no admissions or collateral information to support the polygraph findings?

This is an important question that must be considered in the context of the larger containment strategy. Invoking consequences should depend on many factors, including the expectation of honesty, the cohesiveness of the containment team, the purpose of the exam, the specificity of the questions, the number of prior deceptive exams, and the length of time the offender has been in treatment.[25]

Generally, the threat of consequences increases the stake the offender has in the outcome of the examination. Increasing the stakes increases accuracy. Polygraph studies of accuracy consistently find field tests (actual cases) to be significantly more accurate than lab (mock crime) experiments. Increasing the stakes also increases the nondeceptive rate among offenders, as shown in a pilot study (Heil et al., 2004).

Consequences can be clearly spelled out. Members of the sex offender treatment team at the Colorado Department of Corrections joined with parole officers and local treatment providers to develop a "sanctions grid." Low-level sanctions include start-ing regular urinalysis testing, restricting community activities, requiring additional treatment homework, and imposing a curfew or geographic restrictions. Medium-level sanctions include withdrawing driving privileges and travel permits for vacation, more visits with supervising officer, searching the residence, and prohibiting community activities. High-level sanctions include moving the offender to intensive supervision status, contacting law enforcement for surveillance, requiring community service, and imposing a curfew with daily scheduled call-ins to the officer. All sanctions include increased supervision. The sanctions grid is discussed with every offender, and the form requires the signatures of the therapist, supervising officer, and offender. The grid is an excellent example of coordination and collaboration among stakeholders who wanted to be clear and consistent regarding the use of sanctions related to poly-graph testing.[26]

At a minimum, a deceptive polygraph exam should result in significantly increased surveillance along with other efforts to obtain additional information about the offender, but accuracy problems mean that even those who "pass" the polygraph require intense supervision. These efforts should include interviews with potential victims, the victim's therapist, employers, and discussions with law enforcement offi-cers. A deceptive finding on the examination reflects the offender's lack of coopera-tion with the containment approach and his or her lack of commitment to the honesty necessary to make the life changes expected by the containment team.

DISCLOSURE OF PREVIOUS CRIMES

What About Self-Incrimination?

Respecting and upholding the dignity and constitutional rights of incarcerated individuals is a priority in a free society. Self-incrimination is a serious concern and is often mentioned as such by those who question the use of the sex offender post-conviction polygraph examination. This concern has a long history in case law, how-ever, for the courts have been invoked to review the use of the polygraph time and time again. Most important for the discussion here is the review by legal scholars Winick and La Fond (2003). They refer to *Minnesota v. Murphy*,[27] in which the U.S. Supreme Court upheld the use of the power of the state to compel answers to incriminating questions without violating an individuals Fifth Amendment rights, under two condi-tions: (1) the probationer agreed to answer questions as a condition of supervision, and (2) the information would not be used in a criminal proceeding. This case did not involve the use of the polygraph but Winick and La Fond (2003) argue that it would apply equally if the offender agreed to submit to polygraph testing as a condition of probation, parole, or sexually violent predator (SVP) release. *McKune v. Lile*[28] found that an agreement to participate in treatment that includes polygraph testing does not result in compulsory self-incrimination. Similarly, *Patton v. State*[29] found that "the rehabilitative benefits of the polygraph examination condition must be obtained with-out the examination results being admissible in any subsequent court proceeding."[30]

However, refusal to respond to the polygraph examiner's questions after agreeing to do so, by agreeing to participate in treatment, is admissible in a hearing to deter-mine if the offender's supervision should be revoked: "While the offender could invoke his Fifth Amendment privilege to refuse to answer a particular question in a polygraph examination, if his refusal to respond is itself a violation of an agreed-upon condition of release, his invocation of the privilege can serve as a basis for revoking his probation or parole" (Winick & La Fond, 2003, p. 317).

Limited Immunity

The polygraph is sometimes criticized because information gained about past crimes can be used in new prosecutions against the individual. One solution to avoid self-incrimination and prosecution for crimes disclosed during the polygraph examination is to provide limited immunity for crimes similar to the crime of conviction as long as the offender fully complies with treatment and supervision, including complete cooperation with the polygraph examination. Immunity can be offered only by the prosecutor's office. Some prosecutors offer immunity when they believe that learning about prior victims in treatment is more important than prosecuting offenders for crimes that—without treatment—would remain unknown. However, a blanket exception to immunity involves instances in which victims come forward to report the crime and desire prosecution. In this case, it is not the offender's disclosure that leads to prosecution.

Limited immunity can take many forms but it always requires collaboration with the local prosecutor. In some communities, immunity is decided on a case-by-case basis. In others, it remains a broad assurance as long as the offender is completely engaged in treatment, including passing polygraph examinations. By far the most common solution to the issue of immunity is asking the offender to refrain from disclosing details that would identify a specific victim. This involves informing the offender that he is *not* to reveal identifying information about past victim(s). He can reveal the victim's age, sex, and general relationship to the offender; the method of victim selection; how he planned to avoid getting caught (how he groomed the victim); and the circumstances that allowed for access to each victim. Offenders should not reveal the location of the assault or the name of the victim. Without using identifying information, the offender is expected to acknowledge and take responsibility for all harms committed in the past and present.

In January 2005, in *United States v. Antelope*[31] (see Appendix 1, this volume), the Court of Appeals for the Ninth Circuit ruled that Antelope had been unjustly denied his constitutional right against self-incrimination when a Montana district court judge required that he undergo treatment and disclose past crimes as a condition of probation supervision. The court found that Antelope could not be forced to participate in treatment unless he was promised that he would not be prosecuted for past crimes. This ruling, while applicable only to the jurisdiction covered by the Ninth Circuit, marks the critical need to clarify with offenders and the containment team exactly how the information obtained during therapy and polygraph examinations will be used. It underscores the value of the strategy, described previously, that precludes professionals from obtaining from offenders specific details necessary for prosecution (name of victim, geographic location, and date/time of offense).

Note that new crimes committed while under supervision and disclosed during a polygraph examination should include identifying information and should result in prosecution. Clearly there is no immunity for crimes committed while the offender is under supervision or in treatment. Current crimes disclosed by those in civil commitment institutions, particularly sex crimes, must be prosecuted. This communicates to offenders the goal of community/facility safety.

Officials Must Establish How Much Information Offenders Are Expected to Disclose

This is often a difficult discussion to complete with satisfaction. Some jurisdictions implement only the monitoring or maintenance polygraph test in order to avoid the obvious problems associated with full disclosure required for the sexual history examination.[32] Implementing this type of polygraph examination is certainly easier than including the sex history exam, and it is usually accompanied with a high level of comfort on the part of professionals. In fact, given that an offender has been civilly committed, sometimes professionals will assume that these offenders are naturally "high risk." In this case, perhaps some professionals believe that they have acquired enough information and so full disclosure of past crimes is unnecessary.

Unfortunately, excluding the sex history examination results in a reliance on the offender's self-report of past crimes. Often a "high risk" or civil commitment designation is derived from a heinous current crime and little may be known about the entire scope of the offender's deviant past. Additional information received in the course of traditional treatment—while sometimes expansive—will reflect only what the offender intends for others to know. But the emotional relief and full acceptance of responsibility for significant harm done that can follow complete disclosure often remains an untapped treatment domain.

The decision to implement the sex history examination is complex in jurisdictions with civil commitment or lifetime supervision where the disclosed information might be used to incarcerate the offender indefinitely. The information becomes part of the offender's file and becomes available to those who make the commitment and release decisions. In many ways, however, this dilemma occurs in other jurisdictions. In Colorado, for example, state statute requires that offenders sentenced to prison under the lifetime statute[33] participate in sex offender treatment prior to being approved for parole supervision; other inmates incarcerated for sex crimes are required by informal policy to participate in treatment before the parole board will approve release. Even in locations in which indeterminate sentencing is not a looming concern, there are ethical issues associated with making decisions about a person's liberty based on crimes for which one was never convicted.

The most important issue regarding information disclosed during polygraph examinations is this: Officials in jurisdictions using the polygraph must agree on what they expect from the offender, what they intend to do in response to various types of disclosures, and how they will manage sharing the information obtained. The answers to these questions will vary from jurisdiction to jurisdiction; local written agreements and consistency in practice are necessary for successful implementation.

The key to managing the disclosure of additional information is for decision makers to become knowledgeable about sex offender management. They need to understand that the disclosure of this information is an indication of treatment cooperation; that nearly all convicted sex offenders have long histories but not all of them work with the therapist to take responsibility for past abusive behaviors. The information

made available to release authorities must be reviewed in the context of an understanding of sexual abuse. Often release authorities are not familiar with the lifestyle
of abusing that most offenders disclose, and some officials experience revulsion at the
information that is obtained for the purpose of preventing future abuses. Education
can help these officials understand the value of the information for treatment and
release planning.

Educating Decision Makers

Authorities are sometimes reluctant to release certain sex offenders into the community because of past crimes they have disclosed in the process of treatment. Release
authorities should be informed of the extent of supervision and behavioral monitoring
that will occur in the offender's release environment. When a supervision plan is
developed based on the offender's assault history, decision makers begin to understand
how the details about prior crimes can be used to increase public safety. Ideally, the
release plan will delineate how the release environment will be systematically monitored and structured to identify preoffending behaviors, and interventions that can be
employed to prevent opportunities for offenders to commit new crimes. This plan can
be shared with release authorities and family members.

Further, summaries and reviews of relevant research can be helpful for many decision makers. It is important for officials to understand that, according to research,
most sex offenders have long histories of sex crimes with multiple victims, and that
having this information on individual offenders makes it more likely that meaningful
community-based treatment and supervision will occur. Important studies include, for
example, one by Ahlmeyer et al. (2000), who studied the use of the polygraph with
prisoners and reported over 100 hands-on and hands-off sex crimes for every arrest in
official records. Abel et al. (1987) found incest offenders repeatedly molested the
same child (reporting means of thirty-seven incidents per boy victims and forty-five
incidents for girl victims; sadists averaged forty-three incidents per victim). In a study
of hands-on sex crime by inmates and parolees, Heil et al. (2004) reported that, among
the inmates, 80 percent assaulted both adults and children and 70 percent assaulted
relatives and nonrelatives. English et al. (2000; English et al., 2003b) report findings
from community samples (probation and parole) obtained from four states. Analyses
of disclosure information obtained from polygraph examination reports revealed that
two-thirds of the offenders disclosed victims of multiple age groups, gender, and relationships. Only 30 percent of the offenders in this study were considered by the examiner to be truthful, so the information obtained by researchers likely reflects an underestimate of the proportion engaging in these activities. O'Connell (1998) studied a
community sample and found two-thirds of the rapists reported assaulting children.

These studies provide generally a robust picture of the sexual histories of convicted offenders across different criminal justice samples. The frequency with which
offenders commit these crimes is consistent with victimization studies that report that
one out of six U.S. women and one out of thirty-three U.S. men have been victims of
a completed or attempted rape (see Tjaden & Thoennes, 2000a).[34]

This information must be packaged and continually delivered to decision makers
so that the information in case files is observed as evidence of cooperation with treatment. The information allows community supervision officials to develop very spe-

cific safety plans for family members and specific restriction plans for offenders. The polygraph can then be used to monitor the offender's adherence to this plan.

POLYGRAPH ACCURACY

Opponents of the use of the polygraph in sex offender management often question the accuracy of the instrument. The National Research Council (NRC; 2003) explored the use of the polygraph in the detection of espionage and, despite criticizing the paucity of well-controlled research on the instrument, concluded that "specific incident polygraph tests can discriminate lying from truth telling at rates well above chance, though well below perfection. Because the studies of acceptable quality all focus on specific incidents, generalization from them to uses for screening is not justified" (p. 4).

But the polygraph is not used for screening in sex offender testing. Postconviction polygraphs are quite specific in focus. Communication between the examiner, therapist, and supervising officers results in the identification of areas of concern. Further, the examiner should review past examination reports so he or she knows what has and has not been covered. If an offender is living at home with children—not an uncommon scenario, given the scarcity of housing for this population—the examiner will nearly always ask about sexual contact with those children. The focus will be on the offender's vulnerabilities: drinking, driving "aimlessly," masturbating to inappropriate sexual fantasies, and specific precursor behaviors such as stalking.

Likewise, the sexual history examination is not a screening test. Examiners should never test on written material, such as "have you left anything important out of your journal?" Such questions are too vague, making it easy for the offender to rationalize a "no" answer. The examiner will read case materials, the sexual history journals, and prior polygraph examination reports and will have talked with the therapist and supervising officer. A well-trained and experienced examiner will incorporate all the information into test questions that target relevant concerns.

As noted by the NRC, research on polygraph accuracy is difficult to conduct.[35] Validity can be checked under two conditions: a mock crime scenario or field tests that are cleared by a confession. Field tests are considered to be more accurate because they occur under "real-life" situations where the stakes are high, as compared to mock crimes where participants have nothing at stake and physiological measures are less reactive because fear of detection is difficult to manufacture. The error rate is expected to be higher in mock crime scenario studies compared to field studies.

Forensic Research, Inc., of Severna Park, Maryland, reviewed nearly two dozen polygraph reliability and validity studies for the American Polygraph Association in 1997. Validity reviews of twelve field studies involving 2,174 charts indicated that between 96 and 98 percent of exams correctly identified deception. Specifically, accuracy for the truthful person averaged 96 percent and accuracy for the deceptive person averaged 98 percent.

Reliability assessments require retesting or reanalysis of field charts by quality control examiner. The Department of Defense regularly employs retesting or reviewing of charts as a method of quality control. According to Forensic Research, the test-retest reliability of eleven field examination studies that involved 1,609 charts averaged 92 percent. The reliability rates were 90 percent for nondeceptive charts and 95 percent for those scored deceptive. However, for nearly all studies, inconclusive results—meaning insufficient information was available to score the exam—are excluded from the averages, and this may inflate accuracy rates.

Krapohl and Stern (2003), researchers at the Department of Defense Polygraph Institute, compared counterintelligence testing with postconviction sex offender testing. In espionage testing, the assumption is that there may be 1 out of 1,000 or 10,000 tested subjects engaged in espionage. However, in sex offender testing, the situation is reversed: It is likely that 500 or 800 or 950 offenders out of 1,000 are hiding important information.[36] Thus for sex offender testing, when 950 out of 1,000 offenders have something to hide, and accuracy is (conservatively) 80 percent, then for every 1,000 offenders tested, only 40 will be correctly found to be truthful. The error is in the direction of *missing* the deceptive individuals because 190 deceptive offenders will be called truthful. Ten truthful individuals will be called deceptive, assuming accuracy at 80 percent. These errors reflect the need for ongoing intensive supervision and vigilance on the part of the treatment provider and supervising officer.

One of the most important findings of this exercise, however, is that 760 of the 1,000 sex offenders will be correctly identified as deceptive on the exam. Nearly all of these offenders will disclose extremely important risk-related information to the polygraph examiner during the course of the examination. The information may not be complete, and deceptive exam findings require additional testing to clarify risk information, but significantly more information now exists for treatment and supervision purposes.

This information is simply not available in jurisdictions in which efforts to implement the polygraph have stalled or were never pursued. The value of the post conviction polygraph is obtaining information about dangerous behavior that otherwise would remain unknown.

"Accuracy versus utility" is a phrase used to explain that the polygraph examination is very useful, if not always accurate. However, accuracy concerns have begun to trump the value of utility examinations. Utility exams often include question sets that target a general area. Common practice in many jurisdictions, however, is leading to the use of very focused specific-issue examinations so that accuracy is at its highest levels. Deceptive exam results should be followed by another examination that is completely specific. This trend toward increasing the use of specific-issue exams is to increase accuracy in postconviction sex offender testing.

Choose Skilled Examiners

Probation and parole supervisors reported that "choosing skilled examiners" was the most important consideration in the successful implementation of the polygraph (English et al., 2000). Examiners must follow established practices to maximize accuracy and reliability. The American Polygraph Association has published standards of practice for examiners conducting post-conviction sex offender examinations, and these standards are intended to limit variation in practice across examiners (Dutton, 2000).

Question construction is a critical component of the polygraph examination. Inconclusive test results are often linked to errors in question construction. Questions must be short and direct, exclude legal terminology, and be easily answered with yes or no. Test questions must focus on behavior, not intent or motivation. Question construction for sex offender testing is a skill that requires specialized training. The American Polygraph Association requires forty hours of sex offender testing training. The Colorado Sex Offender Management Board requires examiners to be supervised when they have conducted fewer than 100 sex offender postconviction examinations.

"I Had to Lie to Pass the Test"

It is very common for offenders to say, "I had to lie to pass the test." Ironically, this usually results in a deceptive test rather than a clean exam, but professionals who are reluctant to accept the use of the polygraph often overlook the details of the examination. Nevertheless, this disclaimer usually occurs when the polygraph information is provided to parents and the therapist, and the offender is ashamed of the disclosed behaviors, fears the consequences, or both. This is clearly an important time for the therapist to intervene in the offender's emotional life. Opportunities are lost when the therapist joins with the offender to question the findings of the polygraph examiner. Indeed, many offenders recant the information, or say the examiner lied or forced them to report untruths. It is essential that polygraph examinations be videotaped from beginning (when the door to the office is closed) to the end (when the offender leaves the office). Therapists should view the videotape with the offender, preferably in group therapy, to discuss the behavior of the offender during the examination. Questions about the examination should be discussed directly with the examiner. Manipulations on the part of the offender decrease considerably after the team coalesces and the offender experiences that life goes on after the disclosure of closely held secrets.

Polygraphy and Psychopathy

Can psychopaths beat the polygraph exam? Surely the best of liars can pass a polygraph examination. Apparently this is not the case. Stern and Krapohl (2004) express the concern raised when known psychopaths are the subjects of polygraph examinations:

> . . . as the habitual liar continues his manipulative behavior, he becomes progressively desensitized to lying. If the liar becomes desensitized, it is argued, he would have a correspondingly diminished autonomic nervous system response when telling a lie and therefore more difficult to detect through use of the polygraph. (p. 205)

However, the psychopath is highly motivated to continue the deceptions and deeply invested in "winning." This population is likely to attempt to control their physical responses during an examination. Examiners will recognize these attempts as countermeasures, a topic about which examiners receive significant training, and the examiner will terminate the exam.

The NRC (2003) reviewed three studies comparing psychopaths to nonpsychopaths. Hammond (1980) used mock crime scenarios with "normal" individuals and examiners who in the final weeks of polygraph training; Raskin and Hare (1978) and Patrick and Iacono (1989) studied prison inmates. All three studies involved specific-incident scenarios involving mock thefts of $10 to $20. Specific-issue polygraph test have the highest accuracy rate. These studies found high rates of accuracy in the crime scenario subjects and no differences between the psychopaths and nonpsychopaths.[37]

In sum, the empirical evidence generally shows no difference in the polygraph response between psychopaths and nonpsychopaths. This may seem counterintuitive as psychopaths are well practiced at lying and living a life of deceit. Indeed, they seem to be immune from anxiety regarding lying. But their level of self-interest, need for control, and determination to "beat" the examiner may be reasons for high accuracy rates for tests involving this group of offenders. Also, like other offenders, psychopaths are concerned that the outcome of the test could result in a loss of privileges, and having a stake in the outcome of the examination is necessary for a physiological response. Even psychopaths cannot control their autonomic nervous systems. Ultimately, however, the reasons psychopaths make good examination subjects remain theoretical, as does much of the reasoning that the polygraph works on the rest of us.

IS THE POLYGRAPH THERAPEUTIC FOR THE THERAPIST?

The use of the polygraph examination can be very disturbing to some therapists. Many therapists feel the polygraph is intrusive and unreliable. However there is a tradition in criminal justice of sampling bodily fluids (urinalysis and DNA testing, for example), and using intense surveillance tools such as GPS tracking. Even in sex offender treatment the use of the plethsymograph might be considered particularly intrusive. Further, it is important to remember that the reliability of the polygraph exam is not in question when the offender self-reports additional or new victims.

Most troubling for some therapists is when a "star client" fails a polygraph examination, and then fails a retest a few weeks later. Sometimes these exams involve disclosures by the offender of high-risk or actual offending behaviors. When the offender fails to disclose new information—and sometimes when he does—the situation can give rise to professionals' concerns that the polygraph is not accurate or the examiner is not competent. Sometimes this leads to significant conflict between the therapist and the supervising officer who will act on the information by increasing surveillance and restricting the offender's lifestyle. If the offender discloses new criminal behavior, the officer may pursue an arrest.

This series of events can be extremely difficult for the therapist and can create considerable tension among the examiner, officer, therapist, and offender. Unfortunately, sometimes therapists are more bonded with the offenders rather than the containment team, especially as they interact with the offender more often than the other professionals. But offenders often groom the therapist as they did their victims, and so using the polygraph and relying on the containment team members can be a "reality check" that can be very helpful to those working with this population. The development of policies, protocols, and agreements regarding the use of the polygraph will be especially helpful at this time.

Polygraph examiners and supervising officers frequently reported to us during dozens of interviews that some therapists were resistant to the examination findings. In these cases, therapists did not return phone calls from the examiner, and when they did speak on the phone, the therapist was incredulous rather than feeling relief at getting to the offender's core secrets. Research at the prison in Colorado is showing that offenders were more likely to fail polygraphs when the therapist was rated as ambivalent about the use of the tool,[38] and when there were no consequences for findings of deception (Heil, Simons, & Ahlmeyer, 2003). Unless a therapist has a goal of *obtaining information so he or she can help the offender and protect the public,* the therapist may be uncomfortable using the polygraph.

In the end, it may be helpful to those who find themselves uncomfortable with the polygraph process to consider that the examination is intended to help prevent the offender from harming again. This is a humane undertaking. Offenders reluctantly report that the use of the polygraph is valuable, even as they dislike taking the exam. Therapists who dislike the use of the polygraph may benefit from visiting the examiner at his office, observing an exam via short-circuit television or videotape, talking with other therapists who use the polygraph, and obtaining training that specifically focuses on how best to use postconviction polygraph results.

A WORD ABOUT LOW-RISK OFFENDERS

It is important to synthesize some of the information presented here in terms of what "low risk" really represents, particularly as officials in some jurisdictions target only the highest-risk offenders for polygraph testing. This practice should be carefully evaluated in light of the reliance on official records to score risk assessment instruments and the research (described earlier) that indicates that few victims report this crime to authorities. Known sex offenders may be particularly dangerous because research suggests that most are convicted eventually of a new sex crime (Prentky et al., 1997).

When resource limitations warrant selection of polygraph subjects, officials may want to identify ten or fifteen low-risk offenders for testing. Taking the information gained from these examinations to policymakers, including legislative budget committees, might result in increased funding for polygraph examinations for all sex offenders in treatment, as it did for Colorado's prison treatment program in the mid-1990s.

SUMMARY

Those who rely on official records and self-report obtained from offenders in the course of treatment are unlikely to have enough information to have a positive impact on the offender and community safety. Accurate risk information remains outside the reach of professionals. Overreliance on treatment and actuarial risk assessment instruments is unlikely to serve the offender or the public. Without the polygraph examination to facilitate the acquisition of individual risk information, offenders are allowed to continue to live secret lives and cannot experience the relief and healing associated with full disclosure.

Footnotes

---

[1] Sixty percent of community-based adult treatment programs and one-third of adolescent treatment programs reported using the postconviction polygraph, according to the 1999–2000 Safer

Society survey of treatment providers; one-third of residential adult programs and between 19 and 30 percent of juvenile treatment programs (male and female programs, respectively) reported using the polygraph in the survey. Results presented here are from a special analysis performed by David Burton.

[2] "Deterrence is distinct from the validity of polygraph testing because the polygraph can be an effective deterrent even if it does not provide valid information about deception" (National Research Council, 2003, p. 54).

[3] The extent to which errors and omissions in criminal history records are random or biased remains an empirical question. Many researchers assume that, in general, the errors are equally distributed across offenders and crime situations. However, the differential treatment of subgroups of the offender population has been well documented in the literature (e.g., issues related to the minority overrepresentation in the juvenile and criminal justice systems). Regarding sex offenders, research has found that young victims who know the offenders are least likely to report the crime (Smith et al., 2000), meaning offenders who target children will be least likely to acquire a criminal record.

[4] For example, this is the sentiment of a long-time probation officer who worked in the Maricopa County Sex Offender Program: "Following the terms and conditions will protect them from going to prison" (English et al., 1996, pp. 6–10).

[5] For example, in one polygraph study of 116 juveniles ages 13–18 with sexual behavior problems, all of whom were either in residential placement or under the supervision of a probation officer (or both), over 40 percent of the youth reported 141 new victims, 8 of whom were siblings who had not reported the assault to anyone despite the fact that the perpetrator had been identified by other victims (English et al., 2002a).

[6] Miner (1997) summarized the methodological problems associated with treatment outcome research. In addition, Barbaree (1997) identified statistical challenges associated with establishing treatment effectiveness.

[7] For example, denial of the offense has been found to lack predictive power in meta-analyses (Hanson & Bussière, 1998; Hanson & Morton-Bourgon, 2004). Lund (2000) questioned the 1998 study findings and reviewed the eight studies in the meta-analysis that included denial as a dependent variable. The subsequent 2004 meta-analysis dropped five of the original eight studies from inclusion in the analysis. Perhaps measurement problems explain why denial has not been found to be associated with recidivism (see Lund, 2000). A study by English, Retzlaff, and Kleinsasser (2002b) found an explicit and reliable measure of denial at the onset of treatment to correlate with treatment/supervision failure. See Schneider and Wright (2004) and Levenson and MacGowan (2004) for recent discussions of this treatment complication.

[8] This study combined probationers and parolees after a comprehensive analysis found no differences between the two groups on several domains including demographics, self-reported paraphilias, and the number and types of self-reported victims. Parolees were significantly more likely to have accrued an arrest for domestic violence and, in general, had a more extensive official record of criminal history.

[9] Because nearly all the offenders in this sample assaulted females, the item on actuarial scales pertaining to male victims is likely measuring gender crossover.

[10] Grove and Meehl (1996) note that despite nearly seven decades of findings about the superiority of actuarial methods over clinical opinions, clinicians remain reluctant to replace their judgment with scientific tools.

[11] The long-term follow-up periods used in Hanson and Harris (2000) and Prentky et al. (1997) contrast with a frequently quoted study recently published by the Bureau of Justice Statistics, the statistical agency of the U.S. Department of Justice. This study by Langan, Schmitt, and Durose (2003) studied 272,111 prisoners released in fifteen states in 1994. Nearly 9,691 (3 percent) of these were male sex offenders (this group represented two-thirds of all the male sex offenders released from state prisons in 1994.) The study found that within the first three years following release from prison in 1994, 5.3 percent were rearrested for a sex crime. Forty-six percent of the rapists were rearrested for a new crime in the three-year follow-up period.

[12] The study used a definition of rape that included attempted or completed forced vaginal, oral

and anal sex, the same definition used by the Federal Bureau of Investigation. These figures are likely underestimates because children and adolescents were excluded from the samples, as were men and women who were homeless, living in institutions, group facilities, or households without telephones.

[13] We recommend caseload sizes of twenty-five and, even in times of shrinking resources, no more than forty. The additional information obtained in the course of treatment combined with the polygraph requires officers to have the time necessary to make important, ongoing risk management decisions about individual cases.

[14] The Oregon Adolescent Sex Offender Treatment Network began testing all juveniles with sexual behavior problems in all counties in 1985.

[15] The Colorado Sex Offender Management Board (SOMB; 2004) has prepared *Standards and Guidelines for the Assessment, Evaluation, Treatment and Behavioral Monitoring* for juvenile, adult and developmentally disabled sex offenders. It has developed criteria for the lifetime supervision of sex offender, as mandated by the 1998 statute that enacted lifetime supervision (probation or parole) for certain sex crimes. The SOMB administrator and staff collaborate with the state's Division of Probation Services and the Department of Corrections to prepare an annual report to the legislature on the status of offenders sentenced under the lifetime statute. These documents reflect the thoughtful dialogue of dozens of professionals in the field of sex offender management and provide an extraordinary resource to sex offender treatment and management professionals in other jurisdictions. These and other relevant materials are available at *http://dcj.state.co.us/odvsm/*.

[16] Many strategies can be added to enhance the value of the containment approach, such as the use of certain mood-stabilizing medications and providing significant support for the nonoffending spouse in incest cases.

[17] Lowden et al.'s (2003) study of the Colorado Department of Corrections' therapeutic community for sex offenders found that for every additional month offenders spent in the therapeutic community, recidivism (rearrest) probabilities decreased by 1 percent.

[18] For an excellent discussion of sex offender group therapy, see Jennings and Sawyer (2003).

[19] Offenders will take as long as therapists allow to successfully complete the sex history polygraph examination (English et al., 2000).

[20] Recidivists committed a new sexual offense while on community supervision; data were collected from interviews and focus groups conducted with more than sixty community supervision officers and file reviews of 208 recidivists and 201 nonrecidivists. Incest offenders (targeting step or biological children) were excluded from the study. Given that a least two-thirds of incest offenders "crossover" and abuse children outside the family (Abel et al., 1988; English et al., 2000; Heil et al., 2003; Heil et al., 2004) the results from Hanson and Harris (2000) are probably generalizable to incest perpetrators.

[21] Deceptive questions require that the entire exam be considered deceptive. This is because not all questions may cause the same level of anxiety or discomfort. The examiner cannot be sure that the questions for which the offender seemed to be forthcoming were not simply perceived by the offender as a lesser threat.

[22] In our field research involving five sites in four states (English et al., 2000), we found that jurisdictions that had a tight containment team—meaning good communication among the examiner, officer and therapist—had few deceptive and inclusive test results. We heard this was the case during interviews, but quantitative analysis of information contained in polygraph examiner reports and probation supervision files confirmed that established teams that met regularly had 80 percent nondeceptive tests. In a site that had recently implemented the polygraph, 30 percent of the tests were nondeceptive.

[23] Mental countermeasures were usually rationalizations ("I did not steal the money, I was told to take it as part of a study") or disassociation (the subject imagined they were elsewhere).

[24] Both inconclusive and deceptive exams should result in a retest, but scheduling an exam may take several weeks, so surveillance should be increased immediately.

[25] Heil, Ahlmeyer, Heil, McCullar, and McKee (2000) found that sex offenders tended to be found non-deceptive as they disclosed more victims over time.

[26] A copy of the Colorado Polygraph Sanctions Grid may be found on pages 138–140 of the Colorado Sex Offender Management Board's (2004) *Standards and Guidelines for the Assessment, Evaluation, Treatment and Monitoring of Adult Sex Offenders*. This document is available from the Colorado Division of Criminal Justice or online at *http://dcj.state.co.us/ odvsom/Sex_Offender/SO_Pdfs/ADULTSDJUNE2004.pdf.*

[27] 465 U.S. 420, 104 S. Ct.1932 (1984).

[28] Westlaw 1270605 (U.S.) (2002).

[29] 580 N.E.2d 693 (Ind. Ct. App. 1992).

[30] Id. at 29.

[31] 05 C.D.O.S. 745 (9th Cir. 2005).

[32] A 1998 telephone survey of more than 600 probation and parole supervisors found that half of the agencies that frequently used the polygraph exam with sex offenders used only the monitoring/maintenance exam (English et al., 2000).

[33] Offenders convicted of Class 2, 3, or 4 felony sex crimes, in a classification scheme that includes Class 1 (most serious) to Class 6 (least serious), are required to receive lifetime sentences, but the offender may receive a probation or prison sentence. See Colo. Rev. Stat. §§ 18.1.3–1001.

[34] The study used a definition of rape that included attempted or completed forced vaginal, oral, and anal sex, the same definition used by the Federal Bureau of Investigation. These figures are likely underestimates because children and adolescents were excluded from the samples, as were men and women who were homeless, living in institutions, group facilities, or households without telephones.

[35] One of the major criticisms of the polygraph is the lack of theoretical basis for instrument. There is nothing to substantiate that lying is, in fact, linked to responses in the autonomic nervous system. Despite this theoretical problem, the Department of Defense Polygraph Institute continues to conduct research that can clarify and improve the practice of polygraph testing.

[36] The base rate will depend on many factors (e.g., whether the exam is focused on the sex history vs. monitoring the last six months in treatment, whether the treatment provider believes the polygraph examination is useful (Heil et al., 2004), and the use of positive and negative sanctions for the polygraph outcomes).

[37] Stern and Krapohl (2004) cite another study by Raskin, Barland, and Podlesny (1977) that tested twenty-four psychopaths and twenty-four nonpsychopaths. The accuracy rate for the psychopaths was 96 percent compared to 79 percent for the nonpsychopathic group. Four examinations were inconclusive.

[38] Ratings of "buy-in" were obtained from polygraph examiners and other therapists.

References

Abel, G. G., Becker, J. V., Cunningham-Rathner, J., Mittelman, M. S., & Rouleau, J.-L. (1988). Multiple paraphilic diagnoses among sex offenders. *Bulletin of the American Academy of Psychiatry and Law, 16,* 153–168.

Abel, G. G., Becker, J. V., Mittelman, M. S., Cunningham-Rathner, J., Rouleau, J.-L., & Murphy, W. D. (1987). Self-reported sex crimes of nonincarcerated paraphiliacs. *Journal of Interpersonal Violence, 2,* 3–25.

Abel, G. G., & Rouleau, J.-L. (1990). The nature and extent of sexual assault. In W. L. Marshall, D. R. Laws, & H. E. Barbaree (Eds.), *Handbook of sexual assault: Issues, theories and treatment of the offender* (pp. 9–22). New York: Plenum Press.

Abrams, S., & Abrams, J. B. (1993). *Polygraph testing of the pedophile.* Portland, OR: Ryan Gwinner Press.

Ahlmeyer, S., Heil, P., & English, K. (1998). *The value of the polygraph: An exploratory study.* Paper presented at the annual conference of the Association of the Treatment of Sexual Abusers, Vancouver, British Columbia.

Ahlmeyer, S., Heil, P., McKee, B., & English, K. (2000). The impact of polygraphy on admissions of victims and offenses in adult sex offenders. *Sexual Abuse: A Journal of Research and Treatment, 12,* 123–138.

Amato-Henderson, S. L. (1996). *Effects of misinformation on the concealed knowledge test* (Report No. DoDPI97-R-0001). Ft. McClellan, AL: Department of Defense Polygraph Institute.

Anglin, M. D., & Hser, Y-I. (1990). Treatment of drug abuse. In M. Tonry & J. Q. Wilson (Eds.), *Drugs and crime* (pp. 393–460). Chicago: University of Chicago Press.

Barbaree. H. E. (1997). Evaluating treatment efficacy with sex offenders: The insensitivity of recidivism studies to treatment effects. *Sexual Abuse: A Journal of Research and Treatment, 9,* 111–128.

Barrett, M., Wilson, R. J., & Long, C. (2003). Measuring motivation to change in sexual offenders from institutional intake to community treatment. *Sexual Abuse: A Journal of Research and Treatment, 15,* 269–283.

Berliner, L. (2002). Commentary. *Sexual Abuse: A Journal of Research and Treatment, 14,* 195–197.

Blumstein, A., Cohen, J., Roth, J. A., & Visher, C. A. (Eds.). (1986). *Criminal careers and "career criminals": Vol. II.* Washington, DC: National Academy Press.

Bureau of Justice Statistics. (1994). *Tracking offenders, 1990.* (NCJ 148200). Washington, DC: U.S. Office of Justice Programs, Department of Justice.

Burton, D. (2004). *1999–2000 National Safer Society Survey: A survey of treatment programs and models serving children with sexual behavioral problems, adolescent sex offenders, and adult sex offenders* [Special analysis on the polygraph, on file with the authors]. Brandon, VT: Safer Society Press.

Catalano, S. M. (2004). *The National Crime Victimization Survey: Criminal Victimization, 2003* (NCJ 205455). Washington, DC: U.S. Department of Justice, Office of Justice Programs, Bureau of Justice Statistics.

Chaiken, J., & Chaiken, M. (1982). *Varieties of criminal behavior.* Santa Monica, CA: Rand Corporation.

Colorado Sex Offender Management Board. (2004). *Standards and guidelines for the assessment, evaluation, treatment and behavioral monitoring of adult sex offenders.* Denver: Colorado Department of Public Safety, Division of Criminal Justice.

Craig, L. A., Browne, K. D., & Stringer, I. (2003). Treatment and sexual recidivism. *Trauma, Violence and Abuse, 4,* 70–89.

Doren, D. M. (2002). *Evaluating sex offenders: A manual for civil commitment and beyond.* Thousand Oaks, CA: Sage.

Dutton D. W. (2000). Introduction to the special issue: Post conviction sex offender testing. *Polygraph, 29,* 1–5.

Elliott, D., Ageton, S., & Huizinga, D. (1980). *The National Youth Survey: 1976 self-reported delinquency estimates.* Boulder, CO: Behavioral Research Institute.

Emerick, R. L., & Dutton, W. A. (1993). The effect of polygraphy on the self-report of adolescent sex offenders: Implications for risk assessment. *Annals of Sex Research, 6*(2), 83–103.

English, K. (1989). *The quality of data obtained from inmate self-reports.* Master's thesis. University of Colorado, Boulder.

English, K. (1998). The containment approach: An aggressive strategy for the community management of adult sex offenders. *Psychology, Public Policy and the Law, 14*(2/1), 218–235.

English, K. (2004). The containment approach to managing sex offenders. *Seton Hall Law Journal, 989,* 1255–1272.

English, K., Jones, L., Pasini-Hill, D., Patrick, D., & Cooley-Towell, S. (2000). *The value of polygraph testing in sex offender management* (Research report submitted to the National Institute of Justice, Grant No. D97LBVX0034). Denver: Colorado Department of Public Safety, Division of Criminal Justice, Office of Research and Statistics.

English, K., Jones, L., & Patrick, D. (2003a). Risk management of adult sex offenders. In B. J. Winick & J. Q. La Fond, (Eds.), *Sexually violent offenders: Law and policy in North America* (pp. 265–280). Hyattsville, MD: American Psychological Association.

English, K., Jones, L., Patrick, D., & Pasini-Hill, D. (2003b). Sex offender containment: Use of the post-conviction polygraph. *Annals of the New York Academy of Sciences, 989,* 411–427.

English, K., Lowden, K., DiTrolio, E., Harrison, L., Hagler L., & Nelson, R. (2002a, February 15). *Analysis of disclosures documented in the polygraph reports of 116 youth with sexual behavior problems.* Study undertaken on behalf of the Colorado Sex Offender Management Board, Denver.

English, K., & Mande, M. (1992). *Measuring crime rates of prisoner* (Report to the National Institute of Justice, Grant No. 87IJJCX0048). Denver: Colorado Department of Public Safety, Division of Criminal Justice, Office of Research and Statistics

English, K., Pullen, S., & Jones, L. (1996). *Managing adult sex offenders: A containment approach.* Lexington, KY: American Probation and Parole Association.

English, K., Retzlaff, P., & Kleinsasser, D. (2002b). The Colorado Sex Offender Risk Scale. *Journal of Child Sexual Abuse, 11,* 77–96

Farrington, D. P. (1979). Environmental stress, delinquent behavior and convictions. In I. G. Sarason & C. D. Pielberger (Eds.), *Stress and anxiety* (Vol. 6, pp. 320–341). Washington, DC: Hemisphere.

Finkelhor, D. (1988). The trauma of child sexual abuse: Two models. In G. Wyatt, & G. Powell (Eds.), *The lasting effects of child sex abuse* (pp. 61–82). Newbury Park, CA: Sage.

Finkelhor, D., Hotaling, G. T., Lewis, I. A., & Smith, C. (1990). Sexual abuse in a national survey of adult men and women: Prevalence, characteristics and risk factors. *Child Abuse and Neglect, 14,* 12–28.

Forensic Research, Inc. (1997). *Polygraph reliability and validity: A review of the research.* Chattanooga, TN: American Polygraph Association National Office.

Gallagher, C. A., Watson, D. B., Hirschfield, P., Coggenshall, M. B., MacKenzie, D. L. (1999). A quantitative review of the effects of sex offender treatment on sexual reoffending. *Corrections Management Quarterly, 3,* 19–29.

Gaschler, W. J., McGettigan, J. P., Menges, P. M., & Waller, J. F. (2001). Review of polygraph screening assessment method. *Polygraph, 30,* 254–259.

Gold, M. (1970). *Delinquent behavior in an American city.* Belmont, CA: Brooks/Cole.

Goodwin, J. M. (1988). Obstacles to policymaking about incest: Some cautionary folktales. In G. E. Wyatt & G. J. Powell (Eds.), *Lasting effects of child sexual abuse* (pp. 21–39). Newbury Park, CA: Sage.

Gottfredson, D. M., & Tonry, M. (1987). *Prediction and classification: Criminal justice decision making. Vol. 9: Crime and justice: A review of research.* Chicago: University of Chicago Press.

Greenwood, P. W., Chaiken, J. M., Petersilia, J. R., & Peterson, M. A. (1978). T*he RAND Habitual Offender Project: Summary of research findings to date* (P-5957). Santa Monica, CA: Rand Corporation.

Groth, A. N. (1979). *Men who rape: The psychology of the offender.* New York: Plenum Press.

Grove, W. M., & Meehl, P. E. (1996). Comparative efficiency of informal (subjective, impressionistic) and formal (mechanical, algorithmic) prediction procedures: The clinical-statistical controversy, *Psychology, Public Policy and the Law, 293,* 296–299.

Hall, G. C. N. (1995). Sexual offender recidivism revisited: A meta-analysis of recent treatment studies. *Journal of Consulting and Clinical Psychology, 63,* 802–809.

Hammond, D. L. (1980). The responding of normals, alcoholics, and psychopaths in a laboratory lie detection experiment. *Dissertation Abstracts International* (UMI No. AAD8–28678).

Hansen, R. F., Resnick, H. S., Saunders, B. E., Kilpatrick, D. G., & Best, C. (1999). Factors related to the reporting of childhood rape. *Child Abuse and Neglect, 23,* 559–569.

Hanson, R. K. (1997a). How to know what works with sex offenders. *Sexual Abuse: A Journal of Research and Treatment, 9,* 129–143.

Hanson, R. K. (1997b). *The development of a brief actuarial risk scale for sexual offense recidivism* [Online]. Ottawa, Ontario: Department of the Solicitor General of Canada. Available: *www.psepc-sppcc.gc.ca/publications/corrections/199704_e.pdf.*

Hanson, R. K. (1998). What do we know about sex offender risk assessment? *Psychology, Public Policy and Law, 4*(1/2), 50–72.

Hanson, R. K., & Bussière, M. T. (1998). Predicting relapse: A meta-analysis of sexual offender recidivism studies. *Journal of Consulting and Clinical Psychology, 66*(2), 348–362.

Hanson, R. K, Gordon, A., Harris, A. J., Marques, J. K., Murphy, W., Quinsey, V. L., et al. (2002). First report of the collaborative outcome data project on the effectiveness of psychological treatment for sex offenders. *Sexual Abuse: Journal of Research and Treatment, 14*(2), 169–194.

Hanson, R. K., & Harris, A. J. R. (2000). Where should we intervene: Dynamic predictors of sexual assault recidivism. *Criminal Justice and Behavior, 27*(1), 6–35.

Hanson, R. K., Morton, K. E., Harris, A. J. R. (2003). Sexual offender recidivism risk: What we know and what we need to know. *Annals of the New York Academy of Sciences, 989*, 154–166.

Hanson, R. K., & Morton-Bourgon, K. (2004). *Predictors of sexual recidivism: An updated meta-analysis.* Ottawa, Ontario, Canada: Public Works and Government Services. Available: *www.psepc.gc.ca/publications/corrections/pdf/200402_E.pdf.*

Hanson, R. K., & Thornton, D. (2000). Improving risk assessments for sex offenders: A comparison of three actuarial scales. *Law and Human Behavior, 24*, 119–136.

Harris, G. T., Rice, M. E., & Quinsey, V. L. (1993). Violent recidivism of mentally disordered offenders: The development of a statistical prediction instrument. *Criminal Justice and Behavior, 20*, 315–395.

Harris, G. T., Rice, M. E., & Quinsey, V. L. (1998). Appraisal and risk management of risk in sexual aggressors: Implications for criminal justice policy. *Psychology, Public Policy and the Law, 14*(2/1), 73–115.

Harrison, J. S., & Kirkpatrick, B. (2000). Polygraph testing and behavioral change with sex offenders in an outpatient setting: An exploratory study. *Polygraph, 29*, 6–19.

Heil, P., Ahlmeyer, S., McCullar, B., & McKee, B. (2000). Integration of polygraph testing with sexual offenders in the Colorado Department of Corrections. *Polygraph: Special Edition, Post-Conviction Sex Offender Testing, 29*(1), 26–35.

Heil, P., Simons, D., & Ahlmeyer, S. (2003). Cross-over sexual offense. *Sexual Abuse: A Journal of Research and Treatment, 15*(4), 221–236.

Heil, P., Simons, D., & English, K. (2004, October 22). *Cross-over sexual offenses disclosed by offenders found non-deceptive on the post-conviction polygraph examination.* Paper presented at the annual conference of the Association for the Treatment of Sexual Abusers, Albuquerque, NM.

Herman, J. L. (1992). *Trauma and recovery.* New York: Basic Books.

Hindelang, M. J. (1974). The Uniform Crime Reports revisited. *Journal of Criminal Justice, 1*(1), 1–18.

Hindelang, M. J., Hirschi, T., & Weis, J. (1981). *Measuring delinquency.* Newbury Park, CA: Sage.

Honts, C. R., Amato, S. L., & Gordon, G. K. (2001). Effects of spontaneous countermeasures used against the comparison question test, *Polygraph, 30*, 1–9.

Honts, C. R., Hodes, R. L., & Raskin, D. C. (1985). Effects of physical countermeasures on the physiological detection of deception. *Journal of Applied Psychology, 70*, 177–187.

Honts, C. R., Raskin, D. C., & Kircher, J. C. (1994). Mental and physical countermeasures and their electromyographic detection during polygraph tests for deception. *Journal of Psychophysiology, 1*, 241–247.

Honts, C. R., Raskin, D. C., Kircher, J. C., & Hodes, R. L. (1988). Effects of spontaneous countermeasures on the physiological detection of deception. *Journal of Police Science and Administration, 16*, 91–94.

Horney, J., & Marshall, I. H. (1991). Measuring lambda through self-reports. *Criminology, 29*, 471–496.

Janus, E. S. (2004). Closing Pandora's box: Sexual predators and the politics of sexual violence. *Seton Hall Law Review, 34*(4), 1233–1253.

Janus, E. S., & Prentky, R. A. (2003). Forensic use of actuarial risk assessment with sex offenders: Accuracy, admissibility and accountability. *American Criminal Law Review, 40*(4), 1443–1499.

Jennings, J. L., & Sawyer, S. (2003). Principles and techniques for maximizing the effectiveness of group therapy with sex offenders. *Sexual Abuse: A Journal of Research and Treatment, 15*, 251–268.

Kilpatrick, D. G., Edmunds, C. N., & Seymour, A. K. (1992). *Rape in America: A report to the nation.* Charleston: National Victim Center and the University of South Carolina Medical Center.

Kindermann, C., Lynch, J., & Cantor, P. (1997). *National Crime Victimization Survey: Effects of the Redesign on Victimization Estimates* (NCJ-164381). Washington, DC: U.S. Department of Justice, Office of Justice Programs, Bureau of Justice Statistics.

Kitsuse, J. I., & Cicourel, A. V. (1963). A note on the uses of official statistics. *Social Problems, 2*(2), 131–139.

Knapp, M. (1996). Treatment of sex offenders. In K. English, S. Pullen, & L. Jones (Eds.), *Managing adult sex offenders: A containment approach* (pp. 13-1–13-15). Lexington, KY: American Probation and Parole Association.

Krapohl, D. J., & Stern, B. A. (2003). Principles of multiple-issue polygraph screening: A model for applicant, post-conviction offender, and counterintelligence testing. *Polygraph, 30,* 201–210.

La Fond, J. Q. (2003). The costs of enacting a sexual predator law and recommendations for keeping them from skyrocketing. In B. J. Winick & J. Q. La Fond (Eds.), *Protecting society from sexually dangerous offenders: Law, justice and therapy* (pp. 283–300). Washington, DC: American Psychological Association.

Lamb, S., & Edgar-Smith, S. (1994). Aspects of disclosure: Mediators of outcome in childhood sexual abuse. *Journal of Interpersonal Violence, 9*, 307–326.

Langan, P. A., Schmitt, E. L., & Durose, M. R. (2003, November). *Recidivism of sex offenders released from prison in 1994* (NCJ 198281). Washington, DC: U.S. Department of Justice, Office of Justice Programs, Bureau of Justice Statistics,

Levenson, J. S., & Macgowan, M. J. (2004). Engagement, denial, and treatment progress among sex offenders in group therapy. *Sexual Abuse: A Journal of Research and Treatment, 16*, 49–63.

Lowden, K., Hetz, N., Patrick, D., Pasini-Hill, D., Harrison, L., & English, K. (2003). *Evaluation of Colorado's prison therapeutic community for sex offenders: A report of findings.* Denver: Colorado Department of Public Safety, Division of Criminal Justice, Office of Research and Statistics.

Lund, C. A. (2000). Predictors of sexual recidivism: Did meta-analysis clarify the role and relevance of denial? *Sexual Abuse: A Journal of Research and Treatment, 12*, 275–288.

Maltz, M. D. (1977). Crime statistics in a historical perspective. *Crime and Delinquency, 23*, 32–40.

Maltz, M. D. (1999). *Bridging gaps in police crime data* (NCJ-176365). Washington, DC: Bureau of Justice Statistics, Office of Justice Programs, U.S. Department of Justice.

Mande, M., & English, K. (1988). *Crime rates of Colorado prisoners* (Report to the National Institue of Justice, Grant No. 84IJCX0034). Denver: Colorado Department of Public Safety, Division of Criminal Justice, Office of Research and Statistics.

Marshall, W. L., Thornton, D., Marshall, L. E., Fernandez, Y., & Mann, R. (2001). Treatment of sexual offenders who are in categorical denial: A pilot project. *Journal of Research and Treatment, 13*(3), 205–215.

Miner, M. H. (1997). How can we conduct treatment outcome research? *Sexual Abuse: A Journal of Research and Treatment, 9*(2), 95–110.

Moore, M. H. (1986). Purblind justice: Normative issues in the use of prediction in the criminal justice system. In A. Blumstein, J. Cohen, J. A. Roth, & C. A. Visher (Eds.), *Criminal careers and "career criminals"* (Vol. 2, pp. 314–355). Washington, DC: National Academies Press.

National Research Council. (2003). *The polygraph and lie detection. Committee to review the scientific evidence on the polygraph.* Washington, DC: Division of Behavioral and Social Sciences and Education, National Academy of Sciences Press.

O'Connell, M. A. (1998). Using polygraph testing to assess deviant sexual history of sex offenders (UMI 48106). *Dissertation Abstracts International, 49.*

Patrick, C. J., & Iacono, W.G. (1989). Psychopathy, threat and polygraph test accuracy. *Journal of Applied Psychology, 74*, 347–355.

Petersilia, J. R. (1977). *The validity of criminality data derived from personal interviews.* Santa Monica, CA: Rand Corporation.

Petersilia, J., Greenwood, P., & Lavin, M. (1977). *Criminal careers of habitual felons.* Santa Monica, CA: Rand Corporation.

Peterson, M. A. (1978). *The Rand Habitual Offender Project: Summary of research findings to date* (P-5957). Santa Monica, CA: Rand Corporation.

Peterson, M. A., & Braiker, H. B. (1980). *Doing crime: A survey of California prison inmates.* Santa Monica, CA: Rand Corporation.

Prentky, R. A. (2003). A 15-year retrospective on sexual coercion: Advancements and projections. *Annals of the New York Academy of Sciences, 989*, 13–31.

Prentky, R. A., Lee, A. F. S., Knight, R. A., & Cerce, D. (1997). Recidivism rates among child molesters and rapists: A methodological anlaysis. *Law and Human Behavior, 21*, 635–659.

Quinsey, V. L., Harris, G. T., Rice, M. E., & Cormier, C. A. (1998). *Violent offenders: Appraising and managing risk.* Washington, DC: American Psychological Association.

Quinsey, V. L., Khanna, A., & Malcolm, B. (1998). A retrospective evaluation of the Regional Treatment Centre Sex Offender Programme. *Journal of Interpersonal Violence, 13*, 21–644.

Raskin, D. C., Barland, G. H., & Podlesny, I. A. (1977). Validity and reliability of detection of deception. *Polygraph, 6*, 1–39.

Raskin, D. C., & Hare, R. D. (1978). Psychopathy and detection of deception in a prison population. *Psychophysiology, 15*, 126–135.

Rice, M. E., & Harris, G. T. (1997). Cross-validation and extension of violence risk appraisal guide for child molesters and rapists. *Law and Human Behavior, 21*, 231–241.

Rice, M. E., & Harris, G. T. (2003a). The size and sign of treatment effects in sex offender therapy. *Annals of the New York Academy of Sciences, 989,* 428–440.

Rice, M. E., & Harris, G. T. (2003b). What we know and don't know about treating adult sex offenders. In B. J. Winick & J. Q. La Fond (Eds.), *Protecting society from sexually dangerous offenders: Law, justice and therapy* (pp. 101–118). Washington, DC: American Psychological Association.

Roesler, T. A., & Wind, W. T. (1994). Telling the secret: Adult women describe their disclosure of incest. *Journal of Interpersonal Violence, 9*, 307–326.

Russell, D. E. H. (1986). *The secret trauma: Incest in the lives of girls and women.* New York: Basic Books.

Schneider, S. L., & Wright, R. C. (2004) Understanding denial in sexual offenders: A review of cognitive and motivational processes to avoid responsibility. *Trauma, Violence and Abuse, 5*, 3–20.

Sellin, T., & Wolfgang, M. (1964). *The measurement of delinquency.* New York: Wiley.

Serin, R. C., & Mailloux, D. L. (2003). Assessment of sex offenders: Lessons learned from the assessment of non-sex offenders. *Annals of the New York Academy of Sciences, 989*, 185–197.

Smith, D. W., Letourneau, E. J., Saunders, B. E., Kilpatrick, D. G., Resnick, H. S., & Best, C. (2000). Delay in disclosure of childhood rape: Results from a national survey. *Child Abuse and Neglect, 24*, 273–287.

Snyder, H. (2000). *Sexual assault of young children as reported to law enforcement: Victim, incident, and offender characteristics.* Washington, DC: U.S. Department of Justice, Bureau of Justice Statistics.

Stern, B. A., & Krapohl, D. J. (2004). The efficacy of detecting deception in psychopaths using a polygraph. *Polygraph, 33*, 201–213.

Tjaden, P., & Thoennes, N. (2000a, July). *Extent, nature and consequences of intimate partner violence* (NCJ Publication No. 181867). Washington, DC: U.S. Department of Justice, Office of Justice Programs.

Tjaden, P., & Thoennes, N. (2000b, November). *Full report of the prevalence, incidence, and consequences of violence against women: Findings from the National Violence Against Women Survey* (NCJ Publication No. 183781). Washington, DC: U.S. Department of Justice, Office of Justice Programs.

Weis, J. G. (1986). Issues in the measurement of criminal careers. In A. Blumstein, J. Cohen, J. A. Roth, & C. A. Visher (Eds,), *Criminal careers and "career criminals"* (Vol. 2, pp. 1–51). Washington, DC: National Academies Press.

Winick, B. J., & La Fond, J. Q. (Eds.). (2003). *Protecting society from sexually dangerous offenders: Law, justice and therapy.* Washington, DC: American Psychological Association.

Chapter 10

The Use of Ethics and Drama-Based Techniques to Modify Security Staff's Beliefs About Working With Sex Offenders

by John Bergman, M.A., R.D.T., M.T.

INTRODUCTION

Correctional officers are gradually being acknowledged as a critical part of the work force that supports rehabilitative offender change in correctional systems. It is believed that successful motivation and maintenance of offender change can be accomplished by correctional officers. "Because correctional officers play such a crucial part in carrying out correctional objectives, an expansion of the correctional officers' role to include elements of treatment and rehabilitation has been suggested. Currently, in many correctional jurisdictions around the world, in addition to the custodial functions, correctional officers have also a human service role" (Tellier & Serrin, 2001, p. 6).

The same is believed to be true about the line staff, who are responsible for maintaining the secure environment in the treatment programs for the civilly committed sexual offenders. These staff members are often recruited from a pool of individuals who have previously worked as correctional officers in jails or prisons; however, in the civil commitment programs their job descriptions are more likely to recognize their therapeutic influence on the residents. This influence is reflected even in the job titles, with classifications such as "security counselor" and "residential rehabilitation counselor." Most residential treatment programs recognize that the security/residential line staff are necessary to reinforce and bolster successful treatment (Poole & Regoli, 1980; Paboojian & Teske, 1997). After all, these staff members are the dominant force in terms of numbers in any institution, and they have the largest percentage of interactions with the offenders (Jurik & Musheno, 1986); therefore, their influence on the therapeutic environment is quite powerful.

Practically we have seen this borne out in Corrections Victoria (Victoria State, Australia) where officers are gradually adopting and adapting to change strategies that practice rehabilitation and forming rehabilitative offender relationships as part of the daily fabric of corrections. But these changes to Corrections Victoria's correctional officers and community officers have not come easily. It is well known that many of the issues and actions in contemporary corrections theory and policy create intense resistance in some officers. It is such resistance that any trainer of correctional officers, or any would-be change agents in any correctional system, must learn how to address.

The central question considered here is whether or not security staff can be trained to become a vital part of therapeutic change initiatives with offenders who have been found guilty of sexual offenses. Or, if we reframe this question just a little, the issue becomes whether some of the institutional-based behaviors and attitudinal pressures typically expressed by security staff about rehabilitation are simply too great to overcome when they are also dealing with the institutional and sociocultural perceived "otherness" of sexual offenders. And, for the trainer, the issue is what training strategies could possibly help to facilitate the attitudinal change of line staff and encourage them to take on assisting and supporting sexual offender rehabilitation?

THE PROBLEM

In some of the studies of prison officers' attitudes regarding sexual offenders it is clear that there is some strong officer support for negative attitudes and beliefs toward men who sexually abuse. For example, in a voluntary study of male and female officers, it was found that many officers saw sex offenders as significantly more dangerous, harmful, violent, tense, unpredictable, unchangeable, aggressive, weak, irrational, and afraid than non-sex offenders (Correctional Service of Canada, n.d.). This Canadian study indicated that there was a potent degree of dislike and much negative emotion concerning these types of offenders. And, the intensity of the officers' negative emotional responses was even greater for sexual offenders who had offended against children. (This type of analysis accurately reflects Stonewall Arts Project Inc.'s twenty-five years of experiences and interactions working in prisons and criminal justice facilities with correctional staff.) Yet another Canadian study (Weekes, Pelletier, & Beaudette, 1995) supported the notion that officers have rejecting attitudes to sex offenders. In that study it was found that just over half the officers thought that general offenders could be rehabilitated, but only one in five officers thought that sex offenders could be similarly changed. Again, this correlates to Stonewall Art's practical experience with officers who expressed over the years quite emphatically held beliefs that sexual offenders cannot change. We have, at times, actually heard officers call these men "monsters" during our training seminars.

Indeed, Crawley (2004) notes that sex offenders create in officers a wide number of highly charged emotional responses. Crawley (2004) provides an example in her discussion of the performative elements of the officer's role in the U.K. correctional system. The Home Office employs correctional officers to deliver parts of the national prison sex offender program. These officers are also referred to as tutors. Some officers debrief after the sessions with the offenders, and Crawley surmises in her perceptions of the staff that officers who do this work "may experience feelings that threaten their own sense of self, namely that they have been 'contaminated' by their contact with sex offenders." In other words, "that they have caught perversive thoughts from those they are trying to treat" (p. 421). Crawley also hints that these officers engage in public expressions of disgust toward the offenders in order to show that they also still hold "normal" or general officer derived attitudes: "See, I find sex offenders disgusting, just like you" (Crawley, 2004, p. 421). The officer who wants to work in a nonadversarial relationship with the sex offender must navigate a complex path through beliefs about role, performative peer role presentations, and the anxiety generated by his perception of an implied psychological threat from these offenders.

Beliefs About Role

The "new" style correctional officer is under very "new" pressures. Despite the training of such organizations as the American Correctional Association and the overt use of the word "professionalism" in corrections' circles, few training seminars can impart the natural or even learned skills of emotionally coping with people's perceived "otherness." In new prisons, the past tactic of authoritarian control alone is understood to be ineffective in producing offender change. Criminal sanctions and "scared straight" processes are just not effective in reducing recidivism (McGuire, 2002).

Prison officers who experience stress are much less likely to support rehabilitation and are instead much more likely to support punitive notions of prison (Larivière & Robinson, 1996; Robinson, Porporino, & Simourd, 1993; Tellier & Robinson, 1995). Prison officers and supervisors, even head office staff, may therefore not have the experience nor the backing to put in place new initiatives. Where there is resistance, active resentment, even sabotage from officers and the system, new initiatives will founder.

Yet the "new" officers must still carry out their role tasks. They must carry out the new or old agreed role of the officer, including the daily work of musters, conflict resolution, and the endless watching to ensure that they, their peers, and the offenders in the facility are safe. And, the new concepts of the correctional officer's role comes with the the theoretical expectation is that he or she must also try to be a motivator and an on-the-spot counselor (Birgden, 2004).

For the "new" prison officers to be effective in new ways of working it is our experience that they may first have to understand, accept, or change their own attitudes to prisoners, incarceration, punishment, and the nature of social responsibility versus the individual's accountability (Bergman, 2000). Some studies show that officers who believe that the offenders are not punished enough, or who believe that offenders can never change, are often more likely to resist working with therapeutic or rehabilitative processes, even when they have been directed to do so.

Peer Influence

The problem for the contemporary officer may be further exacerbated in that the officers' mandate, objectives, and demands keep changing, yet the realities of incarceration and the cross-pressures of being both the guardian and the guard can easily complicate the new roles.

Prison is a closed box in which officers and offenders interact intensively, even intimately, every minute of every hour. Only a limited number of those interactions are truly governed by any concrete rules. The prison officer makes decisions from moment to moment based in part on his or her own automatic sense of what is right. Each one of these decisions can be further influenced by a wide variety of pressures and peer pressures. Commonly, these pressures include the degree of stress the officer is experiencing either in the institution, at home, or in relationships with others. In addition, the officer is influenced by the potency of any of the peer groups in the facility and the degree of dangerousness in the institution. The officers' actions are influenced, therefore, by a complex personal and institutional script. This script is hardened through practice and acquired skill over time. Studies show that officers begin to establish role scripts as early as one year into the job. In reality, though, a correctional officer's life in a prison is both arbitrary and fixed. That is, the role of the officer is strictly defined, yet more arbitrarily performed and far more complex, than is conceived in most pencil-and-paper lecture/trainings

The pressure for or against new strategies of offender/officer relationships can be very intense. Officer peer groups, for example, can use a range of strategies to induce officers to make decisions on a unit in particular ways that include highly coercive techniques such as shaming and exclusion, bullying, and sabotage. This peer influence can often target officer involvement in rehabilitation efforts. In the 1980s, Stonewall Arts Project was co-involved in setting up a violence unit in a New England prison. The unit and its treatment modalities were to be organized and administered by the prison officers. It was not until the unit had been running for some time that a few officers told us of the intense harassment they had received from other officers. It is now widely accepted that effective changes in officer roles should and must target not just a few staff but all staff, throughout an entire system (Gendreau, Goggins, & Smith, 1999).

But this problem is not merely an issue of officer resistance. The same coercive pressures are often exerted by supervisors, who, in their failure to take responsible action, send covert or overt lack-of-support signal messages that negate rehabilitative or motivational relationships with offenders (Bergman, 2000). In Stonewall Arts Project's "Setting the Scene" systemwide information and change program with Corrections Victoria, resistance (when it was expressed) was just as likely to come from supervisory staff as it was from line officers or community corrections staff.

From the "old practice" prison officers' perspectives, rehabilitation is simply poor prison praxis. In many systems in which we have worked, including the Romanian prison system, the concept of rehabilitation is still considered foreign, risible, and a mark that signifies dangerousness. And, if practiced by officers, it signifies their dangerousness to the group as well as to the institution. Paradoxically, officers who are trained and adept in "new" techniques seem more comfortable with offenders.The officers who we have partly trained in "new" techniques to run a therapeutic community called Descatusarea in Rahova, Romania, are often poached by other parts of the prison because of their comfortable interaction and skilled rapport with dangerous offenders of all types. Aggressive, intolerant officers appear to create more rather than less trouble in prisons.

It is often difficult to convince officers of the effectiveness of rehabilitative practices. Contrary to the Canadian officers' expectations, some recidivism studies in the field of sexual offending suggest that sex offender treatment is effective (Hanson et al., 2002; Nagayama-Hall, 1995). In these studies there is a strong suggestion that the treatment and the ecological management of offenders (both in the facility and in the community) can really work. Yet, the antipathy to sexual offenders has often blurred the possible effectiveness of the treatment.

Expression of Negative Emotions

We have, as part of our trainings, always included some of the latest, favorable statistical evidence, often to the sheer disbelief of the officers. Sexual offenders can cause very strong, even contradictory emotions in therapists and treatment providers. Adequate supervision for treatment providers invariably includes attention to issues of vicarious traumatization. Prison officers are equally prey to these enormous emotional forces and, in our trainings in Australia over the last six years, we have privately discussed these issues with officers involved in working closely with sexual offenders. It seems clear that some officers appear to have to work hard to control the intense emotions generated by working with people who have violated precious norms and beliefs This self-control can create what clearly appears to be an intensely suppressed affect. It can look to the untrained eye like barely suppressed disgust, or sarcasm, or disaffection. This constricted affective expression, is well known to any trainers in corrections. It can range in a training session from constant needling to passive-aggressive displays of indifference to open expressions of disinterest and anger. In training seminars about treatment, disgusted officers are well known for doing such things as wearing dark glasses, sitting with their arms folded throughout a day, refusing to answer, and even reading the day's newspaper in front of the trainers. Such rage can obviously intensely reduce common empathy for any types of offenders.

In addition, the very norms and beliefs of institutional staff can contribute to countertherapeutic acts. These norms are hard to challenge but are part and parcel of the fabric of prison officer life. Crawley notes, in her ethnographic study of selected U.K. prison officers, that the officers discussed six prison norms that we also have found common to officers in other prison systems especially Australia, the United States, and to some degree Romania. These norms include the following:

- Total public support for fellow officers, no matter what they may have seen another officer do or say.

- Not engaging in any criticism of a fellow officer no matter how much in the wrong the officer might be.

- Not showing any positive regard for an offender, especially in front of other staff. This applies especially to women officers.

Though these are not hard and fast rules, they are rules that are an underlying fact of most penitentiary life. They are a challenge, in themselves, to transparency, democracy, and good use of criticism for gradual behavior change, and they also mimic the secrecy that is so endemic in antisocial offenders' lives. For the sexual offender, secrecy is at the heart of remaining safe, maintaining dangerous feelings, and trying to forget the dangerous past.

When these "rules" become norms and beliefs, then officers who find it hard to accept the juxtaposition of rule versus personal belief may resolve the tension by engaging in a degree of affective as well as cognitive, self-control. The strong prohibition of "informing" supervisors of possible behavioral irregularities by other officers means that to survive it is necessary to maintain a detached and even tightly structured set of attitudes and feelings in order to maintain a sense of integrity. Some prison officers, therefore, present images that give the impression that they are tough; judgmental toward weakness, including that of officers; conservative about any change; and dismissive of feminized emotions such as despair, shared insight, or feelings of insecurity.

Anxiety of Implied Threat

Yet in many of our discussions with Australian prison officer staff, there were quiet but intense allusions to the emotional pain of being bullied and controlled by other staff, including supervisors, of being threatened physically by staff, and of course the unspoken stress of being threatened by the few unpredictable but dangerous offenders.

The Role of Change

There were also shared moments of generous discussion of the hard lives of some of the offenders, and of the need for offenders to be motivated to change. We have not been able to find any studies of traumatization in officers due to changes in an entire prison system. We hypothesize that institutional change that is global in a system may be traumatic for sensitive officers in that change represents a huge danger. For those officers who have already experienced traumatic reactions to previous dangerous situations, resistance to change will be automatic, indicative of the hyperalert traumatized brain. For officers who are true to the prison officer norms, change, especially institutional change, is a threat not just to the code of understanding the job, other officers, and issues such as courage and faithfulness to other officers but to a very core fabric of living that may even include family relationships and relationships with other officers' families.

Because of the intensity of many of these shared private discussions, as trainers, we maintain the fiction during our work that these are merely training discussions and that these affectively dense experiences are not part of the correctional experience. "Prison officers are acutely aware that they must play parts and stage manage their actions if they are to control the impressions they convey to prisoners and, just as importantly to fellow staff" (Crawley, 2004, p. 414).

At times, it seems as if officers must appear to be equally unmoved by an offender suicide as by a supervisor's institutional cruelty. Interestingly the "literature" on officer attitudes toward offenders is quite contradictory. Although many officers during our international trainings have spoken of how hard it is to do new correctional programming when the "old guard" of officers is so powerful and repressive, there is contradictory evidence that older officers are more open to rehabilitation programs (Farkas, 1999; Larivière & Robinson, 1996) and more comfortable with offenders (Larivière & Robinson, 1996).

CASE STUDY: ATTITUDINAL CHANGE TRAINING FOR A LARGE CORRECTIONAL STAFF

The Company

Stonewall Arts Project Inc. is a twenty-four-year-old drama-based change organization that has worked in international corrections in countries as diverse as Romania, Bulgaria, Brazil, the United States, and Australia. The company has worked to create and perform interactive educational productions on violence, family relationships, and survival in the free world. Further, the company has worked intensively with violent offenders and sexual offenders using dramatherapy, experiential therapy, and intensive cognitive-behavioral treatment. In the last ten years, this company has taught and trained a number of correctional officers and police to work in more "therapeutic" modes with their wards.

Stonewall Arts Project has been involved extensively in preparing officers to take on more intensive therapeutic roles in both adolescent and adult corrections. Thus, in 2000, the Stonewall Arts Project worked with youth workers in Melbourne to prepare them to run a therapeutic community for violent adolescents. During this time the company also worked with the Romanian prison system to train officers and psychologists together to create an extensive therapeutic community of incarcerated violent offenders (Bergman, 2002). In 2004, Stonewall Arts Project also worked with Australian prison officers to prepare them for working with adult sex offenders in a therapeutic community environment and social workers and psychologists in the Bulgarian prison system.

Officers and psychologists from many of these training sessions are still involved in delivering basic treatment strategies such as cognitive skills, anger management, and antisocial self-change programs. In a surprisingly similar way, most of the leaders in these programs eventually had to confront many of the same issues: officer resistance to working with offenders whose crimes seemed heinous; the impact of significant negative officer and administrator peer groups; anxiety in taking on helper roles rather than the more traditional authority role; covert sabotage from a variety of staff and bureaucratic functions, some of them bordering on violence.

The Techniques

Many of the strategies which we believe are effective for system change are also strategies that we have used to train officers to work more effectively with sexual offenders. Here we examine, in some detail, a change process that Stonewall Arts

Project accomplished over an eighteen-month period with Corrections Victoria, to see how the basic strategies were implemented in a more global way.

During 2002–2004, I was the director of Stonewall Arts Project Inc./Geese Company, which worked with close to 1,000 prison officers and community corrections officers in a training called "Setting the Scene" (originally called "Ethics In Action"). Each of the many three-day trainings for Corrections Victoria, Melbourne was intended to prepare officers, supervisors, central office staff, and the whole gamut of community corrections to change their beliefs about offenders and to work in an increasingly supportive and ethical way in order to motivate offenders to consider challenging their lifestyles. This objective was one of many that added up to a new focus on using the system's resources in a novel way to reduce the risk levels of its medium- and high-risk offenders using "world's best practices." The underlying notion was to encourage all staff to become enthusiastic supporters of system change and of the potential for their personal efforts to lead toward motivating prisoners and intervening in their lives no matter how heinous their crime.

The training was delivered to officers and administrators, psychologists, social workers, and correctional industry representatives throughout the system, as well as community corrections staff at all levels. Staff members were often chosen based on availability, but the primary emphasis was to get the training and its messages to as many people as possible in the system. It made no difference whether the staff were working in the gatehouse, in the dorm, in offender units, or on the graveyard shift. Staff participants included union men and women, staff who had literally arrived in corrections only three days before the training seminar, and staff who had already announced their retirement.

Staff ranged in age from heir late teens to their early 60s, and therefore they had a variety of experiences. Some of the staff were from private prisons, some were from the state prisons, and some had worked in private enterprise before entering the prison system. In some cases staff had had extensive experience with very difficult clients and in some cases they had been in support roles in finance or planning and had very limited offender contact.

Although this change had been in the offing for some time, and the system certainly seemed to be ready for such a change, the breadth of the proposed change according to the program architect was very great.

> The mission for Corrections Victoria is to *deliver a safe and secure corrections system in which we actively engage offenders and the community to promote positive behaviour change. . . .* The aim is to commence a service system approach to reducing re-offending. . . . In October 2001 the Expenditure Review Committee (ERC) provided substantial state government funding for the Corrections Long Term Management's Strategy . . . including the delivery of a framework to reduce re-offending. (Birgden & McLachlan, 2002, p. 20)

The Victorian system was, unlike our experiences in other international prison systems, ready for change. Though we certainly faced many classic negative stances, they were not the overwhelming majority. We had had an earlier experience with the Victorian Sex Offender Program in co-training correctional officers at Ararat prison in support of the therapeutic community for sex offenders. The officers' participation and running of the community was of the highest quality. But this was a small facility and a very small percentage of officers.

Corrections Victoria had clearly thought through the theoretical support for using Stonewall Arts Project to do the cultural change part of the work of system change. It was understood by the department's theoreticians that for rehabilitation programs to be effective there had to first be a clear and responsive mechanism to deal with issues of resistance throughout the department. Drama-based techniques are strongly indicated for external responsivity strategies including being participatory, interactive and engaging.

There is very little research on how to effect change that is enduring, though Gendreau et al. (1999) have researched and defined four necessary foci for any programmatic and systemic change that critically include a successful change agent and an experienced use of adequate responsivity factors. As Birgden and McLachlan (2002) note, the change agent needs to have real support all the way up the line, be believable as a professional in the field, understand how the system and its staff interact and relate, demonstrate that he or she has comparable value stances with the system, and be able to use a flexible set of training tools, including responsivity-based tools such as drawing, role play, and simulations, as well as to motivate, persuade, listen intensively, model, and reinforce. The staff members were trained in blocks of twenty, mostly offsite, for a period of three days. Those who missed any part of the training made up the time on other days.

The Curriculum

Though our approach to officer change is by no means exclusive, we used a general set of strategies that included, in the early stages of the training, how to change or affect your ethical environment, with a special emphasis on focusing on right/good decision making. This process included simulated ethical dilemmas (a basic set of five principles for solving ethical dilemmas) and then the "meat of the day," dealing with ethical dilemmas on the job but using the ethical principles to solve the problems rather than the cultural- or institution-based solutions. On the first day, we used a combination of group simulations, role plays, group discussions, goal-based forum strategies, and basic flipchart and felt pen.

The notion of the day was to challenge the ethical status quo of the staff, provoke staff into presenting their real attitudes, and provide them a teacher who felt safe to them as well as knowledgeable about corrections. Some of this was also achieved in the first check-in. The day began by simply going slowly around to all participants, meeting them, asking them what they wanted or expected from the training, what they had heard, whether they had been forced to come, and what they felt about the new changes in the system.

In some cases it was already necessary to deal with their antagonism, distrust, and sometimes barely disguised sarcasm and anger. Many staff had been told only a few days before that they would be at the trainings, and in the early days, there was just not enough evidence of the safety of the training. It is interesting to note that there is little difference in doing a training seminar and doing treatment with clients. The issues are still safeness, whether there can be a safe flow of information, and whether the trainers will really listen to the participants or are merely a tool for the new propaganda.

We at Stonewall Arts Project also suggest that any trainings that directly lead to system change have the imprimatur of the system. We rarely began a three-day session without high-level representatives from the system introducing us, our purpose, and the purpose of the entire change. Each participant received a systemic change map of the proposed new directions and relationships of staff with each other and the offenders. We operated, as the principles suggest, inside this box.

The ethical dilemmas allowed staff to discuss helping, the sanctity of life, the notion of doing altruistic acts, and the "specialness" of life and death. Sometimes staff acted out these dilemmas, which gradually sensitized them, thereby reducing the aggressive or callous discourse.

Liebling (2003) clearly notes the importance of discussing these types of issues. She explores the issue of the constant shift in meaning of such terms as good and justice: "One of the problems of recent prison life has been a lack of clarity, by those working in and managing prisons, about what terms like "justice," "liberal," and "care" might mean *in practice*. . . . How are prison officers, the key translators of important terminology into practice, supposed to grasp the meaning of open textured terminology like justice and respect without clear guidance, or consensus, or clarity from those above them?" (p. 3).

It is our belief that prison officers can be moved from their fairly rigid concepts of offenders in part by discussions of what constitutes good actions, by getting agreement about right and wrong actions, which allow the facilitator small windows of opportunity to support the staff in changing their basic narrative of the debate about the "humanness" of offenders, especially sex offenders. Sex offenders, like many other types of offenders, strike very deep chords of distress—especially in personal areas of officers' experience such as parenting, justice, and punishment. Beliefs about sex offenders and other offenders can be loosened when the officers have an opportunity to change, if only temporarily, their narratives about these critical issues.

On the second day we reinforce these windows for making new narrative by focusing on treatment, how some offenders get to do what they do, and basic attachment theory. The latter has proved to be a critical tool for officers on which to hang their own theories of offending. We use no experiential strategies here, merely two circles representing the first and second year of child/parent attachment. We focus on the basics: the child's cries, the parents' immediate response, attunement, and symptom relief for the parent and the fact of its multiple repetition during the first year of the child's life. In the second year the focus is on the outward curiosity and reaching of the child, the intervention of the parent when the child becomes unsafe or breaks a rule, and the child's acceptance of the authority of the parent. The parent is the model in some ways for much of the child's attitudes to authority later on his or her life.

We then discuss what happens if no one comes, or comes intermittently in the first year, and what happens if no one disciplines the child or if the parent interventions in the second year are dangerous or frightening. Often in answer to the question, What does the child learn in a healthy first-year attachment? The answer from officers is that the child learns how to manipulate others. But it is also equally common to see officer staff members who are distressed by this segment or ask questions about their own parenting or the parenting they are giving their children. They suddenly have a clearer picture of why someone might be set on course to offend. It is often a seminal moment on the road to *temporarily* relaxing the staff's beliefs and attitudes about offenders. We stress "temporary" because we have no evidence that these simple strategies alone will cause permanent change.

This day is buttressed by a detailed and interactive training on cognitive-behavioral therapy (CBT), including the reason CBT is used so extensively in the field of correctional treatment and a discussion of the effectiveness of the different treatments. Dialectical behavior therapy (DBT) techniques are also discussed, and it is noted that one of the goals is to promote core mindfulness, a really strong and grounded self-awareness. In conjunction with other training components on the second day, we also focus on giving the officers an experience with their own thoughts in order to begin the process with of a more overt self-awareness. We believe that staff members who are more self-reflective are more likely to find it easier to be empathic with the offenders they are trying to motivate to change.

To encourage this knowledge, we ask staff members to complete a cognitive and affective report on the experience of doing one less of something that they usually do as a daily habit. For example, if the individual walked three miles every day, we would make him do one mile less and record all the sensations he had. It is a very effective shortcut to understanding the notion of the intense power of thoughts and adding to the perception that (1) that offenders mostly are "created"; (2) treatment works; and (3) each of the officers has the potential to change his or her own behavior.

Changing the Culture Using Drama-Based Techniques

The culture cannot shift if attitudes toward change do not evolve. If staff members are cynical and unbelieving, any change will be short-circuited as soon as any new rehabilitation strategy is announced. Change efforts must include security staff, supervisors, parole officers, central office staff, cooks and support staff, and eventually the offenders. Culture change can make staff vulnerable and they must be protected from interstaff bullying and the potential sabotage of the systems supporting the new culture.

New beliefs are vulnerable to old bullies and repressive peers. Thus, the third training day with the correctional staff in Victoria always emphasized the terrible impact of officer-to-officer bullying and, therefore, how vulnerable the new directions, including the new interactions with offenders, were. It was our experience in Victoria that all staff at all levels had something to say about sabotage and bullying and many had had painful experiences with it. The techniques had to be dynamic enough to deflect the tense resentment of old cultures and especially old beliefs about offenders as staff considered the validity of the new cultural meanings.

As this chapter stated earlier, prison officers are often under enormous stress—especially to prove to other staff that they are "with" the group, support a shared anti-offender stance, and are not going to follow any new processes that might weaken this position. Resistance can be fierce. Old system change techniques, such as ordering people to change, just cannot compete in effectiveness with teaching staff to consider and argue the old issues in a new way.

The basis for any cultural change in a prison system must include a shared vision of realistic strategies for offender change and shared beliefs in their effectiveness, as well as agreeing to timely consequences for corrupt behavior, a shared understanding of ethical behavior, and supportive prison environments. Culture change is dynamic and filled with unknown consequences. Culture change is an act of suasion, of confrontation, of rooting out the old beliefs and asking every staff member to make the step into a new culture. It is a therefore a dramatic moment, a little like taking "the pledge." The officers may have to publicly renounce the old pressure group, step away from officers who either distrust or dislike administration and offenders alike. In the training we asked officers and administrative staff to publicly practice thinking about what is right, what is the good thing to do for offenders, and what might harm the environment of the prison as a change place. In the focus on ethical practices we asked trainees to enact or discuss such old prison cultural issues as being drunk on the job, having affairs, using violence, and publicly using new and sensitive strategies to deal with hitherto hidden problems.

In the new culture of Corrections Victoria, it was proposed that staff see themselves as change agents. This meant that we emphasized, repeated, and questioned the central message to the staff that offenders are human, capable of change, and responsive to new techniques of treatment. In any culture change this belief must be repeated, experienced, discussed, and publicly argued. We must prove that what we believe is believable. Correctional system training is never just a matter of rote procedures.

For the culture change to be effective, the message must be given in every way that the staff can understand—it must match each staff members' most potent way of understanding and remembering. Many of us learn better through action: through making a sculpture or a drawing of an idea or a thought, through pictures, by watching, or through listening. In our work to reduce the dangerous perceptions of sex offenders we have always used masks or dolls that portray some of the early experiences that many of these men go through: the neglect, the loneliness, the frozen shame. For many officers this is the first time they have been close to a live drama of the family life of one inmate. Suddenly, the violent antipathy of a few peers pales against the unveiling of the true past of the men who the officers jail every day.

"Role playing through psychodrama or dramatherapy techniques allows a situation to be viewed from another's perspective and increase the likelihood that staff will perceive new information as relevant" (Birgden & MacLachlan, 2002, p. 292). There are those practitioners such as Reiss, Quayle, Brett, and Meux (1998) who very clearly perceive that dramatherapy and theater games can play a critical part in meeting the needs of culture change. That is, for change to occur the teaching must be educational but available to all the participants. It must give staff a learning experience that automatically connects thoughts and feelings in such a way that the experience can challenge effectively the older cultural meanings, and in a public space. It is why Stonewall Arts and Geese Company have always used this potent combination of experiential learning, art, role play, culturally relevant strategies, and didactic teaching.

In 1980, Geese Company focused on how to acquire and convert prisoner images and metaphors (Bergman & Hewish 1996) to drama-based techniques. This led, in one instance, to creating masks that represented many types of resistance, deception, and affective control. It came about simply as a result of matching the input of the offenders with the available parallels in dramatherapy. Felicitously the masks have continued to be an extraordinary tool for offender self-knowledge and staff understanding.

Dramatherapy can and does actively teach people about who and what they believe they are. Dramatherapy and drama games give participants a type of temporary visa to new or forbidden territory. These territories are intended to be a drastic alternative to the way in which the participant currently thinks. These experiences are not easily forgotten, and because they occur in a safe environment they can therefore be summoned up in the future without fear of traumatic abreaction.

These mnemonic devices allow for old and new information to be rearranged in ways that lead to new ways of making sense of experiences. That is, the participant can reexamine his or her reactions and beliefs about sex offenders through a new lens of meaning. The officer participant in dramatherapy can see the offender in the same way that he or she might have experienced the offender in a role play, perhaps, depending on the training experience, remembering seeing the role player of the sex offender being rejected from a football team and feeling empathy for him for the first time.

The dramatherapy tool gives people a chance to describe the indescribable in manner that may make more sense to them than using a paper-and-pencil lecture or in words. Drawing disgust with a sex offender may be a more profoundly "real" experience than saying that sexual offenders are disgusting. It is a short jump to asking the offender to imagine why he made the staff person feel that way and then setting this up as a role play. Even a role reversal for someone who has never been at the mercy of himself may have a deeply liberating impact on a callous, jaded, or angry administrator or officer. Also, in the final day of the Victoria training, we set up simple role plays in a forum-based style, where officers had to find ways to deal with future sabotage strategies. The staff members were all quick to come up with the sabotage that they thought would occur. In quick succession we asked other staff to rotate into the scene to come up with new ways to circumvent the attacks on these new system approaches. It was enlightening for all the staff to see that the hopelessness they envisaged was, at least in these scenarios, significantly reduced. Staff could act using affect and new modified cognitions, memory, and new teachings to present significantly modified behaviors.

FUTURE DIRECTIONS

The concepts of using ethics and dramatherapy to obtain culture change (or to initially set a positive culture in a new program) could also be extremely beneficial when applied to the civil commitment programs for sexual offenders in the United States. This practice was begun, to some degree, in the Minnesota program, where all staff (including security, support staff, and maintenance workers) were trained in the principles of sex offender treatment and encouraged to play a major role in observing and documenting behavior change in the offenders (Schlank, Harry, & Farnsworth, 1999). In addition, the Stonewall Arts Project/Geese Company was brought in on a contractual basis to provide training (using role-play exercises) for the newly hired staff members in that program.

We are also currently considering how to take these concepts into the community to build bridges for the sexual offenders on their release from prison. We are still trying to create short repeatable scenes of stereotypical characters to which we can fit behaviors and to more accurately mimic the staff's more feared offenders. We are still looking for videos done by sexual offenders and violent offenders where it is clear that they are honestly showing us their successes. We are trying to see whether there is any need for different types of training vehicles at certain times of the trainings. We believe that forty-minute performances highlighting the issues and seen by many participants is an apt way to begin. It is a matter of making connection.

In our work with the officers in the Victoria prison system we had occasionally to deal with suspicion, disbelief, and a sense that nothing would work, as well as interest, relief, and a great pride that finally the "system" was beginning to ask the prison officers for their ideas, their help, and their advice. At the heart of the "Ethics in Action" training was not only the "what works" information but a vital change in the relationship with the offenders. It is the apparent success of this, the clear evidence of more officers being involved in rehabilitative efforts with therapists, that leads us to believe that the entire training series and the methodology of change that the system adopted can support increased sensitivity for all types of security staff who might work with sex offenders.

Over and over in our teaching we stressed that we were part of a systemwide approach. When a security staff member knows that his or her work will be watched, that accountability will be enforced, that the supervisor will try to help, and that there is a direction to all the work in the system, the change will be more widespread, and staff will begin to change their beliefs more publicly.

But, beliefs can be easily dispelled. Trust between security and supervisory staff can sometimes be the casualty most often seen on the road to change. Staff look for meaning, and they must check that new meaning against what they now believe. Training is a matter not just of facts and skills but of belief and will. The platform for cultural change in sex offender program includes ethical action, potent training strategies that leave a lasting experience of altered beliefs about dangerous offenders, a realistic discussion and even acceptance of all staff beliefs and attitudes, a believable systemic change, and reassurance that getting close to sexual offenders cannot affect one's heterosexual or taboo beliefs and actions. It is our experience that the security staff who come to work with the sexual offender are the ones who achieve lasting institutional satisfaction.

References

Bergman, J. (2000). Creating new cultures: Using drama therapy to build therapeutic communities in prison. In P. Lewis & D. R. Johnson (Eds.), *Current approaches in drama therapy* (pp. 303–330). Springfield, IL: Charles C. Thomas.

Bergman, J., & Hewish, S. (1996). The violent illusion: Drama therapy and the dangerous voyage to the heart of change. In M. Liebmann (Ed.), *Arts approaches to conflict* (pp. 92–117). London: Jessica Kingsley.

Birgden, A. (2004). Therapeutic jurisprudence and responsivity: Finding the will and the way in offender rehabilitation. *Psychology, Crime and Law, 10*(3), 283–295.

Birgden, A., & McLachlan, C. (2002), *Reducing reoffending framework: Setting the scene* (Paper No 1). Melbourne, Australia: Office of the Correctional Services Minister, Victoria.

Correctional Service of Canada. (n.d.). *What do correctional officers think of sexual offenders?* Available: www.csc-scc.gc.ca/text/pblct/forum/e04/e041g_e.shtml.

Crawley, E. M. (2004). Emotion and performance: Prison officers and the presentation of self in prisons. *Punishment and Society, 6*, 411–427.

Farkas, M. A. (1999). Correctional officers attitudes toward inmates and working with inmates in a "get tough" era. *Journal of Criminal Justice, 27*(6), 495–506.

Gendreau, P., Goggin, C., & Smith, P. (1999). The Gendreau, Goggin, and Smith checklist for implementing effective correctional treatment programs. *International Journal of Offender Therapy and Comparative Criminology, 43*(2), 180–187.

Hanson, R. K, Gordon, A., Harris, A. J., Marques, J. K., Murphy, W., Quinsey, V. L., et al. (2002).

First report of the collaborative outcome data project on the effectiveness of psychological treatment for sex offenders. *Sexual Abuse: Journal of Research and Treatment, 14*(2), 169–194.

Jurik, N. C., & Musheno, M. C. (1986). The internal crisis of corrections: Professionalization and the work environment. *Justice Quarterly, 3*(4), 457–480.

Larivière, M., & Robinson, D. (1996). *Attitudes of correctional officers towards offenders (Executive summary)*. Toronto, Ontario, Canada: Price Waterhouse.

Liebling, A. (2003). *Moral values, prison performance and the problem of quality: A summary and discussion paper.* Cambridge, UK: Institute of Criminology.

McGuire, J. (Ed.). (2002). *Offender rehabilitation and treatment-effective programs and policies to reduce re-offending.* London: Wiley.

Nagayama-Hall, G. C. (1995). Sexual offender recidivism revisited: A meta-analysis of recent treatment studies. *Journal of Consulting and Clinical Psychology, 63*, 802–809.

Paboojian, A., & Teske, R. H. C. (1997). Pre-service correctional officers: What do They think about treatment? *Journal of Criminal Justice, 25*(5), 425–433.

Poole, E. D., & Regoli, R. M. (1980). Role stress, custody orientation, and disciplinary actions: A study of prison guards. *Criminology, 18*(2), 215–226.

Reiss, D., Quayle, M., Brett, T., & Meux, C. (1998). Dramatherapy for mentally disordered offenders: changes in levels of anger. *Criminal Behaviour and Mental Health, 8*, 139–153.

Robinson, D., Porporino, F. J., & Simourd, L. (1993). The influence of career orientation on support for rehabilitation among correctional staff. *Prison Journal, 73*, 162–177.

Schlank, A., Harry, R., & Farnsworth, M. (1999). The Minnesota Sex Offender Program. In A. Schlank & F. Cohen (Eds.), *The sexual predator: Legal issues, commitment proceedings, evaluation and treatment* (pp. 10-1–10-18). Kingston, NJ: Civic Research Institute.

Tellier, C., & Robinson, D. (1995). *Correlates of job stress among front-line correctional staff.* Paper presented at the annual convention of the Canadian Psychological Association, Charlottetown, PEI.

Tellier, C., & Serin, R. C. (2001). *The role of staff in effective program delivery* (Compendium 2000, vol. 1). Ottawa, Ontario: Correctional Service of Canada.

Weekes, J., Pelletier, G., & Beaudette, D. (1995). Correctional officers: How do they perceive sex offenders? *International Journal of Offender Therapy and Comparative Criminology, 39*, 55–61.

Chapter 11

Assessing Treatment Progress in Civilly Committed Sex Offenders— The New Jersey Approach

by Glenn Ferguson, Ph.D., Merrill Main, Ph.D. and Jennifer Schneider, Ph.D.

Note: The views expressed here are those of the authors and not necessarily the New Jersey Department of Human Services.

INTRODUCTION

Historically, sex offender treatment services have been provided in a variety of settings, ranging from outpatient to inpatient and prison based to hospital based. Therefore, the importance of assessing sex offender treatment progress can be viewed from a variety of clinical, legal, and public safety perspectives. Even in the rare instance in which an individual seeks voluntary treatment for his or her sexually abusive behavior, the clinician providing such treatment takes on a role with significant legal implications (duty to warn, child abuse reporting, assessing dangerousness). Likewise, clinicians engaged in postconviction sex offender services take on forensic roles in performing assessment and treatment (presentence evaluations, preparole evaluations, treatment progress reports, and treatment termination reports, as well as at several points in the civil commitment process, referral, commitment, and discharge decision making). Thus, current forensic mental health guidelines must be considered when establishing clinical procedures for sex offender treatment.

The relatively low-frequency but high-stakes failures inherent in treating this population has led to the enactment of two generations of civil commitment laws in the United States. The majority of the so-called sexual psychopath laws of the 1930s and 1940s were repealed largely on constitutional grounds and in part due to the lack of evidence that mental health professionals could accurately predict which known sex offenders were likely to recidivate (Prentky & Burgess, 2000). The second generation of postincarceration civil commitment laws for high-risk sex offenders came in the wake of the U.S. Supreme Court's decision in *Kansas v. Hendricks*,[1] which established the constitutionality of the Kansas Sexually Violent Predator (SVP) Act.

The development of empirically based sex offender risk assessment instruments over the past two decades has enhanced the selection process involved in implementing today's sexual predator laws. To date, the use of actuarial methods has met the legal standard for admissibility of scientific evidence in the jurisdictions in which their use has been challenged. However, these scales are predominantly based on static/historical risk factors that do not take into account the mitigating effects of treatment on an offender's recidivism risk. While the focus of sex offender recidivism research has recently shifted to the development of dynamic risk assessment scales (Hanson & Harris, 2000b), those clinicians engaged in the evaluation and treatment of civilly committed sex offenders have been left largely to their own devices in attempting to answer the frequently asked question at subsequent commitment review hearings, "Has the offender sufficiently benefited from treatment so that he or she is no longer likely to reoffend?" or simply put, "When is enough treatment really enough?"

This debate has contributed to increased interest in the assessment of sex offender treatment progress by those in the clinical and legal professions. This chapter provides a review of the literature related to the assessment of sex offender treatment progress, a clinical perspective on empirically based assessment of treatment gains, and a discussion of the methods adopted by the clinical administration of the Special Treatment Unit, New Jersey's postincarceration civil commitment program for adult sex offenders.

THE IMPORTANCE OF MEASURING TREATMENT PROGRESS

Treatment for sex offenders is intended to reduce an individual's risk for reoffending, whether the offender is in an institutional or community-based setting. Measuring the treatment progress of individual sex offenders is an essential component of the treatment process because it allows clinicians to determine whether the individual is actively making advances in treatment. Measures of treatment progress are intended to provide objective, quantifiable criteria for clinicians to assess treatment gains over time. Information about treatment performance is used to guide decisions at several stages of the criminal justice system, including decisions regarding sentencing, institutional placement, conditional release, and level of community supervision.

Sex offenders commonly deny they have a problem, blame others for their behavior, and tend to minimize the impact of their offense on the victim. Most sex offenders enter treatment not by choice but because they are mandated to do so by the courts or a similar agency. Thus they are frequently reluctant to participate in treatment and to discuss their deviant sexual behavior. For these reasons, assessing progress, the impact of denial, and the influence of coercion on participation in treatment play a role in the accurate measurement of treatment progress.

DEFINING TREATMENT PROGRESS

Measurements

One difficulty in measuring treatment progress is that definitions of treatment progress and measures used to assess progress vary across programs. Several scales were developed to measure treatment progress in treatment programs; however, each scale takes different factors into consideration. For example, Seto (2003) measured treatment progress through an evaluation of three concepts: involvement in treatment (including attendance, motivation, and level of participation), compliance with treatment rules and expectations, and attainment of treatment goals (measured through successful learning of treatment principles, understanding of treatment concepts, and the development of new skills).

According to Seto (2003), measures of treatment progress should incorporate both specific and nonspecific aspects of treatment performance.

Specific Aspects of Treatment Performance. Specific aspects of treatment performance include factors such as skills acquisition, quality of homework, understanding of offense cycle, and development of a relapse prevention plan.

Nonspecific Aspects of Treatment Performance. Nonspecific aspects of treatment performance include measures of motivation, compliance with rules, attendance, and level of participation in treatment. Consideration of both specific and nonspecific aspects of treatment performance provides a more comprehensive evaluation of the offender's overall progress.

EXISTING MEASURES OF TREATMENT PROGRESS

Sex Offender Treatment Rating Scale

The Sex Offender Treatment Rating Scale (SOTRS) was designed as both a process and an outcome measure for a sex offender treatment program in Connecticut (Anderson, Gibeau, & D'Amora, 1995). The scale was developed to provide therapist ratings of progress for offenders participating in cognitive-behavioral sex offender treatment. The original version of the scale consisted of twelve categories; the revised edition of the scale was condensed to six categories to facilitate and clarify the scoring process. Categories included (1) insight, (2) deviant thoughts, (3) awareness of situational risks, (4) motivation, (5) victim empathy, and (6) offense disclosure. A reliability study based on a sample of 122 sex offenders referred to outpatient treatment through probation or parole suggested that the scale had high internal consistency. The authors recommended a follow-up validity study to assess the utility of the scale in predicting recidivism.

Goal Attainment Scaling

Stripe, Wilson, and Long (2001) developed Goal Attainment Scaling (GAS) to objectively assess the impact of clinical and motivational elements of treatment for sex offenders on conditional release. The GAS consisted of twelve subscales divided into three major areas. The three areas included non-relapse prevention clinical dimensions, relapse prevention clinical dimensions, and motivational dimensions. Non-relapse clinical dimensions included (1) acceptance of guilt for the offense, (2) showing insight into victim issues, (3) showing empathy for one's victims, (4) acceptance of personal responsibility, (5) recognizing cognitive distortions, and (6) minimization of consequences. Relapse prevention clinical dimensions included (7) understanding of lifestyle dynamics, (8) understanding the offense cycle, and (9) identification of relapse prevention concepts. Motivational dimensions included (10) disclosure of personal information, (11) participation in treatment, and (12) motivation to change.

To assess the utility of the scale, information was collected from psychological reports written pre- and posttreatment and again after three months of follow-up in the community on a sample of forty-eight offenders on conditional release. For the purpose of the study offenders were divided into two groups: low to moderate risk and high risk. As anticipated, individuals with positive attitudes were more likely to complete the treatment program, whereas offenders with negative attitudes were less likely to complete the program. Although both groups made gains between pretreatment and follow-up in the community, comparisons between the three stages of treatment demonstrated that the low-risk group consistently outperformed the high-risk group in terms of total score. The GAS was developed as a measure of treatment effectiveness to provide an increased understanding of variables associated with treatment responsiveness.

Regional Treatment Center

Quinsey et al. (1998) examined the contribution of dynamic variables *including* a measure of therapeutic change to the prediction of recidivism among 193 sex offenders treated at the Regional Treatment Center in Canada. Therapists rated gains in treatment on a 4-point scale ranging from poor to very good. Treatment gain was found to be unrelated to either sexual or sexual and violent arrests. The study demonstrated a lack of a relationship between treatment gains as measured and recidivism rates, contrary to the theoretical expectation that treatment would reduce recidivism. The authors argue that the findings mirror those of previous research and indicate that despite advances in sex offender treatment, we are more capable of measuring risk for reoffending than actually modifying risk.

Treatment Progress Scale

The Treatment Needs and Progress Scale (TPS) is composed of risk factors linked to sexual offending that are both amenable to change and can be used as targets for intervention in a treatment program. The scale contains a total of twenty-two risk factors scored on a 4-point scale to evaluate initial treatment need as well as progress in treatment when administered regularly at six-month intervals. The TPS was developed based on a sample of 329 adult male sex offenders enrolled in outpatient treatment programs under community correctional supervision in Vermont. The initial validity study suggested that the TPS has predictive validity in terms of measuring both treatment progress and risk for reoffending. TPS scores demonstrated a moderate correlation with existing risk scales known to have predictive validity including the Rapid Risk Assessment for Sex Offender Recidivism (RRASOR; Hanson, 1997), the Static-99 (Hanson & Thornton, 1999) and Vermont Assessment of Sex-Offender Risk (VASOR; McGrath, Hoke, Livingston, & Cumming, 2001). In addition, differences were found among total mean scores of participants at various stages of treatment, providing further evidence of the validity of the instrument. For example, offenders at the beginning of treatment had higher scores as compared to offenders at the middle or end stages of treatment (McGrath, Livingston, & Cumming, 2002). The TPS is intended to serve as a treatment planning and program monitoring tool for sex offenders under community supervision.

Sex Offender Needs Assessment Rating

The Sex Offender Needs Assessment Rating (SONAR; Hanson & Harris, 2000a) evaluates change in risk among sexual offenders. The scale is composed of five stable factors (intimacy deficits, negative social influences, attitudes tolerant of sex offending, sexual self-regulation, and general self-regulation) and four acute factors (substance abuse, negative mood, anger, and victim access). The SONAR demonstrated adequate internal consistency and moderate ability to distinguish between recidivists and nonrecidivists in a sample of 409 nonincestuous offenders on community supervision. In addition SONAR scores were correlated with static measures of risk including the Violence Risk Appraisal Guide (VRAG; Quinsey, 2000) and the Static-99 (Hanson & Harris, 2000a). The authors note the extent to which changes in SONAR scores are indicative of changes in recidivism risk requires further testing of the instrument beyond the retrospective design of the present study. Although the SONAR was not designed to specifically measure treatment progress, it consists of risk factors similar to those found in existing scales of treatment progress that serve as the principal targets of sex offender treatment.

THE ROLE OF MOTIVATION IN TREATMENT

The Influence of Coercion

Sexual offenders do not typically agree to participate in treatment voluntarily; instead, they are frequently mandated or coerced to attend a specialized treatment program. Research regarding the influence of coercion on treatment has focused on substance-abusing or mentally ill offenders. Therefore, little is known about whether coercion influences the treatment and management of sex offenders (Burdon & Gallager, 2002). Coercion is categorized as either external or internal in terms of its origin. External coercion is typically exerted by a criminal justice agency such as the court, probation or parole agency, or the offender's friends or family members. Internal coercion is considered to be a product of the offender's guilt resulting from his deviant sexual offending behavior.

Coercion serves two purposes: It incapacitates the offender through the use of incarceration and civil commitment, while at the same time ensuring participation and retention in treatment. Burdon and Gallager (2002) argue that because coerced clients are less motivated they are more likely to drop out of treatment if the opportunity arises. Although coerced clients are less motivated, the rationale behind the use of coercion is that over time attendance in treatment will eventually influence coerced clients to engage in and successfully complete a treatment program. In other words, coercion is used to persuade an offender to enter into treatment in the hope that treatment will eventually result in desired long-term behavioral changes.

A study of drug addicted offenders in a prison-based drug treatment program in California examined psychosocial changes during and posttreatment through a comparison of inmates admitted voluntarily versus involuntarily to the program (Prendergrast, Farabee, Cartier, & Henkin, 2002). The researchers were also concerned with the broader policy issue surrounding the appropriateness and effectiveness of coercing incarcerated offenders to enter and continue in drug treatment. A comparison of scores on the Self-Rating form (Simpson & Knight, 1998), a tool used to assess psychological and social functioning, found that inmates exhibited significant change on most of the scales of the form regardless of whether they were admitted voluntarily or involuntarily to the treatment program. The study also showed that inmates involuntarily referred to the program did not differ in terms of motivation for treatment. The findings demonstrated that external pressure to engage in treatment did not negatively influence change, suggesting that the use of coercion to pressure inmates to enter treatment may serve to increase treatment retention and outcome.

Motivational Factors

According to Jenkins-Hall (1994), sex offenders who experience external pressure to engage in treatment or those who are mandated to attend treatment are less motivated to change. Motivation to participate in treatment that is external (such as court mandated treatment) rather than internal in nature is criticized as less genuine or sincere. Motivation for treatment among sex offenders is difficult to quantify but can be assessed through the offender's acceptance of responsibility for his crime as well as attendance in treatment and level of participation.

In a study of motivational factors among child molesters attending outpatient therapy, Jenkins-Hall (1994) found evidence that client motivation was related to treatment outcome. The study examined four motivational factors: acceptance of problems with sexual deviancy, attendance in treatment, level of participation in therapy, and number of times the client was tardy to treatment. The four motivational factors were found to be correlated with treatment effectiveness as measured through changes in deviant sexual arousal and mastery of cognitive-behavioral concepts and strategies. Although all four measures were found to be related to treatment outcome, the variable measuring client acceptance of problems with sexual deviancy proved to be the most statistically powerful predictor of treatment outcome.

MEASUREMENT OF TREATMENT PROGRESS

Although measures of treatment progress assess gains made as a result of participation in treatment, some offenders fail to apply concepts learned in treatment following release from incarceration. Therefore, it is necessary to distinguish genuine treatment performance from manipulation when it is used to make the offender appear to be at a lower risk for reoffending. Miner (2000) developed a test of behavioral competency measures designed to assess the sincerity of treatment performance. Prevention assists in the development of specific skills and knowledge. Competency-based assessment evaluates progress made during treatment through an assessment of whether the client simply "talks the talk" to appease the therapist during treatment or truly "walks the walk" by actually applying the concepts learned over the course of treatment to real-life situations outside a restricted environment. Although the study identified a number of indicators related to behavioral competency, the assessment instrument itself requires additional testing to establish its predictive accuracy.

Linking Treatment Progress to Treatment Completion

Treatment performance is typically measured during or following completion of a sex offender treatment program to assess mastery of basic concepts and to assist in release decisions. Hanson and Bussière (1998) conducted a meta-analysis of sixty-one sex offender recidivism studies to determine which factors were strongly related to reoffending. The authors hypothesized that offenders who accepted responsibility for their crimes, demonstrated motivation, and complied with treatment should represent a lower risk than those offenders who denied problems or resisted change. The analysis demonstrated that failure to complete a treatment program was a moderate predictor of sexual recidivism. Lack of treatment completion increases an individual's risk for reoffending; therefore, offenders who successfully complete treatment are less likely to reoffend.

Relationship Between Treatment Progress and Outcome

In a study of 224 sex offenders treated at the Warkworth Sexual Behavior Clinic in Canada, Seto and Barbaree developed a treatment performance measure that included both specific and nonspecific measures of treatment progress. The measure focused on (1) behavior in group, (2) treatment progress, and (3) clinician ratings. The study predicted that good treatment behavior would be associated with success on parole supervision and reduced recidivism. Contrary to expectations, good treatment performance was not associated with lower rates of recidivism during the initial thirty-two-month follow-up period; in contrast, good treatment performance was associated with higher rates of recidivism. This finding suggests that treatment performance is not a static risk factor and that good treatment performance is not indicative of lower risk over time. However, the authors suggest that treatment performance be considered a dynamic risk factor used to signal the imminence of recidivism rather than to predict reoffending. Two possible explanations offered for the findings were that the measure of treatment behavior identified a group of offenders who are good at manipulation and exploitation or that offenders learned manipulative skills in treatment which in turn increased their risk for recidivism.

A second follow-up of the same subjects in which the total time at risk was increased from thirty-two to sixty-two months also demonstrated that treatment performance was unrelated to recidivism (Seto & Barbaree, 2003). One possible explanation for the contradictory findings was that the design of the original follow-up period excluded certain sentences; new provincial sentences of less than two years in length were not captured in the original analysis. The second study included shorter provincial sentences in the calculation of recidivism, thereby providing a more accurate indicator of the true recidivism rate.

CLINICAL PERSPECTIVES ON MEASURING TREATMENT GAINS

Assessing treatment progress in sexual offenders is complex, multifaceted, and interactive. Therefore, any discussion of treatment progress must reduce the complexity by assuming that certain variables are held constant while others are measured. That is, many of the following statements regarding reoffense risk assume "all else being equal." Another caution is that much of evaluation via interview relies on self-report. Self-report is often adapted to foster a desired, though not necessarily factual, view of the individual.

Reviewing Available Treatment Reports

The evaluator should review any available treatment reports. Reports of single treatment contacts should be considered cautiously as they may not reflect overall or sustained treatment progress. Similarly, synopses by treating clinicians of more relevant time periods—such as three-month, six-month, or one-year periods—may be influenced by extraneous variables. These variables include such things as appearance, verbal skills, social skills, and more. A body of literature exploring constructs such as the "halo effect" exists (Doren, 2005) and should be very familiar to the examiner. A rule of thumb is that the more contact one has with an individual, the more one may be influenced by extraneous variables. In addition, group treatment is the preferred modality of treatment for sexual offenders (Schwartz, 1995). It should be expected that treating clinicians will be influenced by the performance of an offender relative to the other group members. Thus, a mildly resistant individual will be viewed more positively in a very resistant group and more negatively in a very motivated group. For these and more reasons, the evaluator must independently assess treatment progress while seriously considering the treatment synopsis provided by the treating clinicians. The primary assessment tool available to the evaluator is the clinical interview.

The Acquisition of Relapse Prevention Skills

Cognitive-behavioral, relapse prevention-focused treatment seems to have the greatest demonstrable efficacy in reducing sexual recidivism rates among sexual offenders (Hanson & Bussière, 1998). Therefore, a primary focus in assessing treatment progress is the sound acquisition of relapse prevention skills. Relapse prevention may be conceptualized as a set of life skills. Assessment of treatment progress also includes the assessment of additional life skills such as affect management, insight, social skills, and vocational skills. Progress in treatment involves acquiring relevant constructs and soundly applying those constructs in a wide range of situations and over a meaningful span of time. In advanced stages of treatment, "overlearning" of the constructs is expected to have occurred. Overlearned information should be readily accessed in nearly any setting and state. Thus the offender should be able to recall substantial segments of offense cycle and relapse prevention plan while depressed, in anxiety-provoking situations, in both familiar and unfamiliar environments, and so on. Overlearned information should also be accessible using few, if any, memory cues.

Relapse prevention is predicated on the premise that sexual offenders have authentic intentions to avert reoffending. The primary tenet of relapse prevention is that good intentions are necessary but not sufficient to avert reoffense. Relapse prevention is a process wherein detailed plans to accomplish the intentions to avert relapse are devised. Similar life skills are relevant to many areas of human functioning. An example might be that a student who intends to earn good grades still requires skills needed to accomplish the goal. In such an example, the student needs some study skills along with a plan of when to study, how much to study, how to deal with the inevitable distractions, how to deal with internal states such as tedium, how to deal with external situations such as parties, when to seek assistance, and so on. Much of this planning can be found in prior situations wherein failure ensued despite the good intentions. Readers who are versed in relapse prevention will readily assign relapse prevention-specific labels such as high-risk factors, triggers, seemingly unimportant decisions, desire for immediate gratification, and so forth, to the items in the preceding sentences.

Mastery of relapse prevention is assessed by reviewing the individual's relapse prevention plan and via clinical interview. Understanding the chain of behaviors preceding an offense; the offense cycle; or the thoughts, feelings, behaviors, and situations that foster offending should be readily delineated in the relapse prevention plan and verbally by the offender. As always, less directive questions should precede the more specific questions. A question such as "If you were to reoffend, how would it probably happen?" should precede a request that the individual draw his offense cycle for the evaluator. If the offender has not thought about the manner in which he would most likely reoffend, relapse prevention was merely an academic exercise. Indeed, the entire relapse prevention process is actually focused on dealing with the answer to that question. The "correct" answer to that question must be plausible and sufficiently detailed in terms of both victim and offense profile. Reflected but not blamed in the answer should be the thoughts, feelings, behaviors, and situations that facilitate or precipitate the offense. Common examples of implausible answers are those that focus on victims who will never again be available and situations that are very unlikely to occur (such as an offender who sexually molested his youngest niece ten years ago when she was 10 years old who says that the most likely reoffense scenario is "I'm asked to babysit my niece . . .").

Lying, denial, minimization, and justification are constructs that are relevant to treatment motivation and progress. In general, the greatest motivation to acquire relapse prevention skills stems from the offender's acknowledgment that he has a problem. A form of relapse prevention is still possible in the absence of such an acknowledgement in that the offender can make detailed plans to avoid false accusations in the future. While this seems countertherapeutic, the offender who diligently avoids situations wherein he can be accused of a sexual offense is unlikely to be able to commit a sexual offense. However, the patient who does not take responsibility for the offending behaviors cannot readily address his internal states in the detailed relapse prevention planning. For the sake of clarity, let us define lying as the deliberate telling of false information, denial as a process of self deception, minimization as a mixture of truth and deliberate omission of more damning details, and justification as the inclusion of irrelevant or erroneous explanations for offending behaviors.

Lying, denial, minimization, and justification are best assessed by asking about the sexual offending behaviors in as nondirective a manner as possible; for instance, "Help me get to know about you; how about starting with what got you in this situation." In general, treatment progress is reflected in how readily the offender takes responsibility for the offending behaviors. Conceptually, an offender who has made substantial progress in treatment will need little prompting to give a rendition of events surrounding the offense that is sufficiently detailed so as to allow the assessor to have a realistic impression of what the offender and the victim experienced. Revealed in that rendition will be many of the constituents of the relapse prevention cycle such as internal and external triggers. Also apparent will be deviant sexual arousal pattern and capacity for empathy for the victim.

In all phases of the clinical interview, it is important that the evaluator avoid ascribing more meaning to answers they clearly convey. It is not unusual that an offender will say, "I take full responsibility for the offense," but when questioned in detail, he really means that he takes full responsibility for not being smart enough to avoid becoming the victim of false accusations. Similarly, statements, such as "I touched her on her privates," often overlie claims of accidentally touching a child's buttocks while engaging in some innocuous behavior. The evaluator must ask increasingly more direct and specific questions to elicit sufficient details. Again, all else being equal, less progress in treatment is suggested by the need for more direct and more specific questions.

Assessing the Constructs of Empathy and Self-Esteem

Empathy Training. Empathy training is often seen as a core ingredient in sex offender treatment. Some research suggests that a significant portion of sexual offenders were not aware that they were hurting their victims. Some such offenders were sexually molested as children and focused on the pleasurable aspects of the sexual interactions while convincing themselves that the harmful aspects did not exist. Another segment of the offender population seems to have had the capacity to feel empathy but deliberately averted their attention from the harmful effects on the victim. For such offenders, empathy training seems likely to reduce recidivism.

Despite the clinical logic, there is a lack of empirical evidence that empathy training has a measurable effect of recidivism. Empathy may be conceptualized in several ways and can be exceedingly difficult to quantify. One conceptualization is that empathy is the ability to understand what another person is experiencing. A second conceptualization is that empathy is the voluntary ability to feel emotions that are similar to what another person is experiencing. Yet a third conceptualization is that empathy is the involuntary tendency to feel emotions that are similar to what others feel. Almost certainly, the goal of empathy training is to have the offender attain the latter state wherein he experiences distress any time someone else does. One problem is the apparent fragility of empathy in the face of anger, entitlement, or personal suffering. Another problem is that sadistic offenders often have an impressive ability to understand the suffering of their victims and to enjoy that suffering.

In the recent past, concerns were raised about the possibility that treatment in general and empathy training in particular served to increase reoffense risk among psychopaths. Rice, Harris, and Cormier (1992) were sometimes cited in support of this perspective, but D'Silva, Duggan, and McCarthy (2004) cogently argued that the Rice study lacked external validity. The most supportable perspective seems to be that empathy training does little harm but likely does not help with psychopaths. It should also be noted that higher levels of social adeptness, fearlessness, and antisocial tendencies in an individual should raise questions about the tendency to fake empathic emotional responses.

To the degree that empathy is conceptualized as a likely reoffense deterrent in the case being considered, assessing empathy skills is part of the assessment of treatment progress. To the degree that the offender has made gains in treatment, some empathy for the victim or victims will be evident in his rendition of the offending behaviors. The more prompting one has to do to evoke an empathic response to the victim's suffering, the less progress the offender has made in treatment. Details of the offense should be sufficient to display awareness of the victim's suffering, and the offender is expected to display a reasonable amount of affect that is commensurate with that suffering. Assessing the authenticity of the empathic response is exceedingly difficult to objectively define. In the absence of such a definition, it may be useful to refer to the psychodynamic literature wherein it is sometimes suggested that authentic emotions displayed by the patient evoke empathic responses from the therapist while unauthentic emotions evoke detachment or boredom.

After assessing empathy via the less directive approach, the offender's intellectual empathy skills may be further assessed by asking a question such as, "How do you think your victim was affected?" Some of the literature on empathy training suggests that the offender should neither overstate nor understate the likely trauma. Thus, "I ruined her life" may be more a statement of the offender's desire to permanently possess the victim or to have left a permanent mark on the victim. Even if the stated level of trauma is likely to be accurate, the offender should be able to explain probable affective, social, and behavioral effects of the offense on the victim. Lying, denial, minimization, and justification may readily be conceptualized as evidence of deficient empathy. This is because it should feel disrespectful and hurtful to the victim to deny the reality of the traumatic event even when the victim is not present. Especially in the assessment of empathy, the evaluator must not assume that generalizations are meaningful. The offender who says "I know I really hurt my victim" may, upon closer examination, mean that he hurt the victim by not engaging the victim in additional sexual interactions. More frequently, such a statement is exposed as being a shallow response when the offender is at a loss to explain how he "really hurt" the victim.

Self-Esteem. Similar to the construct of empathy is the construct of self-esteem. Research on the effect of self-esteem on sexual recidivism is, at best ambiguous. Gains in self-esteem may be assessed in the course of the clinical interview. The offender's statements regarding internal states that preceded offending often relate to self-esteem deficits. These statements should be followed by questions designed to evoke comparison between past and present self-esteem. The development or enhancement of a self-image that is not conducive to offending is a product of treatment gains. Unrealistically positive, and thus fragile, self-esteem is expected in early treatment stages. Later treatment stages should instill realistic self-image along with sound coping strategies for times at which self-esteem is waning. Included should be indications of resiliency at such times. Concrete responses should include references to the use of appropriate professional and social supports when depressed. Insight such as "even when I'm feeling really bad about myself, I know that the worst thing I could do would be to reoffend" should be overlearned.

Acknowledgment of the Risk of Reoffending

A realistic acknowledgment of the risk of reoffending also suggests that progress has been made in treatment. The difficulty here is arriving at an empirically supported consensus of what constitutes realistic. It seems safe to assume that an offender who believes that there is zero possibility of reoffending will not be sufficiently vigilant and cautious. It is very unlikely that such an individual will diligently follow any elements of his relapse prevention plan. Conversely, the offender who indicates that his reoffense probability is 100 percent is almost certainly highly likely to reoffend. The "correct" answer should reflect that the offender acknowledges a level of risk that will foster caution but not so high as to reflect potentially destabilizing anxiety or, worse, resignation. A major confounding variable when asking an offender about his reoffense risk is that the answer is likely to be greatly influenced by what he believes the examiner wants to hear. This is true of all questions, but simpler answers are more readily adapted.

Knowledge of Methods to Change Sexual Arousal Pattern

Sexual arousal pattern and knowledge of the methods used to change that pattern should also be assessed. Most assessments will not include behavioral measures such as the polygraph or, more specific, the plethysmograph or the Abel Assessment for Sexual Interest screen (Abel, Jordan, Hand, Holland, & Phipps, 2001). Such tools should be used whenever possible. However, the evaluator should be well versed in the psychometric properties of such tests. The tests mentioned use sophisticated electronics and are readily perceived as having greater validity and reliability than empirical measures suggest.

The pretreatment sexual arousal pattern is likely to be reflected in the history of the offender. The term "deviant sexual arousal" is often used, but "criminal sexual arousal" may be a less ambiguous term. Research suggests that the presence and magnitude of criminal sexual arousal patterns are robust predictors of reoffending. Similarly, legal sexual arousal patterns negatively correlate with recidivism.

The reason for caution regarding the use of the term "deviant sexual arousal" is that legal sexual behavior may be viewed as deviant. Treatment progress, defined as mitigation of reoffense risk, must consider legal sexual behaviors in terms of whether they are likely to increase or decrease reoffense risk. For example, autoerotic behaviors using inanimate objects for stimulation are often regarded as "deviant" but are rarely illegal. If illegal, such behaviors constitute essentially victimless crimes. Should an offender reveal a propensity or desire to engage in such behaviors, an attempt to answer the question of whether reoffense risk is exacerbated or mitigated must be made. Such answers are likely to be highly idiosyncratic and multifaceted if not theoretical. The behavior of some sexual offenders seems to fit an addictions model wherein engaging in almost any sexual behavior seems to increase the drive to engage in many more sexual behaviors. Conversely, some offenders seem to become less likely to engage in illegal sexual behaviors if sexual release is obtained via legal means.

Assessing treatment progress involves determining how offenders have changed or learned to manage their sexual arousal patterns. The evaluator should be well versed in arousal reconditioning methods. Offenders should have the use of relevant arousal reconditioning techniques noted in their relapse prevention plans. Their ability to access such knowledge may be assessed via less specific questions such as "What would you do if you saw a child on television and felt some of the old sexual arousal again?" The "correct" answer should reflect the application of a covert or overt aversive stimulus, escaping and avoiding the stimulus, and processing the situation with appropriate social supports and treating clinicians. A more specific statement would be, "Tell me how you have managed sexual arousal." Yet more specific would be to ask the individual what he knows about arousal reconditioning. Again, "better" answers in response to less specific questioning indicate greater progress in treatment.

Generic Mental Health Treatment

Much of the preceding focused on the sex offender-specific elements of treatment. However, much, if not most, of sex offender treatment is generic mental health treatment. Such treatment focuses on numerous and varied life skills, such as the ability to form and maintain relationships, including intimate relationships, obtain and retain employment, manage finances, balance work versus recreation versus relaxation, manage and tolerate affect, mourn losses, control impulses, appropriately and purposefully delay gratification, resolve trauma, communicate effectively, avoid abuse of psychoactive substances, maintain psychological resilience, seek and use assistance, and much more. Realistic plans and skills that will allow the offender to avoid or effectively cope with destabilizing or disinhibiting events should be the focus. Perfect mastery of the sex offender-specific elements of treatment is of no value if the individual cannot maintain adequate behavioral stability. Indeed, for a significant subset of offenders, aftercare focused on mental health will be more important than aftercare focused on sexual offending.

NEW JERSEY'S APPROACH TO THE ASSESSMENT OF TREATMENT PROGRESS

As discussed throughout this chapter, the accurate and reliable assessment of progress in treatment is the cornerstone of effective sex offender treatment. The forensic nature of sex offender treatment services is rarely as evident as when delivered in civil commitment settings, where offenders may be involved in court proceedings several times a year.

In their discussion of emerging principles in forensic treatment programs, Heilbrun and Griffin (1999), make the following recommendation, "Use of review boards and other administrative review mechanisms should improve decision making regarding privileging and release." Although some states have legislated the committee-based discharge decision-making model (see Minnesota and Massachusetts SVP laws, for example), the Special Treatment Unit, New Jersey's SVP program, has established a system of clinical oversight incorporating both internal and external review bodies. This system of checks and balances serves not only to inform the judicial decision-making process but also to preserve the therapeutic relationships so difficult to establish in civil commitment settings. Shuman, Greenberg, Heilbrun, and Foote (1998) go so far as to recommend that treating clinicians be barred from testifying about their patients in an effort to reduce the ethical conflicts inherent in the dual roles of forensic evaluator and therapist.

It is for this reason the Special Treatment Unit has established the Treatment Progress Review Committee (TPRC). The mission of this committee is to assess the treatment progress of each resident committed under the New Jersey Sexually Violent Predator Act. The committee's assessment is detailed in a written report and disseminated to the offender, his treatment team, the Clinical Assessment and Review Panel (CARP) and the court. As these evaluations are routinely submitted as evidence in court, it is imperative that the psychologists engaged in this practice follow accepted standards for conducting forensic psychological evaluations (Committee on Ethical

Guidelines for Forensic Psychologists, 1991). This includes a thorough review of available clinical and legal data, as well as consulting collateral sources of information to verify the offender's self-report.

The review conducted by the TPRC is the second of four levels of review. The first level of review is conducted by the resident's multidisciplinary treatment team. The third level is conducted by the CARP. CARP advises the medical director of the New Jersey Division of Mental Health Services, who is responsible for reviewing all recommendations for changes in privileging and conditional discharge of forensic patients from the Division of Mental Health Services facilities. The TPRC makes recommendations to the CARP as to progress in treatment, including current level of treatment. The fourth level of review is conducted by the court at the resident's commitment review hearing.

The TPRC will consist of at least three psychologists from the Special Treatment Unit staff. A committee chair for the TPRC, who also serves as a TPRC member, is appointed by the clinical director of the Special Treatment Unit.

Each resident is scheduled for in-person review by the TPRC at least once a year. At the conclusion of the review, the TPRC makes written recommendations in a report to CARP within thirty days of the TPRC meeting.

If the TPRC recommends that a resident be placed in Treatment Phase III (the core phase of treatment) or higher, final approval for this recommendation must be made by the CARP. The CARP notifies the TPRC of the final treatment phase determination within thirty days of receipt of the TPRC report.

In cases that are exceedingly complex, there may be disparate recommendations regarding treatment phase among TPRC members. In such cases, two reports will be written expressing the differing opinions and both reports will be sent to the CARP. The division medical director, in appropriate consultation with all relevant parties including CARP and the Special Treatment Unit administration, is responsible for making the final decision regarding the appropriate treatment phase. It is understood that placement into Phases III, IV, and V always require CARP approval. Thus, residents cannot progress into or through these phases of treatment without an in-person review by the TPRC and subsequent approval of the division medical director.

Assessment of a resident's progress through treatment is via a multidisciplinary, multilevel process. The first level of assessment occurs with the resident's multidisciplinary treatment team. Every six months, the treatment team will compile a TPRC that synopsizes the resident's treatment gains and goals. The first such report will be generated in six-month intervals after the beginning of treatment. TPRC reports address the following areas:

1. Major issues the resident has been discussing in treatment.

2. Quantity and quality of participation to address his own relevant treatment issues.

3. Quantity and quality of participation to help other group members.

4. Psychoeducational modules successfully completed, failed, to be retaken, feedback, etc.

5. Quantity and quality of participation in recreational activities.

6. Quantity and quality of participation in educational/rehabilitative activities.

7. Quantity and quality of participation in occupational activities including institutional job.

8. Quality of institutional adjustment especially regarding functioning on the housing unit.

9. Degree to which resident presents as having mastered sex offender-specific treatment goals.

10. Degree to which resident appears to take responsibility for offenses.

11. Degree to which resident displays remorse, empathy, relapse prevention skills, etc.

12. Degree to which progress in treatment seems likely to ameliorate the risk factors that initially resulted in civil commitment.

13. Goals for next six-month period and beyond.

14. Any other clinically relevant issues.

It is important to note that TPRCs are the product of the resident's multidisciplinary treatment team. Thus, all multidisciplinary treatment team members must participate in the writing of the report and sign to indicate that it meets their approval.

The resident's multidisciplinary treatment team may recommend advancement in phases in these reports or the resident's progress may speak for itself. At least once per year, each resident will be scheduled for in-person review by the TPRC. The TPRC will then evaluate the resident's progress in treatment using the TPR, consultations with treating clinicians, clinical interview of the resident, and any other relevant methods.

At the conclusion of an in-person evaluation, the TPRC will give verbal feedback to residents and treating clinicians regarding elements of treatment progress and treatment recommendations. Recommendations regarding the appropriate treatment phase, however, will only be made via written report.

It must be recognized that healthy functioning for the sexual offender, as for anyone, may vary on a moment-to-moment basis. In contrast, the goal of treatment is for the resident to achieve treatment gains that are sustainable and relatively stable over a lifetime. It must also be recognized that intellectual mastery of treatment concepts is necessary but not sufficient. Residents are expected to consistently "walk-the-walk" as well as they "talk-the-talk." Considering that any evaluative period is likely to be relatively short compared to the lifetime goal, setbacks will sometimes be encountered. Such therapeutic "decompensating" or "backsliding" may appropriately result in a resident being reverted to an earlier phase of treatment.

As is the case with all residents' records, TPRC reports are discoverable and all reasonable efforts will be made to have committee members available for providing testimony if required by either the attorney general or defense attorneys.

Procedures for TPRC Reviews

1. One week prior to the TPRC meeting, each TPRC member receives a packet of information which includes the resident's history (documents taken from the discov-

ery materials available on a resident,) as well as his treatment records and assessment team reports.

2. The resident is notified in writing one week in advance as to when he is scheduled to be interviewed by the TPRC.

3. At the meeting, the TPRC has a preliminary discussion of the case with a representative of the resident's treatment team for the purpose of obtaining his input, perspective, insight, and opinion.

4. When the TPRC is ready to interview the resident, he is provided with information on which to base whether or not he will consent to be interviewed by the committee. He can have a member of his treatment team present during the interview. He is told that he has the right not to be interviewed but should he not participate, that fact will be reflected in the TPRC's report. If the resident is not willing to be interviewed, the TPRC shall nevertheless make its assessment and issue a report.

5. After interviewing the resident, the TPRC confers with the treatment team representative(s). The TPRC then discusses with the treatment team representative(s) the resident's general progress in treatment, areas that the resident needs to address in treatment both short term and, where appropriate, long term, and a clinical case formulation. However, recommendations regarding treatment phase are not shared with either the resident or treatment team members until these recommendations are reviewed by the CARP. The exception to this is when Phase I or Phase II is recommended unanimously by the TPRC members. In such cases, the TPRC also communicates the treatment phase recommendation to the treatment team representative(s).

6. Subsequent to conferring with the treatment team representative(s), the TPRC deliberates in private regarding the appropriate treatment phase. It is important that TPRC treatment phase recommendations not be disclosed until the CARP has had a chance to complete its review. Recommendations about treatment phase are made via a multidisciplinary, hierarchical review process. Premature disclosure of TPRC recommendation of treatment phase fosters confusion and divisiveness. It can lead to a resident's feeling discouraged and unfairly treated.

7. Also in private, the TPRC considers other clinically sensitive issues such as the therapeutic relationship between treating clinicians and the resident and the overall quality of treatment. These clinically sensitive issues are generally not included in the TPRC report because such issues are more appropriately addressed in clinical supervision.

8. An individual TPRC member takes responsibility for synopsizing the TPRC assessment and recommendations in a report written on behalf of the TPRC. Upon completion of the report, it is reviewed by the committee chairperson and revised as appropriate. Copies of the report are distributed to the other TPRC members for their review and comments. Such comments, if any, are submitted to the primary author of the report as soon as possible and within one week.

9. After the TPRC and CARP reports are completed, the treatment team representative(s) are notified and copies of the reports are made available. Copies of the completed TPRC and CARP reports are also placed in the resident's chart.

The TPRC Report

The TPRC report is structured around three broad classifications of information:

1. Clinical and legal data.

2. Clinical case formulation and recommendations.

3. Clinical and factual support for the TPRC formulation and recommendations.

TPRC members are experts in understanding the differences between these classes of information. Such information is entered in the appropriate section of the TPRC report. Clinical and legal data will be documented in the sections titled Relevant Personal History, History of Sexual Behavior, Official Version of the Index Offense, Resident's Version of the Index Offense, and Course of Treatment to Date.

The clinical case formulation along with the clinical and factual support for the formulation and the recommendations are recorded in the sections titled Clinical Formulation and Treatment Recommendations.

A TPRC report includes the relevant data on which any inference or opinion is based. Generally, these data (and only data) appear in sections of the report devoted to history, past and present progress in treatment, and the examination of the resident. The report indicates which data were reported to the TPRC by the resident and which were reported by the treatment team. References to other clinical reports or opinions are clearly labeled and referenced. Only the data necessary to make the inferences which form the opinions expressed in the clinical formulation are included in the report.

CONCLUSION

In a variety of settings and from several perspectives, it is well established that the process of assessing sex offender treatment progress is important. In situations involving civil commitment, assessing treatment progress may readily be seen as being critical. This is evident in the pronounced need to balance public safety with individual liberties in such situations. Also to be considered in the process are general assessment issues such as validity, reliability, standards of practice, ethics, and more.

Currently, efforts to define treatment progress seem to be in their early stages. In even earlier stages are attempts to standardize the assessment of such progress. Continuing efforts are needed in both areas. Pending further progress in these areas, clinicians must use the available empirical evidence to best define treatment progress and to assess such progress. It is likely that useful sources of guidance may be found in assessment instruments that are currently undergoing validation such as the SOTRS, GAS, and TPS. Absent a well-standardized assessment instrument, it is recommended that clinicians rely on empirical evidence of factors that seem to contribute to reoffense risk. It is suggested that the best current practice is to use this empirical evidence along with sound clinical interviewing techniques to assess progress in treatment.

Future research efforts may wish to address the relationship between treatment progress and successful completion of treatment as well as outcome. Another area in need of empirical exploration is the synergistic effects of combining sex offender specific psychotherapy and community supervision as part of a comprehensive sex offender risk management approach.

Footnotes

[1] Kansas v. Hendricks, 521 U.S. 346 (1997).

References

Abel, G., Jordan, A., Hand, C. G., Holland, L. A., & Phipps, A. (2001). Classification models of child molesters utilizing the Abel Assessment for Sexual Interest. *Child Abuse and Neglect: The International Journal, 25*(5), 703–718.

Anderson, R. D., Gibeau, D., & D'Amora, B. A. (1995). The Sex Offender Treatment Rating Scale: Initial reliability data. *Sexual Abuse: A Journal of Research and Treatment, 7*(3), 221–227.

Burdon, W. M., & Gallagher, C. A. (2002). Coercion and sex offenders: Controlling sex-offending behavior through incapacitation and treatment. *Criminal Justice and Behavior, 29*(1), 87–109.

Committee on Ethical Guidelines for Forensic Psychologists. (1991). Specialty guidelines for forensic psychologists. *Law and Human Behavior, 15*(6), 655–665.

D'Silva, K., Duggan, C., & McCarthy, L. (2004). Does treatment really make psychopaths worse? A review of the evidence. *Journal of Personality Disorders, 18*(2), 163–177.

Doren, D. M. (2005). What weight should courts give to treaters' testimony concerning recidivism risk? *Sex Offender Law Report, 6*(1), 1–2 & 15.

Hanson, R. K. (1997). *The development of a brief actuarial risk scale for sexual offense recidivism* [Online]. Ottawa, Ontario: Department of the Solicitor General of Canada. Available: *www.psepc-sppcc.gc.ca/publications/corrections/199704_e.pdf*.

Hanson, R. K., & Bussière, M. T. (1998). Predicting relapse: A meta-analysis of sexual offender recidivism studies. *Journal of Consulting and Clinical Psychology, 66*(2), 348–362.

Hanson, R. K., & Harris, A. (2000a). *The Sex Offender Need Assessment Rating (SONAR): A method for measuring change in risk levels.* Ontario: Department of the Solicitor General of Canada.

Hanson, R. K., & Harris, A. (2000b). Where should we intervene? Dynamic predictors of sexual offense recidivism. *Criminal Justice and Behavior, 27*(1), 6–35.

Hanson, R. K., & Thornton, D. (1999). *Static 99: Improving actuarial risk assessment for sex offenders.* Ottawa, Ontario: Department of the Solicitor General of Canada.

Heilbrun, K., & Griffin, P. (1999). Forensic treatment: A review of programs and research. In R. Roesch, S. D. Hart, & J. R. P. Ogloff (Eds.), *Psychology and law: The state of the discipline* (pp. 241–374). New York: Kluwer.

Jenkins-Hall, K. (1994). Outpatient treatment of child molesters: Motivational factors and outcome. *Journal of Offender Rehabilitation, 21*, 139–150.

McGrath, R. J., Hoke, S. E., Livingston, S. A., & Cumming, G. (2001). *The Vermont Assessment of Sex-Offender Risk (VASOR): An initial reliability and validity study.* Paper presented at the 20th annual conference of the Association for the Treatment of Sexual Abusers, San Antonio, TX.

McGrath, R. J., Livingston, J., & Cumming, G. F. (2002). *Development of a treatment needs and progress scale for adult sex offenders.* Washington, DC: U.S. Department of Justice, Office of Justice Programs.

Miner, M. H. (2000). Competency-based Assessment. In D. R. Laws, S. M. Hudson, & T. Ward (Eds.), *Remaking relapse prevention with sex offenders: A sourcebook* (pp. 213–224). Thousand Oaks, CA: Sage.

Prendergrast, M. L., Farabee, D., Cartier, J., & Henkin, S. (2002). Involuntary treatment within a prison setting: Impact on psychosocial change during treatment. *Criminal Justice and Behavior, 29*(1), 5–26.

Prentky, R. A., & Burgess, A. W. (2000). *Forensic management of sexual offenders.* New York: Kluwer/Plenum Press.

Quinsey, V. L. (2000, March). *The Violence Risk Appraisal Guide.* Paper presented at Sinclair Seminars' Sex Offender Re-Offense Risk Prediction Symposium, Madison, Wisconsin. Available: *www.sinclairseminars.com*.

Rice, M. E., Harris, T. T., & Cormier, C. A. (1992). An evaluation of a maximum security therapeutic community for psychopaths and other mentally disordered offenders. *Law and Human Behavior, 16*, 399–412.

Schwartz, B. K. (1995). Group therapy. In B. K. Schwartz & H. R. Cellini (Eds.), *The sex offender: Corrections, treatment, and legal practice* (pp. 14-1–14-16). Kingston, NJ: Civic Research Institute.

Seto, M. C. (2003). Interpreting the treatment performance of sex offenders. In A. Matravers (Ed.), (2003). *Sex offenders in the community: Managing and reducing the risks.* Portland, OR: Willian.

Seto, M. C., & Barbaree, H. E. (1999). Psychopathy, treatment behavior, and sex offender recidivism. *Journal of Interpersonal Violence, 14*(12), 1235–1248.

Seto, M. C., & Barbaree, H. E. (2003). *Psychopathy, treatment behavior, and recidivism: An extended follow-up of Seto and Barbaree (1999).* Manuscript submitted for publication.

Shuman, D. W., Greenberg, S., Heilbrun, K., & Foote, W. E. (1998). Special perspective an immodest proposal: Should treating mental health professionals be barred from testifying about their patients? *Behavioral Sciences and the Law, 16,* 509–523.

Simpson, D. D., & Knight, K., (1998). *TCU data collection forms for correctional residential treatment.* Fort Worth: Texas Christian University, Institute of Behavioral Research.

Stripe, T. S., Wilson, R. J., & Long, C. (2001). Goal attainment scaling with sexual offenders: A measure of clinical impact at post-treatment and at community follow-up. *Sexual Abuse: A Journal of Research and Treatment, 13,* 65–77.

Appendix A
TPRC Report Protocol
Treatment Progress Review Committee
Annual Review Report

A. Name: SVP #

B. Date of Birth:

C. Date of Initial Commitment:

D. Date of Present Assessment:

E. Phase of Treatment Recommendation:

Must include recommendation of committee. If there is a split decision, the decision of each member must be noted.

F. Action To Be Taken:

Should include a description of what needs to happen next.

1. If TPRC's decision is unanimous and recommends placement in Phase One or Two, this Phase of treatment placement is finalized and listed in the resident's chart.

2. If TPRC's decision is unanimous and recommends placement above Phase II, the report and recommendation shall be submitted to CARP for review. CARP will issue a written decision regarding the resident's Treatment Phase placement and that decision will be noted in the resident's chart.

3. If TPRC's decision is unanimous and recommends that the resident be moved from a higher to a lower Phase, the report and recommendation shall be submitted to CARP for review. CARP will issue a written decision regarding the resident's Treatment Phase placement and that decision will be noted in the resident's chart.

4. If TPRC's decision is a split decision, the two reports and recommendations shall be submitted to CARP for review. CARP will issue a written decision regarding the resident's Treatment Phase placement and that decision will be noted in the resident's chart.

G. Committee Members:

Must include name and title of each committee member.

H. Treatment Team Members Present:

Must include name and title of each treatment team member present and indication of whether the treatment team member was interviewed.

I. Informed Consent:

1. In this section the TPRC must confirm that it explained to the resident that:

a. the individuals present were members of the TPRC and employees of the Department of Human Services at the STU.

b. the purpose of the TPRC is to review the resident's progress in treatment and to make recommendations regarding the resident's Phase-of-treatment placement.

c. the resident has the right to refuse to participate in the interview and that, if he chooses not to participate this will be noted in the report and the TPRC will issue a report without the benefit of his input.

d. the resident has the right to refuse to answer specific questions or to terminate the interview at any time.

e. the resident will be given verbal feedback at the end of the review and a copy of the report when finalized, and that the TPRC's report will be filed in his record and that members of the TPRC may be called to testify about their findings by the defense attorney or Deputy Attorney General, and

2. The TPRC must also confirm in writing that the resident was asked to repeat in his own words the above statement of informed consent and, after doing so to the satisfaction of the TPRC, the interview commenced.

J. Sources of Information:

K. Relevant Personal History:

1. In this section the TPRC may quote from prior STU Assessment Team reports, for example:

"According to Dr. X's psychological assessment report dated April 1, 2000: [Insert entire history section from the prior report.]"

2. Attention should be given to the following areas:

a. History of mental functioning and psycho social adaptation (developmental, family, educational, military, employment, marital, psychiatric and relevant medical history).

b. Substance abuse.

c. Treatment history prior to commitment at the STU.

d. History of aggressive, antisocial or harmful behavior to others, whether or not criminal justice system was involved.

L. History of Sexual Behavior:

1. Sexual History:

In this section the TPRC should discuss (or set out) the nature, quality and quantity of the resident's sexual experiences for example including age of resident when the offenses were committed and type of sexual encounter, nature of masturbatory fantasies, evidence of (additional) paraphilias, use of pornography, history of sexual trauma and victimization.

2. Sex Offense History:

This section should include information about sexually aggressive behavior (whether or not the criminal justice system was involved). Although it does not have to be an exhaustive recitation, it should include the most relevant data regarding behavior topographies, victim-seeing behaviors, victim characteristics, use of violence, extent to which violence was eroticized, associated frequency(ies), recency and trend(s) of behavior (s), and specific situational factors (i.e. employment and living circumstances, lifestyle, mental status, use of disinhibiting substances, recent losses or other stresses believed to be related to the offending behavior.

Again, segments from prior assessment reports where appropriate may be quoted.

M. Official Version of the Index Offense:

This must be taken from police or court records or the Petition for Civil Commitment.

N. Resident's Version of the Index Offense:

This must be based on the TPRC's interview of the resident or, if he refuses to be interviewed, on his most recent treatment records.

O. Course of Treatment at the STU to Date:

A description of relevant treatment experiences and the resident's response should be set out in this section. Current treatment issues and needs should also be identified. When possible, issues related to the resident's relapse prevention knowledge and abilities should be addressed. At a minimum, you must:

1. Document Modules and Treatment Groups

2. Provide a Summary of the Treatment Team's Presentation of Treatment Progress and

3. Provide a Summary of the Resident's Presentation of Treatment Progress.

P. Clinical Formulation and Treatment Recommendations:

The clinical formulation should refer to the previously cited empirical data and clearly state the rationale for opinions regarding appropriate Phase of treatment and specific treatment recommendations. In all cases, a summary of DSM-IV diagnoses and sex offender risk assessment scales is incorporated into the clinical formulation.

An example of what should be included in this section would be as follows:

"Based on today's review, Mr. X presented negligible familiarity with events which trigger him to assault female children over an extended (15 year) period of time. He downplayed the role of mind altering substances in his offending behavior while his history suggests the presence of alcohol and other drugs such as cocaine in his system while luring children from a play ground to his car. He denies any past or continuing sexual arousal to children and instead blames his behavior on deteriorating relationships with adult females. To this end, there is no evidence that he has developed a Relapse Prevention plan that will assist him to abstain from drinking when under pressure and he continues to minimize the role deviant arousal played in his offenses.

Based on today's review the resident's progress in treatment, Phase 2 seems appropriate for this man. In this Phase, Mr. X is encouraged to,

(make specific treatment recommendations)."

Respectfully submitted on behalf of the TPRC,

_____

Clinician authoring report

Chapter 12

Implications of Cognitive Rigidity in the Civilly Committed Sex Offender Population

by Anita Schlank, Ph.D.

INTRODUCTION

Many treatment providers who work with repeat sexual offenders have often observed evidence of neuropsychological deficits, although they might not routinely study these observations. Some providers have noted a specific tendency for cognitive rigidity in these offenders, as evidenced by their difficulty in generalizing information from group to another setting. In addition, repeat sexual offenders often appear to have a tendency to consider only one or two alternative solutions to problems and a tendency to view a situation from only one perspective (Bergman & Schlank, 2004). Such cognitive rigidity can interfere with an offender's progress in treatment, which becomes of particular concern in civil commitment programs. In those programs, a lack of progress by residents may lead to administrative pressure due to the cost of the program, and it may lead to hopelessness on the part of new residents because successful discharges are slow. Therefore, it is an area that deserves more detailed investigation.

NEUROPSYCHOLOGICAL FINDINGS IN SEX OFFENDER POPULATIONS

Many researchers have noted the correlation between neuropsychological deficits and general violent behavior (Foster, Hillbrand, & Silverstein, 1993; Krynicki, 1978; Spellacy, 1977), and the question of whether sexually deviant behavior is linked with brain pathology has also been the subject of many studies (Lang, 1993; Langevin, Ben-Aron, Wortzman, Dickey, & Handy, 1987; Regestein & Reich, 1978; Scott, Cole, McKay, Golden, & Liggett, 1984; Tarter, Hegedus, Alterman, & Katz-Garris, 1983). The role of possible dysfunction of the frontal lobes has been of particular interest. For example, Yeudall and Fromm-Auch (1979) investigated neuropsychological impairments in several populations, including sexual offenders, and found that 96 percent of the sex offenders had abnormal results in neuropsychological testing. The abnormality they found appeared to be localized exclusively in the frontotemporal regions of the brain. Lishman (1968) found a link between frontal lobe damage and hypersexuality, criminality, and sexual offenses. In 1990, Galski, Thornton, and Shumsky gave a neuropsychological test battery to incarcerated sexual offenders. In their study, a high percentage (49 percent) showed neuropsychological impairment according to the criteria for interpretation of the Luria-Nebraska Neuropsychological Battery (Golden, Hammeke, & Purisch, 1980), and others showed significant elevations on one or two scales of the battery. They also found that violent sexual offenses were found to be predicted by deficits in neuropsychological functioning, at a statistically significant level. It was also noted that these subjects did not demonstrate any gross evidence of neurological disorders, so their organic brain impairment appeared to be "subclinical." Stone and Thompson (2001) found similar deficits in executive functioning in their study of sixty-three sexual offenders.

EXECUTIVE FUNCTIONING

There is some disagreement about which cognitive processes are truly "executive functions"; however, there appears to be some consensus that executive functions include the processes that enable us to plan behavior and work toward some goal, incorporating feedback and making adjustments along the way. They include the ability to plan for the future, the ability to inhibit or delay responding, and the ability to shift between activities flexibly. Self-monitoring and emotional control are also often included as part of the executive functions. Michaels (2001) notes that one of the most complex of the executive functions is the ability to apply rules of social interactions, such as reading facial expressions, interpreting behavior inappropriately, or being unable to make appropriate decisions based on observations of other's behavior. Luria (1966) believed that executive functions allowed a person to evaluate the success or failure of their behaviors, and Lezak (1982) believed that executive functions were the core of all socially useful abilities. She also believed that deficient executive functioning may result in a lack of self-control, irritability, impulsivity rigidity, and difficulty in shifting attention. These "executive" processes are most often associated with the frontal or prefrontal lobe. Disorders such as attention deficit hyperactivity disorder, obsessive-compulsive disorder, and depression are known to be associated with deficits of executive functioning.

EXECUTIVE FUNCTIONING AND CIVILLY COMMITTED SEXUAL OFFENDERS

Given that many sexual offenders appear to show some deficits in executive functioning, it seemed likely that those assessed to be the most dangerous, most disordered, and most treatment resistant would show significant deficits in that area. Bergman and Schlank (2004) presented on the prevalence of mild deficits in executive functioning in a population of civilly committed sexual offenders. In that study, all new admissions to a civil commitment program for sexual offenders over a period of approximately seven years who agreed to be evaluated for treatment planning purposes were assessed using many different tests and tools, including the Shipley Institute of Living Scale (Shipley & Zachary, 1940/1986), the COGNISTAT (Neurobehavioral Cognitive Status Exam; Kiernan, Mueller, & Langston, 2002) and the Wisconsin Card Sorting Test (WCST; Kongs, Thompson, Iverson, & Heaton, 1993).

The Shipley Institute of Living Scale is a very brief screening test that provides an estimate of intellectual functioning. If this screening test suggests functioning in the borderline or mentally retarded range, it is often beneficial to then use a more comprehensive assessment of intellectual abilities.

The COGNISTAT is a brief screening test that separately assesses ten different domains of cognitive functioning. Subscales include assessments of attention, orientation, comprehension, language repetition, word finding, memory, arithmetic, abstract reasoning, and logical problem-solving.

The WCST is a measure of executive functioning and is particularly sensitive to frontal lobe deficits. The test consists of 4 stimulus cards and 128 response cards. The response cards depict figures of varying forms (crosses, circles, triangles, or stars). These cards differ in shape, color of the forms, and the number of figures on each card (one, two, three, or four). The stimulus cards are placed in front of the subject and the client is then asked to match each consecutive card from the deck with one of the four stimulus cards. The client is told only whether each response is right or wrong, but no information about the sorting principle used is provided, and the sorting principle changes without warning to the client. Successful completion of the test requires concentration, abstract reasoning, problem-solving abilities, and the ability to inhibit impulsive responding. In addition, performance on this test assesses the client's ability to incorporate feedback form the environment into adaptations of his or her problem-solving approach.

For the newly admitted civilly committed sexual offenders, test scores for any offender who fell in the mentally retarded range of intellectual functioning were not included in the study, as deficits in executive functioning would be expected due to their intellectual deficits. In addition, offenders who reported a history of serious head injury with subsequent cognitive impairments or who showed serious impairment on the COGNISTAT were also not considered for this study, as their head injury would provide a confounding variable. The scores on the WCST for the remaining seventy-seven offenders were compared to the means obtained from the population on which this test was normed. It was hypothesized that the sexual offenders who were committed would differ significantly in their scores on the WCST, and results did support this hypothesis. When analyzed using a one-sample *t*-test, the civilly committed sexual offenders scored significantly worse on many aspects of the WCST.

One aspect of the WCST on which the civilly committed sexual offenders showed impairment was the number of categories completed. In the WCST, the test ends when the client has successfully sorted six categories, or after the last of the 128 cards has been used. Those clients who are rigid in their thinking, have impulsive responding, and/or have poor abstract reasoning and problem solving skills will have completed

Figure 12.1
Comparison on Wisconsin Card Sorting Test

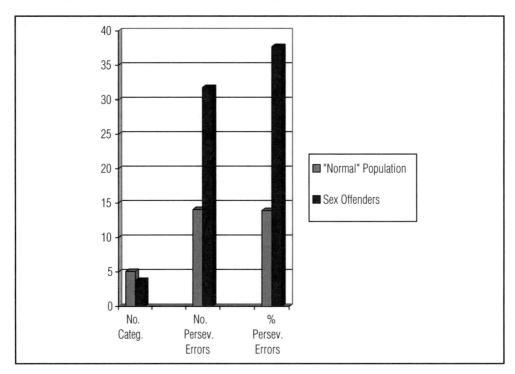

fewer categories by the end of the test. In the "normal" population, the mean number of categories completed was 5.07, but the mean for the civilly committed sex offender population was only 3.77, which was significantly lower (see Figure 12.1).

In the WCST, "perseverative errors" are repetitive errors made when a client continues to sort according to one sorting rule after being informed that such an effort is incorrect. Frequent perseverative errors are suggestive of cognitive rigidity and difficulty "shifting set" from one way of looking at things to another. In the study presented, the "normal" population had a mean of 14.05 perseverative errors (or 13.9 percent of their errors), while the civilly committed sex offender population had a mean of 31.77 perseverative errors (or 49.34 percent of their errors). These numbers were highly significant (using a T-test) and indicated far more rigid thinking on the part of the sexual offenders (see Figure 12.1).

IMPACT ON TREATMENT PROGRESS

The identification of mild neuropsychological deficits in sexual offenders could be extremely important for treatment planning. Because the main orientation of most sex offender treatment programs is cognitive-behavioral (Freeman-Longo & Knopp, 1992, Knopp, Stevenson, & Freeman-Longo, 1992; Marshall, Laws, & Barbaree, 1990; Marshall & Pithers, 1994), and because most programs focus on the improvement of cognitive skills such as problem solving (Neidigh, 1991), the presence of cognitive deficits in sex offenders could have significant implications for progress in treatment. This is particularly important in the population of civilly committed sexual offenders, as successful treatment of those offenders who have been identified as the highest risk and most disordered in a prison population is likely to take an extensive amount of time, even without barriers to their response to treatment.

Relapse prevention is a model that has been demonstrated to be effective in the treatment of some sexual offenders. It is a model that focuses on analyzing past behavior, identifying factors that can contribute to reoffending, and incorporating both cognitive and behavioral strategies to prevent future offending. For treatment to have long-term benefit, the client must be able to process the new information and integrate it with existing knowledge about his history. The ability to see a situation from more than one perspective is important, as is the ability to generate alternative approaches to problem situations. A client with deficits of executive functions will have more difficulty using this approach. For example, one sexual offender who suffered from mild mental retardation stated that he had been struggling with deviant sexual urges for many years. He indicated that he had dealt with these urges by forcing himself to leave the situation and go to the bar and drink himself nearly to the point of unconsciousness. When discussing why he had finally acted on the deviant urges and committed a sexual offense, he stated that he had stopped drinking and was avoiding bars, and could not think of anywhere else to go. In that case a client with limited intellectual abilities had been naturally attempting to use a principle of relapse prevention (removing himself from the environment that triggers the deviant urges), but his cognitive deficits interfered with the effectiveness of his control attempts. If similar cognitive deficits such as rigidity are identified in sexual offenders who are not intellectually deficient, specific interventions to address those deficits are likely to enhance the client's ability to use all other techniques espoused in treatment.

TREATMENTS TO ADDRESS COGNITIVE DEFICITS

There is good reason to believe that cognitive deficits in sexual offenders can be addressed through cognitive remediation, based on the literature available regarding individuals with severe and persistent mental illness (SPMI). There is a vast literature describing the variety and severity of cognitive deficits present in patients suffering from SPMI, particularly schizophrenic spectrum disorders. Most rehabilitation efforts to address these deficits use "mental exercises," focusing on specific cognitive tasks, such as attentional abilities. There is evidence that cognitive remediation programs, such as those used with the head-injured populations, can significantly help improve areas of concentration, attention and generalization of skills in the SPMI population. (Cassidy, Easton, Capelli, Singer, & Bilodeau, 1996; Schlank, 1987; de la Higuera Romero, 2003; Silverstein, Hitzel, & Schenkel, 1998; Spaulding et al., 1999).

Even some very simple cognitive-behavioral techniques appear to be successful at addressing some cognitive deficits. For example, Schlank (1987) studied a method for improving the problem solving of individuals who were psychiatrically hospitalized with SPMI. Eight members of a problem-solving therapy group in a state psychiatric facility in Nebraska were evaluated weekly, with a numerical rating assigned to their problem-solving abilities each week. Members of this group were also randomly assigned to one of two subgroups. One group received cognitive-behavioral interven-

tions to additionally improve their problem-solving abilities. The examiner did not
inform the group leaders of the makeup of each subgroup. Subgroup One met weekly for eight sessions of thirty minutes. During those sessions, they were instructed to
create as many different stories as they could for each card in the Thematic
Apperception Test (TAT), a widely used projective test that helps assess an individual's
perceptions of interpersonal relationships (Murray, 1943/1971). Throughout the sessions, the trainer used investigator modeling, feedback, and assistance in self-instructional statements in an effort to help the subject improve his or her performance (i.e.,
create more stories with fewer perseverated items). Self-instructional statements
included such questions as "how can I make this story different?," "What else could
this person be doing?" or "How else could they know each other." The second subgroup also met weekly for eight thirty-minute sessions; however, for the first four
weeks they did not participate in the cognitive training exercise but instead received
nondirective, supportive counseling, in order to control for the Hawthorne Effect (a
positive programmatic response that is due to the attention received by the program
participants rather than to the content of the program). During the final four weeks,
they too began the previously described cognitive training exercise. Scores were
recorded on members for each subgroup for the number of stories created for each
card and the number of perseverative items. In addition to these scores, the rating
received from each subject's problem-solving therapy group and a weekly evaluation
of ward behavior was also recorded. The weekly evaluation of ward behavior was not
expected to have shown significant changes following the initiation of the cognitive
training exercises.

Results were analyzed using a repeated analysis of variance (ANOVA) measure
(see Figure 12.2) and showed a marginally significant finding for increase in mean
number of stories following the cognitive retraining. Even more significant, however,
was the effect this intervention appeared to have on general problem-solving ability.
Figure 12.3 shows the mean progress rating received in the problem-solving therapy
group by each subgroup over the twelve-week period during which they attended their
problem-solving group sessions. To analyze the specific effect of the individual cog-

Figure 12.2
Number of TAT Stories Generated

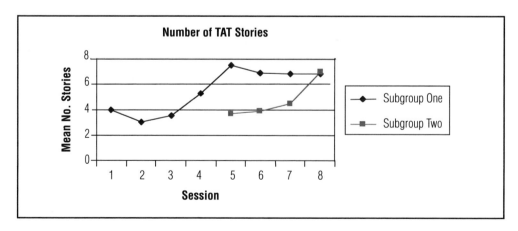

Figure 12.3
Problem-Solving Group Progress Rating

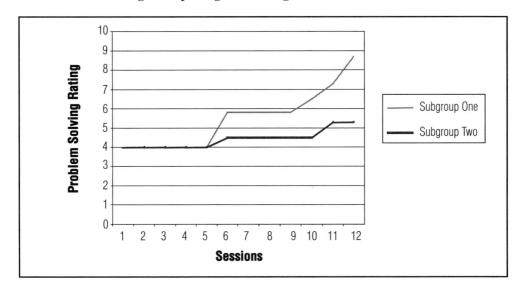

Figure 12.4
Problem-Solving Ratings

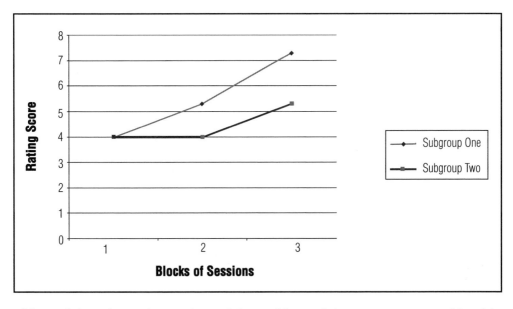

nitive training, the twelve sessions of the problem solving group were considered in terms of three blocks of four sessions each. The first block consisted of four sessions during which neither group received any cognitive therapy exercises. Block two consisted of four sessions during which only Subgroup One was involved in cognitive therapy exercises, and the final block consisted of sessions during which both subgroups received cognitive therapy. Data analysis showed a significant difference for Subgroup One in the ratings received when comparing block one to block two and also when comparing block two to block three. Subgroup Two showed no significant difference in their problem-solving ratings from block one to block two but did show a significant difference in problem-solving ratings when comparing block two to block three, after cognitive therapy exercises began (see Figure 12.4). The independent measure of the nurses' observation of ward behavior showed no significant changes during the period studied, which indicated that the improvements seen on the problem-solving measure were not the result of nonspecific improvement in the patients' condition. The data showed that the treatment effect was highly specific, detectible in the block in which it was delivered, and it exerted an effect over the four subsequent weeks within the block. The cognitive retraining sessions did appear to greatly improve patients' overall problem-solving ability.

If individuals suffering from severe and persistent mental illness can show relatively rapid improvement in their cognitive rigidity through specialized interventions, it appears likely that similar progress can be seen with sexual offenders who also suffer such a deficit. One tool available for addressing such deficits, but not likely to be found in most sex offender treatment programs is the Whole Brain Game (Creative Mind Games, 1989). This is a game for two or more players (age 11 and older), which takes two or more very different words or situations and forces the player to see similarities. Creativity and generation of the most alternatives are rewarded. It is a fast-paced game, and proficiency at this game appears likely to generalize to an ability to "think on one's feet" in daily life.

Another method for addressing cognitive rigidity is the use of dramatherapy techniques. Lang (1993) has suggested that role-play techniques, right-brain imagery, and other action-oriented therapies which rely on right-brain strategies can be used with offenders suffering from frontal-lobe deficits, including cognitive rigidity. Bergman and Hewish (2003) suggest some specific dramatherapy techniques for improving cognitive flexibility, such as the "Fortunately/Unfortunately," "Sleep Interruptions," "The Room that Spoke," and "Curiosity Kaleidoscope" exercises. Utilization of such techniques appears likely to stimulate movement in the "stuck" offender, and assist with the incorporation of other tools learned in therapy. It is noted that from 1996 to 2003, all residents who had earned their way to the transition stage of the Minnesota Sexual Offender Program had participated in the voluntary intensive dramatherapy sessions that were conducted several times a year by John Bergman, M.A., R.D.T.

SUMMARY AND FUTURE DIRECTIONS

Many sexual offenders appear to suffer from mild deficits in their executive functioning. These deficits are likely to interfere with their ability to fully benefit from the cognitive-behavioral techniques that are used in treatment programs. This is of particular concern with the population of civilly committed sexual offenders, as there is evidence that this population is particularly slow in meeting treatment goals. Fortunately, there are interventions available that are effective in addressing such deficits. Cognitive restructuring techniques aimed specifically at these deficits and the use of dramatherapy exercises can be helpful adjuncts to a sex offender treatment program. Treatment providers of civil commitment programs for sexual offenders are likely to see better results if new admissions are screened for deficits in executive functioning, and interventions aimed specifically at any identified deficits become a standard part of the residents' individualized treatment plans.

References

Bergman, J., & Hewish, S. (2003). *Challenging experience: An experiential approach to offender treatment.* Oklahoma City, OK: Wood 'N Barnes.

Bergman, J., & Schlank, A. (2004). *Addressing cognitive inflexibility in sexual offenders.* Workshop presented at the 22nd annual Research and Treatment Conference of the Association for the Treatment of Sexual Abusers, Albuquerque, NM.

Cassidy, J. J., Easton, M., Capelli, C., Singer, A., & Bilodeau, A. (1996, Winter). Cognitive remediation of persons with severe and persistent mental illness. *Psychiatric Quarterly, 67*(4), 313–321.

Creative Mind Games. (1989). *The whole brain game* [Online]. Available: *www.creative mindgames.com.*

de la Higuera Romero, J. (2003). Rehabilitation of cognitive function in patients with severe mental disorder: A pilot study using the cognitive modules of the IPT program. *Psychology in Spain, 79*(1), 77–85.

Foster, H.G., Hillbrand, M. & Silverstein, M. (1993). Neuropsychological deficit and aggressive behavior: A prospective study. *Progress in Neuropsychopharmacological Biological Psychiatry, 17*(6), 939–946.

Freeman-Longo, R. E., & Knopp, F. H. (1992). State-of-the-art sex offender treatment: Outcome and issues. *Annals of Sex Research, 5*, 141–160.

Galski, T., Thornton, K., & Shumsky, D. (1990). Brain dysfunction in sex offenders. *Journal of Offender Rehabilitation, 16*, 65–80.

Golden, C. J., Hammeke, T. A., & Purisch, A. D. (1980). *The Luria-Nebraska Neuropsychological Battery manual.* Available: Western Psychological Services, 12031 Wilshire Boulevard, Los Angeles, California 90025.

Kiernan, R. J., Mueller, J., & Langston, J. W. (2002). *COGNISTAT: Neurobehavioral Cognitive Status Exam* [Online]. Available: *www.parinc.com.*

Knopp, F. H., Stevenson, W. F., & Freeman-Longo, R. E. (1992). *Nationwide Survey of Adolescent and Adult Sex Offender Treatment Programs and Models.* Orwell, VT: Safer Society Press.

Kong, S. K., Thompson, L. L., Iverson, G. L., & Heaton, R. K. (1993). *Wisconsin Card Sorting Test—64 card version* [Online]. Available: *www.parinc.com.*

Krynicki, V. (1978). Cerebral dysfunction in repetitively assaultive adolescents. *Journal of Nervous and Mental Disease, 166*, 59–67.

Lang, R. A. (1993). Neuropsychological deficits in sexual offenders: Implications for treatment. *Sexual and Marital Therapy, 6*(2), 181–200.

Langevin, R., Ben-Aron, M., Wortzman, G., Dickey, R., & Handy, L. (1987). Brain damage, diagnosis, and substance abuse among violent offenders. *Behavioral Sciences and the Law, 5*(1), 77–94.

Lezak, M. D. (1982). The problem of assessing executive functions. *International Journal of Psychology.* 17, 281–297.

Lishman, M. (1968). Brain damage in relation to psychiatric disability after head injury. *British Journal of Psychiatry, 114*(509), 373–410.

Marshall, W. L., Laws, D. R., & Barbaree, H. E. (1900). *The handbook of sexual assault: Issues, theories, and treatment of the offender.* New York: Plenum Press.

Marshall, W. L., & Pithers, W. D. (1994). A reconsideration of treatment outcome with sex offenders. *Criminal Justice and Behavior, 21*(1), 10–27.

Michaels, A. (2001). *Executive functioning* [Online]. Available: *www.aspennj.org/executive.html.*

Murray, H. A. (1971). *Thematic Apperception Test* [Online]. Available: *www.pearson assessments.com.* (Original work published 1943)

Neidigh, L., & Tomiko, R. (1991). The coping strategies of sexual abusers. *Journal of Sex Education and Therapy, 17*, 103–110.

Regestein, Q. R., & Reich, P. (1978) Pedophilia occurring after onset of cognitive impairment. *Journal of Nervous and Mental Disease, 166,* 794–798.

Schlank, A. (1987). *Improving schizophrenic inpatients' problem solving skills: A cognitive-behavioral approach.* Unpublished research-other-than-thesis project submitted in partial fulfillment of a Ph.D. in clinical psychology, University of Nebraska-Lincoln.

Scott, M. L., Cole, J. K., McKay, S. E., Golden, C. J., & Liggett, K. R. (1984). Neuropsychological performance of sexual assaulters and pedophiles. *Journal of Forensic Sciences, 29,* 1114–1118.

Shipley, W. C., & Zachary, R. A. (1986). *Shipley Institute of Living Scale* [Online]. Available: *www.wpspublish.com.* (Original work published 1940)

Silverstein, S. M., Hitzel, H., & Schenkel, L. (1998). Rehab rounds: Identifying and addressing cognitive barriers to rehabilitation readiness. *Psychiatric Services, 49,* 34–36.

Spaulding, W., Fleming, S. K., Reed, D., Sullivan, M. Storzbach, D., & Lam, M. (1999). Cognitive functioning in schizophrenia: Implications for psychiatric rehabilitation. *Schizophrenia Bulletin, 25,* 275–289.

Spellacy, F. (1977). Neuropsychological differences between violent and nonviolent adolescents. *Journal of Clinical Psychology, 23,* 965–969.

Stone, M. H., & Thompson, E. H. (2001). Executive function impairment in sexual offenders. *Journal of Individual Psychology, 57*(1).

Tarter, R. E., Hegedus, A. M., Alterman, A. I., & Katz-Garris, L. (1983). Cognitive capacities of juvenile violent, nonviolent and sexual offenders. *Journal of Nervous and Mental Disease, 171,* 564–567

Yeudall, L. T., & Fromm-Auch, D. (1979). Neuropsychological impairment in various psychopathological populations. In J. Gruzelier & P. Flor-Henry (Eds.), *Hemisphere assymmetries of function and psychopathology* (pp. 5–13). New York: Elsevier.

Chapter 13

Evolution of the Special Commitment Center Program

by Vince Gollogly, Ph.D.

INTRODUCTION

Washington State passed its law for sexually violent predators in 1990, making it one of the first in the new wave of civil commitment statutes. Since that time, several states have modeled their laws on Washington's statute. Washington also gained national attention when the federal district court placed the state's program under injunction, and appointed a Special Master to ensure that the state improve deficiencies in the program. This chapter provided a detailed chronological account of the events surrounding the evolution of this high-profile treatment program. Although this account is specific to the Washington program, it will be useful for readers in other jurisdictions as well.

CIVIL COMMITMENT TASK FORCE

The outrage over a horrendous sexual mutilation murder of a 7-year-old boy in 1989 led to the governor of Washington appointing a task force on community protection to examine the shortcomings of the law and make recommendations regarding perceived weaknesses in the laws concerning sexual offenders.

The task force recommended the use of civil commitment procedures to confine and provide treatment for offenders with histories of violent and predatory sexual offenses who had reached the end of their maximum prison term and were not suitable for confinement under the provisions of state mental health law. In 1990 the Washington State Legislature adopted the recommendations and passed the Community Protection Act,[1] which allowed civil commitment for a small but extremely dangerous group of inmates found to meet the definition of sexually violent predator (SVP). This act also created the Special Commitment Center (SCC) and additionally mandated the registration of all sex offenders who are released from prison and stiffer penalties for sexual offenders. Under the Community Protection Act, persons judged to be SVPs are subject to indefinite commitment at the SCC after completion of their criminal sentences. For an individual to be confined at SCC as an SVP he had to have been convicted of a sexually violent offense or charged with a crime of sexual violence. He also needed to suffer from either a mental abnormality or personality disorder affecting his volitional capacity which predisposes the person to commit criminal and sexual acts if not confined in a secure facility.

OPENING OF THE SPECIAL COMMITMENT CENTER

In 1991 it was determined that the Special Commitment Center should be operated by the Department of Social and Health Services (DSHS), because it is a public mental health treatment program, not a criminal justice program. Initially, the SCC program was located in Monroe, Washington, and was housed in one of the four wings of the Special Offender Unit of the Department of Corrections (DOC), where psychiatrically decompensating mentally ill residents were detained. DSHS hired the unit staff to run the SCC program, but security, meals, and transportation were provided under contract by the DOC.

The first SCC superintendent was appointed in 1990. The first resident came to SCC in the fall of 1990. This resident was placed in the wing designated for SCC, but the DOC still maintained in this wing a program for developmentally disabled offenders who were violent and mentally ill. As more SCC residents entered onto the unit, friction between residents and inmates was inevitable. SCC residents complained that some inmates were screaming all night, preventing them from sleeping. Eventually, the DOC terminated its program and the inmates were moved to different prisons in the state.

There was a rather slow growth in the number of residents placed into SCC, with six or seven residents only in the first two or three years. Procedures and policies were written for SCC and were based on DOC policies and on policies obtained from Atascadero State Hospital in California, which had a sex offender treatment program.

Roxanne Lieb (2003), director of the Washington State Institute for Public Policy, noted that Dr. Vernon Quinsey visited the program in 1992 at the request of the Washington State Institute for Public Policy (an agency mandated by the 1990 Community Protection Act to evaluate the effectiveness of state supported programs for sexual offenders). At that time, there were nine residents, with only three of those residents engaged in the treatment program. Quinsey noted that the ambiguous constitutional status of the law created great uncertainty and many residents were waiting to see if the law would be declared unconstitutional. He concluded that everything was "on hold" until the legal issues were addressed more definitely. He stated that residents have particular reasons to perceive the law as arbitrary and excessive, as they had completed their criminal sentence, and that this made it extremely difficult for program staff to form a therapeutic alliance with "an embittered clientele" (Quinsey, 1992). Most of the residents considered that they would get released through litigation rather than through completing a treatment program. Quinsey recommended separation between residents awaiting a commitment trial and those already committed, and separation between those residents in treatment and those not participating in treatment, because otherwise there would be a negative effect on treatment participation. For those residents not in treatment, long-term living arrangements were needed that offered opportunities for education, recreation, and personal development. He recommended that the state change the law and allow for a gradual release mechanism, so residents who had progressed in treatment could be tested for release readiness in stages.

At that time, clinical staff members consisted of psychologists and forensic therapists (FTs), who typically had a master's degree. Nonclinical staff members were hired as psychiatric security attendants (PSAs). It was not until 1996 that it was decided to change the title of the psychiatric security attendant to residential rehabilitation counselor. The FT made all the decisions on the unit and could authorize PSAs to conduct strip searches of residents if they had cause for suspicion.

The clinical staff had very limited experience in working with sex offenders. They used manuals from the Atascadero Hospital Sex Offender Treatment Program and the Colorado Sex Offender Program and commenced running groups. It was not until September 1994 that the FT supervisor was hired, and he was the first person hired with any specific sex offender experience. At the time he joined the SCC there were twenty residents, but only five or six were involved in treatment. This supervisor, who still works for SCC, reports that when he joined SCC, the treatment program consisted of treatment groups held three times per week and a few psychoeducational modules and a relapse prevention class. An evaluation team was set up comprising two psychologists, a social worker, and a registered nurse. The treatment program was very primitive and there was no impetus to change it until one of the residents was successful in filing a lawsuit challenging the program.

TURAY LAWSUIT

In 1991, one of the SCC residents, Richard Turay, brought an action against SCC employees[2] complaining that the following deprived residents of their constitutional rights: inadequate policies regarding security, physical movement, visitation, and mail; failure to provide adequate mental health treatment; and failure to provide educational, vocational, exercise, and recreational opportunities. He also complained that he had been subjected to an unlawful probe search.

The residents fully supported Turay and, as a sign of solidarity, just prior to the court hearing, all residents at SCC dropped out of treatment. They expected him to prevail in his case. However, at trial in 1994, he prevailed on only one issue—denial of access to constitutionally adequate mental health treatment. In June 1994, Judge William Dwyer of the federal district court in King County subsequently ordered an Order and Injunction to provide Turay with access to mental health treatment that would give him a realistic opportunity to be cured or to improve the mental condition for which he was confined. Judge Dwyer noted that trial testimony had revealed that most of the program's clinical staff members were inexperienced with a sexual offender population, without a supervising psychologist or psychiatrist available to staff for the majority of the program's operation. Staff and residents were unable to assess treatment progress with any objective measures of improvement.

The SCC was enjoined to undertake the following:

• Adapt and implement a plan for initial and ongoing training and/or hiring competent sex offender therapists.

- Implement strategies to rectify the lack of trust and rapport between residents and treatment providers.

- Implement a treatment program for residents which includes all therapy components recognized as necessary by prevailing professional standards in comparable programs where participation is coerced, including the involvement of spouses and family members in the treatment of residents and plans for encouraging the visitation and support of the family members.

- Develop and maintain individual treatment plans for residents that include objective benchmarks of improvement to document, measure and guide an individual's progress in therapy.

- Provide a psychologist or psychiatrist expert with diagnosis and treatment of sex offenders to supervise the clinical work of treatment staff, including monitoring of the treatment plans of individual residents, and consult with staff regarding specific issues of concerns about therapy which may arise.

Judge Dwyer enjoined the SCC to take these steps by July 20, to alter the program to satisfy the injunction and ensure constitutionally adequate mental health treatment was available to residents.

On August 22, 1994, Judge Dwyer found the state's plans insufficient and ordered the parties to submit nominations for a "Special Master" to offer expert advice to the state, to help the state in complying with the injunction, and to report to the court. On September 22, 2004, Dr. Janice Marques of the California Department of Mental Health (who had previously directed a treatment program for sexual offenders at Atascadero State Hospital) was appointed Special Master.

At the time of Marques's appointment there were no published standards that specifically defined adequate mental health treatment for sexual offenders under civil commitment period. Marques (2001) previously reported that she saw her role as to document professional standards of the applicable professional standard and help build a program that met these standards. She noted that in the year following the issuing of the instructions in the case, the court regularly conducted hearings on compliance and issued many additional orders. These orders addressed specific issues raised by Marques and other witnesses.

From my viewpoint the Injunction hearing process went as follows: Marques would visit the SCC and evaluate the program and write a report. The SCC would not contest her report and the court would accept this report at the hearing and adopt the recommendations put forth by Dr. Marques. The court would set another hearing date by which time the court expected the SCC to meet the recommendations put forth by Marques. Before the next hearing, Marques would visit the SCC to evaluate whether the SCC had made progress in meeting her recommendations, and she would suggest further recommendations to improve the program.

Marques's reports were critical to the development of the treatment program at the SCC. Her reports, because they were accepted by the court, drove the program in the early years and they forced the SCC to make dramatic changes in the treatment program and how they changed the SCC from a correctional-type facility to a state-of-the-art mental health facility. They provide a detailed history of developments in the treatment program at SCC, and to understand how the program evolved, we need to look at the details in these reports.

Thus I am going to review these reports in detail. In addition, I am going to address some significant events during these early years that had a major impact on the SCC.

REPORTS OF THE SPECIAL MASTER

Under each report I have summarized information authored by Janice Marques. Some of this information is taken verbatim from her report; some of it is a summary of what she recommended.

First Report: Five Requirements of Injunction

After her appointment as Special Master, Marques visited the SCC in November 1994. She reported (Marques, 1994) on the five requirements of the injunction:

- There was no adequate plan for ensuring that the program staff has the specific skills required for effective sex offender treatment. A training needs analysis needed to be done and a plan developed for hiring training specialists.

- There was a serious level of distrust and lack of rapport between SCC residents and staff, which negatively affected treatment. A plan was needed that specified a series of changes in the program structure and operations that could be implemented over the next year to build and maintain trust between the parties.

- Spousal/family and conditional release/aftercare components were missing from the SCC treatment program, as were victim empathy/awareness. The SCC needed to articulate how its treatment model, structure, and components work together to provide a comprehensive program or develop standardized treatment manuals that establish overall goals for each group and specify the procedures and objectives for each session or week.

- Individual treatment plans were in place but they addressed early treatment goals and not objectives related to specific skills needed to avoid reoffending.

- The SCC did not yet have a strong clinical leader.

Marques's first report confirmed that there were clear deficiencies in the treatment program, which had an impact on the twenty-eight residents at SCC.

Second Report: Deficiencies in Treatment Program and Environment

This report (Marques, 1995a) was submitted after a one-week visit in late January by Marques and by Dr. Craig Nelson, clinical director of Atascadero State Hospital's sex offender program. Marques noted the following:

- *Staff competence.* There was no comprehensive training plan to ensure that all staff attain competence in their roles. No therapists or supervisors have been certified by the Washington State as sex offender treatment providers, which would enhance the programs credibility. The SCC should hire competent sex offender therapists.

- *Treatment environment.* There was a litigious atmosphere; residents were bored, idle, and impatient and had no hope of release through treatment. Staff members were stressed. Their decisions were constantly challenged by the residents and their efforts criticized. Supervision and training of front-line staff needed to be increased; managers and supervisors should spend more time on the unit. The program should emphasize release criteria so residents will be able to see a light at the end of the tunnel. Evaluations needed to be streamlined and reports completed in a more timely fashion. Residents must complete their treatment evaluations before entering treatment and should be encouraged to enter while in the process of being evaluated. Therapists supervised the PSAs and their dual role did not allow them adequate time to do this.

- *Treatment components.* SCC management should proactively contribute to the development of legislation to ensure conditional release was a viable option for residents successfully completing the treatment program. Efforts should be made to determine the effectiveness of the treatment programs components. There were no objective measures of treatment progress in place. Psychoeducational modules needed work and there was no module on victim awareness or victim empathy.

- *Treatment plans.* Long-range targets for treatment should be included in treatment plans. Short-term targets emphasize goals that are steps leading to release criteria.

- *Clinical direction/supervision.* A sex offender treatment expert needed to be hired, preferably a state-certified sex offender treatment provider. Until a full-time expert is recruited, a state-certified sex offender treatment provider should be hired to work at least one day per week at the program.

There were obvious deficiencies in the treatment program and environment, but Marques (1995a) noted: "SCC's program staff appeared cohesive, a significant amount of the program development work had been completed, and in spite of the considerable resistance they face, the staff are interested in improving their skills and making the program work. The pace of implementation, however, has been slow and has incorrectly communicated a message of incompetence" (p. 4).

Third Report: Still Work to Be Done

In her third report, Marques (1995b) noted the following:

- *Staff competence.* There was still no comprehensive training plan to ensure that all staff attain competence in their roles. A certified sex offender treatment provider had been hired to lead the clinical team, who would provide training and help plan training curriculum.

- *Treatment environment.* Steps had been taken but residents still perceived staff as being untrustworthy and uncaring. There was a significant split between residents in treatment and those not in treatment, with the latter dominating the environment. The unit living space was reorganized. Residents' rooms were reassigned and new house rules defined which areas of the unit are accessible to the four subgroups of residents: Tier 1—residents in treatment; Tiers 2 and 3—residents interested in treatment who are taking some classes but who are not yet participating fully and residents not yet committed who are unsure whether to enter treatment; Tier 4—residents refusing treatment or presenting significant management problems.

- *Treatment components.* Program staff had failed to complete the evaluation reports, but other treatment objectives were met. Couples counseling had been initiated with one resident. However, there was no conditional release program and the fate of the enabling legislation was uncertain.

- *Treatment plans.* Release criteria had been included in treatment plans but needed to be individualized. Measures of progress needed to be developed for components involving psychoeducational modules and group therapies.

- *Clinical direction/supervision.* The SCC had contracted with a state-certified sex offender treatment provider, to provide clinical supervision. However, efforts to find a permanent, full-time expert should continue.

Overall, it was obvious that progress had been made on several fronts, but there was still a lot of work to be done. Some of the important specific recommendations that Marques made were:

Staff Competence/Training: a. Complete training grid showing which competencies will be required for each employee classification; b. Psychiatric Security Attendant training: start course on Cognitive Behavioral Approach; finish Attitudes and assumptions course plan ; c. Establish top two training priorities for the next year and identify national expert(s) to address these; d. Establish ongoing training in relapse prevention for new staff; Treatment environment: a. Implement plan for maximizing separation between residents in treatment and treatment refusers, making sure that treatment refusers have access to alternative activities; b. With resident assistance, complete simplified resident handbook (summarize policies, explain rules and expectations, set supportive tone) ; c. Train staff and residents on new complaint procedures; d. Based on educational survey results, develop plan to increase the time that residents can spend in educational activities; e. Develop plan to expand hobby program for residents, with emphasis on hobbies that have potential as vocations; f. Continue increased supervision of PSA's by having meetings twice a month with FT's and program management; Treatment Components: a. Complete treatment evaluations for all residents in Core

Therapy Group. Emphasizing succinctness in reports; b. Continue couples counseling for at least one resident; c. Continue to deliver more scheduled individual therapy and reduce the amount of crisis counseling; Treatment Plans / measures of progress: a. Revise the treatment plan for at least one member of the Core Therapy group to include individualized release criteria, and specify short term plans that are clearly related to these longer term goals of treatment; review plan with resident; b. Develop objective measures of progress for the content to be covered in next quarter of the Core Therapy Group; c. Develop objective measures of progress for the human sexuality module. (Marques, 1995b, pp. 9–10)

Fourth Report: Productive Period

In her fourth report, Marques (1995c) noted the following:

- *Staff competence.* Significant progress had been made. Minimum training requirements for each employee classification were developed with a data system for tracking the training that was delivered. An experienced sex offender therapist had filled the role of supervisor and was providing training on sex offender treatment issues to staff on a weekly basis. The SCC had contracted with a local expert to conduct phallometric assessments for the program.

- *Treatment environment.* The unit living space had been reorganized, resident's rooms were reassigned and new house rules defined which areas of the unit were accessible to the four subgroups of residents (those actively opposing treatment or presenting significant management problems; residents in treatment; residents interested in treatment but not yet participating fully; and residents who are not yet committed and unsure of whether to enter treatment); the resident handbook was completed, educational time was increased and a proposal to increase the hobby program was completed; residents were categorized to maximize the separation of those in treatment and those opposing it.

- *Treatment components.* Treatment evaluations were streamlined; individual sessions were being scheduled and structured by the therapists rather than being provided on demand; and couple therapy was taking place. Marques noted that the legislature had authorized a conditional release provision; program staff had failed to complete the evaluation reports but other treatment objectives had been met. Couple counseling had been initiated with one resident. However, there was no conditional release program and the fate of the enabling legislation was uncertain.

- *Treatment plans.* Release criteria had been included in treatment plans but needed to be individualized. Measures of progress needed to be developed for components involving psychoeducational modules and group therapies.

- *Clinical direction/supervision.* The SCC had contracted with a state-certified sex offender treatment provider to provide clinical supervision. However, efforts to find a permanent, full-time expert to serve as clinical director should be continued.

Marques (1995c) reported: "Overall this was a very productive work period. As the above progress report indicates, SCC management and staff accomplished all of the specific objectives that were set" (p. 5).

Fifth Report: Focus on Treatment Environment

In her fifth report, Marques (1995d) noted the following:

- *Staff competence.* All staff needed to be trained to the standards agreed on in the training grid. This should include, for each individual, a list of courses/readings and training priorities, and a schedule should be set for completion of the requirements. All staff should be trained by Dr. Craig Nelson on "effective institutional treatment programs." Other trainings should be given on attitudes and assumptions in dealing with sex offenders, victim empathy and awareness, and developmental issues/interpersonal deficits.

- *Treatment environment.* The SCC should adopt an overall set of rules, fairly communicated to the residents and consistently enforced by the unit staff. Marques noted that some residents wanted to challenge the law, the staff, and the program on a regular basis. If treatment participants and refusers are not separated, it would be difficult to create the possibility of a cohesive therapeutic environment. There should be more intershift meetings and unit supervisors should work at least two swing shifts per month. A more effective and efficient system for managing residents should be developed. A committee should be established of staff and residents with the objective of identifying specific ways to improve resident-staff relations.

- *Treatment components.* The SCC should start a second core therapy group and a second counseling group if there are enough interested residents. The victim empathy/awareness material should be integrated into individual therapy sessions and the core therapy group. An aftercare model should be presented to residents at the community meeting.

- *Treatment plans.* Two measures of progress for the social skills module should be implemented. Relevant measures of progress should be developed for the anger management module. Individual treatment plans should be developed for at least two members of the new core therapy group.

- *Clinical direction/supervision.* The existing contract, schedule, and clinical duties of the treatment supervisor should be continued and recruitment should begin for a permanent, full-time clinician to lead the treatment program.

Marques paid considerable attention to the treatment environment in this report;

she found that residents not in treatment were still harassing those residents in treatment.

Sixth Report: Treatment Environment Still a Major Issue

In her sixth report, Marques (1995e) noted the following:

- *Staff competence.* Progress had been made and staff had attended training with Dr. Nelson on institutional management and treatment of sex offenders; SCC staff and consultants had provided training on attitudes and assumptions in dealing with sex offenders and victim empathy training. Clinical staff should attend training on advanced clinical topics such as differential diagnosis with sex offenders, treatment methods for addressing interpersonal deficits and developmental issues (loneliness/intimacy), and providing individualized treatment within a structured program

- *Treatment environment.* Given the limitations of the current physical plant, not much more could be done to enhance the separation of residents. Residents not in treatment complained that those in treatment were held to lower standards of behavior and were consistently treated better. Residents in treatment wanted more detailed and individualized treatment plans and additional treatment components such as advanced relapse prevention and prerelease classes. The resident management system should be improved and a centralized interdisciplinary team formed to handle the unit's clinical and management decisions, including security classification levels and behavior management plans. An independent objective reviewer was needed to investigate and respond to resident complaints.

- *Treatment components.* A psychoeducational module for victim empathy needs to be developed. Staff should develop a prerelease class. A psychiatrist was present on the unit one day per month, but there was a concern that this might not be an adequate level of service to identify and monitor residents who have some degree of mental illness.

- *Treatment plans.* Some residents were complaining that they had not had the opportunity to review treatment plans. This should be done in individual sessions. More work needed to be done in the area of measuring treatment progress. Appropriate measures had been developed for the social skills module and anger management module but measures needed to be developed for the remaining psychoeducational modules.

- *Clinical direction/supervision.* The SCC was recruiting for a full-time clinical director, but the salary needed to be increased and, given the possible short-term nature of the job if the law was found to be unconstitutional, consideration should be given to recruiting a current practitioner in Washington State who would be willing to work half-time

The SCC had made good strides in the training area, but the treatment environment was still a major issue.

There were approximately thirty-three residents at the SCC in December 1995.

Seventh Report: Phase Structure Recommended for Treatment Environment

In her seventh report, Marques (1996a) noted the following:

• *Staff competence.* Significant progress had been made. Minimal competencies for various staff classifications had been specified and nearly all the basic training requirements had been met. A system for tracking staff training was in use. A plan was needed for providing staff training on an ongoing basis. SCC management proposed to have staff from the Minnesota civil commitment program to provide training and consultation on how to organize, deliver, and monitor treatment services in a comprehensive institutional program; Marques supported this plan and recommended a full week of on-site training and consultation.

• *Treatment environment.* A staff resident team (SRT) had been formed and had met several times a week from mid-November to mid-December to discuss how to improve the living environment. The SRT had come up with twelve recommendations but the superintendent had acted on only one—he refused to give each resident a holiday gift of $10. Management should communicate its position on each of the recommendations by mid-January. A centralized interdisciplinary team had been formed to handle clinical and management decisions. This team had provided additional supervision for the PSA. However, direct care supervisory positions recommended six months ago had not been filled. The hobby/vocational activities had not been expanded. No ombudsman had been hired to respond to and resolve resident complaints at the SCC. An assault had occurred in an enclosed area off the unit, but the resident did not see who hit him and the culprit was never identified. However, management had not discussed the attack with either the victim or the other residents, leading residents to conclude that managers do not care what happens to them.

• *Treatment components.* Most of the objectives in this area were achieved. Plans were underway for the construction of the SCC's Family Visit Unit, to be available for extended or conjugal visits later this year. A community transition class had been prepared and was scheduled to begin this spring. Alcoholics Anonymous meetings had commenced with a community member being present and the SCC treatment supervisor was helping to organize a chapter of Sex Addicts Anonymous. The new interim program director should assess the need for psychiatric services. The treatment program does not have any overall stage or phase structure that serves to organize the components into a meaningful sequence. Decisions regarding which components are offered each quarter should not be based on a resident survey but on the program's curriculum and individual treatment plans. The types and hours of treatment services delivered should be accurately monitored.

- *Treatment plans.* Further work is needed in the area of describing specific criteria that must be attained for each individual to be recommended for conditional release. FTs should go over treatment plans for each resident in an individual session and discuss progress to date with respect to the criteria for release. Staff need to assemble and review their complete curriculum, including the descriptions and manuals for each component, along with measures used to determine resident progress in each.

- *Clinical direction/supervision.* A state-certified sex offender treatment provider was still providing clinical supervision and training on a variety of topics. An interim program director had been hired, working twenty hours per week; however, he had served as a prosecution witness in the commitment trials of some residents and these residents perceived that he would not support the conditional release of any resident. In the meantime, significant progress was being made in recruiting a full-time clinical director.

Overall significant progress had been made, but it is interesting to note that Marques was now recommending a phase structure for the treatment program and that she wanted to see the complete curricula, which included all the manuals.

Eighth Report: Reasonable Measures in Place for Treatment Components

In her eighth report, Marques (1996b) noted the following:

- *Staff competence.* New employees should complete all required clinical training provided on site. There should be interdisciplinary team reviews of all behavior management reports. There should be one training session per month for residential rehabilitation counselors (note the name change from psychiatric security attendants) and two trainings per month for clinical staff. Each FT should attend at least one session of a sex offender treatment group in the community.

- *Treatment environment.* An ombudsman had been hired and management should meet with the ombudsman weekly to discuss complaints and set time frames for resolution to improve staff resident relations. The interdisciplinary team should continue to meet regularly and give residents an opportunity to address the team when changes are proposed in their classification levels. The time residents can spend in the hobby room should be increased by at least two hours per day.

- *Treatment components.* Clinical staff should regularly review their diagnostic impressions of residents with the program psychiatrist. Couple counseling with at least two other residents should begin. The materials and assignments and measures used for the victim awareness module should be expanded. Outlines for introductory and advanced modules should be prepared. A data system should be set up to track the treatment and other structured program services delivered to individual residents.

• *Treatment plans.* FTs should continue case presentations at clinical team meetings with a focus on discussing individualizing treatment plans and release criteria. Treatment plans should be reviewed with residents and they should sign the plans after discussion. A revised proposal should be submitted for organizing the program to include an expanded description of how the postcommitment stage of treatment will be organized.

• *Clinical direction/supervision.* Existing contracts with the interim clinical director (the title was changed from "interim program director") and the treatment supervisor should be continued. A new clinical director should be hired and a contract with the clinical director developed for two consultation/training sessions.

Marques concluded that the SCC now offered the range of treatment components that are typically provided in institutional sex offender treatment programs and has reasonable measures in place for the treatment components.

Ninth Report: Improvement Continues But at a Slow Rate

In her ninth report, Marques (1996c) noted the following:

• *Staff competence.* The SCC had implemented the basic requirements set for staff training and continued the in-service training sessions recommended in the seventh report to the court. FTs were attending groups in the community; weekly clinical meetings continued to include case presentations, with the interim clinical director leading case discussions. The interdisciplinary team should review all behavior management reports in effect. All staff should be trained on the revised proposal for the structure of the SCC treatment program.

• *Treatment environment.* The ombudsman was still being integrated into the operation of the SCC. She had been at SCC for four months and had submitted two reports describing her activities. She had observed staff-resident interactions in a variety of formal and informal activities. She was endeavoring to make sure that resident complaints were heard and addressed in a timely manner. Most of the thirty-three formal complaints tracked during the month of June had been discussed in a timely manner, but in some cases discussion did not lead to resolution. The ombudsman had reviewed and submitted lengthy critiques of current SCC rules and practices. The ombudsman was to establish trust and be seen as a neutral third party. However, because she had criticized staff or questioned their motivation, she was not perceived by staff as neutral. The SCC had also expanded a contract with the Native American chaplain to seventy-nine hours per month.

• *Treatment components.* The program schedule showed a wide range of activities, including two core therapy groups, a pretreatment group, a sexual arousal modification group, and several psychoeducational modules including human sexuality, social skills, relapse prevention, and community transition. More couple counseling had been implemented. A new psychiatrist was on the unit two days a month. Victim awareness had been expanded to two modules—introductory and advanced. Progress was made toward establishing a management information tracking system for program services, and a program sequence for the postcommitment stage of treatment at SCC was developed. There were now four phases: "learning about treatment," "accepting responsibility," "identifying deviant patterns of sexual behavior," and "developing self-control skills." A clinical participation report for tracking and reporting services delivered each month to individual residents was developed.

- *Treatment plans.* The objectives in this area were met during this work period. All residents had individual treatment plans and those residents in the core therapy group had plans that included measurable release criteria. However, the SCC needed to develop release criteria that more specifically describe the needs of individual residents. Feedback should be given to residents regarding their progress in the program. This latter issue arose most often in discussions of annual reviews. Two residents in the core therapy group who thought they were doing well in treatment were surprised by negative reports in their annual reviews. The report writers should be better integrated with treatment teams. The interim clinical director had proposed rating scales for clinicians to use as measures of progress toward various treatment goals. These could be discussed with residents and can be part of the database for annual reviews. Annual reviews should be discussed with residents before being finalized and residents should have the opportunity to discuss the review with the clinical team.

- *Clinical direction/supervision.* The new clinical director was scheduled to commence work in the first week of September 1996. Once on board, he should review the current program description, especially the new, expanded postcommitment stage of treatment, and provide input to the superintendent and interim clinical director.

Marques (1996b) concluded:

As I have indicated before, it is my view that significant improvements in the SCC program will require the presence of an active, full-time Clinical Director to lead the treatment effort. This is not just to provide supervision and expertise regarding sex offender treatment, but to set a positive and therapeutic tone on the unit. It remains my view that a strong, committed, and enthusiastic leader will make it possible for SCC to have a competent and motivated treatment team, and to meet the requirements of the Court's injunction. (p. 9)

However, she also noted that the pace of improvement continued to be slow and the new clinical director was arriving a year after the position was advertised. The organization and delivery of services needed to be improved to have a more coherent program, and it was critical that a database be developed to track services and resident progress. The SCC should move in the direction of a mental health model, becoming more consistent with other programs for civilly committed patients. This required internal monitoring and appropriate ongoing oversight of the program.

Prior to Marques's next report, it should be noted that in October 1996 the superintendent of the SCC was hired and the clinical director was appointed. Both commenced working at SCC on the same date. The new clinical director was given a mandate of developing and writing a comprehensive treatment program.

The new superintendent and the new clinical director faced a daunting task. At that time, the community meetings, which were held weekly, devolved into screaming and yelling matches. The nontreatment residents were still harassing residents who were trying to enter into treatment. These residents dominated the dayroom and many residents in treatment remained in their rooms to avoid harassment. Individuals entering the SCC were resentful and bitter because they had served their prison sentence and felt they were being punished all over again. Many had no interest in treatment, a number had failed treatment previously, and many of their attorneys were advising them not to enter the treatment program.

At the end of 1996, forty-four residents were being held at the SCC.

Tenth Report: Proactive Leadership in Place

In her tenth report, Marques (1997a) noted that she made a site visit to the SCC in October and met with the new superintendent and clinical director. She developed a set of ambitious objectives for them to complete between mid-October and mid-December. She noted the following:

- *Staff competence.* The SCC had implemented a reasonable plan for initial and ongoing training of treatment staff. The training schedules for the next six months included an intensive course on conflict resolution and presentations by outside experts on a variety of clinical topics. Staff training on forensic assessment and report preparation was provided in December by an outside consultant. Training on conflict resolution and mediation was to be provided to residential rehabilitation counselors later in the month. The need at this time was for staff to have more direct experience under expert supervision with offenders who were progressing through treatment.

- *Treatment environment.* The superintendent and clinical director had attended several community meetings and conveyed strong messages of change, fairness, and cooperation, but residents remained skeptical about real improvements. Efforts were underway to adopt a clear set of protreatment values: developing a fair grievance system to encourage resolution of complaints on the unit, overhauling the classification system to incorporate clinical concerns and higher privilege levels, and expanding and improving communication between residents and staff. The new superintendent was active in advocating for new living and program space. A new grievance procedure was written and reviewed by the ombudsman and revised to incorporate her input. Regular meetings were held between program management and the ombudsman. The SCC had done an analysis of the ombudsman's role and proposed options for ensuring existing functions would be continued.

- *Treatment components.* The SCC's program is based on an accepted, cognitive-behavioral treatment approach and offers the basic offense-specific components included in most institutional programs for sex offenders. Psychiatric consultation appeared to be adequate, with the psychiatrist on site one day per week and participating in initial assessments of residents. The new clinical director was reviewing and updating the program's components and measures of progress. A document was drafted defining the community transition component and describing the process used to make less restrictive alternative (LRA) recommendations for residents. A basic data system for tracking resident progress and services should be online by February. More work needs to be done on the community transition component. Clarification is needed on what LRAs are available. Community sex offender treatment providers should be involved to provide information about the community transition process.

- *Treatment plans.* All residents at the SCC for more than forty-five days had a treatment plan and were given an opportunity to discuss the plan with their assigned FT. Plans reviewed were not consistently detailed and comprehensive but were adequate. The clinical team proposed to refine and expand the plan format over the next quarter to provide a more comprehensive assessment of each individual, including life domains such as health, education, vocational and recreational interests, spiritual needs, family relationships, and adjunctive treatment needs such as substance abuse. Residents are now being offered the opportunity to discuss their annual reviews with their treatment team. The clinical director has begun work on improving the annual review process and he planned to finalize the description of the SCC's phases of treatment over the next quarter. The phases should be incorporated into the new classification or resident privileging structure.

- *Clinical direction/supervision.* This requirement of the injunction is being met with the clinical director's arrival. The implementation of the new team structure effective January 1, 1997, with resident management and treatment decisions being made in small team meetings, should result in more thorough case discussions and better supervision. These teams, each of which will have a psychologist, an FT, and three residential rehabilitation counselors, will meet informally each week and will conduct a formal review of each resident's progress each quarter. The clinical director should be on the unit as much as possible in order to set a positive and therapeutic tone and to model therapeutic interactions.

Marques recommended that the superintendent and clinical director improve communication with residents and set up the advocacy, conflict resolution, and independent review functions. They should meet residents and staff and state values, describe new policies that have been developed, describe the new grievance system, and provide information on the community transition process. A contract with an existing dispute resolution service will be used to provide conflict negotiation services as needed. To avoid conflict of interest, an independent line of authority must be established for the resident advocate and ombudsman positions.

Marques (1997a) noted:

[The Superintendent] had begun to provide the active management that the program requires. He set up a formal, agenda-based management team structure, defined the tasks that needed to be done to build a sound foundation for the program, and assigned work groups to complete these tasks. Work groups include those on policy and procedures, communication, clinical organization and services, transitional programming and quality assurance. Each of these groups had made significant progress. (p. 7)

Marques (1997a) also stated:

[The SCC's new clinical director] wrote a plan for reorganizing the clinical team to improve treatment planning, services and reports. Work was also done on clarifying how a resident can move through the transitional program to a less-restrictive alternative, and on pieces that must be in place to allow community release. Finally, the foundation for a quality assurance system was begun with the development of the computer network that will allow on-line tracking of resident participation in services.) From my perspective this proactive leadership represents a significant and positive change in the SCC program. (p. 8)

Eleventh Report: Progress Continues

In her eleventh report, Marques (1997b) noted the following:

• *Staff competence.* The SCC was conducting active in-service training and staff members were attending appropriate conferences. Improvement was needed in the area of staff supervision. Additional management presence was needed on the unit. The superintendent's proposal to schedule weekly office hours for himself, the grievance coordinator, and the leader of the policy work group should be implemented immediately. The clinical director's duties should be restructured to provide the active clinical direction that the program demands, and as an expert clinician he should be on the unit participating in and overseeing the delivery of the program's services. Other administrative duties must not preempt these important tasks. The clinical director should participate in and observe selected groups and classes. He should be on the unit a minimum of ten hours per week.

• *Treatment components.* By September, each resident who has completed a treatment evaluation and is in a core therapy group should have a treatment plan in place addressing all his or her mental health needs. The current review of the manuals used for group therapy and psychoeducational components should continue, and a schedule should be set up to revise the manuals on a regular basis. The major program work to be done is to develop objective benchmarks of improvement to document, measure, and guide an individual's progress in therapy. This requires the development and specification of program phases, from treatment readiness to community placement. By September, the core program structure should be in place and understood by staff and residents. Current rating scales for measuring progress should be included in the clinical database and in the annual review process. Two residents had been released by the court and it is critical for SCC management to finalize policies on LRA and community placement options and to communicate these to residents on the unit as well as in the resident handbook.

• *Treatment environment.* There must be a consistent pattern of communication and follow-through on the part of SCC leadership. Their commitment to the resident welfare and the program's therapeutic values must be evident on the treatment unit. Unit staff must be consistent, therapeutic, and professional. Program policies that have recently undergone review should be clearly posted on the unit, discussed with program managers, and distributed in a revised resident handbook. SCC managers and staff should continue regular meetings with the resident council and by September should have a working draft on how the council will provide ongoing input to program management. Plans to move the program to a better physical plant or expand and improve the present facility should be completed before September.

• *Mental health program model (internal and external oversight).* The court had affirmed in its February 4, 1997, order that objective external oversight will be needed to guarantee that the essential program features that have been developed at the SCC will continue in place. SCC management had done a lot of work in this area. An advisory board should be officially constituted and its first quarterly meeting should be held during the summer. The newly appointed SCC ombudsman must be in place, conducting and reporting on the required policy reviews. The quality assurance work group must develop an initial set of minimum performance standards suitable for internal and external review purposes. Categories for standards should include living environment, treatment plan and process, therapies (individual, group adjunct), and access to resources. These standards should be reviewed by the advisory board and the Special Master prior to their implementation. A basic preliminary quality assurance plan should be written that specifies three initial targets for improvement at the SCC. For external inspection of care (IOC) reviews, a number of measures (checklists and rating scales) will be needed for each of the standards set. The first of the IOC reviews should be completed and a report sent to SCC management, the SCC advisory board and the Special Master for review.

Twelfth Report: Ongoing Problem of SCC Structure

In her twelfth report, Marques (1997c) noted the following:

• *Staff competence.* The SCC had hired an experienced FT and psychologist. The long-standing need for clinical leadership on the treatment unit is still not being met. His on-unit time has varied considerably. Although he has been more available to residents and staff, much of the clinical director's time is spent in management meetings and on administrative tasks off the unit.

- *Treatment components.* Five comprehensive treatment plans have been written providing an individualized assessment of the resident across many life domains, including diagnostic information, strengths and weaknesses, and short- and long-term treatment goals. Treatment components offered this quarter included one pregroup, one core therapy group, relapse prevention, anger management, and social skills. The clinical director had written a detailed outline of the structure of the program specifying seven phases—six inpatient phases and one aftercare phase: (1) orientation/evaluation, (2) treatment readiness, (3) skill acquisition, (4) skill application, (5) skill generalization, (6) discharge readiness, and (7) aftercare. Treatment components for each phase were specified, along with the goals that residents should reach in order to advance to the next phase. The program was based on the relapse prevention model and used cognitive-behavioral techniques. The program was run a trimester format with approximately sixteen weeks per trimester. There were six inpatient phases and the overriding goal is the development of self-regulation in the resident. Individualized treatment planning is undertaken and at the end of every trimester, treatment plans are updated and revised to reflect the changing needs of the resident. Formal reviews of resident progress are scheduled at the end of each trimester. Staff facilitators report on each resident's completion of assignments and demonstration of knowledge and skills. These reports, resident input, and behavioral observations are used as the basis for treatment planning for the next trimester. This program closely paralleled that of the new sex offender commitment program at Atascadero State Hospital in California and included many of the same components, but in several ways it went beyond the California program, including additional phases, levels of groups, and new modules. It clearly represented the state of the art in sex offender treatment and was a plan for the future in that hardly any of the listed components had been developed.

- *Treatment environment.* When policies are revised, they are posted in each day room and a program manager schedules office hours to discuss the changes with residents and staff. The superintendent holds weekly office hours to discuss management decisions, program changes and policies. A new ombudsman commenced working on August 19, 1997. The resident grievance system was fully implemented and an automated system was in place for tracking and reporting the results of grievances. Grievances were being resolved prior to reaching the superintendent. Two mediations had been conducted by the contractor who was providing conflict resolution services. The unit's community meetings, co-chaired by a resident and the unit supervisor and the more structured resident-staff advisory group meetings, were held as scheduled. The overcrowding in the facility necessitated four residents sleeping in a DOC unit at the facility and spending days in the already scarce program space at the SCC. Many residents were unhappy with the decision by the U.S. Supreme Court,[3] which upheld the constitutionality of the SVP laws. Under the injunction, a number of residents are committed to demonstrating the adequacy of the program, its staff, and its managers. Residents were complaining that their input into decisions and policies were not considered and they were dissatisfied with the grievance policy. Residential staff members were complaining that they did not feel supported by program management and felt that communication between them and the programs leaders was poor. They were unclear about the roles of the superintendent and clinical director and the role that the residential rehabilitation counselors should play in the treatment program. They were very concerned about the move of the facility to a distant location.

• *Mental health program model (internal and external oversight).* The SCC superintendent is committed to implementing a mental health model at the facility and required little consultation from the Special Master. Substantial progress had been made in this area. A basic set of standards for the program to meet was developed, along with a ten-page rating guide for use by reviewers. The standards covered four areas of the program: (1) living environment (food, sanitation, disability accommodations, safety features, aesthetics, privacy, space); (2) treatment plans and processes (criteria and goals for revisions, timelines, comprehensiveness, individualization, resident participation, treatment team meetings); (3) therapies (participation and amount, groups and classes based on state of the art, qualified therapists; and (4) access to resources by residents (clinical consultations, training support, cultural support, activities and hobbies). These standards were used by the first IOC, a one-day review conducted by mental health professionals from Western State Hospital. The team consisted of a psychiatrist, a psychologist, a psychiatric nurse, and an FT. Several problems were identified, such as the restrictive environment, inadequate team involvement in treatment planning, disjointed recordkeeping practices, and health care decisions that did not follow DSHS standards. DSHS had also established an advisory board and the first meeting of this group was held on July 15, 1997. The group is diverse and includes community members, representing the legal profession, law enforcement, victim services, community and institutional sex offender treatment providers, and state hospital programs.

Marques (1997c) concluded:

Once again it is my assessment that although the essential pieces were in place, there is not yet an effective clinical team at SCC. The staff appears somewhat disjointed; they do not share a clear vision of the overall program and how the services provide fit into it. Some staff are unsure about or resistant to a mental health treatment model, while others embrace it. It remains my view that the Clinical Directors job must be restructured to reduce his off-unit administrative burdens and to allow him to pull this program together. This means directly supervising treatment activities, actively participating in treatment teams, motivating unit staff and making sure they understand the

treatment program, modeling therapeutic interactions, and building the relationships that are needed to have a strong and coherent treatment team.
Without this active leadership, SCC will continue to have one program on
paper, and one in practice. The program at SCC is based on an accepted cognitive behavioral treatment approach and offers the basic offense specific
components that are provided in most institutional programs for sex offenders. (p. 14)

Marques (1997c) also noted:

[There is] a useful, on-line clinical data base that allows clinicians and managers to track the services delivered to residents. Treatment planning at SCC
has improved significantly. The plans now being developed for residents have
been broadened to include aspects of the individual's mental health needs that
are not related to sexual offending. They are clearly adequate for guiding the
treatment of individual residents. Despite these accomplishments there are
still two areas in which the program in practice does not yet coincide with the
program on paper. First, the conditional release component, although now
developed in terms of policies and procedures, has not yet been implemented.
The one resident who is in community transition is there because of an agreement initiated in court, not because he progressed through SCC's phases of
treatment. It continues to be the case that SCC clinicians have not determined
that any resident has so changed that he or she is ready for community placement. Nonetheless work must be done so that any recommended community
placements can proceed without unnecessary delays. (p. 14)

In addition, Marques (1997c) referred to the ongoing problem of the structure of
the SCC program, including the measured to gauge progress:

A major planning document has been produced, which shows a comprehensive multi-phased program that if implemented would clearly reflect the state
of the art in terms of treatment goals and components. This is not, however,
SCC's current program and I have not seen a plan for how and when the transition to this new model will occur. . . . (p. 15)

Mediation services are being provided by a conflict resolution service from
the community. The resident advocate is providing a broad range of services
and he reports to the new Ombudsman, who reports to the DSHS Assistant
Secretary for Health and Rehabilitative Services. The resident grievance system is in place and most grievable issues are being resolved at the unit staff
level. There are some problems however, in that many of the residents' major
concerns are not eligible for the grievance process. These include treatment
decisions and medical care complaints. . . . A permanent home for this program must be found immediately. . . . Although I have not yet seen the written report of the first external review of the program, my review of the performance standards, rating scales, and exit conference notes from the
Inspection of Care (IOC) team indicates that this was an effective oversight
mechanism. (pp. 16–17).

Moving from Monroe to McNeil Island

Shortly after the September 1997 Injunction hearing in front of Judge Dwyer, DSHS announced that due to the growth in the program the program was relocating from Monroe to McNeil Island, located in the Puget Sound near Steilacoom. The SCC was to move into a wing of McNeil Island Correctional Center, a medium-level prison. DOC would provide medical care, meals, transportation, and external security, while DSHS was responsible for treatment. Planning and preparation for the move began in October and the move took place on April 18, 1998. This was a huge project and the past six months have been dominated by the disruption, uncertainty, and hard work this kind of move entails. Staff morale was down and many of the staff made decisions that they would not relocate to McNeil Island; consequently nearly 90 percent of the SCC's line staff and clinicians left. Residents were angry about the move and concerns that their families would have much greater difficulty in visiting them on McNeil Island. I remember attending a family meeting regarding the move with the SCC superintendent and facing a room full of very angry family members. It was a tumultuous meeting. The superintendent explained the plans were underway to build a new facility on McNeil Island and plans were being developed to build this facility so that the residents would be able to move into this new facility in five years or so.

SCC management anticipated better program space; greatly enhanced resources, including educational vocational opportunities; and proximity to Western State Hospital, which would allow the SCC to share training and clinical resources with a major mental health program. The SCC was set up as a secure mental health treatment facility and its philosophy was out of step with DOC's philosophy which had a more rigid stance on security. SCC residents had to move within the facility, which resulted in conflicts between residents and inmates. SCC management had to negotiate program space with DOC and movement times for residents.

Thirteenth Report: Relocation Has Some Positive Effect

In her thirteenth report, Marques (1998) noted that the program's relocation significantly affected the SCC's ability to make program improvements. A substantial recruitment program to staff the new facility had been underway.

- *Staff competence.* Two new psychologists were hired and three new FTs with forensic mental health backgrounds and experience with cognitive-behavioral treatment. Forty residential rehabilitation counselor (RRC) positions were filled, including six supervisory-level positions. Most new staff were recruited from mental health settings, either state hospitals or community mental health programs. The living unit was managed by a new residential care manager, an individual with a master's degree in social work and substantial management experience. As of June 1998, the FTs will be under the supervision of a clinician who is certified by the Washington State as a sex offender treatment provider. An impressive training curriculum was developed with a two-week orientation training covering institutional rules and procedures as well as the SCC's values, philosophy, and program. A second component, a three-week program on mental health treatment, designed primarily for RRCs, was developed by the SCC in conjunction with the Washington Institute for Training, which is sponsored by the state's major universities as well as by the DSHS mental health division. Staff members were new and did not understand the treatment model and structure.

• *Treatment components.* A treatment program overview was written and distributed to residents during this period. The program's policy on community reentry was given to residents and discussed with those who attended peer group meetings. During the treatment period that had just ended, thirty residents were involved in program modules, including four psychoeducational classes, three treatment groups (orientation, introduction to treatment, and sex offender group which was previously known as the core group). Due largely to staff turnover, numerous sessions were canceled.

• *Treatment environment.* The SCC had shifted from a maximum-security environment to a medium-security environment. SCC residents have individual rooms opening up to a large communal living area. The surrounding prison is a spacious environment with many resources that SCC residents can access with staff escort. These include law and public libraries, chapel, a large exercise yard, and a gymnasium with a weight/hobby area. Treatment services will be provided off the unit in a newly remodeled building with attractive group therapy rooms, staff offices, and a new sexual behavior laboratory. The superintendent of McNeil Island Correctional Center issued and emphasized a policy "zero tolerance" for any harassment or maltreatment of SCC residents. Residents were unhappy being in the middle of a prison and subject to the intrusion of the prison's rules.

• *Mental health program model (internal and external oversight).* Quality assurance activities had been on hold during the recent transitional period, but a new quality assurance manager had been appointed. Two IOCs had now been completed, resulting in a number of program improvements. For example, as recommended by the IOC team, medical and treatment records are combined and kept on the unit and medical care (utilization review) decisions are now following DSHS, not DOC, standards. The SCC advisory board has continued to meet quarterly and suggested a number of program improvements (e.g., to develop a program package for residents not in treatment and to adopt a mental health grievance procedure rather than a correctional model). Relationships between the ombudsman and the superintendent and advisory board were strained. Management and the board see the ombudsman as failing to maintain a neutral position.

Marques noted that her assessment of the program had not changed substantially from what she had written in her twelfth report, assuming that the disruption in the treatment program was temporary. Now that it had a permanent home, the SCC needed to take the lead in developing a network of community treatment providers who will work with the program. These individuals should provide treatment planning and provide services consistent with the SCC program model to residents making the transition to the community. the SCC's treatment program should be fully implemented. The move to McNeil Island clearly improved some aspects of the environment. The atmosphere of the living unit was less oppressive and unit staff members were positive and respectful toward the residents. However, there was still no plan for addressing the needs of residents who are refusing treatment to ensure they have productive activities in their lives. The resident advocate and ombudsman had both indicated that the grievance system was not working adequately and rule infractions were not handled consistently. They also believed hat the behavioral intervention policy was outdated and needed revision. SCC management, with the support of DSHS administration, should strongly advocate for conditions appropriate for civilly committed individuals with DOC. The ombudsman has strained relations with SCC management and the advisory board and this situation needed to be resolved. Marques recommended that the ombudsman report not to the assistant secretary of DSHS, as he is responsible for the SCC program, but to an individual who has a high-level position and who is substantially independent. Marques recommended that the ombudsman's job description be reviewed and some focused consultation be undertaken.

Marques believed there was a considerable amount of work to be done over the next five months and that an intensive, focused, on-site consultation be conducted by two experts on sex offender treatment who direct civil commitment programs. She recommended that Dr. Craig Nelson, clinical director of the Atascadero Sex Offender Program, and Dr. Anita Schlank, clinical director of the Minnesota Sex Offender Program, undertake this consultation in June 1998.

> The purpose of the consultation will be to build on the experience of others in order to resolve some of the problems described in this report, to avoid other possible pitfalls, and to make decisions that are needed to develop a fully operational program as quickly as possible. Topics to be addressed include: (a) staff development (building effective teams, defining the role of the RRC's, motivating therapists, clinical supervision requirements); (b) resident rights, management and input (classification and privileging systems, resident government, behavioral intervention policies, resident advocacy, investigations of abuse, grievance and "due process" standards, separation of resident subgroups); (c) program elements (measuring progress, implementing a conditional release component, provisions for residents who are not active in treatment) and (d) program oversight (advisory board authority and functions, requirements for ombudsman and other independent reviewers). (Marques, 1998, p. 23)

Consultation From Drs. Nelson and Schlank

Dr. Nelson and Dr. Schlank visited the SCC from June 23, 1998, to June 25, 1998. They made several recommendations (Nelson, 1998; Schlank, 1998).

Staff Competence, Training, and Supervision:

- Efforts should be made to fill all staff vacancies as soon as possible and staff should have previous mental health or sex offender treatment experience.

- Arrangements should be made to have staff who have no experience working with sex offenders trained through the British Columbia Justice
  Institute.

- A regular schedule of clinical supervision sessions of FT, psychologists
  and social workers should be established and maintained.

- Efforts should be made to ensure that all staff has a basic understanding of
  the treatment model and structure and their role in the program. New staff
  should not work on the unit until the initial two-week employee orientation
  is completed. Three weeks of training should be provided to the RRCs
  through the Washington Institute on relevant topics.

- Efforts should be made to ensure agreement and consistency across clinicians and teams in how treatment planning and other decisions are made.
  The clinical director should attend all treatment team meetings.

Treatment Components and Measures of Success:

- The SCC's described program is comprehensive, but the number of components and groups seems overly ambitious given the size of the SCC and
  limited clinical resources available. It is recommended that they simplify
  the program by combining various levels of groups on the same topic or
  by combining other specialty groups into the main sex offender treatment
  group.

- Residents should be allowed to progress to an advanced stage of treatment
  despite their legal situation. Residents should be entered into treatment as
  quickly as possible, even if they are still being assessed.

- Each resident should receive information on the basic treatment structure,
  including the phases and the community transition process. They should
  have a trimester review that documents their current phase of treatment
  and the goals they must achieve to reach the next phase. The trimester
  review report should incorporate resident input into his treatment planning, and the resident should have a copy of this document.

- There should be ongoing monitoring of treatment components to ensure
  they are consistent, with written descriptions, and this could be achieved
  by clinical supervisors and the clinical director attending activities on a
  regular basis.

- Measures of progress should accurately reflect the targets of treatment in
  the program and be used consistently across treatment teams.

Treatment Environment:

- The recorded message on the telephone indicating that the call is from a
  correctional institution should be immediately removed. Residents should

be able to receive as well as make calls. Outside yard access adjacent to the unit should be completed as soon as possible. Medication should be dispensed on the unit.

- A binder of all program policies should be placed in the unit dayroom for resident reference. New policies should be posted on a unit bulletin board. Staff should be required to review all new and updated policies.

- Residents should be treated with respect and provided opportunities to have their grievances addressed in a timely manner.

- The program should address the long-term care needs of residents who are not engaged in treatment activities. They should not be allowed to opt out of all treatment but signed up for treatment activities which are not sex-offender specific, and they should also have trimester reviews. They should have similar job assignments, educational opportunities, and leisure activities to other residents.

Mental Health Program Model and Program Oversight:

- The SCC superintendent should have a staff investigator to perform internal reviews and investigations that do not reach the level of resident abuse.

- Program oversight mechanisms (advisory board, IOC, and ombudsman) are working as planned and have resulted in program improvements. Recommendations from the advisory board and the IOC team should be implemented.

Nelson and Schlank made excellent recommendations that were accepted by the SCC. These recommendations were implemented and are still in practice today.

Fourteenth Report: Implementing Consultant Recommendations

Marques (1998) endorsed the recommendations of Drs. Schlank and Nelson and proposed that they be implemented:

- *Staff competence.* Establish a formal schedule for clinical supervision of therapists; ensure that treatment decisions are made consistently across teams and are communicated to residential care staff.

- *Treatment components.* There were numerous deficiencies in treatment planning. Such planning needs to be timely, comprehensive, and consistent. Efforts needed to be made to minimize barriers to treatment; offer a sufficient range of treatment activities to ensure that participants can complete the program's phases in a timely manner.

- *Treatment environment.* Timely internal reviews of behavior management plans need to be provided which involve those residents in segregation. To ensure quality, a formal resident advisory group should be established and timely responses to input from this group should be provided. A social worker should be hired to increase social and family activities.

• *Mental health program model (internal and external oversight).* Oversight proposals should be provided to the advisory board for their input and approval. Oversight provisions should be similar to those in effect for other mental health programs in the state.

Fifteenth Report: Program Not Yet Fully Operational

In her fifteenth report, Marques (1999a) noted the following:

• *Staff competence.* In accordance with recent court orders, considerable efforts were being made with regard to training. Orientation training was required before new residential care staff began working on the unit. RRCs were required to complete forty hours of mental health training within four months of hire. The Justice Institute of British Columbia had provided half of a 120-hour course on treatment of sexual deviance during February and March. Formal supervision schedules were in place for FTs and psychologists. FTs receive one hour per week individual supervision with the FT supervisor and psychologists receive one hour of group supervision per week with the clinical director. The treatment program was understaffed. Three of nine FT positions were vacant, as was one of three psychologist positions. Residential care managers attend the first hour of the clinical meeting. However, the RRCs were not receiving information from the clinical meeting and RRCs did not attend the majority of treatment team meetings. The SCC should implement strategies to reduce clinical and residential staff turnover, document how and when remaining staff training will be completed, structure and document the supervision provided to therapists, and strengthen communication and teamwork between clinical and residential staff.

• *Treatment components.* A model treatment plan had been developed but was not adopted in practice. A number of plans for individuals with developmental disabilities lacked diagnostic information and failed to prescribe interventions to address the special needs of these residents. There was considerable variability in the adequacy of long-term goals in the treatment plans. Trimester reports had not improved significantly; the content varied depending on the FT who wrote them. Summaries lacked information on the resident's current treatment goals, data from rating instruments, and evidence that the resident had reviewed the report. The SCC had begun to collaborate with senior staff of the Washington Institute to develop the program's measures of treatment progress and outcome. However, the new treatment program at McNeil Island was not systematically measuring resident progress toward treatment goals and providing clear feedback to residents. Treatment participation had increased and fifty-six of eighty-five residents were assigned to treatment activities. The level of programming had pushed program space to its limits and additional group rooms were needed. Community release plans had been written for two residents. Residents complained that with a "new" treatment program at the SCC, previous treatment accomplishments were ignored and they had to start over. They also complained about delays in the evaluation process. Treatment plans were outdated and generic. Trimester reports did not inform about progress and psychologists had been ordered to put only negative statements in the annual reviews about them. A family support policy had been drafted and family support meetings were being held quarterly. There were still problems with contacting families in emergencies. Although the program had greatly expanded, there was a lack of individualized mental health treatment for those with special needs, such as development disabilities and chronic mental illness. The SCC should ensure that there are comprehensive, individualized treatment plans that follow a standard format and are approved by the clinical director. Appropriate individualized treatment is to be provided to residents with special needs (major mental disorders, neurological impairments, and developmental disabilities), to include hiring/contracting experts to provide assessment and treatment planning and ensure that family relationships and support are addressed in treatment plans. In addition, timely and appropriate counseling should be provided to further develop the structures required for community transition

- *Treatment environment.* Routine strip searches were eliminated, as ordered by the court, and will only be done where there is suspicion of contraband. Since March, residents leaving visiting are screened by an X-ray body scanner rather than a strip search. SCC management continued to meet regularly with DOC staff to negotiate for improved conditions. However, since the court order banning strip searching, DOC management took the position that security concerns required the total separation of inmates from SCC residents and SCC residents could not participate in choir or other religious activities. In March, the prison closed the "Big Yard" to residents, eliminating baseball and long-distance running. Plans were underway to acquire additional living and programming space. The interim housing plan was not responsive to the court's instruction to acquire more adequate space with the McNeil Island Correctional Complex. The grievance procedure had been simplified. The program had reintroduced a structured "level system" at which higher levels of privileges are afforded to those who make progress in adopting prosocial attitudes and meeting therapeutic goals. Progress had been made in providing better opportunities for educational and recreational activities. The education program coordinator had developed a program that included assessment of literacy skills, adult basic education and high school completion classes, keyboarding, and industrial safety. Despite the closure of the Big Yard, the SCC had implemented a recreation program. It had its own separate recreation center and an ample schedule to accommodate the residents.

Resident jobs are extremely limited, both in scope and in hours. An election had been held to select residents to serve on a formal resident advisory council. The superintendent was conducting monthly focus groups as another way to invite resident input. A social worker was hired but was assigned to the clinical team instead of the living unit, and as a result the SCC had made little progress in improving the program's connection with family members or in developing more social activities for residents. The SCC should implement a system to allow outgoing calls; revise the grievance process to increase its resolution rate and demonstrate the credibility of the appeal process; document that the new package of policies has undergone a professional review; expand educational, vocational, and work opportunities and integrate these domains into the treatment planning process; assign a social worker to the living unit; ensure that residents with disabilities have access to hobby and recreation rooms and the law library; demonstrate that management is responding to resident advisory council and focus group input; negotiate with DOC to improve conditions; and provide a completed facility planning document showing steps for new construction and an end date for overcrowding.

• *Mental health program model (internal and external oversight).* Substantial efforts had been made to implement internal and external review mechanisms. The quality improvement program had developed plans of correction in response to the 1998 IOC report and had completed several quality assurance projects. The resident abuse policy had been revised and clarified the role of the program's new internal Investigator. In addition to internal review, the Washington State Patrol is available to investigate institutional incidents at the request of the secretary of DSHS. The SCC advisory board was meeting quarterly and providing valuable guidance on the program's development, operation and oversight. In February, the SCC superintendent presented a proposal to the mental health governing body that the SCC be included as a program operating under its umbrella. This proposal was accepted and the SCC is now administratively governed by the same group that oversees the state hospital programs. The SCC should fully implement the oversight package recommended by the advisory board. This includes clarifying the ombudsman and investigator roles and non-DSHS participation in IOC reviews, with one external member of the IOC team being a certified sex offender treatment provider.

Marques (1999a) noted:

Planned improvements had occurred in a number of areas. Training had proceeded briskly and the number of treatment components had greatly expanded. New policies had been implemented to make the environment more predictable and to provide administrative review of behavioral interventions. Educational assessments had been completed and a recreation program has been implemented. Proposed oversight mechanisms had been put in place. I have not identified any major areas in which the program had regressed, although current building plans may revive the overcrowding problem that existed at Monroe. A number of steps need to be taken before the program is fully operational. Treatment teams are not yet working as described; residential care staff are not informed of resident's treatment goals and do not regularly attend treatment team meetings. The mental health model espoused by the program is inconsistently followed on the unit. The program has not achieved its standards regarding the timeliness and comprehensive scope of treatment plans and the systematic review of resident progress is not following the procedures that were described to me before the October hearing. The family support and community transition policies have not been fully implemented. Several planned improvements in the treatment environment have not been made, including the PIN system for outgoing calls, better meal schedules, separation of various subgroups of residents, improved vocational and work opportunities and adding a Social Worker to the unit staff. (p. 23).

Sixteenth Report: Still Some Shortcomings

In her sixteenth report, Marques (1999b) noted the following:

• *Staff competence.* The SCC had taken steps to redress staff recruitment and retention problems. Recruitment efforts included continuous open recruitment and periodic newspaper ads for residential and clinical staff. Exit questionnaires were given to determine reasons why staff left. A proposal had been made to increase RRC salaries and clinical staff members were allowed more flexible work schedules. The Justice Institute of British Columbia had been providing advanced sex offender training for clinical and selected residential staff. Clinical supervision schedules were in place, but no evaluative data on the delivery of groups and classes were available. Communication and teamwork between clinical and residential staff was improving, RRC attendance at treatment team meetings had increased. Documentation of these meetings had greatly improved. RRCs were requesting additional training on how to work effectively with residents. In August, the clinical director resigned and an acting clinical director was appointed. The SCC should recruit nationally for the clinical director position; residential staff should complete orientation before beginning work on the unit; there should be RRC attendance at 90 percent of the treatment team meetings.

• *Treatment components.* A new standardized treatment plan format was implemented on June 1, 1999, and since then all new plans and updates follow this format. Each plan requires diagnostic information, treatment goals, residents' strengths, and an assessment of treatment needs across a variety of life domains and treatment interventions and objectives. Plans reviewed appeared adequate for guiding treatment. However, there were still many incomplete or out-of-date planning documents. The new plan format may not be suitable for special needs residents. The SCC was developing contracts with two experts to assist in developing a treatment program for special needs residents. Their work will need to be documented. Attendance records were being kept but data were not available. A new format for trimester reports was implemented and, at the end of last trimester, a progress report was prepared for all residents documenting the resident's treatment phase, trimester goals, overall level of participation, and treatment progress. Also included in the progress report were treatment team recommendations regarding phase advancement and treatment plan changes. There were no rating scales to guide the FT's assessment of resident progress. These were being developed by the Washington Institute for Mental Health Research and Training. Family relationships and support were being addressed in treatment plans. However, the need for this should be assessed among advanced treatment participants.

• *Treatment environment.* The SCC was still pursuing a number of options to allow residents to make outgoing calls at an acceptable cost. The grievance system is streamlined; a response from a unit supervisor is required in seven working days, and if appealed, a response from an SCC manager is required in ten working days. The SCC was planning to implement a professional review of policies to include feedback from staff, residents, the resident advocate and ombudsman. A new dining hall solely for SCC residents was opened in July and twenty-one food handing jobs were added to the vocational program. Complaints about access to religious services had decreased. A social worker will work half time on the living unit and half time in the clinical department, but he should focus fully 50 percent of his time on increasing family activities, performing family outreach, and building support networks for residents. A recreation specialist had increased social activities on the unit such as board tournaments, bingo, a Fourth of July party, and a summer social. SCC management was still meeting with DOC management to improve conditions. They had acquired space for a new dining hall and meal schedules had been improved. Disabled residents have access to the DOC gym and leisure opportunities and hobbies are provided to them on the unit. It had been agreed that the SCC could take over more space by October 4, 1999, to avoid overcrowding, have more program space, and move key staff back to the living unit.

• *Mental health program model (internal and external oversight).* The internal and external oversight structures recommended by the advisory board and Special Master had been implemented. The quality assurance department had been undertaking chart audits and reorganizing charts so there would be leaner and better organized charts on the unit. They had developed a detailed data collection instrument for the IOC team that included a certified sex offender treatment provider. The role of the internal investigator was clarified in policy. There were still problems between the ombudsman and SCC, with poor communication and cooperation, and the SCC disagreed with the scope of his role. The SCC governing body (composed of the secretary of DSHS and other high-level administrators, chaired by the director of the Division of Mental Health) toured the SCC on July 16, 1999, to review the program's work plans in response to the court's injunction and discuss performance indicators which will be reviewed quarterly. The SCC's highly qualified advisory board continued to provide valuable input actively contributing to the development of the SCC's program. They gave advice on facility improvements, measures of treatment progress, and community release provisions.

Marques noted that one-third of the residents were in treatment and some conditions had improved, but there were still serious shortcomings. The SCC was located within a prison and she considered the prison's influence to be pervasive and damaging. The IOC committee submitted a report in October 1999, found deficiencies similar to those in the Special Master's report, and characterized the program as operating more like a correctional facility than a treatment center or program.

November 1999 Injunction Hearing

At the court hearing on November 15, 1999, considerable time was devoted to the problems that the SCC was facing in a prison setting. The hearing did not go well for the SCC. The court adopted the Special Master's sixteenth report (Marques, 1999b) as a statement of work that needed to be done. Judge Dwyer issued a court order which expressed his displeasure as to what had transpired since the SCC had relocated to McNeil Island. He described the program as an "unwanted stepchild of a medium-security prison" (Dwyer, 1999, p. 16). He found the SCC to be in contempt for failure to comply with injunctions in both the *Sharp*[4] and the *Turay*[5] cases. He identified three main causes for failure to meet compliance: (1) inadequate resources—the state had failed to devote adequate resources to achieve compliance; (2) entrenched resistance to the injunction (the defendants deny anything is amiss, then just before the next court hearing there is a flurry of activity to make improvements); and (3) the prison's dominating influence and the placement of the SCC in the prison made it difficult to achieve a treatment-oriented environment.

The court imposed a $50 per day per resident fine commencing in May 1, 2000, if the court-ordered improvements were not made, with payment deferred for six months. Judge Dwyer would determine whether improvements had been made at the next hearing scheduled for April 18, 2000.

There was considerable concern about sanctions imposed upon the SCC. This was a blow to the management and staff at the SCC who worked so hard to ensure they were in compliance with the injunction. However, there was a silver lining. Judge Dwyer's ruling forced political action. Governor Locke asked the legislature for $19 million to improve the program and make statutory changes necessary to meet the court's order for a transitional facility in the community. Within a short time the SCC received $3 million for staff hiring and training and the legislature budgeted $14 million for the first stage of a brand-new stand-alone facility to be built on McNeil Island outside the McNeil Island Correctional Center.

The SCC immediately began to hire staff and improve treatment conditions.

Seventeenth Report: Sincere Efforts Being Made

In her seventeenth report Marques (2000) documented the sincere efforts that SCC was making to comply with the injunction. She noted:

The work period involved in this report (11/99 to 3/00) was an exceptional one for the SCC program. Following the October hearing and subsequent (November 15, 1999) Court order, DSHS management declared that they would make every effort not only to bring SCC into compliance with the injunction, but to build a model civil commitment program. Ongoing management consultation was provided to develop an extensive "Injunction Response Report," a comprehensive and well organized presentation of the program's goals, objectives, action plans, and achievements. Substantial resources were made available to expand SCC's management team, increase clinical and residential staffing, improve the facility and conditions, and provide the Superintendent and the Clinical Director with the expertise and personnel needed to accomplish the program improvements required by the Court. Consultants and new staff were brought in to address specific program needs such as training, treatment planning, adaptation of the curriculum for individuals with special needs, policy review and the development of a strategic plan for SCC." (p. 2)

Marques concluded that a significant amount of program development had been accomplished by SCC management and staff. She reported:

SCC has a comprehensive training plan and has made a significant effort to ensure that both existing and incoming staff complete the required courses. It also has a vigorous staff recruitment program and adequate candidate pools to allow vacancies to be filled promptly. The program is close to fully staffed, with the obvious exceptions that the Resident Advocate and permanent Clinical Director positions are vacant. The active Clinical Director has accomplished a great deal, particularly with respect to improving the program's treatment planning and clinical decision-making procedures. As a result of turnover and expansion, many of the clinical staff are new, and vary considerable with respect to their training and experience. Some have worked with sexual offenders before; others have come from different specialties such as addictions or child abuse investigation. As a result on the job training and ongoing clinical supervision are needed to ensure that all staff are providing the program's components accordingly. (Marques, 2000, p. 8)

Marques also noted that "substantial efforts had been made to improve treatment planning at SCC. Qualified consultants were retained to evaluate existing plans, suggest improvements, and train staff in writing plans that are individualized and comprehensive. . . . At the time of my visit, all treatment plans were up to date and had been approved by the acting Clinical Director" (p. 10).

In addition, Marques noted that the number of residents participating in treatment had increased, with over two-thirds of residents signing treatment consent forms during that trimester.

Record-keeping at SCC had improved considerably. A records clerk was added to the staff in January in order to improve maintenance of resident treatment records. There is now a chart room in each of the unit's three living areas, allowing staff ready access to the charts they need. Having office space on the units for Ft's has also improved their access to resident charts for recording their entries as well as reading entries by residential care staff. The charts I reviewed were well organized and each had a current treatment plan and trimester review, along with progress notes by both residential and clinical staff. . . . Trimester reports were completed on all residents at the end of the last trimester and feedback was provided to those who agreed to meet with their treatment teams. In addition treatment teams had begun to review residents at mid-trimester, in order to determine if changes in their treatment regimens are needed and to give residents earlier feedback on their progress. . . . Clear phase promotion guidelines were developed and put into practice during the last trimester break. (Marques, 2000, p. 15)

Marques continued with the following comments:

As noted in my last report, senior staff of the Washington Institute for Mental Health Research and Training were developing a general set of rating scales for measuring treatment progress. These "Measures of Treatment Progress" consist of a set of anchored ratings grouped into four broad program areas (treatment participation, residential functioning, accountability and relapse prevention). The measures are relevant to the targets of the program, provide clinically useful information, and should enable treatment teams to be consistent in their judgments regarding treatment progress. They were first used in the January trimester break; a slightly revised set of the measures will be used at the end of the current trimester. Guidelines for using these new measures to determine readiness for phase promotion have also been developed and will be incorporated into the next trimester reviews. (pp. 18–19)

Marques also noted that the SCC addressed the importance of family relationships and support, but although twelve residents have family counseling in their treatment plans, the number of sessions with family members is small.

With regard to community transition, the SCC had hired a community transition manager, written policy and procedures for community placement, described service system components, and conducted site visits of available off-island facilities that would be suitable for placing some of SCC's residents.

Major concerns for the clinical department were outlined in the following criticisms. This author's response to these is set out in italics:

- There should be ongoing monitoring of treatment components to ensure they are consistent with written descriptions and this could be achieved by clinical supervisors and psychologists observing modules and groups but this was being done infrequently.

  We had been very busy and had only observed eleven groups and classes during the third trimester. I assigned six psychologists and managers to observe groups and classes.

- The SCC should ensure that appropriate individualized treatment is provided to residents with special needs.

We had reviewed every treatment plan for special needs residents with Western State Hospital staff including psychologists, recreational thera-pists, and forensic therapists who worked with special needs staff and incorporated their input.

- Resident attendance in treatment activities is being tracked but there was no information regarding this in the clinical charts.

We tracked this information and recorded this in the form of the Measures of Change instrument, which was now formally incorporated in the trimester review process and was placed in the clinical chart.

- The psychiatric social worker assigned to develop family relationships and support and who provided families and couple counseling worked only 50 percent on the unit.

Currently there was not sufficient demand for him to be there full-time, but as soon as the demand increased he would be assigned there full time. He was spending a lot of time on the unit talking to residents about using his services.

- There is still tension between clinical staff and residential staff particular-ly with respect as to how behavioral incidents were handled.

We were arranging team building training between residential and clinical staff and planned to send a schedule to the Special Master.

- The community transition manager was involved in transition planning for three advanced residents. The community placement of these individuals was progressing without the endorsement of the treatment team.

This was incorrect. SCC was endorsing community placement for two indi-viduals and had been supporting the community placement of a third indi-vidual, but it was recently discovered he had smoked marijuana and in view of the fact that this was a dynamic risk factor for him, we could not support him for community placement until he had dealt with this issue in treatment.

- The SCC failed to acknowledge the progress made by residents in prior treatment programs.

We were setting up an evaluation team to assess such individuals and place them into the appropriate phase of treatment.

May 2000 Injunction Hearing

Judge Dwyer issued an order in which he found that the state had been making a genuine and sustained effort to comply with the injunction but was still not in full compliance. He ordered that sanctions to be stayed but to continue to accrue. He fur-ther ordered the state to file a monthly progress and accounting report on the 15th of each month. Another hearing was set for December 5, 2000.

Eighteenth Report: More Family Involvement Necessary

In her eighteenth report, Marques (2000b) noted the following:

- *Staff competence.* Staff supervision was scheduled on a regular basis; most of it was informal and did not include structured assessment of the employees' competencies or provide written feedback to employees. Performance evaluations were not consistently being completed. Or provided to staff on time. Systematic tracking of staff training had begun but transcripts for current staff were not yet complete. Residential care staff had not been incorporated into the treatment program. Although their participation on treatment team meetings had increased, some RRCs attended meetings for many residents and some attended none. Residents complained that FTs and RRCs have openly disagreed on the handling of behavioral incidents and security concerns. It is recommended that more work be done on role clarification; more collaborative assignments and additional clinical-residential training experiences should be provided to develop a more cohesive interdisciplinary team. The unit staffing model should be implemented to improve team effectiveness. Ongoing guidance and supervision must be provided by clinical and residential team leaders.

- *Treatment components.* The program lost the services of the two consultants working with the special needs treatment team and the SCC contracted with James Haaven who ran a similar program at the Oregon State Hospital. Progress notes needed to be improved. Many charts had only two per month. Few entries addressed the resident's treatment plan or goals. More frequent and detailed notes were found in the charts of residents with special needs. Family contacts had increased, but the SCC should do more work to encourage family involvement and support. Family members continued to report that they are not contacted regularly or informed about support meetings on a timely basis. The SCC should develop a database of family contact information and ensure that these individuals are informed as to what is happening. The SCC should continue its efforts in including medical and psychiatric concerns in treatment plans. Clinical experts in the field of developmental disabilities should be on staff or available to consult with the special needs treatment team. The SCC has a community transition manager who is working on transition plans for the SCC's most advanced treatment residents, but an appropriate LRA facility is not available. DSHS is in the process of creating a thirty-bed stepdown facility.

- *Treatment environment.* DOC was still involved in resident management activities. A number of treatment activities had been canceled or delayed because they were scheduled at the same time as DOC movements. Expansion of vocational and work opportunities was delayed because of a lack of programming space. Additional resources are needed to provide meaningful vocational training. Residents were complaining that drugs and alcohol were on the unit and some staff members were unprofessional and disrespectful. Residents were complaining of problems in the area of medical care, including accessibility, quality of service, and the need to get medications via the DOC pill line. The SCC should follow through on its plans to have more of theses services provided by its own medical professionals, such as having medications dispensed by staff on the unit. Work should be done to clarify the use of restraints and seclusion. The proposed "unit staffing model" should still be implemented in February 2001 to encourage more consistent and individualized care.

• *Mental health program model (internal and external oversight).* A well-qualified advisory board does not meet often enough to provide advice and assistance on the wide range of developments that are taking place in the program. The SCC program is inspected annually by outside professionals who use a comprehensive survey instrument that is based on current professional standards. Plans of correction for deficiencies noted in the IOC report are required by the program's governing body.

December 2000 Injunction Hearing

The injunction hearing that took place on December 5, 2000, determined that there were a number of remaining issues to be dealt with, such as selecting a site for a new facility; reducing the McNeil Island Correctional Center negative impact at the SCC; developing individualized treatment plans with discharge criteria included; and to "show a light at the end of the tunnel," establishing LRA facilities for residents on McNeil Island and off McNeil Island. Judge Dwyer issued an order continuing the sanctions and setting the next hearing for July 2001. Monthly reports were to continue.

Inspection of Care Review

The IOC team conducted an interim review and made the following recommendations:

• *Staff competence.* Work should continue to ensure that all performance evaluations are up to date and continue to be performed yearly

• *Treatment components.* Staff understood charting requirements, but this did not extend to goal-oriented charting methods and procedures. Residential staff wanted to become more involved in behavioral management issues, specifically administrative reviews of behavior management reports (BMRs). Staff complained that results of BMRs were not divulged to residential staff, who often initiated the process. This vacuum reportedly results in suspicions that clinical staff "side" with residents against the involved residential staff. Some manner of information sharing about the clinician's determinations may represent an opportunity to develop a unified and cohesive approach to therapeutically defined behavioral expectations and consequences. Treatment plans did not specifically identify what residents needed to do to be discharged. The discharge plan statement should outline to some extent what needs to be accomplished for discharge. More work and training needed to be done on goal-based charting. The charting system needed to be improved. Medical and clinical charts were housed off the unit and desk chart was available on the unit. Progress notes were written on the unit, then filed off-unit. As a result, unit staff members did not have ready access to relevant background and prior notes, and there was only limited continuity to charting. Chart notes were incomplete and lacked fundamental data. The method of managing records/documentation still needs improvement and refinement. Medical and clinical charts should be kept on the unit. The SCC should consult with a medical records technician, establish a chart-user committee, and hire a medical records specialist.

- *Treatment environment.* Work should continue to provide offices for clinical staff on the living units. The SCC should continue with its plans to provide insulin injection and delivery of all medications on the unit. The SCC should continue its work to develop a medical database. The program should continue efforts toward achieving medical independence.

Nineteenth Report: Final Recap of the Special Master

In her nineteenth report, Marques (2001a) noted the following:

- *Staff competence.* Training transcripts for all SCC staff were completed and were being updated regularly. Seventy-three staff members had received training on professional boundaries and teamwork. Training on goal-oriented charting was provided to forty-three residential staff. Clinical supervision was provided in regularly scheduled individual and group meetings. During the current trimester, four groups or classes per week were observed by senior clinical staff. Some 86 percent of annual evaluations due by May 1, 2002, had been completed (compared with 37 percent at this time the previous year). Teamwork between residential and clinical staff had improved. Some treatment team leaders were present at the biweekly meetings of the residential care managers and supervisors. Most treatment plans and trimester reviews had documentation of residential staff involvement. The "unit staffing model" was fully implemented on the SCC's special needs unit and the FTs and residential care supervisors had offices on the unit. Both clinical and residential staff members attended the team meetings held on the unit three days per week. However, residential staff needed to make more entries in the charts and some communication problems existed between clinical and residential staff, particularly around behavioral management decisions. Programwide implementation of the unit staffing model had taken longer than expected due to a number of factors including physical plant. A need for further staff training in crisis intervention and managing aggressive behavior had recently been identified but the training had not yet occurred.

- *Treatment components.* There had been recent improvements in the extent to which treatment plans include resident's medical and psychiatric concerns—efforts in this area needed to continue. The special needs program must ensure that individuals with expertise in developmental disabilities are on staff. Ongoing consultation should be provided on individual cases as well as on treatment planning and curriculum development. In this respect the SCC had retained the services of a nationally recognized expert from Oregon State Hospital (James Haaven) to give advice on program structure, assessment, treatment planning, treatment milieu, and how to build effective interdisciplinary teams. A developmental disabilities specialist from Western State Hospital had been contracted to meet with the special needs team for several hours twice a month to develop and refine treatment plans. Improvements in progress notes were still needed to make these more useful in evaluating resident's progress toward treatment goals. To improve family involvement, the SCC needed to develop a complete and accurate database of family contact information and ensure that these individuals have clear opportunities to stay informed and involved. The SCC had also taken action to address issues noted in the IOC report: Each treatment plan included a paragraph describing what the resident must do to be considered for discharge; a new progress note was developed to encourage goal-oriented charting by RRCs, and a medical records specialist position was included in the new budget. An appropriate LRA facility was still not available, due to public resistance, although DSHS had recently launched a comprehensive and well-managed effort to create LRA options. Legislation was passed that would allow the immediate siting of an LRA facility at the North Complex on McNeil Island. However, this did not complete the community transition element of the program. The next step into the community still needed to be taken. This was the most important piece of unfinished business.

- *Treatment environment.* More therapist offices had been moved to the residential units, with fourteen offices on the units. The unit staffing model (in which RRCs are assigned to a specific living area and resident group, and are expected to work with therapists as part of the treatment team) was fully implemented in the special needs unit and partially implemented in other program areas. The North Complex on McNeil Island had been selected as the site for the SCCs permanent new facility and planning was underway to complete renovations—build new wings so that eventually the SCC would be able to operate independently of the prison, though marine transportation and perimeter security would still continue to be provided by DOC. Significant improvements had been made in the SCC's medical services: A "may carry meds" program had been implemented for responsible residents; a small clinic had been opened on a unit; the nursing service had been restructured so each nurse had a caseload and regular service responsibilities; a weekly chronic care clinic staffed by an internist had been initiated; and a medical database had been established. Resources for Native American cultural and spiritual activities had increased. A Native American culturalist had been contracted with. The SCC had completed a number of improvements to be compliant with the Americans With Disabilities Act. The SCC policy analyst had completed the first draft of a set of policies addressing the restraint, isolation, and seclusion of residents. Once adopted, along with revision of existing policies on behavioral management and use of restraints, it will provide a graduated comprehensive approach to behavioral intervention. Marques noted some issues that needed to be addressed: time frames for responding to grievances, grievance appeals, and the fact that requests for administrative reviews and appeals of administrative review decisions were being ignored. Only five room searches had been conducted since the first quarter of 2001, well below the five searches per week the program had set as its standard. The SCC ombudsman complained that program managers had failed to adequately investigate a number of resident abuse allegations. There were concerns about the SCC's housing of youthful offenders with adults, and that the SCC should provide additional protections for its vulnerable residents. Residents complained that the surrounding prison had some impact on the program. Residents encountered inmates and inmate workers have regularly been in the SCC unit doing plumbing, electrical, and woodworking tasks. The current resident advisory structure was not seen as an effective way to incorporate resident input into the program and should be replaced with other methods for accomplishing these goals. There was no room for a vocational program and the visiting area was crowded on weekends. The new draft policies on the use of restrictive interventions should be approved for implementation.

July 2001 Injunction Hearing

The injunction hearing took place from July 9–11, 2001, and was held before Magistrate Weinberg who made a report and recommendation to Judge Dwyer. Judge Dwyer accepted these recommendations and issued an order on August 14, 2001. The order stated that the remaining issues for the SCC to meet injunction compliance was to establish a temporary LRA on McNeil Island and to commit to establishing a permanent LRA adjacent to the projected SCC facility at the northern part of the Island; to establish one or more LRA facilities other than McNeil Island; to commit to building a new SCC facility outside the perimeter of McNeil Island Correctional Center; to fill the resident advocate position and fill vacancies in the advisory board; to appoint a new ombudsman; to develop vocational training facilities in the existing facility; and to formulate plans for adequate space, staff, and program at the new SCC facility. Although significant process had been made, the state was not in full compliance and sanctions will continue to accrue.

Janice Marques requested that she step down as Special Master and the court deemed it unnecessary to appoint a new one. Judge Dwyer commended her for her valuable role and informed her that her work and reports were of great benefit to all involved, including the court, the parties, the public, and all institutions in the United States that are devoted to the treatment of persons civilly committed as SVPs.

By the time Marques resigned as Special Master, the SCC had in place a state-of-the-art treatment program. There is no doubt that she was the driving force behind most of the changes that took place at the SCC. She had recommended that in order for the program to become similar to a mental health facility, the SCC put in place oversight mechanisms, an advisory board, and an IOC team. In some ways the IOC team began to take over her role in ensuring that the SCC maintained a dynamic treatment program. The Federal Court began to rely on the reports of the IOC.

February 2002 Injunction Hearing

As a result of Judge Dwyer's declining health, the case was reassigned to Judge Barbara Rothstein in 2002. Judge Rothstein signed the order from the February 25 evidentiary hearing on April 17, 2002. The ruling provided for the denial of the defendant's motion to dismiss the injunction and denial of the plaintiffs' motion for sanctions in part. The elements for the SCC to accomplish were as follows: fund and establish LRA facilities in locations other than McNeil Island; develop additional LRA space; appoint a new ombudsman; develop vocational training facilities and programs as soon and as fully as possible in the SCC's current location and formulate plans for adequate space, staff, and program at the new SCC facility; fully implement effective grievance procedures; revise and continue regular consultations for the special needs program; and finalize measures of progress for the special needs population

December 2002 Injunction Hearing

Judge Barbara Rothstein signed the order from the December 13 and December 16 evidentiary hearings on February 26, 2003. Judge Rothstein reported:

> Since the February 2002 hearing, defendants have continued to make progress towards injunction compliance in several important areas. The permanent LRA facility on McNeil Island is near completion; occupancy is scheduled for sometime in early 2003. Defendants have also identified several potential sites for an off-Island LRA. Defendants had hired an Ombudsman, Penny Rarick. Defendants have advanced the treatment program for SCC Special Needs residents by developing Measures of Progress. The evidence continues to show however, that much of the defendant's progress appears influenced by the impending date of the compliance hearing. Just as before the last compliance hearing in February 2002, a flurry of activity is concentrated within weeks, or even days of the hearing. It is therefore evident that the improvements defendants have made, come in small part, in response to the court's contempt orders and to the accrual of sanctions. (pp. 4–5)

Judge Rothstein noted that collaboration between residential and clinical staff had improved, resulting in a better treatment environment, especially in the special needs program. The SCC had made progress in improving vocational programming and had hired a manager with numerous years of experience in the vocational rehabilitation field to supervise and develop vocational programs at the SCC and the Secure Community Transitional Facility (SCTF). The new manager had made considerable headway in developing vocational programs for both regular track and special needs residents and redesigning the jobs program at the SCC. The SCC had significantly improved the grievance process. Revisions to policy were made and a full-time grievance investigator hired.

Judge Rothstein pointed out, however, the "while defendants have indeed made progress in achieving several goals of the injunction, there is evidence of backsliding in at least one critical area: the adequacy of the SCC's charting of resident's treatment plan and progress, as documented by the IOC" (p. 16).

Judge Rothstein concluded:

> Defendants continue to make great strides towards compliance with the injunction and purging the contempt. . . . They will be in full compliance with the injunction when they accomplish the following steps: (a): develop and fund off-Island LRA's; (b) develop and fund adequate LRA capacity space soon enough to ensure that there will be sufficient available capacity so that residents can apply for LRA status and receive prompt placement if they are found to qualify; (c) continue progress in the development of vocational training programs and apply for funding where there is a perceived need; (d) continue progress in the special needs program and apply for funding where there is a perceived need, and (e) correct the long-standing deficiencies in the treatment program so as to provide SCC residents with a clear roadmap to release. (p. 19)

It can be seen from this report that the court is using the IOC report to guide its judgment, similar to the way that the Special Master's reports were used.

The program has demonstrated that release is possible through treatment. The SCC has released a number of residents to LRAs. Three residents live in a group home, three are living in heir own homes, and four are in the SCTF at the North Complex at McNeil Island opened in the spring of 2003. As provided in the law, the SCC program must develop SCTFs in mainland locations. Following an extensive search for property meeting the statutory siting requirements, the SCC program selected a site that is an existing commercial property in South Seattle. After extensive remodeling has been completed, the building is projected to open in August 2005 as the new SCTF in King County. Eventually, as needed, state law provides the option to site SCTFs in five other counties besides King County. The SCC has almost met the court requirements to lift the injunction

OTHER FACTORS AFFECTING THE DEVELOPMENT OF THE SCC PROGRAM

New SCC Facility

In May 2004, the SCC moved to a newly constructed facility on McNeil Island at the island's North Complex location. This modern facility has a capacity of 268 beds. Design plans provide for expansion in phases as needed to accommodate up to a maximum of 450 adults. There is adequate programming space, a gymnasium, music rooms, and a library, and it is designed as an open campus.

Use of Consultants

A number of individuals were vital to the development of the SCC program. SCC staff have worked incredibly hard over the years to meet the demands of the court and to develop a state-of-the-art program. We owe a great a great debt to Dr. Marques and all the consultants who have given the SCC their skills and advice to develop a professional program recognized as being one of the most advanced in states with such programs. These consultants include Dr. Robert Prentky who had worked in the Massachusetts sex offender program; Dr. Anita Schlank, former clinical director of the Minnesota Sex Offender Program; Dr. Ray Wood, clinical director of the Illinois SVP program; Dr. Craig Nelson, former clinical director of the Atascadero State Hospital; Dr. Gary Johnson of the Washington Institute, who helped the SCC develop measures of progress for residents participating in the treatment program; Dr. Chuck Lund and Donna Dykstra, who worked with developmentally disabled sex offenders and helped the SCC to set up a program for special needs residents; James Haaven, M.S., who ran the program for developmentally disabled sex offenders at Oregon State Hospital, and accepted a contract to continue the work of Dr. Lund and assist the SCC to further develop the special needs program; Dr. Walter Tunstall, who provides consultation on special need treatment plans; Dr. John Turner, who had taught staff to write treatment plans at Western State Hospital and was hired to train clinical staff in writing effective treatment plans; Dr. Henry Cellini, who was hired to train residential and clinical staff in boundary issues and mental health training; staff from the Justice Institute of British Columbia who provided the SCC with a 120-hour advanced sex offender treatment training program; and Dr. Henry Richards, who developed a severe personality disorder track and trained clinical staff in group counseling skills and in scoring the Psychopathy Checklist—Revised (Hare, 1991). He is the current superintendent of the SCC.

Inspection of Care Team

This team of outside professionals is now filling a role that the Special Master had—conducting regular inspections of the SCC to ensure that it is meeting the professional standards for adequate mental health treatment for sexual offenders under civil commitment. The SCC has a core team consisting of Robert Briody, Ph.D, who was until recently the executive director of the Florida SVP program; Maureen Saylor, a state-certified sex offender therapist and who was previously the director of the Sexual Psychopathy Program at Western State Hospital; and Dorcas Dobie, M.D., a psychiatrist with the Veterans Administration. Dr. Dobie recently resigned after taking another appointment, and the team has now been joined by two experienced health facility surveyors, one who is an expert in reviewing medical care and the other an expert in reviewing facility management and the operation of food services. Dr. Briody and Ms. Saylor have considerable experience in running sex offense treatment programs in institutions and provide a valuable service to the SCC.

Impact of Attorneys

Prosecutors and defense attorneys greatly affected the way that the SCC undertook forensic evaluations of SCC residents. The resident was to be sent for evaluation and treatment services to the same facility. By statute within forty-five days after admission, commitment evaluations are to be completed. The evaluation process was expensive and cumbersome. The defense attorneys hired their own expert to evaluate the resident. The prosecuting attorneys hired their own expert and SCC psychologists also conducted evaluations of the resident.

SCC psychologists who undertook these evaluations also provided treatment services to residents. It was rapidly realized that if a psychologist undertook an evaluation and testified in court, and the resident was civilly committed as an SVP, the resident typically held considerable animosity toward the psychologist. This made for some interesting group dynamics when the resident became a member of the group the psychologist was running. Due to staff shortages it was not always possible to assign the resident to a different group.

It was decided to set up a forensic unit composed of psychologists whose duties would consist solely of undertaking commitment evaluations and completing annual reviews of the residents who were committed to the SCC to report on their progress to the court and determine whether their mental abnormality had so changed that they could be released to a least restrictive alternative. The SCC was fortunate in that it is located next to Western State Hospital which had a forensic postdoctoral program. These students provided a pool of recruits for the the SCC clinical department. The SCC was eventually able to get a staff member appointed the internship committee and, within a couple of years, the SCC was able to negotiate that the residents completed one of their three rotations at the SCC. This gave the SCC the opportunity to evaluate the interns while they worked at the SCC. As a result, the SCC was able to hire some outstanding young psychologists. Due to the fact that the SCC had a backlog of evaluations, new forensic psychologists were hired and put them to work immediately writing evaluations. These evaluators were based in the administrative offices in Steilacoom and not on McNeil Island. As soon as possible, however, this practice was changed to ensure that those psychologists hired to be forensic psychologists had to spend at least a year delivering treatment services to residents, to ensure they were familiar with the treatment program and the treatment process, before they were transferred to the forensic unit.

It takes time to train competent forensic psychologists who have the knowledge, skills, and abilities to write excellent reports and testify in court as an expert witness. Due to the growth of the SCC, we were falling behind on the annual review reports. There was pressure from prosecuting and defense attorneys to improve and change the system so that reports could be completed more quickly. We had recognized that the evaluation process was cumbersome and expensive, and in 2002 a committee was set up to make changes to this process. The committee consisted of representatives from the SCC, DOC, King County prosecutors, assistant attorney general's SVP prosecution unit, and the public defenders association. It was decided that the commitment evaluations would be undertaken by psychologists who would be selected to be part of a joint forensic unit and that SCC psychologists would not undertake commitment evaluations but concentrate their efforts on undertaking annual review reports of those residents committed to the SCC. This is the system in operation today.

SUMMARY

Taking a position as clinical director enabled me to see, firsthand, how difficult it is to develop an effective treatment program without adequate resources. When the legislature passed the SVP law in 1990, many legislators saw this as a way to keep dangerous sex offenders off the streets indefinitely. There were no clear standards for treating such offenders and the SCC's initial treatment program was inadequate. The

SCC was found to have violated the civil rights of a resident by not providing him with access to minimally adequate mental health treatment offering a realistic opportunity for cure or improvement in the mental condition that caused the confinement. Without a doubt the SCC program benefited from the federal injunction imposed because of this situation. The SCC would not have the resources to hire so many excellent consultants to help us develop this treatment program and train our staff, nor would we have had the resources move in to a newly constructed mental health facility.

After the SVP law was enacted no one knew whether it was constitutional. It took decisions from Washington Superior Court and the U.S. Supreme Court to resolve that issue. It was at this point that SCC residents chose to enter treatment hoping that it was a way to get released. The SCC was forced by the court to develop a viable treatment program to ensure that residents could be conditionally released after successfully completing the phases of the treatment program. I know that when we were developing this program, the SCC management team felt that we were serving many masters, all of whom were telling us how to improve the SCC program. These included the court, the Special Master, the advisory board, and the IOC team. Residents have been released into the community after successfully completing the treatment program. However, there are many challenges still to face. There are unique issues associated with this highly dangerous population, which will call for flexibility in developing and changing the treatment program to meet these challenges.

Footnotes

[1] Wash. Rev. Code § 71.09 (2000).

[2] Turay v. Weston, No. C91–664WD (unpub. op., W.D. Wash. 1994), later known as Turay v. Seling, No. C91–664WD (unpub. op. W.D. Wash. 1997).

[3] Kansas v. Hendricks, 521 U.S. 346 (1997).

[4] Sharp v. Weston, 233 F.3d 1166 (9th Cir. 2000).

[5] Turay v. Seling, 108 F. Supp. 2d 1154–1155 (W.D. Wash. 1994).

References

Dwyer, W. (1999). *Findings of fact, conclusions of law and order re: hearing on November 15, 1999. Turay v. Weston.* U.S. District Court Western District of Washington at Seattle.

Hare, R. (1991). *Psychopathy Checklist—Revised.* Toronto, Ontario, Canada: Multi-Health Systems.

Lieb, R. (2003). After *Hendricks*: Defining constitutional treatment for Washington State's civil commitment program. *Annals of the New York Academy of Sciences, 989*(1), 474–488.

Marques, J. K. (1994, December 13). *First, preliminary report of the Special Master, Turay v. Weston.*

Marques, J. K. (1995a, February 13). *Second report of the Special Master, Turay v. Weston.*

Marques, J. K. (1995b, April 13). *Third report of the Special Master, Turay v. Weston.*

Marques, J. K. (1995c, June 13). *Fourth report of the Special Master, Turay v. Weston.*

Marques, J. K. (1995d, August 14). *Fifth report of the Special Master, Turay v. Weston.*

Marques, J. K. (1995e, November 13). *Sixth report of the Special Master, Turay v. Weston.*

Marques, J. K. (1996a, January 15). *Seventh report of the Special Master, Turay v. Weston.*

Marques, J. K. (1996b, May 30). *Eighth report of the Special Master, Turay v. Weston.*

Marques, J. K. (1996c, July 30). *Ninth report of the Special Master, Turay v. Weston.*

Marques, J. K. (1997a, January 5). *Tenth report of the Special Master, Turay v. Weston.*

Marques, J. K. (1997b, May 2). *Eleventh report of the Special Master, Turay v. Weston.*

Marques, J. K. (1997c, September 12). *Twelfth report of the Special Master,* Turay v. Seling.

Marques, J. K. (1998, May 1). *Thirteenth report of the Special Master,* Turay v. Seling.

Marques, J. K. (1998, September 25). *Fourteenth report of the Special Master,* Turay v. Seling.

Marques, J. K. (1999a, May 6). *Fifteenth report of the Special Master,* Turay v. Seling.

Marques, J. K. (1999b, September 9). *Sixteenth report of the Special Master,* Turay v. Seling.

Marques, J. K. (2000a, April 11). *Seventeenth report of the Special Master,* Turay v. Seling.

Marques, J. K. (2000b, November 27). *Eighteenth report of the Special Master,* Turay v. Seling.

Marques, J. K. (2001a, June 25). *Nineteenth report of the Special Master,* Turay v. Seling.

Marques, J. K. (2001b). Professional standards for civil commitment programs. In A. Schlank (Ed.), *The sexual predator: Legal issues, clinical issues, special populations* (pp. 2-1–2-15). Kingston, NJ: Civic Research Institute.

Nelson, C. (1998). *Consultation report: Special Commitment Center,* Turay v. Seling.

Quinsey, V. L. (1992). *Review of the Washington State Special Commitment Center program for sexually violent predators* (appendix to *Review of sexual predator program: Community Protection Research Project*). Olympia: Washington State Institute for Public Policy.

Rothstein, B. (2003, February 26). *Findings of fact, conclusions of law, and order re: hearing held December 13 and 16, 2002). Richard G. Turay, Plaintiff v. Mark Seling et al., Defendants,* No. C91-664R. *Jerry R. Sharp et al., Plaintiffs v. David B. Weston et al.,* Defendants, No. C94-121R. *Randy Pederson et al., Plaintiffs v. Tim Hill et al., Defendants,* No. C94-211R. *John F. Hall et al., Plaintiffs v. Lyle Quasim, et al., Defendants,* No. C95-1111R.

Schlank, A. (1998). *Consultation report: Special Commitment Center,* Turay v. Seling.

Part 3
Special Populations

Certain specific subgroups of sexual offenders always present special concerns for treatment providers, given their unique treatment needs. The problems raised by residents who score high on psychopathy have been the focus of many debates, as have the issues raised by juveniles and young adults whose offenses have only occurred while in the juvenile courts. In addition, the question of how to best meet the chemical dependency treatment needs of sexual offenders remains a significant concern.

John Edens has written extensively about the classification and treatment of psychopathic individuals. In Chapter 14, Dr. Edens and Anita Schlank collaborate to discuss the issues surrounding efforts to treat psychopathic sexual offenders, beginning with the debate about the amenability to treatment of such individuals.

In Chapter 15, Janis Bremer provides an update on the issues surrounding juveniles who are civilly committed as sexual offenders, as well as young adults whose sexual offenses occurred only while they were still in the juvenile court system.

In Volume II of *The Sexual Predator*, William Plum provided a general discussion of the chemical dependency needs of the SVP population. In Chapter 16 of this volume, he focuses on the specific issues of how substance abuse relates to disordered sexual arousal and the need for experiential techniques to address the problem of euphoric recall of substance abuse.

Chapter 14

Psychopathy in the Civilly Committed Population of Sexual Offenders— Treatment Issues

by Anita Schlank, Ph.D. and John Edens, Ph.D.

INTRODUCTION

While significant disagreement occurs regarding whether or not treatment for sexual offenders is effective (or "effective enough"), even more conflict emerges when the discussion turns to those sexual offenders who also happen to be high in psychopathic traits. Some experts have suggested that there is no successful treatment for psychopathy. They believe treatment providers can do little more than effectively manage psychopaths in institutional settings (Reid & Gacono, 2000) and that treatment might actually make psychopaths even more dangerous (D'Silva, Duggan, & McCarthy, 2004). In their meta-analysis, D'Silva et al. also note that some offenders have even been refused entry into some programs on the grounds of their high score on the Hare Psychopathy Checklist—Revised (PCL-R; Hare, 1991), whereas other programs (L. Sinclair, personal communication, December 1, 2003; Wong & Hare, 2005) divert psychopathic sexual offenders into a different "track" of treatment. The population of civilly committed sexual offenders tends to have a relatively high number of residents who score high on psychopathic traits. This is not surprising, given that the presence of psychopathic traits is often a very influential factor in determining an individual's risk and need for possible civil commitment. Both the Violence Risk Appraisal Guide (VRAG; Quinsey, Harris, Rice, & Cormier, 1998) and the Historical Clinical/Risk Management 20-Item instrument (HCR-20; Webster, Douglas, Eaves, & Hart, 1997) rely on the PCL-R, among other factors, for assessing risk. And, Rice and Harris (1997) reported that the combination of psychopathic traits and sexual deviancy resulted in the highest recidivism rate in their sample of sex offenders. Therefore, questions regarding psychopathic individuals' amenability to treatment are of particular importance to those administering civil commitment programs.

PSYCHOPATHY AS A CONSTRUCT

The term "psychopath" that historically has been used in sexually violent predator (SVP) legislation is quite different from the way it is used currently by diagnosticians and researchers to refer to a clinical designation (Edens & Petrila, in press). In SVP statutes, the term refers to an inability to control one's behavior, making the individual more likely to engage in predatory sexual violence. Gacono (1998) offered a historical perspective of the construct of the "psychopath," noting that nearly 200 years ago a French physician encountered a number of cases that did not readily fit into any contemporary classification. These individuals were believed to have normal intellect but also suffered profound affective abnormalities and were prone to acts of violence. However, for most clinicians, the term "psychopath" refers to a person with a cluster of traits that overlaps with, but is not identical to, the diagnosis of antisocial personality disorder (APD). The diagnosis of APD is largely behavioral in nature and captures the antisocial acts and attitudes that are often seen in psychopaths; however, it does not appear to adequately capture the psychopath's emotional functioning and relationships with others. Cleckley (1976) described a psychopath as showing the following traits:

- Superficial charm;
- Absence of delusions and other irrational thinking;
- Absence of nervousness;
- Unreliability;
- Untruthfulness;
- Insincerity;
- Lack of remorse;
- Antisocial behavior;
- Poor judgment;
- Failure to learn from experience;
- Pathological egocentricity;
- Incapacity for love; and
- General poverty in major affective reactions.

Hare (1991) agreed with Cleckley's basic formulation, arguing that the deficient affective response toward other people is one of the essential features of a psychopath.

The PCL-R (Hare, 1991) is currently the most widely accepted tool for assessing core psychopathic personality characteristics. The PCL-R is a twenty-item scale consisting of two factors. Factor 1 identifies a combination of interpersonal and affective traits that generally describes a tendency to be selfish, callous, lacking in remorse, and exploitative of others. Factor 2 identifies socially deviant features that reflect a chronically unstable, impulsive, irresponsible, and antisocial lifestyle. Although more recent factor-analytic research has examined three- and four-factor models (Cooke & Michie, 2001; Hare, 2003), the vast majority of the existing research has focused on the correlates of the original two factors. Each of the twenty items on the PCL-R may be scored between 0 and 2, allowing for a possible overall score between 0 and 40. A score of 30 and above is most often considered as the "cutoff" for a designation as a psychopath, although many research studies have used lower or higher numbers.

There is considerable debate about whether psychopathy is best understood as a taxon (i.e., a natural class), or whether it is better conceptualized as a continuous personality dimension. Using sophisticated taxometric analyses first developed by Meehl and colleagues, Harris, Rice, and Quinsey (1994) argued that they identified a latent psychopathy taxon in a large Canadian sample of offenders. Other researchers, (Edens, Marcus, Lilienfeld, & Poythress, 2005; Guay, Ruscio, Hare, & Knight, 2004; Marcus, John, & Edens, 2004) have failed to replicate these findings and have argued that psychopathy refers to a combination of features that occurs in many individuals to some degree, and that dichotomous distinctions between "psychopaths" and "non-psychopaths" reflect arbitrary cut points lacking any strong scientific justification. This debate is not settled, and future studies will continue to attempt to clarify that issue.

"TREATABILITY" OF PSYCHOPATHS

Individuals who score high on psychopathic traits are often viewed as a class of individuals who are not amenable for treatment. For example, Reid and Gacono (2000) describe how "normal" individuals develop a motivation for change to avoid the return of pain and anxiety and indicate their belief that these motivators are often absent in psychopaths. Others have claimed that psychopaths are unable to learn from experience, although Schopp and Slain (2000) argue that this belief is an oversimplification of basic learning principles. They point out that psychopaths must have learned from experience in order to drive cars, work at various professions, and develop many skills. They note that this claim of failure to learn is usually made in reference to the psychopath's self-defeating antisocial behavior, but what is ignored is that to psychopaths, the benefits from the times they were not caught might outweigh the consequences when they do get caught. In addition, they note that Schmauk (1970) revealed a significant insight into a psychopath's learning when he discovered that psychopaths showed no deficit in passive avoidance when monetary punishment was used. It appeared that psychopaths were not motivated to refrain from behaviors in order to avoid relatively mild punishments. However, when presented with a punishment that was relevant to their value system, they would engage in the desired behavior to avoid it.

With regard to studies of treatment outcome with psychopaths, a survey of the research shows conflicting information. Much attention as been paid to a study in which those judged to be "psychopaths" had a poorer outcome after completing a particular Canadian treatment program (Rice, Harris, & Cormier, 1992). It should be noted, however, that this program was almost entirely run by offenders, with inmates given the power to make important decisions regarding other offenders, such as whether they were released. In addition, techniques used in the program are now considered ethically questionable (such as nude marathon encounter sessions and LSD treatment), and do not resemble current treatment programs. Finally, the method for classifying program members as a psychopath was with a PCL-R cutoff score that is far lower than what is generally accepted as the cutoff score by most clinicians. Another study of residents who scored at or above 30 on the PCL-R (Hitchcock, 1995) evaluated the effect of a twice weekly criminal thinking group that lasted for twelve weeks. That study found no significant differences between the treatment and control group. However, the number of subjects was so small that little could be assumed from the results.

Ogloff, Wong, and Greenwood (1990) compared the treatment outcomes of psychopaths, nonpsychopaths, and a mixed group in a therapeutic community treatment program. They found that psychopaths remained in the program for a shorter period of time and showed less motivation and improvement than either of the other two groups. (Interestingly, the mixed group did demonstrate improvement, suggesting possible negative effects of segregating treatment clients based on PCL-R score.) However, Salekin, (2002) conducted a meta-analysis and concluded that highly structured, intensive treatment programs might be successful in treating offenders who score high on psychopathic traits.

An article by Seto and Barbaree (1999) also gained considerable attention due to its study of the association between psychopathy, treatment-behavior, and sex offender recidivism. In that study, offenders who scored high on psychopathic traits (by the PCL-R) and who were also assessed by staff to show positive treatment behavior were more likely to commit a new serious offense. This study is often cited by those wishing to point out the perceived dangers of treating psychopathic offenders (such as staff potentially being conned by positive treatment behavior) and to support the perception that treatment might make such individuals somehow "worse." However, it is important to note that a subsequent study on the same sample with a longer follow-up period showed that perceptions of treatment behavior were not related to outcome at all. In that study, individuals with higher PCL-R scores were more likely to be rearrested for any reoffense, regardless of perceived performance in treatment (Barbaree, Seto, & Langton, 2001). This same finding was replicated in a study by Looman, Abracen, Serin, and Marquis (2005). In their study of high-risk offenders in the Canadian system, sexual offenders with high PCL-R scores reoffended at a higher rate than low psychopathy offenders, regardless of perceived treatment behavior. However, those men who scored high on psychopathy but who were rated by clinicians as having lowered their risk at posttreatment did reoffend at a lower rate, suggesting that "some psychopaths may be responsive to a highly structured, intensive, cognitive-behaviorally based treatment program" (p. 563).

Although some have argued that high PCL-R scores are associated with higher rates of violence and other forms of misconduct in institutional settings (Gacono, Meloy, Speth, & Roske, 1997; Heilbrun et al., 1988; Young, Justice, Edberg, & Gacono, 2000), a recent meta-analysis of this literature (Guy, Edens, Anthony, & Douglas, in press) indicated that this association was much weaker than typically thought, with PCL-R scores correlating only marginally with institutional aggression and violence in U.S. studies.

Some investigators have uncovered some possible reasons why these treatment outcome differences might occur. For example, Hare et al. (1997) used single photon emission computerized tomography (SPECT) imaging, (a method for observing blood flow to different parts of the brain) and found differences in the way psychopaths and nonpsychopaths process emotional and neutral emotional words. Kiehl, Smith, Hare, and Liddle (2000) also found differences between psychopaths and "normals" in recognizing negative emotional words using functional magnetic resonance imaging (fMRI). These studies suggest that psychopaths might respond to "emotional" stimuli in a superficial manner through brain areas used for language rather than emotion. Because psychopaths appear less attuned to both their own emotional experiences and those of others, they may be believed to be less affected by emotional cues related to guilt or anxiety (Loving, 2002).

An important qualification to the preceding findings relates to the methodological quality of the research examining the relationship between psychopathy and treatment. For example, Looman et al. (2005) point out that Salekin included in his meta-analysis a number of publications rejected by previous authors because they were believed to be unsound, and that the majority of studies in that meta-analysis did not use recidivism as their criterion for success. D'Silva et al. (2004) recently evaluated all available research studies that assessed psychopathy and treatment outcome. They found that only three studies had a control group consisting of high-scoring psychopaths who were untreated, and all studies had methodological flaws. Given the small number of appropriately designed studies, the researchers were unable to perform a meta-analysis. Their examination of the available research studies showed inconsistent findings. They noted that four studies suggested that high-scoring psychopaths had a negative response to treatment, but four suggested the opposite. Overall, they found that there was insufficient evidence to conclude that treatment makes psychopaths worse. Also, although there was some evidence to suggest that psychopaths may be somewhat less likely to benefit from some types of treatment, that information was not believed to be proof that psychopathy is "untreatable."

SVP PROGRAMS AND PSYCHOPATHY

Most SVP programs have made a decision to incorporate residents who are high on psychopathic traits into the population with the rest of the participants, providing additional interventions intended to correct the increased cognitive distortions and criminal attitudes that these offenders tend to hold. However, the civil commitment sex offender treatment program in Wisconsin has decided to provide an entirely separate track for such residents, including a separate living unit. Wisconsin's "Corrective Thinking" track is designed especially for civilly committed residents who score 25 or higher on the PCL-R. The style of the therapists is different than the style of the therapists in the general SVP program. For example, questioning is more Socratic in the regular track; however, therapists in the Corrective Thinking track will interrupt residents who are avoiding responsibility for their behavior. The Corrective Thinking track therapists are also firmer and provide more challenging statements to the participants (Sinclair, 2003). It is still too early in the evolution of this special treatment track to determine if such separation will lead to improved treatment outcome

SUMMARY AND FUTURE DIRECTIONS

Many offender treatment programs have debated whether a different approach is necessary for those offenders who are assessed to be high on psychopathic traits. Some treatment providers reacted quickly to studies that suggested that psychopaths might be untreatable, or that treatment might even make them worse; however, there is insufficient data to support such an assumption at this time. Although there is a lack of evidence to suggest that psychopaths are untreatable, there is sufficient evidence to suggest that sexual offenders who score high on the PCL-R are likely to be more difficult to treat, and their attitudes may have a detrimental effect on the progress of other residents. This issue of amenability of psychopaths for treatment becomes particularly important for SVP programs, where it is generally reported that approximately one-fifth of the residents score 30 or higher on the PCL-R. One program has developed a separate track for treating the psychopathic offenders, and sexual offender treatment providers are eagerly awaiting results to determine whether this separation of residents and difference in approach will lead to increased success rates in treatment. Additional research is also needed to determine how SVP programs can be adapted to incorporate interventions more closely related to the psychopaths' learning style, and to also use behavioral consequences for problem behavior that will be more relevant to the value system of a psychopath. It has been suggested that increasing the focus on assisting the psychopath to see "what's in it for me" (Loving, 2002; Young et al., 2000) might lead to improved treatment outcome. In addition, there is some evidence to suggest that a more detailed assessment of the two different factors on the PCL-R could lead to a richer understanding of the client and more effective treatment planning, and item analysis may identify specific strengths that can be capitalized on in treatment (Loving, 2002).

References

Barbaree, H. E., Seto, M. C., & Langton, C. M. (2001, October). *Psychopathy, treatment behavior and sex offender recidivism: Extended follow-up.* Paper presented at the annual meeting of the Association for the Treatment of Sexual Abusers, San Antonio, TX.

Cleckley, H. (1976). *The mask of sanity.* St. Louis, MO: Mosby.

Cooke, D. J., & Michie, C. (2001). Refining the construct of psychopathy: Towards a hierarchical model. *Psychological Assessment, 13,* 171–188.

D'Silva, K., Duggan, C., & McCarthy, L. (2004). Does treatment really make psychopaths worse? A review of the evidence. *Journal of Personality Disorders, 18*(2), 163–177.

Edens, J. F., Marcus, D. K., Lilienfeld, S. O., & Poythress, N. G. (2005). *Psychopathic, not psychopath: Taxometric evidence for the dimensional structure of psychopathy.* Manuscript submitted for publication.

Edens, J .F., & Petrila, J. (in press). Legal and ethical issues in the assessment and treatment of psychopath. In C. Patrick (Ed.), *Handbook of psychopathy.* New York: Guilford Press.

Gacono, C. (1998) The use of the Psychopathy Checklist—Revised (PCL-R) and Rorschach in treatment planning with antisocial personality disordered patients. *International Journal of Offender Therapy and Comparative Criminology, 42*(1), 49–64.

Gacono. C., Meloy, J. R., Speth, E., & Roske, A. (1997). Above the law: Escapees from a maximum-security forensic hospital. *Bulletin of the American Academy of Psychiatry and the Law, 23*(3), 547–550.

Guay, J., Ruscio, J., Hare, R., & Knight, R. A. (2004, October). *The latent structure of psychopathy: When more is simply more.* Paper presented at the annual meeting of the Society for Research in Psychopathology, St. Louis, MO.

Guy, L. G., Edens, J. F., Anthony, C., & Douglas, K. S. (in press). Does psychopathy predict institutional misconduct among adults? A meta-analytic investigation. *Journal of Consulting and Clinical Psychology.*

Hare, R. (1991). *The Hare Psychopathy Checklist—Revised.* Toronto, Ontario, Canada: Multi-Health Systems.

Hare, R. D. (2003). *Hare Psychopathy Checklist—Revised manual* (2nd ed.). Toronto, Ontario, Canada: Multi-Health Systems.

Harris, G., Rice, M., & Quinsey, V. (1994). Psychopathy as a taxon: Evidence that psychopaths are a discrete class. *Journal of Consulting and Clinical Psychology, 62,* 387–397.

Heilbrun, K., Hart, S., Hare, R., Gustafson, D., Nunez, C., & White, A. (1998) Inpatient and post-discharge aggression in mentally disordered offenders: The role of psychopathy. *Journal of Interpersonal Violence, 13,* 514–527.

Hitchcock, G. D. (1995). The efficacy of cognitive group therapy with incarcerated psychopaths. *Dissertation Abstracts International, 56(1-B).* (UMI No. 9514344).

Kiehl, K. A., Smith, A. M., Hare, R. D., & Liddle, P. F. (2000). An event-related potential investigation of response inhibition in schihzophrenia and psychopathy. *Biological Psychiatry, 48,* 210–221.

Looman, J., Abracen, J., Sern, R. & Marquis, P. (2005). Psychopathy, treatment change and recidivism in high risk sexual offenders. *Journal of Interpersonal Violence,* 20(5), 549–568.

Loving, J. L. (2002). Treatment planning with the Psychopathy Checklist—Revised. *International Journal of Offender Therapy and Comparative Criminology, 46*(3), 281–293.

Marcus, D. K., John, S., & Edens, J. F. (2004). A taxometric analysis of psychopathy. *Journal of Abnormal Psychology, 113*, 626–635.

Ogloff, J., Wong, S. & Greenwood, A. (1990). Treating criminal psychopaths in a therapeutic community program. *Behavioral Sciences and the Law, 8,* 81–90.

Quinsey, V. L., Harris, G. T., Rice, M. E., & Cormier, C. A. (1998). *Violent offenders: Appraising and managing risk.* Washington, DC: American Psychological Association.

Reid, W. H., & Gacono, C. (2000) Treatment of antisocial personality, psychopathy, and other characterologic antisocial syndromes. *Behavioral Sciences and the Law, 18,* 647–662.

Rice, M., & Harris, G. (1997). Cross-validation and extension of the violence risk appraisal guide for child molesters and rapists. *Law and Human Behavior, 21*(2), 231–241.

Rice, M., Harris, G., & Cormier, C. (1992). An evaluation of a maximum security therapeutic community for psychopaths and other mentally disordered offenders. *Law and Human Behavior, 16,* 399–412.

Salekin, R. T. (2002). Psychopathy and therapeutic pessimism: Clinical lore or clinical reality? *Clinical Psychology Review, 22,* 79–112.

Schmauk, F. J. (1970). Punishment, arousal and avoidance learning in sociopaths, *Journal of Abnormal Psychology, 76,* 325.

Schopp, R. F., & Slain, A. J. (2000). Psychopathy, criminal responsibility, and civil commitment as a sexual predator. *Behavioral Sciences and the Law, 18*(2–3), 247–274.

Seto, M. C., & Barbaree, H. E. (1999). Psychopathy, treatment behavior, and sex offender recidivism. *Journal of Interpersonal Violence, 14*(12), 1235–1248.

Webster, C., Douglas, K. S., Eaves, E., & Hart, S. D. (1997). *The HCR-20: Assessing risk for violence. Version 2.* Burnaby, British Columbia: Simon Fraser University.

Wong, S., & Hare, R. D. (2005). *Program guidelines for the treatment of psychopaths: Institutional treatment of violent psychopathic offenders.* Toronto, Ontario, Canada: Multi-Health Systems.

Young, M., Justice, J., Erdberg, P., & Gacono, C. (2000). The incarcerated psychopath in psychiatric treatment: Management or treatment? In C. Gacono (Ed.), *The clinical and forensic assessment of psychopathy: A practitioner's guide* (pp. 313–331). Hillsdale, NJ: Erlbaum.

Chapter 15

Juvenile Hazards— What About Civil Commitment?

by Janis F. Bremer, Ph.D.

INTRODUCTION

Twenty five years ago the issue of juveniles who sexually offend was only just beginning to attract attention, and articles from that period (Groth & Loredo, 1981; Groth, 1977) contained only seven or eight references. The recent surge in interest in this topic has been the result of surveys of adult sex offenders in prison, who have reported that their first offenses occurred in early adolescence. It appeared that the prevailing belief in the past was that if an offense was committed by a juvenile, it was "only a mistake" and that "boys will be boys." However, within ten years, every young person crossing sexual boundaries was suddenly considered a risk to become a patterned adult offender (National Task Force on Juvenile Sexual Offending, 1988). Laws proliferated in the 1990s that require that every adjudicated sex offense result in some form of registration or notification. The issue of whether a young adult requires civil commitment proceedings based on juvenile offenses is also now a critical public policy issue.

While we struggle to find the balance between these two extremes, we can keep two touchstones at the ready: (1) that some of our children, for all the wrong reasons (reacting to puberty, the media, peer pressure), behave in an immoral and illegal manner at one point in time only, and (2) that some of our children, with a complex interaction of genetics and experience, are irrefutably and chronically sexually dangerous by early adulthood. What is known that allows us to move a juvenile into an adult system of open-ended commitment based on mental status? How much is there to learn? And, although professional competency develops, how do we ensure the safety of others from the possibility of victimization? All these questions must be addressed.

Many years ago, while directing a correctional program for serious juvenile offenders, I experienced the many sides of this dilemma with 15-year-old "Mike."[1] Mike was 14 years old when he came into the facility. He participated in all aspects of the program yet continued to seem distant, and at times, he lapsed into regressive temper tantrums. Mike developed a significant relationship with his primary social worker, who often "went to bat" for him. He stayed in the program for close to two years, completing the prescribed program goals. Yet there always was a part of Mike that seemed to be missing. In particular, two aspects of Mike's life in the facility were of concern: (1) his professed religious beliefs had him convinced he would not harm children any more; and (2) his ability to relate to others was superficial and awkward. Mike graduated from the program and was released to a juvenile group home. Some four moths later, at age 16, Mike was arrested for the severe, violent sexual abuse of a 4-year-old girl. He was waived to adult court and sent to a young adult correctional facility. At the end of his sentence, he was civilly committed and remains in a secure treatment center some eighteen years after his first correctional placement. Mike showed himself to be too dangerous to live in an open community. It was, and continues to be, important to recognize that for a few, juvenile offenses are a basis for adult civil commitment. It is our job to learn what is necessary to identify and contain the Mikes in our world before they reoffend.

Then there is "Jack." Jack was adjudicated on the most severe criminal sexual conduct law, a first-degree felony. In itself, this would suggest that at age 17, Jack is potentially dangerous. Jack's charge was based on an acquaintance rape scenario that was reported by the girl's parents. As his treatment progressed, contact was made with the teen girl, who clearly stated she had become afraid when her doctor told her mother she had contracted a sexually transmitted disease. She gave her story of her relationship with Jack to his therapist. She told us she was in a consensual sexual relationship with Jack and considered herself to be his girlfriend. She said she did not have any idea what would happen by denying this relationship to her mother. Once the investigation started, she was too scared and confused to admit her involvement with Jack. She wanted to go through reconciliation with him and to tell the truth to her mother. She gave a timeline of their relationship and how she felt about it. She also admitted that she was not even sure she had contracted the sexually transmitted disease from Jack. Her story matched Jack's story quite accurately. Jack, in his assertive stance and request for help even after suffering significant legal consequences, was exonerated from the offense. Jack's story was heard and without judgment thoroughly investigated. It is quite possible that Jack could have gone through a system in which he was waived to adult court, imprisoned, and then considered for civil commitment if he balked at treatment, with authorities looking only at his sexual relationship with this young woman as a rape. Again, it is our job to ensure that young people like Jack are not lost as a result of the fear and anger related to sexually offensive behavior. Adolescent sexuality is a landmine that can only be defused by attending to the one person in front of us.

RISK PREDICTION

Once a sex offense is committed, regardless of the age of the one who offends, the first concern is whether this individual is at risk to continue with sexually harming behaviors. Historically this is related to the fact that juveniles were spotlighted by retrospective studies of imprisoned adult sex offenders who began their offending behaviors during adolescence. Currently it is related to the fact that adolescents commit a very large number of offenses against minors. However, for various reasons, it is very difficult to study juvenile recidivism. Most studies of recidivism for juveniles with recognized sexual offending behavior show low reoffense rates (Righthand & Welch, 2001). Typically, these studies show such low reoffense rates that they become difficult to interpret. In a summary of studies, Alexander (1999) reported a 7 percent rate. Sexual recidivism studies' results for adolescents vary based on both static and dynamic variables. These disparate results argue for a consistent database so that different populations can be combined or compared on the same variables.

It is also notable that there is only one study, with a small number of subjects, which included a control group (Borduin, Henggeler, Blaske, & Stein, 1990), and there are no prospective studies at this point in the field. One significant social factor in conducting good empirical studies is the availability of adolescents outside the legal system to serve as control groups in large-scale research projects.

Studies of individual factors associated with recidivism have been summarized by Weinrott (1996). These include psychopathy, deviant arousal, cognitive distortions, truancy, a prior known sex offense, blaming the victim, and the use of force or threats. Factors clinically believed to be of importance, such as denial of a known offense or lack of victim empathy, did not rise to significance in these studies. However, it is important to remember that there are numerous clinically noted characteristics that have not been studied at all. Over a twenty-year period less than two dozen studies of juvenile recidivism are available in published form.

Risk Prediction for General Reoffending

Although there are a number of risk assessment instruments for juvenile criminal reoffending, such as the Structured Assessment of Violence Risk in Youth (SAVRY; Borum, Bartel, & Forth, 2002), the Youth Level of Service/Case Management Inventory (YLS/CMI; Hoge & Andrews, 1996), and the Massachusetts Youth Screening Instrument, Second Version (MAYSI-2: Grisso & Barnum, 2000), they do not specifically predict a continuing sex offense pattern into adulthood. Work needs to be done with prospective studies to understand what measures or factors within juvenile measures may indicate what juvenile characteristics carry predictability into adulthood.

Risk Prediction for Sex-Specific Offending

There are two widely used measures of sexual recidivism risk currently in use. The Estimated Risk of Adolescent Sexual Offense Recidivism (ERASOR; Worling & Curwen, 2001) and the Juvenile-Sex Offender Assessment Protocol (J-SOAP; Prentky, Harris, Frizell, & Righthand, 2000) are still in development and undergoing validation. The J-SOAP has gone through a revision and the revised edition is currently available. It is designed as a parallel measure to the actuarial tools in the adult sex offender field. The J-SOAP is constructed with the available juvenile sex offense specific research results as a guide. The ERASOR is a developmentally sensitive tool that is undergoing validity studies (Worling, 2004). The ERASOR uses both available research and best practices beliefs due to the paucity of juvenile research. Both measures extrapolate from the adult sex offender field as a means of supporting face validity. The Juvenile Risk Assessment Tool (J-RAT; Rich, 2003) is a third tool based on empirically guided clinical judgment.

Static vs. Dynamic Factors

There are three generations of risk assessments that have evolved in the corrections system (Bonta, 1996). There is clear evidence that first-generation assessments, based on experiential or expert clinical judgments, are "legally, ethically and pragmatically unacceptable" (Benda, Corwyn, & Toombs, 2001, p. 589).

Second-generation assessments identify static factors to predict future behavior (Bonta, 1996). These static factors do not take into account dynamic factors that reduce risk. It is also important to determine whether there are relevant static factors for recidivism in juveniles. The presence of valid and reliable static factors in the adult population underpins actuarial risk assessment tools; however, the studies available with adolescents do not find these same solid relationships. Worling and Curwen (2001) did not find a relationship between victim characteristics and recidivism, although a quite strong relationship has been found between victim characteristics and recidivism of adults sex offenders (Trivits & Reppucci, 2002). Emerick and Dutton (1993), on the other hand, did find a relationship between victim characteristics and recidivism. These conflicting findings are typical of the results in juvenile studies, including the fact that most of these studies have small sample sizes. It is a significant moral and ethical question whether static factors, although possibly good predictors, should be given weight in immature individuals when there is a good possibility that intervening in dynamic domains may significantly reduce risk for adult criminality (Gottfredson & Tonry, 1987). There is a clear need to support large data analyses that can identify subgroups of adolescents with sexual offenses or a previously unidentified history of sexual offending. Once identified, investigations into the fit with the group of serious juvenile offenders that is studied under the generic corrections rubric can be made.

Dynamic factors are included in third-generation risk assessments. This inclusion of alterable risk factors allow for targeted interventions (Andrews & Bonta, 1995). In a recent study, Benda et al. (2001) investigated the relevance of both static and dynamic factors for predicting adolescents' entry into the adult correctional system. They found dynamic factors significant in predicting entry into the adult system. In a meta-analysis, Gendreau, Little, and Goggin (1996) found dynamic predictor domains performing at least as well as static domains. The direction of research then needs to be on targeted interventions in the area of dynamic predictors.

The potential for dynamic risk factors to take precedence with the juvenile population suggests that with accurate intervention, the vast majority of youth with sexual offenses will not develop chronic deviant sexual preferences. This is a quandary for the research community, as ethics cannot allow for a control group of known juveniles with sexual offenses to remain in the community without any intervention. An effort to identify the specific clusters of factors that may lead to sexual offending and an effort to discover the effective means of changing those pathways must be made. Currently, significant inroads are being made by Sims-Knight, Knight, Schatzel, & Daversa (2004) and Knight (1998, 2005) using a comprehensive data set that includes both static and dynamic factors.

In general, the studies available until recently were used in a manner well beyond their statistical validity. Methodological flaws, small sample sizes, and unreplicated results went unnoticed. Political hay was made by focusing on those results that supported stronger laws and allowing laws that were created for adults to include juveniles. Trivits and Reppucci (2002), in a comprehensive review of juvenile recidivism studies, highlight the difficulty in comparing studies while noting that the vast majority show such low rates of recidivism they support Chaffin, Letourneau, and Silovsky's (2001) proposal that sex offending is discontinuous across juveniles and adults.

SEXUAL AROUSAL PREFERENCES IN ADOLESCENCE

Research of phallometric discriminative validity for adolescents is just developing, and there are ongoing concerns about the use of phallometrics with juveniles. The hormonal fluctuations during puberty make it difficult to distinguish true arousal to a stimulus versus arousal due to hormonal surges. The few available studies show variable results. In a summary of multiple studies, Becker (1998) found that phallometric arousal for adolescents has a weaker relationship with clinical characteristics than for the adult population. This is of interest as deviant sexual arousal in adults is one of the two key markers for predicting recidivism, with the second being psychopathy (Rice & Harris, 1997). This finding suggests that the underlying reasons for juveniles who molest children may be qualitatively different than those for adults. Again, motivation for behavior that looks the same along the life course may be the result of quite different internal processes.

Hunter and Becker (1994) found that adolescents are sexually aroused to a wider range of stimuli than adults. This led them to suggest that due to still open developmental pathways, adolescents do not yet have a stable sexual arousal pattern. More recently, there are results that suggest both that adolescent phallometric studies discriminate the subgroup that are sexually interested in young children and that this group is a different group than the adult pedophilic interest group. Seto, Lalumière, and Blanchard (2000) found that pedophilic index scores of adolescent offenders were associated with multiple victims, male victims, very young victims, and extrafamilial victims. Adolescents with only younger female victims did not tend to show pedophilic interests, whereas with adults with only younger female victims do show pedophilic interest.

There is one valid measure of sexual arousal preference based on visual response time rather than the more intrusive erectile response measure. The Abel Assessment of Sexual Interest (AASI; Abel Screening, 1996) is developing a large juvenile database. The AASI is a valid and reliable measure of sexual interest in adolescents. Recent studies suggest that the AASI does appear to be a valid measure of sexual interest in adolescent male child molesters (Abel et al., 2004).

PSYCHOPATHY IN ADOLESCENCE

There is a strong association between the syndrome of psychopathy and continued sex offending for adult sex offenders. The Psychopathy Checklist—Revised (PCL-R; Hare, 1991) is the most widely used tool to assess psychopathy in adult sex offenders. To consistently investigate the relationship in adolescence with emerging psychopathy, a Psychopathy Checklist—Youth Version (PCL:YV) has been developed (Forth, Kosson, & Hare 2003). Previous studies that used parent and teacher ratings show that children and youth do show psychopathic traits that resemble psychopathic adults. However, parent and teacher ratings are not particularly reliable because of lower agreement rates and the ongoing relationships between these adults and the assessed children. The PCL:YV is designed to be responsive to adolescent roles and situations while providing a valid and reliable measurement of these antisocial traits. Although there are results emerging from PCL:YV studies, much larger samples are needed that address more aspects of the psychopathy construct than antisocial behavior. A study by Kosson, Cyterski, Neumann, Steuerwald, and Walker-Matthews (2002) suggests that the PCL:YV provides evidence for an adolescent psychopathy syndrome. This syndrome is characterized by overt behavior problems and interpersonal and affective anomalies that are similar to those shown by adults. Across the adult and adolescent measures of psychopathy, however, the underlying factor structure may differ in significant ways. Therefore, the use of a psychopathy construct in adolescence must be considered tentative. It will require significant research before a clearer picture emerges and a connection to adult psychopathy is made. The significant issue that requires study is whether a psychopathic character in adolescence leads to adult psychopathic behavior.

ETIOLOGY OF ADOLESCENT SEXUAL OFFENSES

The relevance of etiology to juvenile civil commitment is tied to the relevance of dynamic versus static factors. Etiology is framed in theory rather than the level of specific factors. Given the limited research, theories on juvenile sex offending range from completely environmental (sociocultural) to completely internal (physiological). The nature-nurture argument can be viewed as a distraction. In a policy area as significant as the civil commitment of a young adult who may have lived in a restricted environment from age 13 or 14, the real focus must be on the individual.

There may be individuals who, through a combination of genetic influence on neurotransmitters and cognitive functioning, are a chronic danger to others. Other young people, with no known biological basis, traumatized by early childhood abuse and lack of consistent caretakers, (entirely environmental influences), are a chronic danger to others. A comprehensive literature review (Veneziano & Veneziano, 2002) concludes that treatment should address the specific needs of the individual who offends. Predefined programs are unlikely to apply to the population as a whole, or even certain subgroups. There is simply too little available to develop such "workbook" programs. Thus, although it is somewhat tongue-in-cheek, the "it depends" theory (Worling, 2001) may be our best guide. Worling notes that it is now clear that juveniles who sexually offend are a heterogeneous group, and the number and type of significantly different subgroups remain unclear. In developing training on how to treat these young offenders, Worling developed a list of possible etiological constructs and theories that can be considered in individual cases. Several of these are significant for some youth; for others there may be overlap or a completely different set of etiological factors. Using an "it depends" mind-set provides a guideline for determining a highly individualized treatment plan for the individual youth.

Multiple Pathways

Juveniles who sexually abuse children appear to have little in common besides their offense behavior (Knight & Prentky, 1993). There are notable differences between youth who molest children and youth who offend against peers (Krauth, 1998). Attempts at identifying typologies within the juvenile sex offending population have been made, but none have been empirically validated (Chaffin et al., 2001). Without an empirically based knowledge of the diversity in the juvenile sex offending population, comparison with characteristics of adult sex offenders is impossible. Not only may the characteristics of juveniles who become adult sex offenders differ from their adult counterparts, but what triggers the behavior may have no relationship to how sex offending becomes a chronic behavior.

In their review of the literature on juvenile sex offending, Veneziano and Veneziano (2002) listed thirteen characteristics identified as concomitant with adolescent sex offending. In the 1993 National Task Force report, thirty-six characteristics were listed. To date no individual study has had a large enough sample size to reliably define specific pathways leading to offending behaviors. Research based on a large sample is essential to look at what characteristics "hang together" and whether these characteristics are important in and of themselves or only in combination with other characteristics. A promising tool now undergoing validation is the Multidimensional Inventory of Development, Sex and Aggression (MIDSA). This assessment and research tool (Knight, 2005), whose development has been spearheaded by Raymond Knight, over the last fifteen years, is expected to be available within the next year.

Sexually Harming Behaviors Across the Lifespan

Is there any validity to the "once an offender always an offender" approach to juveniles who sexually offend? It is this type of unfounded belief that leads to perceiving all juveniles with a sex offense as dangerous. When young adults are civilly committed on juvenile offenses, it is often with this belief lurking in the background. Studies examining a relationship between childhood, adolescence and adulthood find developmental discontinuity between these major life phases (Chaffin et al., 2001; Burton, 2000). Juveniles who sexually offend typically do not report their behavior beginning in childhood (Burton, 2000), and the recidivism rate for children is quite low (Alexander, 1999). If there are children who continue offending behaviors into adolescence, and then into adulthood, they are a quite small subgroup of children with sexual behavior problems.

As mentioned earlier, recidivism rates for juveniles are also quite low. These studies are confounded by including both older youth and young adults as part of the follow-up sample and by being based on known juveniles who offended and participated in treatment programs. Again, the lack of solid research allows for a limited knowledge base. The rates available do point to a small number of juveniles likely to re-offend as older juveniles/young adults. A salient move for this field is to begin prospective studies that follow children through adolescence and into adulthood.

Attachment Theory and Psychopathy

Attachment has been described as the base for developing a working model of the world. Meloy (2002) proposes that attachment relations are a "biopsychosocial behavioral system" and that disruption of secure attachment results in characterological traits in adulthood that predispose one to violence. The biological function of attachment is considered to be survival. This means that attachment can be considered as a fundamental behavior (Bowlby, 1988). Research on attachment theory (Ainsworth, 1978) which has led to the classification of various attachment styles provided evidence that attachment style underlies human social emotional development. Attachment styles and their meaning for later childhood, adolescent, and even adult behavior are currently receiving recognition in our field for the development of characterological traits such as that suggested by Meloy. The development of psychopathy and how this presents itself at different ages appears to be a critical aspect of when and how we can request containment for an indeterminate period of time (civil commitment). The ability, or inability, to recognize and respond to others is based on one's initial attachment relationship.

Juveniles who commit sex offenses are clearly disregarding the reality of their victim. Whatever the reason for their lack of social responsivity, it is this aspect of their functioning that must change, in all its complexity, for the safety of others. It is clear that for most juveniles who commit a sexual offense, this is a minor and easily remediated problem. In fact, many of these youth do in fact realize and change their behavior based on the reaction of their first and only victim. For the majority of our youth in treatment, their basic understanding of relationship is sound. They may experience an acute reaction to current events that let them to "forget" and use another for their own interests. For some of our offending youth, the lack of a secure attachment style results in misunderstanding the very basic nature of relationship.

Social messages are all translated by one's attachment style. Ambivalent, anxious, and disorganized attachment styles, for example, may all lead to poor social skills. Research into how psychopathic and other self-focused characterological traits develop from these learned styles may help us understand more clearly these deviations from the normal developmental processes. We need to balance between finding ways to create secure attachments in juveniles who harm others as a matter of course with solid research into how an individual moves from poor attachment relations to the stranglehold of psychopathy in adulthood. The treatment methods for shifting relationship style and to control psychopathic behavior differ significantly. With adolescents, the potential to change attachment style and prevent the permanent shift to callous emotional states is more likely due to their developmental immaturity.

Biology and Development: Emerging Research and Genetic Factors

Research on the interaction between genetic and environmental influences is resulting in specifying the role genetic influence plays on behavior. For example, the results of a prospective birth-to-adulthood study on the cycle of violence reveals the importance of considering genetic influence on emergent antisocial behavior in maltreated or abused children (Caspi et al., 2002). This study tested the influence of a gene that encodes an enzyme that metabolizes neurotransmitters. Deficiencies in the enzyme are linked to aggression. The results of this research confirm that the production of this enzyme moderates antisocial problems in adults who experienced childhood abuse. Low enzyme production in abused children led to later criminal behavior at a highly significant level. This type of research links to the current research on delinquent juveniles with sex offending behavior as more likely to recidivate sexually. Although these are preliminary results in a very new field, the possibility of future pharmacological treatments to prevent the development of violence cannot be ignored.

Zeroing in on human sexual behavior that deviates from the norm, a well-designed study investigated the relevance of a gene associated with Tourette's syndrome (Comings, 1994). Results confirm the relevance of genetic loading for Tourette's and sexual behaviors with obsessive-compulsive characteristics. The genetic impact again is in the production of neurotransmitters. The use of serotonergic antidepressants is now considered a useful medical intervention with this genetic factor.

This emerging area of medical research suggests that there will be more effective pharmacological responses in the future. Either as stand-alone interventions or in combination with a psychological therapeutic intervention, medication can be an important tool to allow some of youth who offend remain in their communities as adults.

Neural Development

As with genetic research, the understanding of brain development is undergoing a significant learning curve. The advent of magnetic resonant imaging as a standard research tool is changing our understanding of brain functioning and development. In general, recent research indicates that brain development continues until some point in our 20s. There is a surge of brain reorganization in mid to late adolescence that parallels neurological development in early childhood. An argument is now being made that adolescents' poor decision making and impulsiveness may be a direct result of immature neurological functioning (Sowell & Peterson, 2003). Researchers are suggesting that with continued study, adolescents will be shown to have reduced legal culpability due to immature brain development. Currently, this argument is being presented in regard the most severe legal penalty, the death penalty for adolescents.

This emerging research suggests that juveniles are not in a position to receive indeterminate civil commitments. Rather, an approach that extends juvenile jurisdiction beyond age 18 or 21 to some point in the mid-20s is a more humane and developmentally appropriate response.

JUVENILE CIVIL COMMITMENT: IS THERE SUCH A DETERMINATION?

Civil commitment under sexually violent predator laws allow for the commitment of juveniles based on juvenile offenses in four states (Illinois, South Carolina, Washington, and Wisconsin). Other states (Florida, Minnesota, and Pennsylvania) allow for civil commitment of young adults (over 18 years) based on juvenile offenses. Pennsylvania recently opened the first facility in the country solely for young adults committed on juvenile sex offenses. Many other states civilly commit on juvenile offenses after the juvenile is waived to adult court, serve their adult sentence, and are then evaluated under sexually violent predator Laws. Clearly the definition of "juvenile civil commitment" is a moving target based on state law. The majority of "juvenile civil commitments" are in fact adult commitments made on the basis of juvenile crimes. Given the seriousness of this type of legal procedure, what may essentially translate to a lifetime in locked facilities, it is past time to define federal standards.

Until the 2004 opening of the Pennsylvania program, young adults were placed in general population facilities (adult). They are clear that the facility and program are for young adult *violent sexual* offenders, not adolescent sex offenders. Pennsylvania's program, and its ability to develop treatment applicable to these young men, bears watching. One of the significant concerns with committing a young adult on a juvenile offense is housing and treating them within an adult milieu. The programming may not address those concerns relevant to juvenile offending and the milieu places them in a vulnerable position in terms of age and general maturity.

The varying state legal requirements related to civil commitment are only one engine driving this moving target. Another is the lack of any predictive assessment tools that are valid and reliable (Shaw, Heesacker, & Delgado-Romero, 2001). The determination of dangerousness for individuals with only juvenile sex offenses is made primarily on clinical judgment. Clinical judgment is notably unreliable. Clinicians tend to overestimate recidivism in the juvenile population (Oregon Juvenile Sex Offender Task Force, 1986). Although adult actuarial tools are used with young adults, Shaw et al. (2001) point out that the standardization sample actually makes the results highly suspect. It is an open question whether actuarial measures can be developed for a population who are continuing to work through developmental milestones.

Now that the PCL: YV is available (Forth et al., 2003), ideally it will prove useful as one component in a battery that will be developed in the future. At this time, the PCL:YV bases itself in a particular theory that hypothesizes specific factors as relevant to reoffending. As reviewed earlier, the field of adolescent sex offending itself is unable to offer solid research about the etiology of juvenile sexual offending. The recent research identifying developmental discontinuity between age groupings strongly directs our attention to the need for significant research yet to be done.

In summary, there is no definitive method for determining which juveniles are in need of civil commitment to keep our communities safe. There are, however, a small number of juveniles who, left unchecked, will continue commit heinous sex crimes. This creates a significant dilemma. It is not enough to ameliorate the notion of juvenile civil commitment based on numbers; "allowing" any number (however small) of juveniles to offend as adults is immoral and unethical. The solution may rest in a twofold approach:

1. *To operate juvenile civil commitment at a federal level.* Given the small numbers, it is entirely feasible to operate in a consistent manner. As an example, the newly opened Pennsylvania program is a twelve-bed facility. If there are that many juveniles in every state, there are only 600 juveniles nationally within about a year's span that require this level of intervention. It is quite likely that there are significantly fewer in many states, with only a few states like New York and California that may exceed that number.

2. *To operate a program that is specifically designed for older juveniles with the goal of successful treatment for the majority of committed young adults.*

Shaw et al. (2001) concluded that the current civil commitment system is not a response designed for juveniles. Their determination that this response is irrational and short-sighted, based more on political gain than the needs of the public or the juveniles who sexually offend, can be seen to continue to be quite accurate. When we stop to consider newly learned information in the past few years, as well as the recognition that we successfully treat the majority on the continuum of youthful offenders, it is essential to look for an accurate and adequate response to those few serious chronic offenders.

Pro and Con: Is There a Fulcrum?

There are, retrospectively, a small number of children who start young and keep on harming others with their sexual behavior. There are also some juveniles who begin their offending behaviors in adolescence and maintain their offending into adulthood. These two particular paths to adult offending are not in dispute. What is in dispute is the numbers and significance as a social issue for life-course sexual offending. How we determine who, in late adolescence, poses a serious community risk as an adult is at the core of the civil commitment debate.

"Group think" and simplistic responses clearly mean we will entrap and contain a significant number of youth who would not reoffend. If the literature agrees on anything, it is that there are multiple pathways to serious juvenile sex offending and that the exact sex offense behavior itself is not a strong indicator for future sexual offending. Further complicating the picture is the fact that clinical judgment is a notably unreliable means of determining dangerousness. In fact, clinicians predicting the success of their own sex-offending clients tend to overestimate the number who will continue to have difficulties with their sexual behavior (Smith & Monastersky, 1986).

In terms of public policy, how do we create a system in which we can identify, contain, and potentially rehabilitate youth at risk for adult sex offenses? It is critical to keep the issue of civil commitment at one end of the juvenile offending continuum, with the issue of *no* sex offense-specific intervention at the other end. Only in this way can we maintain a balance that accounts for the full spectrum of diversity in this population.

Recommendations

There are two means of providing reasoned public policy on juveniles and the issue of civil commitment. One is to accept the need to conduct prospective epidemiological studies that will provide a clearer picture of how and when to intervene. The current political climate will not allow for this as there would be a group of youth identifying themselves as offending without a potential consequence or intervention. As the field continues to collect very low recidivism statistics, the more able we are to make a valid argument for epidemiological research. The second method is to create a model program now for those youth who to the best of our knowledge, will continue to victimize others.

Prospective epidemiological research requires a searching look at current public policy strategies. The work cannot be done currently because of the concerns about asking large numbers of minors about their sexual practices, including behaviors that harm others. Although the ethical issue of "identifying" without the ability to intervene both those victimized and those who offend is a valid point, so is the ethical issue of iatrogenic abuse by assuming the worst after an illegal sexual behavior event. There is also the difficulty of getting consent from parents of children to follow them for twenty years, specifically focusing on details of their sexuality in all its varied aspects. This may actually be the more difficult task. The concern over ignoring known harm to others is likely to be a small risk as those youth who commit serious offenses will be identified through normal channels (victim reporting, other delinquent activities) and dealt with appropriately.

Restorative justice is a concept that incorporates a way to create unique yet safe living environments for these young people. With appropriate safeguards, in terms of both the physical environment and the adults who care for them, a setting can be designed that addresses the needs of these youth without an entirely artificial environment. Correctional facilities and locked psychiatric hospitals cannot promote normative development. Only a community setting, in which the structure is social rather than physical, can promote normal development. One such notion is in the "circle of support," in which a group of trained community members commit to providing a safety net so that the offending youth may remain in the open community. The oft repeated "it takes a village to raise a child" is truly actualized with a circle of support. Restorative justice aims to repair the damage done by a criminal act through taking into account the direct victim, the community, and the person who offends. This perspective is essential in regaining the personal and social balance necessary to stop offending behavior.

Perhaps the question is not whether young adults require civil commitment (based on juvenile offenses) as one option to contain their behavior. Instead, we should ask if we, as adults charged with raising our children to become constructive adults in our communities, can create a different response model that is focused on a positive outcome for our communities?

Footnote

[1] Names used in case examples in this chapter are not the individuals' real names.

References

Abel, G. G., Jordan, A., Rouleau, J. L., Emerick, R., Barboza-Whitehead, S., & Osborn, C. (2004). Use of visual reaction time to assess male adolescents who molest children. *Sexual Abuse: A Journal of Research and Treatment, 16*(3), 255–265.

Abel Screening. (1996). *Abel assessment for sexual interest: Juvenile sex offenders* [Therapist product information brochure]. Atlanta, GA: Author.

Ainsworth, M., Blehar, M., Waters, E., & Wall, S. (1978). *Patterns of attachment.* Mahwah, NJ: Erlbaum.

Alexander, M. (1999). Sexual offender treatment efficacy revisited. *Sexual Abuse: Journal of Research & Treatment, 11*(2), 101–116.

Andrews, D. A., & Bonta, J. (1995). *The Level of Service Inventory—Revised.* Toronto, Ontario, Canada: Multi-HealthSystems.

Becker, J. V. (1998). What we know about the characteristics and treatment of adolescents who have committed sexual offenses. *Child Maltreatment, 3*(4), 317–329.

Benda, B., Corwyn, R. F., & Toombs, N. (2001). Recidivism among adolescent serious offenders. *Criminal Justice and Behavior, 28*(5), 588–614.

Bonta, J. (1996). Risk-needs assessment and treatment. In A. Harland (Ed.), *Choosing correctional options that work: Defining the demand and evaluating the supply* (pp.18–68). Thousand Oaks, CA: Sage.

Borum, R., Bartel, P., & Forth, A. (2002). *The Structured Assessment of Violence Risk in Youth (SAVRY).* Available from Specialized Training Services, Inc., P.O. Box 28181, San Diego, CA 92198 (tel. 1–800–848–1226).

Bourduin, C., Blaske, D., Henggeler, S., & Stein, R. (1990). Multisystemic treatment of adolescent sexual offenders. *International Journal of Offender Therapy and Comparative Criminology,* 105–113.

Bowlby, J. (1988). *A secure base: Clinical applications of attachment theory.* London: Routledge.

Burton, D. (2000). Were adolescent sexual offenders children with sexual behavior problems? *Sexual Abuse: A Journal of Research and Treatment, 12,* 37–48.

Caspi, A., McClay, J., Moffitt, T., Mill, J., Martin, J., Craig, I., et al. (2002). Role of genotype in the cycle of violence in maltreated children. *Science, 297,* 851–854.

Chaffin, M., Letourneau, E., & Silovsky, J. (2001). Adults, adolescents and children who sexually abuse children: A developmental perspective. In J. B. Myers, L. Berliner, J. Briere, C. T. Hendrix, T. Reid, & C. Jenny (Eds.), *APSAC handbook on child maltreatment* (2nd ed., pp. 205–232). Thousand Oaks, CA: Sage.

Comings, D. (1994) Role of genetic factors in human sexual behavior based on studies of Tourette syndrome and ADHD probands and their relatives. *American Journal of Medical Genetics, 54,* 227–241.

Emerick, R. L., & Dutton, W. A. (1993). The effect of polygraphy on the self report of adolescent sex offenders: Implications for risk assessment. *Annals of Sex Research, 6*(2), 83–103.

Forth, A. E., Kosson, D. S., & Hare, R. D. (2003). *The Psychopathy Checklist: Youth Version—Manual.* Toronto, Ontario, Canada: Multi-Health Systems.

Gendreau, P., Little, T., & Goggin, C. (1996) A meta-analysis of the predictors of adult offender recidivism: What works! *Criminology, 34,* 575–607.

Gottfredson, D. M., & Tonry, M. (1987). *Prediction and classification: Criminal justice decision making. Vol. 9: Crime and justice: A review of research.* Chicago: University of Chicago Press.

Grisso, T., & Barnum, R. (2000). *Massachusetts Youth Screening Instrument—2: User's manual and technical report.* Worcester: University of Massachusetts Medical School.

Groth, A. N. (1977). The adolescent sexual offender and his prey. *International Journal of Offender Therapy and Comparative Criminology, 21*(3), 249–254.

Groth, A. N., & Loredo, C. M. (1981). Juvenile sexual offenders: Guidelines for assessment. *International Journal of Offender Therapy and Comparative Criminology, 25*(1), 31–39.

Hare, R. (1991). *The Hare Psychopathy Checklist—Revised.* Toronto, Ontario, Canada: Multi-Health Systems.

Hoge, R., & Andrews, D. (1996). *The Youth Level of Service/Case Management Inventory (YLS/CMI).* Ottawa, Ontario, Canada: Carleton University.

Hunter, J. A., Jr., & Becker, J. V. (1994). The role of deviant sexual arousal in juvenile sexual offending: Etiology, evaluation, and treatment. *Criminal Justice and Behavior, 21*(1), 132–149.

Knight, R. (1998). *Using a new computerized developmental inventory to examine the family and early behavioral antecedents of sexual coercion.* Paper presented at the meeting of the Association for the Treatment of Sexual Abusers, Vancouver, British Columbia, Canada.

Knight, R. (2005, April). *Assessing adults who sexually offend: Using the Multidimensional Inventory of Development, Sex and Aggression (MIDSA).* Paper presented at the seventh annual Joint Conference on Sex Offense-Specific Assessment, Treatment and Safe Management of Children, Adolescents and Adults, Marlborough, MA.

Knight, R. A., & Prentky, R. A. (1993). Exploring characteristics for classifying juvenile sex offenders. In H. E. Barbaree, W. L. Marshall, & S. M. Hudson (Eds.), *The juvenile sex offender* (pp. 45–83). New York: Guilford Press.

Kosson, D., Cyterski, T., Steuerwald, B., Neumann, C., & Walker-Matthews, S. (2002). The reliability and validity of the psychopathy checklist: Youth version (PCL:YV) in nonincarcerated adolescent males. *Psychological Assessment, 14*(1), 97–109.

Krauth, A. A. (1998). A comparative study of male juvenile sex offenders. *Dissertation Abstracts International: Section B: The Sciences and Engineering, 58,* 44–55.

Meloy, J. R. (2002). Normative attachment and object relations theory. In J. R. Meloy (Ed.), *Violent attachments* (pp. 3-18). Northvale, NJ: Jason Aronson.

National Resource Center on Child Sexual Abuse. (1994). *Statistics in child abuse.* Huntsville, AL: Author.

National Task Force on Juvenile Sexual Offending. (1988). The preliminary report. *Juvenile and Family Court Journal, 39*(2).

National Task Force on Juvenile Sexual Offending. (1993). The revised report from the National Task Force on juvenile sexual offending. *Juvenile and Family Court Journal, 44*(4).

Oregon Juvenile Sex Offender Task Force. (1986). *An executive summary of the Oregon Report on Juvenile Offenders.* Salem, OR: Children's Services Division, Department of Human Resources.

Prentky, R., Harris, B., Frizzell, K., & Righthand, S. (2000). An actuarial procedure for assessing risk with juvenile sex offenders. *Sexual Abuse: A Journal of Research and Treatment, 12*(2), 71–93.

Rice, M. E., & Harris, G. T. (1997). Cross-validation and extension of the violence risk appraisal guide for child molesters and rapists. *Law and Human Behavior, 21,* 231–241.

Rich, P. (2003). *Understanding, assessing, and rehabilitating juvenile sexual offenders.* Hoboken, NJ: Wiley.

Righthand, S., & Welch, C. (2001). *Juveniles who have sexually offended: A review of the professional literature.* Washington, DC: U.S. Department of Justice.

Seto, M., Lalumière, M., & Blanchard, R. (2000). The discriminative validity of a phallometric test for pedophilic interests among adolescent sex offenders against children. *Psychological Assessment, 12*(3), 319–327.

Shaw, T., Heesacker, A., & Delgado-Romero, E. (2001). Implications of sexually violent predator laws for youthful offenders. In A. Schlank (Ed.), *The sexual predator* (pp. 12-1–12-10). Kingston, NJ: Civic Research Institute.

Sims-Knight, J., Knight, R., Schatzel, E., & Daversa, M. (2004). *Using the MIDSA to assess juvenile sexual offenders.* Paper presented at the annual conference of the Association for the Treatment of Sexual Abusers, Albuquerque, NM.

Smith, W. R., & Monastersky, C. (1986). Assessing juvenile sex offenders' risk for reoffending. *Criminal Justice and Behavior, 13*, 115–140.

Sowell, E. R., & Peterson, B. S. (2003). Mapping cortical change across the human life span. *Nature Neuroscience, 6*, 309–315.

Trivits, L., & Reppucci, N. (2002). Application of Megan's Law to juveniles. *American Psychologist, 57*(9), 690–704.

Veneziano, C., & Veneziano, L. (2002). Adolescent sex offenders: A review of the literature. *Trauma, Violence and Abuse, 3*(4), 247–260.

Weinrott, M. (1996). *Juvenile sexual aggression: A critical review* Portland, OR: Center for the Study and Prevention of Violence.

Worling, J. (2001). *Popular theories regarding the etiology of adolescent sexual offending behaviour.* Unpublished manuscript.

Worling, J. R. (2004). The estimate of risk of adolescent sexual offense recidivism (ERASOR): Preliminary psychometric data. *Sexual Abuse: A Journal of Research and Treatment, 16*(3), 235–254.

Worling, J., & Curwen, T. (2001). *The ERASOR: Estimate of Risk of Adolescent Sexual Offense Recidivism. Manual.* Toronto, Ontario, Canada: Ministry of Community and Social Services, Sexual Abuse, Family Education & Treatment Program, Thistletown Regional Centre.

Chapter 16

Substance Abuse—
Euphoric Recall and
Deviant Sexual Fantasy

by William Plum, L.A.D.C.

INTRODUCTION

Substance abuse and alcoholism are well represented within the sex offender population (Langevin & Lang, 1990). Valliere (1997) found that the incidence of alcohol use and alcohol dependence in the sexual offending population exceeds that which is found in the general population. Marques, Day, Nelson, Miner, and West (1992) noted that more than one-third of their study sample had been under the influence of drugs or alcohol at the time of their offense. Marques et al. (1992), in the same study, showed that 50 percent of those subjects who met criteria for substance abuse or dependence and who had completed treatment for substance abuse relapsed back to substance use. The Community-Based Sex Offender Program Evaluation Project in Minnesota (2000) concluded that a history of alcohol or drug use was positively related to reoffending. And Langstrom, Sjotedt, and Grann (2004) determined that alcohol use disorder and drug use disorder increased the risk of sexual recidivism.

In addition to the high representation of substance abuse and alcoholism within the sexual offending population, it has also been observed that deviant sexual fantasy plays a major role in offending. Holmes and Holmes (1994), in writing about a sexual homicide, stated: "We have found that in every case the killers attempted to carry their fantasies out on the victims" (p. 157). Other researchers have noted that pairing the pleasure of masturbation and climax with deviant sexual imagery strongly reinforces deviant sexual arousal (Ball & Seghorn, 1999; Hunter, Goodwin, & Becker, 1994; Maletzky, 1991), and behavioral therapies for pedophiles often rely on the ability of the subject to fantasize (Barbaree & Seto, 1997; Grossman, Martis, & Fichtner, 1999; Maletzky, 1991). Likewise, relapse prevention techniques both for substance abuse and sexual offending use methods, such as guided imagery, that are based on the client's ability to imagine (Marlatt, 1983). Marlatt makes a case for a balance between linear verbal communication channels with metaphor and imagery because it improves the processing and storage of information. The connection between substance abuse and deviant fantasy is important because alcohol and other mood-altering chemicals often play a role in intensifying the deviant fantasy involved in the buildup to sexual offending (Plum, 2001).

As much as indulgence in deviant sexual fantasy contributes to a sexual offender's relapse process, or behavioral chain (Maletzky, 1991), euphoric recall of past substance use can contribute to relapse to substance use with addict. Rosenfeld and Webber (2000) maintain that mood-altering substances "hijack" the pleasure centers of the brain in the addict causing a powerful pairing of memory, substance, and mood state. Vaillant (1983) writes that because of "the fact alcohol nonspecifically alters an individual's feeling state makes it a powerful reinforcer" (p. 175). Marlatt and Rohsenow (1980) describe how the individual's culturally conditioned expectancies may be far more specific than the actual pharmacological effects of alcohol. The combination of expectancy, euphoric recall, and the effects of mood-altering substances build, in part, a sturdy matrix of internal and external high risk factors for substance abusers.

Some substance-abusing sexual offenders have difficulty establishing an interrelationship between these two behaviors. The tendency for some clients to compartmentalize, minimize, or otherwise distort their behavior makes it difficult for the client to recognize a buildup to both substance abuse and sexual offending. One program for civilly committed sexual offenders (the Minnesota Sex Offender Program) conceptualized two potential interactions of substance abuse and sexual offending and one principal of treatment:

1. Alcohol and/or drug abuse has either intensified the offenders' behavior or served as a means to support the offenders' behavior.

2. Alcohol and/or drug abuse presents a high-risk factor that can promote relapse to offending behavior.

3. Treatment for substance abuse or dependency must focus on the interrelationship of the offenders' substance use pattern and their offense history. (Plum, 2001, p. 14-2)

Clients frequently expressed on the Plum Sexual Offender Inventory for Chemical Abuse (see Appendix 16.1; Plum, 2001) that their substance abuse was not related to their sexual offending, or that only certain substances were related to sexual offending. They often put forth robust and resilient explanations as to why or how one substance or another does not relate to their sexual offending. In addition, civilly committed sexual offenders often have been incarcerated for long periods of time and embroiled in long legal arguments about the nature and extent of their crimes they often are deeply committed a particular version of their "story." The approach described in this chapter is designed to help clients explore the overt and covert interrelationships of their sexual offending and substance abuse.

NARRATIVE ANALYSIS

Sexual offenders during treatment often distort chronologically and behaviorally the impact of their substance abuse as a contributing factor in their offenses. Clients may say that substances could not have played a role in their sexual offenses because "I wasn't drunk at the time," or "I never used when I raped someone." In addition, sexual offenders deny or minimize their offenses. In a sense, sexual offenders use the same processes to deny two distinct behaviors (e.g., substance abuse and sexual offending). Effective clinical interventions that reduce the risk of clients simply learning what to say to please clinicians will need to explore the emotional components of their relapse process in a powerful manner, as demonstrated in the following case example.

> *"K." was a 45-year-old white male who had been civilly committed as a sexually dangerous person. His offenses were sadistic rapes of adult women. K. openly admitted to being an "alcoholic" but steadfastly denied that his drinking was at all related to his offending behavior.*

For this client, a typical course of addictions treatment was implemented with little or no change in his attitude toward alcohol. In K.'s case, it was important to create a very powerful experience that would help him make the connection between his attitude toward alcohol and his risk for continued sexual offending.

Clients who might be determined to be in "denial" or "resistant" might also be regarded as simply not aware of the various relationships of one behavior to another (Prochaska & DiClemente, 1994). The question is how to develop enough rapport with clients to be able to journey into an undiscovered land with them. In K.'s case, several steps were taken to create an experience of sufficient intensity for him to "feel" the interrelationship of his substance abuse with his sexual offending.

K. had had a pattern of sexual assault against his wife (as well as other victims). K.'s robust religiosity held that God had given him dominion over their home and he could not "rape" his wife because he viewed her as essentially chattel. The following is a quote from K. when discussing the buildup to his sexual offending:

> *"I would drive around in my car drinking beer. I preferred to drink alone, just sitting in my car smoking cigarettes and drinking. Sometimes this would go on late into the night. Sometimes, I just felt restless and did not want to be home."*

The foregoing quote describes obvious high-risk factors to any listener: substance use, negative emotional state, and isolation. However, for K. they were not obvious or necessarily accessible. For K., he was simply "having a few beers."

> *"She knows that I am the man of the house and if I want sex she was going to give to me. Anyhow she liked it when I took control."*

The objectification of his wife, combined with his veneer of religiosity, allowed K. to perceive that he was in control of his "house" and "wife." For K., an experience needed to be created that would bypass his distortions and give him a unique experience that would help him understand the interrelationship of alcohol to his sexual offending.

The process used with K. was to connect the verbal description of his alcohol use pattern with as many sights, sounds, smells, and sensations as possible to an actual offense. In K.'s case, he did not see any connection between his drinking and his sexual assaults against his wife. The following transcript of a portion of a session is an example of narrative analysis:

THERAPIST:	So you are sitting in your car. What are you doing?
K.:	Drinking beer and smoking cigarettes. It's feeling pretty good.
THERAPIST:	Where are you parked?
K.:	At this rest area I liked.
THERAPIST:	How are sitting in the car in what way are you making yourself comfortable?
K.:	I would lay back the seat and turn on the radio.
THERAPIST:	So there you are smoking, listening to the radio, and drinking beer. What else is going on?
K.:	I find myself getting bored after awhile. I would be a little drunk and bored and so I would start to drive.
THERAPIST:	So there you are a little drunk and driving around. Did you know where you were going?
K.:	No. I would just drive and take any turn. Just looking around, you know.
THERAPIST:	What would you be thinking?
K.:	Nothing much sometimes I would feel resentful and angry about being bored with no place to hang out.
THERAPIST:	Resentful and angry, driving around, a little drunk. What would help you to decide to go home?
K.:	I don't know. I just figured it is my home and could drink there if I wanted to.
THERAPIST:	So would it be late when you got home?
K.:	Yeah, 1 or 2 in the morning.
THERAPIST:	So would you try to quiet or not? When you came in the house, would your wife be asleep?
K.:	She went to bed early. I did not think about being quiet. I would go and sit and chair maybe watch TV and have a beer.
THERAPIST:	I am just wondering if you were smoking cigarettes too and if you had a chance to change from your work clothes before you went out?
K.:	Naw, I wouldn't change and I always would smoke when I drank.
THERAPIST:	OK. So what are you thinking? Sitting there in your chair, bored, resentful, a little more drunk, smoking cigarettes, is that right? Thinking that it is your house not really caring if you woke your wife or not. Do you think she heard you come in?
K.:	I am sure she did.

As the client describes his or her behavior the therapist is listening for behaviors, sensations, and experiences to expand on and thereby create within the therapeutic session a powerful facsimile of the client's actually offense and substance abuse pattern.

THERAPIST:	So you must have smelled of alcohol, cigarette smoke, and sweat.
K.:	Yeah, I guess so—not that bad though.
THERAPIST:	OK. So it is getting late and you must be tired. And it seems like you have been doing a lot of thinking—through the evening you been feeling restless, bored, resentful. What kind of thoughts are you having about your wife?
K.:	That she is a bitch sometimes, always bugging me about work.
THERAPIST:	So you are thinking that she is a bitch and a nag. How did you use those words in your head? What other names did you call her?
K.:	I do not know, "a fucking bitch" or "nagging whore."
THERAPIST:	Bored, restless, a little drunk and smelling of alcohol and smoke. Thinking to yourself, "that fucking bitch nagging me all of the time, what a whore?" Drinking some more beer . . . Is that the situation?
K.:	Yes, that is pretty close.
THERAPIST:	OK, so you start walking to bed room. You are aware that she probably heard you come in. When you enter the bedroom what do you see?
K.:	I don't know. She is just laying there.
THERAPIST:	The room is dark?
K.:	Yes.
THERAPIST:	You see her lying there in bed, pretending to sleep, ignoring you. "The fucking bitch." She stays at your house, eating your food, and then nags you about work and your drinking. She can't even get up. Just lying there like some lump,
K.:	Yeah.
THERAPIST:	What are you thinking right now?
K.:	How she needs to know who is boss.

At this point the therapist has brought the client to the moment before a sexual assault. In this case it was important to discover what actually triggered the sexual assault.

THERAPIST:	So what happens next?
K.:	I get into bed with her. I want sex.
THERAPIST:	What does she do?
K.:	She rolls over and turns her back to me.
THERAPIST:	So you get angry.
K.:	Yes.
THERAPIST:	There you are drunk, smelling of sweat and cigarettes, angry, wanting sex and she just turns away from you. So what do you next?

At this point K. describes a sexual assault on his wife. During subsequent therapy sessions K. was able to discuss the assaults on his wife in a more complete manner and could not absolve his use of alcohol from the entire matrix of his offense.

INDUCED EUPHORIC RECALL

The induction of euphoric recall of past substance use can be an effective technique in helping clients understand how substance abuse relates to their sexual offenses. In situations in which clients are living in a controlled and highly structured setting, euphoric recall is safe to use. In outpatient settings this approach has risks associated with it (e.g., clients may leave the therapy session feeling an intense urge to use mood-altering substances). In this case it is important to develop an intensely aversive scene with the client.

"Y." is a civilly committed sexually offender with a history of sexually assaulting adolescent females. He admits to abusing marijuana. In Y.'s case, he firmly maintained that his use of marijuana never played a role in his offenses although he was a daily user of cannabis. Y. had stated throughout therapy that marijuana was not a harmful substance and that he did not think that continued use would place him at risk to committing another sexual offense.

In Y.'s case a strategy of inducing euphoric recall was used for several reasons that were related to his history. Y. was a daily user of marijuana and he tended to use marijuana immediately upon waking in the morning and found his first "high in the morning" the most pleasurable of the whole day.

THERAPIST:	So tell me a little more about your use of marijuana. When, for instance, did you usually start smoking?
Y.:	Usually right away in the morning.
THERAPIST:	Right away in the morning. Does that mean you would be up for a while and then smoke, or would you still be in bed?
Y.:	I would just reach over and then light a joint.
THERAPIST:	Would you use a match or lighter?
Y.:	A lighter.
THERAPIST:	So here you are in bed, you have a joint between your fingers and putting the joint into your mouth you strike the lighter on, moving the flame to the end of the joint. You see it flare and turn red, and then you deeply inhale the smoke. Holding the smoke in, you feel your lungs expand. Exhaling, you blow the smoke out and you see the smoke move across the room and toward the ceiling.
Y.:	Yeah man, I just loved it—it feels really good.
THERAPIST:	Describe "feels good."
Y.:	My body would relax and I could think about a lot of shit.
THERAPIST:	You are feeling high relaxed and you can think and imagine a lot of things. You smell the marijuana and you take another hit. Blowing out the smoke the cloud sort of caresses you like a comforting fog.
Y.:	Yeah, I would like let it happen just feeling high and good.

THERAPIST:	There you are, feeling high and good and your mind drifts and some times you think "Man wouldn't it be nice to have someone there."
Y.:	Sure, you know. You're high and feeling good.
THERAPIST:	And sometimes you get aroused. Laying back, smoking that good weed, feeling good and relaxed.
Y.:	Yeah, I guess. You know you start thinking and playing with stuff in your mind.
THERAPIST:	And sometimes you think of kids.
Y.:	Sure . . .

At this point Y. described how his fantasy evolved into the sexual offending of children. In Y.'s case the linkage between marijuana as a high-risk factor to relapse to sexual offending was covert. In his rather rigid view of his marijuana use, it was not directly coinciding with a sexual offense and it did not "cause" the offense; therefore, it was "safe." One of the mistakes that therapists make in working with substance abusers is the rejection of their client's experience with the mood-altering substance. Another error is to commit a direct frontal assault (Erickson, 1980), attempting in a very confrontational way to convince the client of the correlation between substance abuse and the negative consequences in his or her life. For long-term incarcerated clients, the distance of time will, for many, only enhance their euphoric recall of substance use. By understanding and knowing how to use this state, therapists can help individuals and groups rediscover and reinterpret their relationship with mood altering chemicals to allow for more accountability.

Offender accountability is a central goal of many sexual offender treatment programs (Wright & Schneider, 2004) and is considered an essential aspect for the measurement of progress in treatment. The problem for substance-abusing sexual offenders is the difficulty of integrating two behaviors into a coherent cognitive structure that will lower their risk for offending. For impulsive, cognitively rigid, non-psychologically minded people, the notion of accountability represents a dominate world view of "the problem" (Miller & Duncan, 2004), where direct confrontation about the "the problem" can entrench a client defensive stance. However, if the therapist is aware of the organic processes that support and enhance the client's sexual offending and substance he or she can enter the client's world—no matter how uncomfortable it may be to empathically connect with the client's experience. This does not condone a client's behavior or provide another layer of exegesis explaining it.

COVERT INDUCTION

One aspect for conducting group therapy in civil commitment programs is the ability for staff to promote higher level of emotional arousal than what might be considered appropriate in outpatient settings. An issue that appears common to civil commitment programs is the length of incarceration that clients have served. It is not uncommon for clients to have been in controlled settings for decades, with many years separating them from their last use of mood-altering chemicals (although this may be suspect, in some cases, because some clients are very reluctant to admit to illicit substance use while incarcerated). In a few cases, clients may view themselves as immune to relapse because of the length of time they have abstained from alcohol or other mood-altering substances and the detailed nature of their relapse prevention plans.

Even clients who understand a clear relationship between their use of mood-altering substances and sexual offending may have been so removed from their cues and triggers to relapse that they may develop an overly optimistic stance regarding their ability to cope with them (Childress & McLelland, 1993). It is always difficult to bridge the controlled, artificial, and safe environment of a secure treatment facility with the unpredictability of freedom. The covert induction of euphoric recall and craving may be helpful to clients in appreciating the power of cues and triggers.

The utility for this technique, beyond helping clients reassess their reactivity to cues (American Society of Addiction Medicine, 2004), is to also help staff and clients develop more effective experiential exercises (i.e., role plays where coping skills can be practiced). The strategy is straightforward, for employing it with clients simply involves a discussion around how, when, and where they used mood-altering chemicals. The therapist will simply expand on the discussion with behavioral descriptions of the client's use pattern while paying close attention to changes in client affect.

CLIENT:	I can hang out in bars. I know I won't drink. If I just stay out of strip clubs I will be alright.
THERAPIST:	OK. So there is a difference for you.
CLIENT:	Strip clubs, well if I am in one, it is because I am already really into my cycle—so I will just sit alone and drink, staring at the dancers, getting worked up and frustrated. But a bar, well I would be in there just to talk my friends.
THERAPIST:	Sure you would just hang out and talk. They might be drinking beer having a smoke and telling jokes, listening to music, having something to eat.
CLIENT:	That's right, a social thing.
THERAPIST:	Yeah bars can be so comfortable sometimes.
CLIENT:	Sure, that is where your friends are, drinking beer out of glasses and bottles. Talking and sharing stories.
THERAPIST:	I know the stories, the bottles clinking together, music—sometimes your song comes on, and one of the guys is so fucking funny you think you are going to shit yourself from laughing so hard.
CLIENT:	Man I hate thinking about it—makes me want to drink,
THERAPIST:	How is that?
CLIENT:	You know just thinking about it.

Often, simply getting a client to talk about his or her favorite setting or person will create the sensation for the induction of craving. With the density of embedded environmental triggers, even clients with long periods of enforced abstinence begin to experience a craving.

Craving for alcohol and drugs usually takes form in two basic ways. Clients describe their cravings as either a thought or a feeling. Frequently, the client makes statements such as "I just felt like drinking. I really did not think about it," or, "I just started thinking about using. I couldn't get it off of my mind." Both are abstractions of the same basic process. There is a tendency to minimize the impact of cognitive expressed craving, but the perniciousness of this type of craving often becomes rather a persistent experience. While the intensity of affective/emotional based craving is short-lived, thinking about chemicals can be tormenting. Many civilly committed sexually offenders are loath to admit that they are thinking about using a mood-altering chemical for obvious reasons: fear of being considered treatment resistant and potential loss of "positive progress reports." Induction of craving can help expose a client's internal distress while bypassing their cognitive defenses.

The American Society of Addiction Medicine (2004) committee that developed the Multidimensional Assessment Format for Substance Abuse defined many of essential features of a client's risk to relapse to substance use (to see all six dimensions, refer to Appendix 16.2):

- Current level of awareness of substance related problems

- Chronicity of substance use

- Level and intensity of cravings or thoughts about substances

- Perceived positive or negative benefits of continued substance use

- Reactivity to triggers or cues

- Level of impulsivity

- Internal or external locus of control

- Level of person's aggressiveness or passivity. (p. 155)

Even clients living in controlled environments are still exposed to environmental triggers, such as television, radio, and other media, in addition to other clients who may be rather open about their willingness to continue to use mood-altering substances. Despite the amount of time a client has abstained, if treatment is held in a controlled environment, the risk factors to relapse remain vibrant.

DEBRIEFING

Integrating a therapeutic event into a useful skill set for clients is the central aspect of treatment. Clients who have had cravings induced during group therapy will experience feelings of anxiety, fear, surprise, and sometimes anger. Clients may be rather surprised at the intensity of their response. The debriefing and analysis of the experience of induced craving is absolutely necessary.

Debriefing of craving involves first naming and processing the feelings and then allowing time for the client's arousal to diminish. Second, it involves analyzing, along with the client, the thoughts, feelings, or sensations he or she reacted to during the session. The third step is behavioral analysis to describe previously hidden triggers and cues that correspond with sexual offending and substance use. Finally, the therapist and client identify cognitive-behavioral coping skills to be learned and rehearsed in subsequent therapy sessions.

In addition to debriefing the client, it is important to debrief the other group members. It is not unusual for someone other than the principal client to be affected by the induction process. It is important to recognize this possibility. Therefore, the group therapist must include within the debriefing process as much time as is necessary for members to process their personal experiences during the session. This can be extremely important for not only the principal but also for the group, because it allows for clients to identify potential internal and external high-risk factors. Sometimes it is important for each client to develop an aversive scene after the induction and as part of the debriefing session.

The creation of aversive scenes is similar to induction protocols for euphoric recall. In a sense the therapist helps the client identity and reexperience the thoughts, feelings, and sensations associated with a person's substance use that are of a negative and painful quality. Here as an example of an aversive scene:

THERAPIST: Think of a time when you were so tired, depressed, and disgusted with yourself. You retch at the thought of drinking anymore or using just once more. You are so tired you can't think. Sometimes your right side hurts. And you remember that look of disappointment, or disgust, or coldness of someone who once loved you.

CLIENT: Yeah, I remember sitting in a toilet. I was sick and throwing up. I hadn't showered in days. I was supposed to see my kid and I never showed up for her birthday. I knew I was going to lie to her and tell her some bullshit story. There I was in a toilet. I shot up all my money, the cops were looking for me, and all could think of was how I could get enough heroin.

THERAPIST: OK, there you are vomit in your mouth and thinking of your daughter. Afraid the cops are going to catch you, afraid you won't get enough heroin, and knowing you are going to lie to your daughter about missing her birthday. Is that it?

CLIENT: Yes.

THERAPIST: Visualize your scene as vividly as you can and describe it again with as much detail as you can muster allowing yourself to feel the emotions and sensations associated with it.

CLIENT: I am sitting in a toilet after being sick. My mouth tastes of vomit . . .

The client repeats the scene with the therapist supporting and guiding the imagery, enhancing the image until the client can attribute an aversive emotional state to the scene that is paired to substance use. The therapist then assists the client in creating the mechanism that will help the client to use the aversive scene during therapy sessions.

CONCLUSION

A high percentage of sexual offenders also have histories of substance abuse and the combination of substance abuse and deviant sexual fantasy can serve to strongly influence an offender's choice to reoffend. In treatment programs, it is important for therapists to recognize that there is an interaction between euphoric recall of past substance use and reactivity to cues and triggers with deviant sexual fantasy. The techniques and strategies described in this chapter are similar to those commonly employed by therapists in a variety of settings. For instance, an Abel Assessment of Sexual Interest (Abel, 1997) deliberately exposes a client to variety of evocative images to measure a client's reactivity. And, in substance abuse treatment, exposing clients directly to triggers has been extensively used in a variety of settings. Because of the nature of the civilly committed sexual offender's problems, and his or her level of dangerousness, a very conservative approach that requires a demonstrative and behaviorally oriented stance toward client change is wise. Therefore, use of role play and imagery can be crucial interventions in such treatment programs.

References

Abel, G.G. (1997). *The Abel Assessment for Sexual Interest* [Online]. Available: *www.abelscreen.com.*

American Society of Addiction Medicine. (2004). *Patient placement criteria for the treatment of substance related disorders* (2nd ed.). Available: ASAM Publications Distribution, P.O. Box 101, Annapolis Junction, MD 20701–0101.

Ball, C. J., & Seghorn, T. K. (1999). Diagnosis and treatment of exhibitionism and other sexual compulsive disorders. In B. K. Schwartz (Ed.), *The sex offender: Theoretical advances, treating special populations and legal developments* (pp. 28-1–28-14). Kingston, NJ: Civic Research Institute.

Barbaree, H., & Seto, M. (1997). *Prediction of recidivism among sex offenders.* Power point presentation. Available: *www.mhcp-research.com.*

Childress, A. R., & McLelland, A. T. (1993) *Cue extinction: Handbook for program administrators.* Rockville, MD: National Institute on Drug Abuse.

Erickson, M. (1980). *An introduction to unorthodox therapy; innovative hypnotherapy: Collected papers of Milton H. Erickson* (Vol. IV). New York: Irvington.

Grossman, L. S., Martis, B., & Fichtner, C. G. (1999). Are sex offenders treatable? A research overview. *Psychiatric Services, 50,* 349–361.

Holmes, R. M., & Holmes, S. T. (1994). *Murder in America.* Thousand Oaks, CA: Sage.

Hunter, J. A., Goodwin, D. W., & Becker, J. V. (1994). The relationship between phallometrically measured deviant sexual arousal and clinical characteristics in juvenile sexual offenders. *Behavior Research and Therapy, 32*(5), 533–538.

Langevin, R., & Lang, R. A. (1990). Substance abuse among sex offenders, *Annals of Sex Research, 3,* 397–424.

Langstrom, N., Sjotedt, G., & Grann, M. (2004). Psychiatric disorders and recidivism in sexual offenders. *Sexual Abuse: A Journal of Research and Treatment, 16*(2), 139–150.

Maletzky, B. M. (1991). *Treating the sexual offender.* Newbury Park, CA: Sage.

Marlatt, G. A. (1983). *Relapse prevention: Maintenance strategies in the treatment of addictive behaviors.* New York: Guilford Press.

Marlatt, G. A., & Rohsenow, D. J. (1980). Cognitive processes in alcohol use: Expectancy and the balanced placebo design. In N. K. Mello (Ed.), *Advances in substance abuse: Behavioral and biological research* (Vol. 1, pp.159–199). Greenwich, CT: JAI Press.

Marques, J. K., Day, D. M., Nelson, C., Miner, M., & West, M. A. (1992). Effects of cognitive behavioral treatment on sex offender recidivism: Preliminary results of a longitudinal study. *Criminal Justice and Behavior, 21,* 28–54

Mee-Lee, D. (1995). Matching in addictions treatment: How do we get there from here? *Alcoholism Treatment Quarterly Special Issue: Treatment of the Addictions—Applications of Outcome Research for Clinical Management, 12,* 113–127.

Miller, G. (1994). *Substance Abuse Subtle Screening Inventory (SASSI-3).* Available: 1-88-297-2774.

Miller, S., & Duncan, B. (2004). *The heart and soul of change; What works in therapy.* Washington, DC: American Psychological Association.

Plum, W. (2001). Sex offender and chemical dependency treatment. In A. Schlank (Ed.), *The sexual predator* (pp. 14-1–14-11). Kingston, NJ: Civic Research Institute.

Prochaska, J., & DiClemente, C. (1994) *The transtheoretical approach: Crossing traditional boundaries.* Melbourne, FL: Krieger.

Rosenfeld, J., & Webber, J. R. (2000). *The neuroscience of addiction.* Paper presented at the annual conference of the Illinois Alcohol and Other Drug Abuse Professional Certification Association, Arlington Heights.

Vaillant, G. (1983). *The natural history of alcoholism: Causes, patterns and paths to recovery.* Cambridge MA: Harvard University Press.

Valliere, V. M. (1997). Relationships between alcohol use, alcohol expectancies, and sexual offenses in convicted offenders. In B. K. Schwartz & H. R. Cellini (Eds.), *The sex offender: New insights, treatment interventions, and legal developments* (pp. 3-1–3-14). Kingston NJ: Civic Research Institute.

Wright, R. C., & Schneider, S. L. (2004) Mapping child molester treatment progress with FoSOD: Denial and explanations of accountability. *Sexual Abuse: A Journal of Research and Treatment, 16*(2), 85–106.

Appendix 16.1
Plum Sex Offender Inventory for Chemical Abuse

[Editor's Note: This Inventory appeared as Appendix 14.2 in Plum (2001). That version was printed with some inadvertent errors. Therefore, we are including it again here, printed correctly.]

Answer the following questions only if you have used alcohol or other drugs at some time in your life.

Name: _____

Date: _____

	Strongly Agree	Somewhat Agree	Somewhat Disagree	Strongly Disagree
1. I have used many different mood-altering chemicals.	1	2	3	4
2. I have family members who abuse alcohol and/or drugs.	1	2	3	4
3. My substance abuse is not related to any of my sex offending.	1	2	3	4
4. I believe that if my victim/s were drunk or high that s/he is somewhat responsible for the crime.	1	2	3	4
5. I use mood-altering chemicals as a "weapon" or as a means to "control" my victims.	1	2	3	4
6. I coerced my victims by supplying them with alcohol or other drugs.	1	2	3	4
7. My sexual fantasies increase when I use mood-altering chemicals.	1	2	3	4
8. I like to use mood-altering chemicals alone and watch X-rated movies or read sexually explicit magazines.	1	2	3	4
9. Drinking or drug taking often gave me the courage to do what was on my mind.	1	2	3	4
10. I used criminal behavior to intensify my "high" from mood-altering chemicals.	1	2	3	4
11. I believe that if I did not use mood-altering chemicals I would not have offended.	1	2	3	4

	Strongly Agree	Somewhat Agree	Somewhat Disagree	Strongly Disagree
12. I often used mood-altering chemicals while I sexually offended.	1	2	3	4
13. I often used mood-altering chemicals after I sexually offended.	1	2	3	4
14. I used different substances when I sexually offended than when I was not sexually offending.	1	2	3	4
15. I used my substance abuse as an "excuse" or "reason" to explain my behavior to my victim/s.	1	2	3	4
16. I think that only some types of chemicals are a problem for me.	1	2	3	4
17. I used only a certain type/s of mood-altering chemical/s before my sexual offending.	1	2	3	4
18. I believe that my chemical use has nothing to do with my sexual offending.	1	2	3	4
19. I believe that if I am successful in sex offender treatment, I will be able to safely use mood-altering chemicals.	1	2	3	4
20. I understand that use of mood-altering chemicals could influence my choice to sexually offend.	1	2	3	4
21. I frequently used mood-altering chemicals to cover up my feelings, particularly after I sexually offended.	1	2	3	4
22. I used mood-altering chemicals to stop me from thinking about sexually offending.	1	2	3	4
23. My use of mood-altering chemicals helped me control my behavior by relaxing me.	1	2	3	4
24. Thinking about using mood-altering chemicals is as exciting sometimes as having sexual fantasies.	1	2	3	4

	Strongly Agree	Somewhat Agree	Somewhat Disagree	Strongly Disagree
25. It is hard for me to think of any consequences associated with my alcohol and/or drug use.	1	2	3	4
26. I have committed sexual offenses when I have | been sober.	1	2	3	4
27. I have committed sexual offenses while in or after completing treatment for chemical dependency.	1	2	3	4
28. I think that my sexual offenses were more violent when I was under the influence of alcohol and/or drugs.	1	2	3	4
29. I only started to abuse alcohol and/or drugs after I went to prison.	1	2	3	4
30. I have used alcohol and/or drugs while going through outpatient sex offender treatment.	1	2	3	4
31. I am confused about the role of my alcohol and/or drug use in my sexual offending.	1	2	3	4

Appendix 16.2
Chemical Use Assessment

The chemical use assessment is a structured interview to gather as much relevant information as possible regarding a client's chemical use pattern. The following outlines a multidimensional risk assessment developed by Dr. David Mee-Lee (1995) and modified by the author.

Dimension One: Acute Intoxication/Withdrawal

- Last chemical used and in what amount

- Chemical use pattern during the six months prior to law use (frequency, types and amounts)

- Onset of chemicals: age for each, types, frequency, and amounts

- History of progression of symptoms; tolerance, loss of control, withdrawal syndrome

- Prior diagnosis of addiction; prior treatment history

Dimension Two: Biomedical Conditions

- Client's current biomedical conditions

- Medications prescribed by physicians

- Does the client suffer from biomedical conditions that were caused by his/her chemical addiction or exacerbated by chemical abuse?

- Client's general health history

Dimension Three: Mental Health

- Client's current mental health status

- Medications prescribed for diagnosed mental health disorders

- Does the client admit to a history of using nonprescribed mood-altering chemicals to medicate mental health symptoms?

- Does the client have a history of mixing psychotropic medication with nonprescribed mood altering chemicals?

Dimension Four: Treatment Acceptance

- Does the client identify a chemical use problem?

- What is the client's characterization of his chemical use history?

- Can the client identify any consequences associated with his chemical use pattern?

- Does the client believe he needs CA treatment?

- Does the client express ambivalence about chemicals, believing that some chemicals are still safe to use while others are not?

Dimension Five: Relapse/Continued Use Potential

- If the client was not in a supervised setting, what is his relapse/continued use potential?

- How aware is the client of external/internal high risk factors?

- What coping skills does the client currently have that would support a change in his chemical use pattern?

Dimension Six: Recovery Environment

- What is the client's current environment?

- Does this environment support change?

- If the client were not in a supervised setting, what type of environment would he return to?

- Can the client identify support people or not?

- What is the client's relationship and family history?

- How prevalent is chemical abuse among his family and friends?

- In addition to the clinical interview, the use of testing can be helpful. The Substance Abuse Subtle Screening Inventory (SASSI; Miller, 1994) is an excellent tool that tests for both alcohol and drug abuse. It is divided into face valid items and empirically based scales. The SASSI also tests for defensiveness and random answering patterns.

Appendix 1

United States v. Antelope

395 F.2d 1128 (9th Cir. 2005)

[*Editor's Note*: This appendix reprints the text of the opinion of the Court of Appeals for the Ninth Circuit in *United States v. Antelope*. Official page numbers for the quoted material are indicated in brackets, in boldface type (e.g., **[1130]**), should you need to cite to the case.]

[1130]

***

McKEOWN, Circuit Judge:

Lawrence Antelope is a convicted sex offender who shows promise of rehabilitation. The terms of his supervised release offer him treatment—but at a price he is not willing to pay. Antelope has repeatedly refused to incriminate himself as part of his sex offender treatment. He declines to detail his sexual history in the absence of any assurance of immunity because of the risk that he may reveal past crimes and that his admissions could then be used to prosecute him. In response, the government has twice revoked his conditional liberty and sent him to prison. The case he now brings requires us to decide whether the government's actions violated his Fifth Amendment right against compelled self-incrimination. Because the Constitution does not countenance the sort of government coercion imposed on Antelope, and **[1131]** because his claim is ripe for adjudication, we reverse the judgment of the district court.

We decide also Antelope's challenge to the release term prohibiting him from possessing "any pornographic, sexually oriented or sexually stimulating materials," which we vacate and remand, as well as his challenge to the term prohibiting him from access to "any 'on-line computer service,' " which we affirm.

Background

The course of events leading to this appeal began when Lawrence Antelope joined an Internet site advertising "Preteen Nude Sex Pics" and started corresponding with someone who, unbeknownst to Antelope, was an undercover law enforcement agent. The sting operation proved fruitful when Antelope ordered a child pornography video over the Internet. Federal agents arranged a controlled delivery, delivered the video, and then promptly arrested Antelope.

Caught red-handed, Antelope pleaded guilty to possessing child pornography in violation of 18 U.S.C. § 2252A(a)(5)(B) and was initially sentenced to five years probation. One of the probation terms required Antelope to participate in the Sexual Abuse Behavior Evaluation and Recovery program ("SABER"), which would subject him to mandatory "periodic and random polygraph examinations." At sentencing, Antelope raised a Fifth Amendment challenge to this requirement, but was told by the district judge that the "use of that information . . . is, I think, subject to the privilege between the counselor and the patient." Antelope was also prohibited from "possess[ing] any pornographic, sexually oriented or sexually stimulating materials" and from "possess[ing] or us[ing] a computer with access to any 'on-line computer service' at any location . . . without the prior written approval of the probation department." Both Antelope and the government promptly appealed the sentence.

While the appeal was pending, the district court revoked Antelope's probation for failure to comply with several probation conditions, including the requirement that he submit to polygraph examinations as part of the treatment program. The district judge re-imposed probation with an additional six months of electronic monitoring and warned that Antelope's continued refusal to submit to the polygraph would result in his incarceration. Antelope appealed this ruling as well.

Immediately following this ruling, Antelope filed a motion in the district court seeking to clarify whether the order included immunity from the use of Antelope's statements made in compliance with SABER to prosecute him. The district court never ruled on this motion, later dismissing it as moot.

While these appeals were pending, the district court again found Antelope in violation of probation. At the probation revocation hearing, Roger Dowty, Antelope's counselor at the sex treatment program, testified that Antelope had failed to complete SABER's sexual history autobiography assignment and "full disclosure polygraph" verifying his "full sexual history." Dowty explained that Antelope had been told that any past criminal offenses he revealed in the course of the program could be released to the authorities. Dowty also testified that he was under a legal obligation to turn over information regarding offenses involving victims under eighteen. Antelope argued that the autobiography and full disclosure polygraph requirements violated his Fifth Amendment right, expressed his desire to continue treatment, and sought immunity for statements made in compliance with the program. The district court rejected his argument, ruling that the fact of probation [1132] nullifies any Fifth Amendment right Antelope might otherwise have to decline to "reveal[ ] information that may incriminate him," and sentenced him to 30 months in prison. Antelope appealed a third time.

All three appeals were consolidated for appellate review, and this court issued a decision reversing in part and remanding for resentencing. The court declined to reach Antelope's First and Fifth Amendment claims. See United States v. Antelope, 65 Fed. Appx. 112 (9th Cir. 2003) (mem.).

Following remand, Antelope was resentenced to twenty months incarceration, followed by three years of supervised release. The district court again imposed the contested conditions as terms of his supervised release. Antelope once again objected, but the court ruled that the objection was not ripe, and would not be ripe until Antelope was "prosecuted or subject to prosecution" for additional crimes. Antelope appealed once more. This fourth appeal is one of the two directly before us now.

Shortly after he was resentenced, Antelope finished serving his prison term and was released under supervision. Antelope reasserted his desire for treatment but continued to refuse to reveal his full sexual history absent an assurance of immunity. When Antelope appeared at a release revocation hearing, he yet again argued the merits of his Fifth Amendment claim. The district judge reiterated his belief that Antelope's admissions would be protected by an "absolute privilege under Montana law between a counselor, psychologist and the patient"; asserted that "given the fact that[Antelope has] not said anything yet, . . . everything is premature [a]nd until this judicial proceeding, where he's compelled to testify, it seems to me, . . . you don't have any legal arguments to be making that are meritorious in my view today"; and declined to rule on whether Antelope's admissions would be protected by use immunity, apparently on ripeness grounds. The district judge suggested that Antelope's proper course would be to "assert[ ] his privilege when he goes to see Mr. [Dowty, the counselor,] and say[ ], *I am doing this because I'm ordered to do it. I am not doing it voluntarily, it's a court order, and I do it only because if I don't do it I'm going to end up in jail.*"

The district court sentenced Antelope to an additional ten months in prison and twenty-six months of supervised release with the same conditions. Antelope appealed a final time, and we consider the issues presented by his consolidated fourth and fifth appeals.

Discussion

I. Ripeness

We turn first to the government's argument that Antelope's Fifth Amendment claim is not yet ripe for review. The constitutional component of ripeness is a jurisdictional prerequisite. *Cal. Pro-Life Council, Inc. v. Getman*, 328 F.3d 1088, 1093-94 & n. 2 (9th cir. 2003) (noting that the question of ripeness often "coincides squarely with standing's injury in fact prong"). Whether Antelope's claim is sufficiently mature to justify appellate review is a question of law we consider de novo. *Laub v. United States Dep't of the Interior*, 342 F.3d 1080, 1084 (9th Cir. 2003).

To determine whether Antelope suffered an injury in fact, we must identify "an invasion of a legally protected interest which is (a) concrete and particularized; and (b) actual or imminent, not conjectural or hypothetical." *Id*. at 1085. Here, Antelope's appeal centers around his claimed right to be free of unconstitutional compulsion: Under his theory, the government violated his Fifth Amendment **[1133]** right when it conditioned his probation and supervised release on the submission of a sexual autobiography that we may assume would have revealed prosecutable offenses. From Antelope's perspective, in whose shoes we stand when deciding this threshold issue of justiciability, he has already suffered the very serious and non-hypothetical injury of imprisonment after he invoked his Fifth Amendment right. In other words,"[i]f his legal argument is correct, he has already suffered constitutional injury." *United States v. Purvis*, 940 F.2d 1276, 1278 (9th cir. 1991) (holding ripe the defendant's challenge to his supervised release condition, which he had been re-incarcerated for violating). Antelope's case history reads like a never-ending loop tape: he asserts his constitutional rights, the district court advises him that surely his statements will be confidential but that he must comply with what he views as a violation of his constitutional rights, he refuses to comply, his release is revoked, and Antelope ends up incarcerated. Indeed, it is difficult to imagine a more paradigmatic "injury in fact" than actual incarceration. We therefore conclude that Antelope's Fifth Amendment claim is ripe for review.

II. The Fifth Amendment Right Against Self-Incrimination

Having determined the question justiciable, we address next Antelope's claim to the Fifth Amendment privilege against compelled self-incrimination, an issue that has dominated the five appeals Antelope has filed throughout the course of these proceedings. Antelope contends that the Fifth Amendment restrains the government from forcing him to admit prior wrongdoing unless his statements are protected by use and derivative use immunity in accordance with *Kastigar v. United States*, 406 U.S. 441, 92 S. Ct. 1653, 32 L.Ed.2d 212 (1927). Whether there is merit to Antelope's argument is a legal matter, which we decide without deference to the judgment of the district court. *See United States v. Rubio-Topete*, 999 F.2d 1334, 1338 (9th Cir. 1993).

We ground our analysis in well-settled principles, starting with the Constitution. The Fifth Amendment guarantees that "[n]o person . . . shall be compelled in any criminal case to be a witness against himself." U.S. Const. amend. V. This right remains available to Antelope despite his conviction. *See Minnesota v. Murphy*, 465 U.S. 420, 426, 104 S. Ct. 1136, 79 L.Ed.2d 409 (1984) ("A defendant does not lose this protection by reason of his conviction of a crime. . . ."); *cf. McKune v. Lile*, 536 U.S. 24, 48-54, 122 S. Ct. 2017, 153 L.Ed.2d 47 (2002) (O'Connor, J., concurring in 4-1-4 decision) (applying the full-blown Fifth Amendment analysis to a prisoner's claim that the prison's requirement that he participate in a sex offender treatment program violated his constitutional right).[1]

[1134] To establish his Fifth Amendment claim, Antelope must prove two things: (1) that the testimony desired by the government carried the risk of incrimination, *see*

---

[1] Abiding by the rule that when "no single rationale explaining the result enjoys the assent of five Justices, the holding of the Court may be viewed as that position taken by those Members who concurred in the judgments on the narrowest grounds," *Marks v. United States*, 430 U.S. 188, 193, 97 S.Ct. 990, 51 L.Ed.2d 260 (1977) (internal quotation marks omitted), we treat Justice O'Connor's opinion in McKune as controlling. Two of our sister circuits considering this question have arrived at the same conclusion. *Ainsworth v. Stanley*, 317 F.3d 1, 4 (1st Cir. 2002) ("Justice O'Connor's concurrence [in *McKune*] is arguably more narrow than the plurality's and therefore constitutes the holding of the Court.") (internal quotation marks omitted); *Searcy v. Simmons*, 299 F.3d 1220, 1225 (10th Cir. 2002) ("Because Justice O'Connor based her conclusion on the narrower ground that the [Kansas] policy was not compulsion under the Fifth Amendment, we view her concurrence as the holding of the Court in *McKune*.").

Murphy, 465 U.S. at 435 n. 7, 104 S.Ct. 1136 (explaining that the state may compel answers "as long as it . . . eliminates the threat of incrimination"); *Minor v. United States*, 396 U.S. 87, 98, 90 S.Ct. 284, 24 L.Ed.2d 283 (1969) (rejecting a Fifth Amendment challenge because the risk of incrimination was "only imaginary and insubstantial . . . rather than . . . real and appreciable" (internal quotation marks omitted)), and (2) that the penalty he suffered amounted to compulsion, *see Lefkowitz v. Cunningham*, 431 U.S. 801, 806, 97 s.Ct. 2132, 53 L.Ed.2d 1 (1977) ("[T]he touchstone of the Fifth Amendment is compulsion. . . ."); *cf. Lile v. McKune*, 224 F.3d 1175, 1179 (10th Cir. 2000) ("The privilege has two components: incrimination and compulsion."), *rev'd*, 536 U.S. 24, 122 S.Ct. 2017, 153 L.Ed.2d 47 (2002) (holding the state-imposed repercussions insufficiently coercive to amount to compulsion).

A. Incrimination

The Fifth Amendment privilege is only properly invoked in the face of "a real and appreciable danger of self-incrimination." *McCoy v. Comm'r*, 696 F.2d 1234, 1236 (9th Cir. 1983) (internal quotation marks omitted). "If the threat is remote, unlikely, or speculative, the privilege does not apply. . . ." *Id*. Thus, the Constitution offers no protection to an individual who, for example, asserts a general intent to refuse to answer any questions at a court hearing. *See United States v. Pierce*, 561 F.2d 735, 741-42 (9th Cir. 1977) (holding that the probationer's Fifth Amendment claim could not be evaluated because he had tendered an unspecific "blanket refusal" to answer any questions at a district court hearing designed to probe his financial condition). Nor does its umbrella shelter statements whose ability to incriminate is "highly unlikely." *Seattle Times Co. v. United States Dist. Court*, 845 F.2d 1513, 1520 (9th Cir. 1988) (Reinhardt, J., concurring); *see also Minor*, 396 U.S. at 98, 90 S.Ct. 284 ("[I]maginary and insubstantial hazards of incrimination . . . [do not] support a Fifth Amendment claim." (internal quotation marks omitted)).

Instead, because the Fifth Amendment's self-incrimination clause was designed "to effect [the] practical and beneficent purpose" of preventing inquisitorial interrogation, *Brown v. Walker*, 161 U.S. 591, 596-97, 16 S.Ct. 644, 40 L.Ed. 819 (1896), it may only be invoked when the threat of future criminal prosecution is reasonably particular and apparent. *Cf. id.* at 598, 16 S.Ct. 644 ("[I]f a prosecution for a crime . . . is barred by the statute of limitations, [a witness] is compellable to answer."); *Neal v. Shimoda*, 131 F.3d 818, 833 (9th Cir. 1997) (holding that a prison treatment program requiring inmates to admit guilt of the crime for which they were imprisoned did not violate the Fifth Amendment because double jeopardy and the terms of their plea agreement insured that "no admission . . . could be used against them").

This is not to say, however, that the prosecutorial sword must actually strike or be poised to strike. To the contrary, an individual "need not incriminate himself in order to invoke the privilege," *McCoy*, 696 F.2d at 1236, but may simply refuse to make any statements that place him at risk. *Accord Seattle Times*, 845 F.2d at 1520 (Reinhardt, J., concurring) ("[I]t is appropriate for a defendant to raise a fifth amendment objection at the time he is required to [make the potentially incriminating statements.]"). And as a general rule, countervailing government interests, such as criminal rehabilitation, do not trump this right. Thus, when **[1135]** "questions put to [a] probationer, however relevant to his probationary status, call for answers that would incriminate him in a pending or later criminal prosecution," he may properly invoke his right to remain silent. *Murphy*, 465 U.S. at 435, 104 S.Ct. 1136.

In this case, Antelope's risk of incrimination was "real and appreciable." The SABER program required Antelope to reveal his full sexual history, including all past sexual criminal offenses. Any attempt to withhold information about past offenses would be stymied by the required complete autobiography and "full disclosure" polygraph examination. Based on the nature of this requirement and Antelope's steadfast refusal to comply, it seems only fair to infer that his sexual autobiography would, in fact, reveal past sex crimes. Such an inference would be consistent with the belief of Roger Dowty, Antelope's SABER counselor, who suspects Antelope of having committed prior sex offenses. The treatment condition placed Antelope at a crossroads—comply and incriminate himself or invoke his right against self-incrimination and be sent to prison. We therefore conclude that Antelope's successful participation in SABER triggered a real danger of self-incrimination, not simply a remote or speculative threat.

We have no doubt that any admissions of past crimes would likely make their way into the hands of prosecutors. Dowty made clear that he would turn over evidence of past sex crimes to the authorities. As he explained at Antelope's probation revocation hearing, Dowty has reported his clients' crimes in the past and his reports have led to additional convictions. The SABER release form, which Antelope signed, specifically authorizes Dowty to make such reports.[2] And, were Antelope to reveal any crimes involving minors, Montana law would *require* Dowty to report to law enforcement. *See* Mont. Code Ann. §§ 41-3201 to -202 (2003) (requiring counselors who suspect child abuse to report to the authorities).

In sum, the evidence shows that, setting the privilege aside, Antelope would have to reveal past sex crimes to the SABER counselor; the counselor would likely report the incidents to the authorities, who could then use Antelope's admissions to prosecute and convict him of the additional crimes. Viewed in this light, very little stands between Antelope's participation in SABER and future prosecution. When he invoked his Fifth Amendment right, Antelope's situation presented a "real and appreciable danger," not a "remote, unlikely, or speculative" risk. *See McCoy*, 696 F.2d at 1236. We conclude that Antelope has shown a sufficiently real possibility of incrimination.

B. Compulsion

The second prong of the self-incrimination inquiry asks whether the government has sought to "impose substantial penalties because a witness elects to exercise his Fifth Amendment right not to give incriminating testimony against himself." *Cunningham*, 431 U.S. at 805, 97 S.Ct. 2132. We are mindful that an individual choosing silence does not get a free pass against all possible repercussions. *See, e.g., Ohio Adult Parole*

---

[2] The SABER release form provides: "I hereby allow SABER to report to the appropriate authorities . . . any and all information concerning my behavior which is related to sexual offending."

Auth. v. Woodard, 523 U.S. 272, 286, 118 S.Ct. 1244, 140 L.Ed.2d 387 (1998) (a state clemency board may draw "adverse inferences" from an inmate's failure to testify on his own behalf at a clemency hearing). Only "some penalties are so great as to 'compel' such testimony, while **[1136]** others do not rise to that level." *McKune*, 536 U.S. at 49, 122 S.Ct. 2017 (O'Connor, J., concurring). The Supreme Court's decision in McKune requires us to conclude that this level has been breached in Antelope's case.

In *McKune*, a plurality of four justices concluded that the penalties faced by the inmate in that case, Robert Lile, for refusing to make disclosures required under Kansas's Sexual Abuse Treatment Program ("SATP") did not amount to compulsion under the Fifth Amendment. *Id.* at 29, 122 S.Ct. 2017. Lile brought a § 1983 action against prison officials, alleging that they had violated his Fifth Amendment privilege against self-incrimination by reducing his privileges and transferring him from medium-security housing to maximum-security housing as a result of his refusal to disclose his sexual history as required by SATP.

The plurality rejected Lile's argument that his case was controlled by "the so-called penalty cases" like *Garrity v. New Jersey*, 385 U.S. 493, 497-98, 87 S.Ct. 616, 17 L.Ed.2d 562 (1967) (striking down state statute forcing public employees "either to forfeit their jobs or to incriminate themselves"), and *Spevack v. Klein*, 385 U.S. 511, 516, 87 S.Ct. 625, 17 L.Ed.2d 574 (1967) ("The threat of disbarment and the loss of professional standing, professional reputation, and of livelihood are powerful forms of compulsion to make a lawyer relinquish the privilege."), where lesser penalties involving the potential loss of economic livelihood were held unconstitutional. The plurality distinguished those cases because they "involved free citizens" and were "not easily extended to the prison context." *McKune*, 536 U.S. at 40-41, 122 S.Ct. 2017. Relying instead on prisoner-specific cases like *Murphy*, 465 U.S. at 434-39, 104 S.Ct. 1136 (concluding that there was no Fifth Amendment violation where petitioner claimed he felt compelled to incriminate himself because he feared absent truthful statements his probation would be revoked), and *Woodard*, 523 U.S. at 286-88, 118 S.Ct. 1244 (concluding that there was no compulsion where a death row inmate had to choose between incriminating himself at a clemency interview and having adverse inferences drawn from his silence), where the Court found no Fifth Amendment violations despite the use of far harsher penalties such as longer incarceration or execution, the plurality wrote that "lawful conviction and incarceration necessarily place limitations on the exercise of a defendant's privilege against self-incrimination." *McKune*, 536 U.S. at 38, 122 S.Ct. 2017.

In her concurrence, Justice O'Connor explained that penalties severe enough to offend the Fifth Amendment privilege include: "termination of employment, [*Uniformed Sanitation Men Ass'n, Inc. v. City of New York*, 392 U.S. 280, 88 S.Ct. 1917, 20 L.Ed.2d 1089 (1968], the loss of a professional license, [*Spevack v. Klein*, 385 U.S. 511, 87 S.Ct. 625, 17 L.Ed.2d 574 (1967)], ineligibility to receive government contracts, [*Lefkowitz v. Turley*, 414 U.S. 70, 94 S.Ct. 316, 38 L.Ed.2d 274 (1973)], and the loss of the right to participate in political associations and to hold public office, [*Lefkowitz v. Cunningham*, 431 U.S. 801, 97 S.Ct. 2132, 53 L.Ed.2d 1 (1977)]." *McKune*, 536 U.S. at 49-50, 122 S.Ct. 2017. In contrast, an inmate's "reduction in incentive level, and a corresponding transfer from a medium-security to a maximum-security part of the prison" were not "serious enough to compel him to be a witness against himself." *Id.* at 50 122 S.Ct. 2017.

Significantly, Justice O'Connor did not attempt to establish the governing standard for all cases, noting that she did not "need [to] resolve this dilemma [of setting forth a comprehensive theory of the self-incrimination privilege] to make [her] **[1137]** judgment in" *McKune*. *Id.* at 54, 122 S.Ct. 2017.

Nevertheless, though Justice O'Connor's concurrence does not delineate the limits of the self-incrimination clause's protections, it makes clear that the Court likely would conclude that the penalty Antelope faced for not participating in SABER was constitutionally impermissible.

Although Justice O'Connor agreed with the plurality that Lile's "reduction in incentive level, and . . . corresponding transfer from a medium-security to a maximum-security part of the prison" were not penalties "sufficiently serious to compel his testimony," Justice O'Connor said that she "d[id] not agree with the suggestion in the plurality opinion that these penalties could permissibly rise to the level of . . . penalties [like] longer incarceration and execution[which] are far greater than those we have already held to constitute unconstitutional compulsion." *Id.* at 50, 52, 122 S.Ct. 2017. Justice O'Connor did not accept the plurality's reasoning that the different outcomes in the "penalty cases" and the Court's decisions in cases like *Murphy* and *Woodard* could be explained on the basis of the citizen-prisoner distinction and that the key factor in assessing a prisoner's self-incrimination claim was whether the disputed penalty, in the plurality's language, amounted to an "atypical and significant hardship" within the prison context. Justice O'Connor explained:

> I believe the proper theory should recognize that it is generally acceptable to impose the risk of punishment, however great, so long as the actual imposition of such punishment is accomplished through a fair criminal process.... Forcing defendants to accept such consequences seems to me very different from imposing penalties for the refusal to incriminate one-self that go beyond the criminal process and appear, starkly, as government attempts to compel testimony. . . .

Id. at 53, 122 S. Ct. 2017 (internal citation omitted).

Thus, under Justice O'Connor's opinion in *McKune*, the compulsion inquiry does not dispositively turn on the status of the person claiming the Fifth Amendment privilege or on the severity of the penalty imposed, although these factors may bear on the analysis. Instead, the controlling issue is the state's purpose in imposing the penalty: Although it may be acceptable for the state to impose harsh penalties on defendants when it has legitimate reasons for doing so consistent with their conviction for their crimes of incarceration, it is a different thing to impose "penalties for the refusal to incriminate oneself that go beyond the criminal process and appear, starkly, as government attempts to compel testimony." *Id.*

Applying these principles here, we reject that the state could sanction Antelope for his self-protective silence about conduct that might constitute other crimes. We do not doubt that SABER's policy of requiring convicted sex offenders to give a sexual history, admitting responsibility for past misconduct to participating counselors, serves an important rehabilitative purpose. *See, e.g., id.* at 33, 122 S.Ct. 2017 (plurality opinion) ("An important component of [sex offender] rehabilitation programs requires participants to confront their past and accept responsibility for their misconduct.... Research indicates that offenders who deny all allegations of sexual abuse are three times more likely to fail in treatment than those who admit even partial complicity.") (*citing* U.S. Dep't of Justice, Nat'l Inst. of Corr., A Practitioner's Guide to Treating the Incarcerated Male Sex Offender 73 (1988) and B. Maletzky & K. McGovern, Treating the Sexual Offender 253-55 (1991)). Often sex offenders repeat their past offenses, and informed counseling can only help protect **[1138]** them, their potential victims, and society. The irreconcilable constitutional problem, however, is that even though the disclosures sought here may serve a valid rehabilitative purpose, they also may be starkly incriminating, and there is no disputing that the government may seek to use such disclosures for prosecutorial purposes. In fact, Antelope's SABER counselor testified that he routinely transmits to authorities any admissions his clients make about past sex crimes, and that such reports have led to more prosecutions and convictions. *Cf. McKune*, 536 U.S. at 40-41, 122 S.Ct. 2017 (plurality opinion) (arguing that a "critical distinction" between McKune and the penalty cases where the Court found Fifth Amendment violations is that "[t]here is no indication that the SATP is an elaborate attempt to avoid the protections offered by the privilege against compelled self-incrimination").

Justice O'Connor made clear in her *McKune* concurrence that she would not have found a penalty of "longer incarceration" such as that here to be constitutionally permissible. *Id.* at 52, 122 S.Ct. 2017. The strength of Justice O'Connor's opinion as precedent is reinforced because it seems certain that the four dissenters in *McKune*, who argued that a loss of discretionary privileges and a transfer to less desirable living quarters under similar circumstances were sufficiently compulsive to violate Lile's privilege against self-incrimination, would find a Fifth Amendment violation where the district court revoked Antelope's conditional liberty and sentenced him to an additional ten months in prison.[3] On the basis of *McKune*, we hold that Antelope's privilege against self-incrimination was violated because Antelope was sentenced to a longer prison term for refusing to comply with SABER's disclosure requirements.[4]

---

[3] Indeed, the *McKune* plurality, even with its more stringent standard, might here hold that the Fifth Amendment's self-incrimination clause was violated, given that the *McKune* plurality declared that Kansas had not used the information gathered in SATP for prosecutorial purposes, *id.* at 34, 122 S.Ct. 2017, and that Lile's refusal to participate in Kansas's SATP did not result in an "exten[sion of] his term of incarceration." *Id.* at 38, 122 S.Ct. 2017.

[4] The Court's pre-*McKune* decision in Murphy is consistent. In *Murphy* the defendant challenged a condition of his probation requiring him to "be truthful with [his] probation officer 'in all matters'" or "return to the sentencing court for a probation revocation hearing," arguing that this condition unconstitutionally forced him to choose between making self-incriminating disclosures or returning to prison. 465 U.S. at 422, 104 S.Ct. 1136. The Court held that there was no Fifth Amendment violation because the defendant "could not reasonably have feared that the assertion of the privilege would have led to revocation," given that the state would have provided a hearing before revocation, and defendant could have

Our holding comports with the case authority in our sister circuits which suggests that the conditions must not only be sufficiently coercive, but also more than merely hypothetical. When probation and supervised release terms are at issue, a court must determine whether the alleged Fifth Amendment problem truly implicates the defendant's conditional liberty. In **[1139]**, *United States v. Lee*, 315 F.3d 206, 212 (3d Cir. 2003), *cert. denied*, 540 U.S. 858, 124 S. Cty. 160, 157 L.Ed.2d 106 (2003), for example, the Third Circuit rejected a defendant's challenge to his supervised released condition because Lee offered "no evidence that [his] ability to remain on probation is conditional on his waiving the Fifth Amendment privilege with respect to future criminal prosecution." In *Lee*, the prosecutor had stipulated that Lee's failure "to pass a polygraph examination, in and of itself, likely would not result in a finding of a supervised release violation." *Id.* Without the real risk of revocation, the polygraph's effect on Lee could not amount to constitutional compulsion.

The First Circuit likewise faced a Fifth Amendment challenge to a supervised release condition imposing a polygraph exam requirement in *United States v. York*, 357 F.3d 14 (1st Cir. 2004). The twist in *York* was an ambiguous provision in the release condition: "When submitting to a polygraph exam, the defendant does not give up his Fifth Amendment rights." *Id.* at 18. The First Circuit grappled with York's Fifth Amendment challenge, acknowledging that "the polygraph requirement may implicate York's Fifth Amendment rights, depending on how the district court's order is understood." *Id.* at 24. The York court carefully avoided interpreting the release condition to mean "that it flatly requires York to submit to polygraph testing as a condition of his supervised release, so that York's refusal to answer any question—even on valid Fifth Amendment grounds—could constitute a basis for revocation." *Id.* Rather than impute this "constitutionally problematic" meaning to the release condition, the First Circuit simply construed it to mean that "York's supervised release shall not be revoked based on his valid assertion of Fifth Amendment privilege during a polygraph examination." *Id.* at 24-25.

Although the First and Third Circuits found an interpretative way around the Fifth Amendment issue, the path of constitutional avoidance taken in *York* and *Lee* is unavailable here. Whether Antelope's supervised release is actually conditioned on his participation in SABER is a question whose answer is certain. Antelope has already suffered repeated revocation of his conditional liberty as a result of invoking his Fifth Amendment right. And, we have no doubt that Antelope's loss of liberty was as "substantial" a penalty as, if not more serious than, the ones imposed upon the litigants in the line of cases from *Spevack* to *Cunningham*—and totally unlike the mere transfer from one part of a prison to another, as in *McKune*.

---

raised the privilege as a reason for noncompliance, and that the defendant could point to no case in which Minnesota revoked probation when a probationer "refused to make nonimmunized disclosures concerning his own criminal conduct." *Id.* at 439, 104 S.Ct. 1136. The Court said that the outcome would have differed if the state "expressly or by implication, assert[ed] that invocation of the privilege would lead to revocation of probation," because this would have resulted in "the classic penalty situation." *Id.* at 435, 104 S.Ct. 1136. Here we have the "classic penalty situation" contemplated in Murphy; Antelope's supervised release ended because he would not make potentially self-incriminating statements as required by SABER.

Here, the district court tried to walk a fine line between the government's absolutist view—that full disclosure without immunity was a condition of release—and Antelope's view—that full disclosure without Fifth Amendment protection was a no-win proposition. Although this effort was laudable and the district court was sensitive in recognizing Antelope's Catch-22 predicament, its ruling left Antelope in legal limbo. Ultimately, the district court revoked Antelope's supervised release as a result of his refusal to disclose his sexual history without receiving immunity from prosecution. Because the government and district court have consistently refused to "recognize[ ] that the required answers may not be used in a criminal proceeding" against Antelope, *Murphy*, 465 U.S. at 435 n. 7, 104 S.Ct. 1136, we hold that the revocation of his probation and supervised release violated his Fifth Amendment right against self-incrimination.

C. Antelope's Entitlement to Kastigar Immunity

The nature of Antelope's entitlement to immunity for incriminating statements **[1140]** is subject to some dispute between the parties. We find it appropriate to resolve their disagreement because the issue is intimately bound up with the resolution of the merits of Antelope's Fifth Amendment claim. The government argues that Antelope has no entitlement to an assurance of immunity before he makes incriminating statements. *See Kastigar*, 406 U.S. at 453, 92 S.Ct. 1653 (holding use and derivative use immunity under 18 U.S.C. §§ 6002-6003 co-extensive with the Fifth Amendment privilege). It contends, in effect, that the government has the right to compel Antelope to incriminate himself, prosecute him, and force him to litigate the admissibility of each piece of evidence in future criminal proceedings. Only then, according to its view, can Antelope properly assert his Fifth Amendment privilege. We disagree.

As the Supreme Court has explained, adoption of the government's position would all but eviscerate the protections the self-incrimination clause was designed to provide. *See, e.g., Turley*, 414 U.S. at 78, 94 S.Ct. 316 ("[A] witness protected by the privilege may rightfully refuse to answer *unless* and *until* he is protected at least against the use of his compelled answers and evidence derived therefrom in any subsequent criminal case in which he is a defendant." (emphasis added)). More recently, Justice Thomas, speaking for four members of the Court, reaffirmed this principle: "By allowing a witness to insist on an immunity agreement *before* being compelled to give incriminating testimony in a noncriminal case, the privilege preserves the core Fifth Amendment right from invasion. . . ." *Chavez v. Martinez*, 538 U.S. 760, 771, 123 S.Ct. 1994, 155 L.Ed.2d 984 (2003) (Thomas, J., in a plurality opinion joined by Rehnquist, C.J., O'Connor, J., and Scalia, J.) (emphasis in original).

That this protection should be the law is only logical; "the failure to assert the privilege will often forfeit the right to exclude the evidence in a subsequent 'criminal case.'" *Id.* (*citing Murphy*, 465 U.S. at 440, 104 S.Ct. 1136). Without a pre-testimonial assurance of immunity, the witness would scarcely be better protected than if there were no privilege at all. See id. ("If the privilege could not be asserted [before making the incriminating disclosure], testimony given in those judicial proceedings would be deemed 'voluntary' . . ."). Our conclusion in this case gives effect to Justice

Thomas's admonition that "it is necessary to allow assertion of the privilege prior to the commencement of a 'criminal case' to safeguard the core Fifth Amendment trial right." *Id.*

In the face of the vast weight of precedent to the contrary, *see, e.g., Murphy*, 465 U.S. at 429-40, 104 S.Ct. 1136 (discussing circumstances where the Fifth Amendment privilege is triggered the moment a defendant is compelled to give statements which might incriminate him in criminal proceedings, even if such proceedings have yet to be initiated), the government contends that *Chavez* stands for the proposition that Antelope may not assert the Fifth Amendment right until the moment a compelled statement is used in a criminal proceeding against him. But *Chavez* did not, as the government suggests, unseat decades of Supreme Court law. Instead, the government's argument reveals a fundamental misunderstanding of *Chavez*.

Chavez was a civil rights suit filed under 42 U.S.C. § 1983 by a plaintiff alleging that a police officer who aggressively questioned him violated his Fifth Amendment right. Six justices agreed with the defendant police officer that the cause of action premised on a Fifth Amendment violation could not survive summary judgment. *See Chavez*, 538 U.S. at 766-67, 123 S.Ct. 1994 **[1141]** (Thomas, J., joined by Rehnquist, C.J., O'Connor, J., and Scalia, J.); *id.* at 777-79, 123 S.Ct. 1994 (Souter, J., concurring, joined by Breyer, J.). But *Chavez* left unaltered the Court's commitment to safeguarding the Fifth Amendment's core guarantee under the circumstances presented here— a point the government chooses to ignore. Critical to the reasoning of all six justices was the simple principle that the scope of the Fifth Amendment's efficacy is narrower when used as a sword in a civil suit than when used as a shield against criminal prosecution. *See id.* at 772-73, 123 S.Ct. 1994 (Thomas, J., joined by Rehnquist, C.J., O'Connor, J., and Scalia, J.) ("Rules designed to safeguard a constitutional right [such as that protected by the self-incrimination clause] do not extend the scope of the constitutional right itself. . . . Accordingly, Chavez's failure to read *Miranda* warnings to Martinez . . . cannot be grounds for a § 1983 action. And the absence of a 'criminal case' in which Martinez was compelled to be a 'witness' against himself defeats his core Fifth Amendment claim." (internal citations omitted)); *id.* at 777-78, 123 S.Ct. 1994 (Souter, J., concurring, joined by Breyer, J.) (explaining that while case law "requiring a grant of immunity in advance of any testimonial proffer . . . is outside the Fifth Amendment's core," the privilege's protections will only be expanded where "the core guarantee, or the judicial capacity to protect it, would be placed at some risk in the absence of such complementary protection," and concluding that it was not "necessary to expand protection of the privilege . . . to . . . civil liability"). Simply stated, the holding of *Chavez* is tightly bound to its § 1983 context.

Were Antelope to turn the tables and sue the government, *Chavez* would direct our inquiry to the "core constitutional right"—and, in such a posture, the government's argument might well prevail. But here, where Antelope is on the defensive, Fifth Amendment case law offers him protection beyond what the *Chavez* plurality called the "core" right. Thus, whether we describe our decision as arising out of a "prophylactic" or "constitutional" rule, the same result obtains: Antelope followed the appropriate course of action by refusing to answer the sexual history question until he was assured that his answers would be protected by immunity.[5]

III. The Prohibition on "Any Pornographic Materials"

Antelope also challenges as unconstitutionally vague the provision of his supervised release prohibiting him from possessing "any pornographic, sexually oriented or sexually stimulating materials." In *United States v. Guagliardo*, 278 F.3d 868 (9th Cir. 2002), we held impermissibly vague a similar supervised release term. Guagliardo was prohibited from possessing " 'any pornography,' including legal adult pornography." *Id.* at 872. Because "a probationer cannot reasonably understand what is encompassed by a blanket prohibition on 'pornography,' " we remanded for clarification. *Id.* We do the same here. The condition imposed on Antelope is indistinguishable from the one imposed on Guagliardo. Here, instead of "any pornography," we have "any pornographic . . . materials."

The government contends that "sexually oriented or sexually stimulating" should be **[1142]** read to define "pornographic." We decline to adopt this grammatically unnatural reading. The release term explicitly lists three types of materials that Antelope may not possess: "any pornographic, sexually oriented or sexually stimulating materials." Because the condition imposed on Antelope suffers from the same defect as the one struck down in *Guagliardo*, we vacate and remand for clarification. Upon reconsideration, the district court may take note of the condition imposed in *United States v. Rearden*, 349 F.3d 608 (9th Cir. 2003), which passed constitutional muster.

IV. The Prohibition on "Access to Any On-Line Computer Service"

Antelope's final argument challenges as overbroad the supervised release term prohibiting him from "possess[ing] or us[ing] a computer with access to any 'on-line computer service' at any location (including employment) without the prior written approval of the probation department."

As Antelope acknowledges, we recently rejected precisely such a challenge in *Rearden. See id.* at 620-21. He argues, however, that his case should be treated differently because his crime involved less use of the Internet and was less severe than Rearden's. Although there is some appeal to this nuance, the Internet was nevertheless essential to the commission of Antelope's crime: He first contacted the federal agents through joining a child pornography-oriented online group. Added to the evidence suggesting that Antelope's crime was one step on a path towards more serious transgressions, there is enough to justify the imposition of the term "to protect the public

---

[5] The scope of the immunity should be consistent with the Supreme Court's opinion in *Kastigar*, 406 U.S. at 453, 92 S.Ct. 1653 (holding that "immunity from use and derivative use [provided by 18 U.S.C. §§ 6002-6003] is coextensive with the scope of the privilege against self-incrimination"). *Kastigar*, of course, does not insulate Antelope from prosecution altogether, just from the "use and derivative use" of compelled admissions in trial against him. *Id.*

from further crimes of the defendant" and "to afford adequate deterrence to criminal conduct." 18 U.S.C. § 3553(a)(2)(B) & (C). We affirm the imposition of this provision of Antelope's supervised release.

Conclusion

Accordingly, the decision of the district court revoking Antelope's supervised release because he invoked his Fifth Amendment rights in connection with the SABER program is **REVERSED**, the imposition of the release term prohibiting access to "any pornographic materials" is **VACATED** and **REMANDED**, and the release term prohibiting "access to any 'on-line computer service'" is **AFFIRMED**.

Appendix 2

Hargett v. Baker

2002 WL 1433729 (N.D. Ill. 2002)

[*Editor's Note*: This appendix reprints the text of the district court opinion in *Hargett v. Baker*, which granted inmates in the Illinois sexually violent predator unit certification to bring a class action suit. Page numbers for the quoted material are indicated in brackets, in boldface type (e.g., **[11]**), should you need to cite to the case.]

Memorandum Opinion and Order

[1] Plaintiffs Jeffery Hargett, Kim A. Overlin, Jimmie Smith, and Loren K. Walker brought this action individually and on behalf of a class of persons similarly situated against Defendants Linda R. Baker, Secretary of the Illinois Department of Human Services, Mary Bass, Head Facility Administrator for the Illinois Department of Human Services, Timothy Budz, Facility Director of the Sexually Violent Persons Unit at the Joliet Correctional Center, Raymond Woods, Clinical Director, and Travis Hinze, Associate Clinical Director. Plaintiffs assert a civil rights action pursuant to 42 U.S.C. § 1983 seeking declaratory and injunctive relief. Before the Court is Plaintiffs' motion for class certification pursuant to FED.R.CIV.P. 23.

Background

Concerned with alarmingly high recidivism rates among sex offenders, states began in the 1990's to enact civil commitment regimes for the detention and treatment of those found to be "sexual predators" or "sexually dangerous." Illinois enacted its version, the Sexually Violent Persons Commitment Act, in 1997. *See* 725 ILCS 207/1 *et seq.* Under Illinois' civil commitment program, a "sexually violent person" ("SVP") is defined as a "person who has been convicted of a sexually violent offense, has been adjudicated delinquent for a sexually violent offense, or has been found not guilty of a sexually violent offense by reason of insanity and who is dangerous because he or she suffers from a mental disorder that makes it substantially probable that the person will engage in acts of sexual violence." 725 ILCS 207/5(f). Once found to qualify as an SVP under the Act, the person is committed to the custody of the Sexually Violent Persons Unit operated by the Illinois Department of Human Services ("DHS") at its Joliet Correctional Center. *See* 725 ILCS 207/40. SVP's confined under the Act remain in DHS custody until such time as "the person is no longer sexually violent." 725 ILCS 207/40(a). Plaintiffs bring this class action to challenge what they characterize as the impermissibly punitive conditions of their confinement and the constitutionally inadequate treatment they receive as detainees in the Sexually Violent Persons Unit in Joliet. Specifically, Plaintiffs contend that the punitive conditions and inadequacies of the treatment program work together to deprive SVP's at the Joliet facility of a realistic opportunity to progress through the treatment program and gain their release. Plaintiffs' class action complaint seeks, inter alia, a declaratory judgment that the conditions of confinement and mental health treatment of the SVP's violates the Fourteenth Amendment and a permanent injunction against the Defendants compelling them to implement a plan correcting the alleged constitutional deficiencies in the current program.

Discussion

The Federal Rules of Civil Procedure set forth a number of prerequisites that must be present before a court may approve a class. First, the Plaintiffs must satisfy the four requirements of Rule 23(a), which include numerosity, typicality, commonality, and adequacy of representation. *Harriston v. Chicago Tribune Co.*, 992 F.2d 697, 703 (7th Cir. 1993). Furthermore, at least one of the subsections of Rule 23(b) must also be satisfied. In making this determination, the Court does not consider the merits of the case but instead, as with a motion to dismiss, takes the allegations in the complaint as true. *Eisen v. Carlisle & Jacquelin*, 417 U.S. 156, 177, 94 S.Ct. 2140, 2152, 40 L.Ed. 732 (1974). The Plaintiffs shoulder the burden of demonstrating that a class exists, and district courts have broad discretion in ruling on a plaintiff's request. *Mira v. Nuclear Measurements Corp.*, 107 F.3d 466, 474 (7th Cir. 1997).

[2] In addition to the four express requirements of Rule 23, there are two implied requirements: first, an identifiable class must exist (the "definiteness" requirement) and second, the named representatives must be members of the class. *Gomez v. Illinois St. Bd. of Educ.*, 117 F.R.D. 394, 397 (N.D. Ill. 1987). An identifiable and definite class exists if "its members can be ascertained by reference to objective criteria." *National Organization for Women v. Scheidler*, 172 F.R.D. 351 (N.D. Ill. 1997), *citing Gomez*, 117 F.R.D. at 397. The parties should not have to delve into the merits of the case to determine membership in the class. *Toney v. Rosewood Care Center, Inc.,* No. 98 C 0693, 1999 WL 199249 *5 (N.D. Ill. Mar. 31, 1999). If a class is amorphous or indefinite, however, the court has broad discretion to limit or redefine the class to bring it within Rule 23. *See Gomez*, 117 F.R.D. at 397 n. 2; 7B Charles A. Wright, Arthur R. Miller, *Federal Practice and Procedure,* § 1760, at 128-29 (2d Ed. 1986).

Plaintiffs seek certification of a class consisting of "all persons who have been, are or will be committed under the [Illinois] Sexually Violent Persons Commitment Act, 725 ULCS 207/1 *et seq.* and placed in the facility in Joliet, Illinois operated by the Illinois Department of Human Services." This class definition relies on sufficiently objective and readily identifiable criteria to meet the definiteness requirement. *See, e.g., Robert E. v. Lane*, 530 F. Supp. 930, 944 (N.D. Ill. 1980) (noting that a civil rights action challenging the constitutional adequacy of mental health treatment offered to inmates is a "prototypical candidate" for class certification).

While not commenting on the definiteness of the proposed class, Defendants do contend that named Plaintiffs Overlin, Hargett and Smith are not members of the class and lack standing to challenge the SVP treatment program because they were not enrolled in "Core treatment" at the time the class action complaint was filed. Core treatment is an intensive individualized therapy program consisting of cognitive restructuring, relapse prevention and journal-keeping that is intended to move the SVP closer to a determination that they are no longer "sexually dangerous." The fact that Overlin, Hargett and Smith are not or were not in the Core treatment phase of the SVP program when the complaint was filed does not deprive them of standing. To have standing to sue as a class representative, one must "possess the same interest and suffer the same injury shared by all members of the class he represents." *Keele v. Wexler*, 149 F.3d 589, 592-93 (7th Cir. 1998), *citing Schlesinger v. Reservists Committe to Stop the War*, 418 U.S. 208, 216 (1974). Here, the essential allegation of the complaint is that all SVP's housed in the DHS Joliet facility are subjected to a constitutionally inadequate treatment program that deprives them of any realistic chance to improve and secure their release. The complaint attacks the program in its entirety, not just the Core treatment component. As SVP's detained at the Joliet facility, Hargett, Overlin, Smith and Walker all possess the same interest and suffer the same injury shared by all members of the class and are properly before the court as members of the proposed class with standing to sue. The named Plaintiffs are members of a definite class and the Court will proceed to the express requirements for maintaining a class action.

Numerosity

[3] The first Rule 23(a) requirement is numerosity, *i.e.*, that the class is so numerous that joinder of all members is impracticable. The proposed class in this case consists of more than 150 individuals. Based on this Court's experience with the management of numerous other cases related to the one at bar, there can be no doubt as to the impracticability of joinder in this case.

Commonality

Second, Rule 23(a)(2) requires that the class representatives' claims possess "questions of law or fact common to the class." The common questions, however, need not be identical, and a "common nucleus of operative fact is usually enough to satisfy the commonality requirement." *Rosario v. Livaditis*, 963 F.2d 1013, 1017-18 (7th Cir. 1992). A common nucleus of operative fact is typically found where "defendants have engaged in standardized conduct towards members of the proposed class." *Keele v. Wexler*, 149 F.3d 589, 594 (7th Cir. 1998). Factual variations among class members' grievances do not defeat a class action. *Id.*

Defendants argue that Plaintiffs fail to meet the commonality requirement because the propriety of injunctive or declaratory relief turns on the individual circumstances of each class member's course of treatment, requiring individualized determinations of liability. Whatever the factual variations among the individual SVP's mental health needs may be, the Plaintiffs' attack on the SVP treatment program is premised on a broad allegation that the Defendants engaged in standardized conduct toward the members of the proposed class that deprives all its members of a meaningful opportunity to secure their release. *See John v. DeLeonardis*, 145 F.R.D. 480, 483 (N.D. Ill. 1992) (stating that where the defendant engages in a single course of conduct that results in injury to the class as a whole, a common core of operative facts is usually present). *See also* FED.R.CIV.P. 23(b)(2), Advisory Comm. Notes (stating that action or inaction is directed to a class within the meaning of subdivision (b)(2) even if it has taken actual effect as to only one or a few members of the class, provided it is based on grounds which have general application to the class as a whole). The Court finds that Plaintiffs have established commonality.

Typicality

The third Rule 23(a) requirement, typicality, is met "[w]hen it is alleged that the same unlawful conduct was directed at or affected both the named plaintiff and the class sought to be represented." *Edmondson v. Simon*, 86 F.R.D. 375, 381 (N.D. Ill. 1980). Whether the Plaintiffs' claims are typical of those of the class members they represent is closely related to the commonality inquiry. *Keele*, 149 F.3d at 595. A "plaintiff's claim is typical if it arises from the same event or practice or course of conduct that gives rise to the claims of other class members and his or her claims are based on the same legal theory." *Id.*, citing *De La Fuente v. Stokely-Van Camp, Inc.*, 713 F.2d 225, 232 (7th Cir. 1983) (citations and internal quotation omitted). The Seventh Circuit has explained that the typicality requirement directs the "district court to focus on whether the named representatives' claims have the same essential characteristics as the claims of the class at large." *De La Fuente*, 713 F.2d at 232.

[4] Defendants argue that Plaintiffs' alleged mistreatment, as it relates to each class member, is unique and that the claims of each individual class member require the application of separate defenses and determinations of liability. The Court disagrees. The named Plaintiffs and the members of the proposed class, while all subjected individually to varying treatment, are united in their allegation that they all receive constitutionally inadequate treatment flowing from the same systematic deficiencies in Defendants' program. Furthermore, even though some of the facts underlying each person's claims may vary, they do not create any conflicts between the members of the proposed class. *See Cook*, 151 F.R.D. at 378. The named representatives' claims share the same essential characteristics as the claims of the class at large and Plaintiffs have satisfied the typicality requirement.

Adequacy

To satisfy the adequacy requirement, the class representatives must demonstrate that: (1) they do not have any antagonistic or conflicting claims with other members of the class; (2) they have a sufficient interest in the outcome of the case to ensure vigorous advocacy; and (3) their counsel is competent, qualified, experienced, and able to vigorously conduct the litigation. *Sebo v. Rubenstein, M.D.*, 188 F.R.D. 310, 316 (N.D. Ill. 1999). Here, Defendants do not challenge certification of the class on adequacy grounds. It appears to the Court that the class representatives possess sufficient interest in the outcome of the case and that they do not have any antagonistic or conflicting claims with other members of the class. The Court notes that Plaintiffs' counsel has extensive experience in this type of institutional litigation and finds Plaintiffs' counsel to be well-qualified to litigate this action on behalf of the class.

Rule 23(b)

Having met the requirements of Rule 23(a), Plaintiffs must also meet at least one of the subsections of Rule 23(b). Plaintiffs' § 1983 action seeks declaratory and injunctive relief to remedy what they perceive as systematic constitutional deficiencies in the treatment program offered to SVP's at the Joliet facility. Rule 23(b)(2) authorizes class actions when "the party opposing the class has acted or refused to act on grounds generally applicable to the class, thereby making appropriate final injunctive relief or corresponding declaratory relief with respect to the class as a whole." Defendants make no arguments in response, and as already noted above, an inmate civil rights action challenging the constitutionality of their treatment is a "prototypical candidate" for class certification under Rule 23(b)(2).

Conclusion

For the foregoing reasons, Plaintiffs motion for class certification pursuant to Rule 23(b)(2) is GRANTED.

IT IS SO ORDERED.

Appendix 3

Seling v. Young

531 U.S. 250 (2001)

[*Editor's Note*: This appendix reprints the text of the U.S. Supreme Court opinion in *Seling v. Young*. Internal cross-references have been omitted. Official page numbers for the quoted material are indicated in brackets, in boldface type (e.g., **[253]**), should you need to cite to the case.]

***

[253] JUSTICE O'CONNOR delivered the opinion of the Court.

Washington State's Community Protection Act of 1990 authorizes the civil commitment of "sexually violent predators," persons who suffer from a mental abnormality or personality disorder that makes them likely to engage in predatory acts of sexual violence. Wash. Rev. Code § 71.09.010 *et seq.* (1992). Respondent, Andre Brigham Young, is confined as a sexually violent predator at the Special Commitment Center (Center), for which petitioner is the superintendent. After respondent's challenges to his commitment in state court proved largely unsuccessful, he instituted a habeas action under 28 U.S.C. § 2254, seeking release from confinement. The Washington Supreme Court had already held that the Act is civil, *In re Young*, 122 Wash.2d 1, 857 P.2d 989 (1993) (en banc), and this Court held a similar commitment scheme for sexually violent predators in Kansas to be civil on its face, *Kansas v. Hendricks*, 521 U.S. 346, 117 S. Ct. 2072, 138 L.Ed.2d 501 (1997). The Court of Appeals for the Ninth Circuit nevertheless concluded that respondent could challenge the statute as being punitive "as applied" to him in violation of the **[254]** Double Jeopardy and *Ex Post Facto* Clauses, and remanded the case to the District Court for an evidentiary hearing.

I

A

Washington State's Community Protection Act of 1990(Act) was a response to citizens' concerns about laws and procedures regarding sexually violent offenders. One of the Act's provisions authorizes civil commitment of such offenders. Wash. Rev. Code § 71,09.010 *et seq.* (1992 and Supp. 2000). The Act defines a sexually violent predator as someone who has been convicted of, or charged with, a crime of sexual violence and who suffers from a mental abnormality or personality disorder that makes the person likely to engage in predatory acts of sexual violence if not confined in a secure facility. § 71.09.020(1) (Supp. 2000). The statute reaches prisoners, juveniles, persons found incompetent to stand trial, persons found not guilty by reason of insanity, and persons at any time convicted of a sexually violent offense who have committed a recent overt act. § 71.09.030. Generally, when it appears that a person who has committed a sexually violent offense is about to be released from confinement, the prosecuting attorney files a petition alleging that that person is a sexually violent predator. *Ibid.* That filing triggers a process for charging and trying the person as a sexually violent predator, during which he is afforded a panoply of protections including counsel and experts (paid for by the State in cases of indigency), a probable cause hearing, and trial by judge or jury at the individual's option. §§ 71.09.040-71.09.050. At trial, the State bears the burden to prove beyond a reasonable doubt that the person is a sexually violent predator. § 71.09.060(1).

Upon the finding that a person is a sexually violent predator, he is committed for control, care, and treatment to the custody of the department of social and health services. *Ibid.* Once confined, the person has a right to adequate care **[255]** and individualized treatment. § 71.09.080(2). The person is also entitled to an annual examination of his mental condition. § 71.09.070. If that examination indicates that the individual's condition is so changed that he is not likely to engage in predatory acts of sexual violence, state officials must authorize the person to petition the court for conditional release or discharge. § 71.09.090(1). The person is entitled to a hearing at which the State again bears the burden of proving beyond a reasonable doubt that he is not safe to be at large. *Ibid.* The person may also independently petition the court for release. § 71.09.090(2). At a show cause hearing, if the court finds probable cause to believe that the person is no longer dangerous, a full hearing will be held at which the State again bears the burden of proof. *Ibid.*

The Act also provides a procedure to petition for conditional release to a less restrictive alternative to confinement. § 71.09.090. Before ordering conditional release, the court must find that the person will be treated by a state certified sexual offender treatment provider, that there is a specific course of treatment, that housing exists that will be sufficiently secure to protect the community, and that the person is willing to comply with the treatment and supervision requirements. § 71.09.092. Conditional release is subject to annual review until the person is unconditionally released. §§ 71.09.096, 71.09.098.

B

Respondent, Andre Brigham Young, was convicted of six rapes over three decades. App. to Pet. for Cert. 33a. Young was scheduled to be released from prison for his most recent conviction in October 1990. One day prior to his scheduled release, the State filed a petition to commit Young as a sexually violent predator. *Id.*, at 32a.

At the commitment hearing, Young's mental health experts testified that there is no mental disorder that makes a person likely to reoffend and that there is no way to predict accurately who will reoffend. The State called an expert **[256]** who testified, based upon a review of Young's records, that Young suffered from a severe personality disorder not otherwise specified with primarily paranoid and antisocial features, and a severe paraphilia, which would be classified as either paraphilia sexual sadism or paraphilia not otherwise specified (rape). See generally American Psychiatric Association, Diagnostic and Statistical Manual of Mental Disorders 522-523, 530, 532, 634, 645-646, 673 (4th ed.1994). In the state expert's opinion, severe paraphilia constituted a mental abnormality under the Act. The State's expert concluded that Young's condition, in combination with the personality disorder, the span of time during which Young committed his crimes, his recidivism, his persistent denial, and his lack of empathy or remorse, made it more likely than not that he would commit further sexually violent acts. The victims of Young's rapes also testified. The jury unanimously concluded that Young was a sexually violent predator.

Young and another individual appealed their commitments in state court, arguing that the Act violated the Double Jeopardy, *Ex Post Facto*, Due Process, and Equal Protection Clauses of the Federal Constitution. In major respects, the Washington Supreme Court held that the Act is constitutional. *In re Young*, 122 Wash.2d 1, 857 P.2d 989 (1993) (en banc). To the extent the court concluded that the Act violated due process and equal protection principles, those rulings are reflected in subsequent amendments to the Act. See Part I-A, *supra*.

The Washington court reasoned that the claimants' double jeopardy and *ex post facto* claims hinged on whether the Act is civil or criminal in nature. Following this Court's precedents, the court examined the language of the Act, the legislative history, and the purpose and effect of the statutory scheme. The court found that the legislature clearly intended to create a civil scheme both in the statutory language and legislative history. The court then turned to **[257]** examine whether the actual impact of the Act is civil or criminal. The Act, the court concluded, is concerned with treating committed persons for a current mental abnormality, and protecting society from the sexually violent acts associated with that abnormality, rather than being concerned with criminal culpability. The court distinguished the goals of incapacitation and treatment from the goal of punishment. The court found that the Washington Act is designed to further legitimate goals of civil confinement and that the claimants had failed to provide proof to the contrary. 122 Wash.2d at 18-25, 857 P.2d, at 996-1000.

The Act spawned several other challenges in state and federal court, two of which bear mention. Richard Turay, committed as a sexually violent predator, filed suit in Federal District Court against Center officials under Rev. Stat. § 1979, 42 U.S.C. § 1983, alleging unconstitutional conditions of confinement and inadequate treatment at the Center. In 1994, a jury concluded that the Center had failed to provide constitutionally adequate mental health treatment. App. 64-68. The court ordered officials at the Center to bring the institution up to constitutional standards, appointing a Special Master to monitor progress at the Center. The Center currently operates under an injunction. *Turay v. Seling*, 108 F. Supp. 2d 1148 (W.D. Wash. 2000). See also Brief for Petitioner 8-9.

Turay also appealed his commitment as a sexually violent predator in state court, claiming, among other things, that the conditions of confinement at the Center rendered the Washington Act punitive "as applied" to him in violation of the Double Jeopardy Clause. The Washington Supreme Court ruled that Turay's commitment was valid. *In re Turay*, 139 Wash.2d 379, 986 P.2d 790 (1999) (en banc). The court explained that in *Young* it had concluded that the Act is civil. 139 Wash.2d, at 415, 986 P.2d, at 809. The court also noted that this Court had recently held Kansas' Sexually Violent Predator Act, nearly identical to Washington's Act, **[258]** to be civil on its face. *Ibid*. The Washington Supreme Court rejected Turay's theory of double jeopardy, reasoning that the double jeopardy claim must be resolved by asking whether the Act itself is civil. *Id*., at 416-417, 986 P.2d, at 810 (citing *Hudson v. United States*, 522 U.S. 93, 118 S. Ct. 488, 139 L.Ed.2d 450 (1997)). The court concluded that Turay's proper remedy for constitutional violations in conditions of confinement at the Center was his § 1983 action for damages and injunctive relief. 139 Wash.2d, at 420, 986 P.2d, at 812.

C

That brings us to the action before this Court. In 1994, after unsuccessful challenges to his confinement in state court, Young filed a habeas action under 28 U.S.C. § 2254 against the superintendent of the Center. Young contended that the Act was unconstitutional and that his confinement was illegal. He sought immediate release. The District Court granted the writ, concluding that the Act violated substantive due process, that the Act was criminal rather than civil, and that it violated the double jeopardy and *ex post facto* guarantees of the Constitution. *Young v. Weston*, 898 F. Supp. 744 (W.D.Wash.1995). The superintendent appealed. While the appeal was pending, this Court decided *Kansas v. Hendricks*, 521 U.S. 346, 117 S. Ct. 2072, 138 L.Ed.2d 501 (1997), which held that Kansas' Sexually Violent Predator Act, on its face, met substantive due process requirements, was nonpunitive, and thus did not violate the Double Jeopardy and *Ex Post Facto* Clauses. The Ninth Circuit Court of Appeals remanded Young's case to the District Court for reconsideration in light of *Hendricks*, 122 F.3d 38 (1997).

On remand, the District Court denied Young's petition. Young appealed and the Ninth Circuit reversed and remanded in part and affirmed in part. 192 F.3d 870 (1999). The Ninth Circuit affirmed the District Court's ruling that Young's confinement did not violate the substantive due process requirement that the State prove mental illness **[259]** and dangerousness to justify confinement. *Id*., at 876. The Court of Appeals also left undisturbed the District Court's conclusion that the Act meets procedural due process and equal protection guarantees, and the District Court's rejection of Young's challenges to his commitment proceedings. *Id*., at 876-877. Young did not seek a petition for a writ of certiorari to the Ninth Circuit for its decision affirming the District Court in these respects, and accordingly, those issues are not before this Court.

The Ninth Circuit reversed the District Court's determination that because the Washington Act is civil, Young's double jeopardy and *ex post facto* claims must fail. The "linchpin" of Young's claims, the court reasoned, was whether the Act was punitive "as applied" to Young. *Id.*, at 873. The court did not read this Court's decision in *Hendricks* to preclude the possibility that the Act could be punitive as applied. The court reasoned that actual conditions of confinement could divest a facially valid statute of its civil label upon a showing by the clearest proof that the statutory scheme is punitive in effect. 192 F.3d, at 874.

The Court of Appeals reviewed Young's claims that conditions of confinement at the Center were punitive and did not comport with due process. *Id.*, at 875. Young alleged that for seven years, he had been subject to conditions more restrictive than those placed on true civil commitment detainees, and even state prisoners. The Center, located wholly within the perimeter of a larger Department of Corrections (DOC) facility, relied on the DOC for a host of essential services, including library services, medical care, food, and security. More recently, Young claimed, the role of the DOC had increased to include daily security "walk-throughs." Young contended that the conditions and restrictions at the Center were not reasonably related to a legitimate nonpunitive goal, as residents were abused, confined to their rooms, subjected to random searches of their rooms and units, and placed under excessive security.

[260] Young also contended that conditions at the Center were incompatible with the Act's treatment purpose. The Center had a policy of videotaping therapy sessions and withholding privileges for refusal to submit to treatment. The Center residents were housed in units that, according to the Special Master in the *Turay* litigation, were clearly inappropriate for persons in a mental health treatment program. The Center still lacked certified sex offender treatment providers. Finally, there was no possibility of release. A court-appointed resident advocate and psychologist concluded in his final report that because the Center had not fundamentally changed over so many years, he had come to suspect that the Center was designed and managed to punish and confine individuals for life without any hope of release to a less restrictive setting. 192 F.3d, at 875. See also Amended Petition for Writ of Habeas Corpus, Supplemental Brief on Remand, and Motion to Alter Judgment 4- 5, 8-9, 11-12, 15, 20, 24-26, in No. C94-480C (WD Wash.), Record, Doc. Nos. 57, 155, and 167.

The Ninth Circuit concluded that "[b]y alleging that [the Washington Act] is punitive as applied, Young alleged facts which, if proved, would entitle him to relief." 192 F.3d, at 875. The court remanded the case to the District Court for a hearing to determine whether the conditions at the Center rendered the Act punitive as applied to Young. *Id.*, at 876.

This Court granted the petition for a writ of certiorari, 529 U.S. 1017, 120 S. Ct. 1416, 146 L.Ed.2d 309 (2000), to resolve the conflict between the Ninth Circuit Court of Appeals and the Washington Supreme Court. Compare 192 F.3d 870 (1999), with *In re Turay*, 139 Wash.2d 379, 986 P.2d 790 (1999).

II

As the Washington Supreme Court held and the Ninth Circuit acknowledged, we proceed on the understanding that the Washington Act is civil in nature. The Washington Act is strikingly similar to a commitment scheme we reviewed **[261]** four Terms ago in *Kansas v. Hendricks*, 521 U.S. 346, 117 S. Ct. 2072, 138 L.Ed.2d 501 (1997). In fact, Kansas patterned its Act after Washington's. See *In re Hendricks*, 259 Kan. 246, 249, 912 P.2d 129, 131 (1996). In *Hendricks* we explained that the question whether an Act is civil or punitive in nature is initially one of statutory construction. 521 U.S., at 361, 117 S. Ct. 2072 (citing *Allen v. Illinois*, 478 U.S. 364, 368, 106 S. Ct. 2988, 92 L.Ed.2d 296 (1986)). A court must ascertain whether the legislature intended the statute to establish civil proceedings. A court will reject the legislature's manifest intent only where a party challenging the Act provides the clearest proof that the statutory scheme is so punitive in either purpose or effect as to negate the State's intention. 521 U.S., at 361, 117 S. Ct. 2072 (citing *United States v. Ward*, 448 U.S. 242, 248-249, 100 S. Ct. 2636, 65 L.Ed.2d 742 (1980)). We concluded that the confined individual in that case had failed to satisfy his burden with respect to the Kansas Act. We noted several factors: The Act did not implicate retribution or deterrence; prior criminal convictions were used as evidence in the commitment proceedings, but were not a prerequisite to confinement; the Act required no finding of scienter to commit a person; the Act was not intended to function as a deterrent; and although the procedural safeguards were similar to those in the criminal context, they did not alter the character of the scheme. 521 U.S., at 361-365, 117 S. Ct. 2072.

We also examined the conditions of confinement provided by the Act. *Id.*, at 363-364, 117 S. Ct. 2072. The Court was aware that sexually violent predators in Kansas were to be held in a segregated unit within the prison system. *Id.*, at 368, 117 S. Ct. 2072. We explained that the Act called for confinement in a secure facility because the persons confined were dangerous to the community. *Id.*, at 363, 117 S. Ct. 2072. We noted, however, that conditions within the unit were essentially the same as conditions for other involuntarily committed persons in mental hospitals. *Ibid.* Moreover, confinement under the Act was not necessarily indefinite in duration. *Id.*, at 364, 117 S. Ct. 2072. Finally, we observed that in addition to protecting the public, the Act also provided treatment for sexually violent predators. **[262]** *Id.*, at 365-368, 117 S. Ct. 2072. We acknowledged that not all mental conditions were treatable. For those individuals with untreatable conditions, however, we explained that there was no federal constitutional bar to their civil confinement, because the State had an interest in protecting the public from dangerous individuals with treatable as well as untreatable conditions. *Id.*, at 366, 117 S. Ct. 2072. Our conclusion that the Kansas Act was "nonpunitive thus remove[d] an essential prerequisite for both Hendricks' double jeopardy and *ex post facto* claims." *Id.*, at 369, 117 S. Ct. 2072.

Since deciding *Hendricks*, this Court has reaffirmed the principle that determining the civil or punitive nature of an Act must begin with reference to its text and legislative history. *Hudson v. United States*, 522 U.S. 93, 118 S. Ct. 488, 139 L.Ed.2d 450 (1997). In *Hudson*, which involved a double jeopardy challenge to monetary penalties and occupational debarment, this Court expressly disapproved of evaluating the civil nature of an Act by reference to the effect that Act has on a single individual. Instead, courts must evaluate the question by reference to a variety of factors "'considered in relation to the statute on its face'"; the clearest proof is required to override legislative intent and conclude that an Act denominated civil is punitive in purpose or effect. *Id.*, at 100, 118 S. Ct. 488 (quoting *Kennedy v. Mendoza-Martinez*, 372 U.S. 144, 169, 83 S. Ct. 554, 9 L.Ed.2d 644 (1963)).

With this in mind, we turn to the Court of Appeals' determination that respondent could raise an "as-applied" challenge to the Act on double jeopardy and *ex post facto* grounds and seek release from confinement. Respondent essentially claims that the conditions of his confinement at the Center are too restrictive, that the conditions are incompatible with treatment, and that the system is designed to result in indefinite confinement. Respondent's claims are in many respects like the claims presented to the Court in *Hendricks*, where we concluded that the conditions of confinement were largely explained by the State's goal to incapacitate, not to punish. *521 U.S.*, at 362-368, 117 S. Ct. 2072. Nevertheless, **[263]** we do not deny that some of respondent's allegations are serious. Nor do we express any view as to how his allegations would bear on a court determining in the first instance whether Washington's confinement scheme is civil. Here, we evaluate respondent's allegations as presented in a double jeopardy and *ex post facto* challenge under the assumption that the Act is civil.

We hold that respondent cannot obtain release through an "as-applied" challenge to the Washington Act on double jeopardy and *ex post facto* grounds. We agree with petitioner that an "as-applied" analysis would prove unworkable. Such an analysis would never conclusively resolve whether a particular scheme is punitive and would thereby prevent a final determination of the scheme's validity under the Double Jeopardy and *Ex Post Facto* Clauses. Brief for Petitioner 30; Reply Brief for Petitioner 9. Unlike a fine, confinement is not a fixed event. As petitioner notes, it extends over time under conditions that are subject to change. The particular features of confinement may affect how a confinement scheme is evaluated to determine whether it is civil rather than punitive, but it remains no less true that the query must be answered definitively. The civil nature of a confinement scheme cannot be altered based merely on vagaries in the implementation of the authorizing statute.

Respondent contends that the Ninth Circuit's "as-applied" analysis comports with this Court's precedents. He points out that this Court has considered conditions of confinement in evaluating the validity of confinement schemes in the past. Brief for Respondent 11-16, 29 (citing *Hendricks, supra*, at 363, 117 S. Ct. 2072; *Reno v. Flores*, 507 U.S. 292, 301-302, 113 S. Ct. 1439, 123 L.Ed.2d 1 (1993); *United States v. Salerno*, 481 U.S. 739, 747-748, 107 S. Ct. 2095, 95 L.Ed.2d 697 (1987); *Allen v. Illinois, supra*, at 373-374, 106 S. Ct. 2988; *Schall v. Martin*, 467 U.S. 253, 269-273, 104 S. Ct. 2403, 81 L.Ed.2d 207 (1984)). All of those cases, however, presented the question whether the Act at issue was punitive. Permitting respondent's as-applied challenge would invite an end run around the Washington Supreme Court's decision that the **[264]** Act is civil in circumstances where a direct attack on that decision is not before this Court.

JUSTICE THOMAS, concurring in the judgment, takes issue with our view that the question before the Court concerns an as-applied challenge to a civil Act. He first contends that respondent's challenge is not a true "as-applied" challenge because respondent does not claim that the statute " 'by its own terms' is unconstitutional as applied . . . but rather that the statute is not being applied according to its terms at all." . . . We respectfully disagree. The Act requires "adequate care and individualized treatment," Wash. Rev. Code § 71.09.080(2) (Supp. 2000), but the Act is silent with respect to the confinement conditions required at the Center, and that is the source of many of respondent's complaints, . . . JUSTICE THOMAS next contends that we incorrectly assume that the Act is civil, instead of viewing the Act as "'*otherwise* . . . civil*,' or civil 'on its face." . . . (emphasis added by THOMAS, J.). However the Washington Act is described, our analysis in this case turns on the prior finding by the Washington Supreme Court that the Act is civil, and this Court's decision in *Hendricks* that a nearly identical Act was civil. Petitioner could not have claimed that the Washington Act is "otherwise" or "facially" civil without relying on those prior decisions.

In dissent, Justice STEVENS argues that we "incorrectly assum[e]" that the Act is "necessarily civil," . . . but the case has reached this Court under that very assumption. The Court of Appeals recognized that the Act is civil, and treated respondent's claim as an individual, "as-applied" challenge to the Act. The Court of Appeals then remanded the case to the District Court for an evidentiary hearing to determine respondent's conditions of confinement. Contrary to the dissent's characterization of the case, the Court of Appeals did not purport to undermine the validity of the Washington Act as a civil confinement scheme. The court did not conclude that respondent's allegations, if substantiated, **[265]** would be sufficient to refute the Washington Supreme Court's conclusion that the Act is civil, and to require the release of all those confined under its authority. The Ninth Circuit addressed only respondent's individual case, and we do not decide claims that are not presented by the decision below. *Matsushita Elec. Industrial Co. v. Epstein*, 516 U.S. 367, 379, 116 S. Ct. 873, 134 L.Ed.2d 6 (1996). We reject the Ninth Circuit's "as-applied" analysis for double jeopardy and *ex post facto* claims as fundamentally flawed.

III

Our decision today does not mean that respondent and others committed as sexually violent predators have no remedy for the alleged conditions and treatment regime at the Center. The text of the Washington Act states that those confined under its authority have the right to adequate care and individualized treatment. Wash. Rev. Code § 71.09.080(2) (Supp. 2000); Brief for Petitioner 14. As petitioner acknowledges, if the Center fails to fulfill its statutory duty, those confined may have a state law cause of action. Tr. of Oral Arg. 6, 10-11, 52. It is for the Washington courts to determine whether the Center is operating in accordance with state law and provide a remedy.

State courts, in addition to federal courts, remain competent to adjudicate and remedy challenges to civil confinement schemes arising under the Federal Constitution. As noted above, the Washington Supreme Court has already held that the Washington Act is civil in nature, designed to incapacitate and to treat. *In re Young*, 122 Wash.2d, at 18-25, 857 P.2d, at 966-1000. Accordingly, due process requires that the conditions and duration of confinement under the Act bear some reasonable relation to the purpose for which persons are committed. *Foucha v. Louisiana*, 504 U.S. 71, 79, 112 S. Ct. 1780, 118 L.Ed.2d 437 (1992); *Youngberg v. Romeo*, 457 U.S. 307, 324, 102 S. Ct. 2452, 73 L.Ed.2d 28 (1982); *Jackson v. Indiana*, 406 U.S. 715, 738, 92 S. Ct. 1845, 32 L.Ed.2d 435 (1972).

Finally, we note that a § 1983 action against the Center is pending in the Western District of Washington. . . . **[266]** The Center operates under an injunction that requires it to adopt and implement a plan for training and hiring competent sex offender therapists; to improve relations between residents and treatment providers; to implement a treatment program for residents containing elements required by prevailing professional standards; to develop individual treatment programs; and to provide a psychologist or psychiatrist expert in the diagnosis and treatment of sex offenders to supervise the staff. App. 67. A Special Master has assisted in bringing the Center into compliance with the injunction. In its most recent published opinion on the matter, the District Court noted some progress at the Center in meeting the requirements of the injunction. *Turay v. Seling*, 108 F.Supp. 2d, at 1154-1155.

This case gives us no occasion to consider how the civil nature of a confinement scheme relates to other constitutional challenges, such as due process, or to consider the extent to which a court may look to actual conditions of confinement and implementation of the statute to determine in the first instance whether a confinement scheme is civil in nature. JUSTICE SCALIA, concurring, contends that conditions of confinement are irrelevant to determining whether an Act is civil unless state courts have interpreted the Act as permitting those conditions. By contrast, JUSTICE STEVENS would consider conditions of confinement at any time in order to gain "full knowledge of the effects of the statute." . . .

Whether a confinement scheme is punitive has been the threshold question for some constitutional challenges. *See, e.g., Kansas v. Hendricks*, 521 U.S. 346, 117 S. Ct. 2072, 138 L.Ed.2d 501 (1997) (double jeopardy and *ex post facto*); *United States v. Salerno*, 481 U.S. 739, 107 S. Ct. 2095, 95 L.Ed.2d 697 (1987) (due process); *Allen v. Illinois*, 478 U.S. 364, 106 S. Ct. 2988, 92 L.Ed.2d 296 (1986) (Fifth Amendment privilege against self-incrimination). Whatever these cases may suggest about the relevance of conditions of confinement, they do not endorse the approach of the dissent, which would render the inquiry into the "effects **[267]** of the statute" . . . completely open ended. In one case, the Court refused to consider alleged confinement conditions because the parties had entered into a consent decree to improve conditions. *Flores*, 507 U.S., at 301, 113 S. Ct. 1439. The Court presumed that conditions were in compliance with the requirements of the consent decree. *Ibid*. In another case, the Court found that anecdotal case histories and a statistical study were insufficient to render a regulatory confinement scheme punitive. *Martin*, 467 U.S., at 272, 104 S. Ct. 2403. In such cases, we have decided whether a confinement scheme is punitive notwithstanding the inherent difficulty in ascertaining current conditions and predicting future events.

We have not squarely addressed the relevance of conditions of confinement to a first instance determination, and that question need not be resolved here. An Act, found to be civil, cannot be deemed punitive "as applied" to a single individual in violation of the Double Jeopardy and *Ex Post Facto* Clauses and provide cause for release.

The judgment of the United States Court of Appeals for the Ninth Circuit is therefore reversed, and the case is remanded for further proceedings consistent with this opinion.

It is so ordered.

JUSTICE SCALIA, with whom JUSTICE SOUTER joins, concurring.

I agree with the Court's holding that a statute, "found to be civil [in nature], cannot be deemed punitive" or criminal "as applied" for purposes of the *Ex Post Facto* and Double Jeopardy Clauses. . . . The Court accurately observes that this holding gives us "no occasion to consider . . . the extent to which a court may look to actual conditions of confinement and implementation of the statute to determine in the first instance whether a confinement scheme is civil in nature." . . . I write separately to dissociate myself from any implication that this reserved point may be an open question. I do not regard it as such since, three **[268]** years ago, we rejected a similar double jeopardy challenge (based upon the statute's implementation "as applied" to the petitioners), where the statute had *not* yet been determined to be civil in nature, and where we *were* making that determination "in the first instance." See *Hudson v. United States*, 522 U.S. 93, 118 S. Ct. 488, 139 L.Ed.2d 450 (1997). To be consistent with the most narrow holding of that case (which, unlike this one, did not involve imposition of confinement), any consideration of subsequent implementation in the course of making a "first instance" determination cannot extend to all subsequent implementation, but must be limited to implementation of confinement, and of other impositions that are "not a fixed event." . . . That, however, would be a peculiar limitation, since even "fixed events" such as the imposition of a fine can, in their implementation, acquire penal aspects—exemplified in *Hudson* by the allegedly punitive size of the fines, and by the availability of reduction for "good-faith" violations, see 522 U.S., at 97-98, 104, 118 S. Ct. 488. Moreover, the language and the reasoning of *Hudson* leave no room for such a peculiar limitation.

In that case, the petitioners contended that the punitive nature of the statute that had been applied to them could be assessed by considering the aforementioned features of the fines. We flatly rejected that contention, which found support in our prior decision in *United States v. Halper*, 490 U.S. 435, 109 S. Ct. 1892, 104 L.Ed.2d 487 (1989). *Halper*, we said, had erroneously made a "significant departure" from our prior jurisprudence, in deciding "to 'asses[s] the character of the actual sanctions imposed,' 490 U.S., at 447, 109 S. Ct. 1892, rather than, as *Kennedy* [*v. Mendoza-Martinez*, 372 U.S. 144, 83 S. Ct. 554, 9 L.Ed.2d 644 (1963),] demanded, evaluating the 'statute on its face' to determine whether it provided for what amounted to a criminal sanction, *[id.]*, at 169, 83 S. Ct. 554." 522 U.S., at 101, 118 S. Ct. 488 The *Kennedy* factors, we said, "'must be considered in relation to the statute on its face,'" 522 U.S., at 100, 118

S. Ct. 488, quoting from *Kennedy v. Mendoza-Martinez*, 372 U.S. 144, 169, 83 S. Ct. 554, 9 L.Ed.2d 644 (1963). We held that "[t]he fact that petitioners' **[269]** 'good faith' was considered in determining the amount of the penalty to be imposed in this case [a circumstance that would normally indicate the assessment is punitive] is irrelevant, as we look only to 'the statute on its face' to determine whether a penalty is criminal in nature." *Hudson, supra,* at 104, 118 S. Ct. 488, quoting *Kennedy, supra,* at 169, 83 S. Ct. 554. We repeated, to be sure, the principle that the statutory scheme would be criminal if it was sufficiently punitive " 'either in purpose *or effect*,'" *Hudson, supra,* at 99, 118 S. Ct. 488 (emphasis added), quoting *United States v. Ward*, 448 U.S. 242, 248-249, 100 S. Ct. 2636, 65 L.Ed.2d 742 (1980), but it was clear from the opinion that this referred to effects apparent upon the face of the statute.

The short of the matter is that, for Double Jeopardy and *Ex Post Facto* Clause purposes, the question of criminal penalty vel non depends upon the intent of the legislature;* and harsh executive implementation cannot "transfor[m] what was clearly intended as a civil remedy into a criminal penalty," *Rex Trailer Co. v. United States*, 350 U.S. 148, 154, 76 S. Ct. 219, 100 L.Ed. 149 (1956), any more than compassionate executive implementation can transform a criminal penalty into a civil remedy. This is not to say that there is no relief from a system that administers a facially civil statute in a fashion that would render it criminal. The remedy, however, is not to invalidate the legislature's handiwork under the Double Jeopardy Clause, but to eliminate whatever excess in administration contradicts the statute's civil character. When, as here, a state statute is at issue, the remedy for implementation that does not comport with the civil nature of the statute is resort to the traditional state proceedings that challenge unlawful executive action; if those proceedings fail, and the state **[270]** courts authoritatively interpret the state statute as permitting impositions that are indeed punitive, then and only then can federal courts pronounce a statute that on its face is civil to be criminal. Such an approach protects federal courts from becoming enmeshed in the sort of intrusive inquiry into local conditions at state institutions that are best left to the State's own judiciary, at least in the first instance. And it avoids federal invalidation of state statutes on the basis of executive implementation that the state courts themselves, given the opportunity, would find to be ultra vires. Only this approach, it seems to me, is in accord with our sound and traditional reluctance to be the initial interpreter of state law. See *Railroad Comm'n of Tex. v. Pullman Co.*, 312 U.S. 496, 500-501, 61 S. Ct. 643, 85 L.Ed. 971 (1941).

With this clarification, I join the opinion of the Court.

JUSTICE THOMAS, concurring in the judgment.

We granted certiorari to decide whether "an *otherwise* valid civil statute can be divest-

---

* Hudson v. United States, 522 U.S. 93, 118 S. Ct. 488, 139 L.Ed.2d 450 (1997) addressed only the Double Jeopardy Clause. Since, however, the very wording of the *Ex Post Facto* Clause—"No State shall . . . pass any . . . ex post facto *Law*," U.S. Const., Art. I, § 10, cl. 1 (emphases added)—leaves no doubt that it is a prohibition upon *legislative* action, the irrelevance of subsequent executive implementation to that constitutional question is, if anything, even clearer.

ed of its civil nature" simply because of an administrative agency's failure to implement the statute according to its terms. Pet. for Cert. i (emphasis added). The majority declines to answer this question. Instead, it assumes that the statute at issue is
civil—rather than "*otherwise . . . civil*," or civil "on its face." *Young v. Weston*, 122
F.3d 38 (C.A.9 1997). And then it merely holds that a statute that is civil cannot be
deemed the opposite of civil—"punitive," as the majority puts it—as applied to a single individual. . . . In explaining this conclusion, the majority expressly reserves judgment on whether the manner of implementation should affect a court's assessment of
a statute as civil in the "first instance." . . . I write separately to express my view, first,
that a statute which is civil on its face cannot be divested of its civil nature simply
because of the manner in which it is implemented, and second, that the distinction
between a challenge in the **[271]** "first instance" and a subsequent challenge is one
without a difference.

Before proceeding, it is important to clarify the issue in this case. The majority adopts
the Ninth Circuit's nomenclature and refers to respondent's claim as an "as-applied"
challenge . . . but that label is at best misleading. Typically an "as-applied" challenge
is a claim that a statute, "*by its own terms*, infringe[s] constitutional freedoms in the
circumstances of [a] particular case." *United States v. Christian Echoes Nat. Ministry,
Inc.*, 404 U.S. 561, 565, 92 S. Ct. 663, 30 L.Ed.2d 716 (1972) (*per curiam*) (emphasis
added). In contrast, respondent's claim is not that Washington's Community Protection
Act of 1990 (Washington Act or Act), Wash. Rev. Code § 71.09.010 *et seq.* (1992), "by
its own terms" is unconstitutional as applied to him,[1] but rather that the statute is not
being applied according to its terms at all.[2] Respondent essentially contends that the
actual conditions of confinement, notwithstanding the text of the statute, are punitive
and incompatible with the Act's treatment purpose. . . .

[272] A challenge, such as this one, to the implementation of a facially civil statute is
not only "unworkable," as the majority puts it . . . but also prohibited by our decision
in *Hudson v. United States*, 522 U.S. 93, 118 S. Ct. 488, 139 L.Ed.2d 450 (1997). In
Hudson we held that, when determining whether a statute is civil or criminal, a court
must examine the "statute on its face." *Id.*, at 101, 118 S. Ct. 488, quoting *Kennedy v.
Mendoza-Martinez*, 372 U.S. 144, 169, 83 S. Ct. 554, 9 L.Ed.2d 644 (1963) (internal
quotation marks omitted). In so holding, we expressly disavowed the approach used in

---

[1] Respondent has made the claim that the terms of the Washington Act are criminal so that his confinement under the Act thus violates the Double Jeopardy and *Ex Post Facto* Clauses, but this claim was
rejected below—first by the Washington Supreme Court, *In re Young*, 122 Wash.2d 1, 18-23, 857 P.2d
989, 996-999 (1993), , and then by the Ninth Circuit, *Young v. Weston*, 192 F.3d 870, 874 (1999)—and
has not been presented to this Court.

[2] Disagreeing with this characterization, the majority contends that the statute is silent with respect
to conditions of confinement. . . . Even if the majority were correct—which it is not, see Wash. Rev. Code
§ 71.09.070 (requiring annual examinations of each person's mental conditions); § 71.09.080(2) (Supp.
2000) (requiring "adequate care and individualized treatment"); see also *In re Young, supra*, at 18-23, 857
P.2d at 996-999 (discussing similar provisions on conditions of confinement in 1990 version of
Washington Act)—the question on which we granted certiorari expressly assumes that the statute "mandate[s]" the "conditions of confinement" that petitioner seeks. See Pet. for Cert. i.

United States v. Halper, 490 U.S. 435, 448, 109 S. Ct. 1892, 104 L.Ed.2d 487 (1989), which evaluated the "actual sanctions imposed." 522 U.S., at 101, 118 S. Ct. 488, quoting *Halper, supra,* at 447, 109 S. Ct. 1892 (internal quotation marks omitted). Respondent's claim is flatly inconsistent with the holding of *Hudson* because respondent asks us to look beyond the face of the Washington Act and to examine instead the actual sanctions imposed on him, that is, the actual conditions of confinement. Respondent argues, and the Ninth Circuit held, that *Hudson*'s reach is limited to the particular sanctions involved in that case—monetary penalties and occupational disbarment—and does not apply here, where the sanction is confinement. *Hudson*, however, contains no indication whatsoever that its holding is limited to the specific sanctions at issue. To the contrary, as we explained in *Hudson,* a court may not elevate to dispositive status any of the factors that it may consider in determining whether a sanction is criminal.[3] 522 U.S., at 101, 118 S. Ct. 488. One of these nondispositive **[273]** factors is confinement. *Id.*, at 99, 118 S. Ct. 488 (stating that one of the factors is "[w]hether the sanction involves an affirmative disability or restraint," quoting *Mendoza-Martinez, supra*, at 168, 83 S. Ct. 554 (internal quotation marks omitted)). Yet elevating confinement to dispositive status is exactly what respondent asks us to do when he advances his distinction between confinement and other sanctions. Because *Hudson* rejects such an argument, respondent's claim fails.

An implementation-based challenge to a facially civil statute would be as inappropriate in reviewing the statute in the "first instance" . . . as it is here. In the first instance, as here, there is no place for such a challenge in the governing jurisprudence. *Hudson*, which requires courts to look at the face of the statute, precludes implementation-based challenges at any time. Moreover, the implementation-based claim would be as "unworkable" . . . in the first instance as in later challenges. Because the actual conditions of confinement may change over time and may vary from facility to facility, an implementation-based challenge, if successful, would serve to invalidate a statute that may be implemented without any constitutional infirmities at a future time or in a separate facility. To use the majority's words, the validity of a statute should not be "based merely on vagaries in the implementation of the authorizing statute." *Ibid.*

And yet the majority suggests that courts may be able to consider conditions of confinement in determining whether a statute is punitive. . . . To the extent that the conditions are actually provided for on the face of the statute, I of course agree. Cf. *Hudson, supra*, at 101, 118 S. Ct. 488 (directing courts to look at "'the statute on its face'"). However, to the extent that the conditions result from the fact that the statute

---

[3] The *Hudson* Court referred to the seven factors listed in *Kennedy v. Mendoza-Martinez*, 372 U.S. 144, 83 S. Ct. 554, 9 L.Ed.2d 644 (1963), as "useful guideposts": "(1) whether the sanction involves an affirmative disability or restraint; (2) whether it has historically been regarded as a punishment; (3) whether it comes into play only on a finding of *scienter*; (4) whether its operation will promote the traditional aims of punishment—retribution and deterrence; (5) whether the behavior to which it applies is already a crime; (6) whether an alternative purpose to which it may rationally be connected is assignable for it; and (7) whether it appears excessive in relation to the alternative purpose assigned." 522 U.S., at 99-100, 118 S. Ct. 488, quoting *Mendoza-Martinez, supra*, at 168-169, 83 S. Ct. 544 (internal quotation marks and alteration omitted).

is not being applied according to its terms, the conditions are not the effect of the statute, but rather the **[274]** effect of its improper implementation.⁴ A suit based on these conditions cannot prevail.

* * *

The Washington Act does not provide on its face for punitive conditions of confinement, and the actual conditions under which the Act is implemented are of no concern to our inquiry. I therefore concur in the judgment of the Court.

JUSTICE STEVENS, dissenting.

A sexual predator may be imprisoned for violating the law, and, if he is mentally ill, he may be committed to an institution until he is cured. Whether a specific statute authorizing the detention of such a person is properly viewed as "criminal" or "civil" in the context of federal constitutional issues is often a question of considerable difficulty. See *Kansas v. Hendricks*, 521 U.S. 346, 117 S. Ct. 2072, 138 L.Ed.2d 501 (1997) (reversing, by a 5-to-4 vote, a decision of the Kansas Supreme Court invalidating **[275]** Kansas' Sexually Violent Predator Act); *Allen v. Illinois*, 478 U.S. 364, 106 S. Ct. 2988, 92 L.Ed.2d 296 (1986) (upholding, by a 5-to-4 vote, Illinois' Sexually Dangerous Persons Act); *In re Young*, 122 Wash.2d 1, 857 P.2d 989 (1993) (en banc) (upholding, by a 5-to-4 vote, the provisions of Washington's Community Protection Act of 1990 dealing with sexually violent predators).

It is settled, however, that the question whether a state statute is civil or criminal in nature for purposes of complying with the demands of the Federal Constitution is a question of federal law. If a detainee comes forward with " 'the clearest proof' that 'the statutory scheme [is] so punitive either in purpose or effect as to negate [the State's] intention' that the proceeding be civil, it must be considered criminal." *Allen*, 478 U.S., at 369, 106 S. Ct. 2988 (quoting *United States v. Ward*, 448 U.S. 242, 248-249, 100 S. Ct. 2636, 65 L.Ed.2d 742 (1980)) (emphasis added). See also *Hudson v. United States*, 522 U.S. 93, 100, 105, 118 S. Ct. 488, 139 L.Ed.2d 450 (1997). Accordingly, we have consistently looked to the conditions of confinement as evidence of both the legislative

---

⁴ The dissent argues that, "under the majority's analysis, there is no inquiry beyond that of statutory construction." . . . Although it is unclear to me whether the dissent is correct on this score, I hope that state and federal courts so interpret the majority opinion. For even if the majority opinion does not preclude venturing beyond the face of the statute, *Hudson* certainly does. See *Hudson*, 522 U.S., at 101, 118 S. Ct. 488 (holding that courts must examine a statute " 'on its face' " and may not consider the "'actual sanctions imposed' "); . . . To dispel any suggestion to the contrary . . . I note that *Kansas v. Hendricks*, 521 U.S. 346, 117 S. Ct. 2072, 138 L.Ed.2d 501 (1997), does not provide support for implementation-based challenges. In *Hendricks*, "none of the parties argue[d] that people institutionalized under the . . . civil commitment statute are subject to punitive conditions." *Id.* at 363, 117 S. Ct. 2072. The viability of an implementation-based challenge was simply not at issue. And significantly, six months after *Hendricks* we held in *Hudson* that inquiries into whether a statute is civil are restricted to the "face" of the statute. *Hudson, supra,* at 101, 118 S. Ct. 488. To the extent that *Hendricks* (or any previous opinion . . .) left a door open by not answering the implementation question, *Hudson* closed that door.

purpose behind the statute and its actual effect. See *Hendricks*, 521 U.S., at 361, 367-369, 117 S. Ct. 2072; *Schall v. Martin*, 467 U.S. 253, 269-271, 104 S. Ct. 2403, 81 L.Ed.2d 207 (1984); *Allen*, 478 U.S., at 369, 373-374, 106 S. Ct. 2988. As we have acknowledged in those cases, the question whether a statute is in fact punitive cannot always be answered solely by reference to the text of the statute.

The majority in this case, however, incorrectly assumes that the Act at issue is necessarily civil. The issue the majority purports to resolve is whether an Act that is otherwise civil in nature can be deemed criminal in a specific instance based on evidence of its application to a particular prisoner. However, respondent Young's petition did not present that issue. Rather, consistent with our case law, Young sought to introduce evidence of the conditions of confinement as evidence of the punitive purpose and effect of the Washington statute. See Amended Pet. for Writ of Habeas Corpus 6 and Supp. Brief on Remand 2, 6, 10-11, in No. C94-480C (WD Wash.), Record, Doc. Nos. 57, 155. As a result, Young in no **[276]** way runs afoul of *Hudson v. United States*, 522 U.S. 93, 118 S. Ct. 488, 139 L.Ed.2d 450 (1997). Properly read, *Hudson* acknowledges that resolving whether an Act is civil or criminal in nature can take into account whether the statutory scheme has a punitive effect.[1] *Id.*, at 99, 118 S. Ct. 488. What *Hudson* rejects is an approach *not* taken by respondent—one that bypasses this threshold question in favor of a dispositive focus on the sanction actually imposed on the specific individual.[2] *Id.*, at 101-102, 118 S. Ct. 488.

To be sure, the question whether an Act is civil or punitive in nature "is initially one of statutory construction." . . . However, under the majority's analysis, there is no inquiry beyond that of statutory construction. . . . In essence, the majority argues that because the constitutional query must be answered definitively and because confinement is not a "fixed event," conditions of confinement should not be considered at all, except in the first challenge to a statute, when, as a practical matter, **[277]** the evidence of such conditions is most likely not to constitute the requisite "clearest proof." This seems to me quite wrong. If conditions of confinement are such that a detainee has

---

[1] In his concurrence, JUSTICE SCALIA concludes that, under the rule of *Hudson v. United States*, 522 U.S. 93, 118 S. Ct. 488, 139 L.Ed.2d 450 (1997), courts may never look to actual conditions of confinement and implementation of the statute to determine in the first instance whether a confinement scheme is civil in nature. . . . JUSTICE THOMAS, concurring in the judgment, would take *Hudson* even further, precluding implementation-based challenges "at any time.". . . However, for the reasons set out above, I believe that both concurrences misread *Hudson*. I also note that *Hudson* did not involve confinement. In cases that do involve confinement, this Court has relied on the principle that a statutory scheme must be deemed criminal if it was sufficiently punitive "'either in purpose or effect.'" See *Kansas v. Hendricks*, 521 U.S. 346, 361, 367-369, 117 S. Ct. 2072, 138 L.Ed.2d 501 (1997); *Schall v. Martin*, 467 U.S. 253, 269-271, 104 S. Ct. 2403, 81 L.Ed.2d 207 (1984); *Allen v. Illinois*, 478 U.S. 364, 369, 373-374, 106 S. Ct. 2988, 92 L.Ed.2d 296 (1986).

[2] In response to my dissent, the Court has made it clear that it is simply holding that respondent may not prevail if he merely proves that the statute is punitive insofar as it has been applied to him. The question whether he may prevail if he can prove that the statute is punitive in its application to everyone confined under its provisions therefore remains open. In sum, the Court has rejected the narrow holding of the Ninth Circuit, but has not addressed the sufficiency of the broadest claim that petitioner has advanced.

been punished twice in violation of the Double Jeopardy Clause, it is irrelevant that the scheme has been previously labeled as civil without full knowledge of the effects of the statute.[3]

In this case, Young has made detailed allegations concerning both the absence of treatment for his alleged mental illness and the starkly punitive character of the conditions of his confinement. If proved, those allegations establish not just that those detained pursuant to the statute are treated like those imprisoned for violations of Washington's criminal laws, but that, in many respects, they receive significantly worse treatment.[4] If those allegations are correct, the statute in question should be characterized as a criminal law for federal constitutional purposes. I therefore agree with the Court of Appeals' conclusion that respondent should be given the opportunity to come forward with the "clearest proof" that his allegations are true.

Accordingly, I respectfully dissent.

---

[3] In this case, those detained pursuant to Washington's statute have sought an improvement in conditions for almost seven years. Their success in the courts, however, has had little practical impact.

[4] Under such conditions, Young has now served longer in prison following the completion of his sentence than he did on the sentence itself.

Appendix 4
Bibliography

Abel, G.G. (1997). *The Abel Assessment for Sexual Interest* [Online]. Available: *www.abelscreen.com.*

Abel, G. G., Becker, J. V., Cunningham-Rathner, J., Mittelman, M. S., & Rouleau, J.-L. (1988). Multiple paraphilic diagnoses among sex offenders. *Bulletin of the American Academy of Psychiatry and Law, 16,* 153–168.

Abel, G. G., Becker, J. V., Mittelman, M. S., Cunningham-Rathner, J., Rouleau, J.-L., & Murphy, W. D. (1987). Self-reported sex crimes of nonincarcerated paraphiliacs. *Journal of Interpersonal Violence, 2,* 3–25.

Abel, G., Jordan, A., Hand, C. G., Holland, L. A., & Phipps, A. (2001). Classification models of child molesters utilizing the Abel Assessment for Sexual Interest. *Child Abuse and Neglect: The International Journal, 25*(5), 703–718.

Abel, G. G., Jordan, A., Rouleau, J. L., Emerick, R., Barboza-Whitehead, S., & Osborn, C. (2004). Use of visual reaction time to assess male adolescents who molest children. *Sexual Abuse: A Journal of Research and Treatment, 16*(3), 255–265.

Abel, G. G., Osborn, C., Anthony, D., & Gardos, P. (1992). Current treatments of paraphiliacs. *Annual Review of Sex Research, 3,* 255–290.

Abel, G. G., & Rouleau, J.-L. (1990). The nature and extent of sexual assault. In W. L. Marshall, D. R. Laws, & H. E. Barbaree (Eds.), *Handbook of sexual assault: Issues, theories and treatment of the offender* (pp. 9–22). New York: Plenum Press.

Abel Screening. (1996). *Abel assessment for sexual interest: Juvenile sex offenders* [Therapist product information brochure]. Atlanta, GA: Author.

Abrams, S., & Abrams, J. B. (1993). *Polygraph testing of the pedophile.* Portland, OR: Ryan Gwinner Press.

Adkins, G., Huff, D., & Stageberg, P. (2000). *The Iowa Sex Offender Registry and recidivism.* Des Moines: Iowa Department of Human Rights, Division of Criminal and Juvenile Justice Planning and Statistical Analysis Center.

Ahlmeyer, S., Heil, P., & English, K. (1998). *The value of the polygraph: An exploratory study.* Paper presented at the annual conference of the Association of the Treatment of Sexual Abusers, Vancouver, British Columbia.

Ahlmeyer, S., Heil, P., McKee, B., & English, K. (2000). The impact of polygraphy on admissions of victims and offenses in adult sex offenders. *Sexual Abuse: A Journal of Research and Treatment, 12,* 123–138.

Ainsworth, M., Blehar, M., Waters, E., & Wall, S. (1978). *Patterns of attachment.* Mahwah, NJ: Erlbaum.

Alexander, M. (1999). Sexual offender treatment efficacy revisited. *Sexual*

Abuse: Journal of Research & Treatment, 11(2), 101–116.

Alexander, R. (2000). Civil commitment of sex offenders to mental institutions: Should the standard be based on serious mental illness or mental disorder? *Journal of Health and Social Policy, 11*(3), 67–79.

Amato-Henderson, S. L. (1996). *Effects of misinformation on the concealed knowledge test* (Report No. DoDPI97-R-0001). Ft. McClellan, AL: Department of Defense Polygraph Institute.

American Civil Liberties Union. (2004). *Class action complaint challenges failure of Illinois officials to provide adequate mental health treatment under the state's Sexually Violent Persons Act.* Available: *www.aclu-il.org/news/press/000064.shtml.*

American Psychiatric Association. (1994). *Diagnostic and statistical manual of mental disorders* (4th ed.). Washington, DC: Author.

American Psychiatric Association. (1999). *Dangerous sex offenders: A Task Force report of the American Psychiatric Association.* Washington, DC: Author.

American Psychiatric Association. (2000). *Diagnostic and statistical manual of mental disorders* (4th ed., text rev.). Washington, DC: Author.

American Society of Addiction Medicine. (2004). *Patient placement criteria for the treatment of substance related disorders* (2nd ed.). Available: ASAM Publications Distribution, P.O. Box 101, Annapolis Junction, MD 20701–0101.

Anderson, R. D., Gibeau, D., & D'Amora, B. A. (1995). The Sex Offender Treatment Rating Scale: Initial reliability data. *Sexual Abuse: A Journal of Research and Treatment, 7*(3), 221–227.

Andrews, D. A. (1982). *The Level of Supervision Inventory (LSI): The first follow-up.* Toronto, Ontario, Canada: Ontario Ministry of Correctional Services.

Andrews, D. A., & Bonta, J. (1995). *The Level of Service Inventory—Revised.* Toronto, Ontario, Canada: Multi-HealthSystems.

Andrews, D. A., & Bonta, J. L. (2001). *The Level of Service Inventory—Revised user's manual.* North Tonawanda, NY: Multi-Health Systems.

Anglin, M. D., & Hser, Y-I. (1990). Treatment of drug abuse. In M. Tonry & J. Q. Wilson (Eds.), *Drugs and crime* (pp. 393–460). Chicago: University of Chicago Press.

Associated Press. (2003, March 15). *State to pay $1 million for sex predator oversight.*

Associated Press. (2003, December 1). *Police arrest Minnesota man in disappearance of missing college student.*

Associated Press. (2004, February 16). *Two sex offenders sue over confinement: Terms over, treatment continues in NJ.*

Associated Press. (2005). Florida governor OK's tough child molester bill: Violators face lifetime of tracking by global positioning technology. Available: *www.msnbc.msn.com/id/7712095/print/1/displaymode/1098.*

Associated Press. (2005, April 20). *Prosecutors: Lunsford raped, buried alive.*

Associated Press. (2005, June 3). *Separate hurricane shelter for sex offenders?*

Association for the Treatment of Sexual Abusers. (2001). *Practice standards and guidelines for members of the Association for the Treatment of Sexual Abusers.* Beaverton, OR: Author.

Ball, C. J., & Seghorn, T. K. (1999). Diagnosis and treatment of exhibitionism and other sexual compulsive disorders. In B. K. Schwartz (Ed.), *The sex offender: Theoretical advances, treating special populations and legal developments* (pp. 28-1–28-14). Kingston, NJ: Civic Research Institute.

Barbaree. H. E. (1997). Evaluating treatment efficacy with sex offenders: The insensitivity of recidivism studies to treatment effects. *Sexual Abuse: A Journal of Research and Treatment, 9,* 111–128.

Barbaree, H. E., & Marshall, W. L. (1989). Erectile responses among heterosexual child molesters, father-daughter incest offenders, and matched non-offenders: Five distinct age preference profiles. *Canadian Journal of Behavioural Science, 21,* 70–82.

Barbaree, H., & Seto, M. (1997). *Prediction of recidivism among sex offenders.* Power point presentation. Available: *www.mhcp-research.com.*

Barbaree, H. E., Seto, M. C., & Langton, C. M. (2001, October). *Psychopathy, treatment behavior and sex offender recidivism: Extended follow-up.* Paper presented at the annual meeting of the Association for the Treatment of Sexual Abusers, San Antonio, TX.

Barbaree, H. E., Seto, M. C., Langton, C., & Peacock, E. (2001). Evaluating the predictive accuracy of six risk assessment instruments for adult sex offenders. *Criminal Justice and Behavior, 28*(4), 490–521.

Barrett, M., Wilson, R. J., & Long, C. (2003). Measuring motivation to change in sexual offenders from institutional intake to community treatment. *Sexual Abuse: A Journal of Research and Treatment, 15,* 269–283.

Bartosh, D. L., Garby, T., Lewis, D., & Gray, S. (2003). Differences in the predictive validity of actuarial risk assessments in relation to sex offender type. *International Journal of Offender Therapy and Comparative Criminology, 47*(4), 422–438.

Becker, J. V. (1998). What we know about the characteristics and treatment of adolescents who have committed sexual offenses. *Child Maltreatment, 3*(4), 317–329.

Becker, J. Marques, J. Nelson, C., & Schlank, A. (2001). *Best practices in civil commitment programs.* Preconference workshop presented at the 20th annual Research and Treatment Conference of the Association for the Treatment of Sexual Abusers. San Antonio, TX.

Benda, B., Corwyn, R. F., & Toombs, N. (2001). Recidivism among adolescent serious offenders. *Criminal Justice and Behavior, 28*(5), 588–614.

Bergman, J. (2000). Creating new cultures: Using drama therapy to build therapeutic communities in prison. In P. Lewis & D. R. Johnson (Eds.), *Current approaches in drama therapy* (pp. 303–330). Springfield, IL: Charles C. Thomas.

Bergman, J., & Hewish, S. (1996). The

violent illusion: Drama therapy and the dangerous voyage to the heart of change. In M. Liebmann (Ed.), *Arts approaches to conflict* (pp. 92–117). London: Jessica Kingsley.

Bergman, J., & Hewish, S. (2003). *Challenging experience: An experiential approach to offender treatment.* Oklahoma City, OK: Wood 'N Barnes.

Bergman, J., & Schlank, A. (2004). *Addressing cognitive inflexibility in sexual offenders.* Workshop presented at the 22nd annual Research and Treatment Conference of the Association for the Treatment of Sexual Abusers, Albuquerque, NM.

Berlin, F. S., Galbreath, N. W., Geary, B., & McGlone, G. (2003). The use of acturials at civil commitment hearings to predict the likelihood of future sexual violence. *Sexual Abuse: A Journal of Research and Treatment, 15*(4), 377–382.

Berliner, L. (2002). Commentary. *Sexual Abuse: A Journal of Research and Treatment, 14,* 195–197.

Bianchi, M. (1990). Fluoxetine treatment of exhibitionism [Letter]. *American Journal of Psychiatry, 147*(8), 1089–1090.

Birgden, A. (2004). Therapeutic jurisprudence and responsivity: Finding the will and the way in offender rehabilitation. *Psychology, Crime and Law, 10*(3), 283–295.

Birgden, A., & McLachlan, C. (2002), *Reducing reoffending framework: Setting the scene* (Paper No 1). Melbourne, Australia: Office of the Correctional Services Minister, Victoria.

Blumstein, A., Cohen, J., Roth, J. A., &

Visher, C. A. (Eds.). (1986). *Criminal careers and "career criminals": Vol. II.* Washington, DC: National Academy Press.

Boer, D. P., Hart, S. D., Kropp, P. R. & Webster, C. D. (1997). *The Sexual Violence Risk—20 Guide (SVR-20).* Burnaby, British Columbia, Canada: The Mental Health, Law and Policy Institute, Simon Fraser University.

Bonta, J. (1996). Risk-needs assessment and treatment. In A. Harland (Ed.), *Choosing correctional options that work: Defining the demand and evaluating the supply* (pp.18–68). Thousand Oaks, CA: Sage.

Borum, R., Bartel, P., & Forth, A. (2002). *The Structured Assessment of Violence Risk in Youth (SAVRY).* Available from Specialized Training Services, Inc., P.O. Box 28181, San Diego, CA 92198 (tel. 1–800–848–1226).

Bourduin, C., Blaske, D., eler, S., & Stein, R. (1990). Multisystemic treatment of adolescent sexual offenders. *International Journal of Offender Therapy and Comparative Criminology,* 105–113.

Bowlby, J. (1988). *A secure base: Clinical applications of attachment theory.* London: Routledge.

Bradford, J. (1985). Organic treatments for the male sexual offender. *Behavioral Sciences & the Law, 3*(4), 355–375.

Bradford, J. M. W. (1991, October 9). *The role of serotonin reuptake inhibitors in forensic psychiatry.* Paper presented at the 4th Congress of European College of Neuropsychopharmacology, The Role of Serotonin in Psychiatric Illness, Monte Carlo, Monaco.

Bradford, J. M. W. (1994). Can pedophilia be treated? *The Harvard Mental Health Letter, 10*(8), 3.

Bradford, J. M. W. (1995). The pharmacological treatment of paraphilias. In J. M. Oldham & M. B. Riba (Eds.), *Review of psychiatry* (Vol. 14, pp. 755–777. Washington, DC: American Psychatric Association Press.

Bradford, J. (1999, Fall). The paraphilias, obsessive compulsive spectrum disorder, and the treatment of sexually deviant behaviors. *Psychiatric Quarterly, 70*(3). Available: *www.brainphysicis. com/ocd/research/ocpara.html.*

Bradford, J., & Harris, V. (2003). *Principles and practice of forensic psychiatry* (2nd ed.). New York: Oxford University Press.

Briken, P., Nika, E., & Berner, W. (2001). Treatment of paraphilia with luteinizing hormone-releasing hormone agonist. *Journal of Sex and Marital Therapy, 27*(1), 45–55.

Briken, P. (2002). Pharmacotherapy of paraphilias with luteinizing hormone-releasing hormone agonists. *Archives of General Psychiatry, 59*(5), 469–470.

Briken, P., Hill, A., & Berner, W. (2003). Pharmacotherapy of paraphilias with long-acting agonists of luteinizing hormone-releasing hormone: A systematic review. *Journal of Clinical Psychiatry, 64*(8), 890–897.

Brunader, R., & Shelton, D. (2002). Radiologic bone assessment in the evaluation of osteoporosis. *American Family Physician, 65*, 1357–1364.

Burdon, W. M., & Gallagher, C. A. (2002). Coercion and sex offenders:

Controlling sex-offending behavior through incapacitation and treatment. *Criminal Justice and Behavior, 29*(1), 87–109.

Bureau of Justice Statistics. (1994). *Tracking offenders, 1990.* (NCJ 148200). Washington, DC: U.S. Office of Justice Programs, Department of Justice.

Burton, D. (2000). Were adolescent sexual offenders children with sexual behavior problems? *Sexual Abuse: A Journal of Research and Treatment, 12,* 37–48.

Burton, D. (2004). *1999–2000 National Safer Society Survey: A survey of treatment programs and models serving children with sexual behavioral problems, adolescent sex offenders, and adult sex offenders* [Special analysis on the polygraph, on file with the authors]. Brandon, VT: Safer Society Press.

California Legislative Analyst's Office. (2004). *Analysis of 2004–05 budget bill: Department of Mental Health.* Sacramento, CA: Author.

Campbell, T. W. (2000). Sexual predator evaluations and phrenology: Considering issues of evidentiary reliability. *Behavioral Sciences and the Law, 18,* 111–130.

Campbell, T. W. (2004). *Assessing sex offenders: Problems and pitfalls.* Springfield, IL: Charles C. Thomas.

Caspi, A., McClay, J., Moffitt, T., Mill, J., Martin, J., Craig, I., et al. (2002). Role of genotype in the cycle of violence in maltreated children. *Science, 297,* 851–854.

Cassidy, J. J., Easton, M., Capelli, C., Singer, A., & Bilodeau, A. (1996, Winter). Cognitive remediation of persons with severe and persistent mental illness. *Psychiatric Quarterly, 67*(4), 313–321.

Catalano, S. M. (2004). *The National Crime Victimization Survey: Criminal Victimization, 2003* (NCJ 205455). Washington, DC: U.S. Department of Justice, Office of Justice Programs, Bureau of Justice Statistics.

Chaffin, M., Letourneau, E., & Silovsky, J. (2001). Adults, adolescents and children who sexually abuse children: A developmental perspective. In J. B. Myers, L. Berliner, J. Briere, C. T. Hendrix, T. Reid, & C. Jenny (Eds.), *APSAC handbook on child maltreatment* (2nd ed., pp. 205–232). Thousand Oaks, CA: Sage.

Chaiken, J., & Chaiken, M. (1982). *Varieties of criminal behavior.* Santa Monica, CA: Rand Corporation.

Chang, S. (2003). Exploring the effects of luteinizing hormone-releasing hormone agonist therapy on bone health: Implications in the management of prostate cancer. *Urology, 62*(Suppl. 6A), 29–35.

Childress, A. R., & McLelland, A. T. (1993) *Cue extinction: Handbook for program administrators.* Rockville, MD: National Institute on Drug Abuse.

Cleckley, H. (1976). *The mask of sanity.* St. Louis, MO: Mosby.

Cohen, F. (1997). Sexually dangerous persons/predators legislation. In B. K. Schwartz & H. R. Cellini (Eds.), *The sex offender: New insights, treatment innovations, and legal developments* (pp. 22-1–22-12). Kingston, NJ: Civic Research Institute.

Coleman, E., Cesnik, J., Moore, A. M.,

& Dwyer, S. M. (1992). An exploratory study of the role of psychotropic medications in treatment of sexual offenders. *Journal of Offender Rehabilitation, 18,* 75–88.

Colorado Sex Offender Management Board. (2004). S*tandards and guidelines for the assessment, evaluation, treatment and behavioral monitoring of adult sex offenders.* Denver: Colorado Department of Public Safety, Division of Criminal Justice.

Comings, D. (1994) Role of genetic factors in human sexual behavior based on studies of Tourette syndrome and ADHD probands and their relatives. *American Journal of Medical Genetics, 54,* 227–241.

Committee on Ethical Guidelines for Forensic Psychologists. (1991). Specialty guidelines for forensic psychologists. *Law and Human Behavior, 15*(6), 655–665.

Cooke, D. J., & Michie, C. (2001). Refining the construct of psychopathy: Towards a hierarchical model. *Psychological Assessment, 13,* 171–188.

Correctional Service of Canada. (n.d.). *What do correctional officers think of sexual offenders?* Available: *www.csc-scc.gc.ca/text/pblct/forum/e04/e041g_e. shtml.*

Craig, L. A., Browne, K. D., & Stringer, I. (2003). Treatment and sexual recidivism. *Trauma, Violence and Abuse, 4,* 70–89.

Creative Mind Games. (1989). *The whole brain game* [Online]. Available: *www.creativemindgames.com.*

Crawley, E. M. (2004). Emotion and performance: Prison officers and the presentation of self in prisons. *Punishment and Society, 6*, 411–427.

de la Higuera Romero, J. (2003). Rehabilitation of cognitive function in patients with severe mental disorder: A pilot study using the cognitive modules of the IPT program. *Psychology in Spain, 79*(1), 77–85.

Doren, D. M. (1998). Recidivism base rates, predictions of sex offender recidivism, and the "sexual predator" commitment laws. *Behavioral Sciences and the Law, 16,* 97–114.

Doren, D. M. (2001). Analyzing the analysis: A response to Wollert (2000). *Behavioral Sciences and the Law, 19,* 185–196.

Doren, D. M. (2002). *Evaluating sex offenders: A manual for civil commitments and beyond.* Thousand Oaks, CA: Sage.

Doren, D. M. (2004). Stability of the interpretative risk percentages for the RRASOR and Static-99. *Sexual Abuse: A Journal of Research and Treatment, 16*(1), 25–36.

Doren, D. M. (2005). Recidivism risk assessments: Making sense of controversies. In W. Marshall, Y. Fernandez, L. Marshall, & G. Serran (Eds.), *Sexual offender treatment: Issues and controversies* (pp. 3–16). West Sussex, UK: Wiley.

Doren, D. M. (2005). What weight should courts give to treaters' testimony concerning recidivism risk? *Sex Offender Law Report, 6*(1), 1–2 & 15.

Doren, D. M., & Dow, E. A. (2003). What "shrinkage" of the MnSOST-R? A response to Wollert (2002). *Journal of Threat Assessment, 2*(4), 49–64.

D'Silva, K., Duggan, C., & McCarthy, L. (2004). Does treatment really make psychopaths worse? A review of the evidence. *Journal of Personality Disorders, 18*(2), 163–177.

Dutton D. W. (2000). Introduction to the special issue: Post conviction sex offender testing. *Polygraph, 29*, 1–5.

Dvoskin, J. A. (1991). Allocating treatment resources for sex offenders. *Hospital and Community Psychiatry,* 42(3), 229.

Dvoskin, J. A., & Patterson, R. F. (1998). Administration of treatment programs for offenders with mental illness. In R. M. Wettstein (Ed.), *Treatment of offenders with mental disorders* (pp. 1–43). New York: Guilford Press.

Dvoskin, J. A., Petrila, J., & Stark-Riemer, S. (1995). Application of the professional judgment rule to prison mental health. *Mental and Physical Disability Law Reporter, 19*(1), 108–114.

Dwyer, W. (1999). *Findings of fact, conclusions of law and order re: hearing on November 15, 1999. Turay v. Weston.* U.S. District Court Western District of Washington at Seattle.

Edens, J. F., Marcus, D. K., Lilienfeld, S. O., & Poythress, N. G. (2005). *Psychopathic, not psychopath: Taxometric evidence for the dimensional structure of psychopathy.* Manuscript submitted for publication.

Edens, J .F., & Petrila, J. (in press). Legal and ethical issues in the assessment and treatment of psychopath. In C. Patrick (Ed.), *Handbook of psychopathy.* New York: Guilford Press.

Elliott, D., Ageton, S., & Huizinga, D.

(1980). *The National Youth Survey: 1976 self-reported delinquency estimates.* Boulder, CO: Behavioral Research Institute.

Emerick, R. L., & Dutton, W. A. (1993). The effect of polygraphy on the self-report of adolescent sex offenders: Implications for risk assessment. *Annals of Sex Research, 6*(2), 83–103.

English, K. (1989). *The quality of data obtained from inmate self-reports.* Master's thesis. University of Colorado, Boulder.

English, K. (1998). The containment approach: An aggressive strategy for the community management of adult sex offenders. *Psychology, Public Policy and the Law, 14*(2/1), 218–235.

English, K. (2004). The containment approach to managing sex offenders. *Seton Hall Law Journal, 989,* 1255–1272.

English, K., Jones, L., Pasini-Hill, D., Patrick, D., & Cooley-Towell, S. (2000). *The value of polygraph testing in sex offender management* (Research report submitted to the National Institute of Justice, Grant No. D97LBVX0034). Denver: Colorado Department of Public Safety, Division of Criminal Justice, Office of Research and Statistics.

English, K., Jones, L., & Patrick, D. (2003). Risk management of adult sex offenders. In B. J. Winick & J. Q. LaFond, (Eds.), *Sexually violent offenders: Law and policy in North America* (pp. 265–280). Hyattsville, MD: American Psychological Association.

English, K., Jones, L., Patrick, D., & Pasini-Hill, D. (2003). Sex offender containment: Use of the post-conviction polygraph. *Annals of the New York Academy of Sciences, 989,* 411–427.

English, K., Lowden, K., DiTrolio, E., Harrison, L., Hagler L., & Nelson, R. (2002, February 15). *Analysis of disclosures documented in the polygraph reports of 116 youth with sexual behavior problems.* Study undertaken on behalf of the Colorado Sex Offender Management Board, Denver.

English, K., & Mande, M. (1992). *Measuring crime rates of prisoner* (Report to the National Institute of Justice, Grant No. 87IJJCX0048). Denver: Colorado Department of Public Safety, Division of Criminal Justice, Office of Research and Statistics.

English, K., Pullen, S., & Jones, L. (1996). *Managing adult sex offenders: A containment approach.* Lexington, KY: American Probation and Parole Association.

English, K., Retzlaff, P., & Kleinsasser, D. (2002). The Colorado Sex Offender Risk Scale. *Journal of Child Sexual Abuse, 11,* 77–96.

Epperson, D. L., Kaul, J. D., Huot, S. J., Hesselton, D., Alexander, W., & Goldman, R. (1999). *Minnesota Sex Offender Screening Tool—Revised (MnSOST-R): Development, performance, and recommended risk level cut scores* [Online]. Available: *www. psychology.iastate.edu/faculty/ epperson/mnsost_download.htm.*

Erickson, M. (1980). *An introduction to unorthodox therapy; innovative hypnotherapy: Collected papers of Milton H. Erickson* (Vol. IV). New York: Irvington.

Faigman, D. L., Kaye, D. H., Saks, M. J., & Sanders, J. (1997). *Modern scientific evidence. The law and science of expert testimony* (Vol. 1). St. Paul, MN: West.

Farkas, M. A. (1999). Correctional officers attitudes toward inmates and working with inmates in a "get tough" era. *Journal of Criminal Justice, 27*(6), 495–506.

Farkas, M. A., & Stichman, A. (2002). Sex offender laws: Can retribution, public safety and treatment be reconciled? *Criminal Justice Policy Review, 27*(2), 256–283.

Farrington, D. P. (1979). Environmental stress, delinquent behavior and convictions. In I. G. Sarason & C. D. Pielberger (Eds.), *Stress and anxiety* (Vol. 6, pp. 320–341). Washington, DC: Hemisphere.

Fava, M., & Rankin, M. (2002). Sexual functioning and SSRIs. *Journal of Clinical Psychiatry, 63*(Suppl. 5), 13–16.

Finkelhor, D. (1988). The trauma of child sexual abuse: Two models. In G. Wyatt, & G. Powell (Eds.). *The Lasting Effects of Child Sex Abuse.* Newbury Park, CA: Sage.

Finkelhor, D., Hotaling, G. T., Lewis, I. A., & Smith, C. (1990). Sexual abuse in a national survey of adult men and women: Prevalence, characteristics and risk factors. *Child Abuse and Neglect, 14*, 12–28.

Fitch, W. L., & Hammen, D. (2004, September). *Sex offender commitment in the United States.* Paper presented at the conference of the National Association of Mental Health Program Directors—Forensic Division, Atlanta.

Florida Department of Children and Families. (2004, September). *Monthly caseflow report.* Tallahassee, FL: Author.

Florida Legislature. (2004). *Sexually violent predator program—Time from referral to DCF to trial.* Tallahassee, FL:

Office of Economic and Demographic Research.

Florida Office of Inspector General. (2004). *Report Summary, Case #2004–0043-WB.* Tallahassee, FL: Department of Children and Families.

Florida Office of Inspector General. (2005). *Report Summary, Case #2004–0083.* Tallahassee, FL: Department of Children and Families.

Florida Office of Program Policy Analysis and Governmental Accountability. (2004). *Sexually violent predator program is reducing backlog, but still not timely* (Report # 04–63). Tallahassee, FL: Author.

Forensic Research, Inc. (1997). *Polygraph reliability and validity: A review of the research.* Chattanooga, TN: American Polygraph Association National Office.

Forth, A. E., Kosson, D. S., & Hare, R. D. (2003). *The Psychopathy Checklist: Youth Version—Manual.* Toronto, Ontario, Canada: Multi-Health Systems.

Foster, H.G., Hillbrand, M. & Silverstein, M. (1993). Neuro-psychological deficit and aggressive behavior: A prospective study. *Progress in Neuropsychopharmacological Biological Psychiatry, 17*(6), 939–946.

Freeman-Longo, R. E., & Knopp, F. H. (1992). State-of-the-art sex offender treatment: Outcome and issues. *Annals of Sex Research, 5*, 141–160.

Gacono, C. (1998) The use of the Psychopathy Checklist—Revised (PCL-R) and Rorschach in treatment planning with antisocial personality disordered patients. *International Journal of Offender Therapy and Comparative Criminology, 42*(1), 49–64.

Gacono. C., Meloy, J. R., Speth, E., & Roske, A. (1997). Above the law: Escapees from a maximum-security forensic hospital. *Bulletin of the American Academy of Psychiatry and the Law, 23*(3), 547–550.

Gagne, P. (1981). Treatment of sex offenders with medrooxyprogesterone acetate. *American Journal of Psychiatry, 138*(5), 644–646.

Gallagher, C. A., Watson, D. B., Hirschfield, P., Coggenshall, M. B., & MacKenzie, D. L. (1999). A quantitative review of the effects of sex offender treatment on sexual reoffending. *Corrections Management Quarterly, 3,* 19–29.

Galski, T., Thornton, K., & Shumsky, D. (1990). Brain dysfunction in sex offenders. *Journal of Offender Rehabilitation, 16,* 65–80.

Gaschler, W. J., McGettigan, J. P., Menges, P. M., & Waller, J. F. (2001). Review of polygraph screening assessment method. *Polygraph, 30,* 254–259.

Gendreau, P., Goggin, C., & Smith, P. (1999). The Gendreau, Goggin, and Smith checklist for implementing effective correctional treatment programs. *International Journal of Offender Therapy and Comparative Criminology, 43*(2), 180–187.

Gendreau, P., Little, T., & Goggin, C. (1996) A meta-analysis of the predictors of adult offender recidivism: What works! *Criminology, 34,* 575–607.

Gold, M. (1970). *Delinquent behavior in an American city.* Belmont, CA: Brooks/Cole.

Golden, C. J., Hammeke, T. A., & Purisch, A. D. (1980). *The Luria-*

Nebraska Neuropsychological Battery manual. Available: Western Psychological Services, 12031 Wilshire Boulevard, Los Angeles, CA 90025.

Goodwin, J. M. (1988). Obstacles to policymaking about incest: Some cautionary folktales. In G. E. Wyatt & G. J. Powell (Eds.), *Lasting effects of child sexual abuse* (pp. 21–39). Newbury Park, CA: Sage.

Gottfredson, D. M., & Tonry, M. (1987). *Prediction and classification: Criminal justice decision making. Vol. 9: Crime and justice: A review of research.* Chicago: University of Chicago Press.

Governor's Commission on Sex Offender Policy. (2005). *Final report.* Available: *www.doc.state.mn.us/ commissionsexoffenderpolicy/ commissionfinalreport.pdf.*

Grasswick, L. J., & Bradford, J. M. W. (2003). Osteoporosis associated with the treatment of paraphilias: A clinical review of seven case reports. *Journal of Forensic Science, 48*(4). Available: *www.astm.org.*

Greenwood, P. W., Chaiken, J. M., Petersilia, J. R., & Peterson, M. A. (1978). T*he RAND Habitual Offender Project: Summary of research findings to date* (P-5957). Santa Monica, CA: Rand Corporation.

Greenberg, D. M., Bradford, J. M., Curry, S., & O'Rourke, A. (1996). A comparison of treatment of paraphilias with three serotonin reuptake inhibitors: A retrospective study. *Bulletin of the American Academy of Psychiatry and the Law, 24*(4), 525–532.

Gregorian, R. S., Golden, K. A., Bahce, A., Goodman, C., Kwong, W. J., & Khan, Z. M. Antidepressant-induced sexual dysfunction. *Annals of Pharmacotherapy, 36*(10), 1577–1589.

Griffin, J., & Wilson, J. (2003) *Williams textbook of endrocrinology* (10th ed.). Philadelphia: Saunders.

Grisso, T. (2003). Risk assessment: Discussion of the section. In R. A. Prentky, E. S. Janus, & M. C. Seto (Eds.), *Understanding and managing sexually coercive behavior* (Vol. 989, pp. 236–245). New York: Annals of the New York Academy of Sciences.

Grisso, T., & Barnum, R. (2000). *Massachusetts Youth Screening Instrument—2: User's manual and technical report.* Worcester: University of Massachusetts Medical School.

Grossman, L. S., Martis, B., & Fichtner, C. G. (1999). Are sex offenders treatable? A research overview. *Psychiatric Services, 50,* 349–361.

Groth, A. N. (1977). The adolescent sexual offender and his prey. *International Journal of Offender Therapy and Comparative Criminology, 21*(3), 249–254.

Groth, A. N. (1979). *Men who rape: The psychology of the offender.* New York: Plenum Press.

Groth, A. N., & Loredo, C. M. (1981). Juvenile sexual offenders: Guidelines for assessment. *International Journal of Offender Therapy and Comparative Criminology, 25*(1), 31–39.

Grove, W. M., & Meehl, P. E. (1996). Comparative efficiency of informal (subjective, impressionistic) and formal (mechanical, algorithmic) prediction procedures: The clinical-statistical controversy, *Psychology, Public Policy and the Law, 293,* 296–299.

Guay, J., Ruscio, J., Hare, R., & Knight, R. A. (2004, October). *The latent structure of psychopathy: When more is simply more.* Paper presented at the annual meeting of the Society for Research in Psychopathology, St. Louis, MO.

Guy, L. G., Edens, J. F., Anthony, C., & Douglas, K. S. (in press). Does psychopathy predict institutional misconduct among adults? A meta-analytic investigation. *Journal of Consulting and Clinical Psychology.*

Hall, G. C. N. (1995). Sexual offender recidivism revisited: A meta-analysis of recent treatment studies. *Journal of Consulting and Clinical Psychology, 63,* 802–809.

Hammond, D. L. (1980). The responding of normals, alcoholics, and psychopaths in a laboratory lie detection experiment. *Dissertation Abstracts International* (UMI No. AAD8–28678).

Hansen, R. F., Resnick, H. S., Saunders, B. E., Kilpatrick, D. G., & Best, C. (1999). Factors related to the reporting of childhood rape. *Child Abuse and Neglect, 23,* 559–569.

Hanson, R. K. (1997). How to know what works with sex offenders. *Sexual Abuse: A Journal of Research and Treatment, 9,* 129–143.

Hanson, R. K. (1998). What do we know about sex offender risk assessment? *Psychology, Public Policy and Law, 4*(1/2), 50–72.

Hanson, R. K. (1997). *The development of a brief actuarial risk scale for sexual offense recidivism.* Ottawa, Ontario: Department of the Solicitor General of Canada. Available: *www.psepcsppcc.gc. ca/publications/corrections/199704-_e.pdf.*

Hanson, R. K., & Bussière, M. T. (1998). Predicting relapse: A meta-analysis of sexual offender recidivism studies. *Journal of Consulting and Clinical Psychology, 66*(2), 348–362.

Hanson, R. K, Gordon, A., Harris, A. J., Marques, J. K., Murphy, W., Quinsey, V. L., et al. (2002). First report of the collaborative outcome data project on the effectiveness of psychological treatment for sex offenders. *Sexual Abuse: Journal of Research and Treatment, 14*(2), 169–194.

Hanson, R. K., & Harris, A. (2000). *The Sex Offender Need Assessment Rating (SONAR): A method for measuring change in risk levels.* Ontario: Department of the Solicitor General of Canada.

Hanson, R. K., & Harris, A. (2000). Where should we intervene? Dynamic predictors of sexual offense recidivism. *Criminal Justice and Behavior, 27*(1), 6–35.

Hanson, R. K., & Harris, A. J. R. (2001). A structured approach to evaluating change among sexual offenders. *Sexual Abuse: A Journal of Research and Treatment, 13*(2), 105–122.

Hanson, R. K., Morton, K. E., Harris, A. J. R. (2003). Sexual offender recidivism risk: What we know and what we need to know. *Annals of the New York Academy of Sciences, 989*, 154–166.

Hanson, R. K., & Morton-Bourgon, K. (2004). *Predictors of sexual recidivism: An updated meta-analysis.* Ottawa, Ontario, Canada: Public Works and Government Services. Available: *www.psepc.gc.ca/publications/ corrections/pdf/200402_E.pdf.*

Hanson, R. K., & Thornton, D. (1999). *Static 99: Improving actuarial risk assessment for sex offenders.* Ottawa, Ontario: Department of the Solicitor General of Canada.

Hanson, R. K., & Thornton, D. (2000). Improving risk assessments for sex offenders: A comparison of three actuarial scales. *Law and Human Behavior, 24*, 119–136.

Hare, R. D. (1991). *The Hare Psychopathy Checklist—Revised.* Toronto, Ontario, Canada: Multi-Health Systems.

Hare, R. D. (2003). *Hare Psychopathy Checklist—Revised manual* (2nd ed.). Toronto, Ontario, Canada: Multi-Health Systems.

Harris, G. (2003). Men in his category have a 50% likelihood, but which half is he in? Comments on Berlin, Galbreath, Geary, and McClone. *Sexual Abuse: A Journal of Research and Treatment, 15*(4), 389–392.

Harris, A. (2005). *Civil commitment of sexual predators: A study in policy implementation.* New York: LFB Scholarly Publications.

Harris, G. T., Rice, M. E., & Quinsey, V. L. (1993). Violent recidivism of mentally disordered offenders: The development of a statistical prediction instrument. *Criminal Justice and Behavior, 20*, 315–395.

Harris, G., Rice, M., & Quinsey, V. (1994). Psychopathy as a taxon: Evidence that psychopaths are a discrete class. *Journal of Consulting and Clinical Psychology, 62*, 387–397.

Harris, G. T., Rice, M. E., & Quinsey, V. L. (1998). Appraisal and risk management of risk in sexual aggressors: Implications for criminal justice policy. *Psychology, Public Policy and the Law, 14*(2/1), 73–115.

Harrison, J. S., & Kirkpatrick, B. (2000). Polygraph testing and behavioral change with sex offenders in an outpatient setting: An exploratory study. *Polygraph, 29*, 6–19.

Hart, S. D. (2003). Actuarial risk assessment: Commentary on Berlin et al. *Sexual Abuse: A Journal of Research and Treatment, 15*(4), 383–388.

Heil, P., Ahlmeyer, S., McCullar, B., & McKee, B. (2000). Integration of polygraph testing with sexual offenders in the Colorado Department of Corrections. *Polygraph: Special Edition, Post-Conviction Sex Offender Testing, 29*(1), 26–35.

Heil, P., Ahlmeyer, S., & Simons, D. (2003). Cross-over sexual offense. *Sexual Abuse: A Journal of Research and Treatment, 15*(4), 221–236.

Heil, P., Simons, D., & English, K. (2004, October 22). *Cross-over sexual offenses disclosed by offenders found non-deceptive on the post-conviction polygraph examination.* Paper presented at the annual conference of the Association for the Treatment of Sexual Abusers, Albuquerque, NM.

Heilbrun, K., & Griffin, P. (1999). Forensic treatment: A review of programs and research. In R. Roesch, S. D. Hart, & J. R. P. Ogloff (Eds.), *Psychology and law: The state of the discipline* (pp. 241–374). New York: Kluwer.

Heilbrun, K., Hart, S., Hare, R., Gustafson, D., Nunez, C., & White, A. (1998) Inpatient and post-discharge aggression in mentally disordered offenders: The role of psychopathy. *Journal of Interpersonal Violence, 13,* 514–527.

Heim, N., & Hursch, C. J. (1977). Castration for sexual offenders: Treatment or punishment? A review and critique of recent European literature. *Archives of Sexual Behavior, 8,* 281–304.

Held, A. (1999). The civil commitment of sexual predators—Experience under Minnesota's law. In A. Schlank & F. Cohen (Eds.), *The sexual predator: Law, policy, evaluation, and treatment* (pp. 2-1–2-54). Kingston, NJ: Civic Research Institute.

Herman, J. L. (1992). *Trauma and recovery.* New York: Basic Books.

Hindelang, M. J. (1974). The Uniform Crime Reports revisited. *Journal of Criminal Justice, 1*(1), 1–18.

Hindelang, M. J., Hirschi, T., & Weis, J. (1981). *Measuring delinquency.* Newbury Park, CA: Sage.

Hitchcock, G. D. (1995). The efficacy of cognitive group therapy with incarcerated psychopaths. *Dissertation Abstracts International, 56(1-B).* (UMI No. 9514344).

Hoge, R., & Andrews, D. (1996). *The Youth Level of Service/Case Management Inventory (YLS/CMI).* Ottawa, Ontario, Canada: Carleton University.

Holmes, R. M., & Holmes, S. T. (1994). *Murder in America.* Thousand Oaks, CA: Sage.

Honts, C. R., Amato, S. L., & Gordon, G. K. (2001). Effects of spontaneous countermeasures used against the comparison question test, *Polygraph, 30,* 1–9.

Honts, C. R., Hodes, R. L., & Raskin, D. C. (1985). Effects of physical countermeasures on the physiological detection of deception. *Journal of Applied Psychology, 70,* 177–187.

Honts, C. R., Raskin, D. C., & Kircher, J. C. (1994). Mental and physical countermeasures and their electromyographic detection during polygraph tests for deception. *Journal of Psychophysiology, 1*, 241–247.

Honts, C. R., Raskin, D. C., Kircher, J. C., & Hodes, R. L. (1988). Effects of spontaneous countermeasures on the physiological detection of deception. *Journal of Police Science and Administration, 16*, 91–94.

Horney, J., & Marshall, I. H. (1991). Measuring lambda through self-reports. *Criminology, 29*, 471–496.

Hunter, J. A., Jr., & Becker, J. V. (1994). The role of deviant sexual arousal in juvenile sexual offending: Etiology, evaluation, and treatment. *Criminal Justice and Behavior, 21*(1), 132–149.

Hunter, J. A., Goodwin, D. W., & Becker, J. V. (1994). The relationship between phallometrically measured deviant sexual arousal and clinical characteristics in juvenile sexual offenders. *Behavior Research and Therapy, 32*(5), 533–538.

Janus, E. S. (2000). Sexual predator commitment laws: Lessons for law and the behavioral sciences. *Behavioral Sciences and the Law, 18*, 5–21.

Janus, E. S. (2004). Closing Pandora's box: Sexual predators and the politics of sexual violence. *Seton Hall Law Review, 34*(4), 1233–1253.

Janus, E. S., & Prentky, R. A. (2003). Forensic use of actuarial risk assessment with sex offenders: Accuracy, admissibility and accountability. *American Criminal Law Review, 40*(4), 1443–1499.

Janus, E. S., & Prentky, R. A. (2004). Forensic use of actuarial risk assessment: How a developing science can enhance accuracy and accountability. *Sex Offender Law Report, 5*(5), 55–56 & 62–63.

Janus, E. S., & Walbeck, N. H. (2000). Sex offender commitments in Minnesota: A descriptive study of second generation commitments. *Behavioral Sciences and the Law, 18*, 343–374.

Jenkins-Hall, K. (1994). Outpatient treatment of child molesters: Motivational factors and outcome. *Journal of Offender Rehabilitation, 21*, 139–150.

Jennings, J. L., & Sawyer, S. (2003). Principles and techniques for maximizing the effectiveness of group therapy with sex offenders. *Sexual Abuse: A Journal of Research and Treatment, 15*, 251–268.

Jurik, N. C., & Musheno, M. C. (1986). The internal crisis of corrections: Professionalization and the work environment. *Justice Quarterly, 3*(4), 457–480.

Kafka, M. P. (1991). Successful treatment of paraphilic coercive disorder (a rapist) with fluoxetine hydrochloride. *British Journal of Psychiatry, 158*, 844–847.

Kafka, M. P. (1994). Sertraline pharmacotherapy for paraphilias and paraphilia-related disorders: An open trial. *Annals of Clinical Psychiatry, 6*(3), 189–195.

Kafka, M. P. (1996). Therapy for sexual impulsivity: The paraphilias and paraphilia-related disorders. *Psychiatric Times, 13*(6). Available: *www.psychiatrictimes.com/p960627.html*.

Kafka, M. P. (2000).

Psychopharmacologic treatments for nonparaphilic compulsive sexual behaviors. *CNS Spectrums, 5*(1), 49–59.

Kafka, M. P., & Prentky, R. (1991a). Comparative study of non-paraphilic sexual addictions and paraphilias in men. *Journal of Clinical Psychiatry, 53*, 345–350.

Kafka, M. P., & Prentky, R. (1991b). Fluoxetine treatment of voyeurism. *American Journal of Psychiatry, 148*, 950.

Keiger, D. (1994). The dark world of Park Dietz. *Johns Hopkins Magazine.* (November) available at *www.jhu.edu/jhumag/1194web/dietz.html.*

Kiehl, K. A., Smith, A. M., Hare, R. D., & Liddle, P. F. (2000). An event-related potential investigation of response inhibition in schihzophrenia and psychopathy. *Biological Psychiatry, 48*, 210–221.

Kiernan, R. J., Mueller, J., & Langston, J. W. (2002). *COGNISTAT: Neurobehavioral Cognitive Status Exam* [Online]. Available: *www.parinc.com.*

Kilpatrick, D. G., Edmunds, C. N., & Seymour, A. K. (1992). *Rape in America: A report to the nation.* Charleston: National Victim Center and the University of South Carolina Medical Center.

Kindermann, C., Lynch, J., & Cantor, P. (1997). *National Crime Victimization Survey: Effects of the Redesign on Victimization Estimates* (NCJ-164381). Washington, DC: U.S. Department of Justice, Office of Justice Programs, Bureau of Justice Statistics.

Kitsuse, J. I., & Cicourel, A. V. (1963). A note on the uses of official statistics. *Social Problems, 2*(2), 131–139.

Knapp, M. (1996). Treatment of sex offenders. In K. English, S. Pullen, & L. Jones (Eds.), *Managing adult sex offenders: A containment approach* (pp. 13-1–13-15). Lexington, KY: American Probation and Parole Association.

Knight, R. (1998). *Using a new computerized developmental inventory to examine the family and early behavioral antecedents of sexual coercion.* Paper presented at the meeting of the Association for the Treatment of Sexual Abusers, Vancouver, British Columbia, Canada.

Knight, R. (2005, April). *Assessing adults who sexually offend: Using the Multidimensional Inventory of Development, Sex and Aggression (MIDSA).* Paper presented at the seventh annual Joint Conference on Sex Offense-Specific Assessment, Treamtent and Safe Management of Children, Adolescents and Adults, Marlborough, MA.

Knight, R. A., & Prentky, R. A. (1993). Exploring characteristics for classifying juvenile sex offenders. In H. E. Barbaree, W. L. Marshall, & S. M. Hudson (Eds.), *The juvenile sex offender* (pp. 45–83). New York: Guilford Press.

Knopp, F. H., Stevenson, W. F., & Freeman-Longo, R. E. (1992). *Nationwide Survey of Adolescent and Adult Sex Offender Treatment Programs and Models.* Orwell, VT: Safer Society Press.

Kong, S. K., Thompson, L. L., Iverson, G. L., & Heaton, R. K. (1993). *Wisconsin Card Sorting Test—64 card version* [Online]. Available: *www.parinc.com.*

Kosson, D., Cyterski, T., Steuerwald, B.,

Neumann, C., & Walker-Matthews, S. (2002). The reliability and validity of the psychopathy checklist: Youth version (PCL:YV) in nonincarcerated adolescent males. *Psychological Assessment, 14*(1), 97–109.

Kozlowski, K. (2001). In the wake of *Hendricks*—States seem "committed" to SVP programs. In A. Schlank & F. Cohen (Eds.), *The sexual predator: Law, policy, evaluation, and treatment* (pp. 4-1–4-24). Kingston, NJ: Civic Research Institute.

Krapohl, D. J., & Stern, B. A. (2003). Principles of multiple-issue polygraph screening: A model for applicant, post-conviction offender, and counterintelligence testing. *Polygraph, 30,* 201–210.

Krauth, A. A. (1998). A comparative study of male juvenile sex offenders. *Dissertation Abstracts International: Section B: The Sciences and Engineering, 58,* 44–55.

Kravitz, H., Haywood, T., Kelly, J., Liles, S., & Cavanaugh, J. (1996). Medroxyprogesterone and paraphiles: Do testosterone levels matter? *Bulletin of the American Academy of Psychiatry and the Law, 24*(1), 73–83.

Kravitz, H., Haywood, T., Kelly, J., Wahlstrom, C., Liles, S., & Cavanaugh, J. (1995). Medroxyprogesterone treatment for paraphiliacs. *Bulletin of the American Academy of Psychiatry and the Law, 23*(1), 19–33.

Krueger, R. B., & Kaplan, M. S., (2001). Depot-leuprolide acetate for treatment of paraphilias: A report of twelve cases. *Archives of Sexual Behavior, 30*(4), 409–422.

Krynicki, V. (1978). Cerebral dysfunction in repetitively assaultive adoles-cents. *Journal of Nervous and Mental Disease, 166,* 59–67.

La Fond, J. Q. (2003). The costs of enacting a sexual predator law and rec-ommendations for keeping them from skyrocketing. In B. J. Winick & J. Q. La Fond (Eds.), *Protecting society from sex-ually dangerous offenders: Law, justice and therapy* (pp. 283–300). Washington, DC: American Psychological Association.

La Fond, J. (2005). *Preventing sexual violence: How society should cope with sex offenders.* Washington, DC: American Psychological Association.

Lalumière, M. L., Quinsey, V. L., Harris, G. T., Rice, M. E., & Trautrimas, C. (2003). Are rapists differentially aroused by coercive sex in phallometric assess-ments? In R. A. Prentky, E. S. Janus, & M. C. Seto (Eds.), *Understanding and managing sexually coercive behavior* (Vol. 989, pp. 211–224). New York: Annals of the New York Academy of Sciences.

Lamb, S., & Edgar-Smith, S. (1994). Aspects of disclosure: Mediators of outcome in childhood sexual abuse. *Journal of Interpsonal Violence, 9,* 307–326.

Lang, R. A. (1993). Neuropsychological deficits in sexual offenders: Implications for treatment. *Sexual and Marital Therapy, 6*(2), 181–200.

Langan, P. A., Schmitt, E. L., & Durose, M. R. (2003, November). *Recidivism of sex offenders released from prison in 1994* (NCJ 198281). Washington, DC: U.S. Department of Justice, Office of Justice Programs, Bureau of Justice Statistics,

Langeluddeke, A. (1963). *Die*

Entmannung von Sittlichkeitsverbrecher. Berlin, Germany: Aldine de Gruyter.

Langevin, R., Ben-Aron, M., Wortzman, G., Dickey, R., & Handy, L. (1987). Brain damage, diagnosis, and substance abuse among violent offenders. *Behavioral Sciences and the Law, 5*(1), 77–94.

Langevin, R., & Lang, R. A. (1990). Substance abuse among sex offenders, *Annals of Sex Research, 3*, 397–424.

Langstrom, N., Sjotedt, G., & Grann, M. (2004). Psychiatric disorders and recidivism in sexual offenders. *Sexual Abuse: A Journal of Research and Treatment, 16*(2), 139–150.

Langton, C. M. (2003). *Contrasting approaches to risk assessment with adult male sexual offenders: An evaluation of recidivism prediction schemes and the utility of supplementary clinical information for enhancing predictive accuracy.* Unpublished doctoral thesis, University of Toronto, Toronto, Ontario, Canada.

Larivière, M., & Robinson, D. (1996). *Attitudes of correctional officers towards offenders (Executive summary).* Toronto, Ontario, Canada: Price Waterhouse.

Laschet, U., & Laschet, L. (1971) Psychopharmacotherapy of sex offenders with cyproterone acetate. *Pharmacopsychiatric and Neuropsychopharmacological Advances in Clinical Research, 4*, 99–110.

Laschet, U., & Laschet, L. (1975) Antiandrogens in the treatment of sexual deviations in men. *Journal of Steroid Biochemistry, 6*(6), 821–826.

Levenson, J. S., & Macgowan, M. J. (2004). Engagement, denial, and treatment progress among sex offenders in group therapy. *Sexual Abuse: A Journal of Research and Treatment, 16*, 49–63.

Lezak, M. D. (1982). The problem of assessing executive functions. *International Journal of Psychology. 17*, 281–297.

Lieb, R. (2003). After *Hendricks*: Defining constitutional treatment for Washington State's civil commitment program. *Annals of the New York Academy of Science, 989*(1), 474–488.

Liebling, A. (2003). *Moral values, prison performance and the problem of quality: A summary and discussion paper.* Cambridge, UK: Institute of Criminology.

Link, B. G., & Phelan, J.C. (1999). The labeling theory of mental disorder (II): The consequences of labeling. In A. V. Horwitz & T. L. Scheid (Eds.), *A handbook for the study of mental health: Social contexts, theories, and systems* (pp. 361–376). New York: Cambridge University Press.

Link, B. G., Phelan, J. C. Bresnahan, M., Stueve, A., & Pescosolido, B. A. (1999). Public concepts of mental illness: Labels, causes, dangerousness, and social distance. *American Journal of Public Health, 89*(9), 1328–1333.

Lishman, M. (1968). Brain damage in relation to psychiatric disability after head injury. *British Journal of Psychiatry, 114*(509), 373–410.

Lloyd, M. D., & Grove, W. M. (2002). *The uselessness of the Minnesota Sex Offender Screening Tool—Revised (MnSOST-R) in commitment decisions.* Manuscript submitted for publication.

Looman, J., Abracen, J., Sern, R. &

Marquis, P. (2005). Psychopathy, treatment change and recidivism in high risk sexual offenders. *Journal of Interpersonal Violence, 20*(5), 549–568.

Loving, J. L. (2002). Treatment planning with the Psychopathy Checklist—Revised. *International Journal of Offender Therapy and Comparative Criminology, 46*(3), 281–293.

Lowden, K., Hetz, N., Patrick, D., Pasini-Hill, D., Harrison, L., & English, K. (2003). *Evaluation of Colorado's prison therapeutic community for sex offenders: A report of findings.* Denver: Colorado Department of Public Safety, Division of Criminal Justice, Office of Research and Statistics.

Lund, C. A. (2000). Predictors of sexual recidivism: Did meta-analysis clarify the role and relevance of denial? *Sexual Abuse: A Journal of Research and Treatment, 12*, 275–288.

Madigan, L. (2005). Madigan unveils lifetime supervision for sex offenders [Illinois Attorney General's press release]. Available: *www.illinoisattorney-general.gov/pressroom/2005_02/20050214c.html.*

Mainwaring, J. P. (1977). Modes of action of antiandrogens: A survey. In L. Martini & M. Motta (Eds.), *Androgens and antiandrogens* (pp. 151–161). New York: Raven Press.

Maletzky, B. M. (1991). *Treating the sexual offender.* Newbury Park, CA: Sage.

Maltz, M. D. (1977). Crime statistics in a historical perspective. *Crime and Delinquency, 23*, 32–40.

Maltz, M. D. (1999). *Bridging gaps in police crime data* (NCJ-176365). Washington, DC: Bureau of Justice Statistics, Office of Justice Programs, U.S. Department of Justice.

Mande, M., & English, K. (1988). *Crime rates of Colorado prisoners* (Report to the National Institue of Justice, Grant No. 84IJCX0034). Denver: Colorado Department of Public Safety, Division of Criminal Justice, Office of Research and Statistics.

Marcus, D. K., John, S., & Edens, J. F. (2004). A taxometric analysis of psychopathy. *Journal of Abnormal Psychology, 113*, 626–635.

Marlatt, G. A. (1983). *Relapse prevention: Maintenance strategies in the treatment of addictive behaviors.* New York: Guilford Press.

Marlatt, G. A., & Rohsenow, D. J. (1980). Cognitive processes in alcohol use: Expectancy and the balanced placebo design. In N. K. Mello (Ed.), *Advances in substance abuse: Behavioral and biological research* (Vol. 1, pp.159–199). Greenwich, CT: JAI Press.

Marques, J. K. (1994, December 13). *First, preliminary report of the Special Master.*

Marques, J. K. (1995, February 13). *Second report of the Special Master,* Turay v. Weston.

Marques, J. K. (1995, April 13). *Third report of the Special Master,* Turay v. Weston.

Marques, J. K. (1995, June 13). *Fourth report of the Special Master,* Turay v. Weston.

Marques, J. K. (1995, August 14). *Fifth report of the Special Master,* Turay v. Weston.

Marques, J. K. (1995, November 13).

Sixth report of the Special Master, Turay v. Weston.

Marques, J. K. (1996, January 15). *Seventh report of the Special Master,* Turay v. Weston.

Marques, J. K. (1996, May 30). *Eighth report of the Special Master,* Turay v. Weston.

Marques, J. K. (1996, July 30). *Ninth report of the Special Master,* Turay v. Weston.

Marques, J. K. (1997, January 5). *Tenth report of the Special Master,* Turay v. Weston.

Marques, J. K. (1997, May 2). *Eleventh report of the Special Master,* Turay v. Weston.

Marques, J. K. (1997, September 12). *Twelfth report of the Special Master,* Turay v. Seling.

Marques, J. K. (1998, May 1). *Thirteenth report of the Special Master,* Turay v. Seling.

Marques, J. K. (1998, September 25). *Fourteenth report of the Special Master,* Turay v. Seling.

Marques, J. K. (1999, May 6). *Fifteenth report of the Special Master,* Turay v. Seling.

Marques, J. K. (1999). How to answer the question, Does sex offender treatment work? *Journal of Interpersonal Violence, 14*(4), 437–451.

Marques, J. K. (1999, September 9). *Sixteenth report of the Special Master,* Turay v. Seling.

Marques, J. K. (2000, April 11). *Seventeenth report of the Special Master,* Turay v. Seling.

Marques, J. K. (2000, November 27). *Eighteenth report of the Special Master,* Turay v. Seling.

Marques, J. K. (2001, June 25). *Nineteenth report of the Special Master,* Turay v. Seling.

Marques, J. K. (2001). Professional standards for civil commitment programs. In A. Schlank (Ed.), *The sexual predator: Legal issues, clinical issues, special populations* (pp. 2-1–2-15). Kingston, NJ: Civic Research Institute.

Marques, J. K., Day, D. M., Nelson, C., Miner, M., & West, M. A. (1992). Effects of cognitive behavioral treatment on sex offender recidivism: Preliminary results of a longitudinal study. *Criminal Justice and Behavior, 21,* 28–54.

Marques, J. K., Wiederanders, M., Day, D. M., Nelson, C., & van Ommeren, A. (2005). Effects of a relapse prevention program on sexual recidivism: Final results from California's Sex Offender Treatment and Evaluation Project (SOTEP). *Sexual Abuse: A Journal of Research and Treatment, 17*(1), 79–107.

Marshall, W. L., & Barbaree, H. E. (1995). *Heterogeneity in the erectile response patterns of rapists and nonoffenders.* Unpublished manuscript, Queen's University, Kingston, Ontario, Canada.

Marshall, W. L., Laws, D. R., & Barbaree, H. E. (1900). *The handbook of sexual assault: Issues, theories, and treatment of the offender.* New York: Plenum Press.

Marshall, W. L., & Pithers, W. D. (1994). A reconsideration of treatment outcome with sex offenders. *Criminal Justice and Behavior, 21*(1), 10–27.

Marshall, W. L., Thornton, D., Marshall, L. E., Fernandez, Y., & Mann, R. (2001). Treatment of sexual offenders who are in categorical denial: A pilot project. *Journal of Research and Treatment, 13*(3), 205–215.

Mazmanian, D. A., & Sabatier, P. A. (1989). *Implementation and public policy; with a new postscript.* Lanham, MD: University Press of America.

McGrath, R. J., Livingston, J., & Cumming, G. F. (2002). *Development of a treatment needs and progress scale for adult sex offenders.* Washington, DC: U.S. Department of Justice, Office of Justice Programs.

McGrath, R. J., Hoke, S. E., Livingston, S. A., & Cumming, G. (2001). *The Vermont Assessment of Sex-Offender Risk (VASOR): An initial reliability and validity study.* Paper presented at the 20th annual conference of the Association for the Treatment of Sexual Abusers, San Antonio, TX.

McGuire, J. (Ed.). (2002). *Offender rehabilitation and treatment-effective programs and policies to reduce re-offending.* London: Wiley.

Mee-Lee, D. (1995). Matching in addictions treatment: How do we get there from here? *Alcoholism Treatment Quarterly Special Issue: Treatment of the Addictions—Applications of Outcome Research for Clinical Management, 12,* 113–127.

Meloy, J. R. (2002). Normative attachment and object relations theory. In J. R. Meloy (Ed.), *Violent attachments* (pp. 3–18). Northvale, NJ: Jason Aronson.

Meyer, G. J., Finn, S. E., Eyde, L. D., Kay, G. G., Moreland, K. L., Dies, R. R.,

et al. (2001). Psychological testing and psychological assessment. *American Psychologist, 56*(2), 128–165.

Michaels, A. (2001). *Executive functioning* [Online]. Available: *www.aspennj.org/executive.html.*

Miller, G. (1994). *Substance Abuse Subtle Screening Inventory (SASSI-3).* Available: 1-88-297-2774.

Miller, H. A., Amenta, A. E., & Conroy, M. A. (2005). Sexually violent predator evaluations: Empirical evidence, strategies for professionals, and research directions. *Law and Human Behavior, 29,* 29–54.

Miller, S., & Duncan, B. (2004). *The heart and soul of change; What works in therapy.* Washington, DC: American Psychological Association.

Milloy, C. (2003). *Six-year follow-up of released sex offenders recommended for commitment under Washington's Sexually Violent Predator law where no petition was filed.* Olympia: Washington State Institute for Public Policy.

Mindes, P. (1995–1996). Tuberculosis quarantine: A review of legal issues in Ohio and other states. *Journal of Law and Health, 10*(2), 403–423.

Miner, M. H. (1997). How can we conduct treatment outcome research? *Sexual Abuse: A Journal of Research and Treatment, 9*(2), 95–110.

Miner, M. H. (2000). Competency-based Assessment. In D. R. Laws, S. M. Hudson, & T. Ward (Eds.), *Remaking relapse prevention with sex offenders: A sourcebook* (pp. 213–224). Thousand Oaks, CA: Sage.

Minnesota Department of Corrections.

(1999). *Civil Commitment Study Group 1998 report to the legislature.* St. Paul, MN: Author.

Moore, M. H. (1986). Purblind justice: Normative issues in the use of prediction in the criminal justice system. In A. Blumstein, J. Cohen, J. A. Roth, & C. A. Visher (Eds.), *Criminal careers and "career criminals"* (Vol. 2, pp. 314–355). Washington, DC: National Academies Press.

Morse, S. J. (1998). Fear of danger, flight from culpability. *Psychology, Public Policy, and Law, 4,* 25–54.

Mulvey, E. P., & Fardella, J. (2000, November/December). Are the mentally ill really Violent? *Psychology Today, 39,* 51.

Murray, H. A. (1971). *Thematic Apperception Test* [Online]. Available: *www.pearson assessments.com.* (Original work published 1943)

Nagayama-Hall, G. C. (1995). Sexual offender recidivism revisited: A meta-analysis of recent treatment studies. *Journal of Consulting and Clinical Psychology, 63,* 802–809.

National Association of State Mental Health Program Directors. (1997). *Position statement on laws providing for the civil commitment of sexually violent criminal offenders.* Available: *www.nasmhpd.org/general_files/position_statement/sexpred.htm.*

National Research Council. (2003). *The polygraph and lie detection. Committee to review the scientific evidence on the polygraph.* Washington, DC: Division of Behavioral and Social Sciences and Education, National Academy of Sciences Press.

National Resource Center on Child Sexual Abuse. (1994). *Statistics in child abuse.* Huntsville, AL: Author.

National Task Force on Juvenile Sexual Offending. (1988). The preliminary report. *Juvenile and Family Court Journal, 39*(2).

National Task Force on Juvenile Sexual Offending. (1993). The revised report from the National Task Force on juvenile sexual offending. *Juvenile and Family Court Journal, 44*(4).

Neidigh, L., & Tomiko, R. (1991). The coping strategies of sexual abusers. *Journal of Sex Education and Therapy, 17,* 103–110.

Nelson, C. (1998). *Consultation report: Special Commitment Center,* Turay v. Seling.

New York Civil Liberties Union. (n.d.). *Legislative memo: Civil commitment of "sexually violent predators.* Available: *www.nyclu.org/violent_off.html.*

Nicholaichuk, T., Templeman, T. L., & Gu, D. (1999, May). *Empirically based screening for sex offender risk.* Paper presented at the conference of the Correctional Services of Canada, Ottawa, Ontario.

Nuffield, J. (1982). *Parole decision making in Canada: Research towards decision guidelines.* Ottawa, Ontario: Solicitor General of Canada.

Oakes, L. (2004). Sex offender continues crime from custody. *Star Tribune,* Dec. 13, 2004.

O'Connell, M. A. (1998). Using polygraph testing to assess deviant sexual history of sex offenders (UMI 48106). *Dissertation Abstracts International, 49.*

Ogloff, J., Wong, S. & Greenwood, A. (1990). Treating criminal psychopaths in a therapeutic community program. *Behavioral Sciences and the Law, 8,* 81–90.

Oregon Juvenile Sex Offender Task Force. (1986). *An executive summary of the Oregon Report on Juvenile Offenders.* Salem, OR: Children's Services Division, Department of Human Resources.

Otto, R. K., & Petrila, J. (2002). Admissibility of testimony based on actuarial scales in sex offender commitments: A reply to Doren. *Sex Offender Law Report, 3*(1), 1, 14–16.

Ozer, D. J. (1985). Correlation and the coefficient of determination. *Psychological Bulletin, 97,* 307–315.

Paboojian, A., & Teske, R. H. C. (1997). Pre-service correctional officers: What do They think about treatment? *Journal of Criminal Justice, 25*(5), 425–433.

Patrick, C. J., & Iacono, W.G. (1989). Psychopathy, threat and polygraph test accuracy. *Journal of Applied Psychology, 74,* 347–355.

Petersilia, J. R. (1977). *The validity of criminality data derived from personal interviews.* Santa Monica, CA: Rand Corporation.

Petersilia, J., Greenwood, P., & Lavin, M. (1977). *Criminal careers of habitual felons.* Santa Monica, CA: Rand Corporation.

Peterson, M. A. (1978). *The Rand Habitual Offender Project: Summary of research findings to date* (P-5957). Santa Monica, CA: Rand Corporation.

Peterson, M. A., & Braiker, H. B.

(1980). *Doing crime: A survey of California prison inmates.* Santa Monica, CA: Rand Corporation.

Petrila, J., & Otto, R. K. (2001). Issues in admissibility of expert testimony in sexually violent predator evaluations. In A. Schlank (Ed.), *The sexual predator: Legal issues, clinical issues, and special populations* (pp. 3-1–3-25). Kingston, NJ: Civic Research Institute.

Plum, W. (2001). Sex offender and chemical dependency treatment. In A. Schlank (Ed.), *The sexual predator* (pp. 14-1–14-11). Kingston, NJ: Civic Research Institute.

Poole, E. D., & Regoli, R. M. (1980). Role stress, custody orientation, and disciplinary actions: A study of prison guards. *Criminology, 18*(2), 215–226.

Prendergrast, M. L., Farabee, D., Cartier, J., & Henkin, S. (2002). Involuntary treatment within a prison setting: Impact on psychosocial change during treatment. *Criminal Justice and Behavior, 29*(1), 5–26.

Prentky, R. A. (2003). A 15-year retrospective on sexual coercion: Advancements and projections. *Annals of the New York Academy of Sciences, 989,* 13–31.

Prentky, R. A., & Burgess, A. W. (2000). *Forensic management of sexual offenders.* New York: Kluwer/Plenum Press.

Prentky, R., Harris, B., Frizzell, K., & Righthand, S. (2000). An actuarial procedure for assessing risk with juvenile sex offenders. *Sexual Abuse: A Journal of Research and Treatment, 12*(2), 71–93.

Prentky, R. A., Lee, A. F. S., Knight, R. A., & Cerce, D. (1997). Recidivism rates among child molesters and rapists: A methodological anlaysis. *Law and Human Behavior, 21*, 635–659.

Prochaska, J., & DiClemente, C. (1994) *The transtheoretical approach: Crossing traditional boundaries.* Melbourne, FL: Krieger.

Quinsey, V. L. (1992). *Review of the Washington State Special Commitment Center program for sexually violent predator* (appendix to *Review of sexual predator program: Community Protection Research Project*). Olympia: Washington State Institute for Public Policy.

Quinsey, V. L. (2000, March). *The Violence Risk Appraisal Guide.* Paper presented at Sinclair Seminars' Sex Offender Re-Offense Risk Prediction Symposium, Madison, Wisconsin. Available: *www.sinclairseminars.com.*

Quinsey, V. L., Harris, G. T., Rice, M. E., & Cormier, C. A. (1998). *Violent offenders: Appraising and managing risk.* Washington, DC: American Psychological Association.

Quinsey, V. L., Khanna, A., & Malcolm, B. (1998). A retrospective evaluation of teh Regional Treatment Centre Sex Offender Programme. *Journal of Interpersonal Violence, 13*, 21–644.

Rainey, J. (2000, August 3, 2000). Coalinga gets its wish. *Los Angeles Times,* p. A3.

Raskin, D. C., Barland, G. H., & Podlesny, I. A. (1977). Validity and reliability of detection of deception. *Polygraph, 6*, 1–39.

Raskin, D. C., & Hare, R. D. (1978). Psychopathy and detection of deception in a prison population. *Psychophysiology, 15*, 126–135.

Regestein, Q. R., & Reich, P. (1978) Pedophilia occurring after onset of cognitive impairment. *Journal of Nervous and Mental Disease, 166*, 794–798.

Reid, W. H., & Gacono, C. (2000) Treatment of antisocial personality, psychopathy, and other characterologic antisocial syndromes. *Behavioral Sciences and the Law, 18,* 647–662.

Reilly, D., Delva, N., & Hudson, R. (2000). Protocols for the use of cyproterone, medroxyprogesterone, and leuprolide in the treatment of paraphilia. *Canadian Journal of Psychiatry, 45*, 559–563.

Reisner, R., Slobogin, C., & Rai, A. (1999*). Law and the mental health system: Civil and criminal aspects.* New York: West Group.

Reiss, D., Quayle, M., Brett, T., & Meux, C. (1998). Dramatherapy for mentally disordered offenders: changes in levels of anger. *Criminal Behaviour and Mental Health, 8*, 139–153.

Rice, M. E., & Harris, G. T. (1997). Cross-validation and extension of the violence risk appraisal guide for child molesters and rapists. *Law and Human Behavior, 21,* 231–241.

Rice, M. E., & Harris, G. T. (2003). The size and sign of treatment effects in sex offender therapy. *Annals of the New York Academy of Sciences, 989,* 428–440.

Rice, M. E., & Harris, G. T. (2003). What we know and don't know about treating adult sex offenders. In B. J. Winick & J. Q. Lafond (Eds.), *Protecting society from sexually danger-*

ous offenders: Law, justice and therapy (pp. 101–118). Washington, DC: American Psychological Association.

Rice, M. E., Harris, T. T., & Cormier, C. A. (1992). An evaluation of a maximum security therapeutic community for psychopaths and other mentally disordered offenders. *Law and Human Behavior, 16*, 399–412.

Rich, P. (2003). *Understanding, assessing, and rehabilitating juvenile sexual offenders.* Hoboken, NJ: Wiley.

Righthand, S., & Welch, C. (2001). *Juveniles who have sexually offended: A review of the professional literature.* Washington, DC: U.S. Department of Justice.

Robinson, D., Porporino, F. J., & Simourd, L. (1993). The influence of career orientation on support for rehabilitation among correctional staff. *Prison Journal, 73*, 162–177.

Roesler, T. A., & Wind, W. T. (1994). Telling the secret: Adult women describe their disclosure of incest. *Journal of Interpersonal Violence, 9*, 307–326.

Rosenfeld, J., & Webber, J. R. (2000). *The neuroscience of addiction.* Paper presented at the annual conference of the Illinois Alcohol and Other Drug Abuse Professional Certification Association, Arlington Heights.

Rosler, A., & Witztum, E. (1998) Treatment of men with paraphilia with a long-acting analogue of gonadotropin releasing hormone. *New England Journal of Medicine, 338*(7), 416–422.

Rosler, A., & Witztum, E. (2000) Pharmacotherapy of paraphilias in the next millenium. *Behavioral Sciences and the Law, 18*, 43–56.

Rothstein, B. (2003, February 26). *Findings of fact, conclusions of law, and order re: hearing held December 13 and 16, 2002). Richard G. Turay, Plaintiff v. Mark Seling et al., Defendants*, No. C91-664R. *Jerry R. Sharp et al., Plaintiffs v. David B. Weston et al.*, Defendants, No. C94-121R. *Randy Pederson et al., Plaintiffs v. Tim Hill et al., Defendants*, No. C94-211R. *John F. Hall et al., Plaintiffs v. Lyle Quasim, et al., Defendants*, No. C95-1111R.

Russell, D. E. H. (1986). *The secret trauma: Incest in the lives of girls and women.* New York: Basic Books.

Saleh, F. M., Niel, T. & Fishman, M. J. (2004). Treatment of paraphilia in young adults with leuprolide acetate: A preliminary case report series. *Journal of Forensic Science, 49*(6). Available: *www.astm.org.*

Salekin, R. T. (2002). Psychopathy and therapeutic pessimism: Clinical lore or clinical reality? *Clinical Psychology Review, 22,* 79–112.

Sarker, S. P. (2003). From *Hendricks* to *Crane:* The sexually violent predator trilogy and the inchoate jurisprudence of the U.S. Supreme Court. *Journal of the American Academy of Psychiatry and the Law, 31*(2), 242–248.

Schlank, A. (1987). *Improving schizophrenic inpatients' problem solving skills: A cognitive-behavioral approach.* Unpublished research-other-than-thesis project submitted in partial fulfillment of a Ph.D. in clinical psychology, University of Nebraska-Lincoln.

Schlank, A. (1998). *Consultation report: Special Commitment Center,* Turay v. Seling.

Schlank, A., & Harry, R. (2003). The

treatment of the civilly committed sex offender in Minnesota: A review of the past ten years. *William Mitchell Law Review, 29*(4), 1221–1239.

Schlank, A., Harry, R., & Farnsworth, M. (1999). The Minnesota Sex Offender Program. In A. Schlank & F. Cohen (Eds.), *The sexual predator: Legal issues, commitment proceedings, evaluation and treatment* (pp. 10-1–10-18). Kingston, NJ: Civic Research Institute.

Schneider, S. L., & Wright, R. C. (2004) Understanding denial in sexual offenders: A review of cognitive and motivational processes to avoid responsibility. *Trauma, Violence and Abuse, 5*, 3–20.

Schmauk, F. J. (1970). Punishment, arousal and avoidance learning in sociopaths, *Journal of Abnormal Psychology, 76*, 325.

Schopp, R. F., & Slain, A. J. (2000). Psychopathy, criminal responsibility, and civil commitment as a sexual predator. *Behavioral Sciences and the Law, 18*(2–3), 247–274.

Schwartz, B. K. (1995). Group therapy. In B. K. Schwartz & H. R. Cellini (Eds.), *The sex offender: Corrections, treatment, and legal practice* (pp. 14-1–14-16). Kingston, NJ: Civic Research Institute.

Schwartz, B. (1999). The case against involuntary commitment. In A. Schlank & F. Cohen (Eds.), *The sexual predator: Law, policy, evaluation, and treatment* (pp. 4-1–4-22). Kingston, NJ: Civic Research Institute.

Scott, M. L., Cole, J. K., McKay, S. E., Golden, C. J., & Liggett, K. R. (1984). Neuropsychological performance of sexual assaulters and pedophiles. *Journal of Forensic Sciences, 29*, 1114–1118.

Sellin, T., & Wolfgang, M. (1964). *The measurement of delinquency*. New York: Wiley.

Serin, R. C., & Mailloux, D. L. (2003). Assessment of sex offenders: Lessons learned from the assessment of non-sex offenders. *Annals of the New York Academy of Sciences, 989*, 185–197.

Seto, M. C. (2003). Interpreting the treatment performance of sex offenders. In A. Matravers (Ed.), (2003). *Sex offenders in the community: Managing and reducing the risks.* Portland, OR: Willian.

Seto, M. C., & Barbaree, H. E. (1999). Psychopathy, treatment behavior, and sex offender recidivism. *Journal of Interpersonal Violence, 14*(12), 1235–1248.

Seto, M. C., & Barbaree, H. E. (2003). *Psychopathy, treatment behavior, and recidivism: An extended follow-up of Seto and Barbaree (1999).* Manuscript submitted for publication.

Seto, M., Lalumière, M., & Blanchard, R. (2000). The discriminative validity of a phallometric test for pedophilic interests among adolescent sex offenders against children. *Psychological Assessment, 12*(3), 319–327.

Shaw, T., & Funderburk, J. R. (1999). Civil commitment of sex offenders as therapeutic jurisprudence—A rational approach to community protection. In A. Schlank & F. Cohen (Eds.), *The sexual predator: Law, policy, evaluation, and treatment* (pp. 5-1–5-8). Kingston, NJ: Civic Research Institute.

Shaw, T., Heesacker, A., & Delgado-Romero, E. (2001). Implications of sexually violent predator laws for youthful offenders. In A. Schlank (Ed.), *The sexu-*

al predator (pp. 12-1–12-10). Kingston, NJ: Civic Research Institute.

Shipley, W. C., & Zachary, R. A. (1986). *Shipley Institute of Living Scale* [Online]. Available: *www.wpspublish.com.* (Original work published 1940)

Shuman, D. W., Greenberg, S., Heilbrun, K., & Foote, W. E. (1998). Special perspective an immodest proposal: Should treating mental health professionals be barred from testifying about their patients? *Behavioral Sciences and the Law, 16*, 509–523.

Silverstein, S. M., Hitzel, H., & Schenkel, L. (1998). Rehab rounds: Identifying and addressing cognitive barriers to rehabilitation readiness. *Psychiatric Services, 49*, 34–36.

Simpson, D. D., & Knight, K., (1998). *TCU data collection forms for correctional residential treatment.* Fort Worth: Texas Christian University, Institute of Behavioral Research.

Sims-Knight, J., Knight, R., Schatzel, E., & Daversa, M. (2004). *Using the MIDSA to assess juvenile sexual offenders.* Paper presented at the annual conference of the Association for the Treatment of Sexual Abusers, Albuquerque, NM.

Smith, D. W., Letourneau, E. J., Saunders, B. E., Kilpatrick, D. G., Resnick, H. S., & Best, C. (2000). Delay in disclosure of childhood rape: Results from a national survey. *Child Abuse and Neglect, 24*, 273–287.

Smith, W. R., & Monastersky, C. (1986). Assessing juvenile sex offenders' risk for reoffending. *Criminal Justice and Behavior, 13*, 115–140.

Snyder, H. (2000). *Sexual assault of young children as reported to law enforcement: Victim, incident, and offender characteristics.* Washington, DC: U.S. Department of Justice, Bureau of Justice Statistics.

Sowell, E. R., & Peterson, B. S. (2003). Mapping cortical change across the human life span. *Nature Neuroscience, 6*, 309–315.

Spaulding, W., Fleming, S. K., Reed, D., Sullivan, M. Storzbach, D., & Lam, M. (1999). Cognitive functioning in schizophrenia: Implications for psychiatric rehabilitation. *Schizophrenia Bulletin, 25*, 275–289.

Spellacy, F. (1977). Neuropsychological differences between violent and nonviolent adolescents. *Journal of Clinical Psychology, 23*, 965–969.

Steering Committee of the Physicians' Heath Study Research Group. (1988). Preliminary report: Findings from the aspirin component of the ongoing physicians' health study. *New England Journal of Medicine, 318*, 262–264.

Stein, D. J., Hollander, E., Anthony, D. T., Schneider, F. R., Fallon, B. A., & Liebowitz, M. R. (1992). Serotonergic medications for sexual obsessions, sexual addictions and paraphilias. *Journal of Clinical Psychiatry, 453*, 267–271.

Stern, B. A., & Krapohl, D. J. (2004). The efficacy of detecting deception in psychopaths using a polygraph. *Polygraph, 33*, 201–213.

Stone, M. H., & Thompson, E. H. (2001). Executive function impairment in sexual offenders. *Journal of Individual Psychology, 57*(1).

Stripe, T. S., Wilson, R. J., & Long, C.

(2001). Goal attainment scaling with sexual offenders: A measure of clinical impact at post-treatment and at community follow-up. *Sexual Abuse: A Journal of Research and Treatment, 13*, 65–77.

Summit on the treatment of the sexually violent predator. (2000). Meeting sponsored by the Sand Ridge Treatment Center, Oshkosh, WI.

Tarter, R. E., Hegedus, A. M., Alterman, A. I., & Katz-Garris, L. (1983). Cognitive capacities of juvenile violent, nonviolent and sexual offenders. *Journal of Nervous and Mental Disease, 171*, 564–567.

Tellier, C., & Robinson, D. (1995). *Correlates of job stress among front-line correctional staff.* Paper presented at the annual convention of the Canadian Psychological Association, Charlottetown, PEI.

Tellier, C., & Serin, R. C. (2001). *The role of staff in effective program delivery* (Compendium 2000, vol. 1). Ottawa, Ontario: Correctional Service of Canada.

Tjaden, P., & Thoennes, N. (2000, July). *Extent, nature and consequences of intimate partner violence* (NCJ Publication No. 181867). Washington, DC: U.S. Department of Justice, Office of Justice Programs.

Tjaden, P., & Thoennes, N. (2000, November). *Full report of the prevalence, incidence, and consequences of violence against women: Findings from the National Violence Against Women Survey* (NCJ Publication No. 183781). Washington, DC: U.S. Department of Justice, Office of Justice Programs.

Tonry, M. (1999). Reconsidering indeterminate and structured sentencing. *Sentencing and corrections* (Vol. 2).

Available: *www.msccsp.org/ resources/reconsidering.pdf.*

Trivits, L., & Reppucci, N. (2002). Application of Megan's Law to juveniles. *American Psychologist, 57*(9), 690–704.

Vaillant, G. (1983). *The natural history of alcoholism: Causes, patterns and paths to recovery.* Cambridge MA: Harvard University Press.

Valliere, V. M. (1997). Relationships between alcohol use, alcohol expectancies, and sexual offenses in convicted offenders. In B. K. Schwartz & H. R. Cellini (Eds.), *The sex offender: New insights, treatment interventions, and legal developments* (pp. 3-1–3-14). Kingston NJ: Civic Research Institute.

Veneziano, C., & Veneziano, L. (2002). Adolescent sex offenders: A review of the literature. *Trauma, Violence and Abuse, 3*(4), 247–260.

Vogel, V. de, Ruiter, C. de, Beek, D. van, & Mead, G.(2004). Predictive validity of the SVR-20 and the Static-99 in a Dutch sample of treated sex offenders. *Law and Human Behavior, 28*(3), 235–251.

Walker, P. A., & Meyer, W. J. (1981). Medroxyprogesterone acetate treatment for paraphiliac sex offenders. In J. R. Hayes, T. K. Roberts, & K. S. Solway (Eds.), *Violence and the violent individual* (pp. 353–373). New York: SP Medical and Scientific Books.

Washington Department of Social and Health Services. (2000). *Special commitment center: Secure community housing criteria and site selection process.* Olympia, WA: Author.

Washington Department of Social and Health Services. (2002). *Allocation of Additional Secure Transition Facility*

Beds Per RCW 71.09.250 (6) and ESSB 6594. Olympia, WA: Author.

Washington Department of Social and Health Services. (2003, April 4, 2003). *DSHS adds a forest area location as a potential sex offender housing site* (Press release). Olympia, WA: Author.

Webster, C., Douglas, K. S., Eaves, E., & Hart, S. D. (1997). *The HCR-20: Assessing risk for violence. Version 2.* Burnaby, British Columbia: Simon Fraser University.

Webster, C. D., Harris, G. T., Rice, M. E., Cormier, C. A., & Quinsey, V. L. (1994). *The violence prediction scheme: Assessing dangerousness in high risk men.* Toronto, Ontario, Canada: Centre of Criminology, University of Toronto.

Webster, C. D., Harris, G. T., Rice, M. E., Cormier, C., & Quinsey, V. L. (1994*). The violence prediction scheme: Assessing dangerousness in high risk men.* Toronto, Ontario, Canada: University of Toronto, Centre of Criminology.

Weekes, J., Pelletier, G., & Beaudette, D. (1995). Correctional officers: How do they perceive sex offenders? *International Journal of Offender Therapy and Comparative Criminology, 39,* 55–61.

Weinrott, M. (1996). *Juvenile sexual aggression: A critical review* Portland, OR: Center for the Study and Prevention of Violence.

Weis, J. G. (1986). Issues in the measurement of criminal careers. In A. Blumstein, J. Cohen, J. A. Roth, & C. A. Visher (Eds,), *Criminal careers and "career criminals"* (Vol. 2, pp. 1–51). Washington, DC: National Academies Press.

Winick, B. J., & La Fond, J. Q. (Eds.). (2003). *Protecting society from sexually dangerous offenders: Law, justice and therapy.* Washington, DC: American Psychological Association.

Wisconsin Building Commission. (2001). *2001–2003 capital budget recommendations.* Madison: Wisconsin Department of Administration.

Wisconsin Legislative Fiscal Bureau. (1999). *Sexually violent person evaluation unit (Paper 335).* Madison, WI: Author.

Wisconsin Legislative Fiscal Bureau. (2001). *Supervised and conditional release (Paper 502).* Madison, WI: Author.

Wollert, R. W. (2002). The importance of cross-validation in actuarial test construction: Shrinkage in the risk estimates for the Minnesota Sex Offender Screening Tool–Revised. *Journal of Threat Assessment, 2,* 87–102.

Wollert, R. W. (2003). Additional flaws in the Minnesota Sex Offender Screening Tool—Revised: A response to Doren and Dow (2002). *Journal of Threat Assessment, 2*(4), 65–78.

Wong, S., & Hare, R. D. (2005). *Program guidelines for the treatment of psychopaths: Institutional treatment of violent psychopathic offenders.* Toronto, Ontario, Canada: Multi-Health Systems.

Worling, J. (2001). *Popular theories regarding the etiology of adolescent sexual offending behaviour.* Unpublished manuscript.

Worling, J. R. (2004). The estimate of risk of adolescent sexual offense recividism (ERASOR): Preliminary psychometric data. *Sexual Abuse: A Journal of Research and Treatment, 16*(3), 235–254.

Worling, J., & Curwen, T. (2001). *The ERASOR: Estimate of Risk of Adolescent Sexual Offense Recidivism. Manual.* Toronto, Ontario, Canada: Ministry of Community and Social Services, Sexual Abuse, Family Education & Treatment Program, Thistletown Regional Centre.

Wright, R. C., & Schneider, S. L. (2004) Mapping child molester treatment progress with FoSOD: Denial and explanations of accountability. *Sexual Abuse: A Journal of Research and Treatment, 16*(2), 85–106.

Yeudall, L. T., & Fromm-Auch, D. (1979). Neuropsychological impairment in various psychopathological populations. In J. Gruzelier & P. Flor-Henry (Eds.), *Hemisphere assymmetries of function and psychopathology* (pp. 5–13). New York: Elsevier.

Young, M., Justice, J., Erdberg, P., & Gacono, C. (2000). The incarcerated psychopath in psychiatric treatment: Management or treatment? In C. Gacono (Ed.), *The clinical and forensic assessment of psychopathy: A practitioner's guide* (pp. 313–331). Hillsdale, NJ: Erlbaum.

Table of Acronyms

AASI	Abel Assessment of Sexual Interest
ANOVA	Analysis of variance
APD	Antisocial personality disorder
BJS	Bureau of Justice Statistics
BMR	Behavior management report
CBT	Cognitive-behavioral therapy
CARP	Clinical Assessment and Review Panel
CNS	Central nervous system
CPA	Cyproterone acetate
DBT	Dialectical behavior therapy
DCF	Department of Children and Families
DHS	Department of Human Services
DMH	Department of Mental Health
DOC	Department of Corrections
DSM-IV-TR	*Diagnostic and Statistical Manual of Mental Disorders* (4th ed., text revision, 2000)
DXA	Dual-energy x-ray absorptiometry
ESRC	End of Sentence Review Committee
ERASOR	Estimated Risk of Adolescent Sexual Offense Recidivism
FDA	Food and Drug Administration
fMRI	Functional magnetic resonance imaging
FT	Forensic therapist
GAS	Goal Attainment Scaling
GnRH	Gonadotropin releasing hormone
GPS	Global positioning system
HCR-20	Historical Clinical Risk Management
HPG	Hypothalamic-pituitary-gonadal
INS	Immigration and Naturalization Service
IOC	Inspection of care
J-SOAP	Juvenile-Sex Offender Assessment Protocol
LH	Luteinizing hormone
LHRH	Luteinizing hormone releasing hormone
LRA	Less restrictive alternatives
LSI-R	Level of Service Inventory—Revised
MAYSI-2	Massachusetts Youth Screening Instrument, Second Version
MDSO	Mentally disordered sexual offenders
MI&D	Mentally ill and dangerous
MIDSA	Multidimensional Inventory of Development, Sex and Aggression
MnSOST	Minnesota Sex Offender Screening Tool
MnSOST–R	Minnesota Sex Offender Screening Tool—Revised
MPA	Medroxyprogesterone acetate
MSOP	Minnesota Sex Offender Program

NCS	National Crime Survey
NCVS	National Crime Victimization Survey
NOS	Not otherwise specified
NRC	National Research Council
PCL-R	Psychopathy Checklist—Revised
PCL:YV	Psychopathy Checklist—Youth Version
PPG	Penile plethysmograph
PPP	Positive predictive power
PSA	Psychiatric security attendant
ROC	Receiver operating characteristic
RRASOR	Rapid Risk Assessment for Sexual Offense Recidivism
RRC	Residential rehabilitation counselor
SABER	Sexual Abuse Behavior Evaluation and Recovery program
SCC	Special Commitment Center
SCTF	Secure Community Transitional Facility
SDP	Sexually Dangerous Person Statute
SIR	Statistical Information on Recidivism scale
SONAR	Sex Offender Needs Assessment Rating
SORAG	Sex Offender Risk Appraisal Guide
SOTRS	Sex Offender Treatment Rating Scale
SPECT	Single photon emission computerized tomography
SPMI	Severe and persistent mental illness
SPP	Sexual Psychopathic Personality Statute
SR	Supervised release
SRB	Special Review Board
SSRIs	Selective serotonin reuptake inhibitors
SVP	Sexually violent predator
SVPA	Sexually Violent Predator Act
SVR-20	Sexual Violence Rating Scale
TAT	Thematic Apperception Test
TPRC	Treatment Progress Review Committee
TPS	Treatment Needs and Progress Scale
VASOR	Vermont Assessment of Sex-Offender Risk
VRAG	Violence Risk Appraisal Guide
WCST	Wisconsin Card Sorting Test
YLS/CMI	Youth Level of Service/Case Management Inventory

Table of Cases and Statutes

[References are to pages and footnotes (n.).]

CASES

[References are to pages and footnotes (n.).]

[References are to pages and footnotes (n.).]

[References are to pages.]

STATUTES

[References are to pages.]

Index

[References are to pages.]

[References are to pages.]

[References are to pages.]

[References are to pages.]

[References are to pages.]

[References are to pages.]

Selective serotonin reuptake inhibitors (SSRIs)
    advantages of, 8-8
    mechanism of action, 8-2
    for obsessive-compulsive behavior, 7-4
    for paraphilias, 8-2–8-3
    side effects, 8-3
Self-esteem assessment, 11-12
Self-incrimination, in polygraph examinations,
        9-21–9-25
    establishing boundaries for disclosure,
        9-23–9-24
    limited immunity and, 9-22–9-23
Self-monitoring, as executive function, 12-2
Self-reports, 9-7–9-8
    criminal career paradigm and, 9-5
    during polygraph examinations, 9-19
    problems with, 9-4–9-5
    therapists and, 9-5–9-6
    unreliability of, 9-5
    vs. polygraph exam data, 9-8–9-9
Sentences, length of, 7-9
Sertraline (Zoloft), 8-3
Sex Offender Needs Assessment Rating
        (SONAR), 3-13, 11-5–11-6
Sex Offender Risk Appraisal Guide (SORAG),
        2-7
Sex offenders. See Sexually violent predators
Sex Offender Treatment Rating Scale (SOTRS),
        11-4
Sexual arousal patterns
    in adolescence, 15-5–15-6
    deviant or criminal, 11-13
    illegal vs. legal, 11-13
    knowledge of methods to change, as treatment
        progress, 11-13
    pretreatment, 11-13
Sexual assault, underreporting of, 9-3–9-4
Sexual deviance problem acceptance, treatment
        efficacy and, 11-7
Sexual fantasies, deviant
    with masturbation and climax, 16-1
    of raping, 3-4
    of sexual sadism, 4-10
    substance abuse and, 16-1–16-2
Sexual history disclosure polygraph examination,
        9-16–9-17
Sexually Dangerous Person statutes, 7-3
Sexually harming behaviors, across lifespan,
        15-7–15-8
Sexually violent predator commitment statutes
        (SVP laws), 1-1–1-13
    See also specific state SVP laws
    adoption/implementation of, 2-2
    challenges to, 1-3–1-4
    implementation, 4-2
    intention of, 4-4–4-5

involuntary psychiatric commitment
        provision, 4-1–4-2
    juvenile civil commitment, 15-10–15-12
    legal challenges, 2-2, 4-11–4-12
        admissibility rulings, 2-2–2-3
        double jeopardy issues, 4-12
        ex post facto issues, 4-12
        implementation, due process and, 4-12
        limitations of reviewing appellate cases,
            2-2
    mental abnormalities/illness laws and, 7-1,
        7-2, 7-9
    mentally disordered sexual offenders statutes,
        7-3
    mentally ill and dangerous statutes, 7-3
    postincarceration for high-risk offenders,
        11-2
    "practical effect" of, 4-4
    requirements for, 2-1–2-2
    resource demands, 5-4
    second generation, 1-10
    Sexually Dangerous Person statutes, 7-3
    sexual psychopath laws, 11-2
    structure of, 7-3
    thresholds, actuarial risk percentages below,
        does not meet criteria, 3-23–3-24
    thresholds for, 3-8
    treatment purpose of, 1-5
    Washington, 1-2–1-3
Sexually violent predators (SVPs)
    adult vs. juvenile sex offenders, 15-7
    attitudes of correctional officers toward,
        10-2–10-3
    civilly committed
        diagnoses of, 7-4
        executive functions in, 12-2–12-4
        right to treatment, 1-4–1-6
        security level for, 1-8, 1-10
    confinement. See Confinement
    control of therapist's impressions, 9-6
    critical issues/distress of, 10-10
    definition of, 1-2
    deliberate concealment of information, 9-6
    good actions of, 10-10
    honesty, polygraph examination and, 9-15
    humanness of, 10-10
    information concealment, countermeasures
        and, 9-19–9-20
    information disclosures
        accurate, need for, 9-7
        self-report vs. polygraph exam data,
            9-8–9-9
    juvenile. See Juvenile sex offenders
    legal recourse
        corrective measures necessary for, 1-11
        Section 1983 claims, 1-11, 1-12–1-13

[References are to pages.]

[References are to pages.]

[References are to pages.]

[References are to pages.]

G